SERGEY PROKOFIEV AND HIS WORLD

SERGEY PROKOFIEV
AND HIS WORLD

EDITED BY SIMON MORRISON

PRINCETON UNIVERSITY PRESS

PRINCETON AND OXFORD

Copyright © 2008 by Princeton University Press

Published by Princeton University Press, 41 William Street,
Princeton, New Jersey 08540
In the United Kingdom: Princeton University Press,
6 Oxford Street, Woodstock, Oxfordshire OX20 1TW

All Rights Reserved

For permissions information, see page 562

Library of Congress Control Number 2008926970

ISBN-13: 978-0-691-13894-7 (cloth)
ISBN-13: 978-0-691-13895-4 (paperback)

British Library Cataloging-in-Publication Data is available

This publication has been produced by the Bard College Publications Office:
Ginger Shore, Director
Kevin Trabucco, Cover design
Natalie Kelly, Design
Text edited by Paul De Angelis and Erin Clermont
Music typeset by Don Giller

This publication has been underwritten in part by a grant from
Furthermore: a program of the J. M. Kaplan Fund.

Printed on acid-free paper. ∞

press.princeton.edu

Printed in the United States of America

1 3 5 7 9 10 8 6 4 2

Contents

For Malcolm Brown

Preface and Acknowledgments

Sergey Prokofiev composed some of the most beloved works in the Western musical canon. *Romeo and Juliet*, the Third Piano Concerto, and *Peter and the Wolf* endure in the orchestral and theatrical repertoire even as that repertoire shrinks, ceding to the popular idioms from which it sprang. Much of Prokofiev's appeal stems from his remarkable talent as a melodicist and his invigoration of traditional genres and forms. We know this composer, yet there is much about his art, and his life, that remains unknown.

The story of Prokofiev's prodigious childhood in tsarist Russia, his maturation in the West, and his rise and fall as a Stalinist-era composer has been greatly illuminated by the Serge Prokofiev Foundation in London which, since 2001, has published a biannual journal, *Three Oranges*, devoted to his career. In 2001, 2004, and 2007, respectively, the Glinka Museum in Moscow published a collection of documents dealing with Prokofiev's Soviet period, and in 2003, David Nice produced a detailed biography of the first half of his career. Crucial questions are unanswered, however, and long-standing debates unresolved. The greatest puzzle concerns Prokofiev's decision to relocate with his family from Paris to Moscow in 1936: the chain of events leading up to that move, and the pressures exerted on the composer by Stalinist cultural and political agencies to undertake it, continue to be matters of informed and uninformed speculation. The precise nature of his existence in the Soviet Union—the chronology of his wartime evacuation, the bureaucratic discussions that resulted in certain works being celebrated (*Alexander Nevsky*, the Fifth Symphony, the First Violin Sonata) and others prohibited (the *Cantata for the Twentieth Anniversary of October*, *Tonya*, *A Story of A Real Man*), the causes of the precipitous decline in his health after 1945, his reactions to the arrest of his longtime collaborator Vsevolod Meyerhold—likewise remains unclear. And whereas the publication in 2003 of Prokofiev's diaries (in Russian) offers fascinating, provocative insight into his career between 1907 and 1933, the chronology of his final creative years in the West is incomplete.

Prokofiev spent much of his composing career in and around Paris and Moscow, but he left traces of his existence as a performer in Buffalo, Casablanca, Denver, Havana, Lisbon, London, Montreal, St. Petersburg/

Leningrad, Tokyo, and dozens of other cities and towns. Letters, manuscripts, and reminiscences are preserved in national archives, municipal
libraries, small-town colleges (Dartmouth and Wheaton), specialized collections (the Mary Baker Eddy Library), and the scrapbooks of friends and
acquaintances. Some of the Prokofiev holdings in Russia are inaccessible,
and others simply unexplored—a consequence of the Soviet practice of
distributing the records of leading cultural and political figures among different federal archives. Rarely do revelations about canonic artists
materialize, but Prokofiev remains fertile ground for scholarly study.

This collection of documents and essays, the companion to the 2008
Bard Music Festival, probes beneath the surface of Prokofiev's career, con-
textualizing his contributions to music on both sides of the nascent Cold
War divide. It contains hitherto unknown documents from the Russian
State Archive of Literature and Art in Moscow, the Russian State Archive of
Social and Political History, the State Archive of the Russian Federation,
the Serge Prokofiev Archive in London, and several smaller holdings in the
United States. Pamela Davidson opens the documents section of this volume with a translation of a literary notebook belonging to Prokofiev's
mother, Mariya Grigoryevna, which attests to her profound and long-lasting
investment in her son's education, especially as it concerned his indoctrination in Schopenhauer and Russian Symbolist poetry. As Davidson explains
in her introductory essay, the notebook is especially valuable for its insights
into the conception of Prokofiev's *Seven, They Are Seven*, an outlandish musical treatment of an ancient (third-century) Akkadian incantation against
malevolent spirits. The little-performed score, which calls for full-sized
orchestra, chorus, and dramatic tenor, sets a Russian translation of the incantation by Konstantin Balmont, a founding member of the Symbolist
movement whose influence on composers greatly exceeded that of his peers.

The second cluster of documents chronicles Prokofiev's interaction
with Sigizmund Krzhizhanovsky (1887–1950), a dramatist and surrealist
fiction writer rediscovered in Russia in the 1990s and only now becoming
appreciated in English translation. Krzhizhanovsky fell out of favor with
Stalinist cultural officials and, by inevitable extension, disappeared from
Soviet-era accounts of Prokofiev's career. Using exclusive archival
materials, Caryl Emerson narrates the conception and reception of
Krzhizhanovsky's ill-starred theatrical adaptation of Pushkin's novel-in-
verse *Eugene Onegin*, a commission by the Moscow Chamber Theater for
which Prokofiev composed incidental music in 1936. The adaptation
went unperformed, leaving the composer free to later reuse parts of his
score. Reactionary politics doomed numerous Pushkin-related commissions in the run-up to the official commemoration of the centennial

of the poet's death. Emerson illuminates the theoretical underpinnings of Krzhizhanovsky's adaptation while also describing the function of the forty-four vocal and instrumental numbers Prokofiev conceived for it. Her complete translation of Krzhizhanovsky's adaptation, keyed to Pushkin's original and accompanied with explanatory notes, is intended for live performance.

Turning to the practicalities of composition, there follows a collection of ninety-eight letters between Prokofiev and his de facto Soviet business partner Levon Atovmyan (1901–73). As Nelly Kravetz explains in her introduction, Atovmyan provided crucial support to Prokofiev throughout his Soviet years, facilitating commissions from the Union of Soviet Composers, contributing technical assistance by preparing orchestral and chamber scores for publication, arranging some of these scores for piano, and attending to requests for personal loans, housing, and medical care. Although Atovmyan took a lead role in encouraging Prokofiev to relocate from Paris to Moscow in 1936, the extent to which the creative and personal consequences of that decision took its toll on their relationship cannot be gleaned from their correspondence. The letters are professional and, with rare exceptions, devoid of sentiment; they are, however, among the most revealing documents on Soviet music yet unearthed, illustrating how scores were policed, performed, and published. The letters also provide an intricate account of Prokofiev's activities during and after the Soviet phase of the Second World War, bridging gaps in the chronology of his evacuation.

The essays in the collection range in focus from musical sketches to Kremlin decrees. Stephen Press and Elizabeth Bergman, respectively, explore Prokofiev's extended first visit and last two visits to the United States, furnishing detailed chronologies of his New York City debut, the Chicago premiere for *The Love for Three Oranges*, his squabbles with producers and promoters, and his flirtation with Hollywood studios. The first visit, from August 1918 to April 1920, finds the headstrong, ambitious composer forging a career in unknown terrain with imperfect English-language skills. The last two visits extended from January–February 1937 and from February–March 1938, after Prokofiev's permanent relocation to Moscow, when, in exchange for the privilege of foreign travel, he was obliged to fulfill the duties of a Soviet cultural envoy. The composer planned other visits to the West after 1938, but they never came to pass, owing to an official change in his status from *vïyezdnoy* (allowed to travel) to *nevïyezdnoy* (disallowed). The shift in creative focus that attended that relocation dominates another three essays. Mark Aranovsky evaluates Prokofiev's working methods in the mid-1930s, documenting, through an analysis of three sketchbooks, Prokofiev's aspiration toward directness and simplicity of expression. Kevin Bartig traces the creation of the score for Alexander Fayntsimmer's film *Lieutenant Kizhe* (1934), which finds Prokofiev seeking maximum emotional and psychological impact with minimal means. This score is best known as a concert suite; Bartig restores it to its original cinematic splendor, showing how it alternately complements and contradicts Fayntsimmer's visuals.

Marina Frolova-Walker explores Prokofiev's decision to rewrite his 1930 Fourth Symphony in 1947, illuminating how politics (the obligation to adhere to Soviet aesthetic doctrine) shaped his creative activities, but also how they did not. She likens Prokofiev's decision to monumentalize a neglected pre-Soviet score to the impulse of the writer Boris Pilnyak to expand his novella *Mahogany* into the hefty socialist realist novel *The Volga Falls to the Caspian Sea*. Prokofiev's and Pilnyak's works are unrelated, but the pressures imposed on them virtually identical.

The contributions of Leonid Maximenkov and Peter Schmelz independently detail Prokofiev's immortalization by Soviet officials, composers, and scholars. Maximenkov's study, part of the documents section, records the bureaucratic chaos precipitated by Stalin's death, which occurred, in a macabre twist, on the same day as Prokofiev's. The author then explores the botched planning of Prokofiev tributes during the Khrushchev, Brezhnev, and Gorbachev eras. Schmelz examines the posthumous tragifarce through a different lens, describing Prokofiev's reception by Soviet composers who came of age in the 1960s and 1970s, and the tendentious debates about his significance in the pages of *Sovetskaya muzïka*, the official journal of the Union of Soviet Composers.

Finally, Leon Botstein examines Prokofiev's belief in Christian Science and the paths it opened for his music, a subject largely overlooked in the literature on the composer, but essential to the understanding of his aesthetics, achievement, and, possibly, survival. Beginning in 1924, long before his Soviet period, Prokofiev and his wife indoctrinated themselves in Christian Science, internalizing the foundational text of the faith, Mary Baker Eddy's *Science and Health with Key to the Scriptures* (1875), and consulting it for treatment of physical ailments. Over time, and in keeping with Christian Science precepts, Prokofiev increasingly came to define his creative activities in spiritual language. His God-given talent came with great responsibilities: his life served his art, rather than the opposite, a situation that obliged him to take risks that defied external, non-artistic logic.

The inspiration for this volume belongs to Leon Botstein, the founder of the Bard Music Festival and the President of Bard College, who contacted me in 2006 with an invitation to participate in a series of events dedicated to Prokofiev in 2008, including a production of the original

1935 version of the ballet *Romeo and Juliet*, three weekends of concerts, and this volume. It also belongs to Tambra Dillon, Christopher Gibbs, Susana Meyer, and Irene Zedlacher, who shared their expertise and experience with me throughout the planning process. The words on these pages are the product of a group of intrepid, inspired scholars with whom it was an exceptional pleasure to collaborate: I owe all of them a debt of gratitude. I am especially grateful to Caryl Emerson for her help with numerous translation questions, to Malcolm Brown for providing primary source materials, to Elizabeth Bergman for her generous editorial assistance, and to Kara Olive, who offered indispensable last-minute fact-checking and proofreading. My thanks as well to Noëlle Mann, longtime curator of the Prokofiev Archive in London, for her encouragement. My editorial education came from a remarkable production team: Paul De Angelis, Erin Clermont, Natalie Kelly, and Ginger Shore. As always, I am grateful to Melanie Feilotter.

Simon Morrison
January 2008

Note on Transliteration, Dates, and Titles

The transliteration system used in this book is the system devised by Gerald Abraham for the *New Grove Dictionary of Music and Musicians* (1980), with the modifications introduced by Richard Taruskin in *Musorgsky: Eight Essays and an Epilogue* (1993). The principal exceptions to the system concern commonly accepted spellings of names and places (Prokofiev rather than Prokof'yev) and suffixes (-*sky* rather than -*skiy*). In the bibliographic citations, however, the transliteration system is respected without exception (Prokof'yev rather than Prokofiev). Surname suffixes are presented intact, and hard and soft signs preserved.

Russia used the Julian calendar until February 1, 1918. On that date, the Gregorian calendar was decreed the official calendar; February 1, accordingly, became February 14. Since the Gregorian calendar had been in use in Europe and America long before 1918, Russians tended to double-date their letters when traveling or communicating abroad. Most of the letters, diary entries, and other primary sources used in this book are dated according to the Gregorian calendar. The literary notebook edited and introduced by Pamela Davidson, however, contains references to material with both Julian and Gregorian dates, separated by a slash.

With the exception of long Russian titles, titles of works are provided in the main text in the language in which they were published or are generally known in the West (original titles of the exceptions can be found in the notes). The corresponding English title of a published composition or translation is provided parenthetically in usual title style. Literal English translations for which no published translations or editions exist are given parenthetically with neither italics nor quote marks, with only the first word and proper names capitalized.

PART I

DOCUMENTS

"Look After Your Son's Talents": The Literary Notebook of Mariya Prokofieva

EDITED, TRANSLATED, AND INTRODUCED
BY PAMELA DAVIDSON

The same parting words were always addressed to me: "Look after your son's talents." I remember them with gratitude to this very day and always followed them, whenever possible.   —*Mariya Prokofieva*

The Serge Prokofiev Archive in London houses a copy of an unusual item from the Serge Prokofiev Estate in Paris: a small notebook, completed at the end of 1917, filled with miscellaneous entries from various sources, including poems, philosophical aphorisms, and notes on a wide range of subjects from mysticism to astronomy. It is not known exactly how this notebook ended up among Prokofiev's papers in France; he may have packed it in his suitcase when he left Russia in May 1918, or his mother may have brought it to him together with his musical papers and diary of 1917 when she joined him in France in June 1920, arriving with just two suitcases after an arduous journey from Kislovodsk via Constantinople.[1] Whichever route was taken, it is clear that the notebook was of considerable importance to Prokofiev, otherwise it would not have been chosen as one of the few items to be taken out of Russia after the Revolution.

For many years it was assumed that the entries in the notebook were all made by Prokofiev. This view was taken for granted because the notebook had been kept with Prokofiev's personal papers and contains materials closely linked with his creative work and pursuits at the time: poems by Zinaida Gippius and Konstantin Balmont that he set to music in 1915 and 1917; excerpts from Edouard Schuré and Schopenhauer, whose works he was reading in 1916 and 1917; and two of his own humorous poems, composed in 1916 and 1917. In the course of recent research, however, it became apparent that only the very last entry in the notebook is in Prokofiev's hand; all the other entries are written in the "beautiful and energetic" handwriting of his mother, Mariya Grigoryevna Prokofieva (1855–1924).[2] This discovery raises several intriguing questions. Why would Prokofiev's mother have recorded in her notebook so many items of relevance to her son's creative work and reading? Was this simply a matter of coincidence, reflecting their shared literary and philosophical interests? Or was she keeping a record of the various poems, aphorisms, and notes on subjects that were of special significance to him? If so, what was the purpose of this record? Was she assisting him, perhaps at his request, by copying out various texts of interest?

Some clarification of these questions can be found in the entries made in the notebook. Before looking at the textual evidence, however, we should first consider the broader context of Mariya Prokofieva's personality and relationship with her son. A fairly consistent picture of her character can be pieced together from her own memoir of her son's formative years, his comments about her in his autobiography and diary, contemporary correspondence and recollections. She was clearly a remarkable woman in her own right. Although she came from a family of peasant origins and modest means, she succeeded in building a different life for herself through a combination of natural talent and sheer determination.[3] As Prokofiev noted with pride in his autobiography, both his parents were the cleverest children in their respective families, with a marriage founded on shared intellectual pursuits and aspirations.[4] Mariya Grigoryevna was an accomplished amateur pianist and a lively conversationalist who always enjoyed good company.[5] When her husband, Sergey Alekseyevich, a trained agronomist, took up his position overseeing their estate at Sontsovka, she became determined (like so many of Chekhov's heroines) not to succumb to the stagnation of provincial life. Her home was full of books; she subscribed to all the latest journals and followed the musical and theatrical life of Moscow and St. Petersburg with interest.[6] Every winter she would journey to the capital for one or two months, leaving her son behind in the care of his father and grandmother.[7] She also made considerable efforts to influence those around her who were less privileged, taking part, for example, in the education of local peasant children.[8]

As the only surviving child of the marriage (two older sisters died in early infancy), Prokofiev naturally became the prime focus of his parents' ambitions. His father gave him lessons in Russian, arithmetic, geography, and history, and later, when he came to visit his son in St. Petersburg, in algebra, geometry, and drawing.[9] Prokofiev did not always find these lessons enjoyable because of "Papa's excessive pedantry."[10] This was certainly not the case with his mother's lessons, which evinced her remarkable pedagogical skills. She taught him languages, first French, then German, and studied the Old and New Testaments with him. Most important, she initiated him into the world of music, shaped his early tastes, and took full responsibility for his initial musical training.[11] As an infant, he responded enthusiastically to her piano playing. When he was a young child of seven, she made sure to keep his music lessons short and fun, never boring him with rote learning. She introduced him to the eighteenth- and nineteenth-century piano repertoire, encouraged him to develop independent opinions of it, arranged for a grand piano to be brought from St. Petersburg to Sontsovka, and took him on his first visits to the opera in Moscow and St. Petersburg.[12] When he began to compose his own pieces, she either wrote them out for him or enlisted others for the task—his French governess, for example, copied out his first opera *The Giant* (*Velikan*, 1900) in calligraphic style.[13] On one occasion, when he tried to destroy a piece that he had given to his mother as a present, she insisted on preserving it.[14] Later, she showed him how to record and organize his work, teaching him the principles of musical notation and the importance of making clean copies of his compositions.[15]

When Prokofiev turned eleven, his mother wisely realized that she needed to enlist professional musicians to develop his precocious talent.[16] In January 1902 she took him to see Sergey Taneyev in Moscow; on his recommendation, she invited Reinhold Glier, a graduate of the Moscow Conservatory and Taneyev's former pupil, to spend the summers of 1902 and 1903 at Sontsovka teaching her son composition and music theory.[17] In 1904, following a visit to Alexander Glazunov, the director of the St. Petersburg Conservatory, she enrolled her son as a first-year student.[18] In order to create the best conditions for his education she rented a modest flat in St. Petersburg and moved in with him, organizing everything to meet his needs.[19] After Sergey Alekseyevich died in the summer of 1910, Prokofiev confessed in his diary that he did not know whether he had loved his father, since they had very little in common.[20] The opposite was true of his relationship with his mother, which only strengthened after his father's death. According to the memoirs of Mariya Morolyova, an old family friend, his mother's moral authority was so great that her firm and calmly expressed opinions were accepted uncritically; she taught her son through the power of her example how to speak and behave with directness and honesty.[21]

Mariya Prokofieva's awareness of her vital role in nurturing and developing her son's musical talent is clearly articulated in the memoir of his early years that she dictated in 1922. Her account of their relationship is borne out by Glier's perceptive observations. In his memoirs he describes her as a "rare mother" who believed in her son's creative potential and did everything possible to develop his talent in optimal conditions. He comments that her love for her only child and pride in his achievements never turned into blind adulation; she remained keenly aware of her responsibility for his upbringing and rose to the challenges it presented.[22]

She succeeded in instilling within him a love for work, creative discipline, and order. Glier also notes that Prokofiev recognized the enormous role that his mother played in his creative development and retained a deep sense of gratitude, love, and loyalty to her teachings throughout his life.[23] This view is confirmed by Prokofiev in his autobiography, begun in the late 1930s, which acknowledges and develops many of the points made in his mother's memoirs.

It is clear from all these sources that Prokofiev's musical career would not have developed as it did without the phenomenal energy and resources that his mother invested in his upbringing. One might well gain the impression from her memoir and Prokofiev's autobiographical writings that her close involvement in his musical life, exceptionally strong during his childhood, receded after he joined the Conservatory. From this point on Prokofiev makes relatively few comments about his mother (most of his references to her are of a factual nature, concerning her travel plans, for example, rather than musical or cultural matters). In many ways this is not surprising; it would have been entirely natural for Prokofiev to gravitate toward his teachers and friends during his years at the Conservatory. After his graduation in 1914, when he was in his mid-twenties and already an independent young man, taking on his first musical engagements and establishing his reputation, one would expect even fewer traces of his mother's influence. Her notebook, however, provides compelling evidence of her continuing close involvement in his literary, philosophical, and musical pursuits. In this respect it is an extremely valuable document, countering the general impression that she no longer actively participated in her son's development at this stage. Throughout this later period she continued to play the role that she had adopted in Prokofiev's early life—the role of copying out his works, preserving them, and keeping a record of his interests. This activity evidently provided her with vicarious self-fulfillment. We know from Prokofiev's autobiography that his mother stopped playing the piano when she saw that her son had overtaken her abilities.[24] In similar fashion it would appear that she preferred to follow in the tracks of his literary and philosophical interests, rather than pursuing her own.

In this way she remained faithful to Taneyev's parting injunction, "Look after your son's talents." She recorded these words in her 1922 memoir, and they assumed special meaning for her son, who quoted them twice in both versions (long and short) of his autobiography: "'The main thing is, look after your son's talents,'—said Sergey Ivanovich, and my mother repeatedly recalled this injunction."[25] Her notebook provides unique evidence of the way in which she continued to follow this advice. It is possible that Prokofiev kept the notebook with him after he left Russia not simply because its contents were useful to him, but also because of its sentimental value as testimony to his mother's involvement in his creative development. In the "Apologetic Introduction" to his long autobiography, he drew attention to the importance of his mother's role in this respect. When he was twelve he observed a music professor keeping a diary and was so impressed that he started writing his own diary in secret, often while sitting on the toilet. His mother then gave him a thick bound notebook and said to him: "Sergushechka, write in it whatever comes into your head: let nothing be lost."[26] It was evidently this desire to preserve her son's work that motivated her to keep a notebook of her own for recording items of interest to him.

What, then, can this notebook contribute to our understanding of Mariya Prokofieva's interests and their relation to her son's creative work in the period from 1914 to 1917? As one turns its pages, one encounters a fascinating, sometimes bewildering medley of different entries. There are poems, some by Prokofiev and some by other writers, aphorisms by Schopenhauer, reflections about the Germans and the English, notes on obscure religious sects, observations on the movements of the planets, and thoughts on art, beauty, and mysticism. What significance can be ascribed to these jottings? Interpreting this type of material is a tricky enterprise. Anyone who has ever kept a notebook knows how many random things of no lasting import can land in it. It would undoubtedly be a mistake to assume that every item in the notebook is of central significance to Prokofieva's interests or her son's work at the time. Although some entries bear direct relation to his work, others are of uncertain origin or significance. Nevertheless, as a whole, the document represents a fascinating kaleidoscope attesting to a diverse and eclectic range of study. The remaining part of this introductory essay will therefore provide a general summary of its contents, paying particular attention to the entries that are clearly connected to Prokofiev's music. For further information on the sources and publication details of the entries, the reader is referred to the detailed notes accompanying the full transcript of the notebook.

The notebook opens rather unpromisingly with the phrase "Tenir un carnet de dépenses" (Keep a notebook of expenses). This resolution was not kept—apart from the prices of a few French books, the notebook contains no record of payments. However, this opening phrase provides a useful clue to the date when the notebook may have been started. The use of French, together with the fact that people tend to keep notes on expenses while traveling, suggests that Prokofieva began the notebook during her trip to France and Switzerland with her son in the summer of 1913. This hypothesis is supported by the next page, which lists various French books with titles such as *Leçons de choses*, *Livre du maître*, *Livre de l'élève*, *Le parfait causeur*, together with a note of prices in francs; Prokofieva may have bought, or planned to buy, some of these books to improve her command of the language during her trip. But although the notebook may have been started in 1913, most of the entries date from around 1914 to the end of 1917.

Two photographs have been glued onto the opening pages. The first is of Prokofiev's father, Sergey Alekseyevich, and appears to have been taken not long before his death in 1910, possibly at Sontsovka. The second is of his mother, Mariya Grigoryevna, and looks as if it was taken in France. The photographs may have been stuck into the notebook at a later date, perhaps by Prokofiev after the notebook came into his possession.

The first substantial entry is an extract headed "Chuvstvo bïtiya" (The sense of being), taken from Sergey Rafalovich's collection *Zhenskiye pis'ma* (Women's letters) published in St. Petersburg in 1906. Rafalovich (1875–1943) was a minor Symbolist poet, prose writer, dramatist, and theater critic who maintained close relations with literary circles in St. Petersburg. *Women's Letters* is one of his earliest works and comprises fifteen fictive prose letters from a variety of women dealing with the problems and moral dilemmas posed by love. Prokofieva has copied out two sections from the first letter, titled "Tyotya Mar'ya" (Aunt Marya). Both passages deal with the "sense of being," extolled as a supreme value and contrasted with the sinful denial of life. Prokofieva's eye may have been caught by the link between her own name and the fictive Aunt Marya; it is also possible that she associated Aunt Marya's description of her nephew's intense love of life and highly developed "sense of being" with her own son's zest for life.

Anyone familiar with literary movements in early twentieth-century Russia can appreciate the extent of the contemporary obsession with the individual's relation to life. For the Symbolists, the *realia* of this world were valued as an echo of the *realiora* of a higher, transcendent reality. The Acmeists reacted against this trend by declaring that they would put the emphasis back on life in this world. Despite their focus on everyday urban life, many of the Futurists' experiments with language and meaning had their origins in the Symbolists' aspirations to transcendence. It is worth noting in this context that Prokofiev was surprisingly eclectic in his literary tastes and had good relations with all three movements—he was on close terms with the Symbolist Balmont, setting several of his poems to music; he cooperated on the ballet *Ala and Lolliy* with the Acmeist Sergey Gorodetsky in 1914; he composed a song cycle to Anna Akhmatova's words in 1916; and he had several lively encounters with the Futurist Vladimir Mayakovsky in 1917 and 1918. His mother's attention to the passage from Rafalovich's collection may have been related to her perception of Prokofiev's own strong "sense of being" as a value in itself. As will be seen below, this did not exclude a growing interest on his part in the transcendent dimension of life, explored through philosophy and mysticism.

The extract from Rafalovich is followed by a few brief reflections on the limitations of knowledge and closeness between people, the clash between the rights of the individual and love, and the supremacy of intensity of experience over its duration. The last thought is illustrated by an aphorism, cited in German: "Life is fullness, not time. And even the final moment is far away." The source of this saying is not identified in the notebook; it is the closing couplet of a historical drama by the Austrian playwright Arthur Schnitzler (1862–1931) titled *The Veil of Beatrice* (*Der Schleier der Beatrice*, 1901). Schnitzler's work enjoyed considerable popularity in Russia from 1900 onward and came to the attention of Prokofiev in 1913, when he attended a rehearsal at the Moscow Free Theater of a mime production based on Schnitzler's *The Veil of Pierette* (*Der Schleier der Pierette*, 1910), performed to music by Ernö Dohnányi. Whether this link played a role in Mariya Prokofieva's interest in Schnitzler's aphorism is not known.

These piecemeal jottings all reflect a developing awareness of emotional relationships and their limitations, as well as an interest in defining the strength of experience outside time. There are several possible parallels with Prokofiev's life and creative work, as can be seen from reflections in his diary on his budding romance with Nina Meshcherskaya and, in musical terms, his attempts to capture the fleeting moment in *Visions fugitives* (*Mimolyotnosti*, 1915–17).

Next comes another extract from Rafalovich's *Women's Letters*, this time based on a passage from the second letter in his collection, "Odinokaya" (The lonely woman), dealing with the feeling of loneliness (a recurrent theme throughout the notebook). Although in the original letter this passage is narrated in the first person by a female protagonist, Prokofieva rewrites it in the third person in her notebook, thereby turning it into a general statement with broad application. We know from Prokofiev's diary of the time how frequently he experienced a strong sense of solitude and pondered the significance of this feeling. The loneliness of the individual was also a prominent theme in his musical setting of *The Ugly Duckling* (*Gadkiy utyonok*) in 1914. It is possible that Prokofieva's interest in recording these comments on loneliness reflected her awareness of her son's experience with it.

The next entry is a romantic, rather decadent short poem on love by Daniil Ratgauz (1868–1937), incorrectly identified by Prokofieva as Ratrauz. In the course of two quatrains love is characterized as a dream, a fleeting instant, a magic vision, a ray of paradise in the gloom of the grave, and identified as the only source of happiness in this world. Though undistinguished, the poem was well known at the time and set to music by several composers, including Glier, who tutored Prokofiev in 1902 and 1903 and turned the poem into a song in 1905. It is possible that Prokofiev also considered setting this text to music, as was the case with the two poems by Gippius and Balmont that appear later in the notebook.

The bizarre beliefs and practices of the Johannites, a religious sect who venerated the popular Russian Orthodox priest Father John of Kronstadt, form the subject of the next entry. The fame of the Johannites spread throughout Russia in the late nineteenth and early twentieth century as a result of their association with Father John (who did not recognize them as his true disciples) and their effective propaganda. In 1912, due to the dangerous spread of their influence, their activities were forbidden by the Holy Synod. In her notebook Prokofieva describes their strange custom of "spiritual marriage" and attitude toward smoking and vodka drinking. This entry is one of the more puzzling in the notebook, since it is not at all clear what aroused Prokofieva's curiosity in the movement or served as her source of information. She may have been influenced by the recent growth of interest among the Russian intelligentsia in religious sects, including their social behavior and sexual practices. Leo Tolstoy, for instance, published *Resurrection* (*Voskreseniye*, 1899) to raise money for the Dukhobors, and his disciple, Vladimir Chertkov, wrote extensively on religious sectarianism in Russia during his period of exile in England from 1897 to 1905. Similar interests informed the work of several contemporaries of Prokofiev, including Andrey Belïy, Nikolay Klyuyev, and Vasiliy Rozanov. Belïy's novel *The Silver Dove* (*Serebryanïy golub'*, 1909), for example, tells the story of a young intellectual, disenchanted with urban life, who joins a group of peasant religious sectarians only to be murdered for failing to sire a new messiah with one of the women.

The notebook contains two unusual poems by the Symbolist Gippius. "Naprasno" (In vain) and "Seroye plat'itse" (The gray dress) first appeared in a cycle of fourteen poems titled *Molchaniya* (Silences), published in 1914 in the St. Petersburg literary almanac *Sirin*. Prokofieva transcribed both poems in black ink (rather than in pencil, more common in the notebook) and in neater handwriting than usual, suggesting that clear copies might be required for musical treatment. As we shall see below, the second poem was set by Prokofiev in 1915; he and his mother were clearly intrigued by the musical possibilities of Gippius's *Silences,* which dwell on the spaces between sounds and unvoiced gaps in communication.

"In Vain," dated February 1913, is the eleventh poem in the cycle and was evidently copied by Prokofieva from the original publication of 1914, as the text in her notebook reproduces variants found only in this source. The poem is a polemical response to Fyodor Tyutchev's well-known "Silentium" (1830) and shares several features with its predecessor, including the advocacy of silence, direct address by the poem's narrator to an unnamed addressee, and iambic meter with exclusively masculine rhymes.

Tyutchev's poem consists of abstract injunctions for silence, addressed to the general reader or perhaps to the poet's own inner self; Gippius's form of address, in contrast, establishes an intimate relationship between the narrator and the addressee. Like Tyutchev, Gippius advocates silence, but for different reasons. Tyutchev counsels silence on the grounds that self-expression and understanding are ineluctably imperfect and unable to convey pristine inner truths:

Молчи, скрывайся и таи
И чувства и мечты свои! [. . .]
Как сердцу высказать себя?
Другому как понять тебя? [. . .]
Взрывая возмутишь ключи:
Питайся ими и молчи!

Be silent, hide yourself and conceal
Both your feelings and your dreams! [. . .]
How can the heart express itself?
How can another person understand you? [. . .]
By stirring you will cloud the springs:
Drink from them and be silent!

Gippius recommends silence on a different basis—although understanding is possible, the "invisible threshold" (nevidimïy porog) between two people should never be crossed as a matter of principle. In reworking the message of "Silentium," she cleverly transforms Tyutchev's reference to klyuchi (the springs of pure water that must not be clouded) using the same word's alternate meaning (the keys of a heart that must not be unlocked):

Я и услышу, и пойму—	I will both hear and understand—
А все-таки молчи.	But all the same be silent.
Будь верен сердцу своему,	Be true to your heart,
Храни его ключи.	Guard its keys.

Why did Prokofieva copy this poem? Apart from its intrinsic interest and value as a possible text for her son to set to music, she may have been intrigued by the way it echoed some of the ideas jotted down earlier in her notebook concerning the inability of the individual to know anything other than subjectively, and consequently on the limitations this condition places on mutual human understanding. In this respect it anticipates a poem by Akhmatova written later in 1913: "True tenderness you will never confuse . . ." (Nastoyashchuyu nezhnost' ne sputayesh'. . .), which twice repeats the same word *naprasno* (in vain) and also emphasizes the futility of utter-ing "submissive words about love" (*slova pokornïye o lyubvi*). Although Prokofiev did not set Gippius's poem to music, he chose this poem, writ-ten on a similar theme, for one of the five Akhmatova lyrics he composed in 1916 in an intimate style (op. 27).[27]

The other poem by Gippius, "The Gray Dress," was written in January 1913, a month before "In Vain," and occupies the ninth position in the *Silences* cycle. It also takes the form of an address, this time extended into a dialogue. The narrator accosts a little girl in a gray dress with matted plaits and vacant eyes and asks her a series of questions in order to deter-mine her identity. The girl turns out to be an orphan and reveals that her favorite pursuits are destructive (she bites through the thread of a string of beads, cuts pages out of books, and breaks the wings of a bird). When asked her name, she offers several possibilities: division, enmity, doubt, depression, boredom, and torment. Her mother, however, who is referred to as *Mama-Smert'* (Mama-Death) calls her *razluka* (separation).

This strange and disturbing poem evokes the very antithesis of the prin-ciple of embracing life in its fullness, the "sense of being" extolled in the passage from Rafalovich quoted at the beginning of the notebook. It shares with "In Vain" the themes of separation and silence, but takes these to a more chilling, sinister extreme, combining a Symbolist taste for abstraction with a flat, pedestrian manner of narration in perfect tune with the "grayness" of its subject. It can be read on two levels: as a poem of social protest about the deprivations of a poor orphaned girl (Harlow Robinson accordingly finds that it "resonates with social awareness"), or as an allegory of the consequences of death and separation.[28] From a musical standpoint, "The Gray Dress" may have appealed to Prokofiev more than "In Vain" because of its two-voiced dialogic character and the intriguing shift from the literal to the allegorical plane, qualities that are reflected in his static, declamatory setting of the poem.

The idea of turning Gippius's poem into a song was suggested to Prokofiev in 1915 by his friend Vladimir Derzhanovsky (1881–1942), a Moscow-based music critic and promoter. On July 25, 1915, Prokofiev jok-ingly wrote to him: "Imagine, I have already finished the upper half of your little dress."[29] By this stage he had evidently completed about half the song, which he dedicated to Derzhanovsky and incorporated into his cycle of five poems set to music (op. 23), first performed in Petrograd in November 1916 and published in 1917 by Gutheil.[30]

Given that Derzhanovsky suggested Gippius's poem to Prokofiev, what significance can we attribute to his mother copying it into her notebook? Was she simply keeping a record of the texts set to music by her son? Or was she perhaps helping him by copying out poems that he was planning to set? This second, more likely hypothesis is buttressed by an important fact. Prokofieva's copy of the poem contains one distinctive feature, absent from the published text of 1914: the adjective in the phrase "devochka v *serom* plat'itse" (girl in a *gray* dress), which is repeated five times by Gippius, has been changed to read "devochka v *seren'kom* plat'itse" (girl in a *grayish* dress). The preservation of this unusual difference in the published text of Prokofiev's song suggests that he used the text copied in his mother's notebook when composing it. There is also evidence that Prokofiev worked with the version of Balmont's incantation transcribed in his mother's notebook when setting this text to music in 1917.

Gippius's two poems are separated in the notebook by five pages of miscellaneous reflections. After a note on the secret of artistic creation comes a maxim on the inverse relationship between material and spiritual wealth, followed by a generalization about the national character of the English (bent on materializing the spiritual), contrasted with the Russians (dedicating to spiritualizing the material). Next comes an entry on a religious sect—not a contemporary sect like the Johannites but an ancient one. The Cainites were a second-century heretical Gnostic movement that regarded the God of the Old Testament as responsible for evil in the world and exalted those who opposed him: Cain, Esau, and Korah. The Cainites are reputed to have had an apocryphal Gospel of Judas, whom they revered for betraying Jesus. The comment in the notebook that the Cainites were right "to underline in the 'Gospel of Judas' that the perfection of an enlightened person cannot express itself in any other way than in the dauntless carrying out of the very highest cruelties" reflects a certain fascination with the connection between enlightenment and cruelty. This observation (of unknown provenance) may have been associated in Prokofieva's mind with the Germans in the First World War; later in the notebooks, she records a note about the German people's misconceived belief in their cultural superiority, their racial arrogance, and their inability to understand anything foreign.

The next fourteen entries in the notebook (apart from Gippius's "The Gray Dress") cover ten pages and consist entirely of quotations or paraphrases of passages from the Russian translation of Schuré's history of esoteric religions, *Les Grands Initiés. Esquisse de l'histoire secrète des religions. Rama— Krishna—Hermès—Moïse—Orphée—Pythagore—Platon—Jésus*, published in Paris in 1889. Schuré (1842–1929), a prominent French theosophist, adhered to the conviction that spirit is the only reality. His wide-ranging survey, based on the belief that the essential truth of all world religions lies in their esoteric content, had great appeal for contemporary audiences in search of nontraditional, syncretic forms of spiritual experience; it was frequently reprinted and translated into several languages. The Russian translation by Elena Pisareva first appeared as an appendix to *Vestnik teosofii* (Bulletin of theosophy) in 1908 and 1909; it was followed by two independent editions published in 1910 and 1914 under the title *Velíkiye posvyashchennïye. Ocherk ezoterizma religiy* (*The Great Initiates. A Study of the Secret History of Religions*).

The appearance of several passages from this work in Prokofieva's notebook is not as odd as it may seem. Many members of the cultural elite in early twentieth-century Russia were attracted to theosophy and admired Schuré's work.[31] His translator was a colleague and friend of the legendary Russian theosophist Anna Mintslova, who exerted a strong influence on Belïy and Vyacheslav Ivanov. Other notable literary figures involved in theosophy were Yekaterina Balmont, Maks Voloshin, and his wife, Margarita Sabashnikova. In the musical world followers of theosophy included Alexander Scriabin (whose unexpected death in April 1915 was widely interpreted as the consummation of his theurgic task in this world), the music critic Leonid Sabaneyev (known to Prokofiev for his scathing reviews of his early work, as well as for his biographies of Scriabin and Taneyev), and the concert pianist Mariya Yudina.

Schuré's friendship with and admiration for Wagner made him popular among Moscow and St. Petersburg music lovers, who read his writings about the composer in translation.[32] Schuré's enthusiasm for Wagner as the herald of the mystery of future art reflected Nietzsche's critical approach to the composer and resonated with the Russian fin-de-siècle Wagner cult.[33] During the 1908 celebrations of the twenty-fifth anniversary of Wagner's death, Prokofiev attended every possible performance of his works, finding himself so overwhelmed that he did not want to listen to anything else afterward.[34]

Finally, note that on the concluding page of his survey of esoteric religions, Schuré singled out Russia and America as devout young nations capable of bringing about the mystical, spiritual revival of the world. This idea would obviously have appealed to Russian readers, as it reinforced their belief in the special mission of their "barbaric" nation, destined to initiate a universal cultural and religious renaissance.

Although Prokofiev is not usually considered to have had much interest in mysticism or philosophy, he was inevitably affected by the atmosphere of his times and keen to expand his intellectual horizons. From 1914 his close friend, the dilettante poet Boris Bashkirov (1891–?, known by his pseudonym Boris Verin), regularly subjected him to long conversations about philosophy and attempted to get him interested in mysticism.[35] Prokofiev's diary provides ample evidence of his exposure to these topics in 1916 and 1917, often under Bashkirov's influence. Shortly before Christmas 1915, for example, he went along with his friend to the flat of an acquaintance surnamed Semyonov, where a young girl told his fortune, predicting that he would soon be robbed. Prokofiev was initially skeptical, but subsequently amazed when he returned home with his mother on New Year's Day to find that their flat had indeed been ransacked by burglars.[36] Bashkirov liked to attend talks on religion given by Lotin, a popular preacher and mesmerist, and tried to persuade Prokofiev to accompany him. In January 1916 the composer recorded in his diary with a touch of pride that Bashkirov had recommended him to Lotin as a person with a "crystal soul" despite his lack of passion for mysticism.[37] When he finally went along to one of Lotin's lectures in March, he was not impressed, describing the preacher as a "magnificent talking machine" and blanching at his public attack against modern music and his own compositions.[38] Nevertheless, despite these reservations, in October 1916 he began to attend the Monday salons hosted by Bashkirov, where mysticism and philosophy were staple topics of discussion; on his first visit he listened admiringly to the discourses of the music critic Vyacheslav Karatïgin.[39] Around this time he began studying Kant and Schopenhauer in some depth, and regularly met up with Bashkirov in early 1917 to read Schopenhauer's *Aphorisms on the Wisdom of Life*.

In this context it is not entirely surprising to discover that Schuré's history of esoteric religions was one of the books Prokofiev chose to take with him in July 1916 when he set off on a boat trip down the Volga with Bashkirov. While traveling on his own between Samara and Astrakhan and conversing with fellow passengers, he amused himself by adopting different identities, including that of a landowner studying theology; on this new persona he commented in his diary: "I was indeed reading Schuré's 'Great Initiates.'"[40] We may well wonder, therefore, about the status and purpose of the extracts from this work in his mother's notebook. Was she reading Schuré's book independently and taking notes from it for her own benefit? Or was she transcribing for her son passages that he had marked or noted down separately during his own reading of the book?

On balance, the evidence points toward the second hypothesis, particularly given the content of the passages chosen for inclusion in the notebook. Two extracts are taken from the introduction, and the remaining twelve come from the sections on Rama (two), Krishna (three), Moses (two), and Plato (five). Among the various topics covered, several are remarkably close to Prokofiev's own interests at the time, as recorded in his diary, and reflect his growing preoccupation with the moral foundations of life and art. Such topics include the relationship between male passion and monogamy, the primary importance of good deeds as the achievement of a righteous person, the link between spiritual greatness and loneliness, romantic love, the superiority of moral good over aesthetic beauty, and the association between eternal youthfulness, intellectual depth, and purity of heart. Besides these extracts, the reference to Julian Ochorowicz's book on mental suggestion, lifted from Schuré's work, reflects the interest in hypnosis that had been inspired by Karatïgin's discussion of this subject at Bashkirov's salon in October 1916.[41]

It is also significant that the next entry in the notebook is a poem composed by Prokofiev (dated July 18, 1916) about a personal incident at the end of the Volga trip. Prokofieva must have transcribed this poem from a copy given to her by her son, since this was not a text that she could otherwise have known. If she was doing this for him, then she might just as well have been copying out passages from Schuré's book on his behalf.

Prokofiev took satisfaction in his poetic prowess and knowledge of versification—in 1922 he commented in his diary that had he not become a composer he would probably have been a writer or poet.[42] His poem, described by him as "the most foolish tale of a sleeping monster" (*preglupaya skazka o spyashchem urode*), is a lighthearted parody of the tale of the sleeping beauty and a remarkably accomplished piece of humorous verse. In the course of twenty-five beautifully crafted rhyming couplets it tells the tale of two friends, the "chatterbox poet Boryunya" and his friend "the dashing Sergunya," who are waiting on the Volga for a ship to carry them across the Caspian Sea the next day to a "land ruled by shahs":[43]

урод-поэт и друг урода
Спокойно ждали парохода,
Который их под «охи-ахи»
Свезет в страну, где правят шахи.

The monster-poet and the monster's friend
Were calmly waiting for a ship
Which to the sound of "ohs" and "ahs"
Would take them to a land ruled by shahs.

Boryunya promises his friend to rise early the next morning to board the ship. However, the "poetic creature" suffers all night from strange eruptions in his stomach. In the morning, when Sergunya, punctual to the minute, arrives to wake him, his friend is in a deep sleep, breathing heavily and even dribbling. Sergunya sprinkles him with cold water but fails to wake him; as a result Sergunya sails across the Caspian Sea while Borya continues to sleep, "curled up like a pretzel."

The background to this amusing poem can be reconstructed from Prokofiev's references to his Volga trip with Bashkirov in his correspondence and diary. By July 16, 1916, the two friends had reached Astrakhan, where they expected to sail the Caspian the following morning. Bashkirov overslept, however, and refused to get up when Prokofiev splashed him with cold water.[44] As a result, Prokofiev sailed alone on July 17 without his friend. He did not travel to Baku as originally planned; instead, he disembarked at Petrovsk at midday on July 18 and caught a train to Tiflis.[45]

Since his poem is dated July 18, he must have written it either at sea or on the train, evidently to exorcise the memory of this unfortunate incident through humor; certainly, when he met up again with Bashkirov in August in Petrograd, no mention was made of their "Astrakhan argument" and their learned conversations resumed as before.[46]

The next couple of entries are drier and more serious in tone; they consist of detailed information about the planet Venus and its relationship to the sun, followed by a note on Galileo's development of Archimedes' teachings on the movements of bodies. We know that Prokofiev developed a passion for astronomy and observation of the stars in 1916 and 1917. In the absence of any evidence of his mother sharing this enthusiasm, these two entries offer further indication that she used her notebook to record materials of primary interest to her son. In October 1916 Prokofiev noted in his diary: "I have become very interested in the stars. Astronomy has always attracted me. I have now got hold of Ignatev's book and have enthusiastically started to study the stars in the sky, learning their names and drawing constellations on paper. Alas, last week the sky was cloudy every evening."[47] Ignatev's book was a popular illustrated guide to astronomy and observation of the stars published that year in Petrograd.[48] In February 1917 Prokofiev recorded once more in his diary that he was reading a book on astronomy and had always been attracted to this subject.[49] In May he remarked on the rapid growth of his enthusiasm; after buying an excellent portable telescope for two hundred rubles, he repeatedly attempted to map the night sky in Petrograd and his country retreat near Sablino.[50] In the same month he wrote to his close friend and colleague Nikolay Myaskovsky: "Having finished twenty *Visions fugitives* and having dashed off a Violin Concerto, I have now lost heart and, having bought a telescope, watch the stars. I'm very engrossed with this pastime."[51] The comments in the notebook on the planet Venus evidently relate to this period; its relative proximity to Earth allowed it to be observed by telescope.

Although Prokofieva's notebook was compiled at the time of the First World War and two Russian revolutions, it is surprisingly free of references to contemporary events. The only two entries alluding to the unsettled historical backdrop occur at this point in the notebook. The details of a second lieutenant in the Life-Guards 1st Rifles Regiment serve as an indirect reminder of Prokofieva's constant worries that her son might be called up to the army.[52] The negative comment on the Germans' false faith in their culture and racial arrogance was no doubt linked to the German advance on Petrograd, and perhaps also to the discussion of national pride in Schopenhauer's *Aphorisms on the Wisdom of Life*, since this work is the source of the next thirteen entries in the notebook.

The next section provides valuable insight into Schopenhauer's place in the development of Prokofiev's worldview. Schopenhauer, both on his own and as filtered through Nietzsche and Wagner, exerted a strong influence on the Russian intelligentsia. His followers included Turgenev, Fet, Tolstoy, and several other turn-of-the-century writers; numerous editions of his works appeared in Russian translation from the 1880s onward.[53] Prokofiev first heard about the philosopher from his close friend Maximilian Schmidthof. He spent the evening of his twenty-second birthday in April 1913 with Max, who captivated him with his account of Schopenhauer's life and thought.[54] As Prokofiev later commented, he was initially wary of following his friend's advice to read the philosopher because of the latter's reputation as "hopelessly pessimistic."[55] The news of Schmidthof's suicide, which reached him on April 27, just over a fortnight after their conversation about Schopenhauer, can only have reinforced this association.[56]

Prokofiev returned to Schopenhauer three years later, this time under the influence of Bashkirov. In September 1916 he noted in his diary that they had embarked on a joint reading of the *Aphorisms on the Wisdom of Life*, which he liked very much and wanted to return to once more, since a cursory reading was insufficient to do it justice.[57] The joint reading carried on throughout the winter during his visits to Bashkirov's home.[58] As his diary entry of February 1917 indicates, reading Schopenhauer provided him with a welcome escape and refuge from the increasingly unsettled political atmosphere: "So, everything passed peacefully and quietly, Boris Verin and I regularly read Schopenhauer, enjoying him, and only vague rumors circulated about strikes and a movement among the workers of Petrograd factories."[59] Two months later, in April 1917, he visited Bashkirov once more "for a traditional reading of Schopenhauer with him. That is to say, strictly speaking, he reads (and very well), while I either sit in a deep armchair by the fireplace or lie on the sofa." On this occasion the presence of other members of the family and guests caused the two friends to retire to the study, preferring the company of Schopenhauer to empty social chatter.[60] In May Prokofiev moved out of Petrograd to the countryside, taking Schopenhauer with him: "On the fourteenth I arrived at the dacha and once more plunged into my musical work, green walks, and reading Schopenhauer. I am reading his 'Aphorisms on the Wisdom of Life,' 'Parerga,' and 'Paralipomena' for the second time; I mark them up in pencil and cannot tear myself away from them."[61] A week later he set off on a two-week trip along the Volga and Kama rivers. En route from Kazan to Perm his main reading was Schopenhauer's *Parerga et Paralipomena*; he particularly enjoyed the "brilliant chapter on fame" and the "subtle one on physiognomy," but found the chapter about women less convincing and insufficiently broad in its aims.[62] As in the case of Schuré's book, studied during the previous summer's trip along the Volga, Prokofiev seemed to find sailing along rivers conducive to the reading of serious works on religion and philosophy.

The same entry for May 1917 contains a remarkable passage, unparalleled in Prokofiev's diary, involving an extended analysis of his response to Schopenhauer's teachings. He comments that reading the philosopher's works had "huge significance" for him, marking a new stage in his life and enabling him to acquire a "most perfect equilibrium," as a result of which he could now stand firmly on his own two feet. Instead of being overwhelmed by Schopenhauer's pessimism, his initial fear, he experienced the opposite: he now saw all phenomena with greater clarity and awareness, knew how to value and enjoy what he had, and fully understood and accepted the principle of the ancients "to consider the absence of the sad as happiness, and to consider anything more as a pleasant surprise." Schopenhauer also taught him how to achieve peace of mind by adopting a philosophical approach to the ups and downs of everyday life. As an example, he cites the equanimity with which he received the news during his river trip that Alexander Kerensky, the Minister of War, was planning to send fresh groups of recruits under forty to the front.[63] A few months later, writing from the Caucasus in November 1917, he explained how he managed to sustain a similar feeling of "spiritual equilibrium" by reading philosophy and composing music, despite disturbing news of the spread of Bolshevik vandalism all over Russia and carnage in Moscow.[64]

In June 1917 Prokofiev tried to read Schopenhauer's *The World as Will and Representation* (1818) but gave up in order to follow the philosopher's advice and tackle his preliminary work instead, *On the Fourfold Root of the Principle of Sufficient Reason* (1813).[65] A year later, in June 1918, while waiting for an American visa in Japan, he resumed reading *The World as Will and Representation* for one or two hours a day (apparently, this was the only book he had with him).[66] He described finishing the book in July as "an event in my life"; although he was smitten with Schopenhauer's ideas, he still found it difficult to accept his pessimism, particularly the idea of life in this world as a form of suffering rather than joy.[67]

As Izraíl Nestyev correctly observed, Prokofiev was more interested in Schopenhauer's maxims for practical life than in his cult of pessimism and views on the Will.[68] Reading the philosopher's works helped him to develop a personal code of behavior, based on heightened introspection and self-awareness. We can see from his diary entry of September 1917 just how conscious he was of the way Schopenhauer had defined his approach to life, and how deliberately he strove to model his own behavior on the philosopher's teachings. Seeking to explain how a young man of call-up age could be so happy and carefree at a time of war, revolution, civil strife, and hunger, he offered: "With his truths Schopenhauer gave me a spiritual world and an awareness of happiness: do not run after happiness—strive to avoid sadness. How many possibilities are promised by this truth! And how many amazing surprises does life prepare for the person who recognizes this truth and immerses himself in it!"[69] Schopenhauer's emphasis on solitude as a positive state to be embraced by the gifted individual, together with his relentless exposure of the illusions of reputation and fame, were doubtless also relevant to the composer's growing awareness of his talent and attempt to define his place in society.

What, then, should the reader make of the aphorisms in Mariya Prokofieva's notebook? Were they copied for her own benefit or as a record of her son's response to reading Schopenhauer? As with the extracts from Schuré's book, the second hypothesis is more persuasive, and in this case the evidence is even more compelling. Since we know that Prokofiev marked his favorite aphorisms in pencil while reading them at his dacha in May 1917, it is not difficult to envisage his mother transcribing them from the copy read by her son. Two factors in particular suggest a close connection between the aphorisms recorded in the notebook and Prokofiev's own reading of the work.

The first, most obvious factor is the overlap between the contents of the notebook and various comments in Prokofiev's diary on his response to Schopenhauer. The passages cited in the notebook are drawn from chapters 2, 4, and 5 of *Aphorisms on the Wisdom of Life* and cover topics close to Prokofiev's heart: the envy of personal qualities, the link between the richness of an individual's inner world and his unsociability, the power of beauty, the closed mind of the philistine, the difference between pride and vanity, the illusion of rank and public opinion, the relationship between suffering and happiness, the way to achieve earthly happiness and peace of mind, the clash between fashionable "good form" and common sense, and the opposition between nature's order of precedence and artificial social hierarchies. Many of these topics are also touched on in Prokofiev's diary. Compare, for example, the discussion of happiness as the absence of pain, introduced in the notebook by a quotation from Aristotle, "The prudent man aims at painlessness not pleasure," with the following comment in Prokofiev's diary from May 1917: "I accepted one principle of the ancients developed by him [Schopenhauer]: not to demand extra happiness, but to consider the absence of the sad as happiness."[70]

The second factor relates to a postcard that Prokofiev sent to his friend Eleonora Damskaya in Petrograd from Kislovodsk on October 10, 1917. After describing his recent travels in the Caucasus and the pleasant room he had occupied in the Grand Hotel of Kislovodsk, where his mother would join him, he added an important request in a postscript: "Be kind, send M[ariya] G[rigoryevna] the little book by Schopenhauer, the one with the aphorisms, as my copy has been borrowed by Diederichs."[71] Andrey Diederichs, the concert promoter and co-owner of the Gebrüder Diederichs piano factory in St. Petersburg, spent a few days with Prokofiev in Kislovodsk at the beginning of October 1917; according to Prokofiev, he was exceptionally friendly but evidently left without returning his copy of the aphorisms.[72] The fact that Prokofiev wanted Damskaya to send his mother another copy of the same work reveals its importance; perhaps he needed his mother to have the book so that she could continue to transcribe his favorite aphorisms.

Prokofiev clearly valued keeping a record of his response to Schopenhauer's aphorisms, not just because of their intrinsic interest but also because of the association in his mind between reading Schopenhauer in the summer of 1917 and working on *Seven, They Are Seven* (*Semero ikh*, 1917–18), his cantata setting of an ancient Akkadian incantation against seven evil spirits, rendered into Russian by Balmont. In his diary for 1917 these two activities are frequently juxtaposed. In April 1917, after noting his plan to spend the summer working on the incantation, he describes reading Schopenhauer together with Bashkirov.[73] In November, now in Kislovodsk, he records in quick succession his joy and sense of reverence at taking up "his beloved Schopenhauer's" *World as Will and Representation* and, in parallel, starting work on November 10 on the detailed outline of *Seven, They Are Seven*.[74] A few years later, with the benefit of hindsight, the casual pairing between Schopenhauer and his cantata crystallized into an underlying causal connection. In December 1922, distraught at the thought that his diary from September 1916 to February 1917 might not have survived, he tried to reconstruct the details of its contents: "In my diary my notes on reading Schopenhauer with B[oris] N[ikolayevich], starting with the 'Aphorisms on the Wisdom of Life' and continuing with *The World as Will and Representation*, have been lost. During that winter I was often at B.N.'s home and we spent our evenings reading Schopenhauer. I was very drawn to this reading and deepened by it. It gave birth to the summer of 1917, spent in solitude—and *Seven, They Are Seven* was the result."[75]

Prokofiev's association of the impact of Schopenhauer with the genesis of *Seven, They Are Seven* is telling. The association is indirectly confirmed by his mother's notebook, where the text of the incantation used in the cantata was copied immediately after the philosopher's aphorisms. The plan to set the incantation to music evolved from Prokofiev's long-standing admiration for Balmont's verse and relationship to him. He set three Balmont poems to music during his student days at the Conservatory (opp. 7 and 9, 1909–10). As in the case of Schopenhauer, Bashkirov subsequently played a significant role in encouraging Prokofiev's enthusiasm for the poet; an ardent fan of Balmont, he knew more of his poems by heart than the author himself, and enjoyed reading his verse aloud to his friend.[76]

Prokofiev first met Balmont on February 5, 1916, at the home of the Russian-born English conductor Albert Coates. He was flattered when the famous poet asked him whether he was indeed "the hope of Russian music" about whom he had heard so much. Prokofiev told him that he had turned two of his poems into songs and played his setting of "Yest' inïye planetï . . ." (There are other planets . . .), op. 9, thereby earning the poet's approval.[77] A few months later, in October 1916, he encountered "le grand Konstantin Balmontin" once more, this time at the home of the singer Ivan Alchevsky; Balmont seemed keen to foster the young composer's musical interest in his verse, for he recited some of his latest sonnets and recommended them as song texts.[78] Soon afterward, on November 7, Balmont invited Prokofiev to visit him at home and gave him a copy of a booklet he had written inscribed "To the magician of sounds, S. S. Prokofiev, in whose lofty talent I believe."[79] Given the inscription, it would appear that the booklet was Balmont's treatise on the links between poetry, magic, and music, *Poeziya kak volshebstvo* (Poetry as magic, 1915), which served as the source of the version of the incantation set by Prokofiev to music, using the same text that his mother copied into her notebook.

In early February 1917 Prokofiev played a recital in Moscow attended by Balmont. At a gathering held afterward in the home of Bashkirov's sister, Prokofiev promised Balmont that he would set his incantation to music for male voice, choir, and orchestra and noted the "strong impression" made on him by this work.[80] As he later recalled in his diary, Balmont laconically responded, "You are daring."[81]

From this much we can already establish that Prokofiev definitely knew the text of the incantation by February 1917, and had almost certainly come across it during the previous year, most probably in November 1916 when Balmont gave him a copy of the booklet in which it was published. This conjecture fits well with the position of the incantation in the notebook; it comes after Prokofiev's humorous poem of July 18, 1916, and follows the excerpts from the aphorisms, which we know he was actively engaged in reading with Bashkirov between September 1916 and February 1917.

In April 1917, amid rumors that the Germans were about to enter Petrograd, Prokofiev noted in his diary a "definite" plan to set the incantation to music "with a large choir" during the summer.[82] He was evidently undeterred by his new acquaintance Mayakovsky, who bluntly informed him at their first meeting earlier in the month that he composed wonderful music, but to "appalling texts" by "all sorts of Balmonts," and promised to introduce him to some "real contemporary poetry."[83]

A few months later, in August 1917, Prokofiev met Balmont in the park in Kislovodsk and discussed his plans for the cantata, including precise details of his setting of the incantation. He wondered whether having the choir repeat the last words sung by the tenor (representing the priest) would work with the words *Zemli oni* (of the Earth they), as this phrase was meaningless on its own. Balmont reassured him that the repetitions would sound natural and should be retained.[84] When the poet had breakfast with Prokofiev and his mother at their dacha a few days later, he read his incantation aloud at the composer's request, placing special emphasis on the horror of its content. Prokofiev listened attentively, but did not find the poet's reading as overwhelming as he had expected. He wanted to incorporate some elements of Balmont's recitation into his setting, in particular his frightening whisper at the beginning and the rhythm and intonation he used for the repetition of the key phrases *semero ikh* (seven they are) and *Zemli oni*. Balmont told Prokofiev that he had published different versions of the incantation in three of his books and that the composer could use any version or combination thereof in his cantata.[85]

At this stage Prokofiev hoped to finish his setting of the incantation by the autumn of 1917.[86] It actually took him another five months. On September 4, 1917, while still in Petrograd, he began to compose, planning the "general outlines" of the cantata before, rather than after, sketching the music. In his diary he provided an unusually detailed chronological breakdown of the initial stages of his work until the completion of the first draft on September 15.[87] On September 23 he arrived in the Caucasus; in the mornings he worked on *Seven, They Are Seven* and then read Kant; at this stage the "skeleton" of the musical setting began to grow "muscles."[88] By November, under the influence of Schopenhauer, the skeleton had grown into a fully developed "body."[89] On December 13 he finished the draft and, at the end of the month, copied it.[90] In early January he was still at work on the cantata, only completing it on January 13/26, 1918.[91] *Seven, They Are Seven* was first published in Moscow in 1922, with the belated premiere taking place in Paris on May 29, 1924, under the direction of Serge Koussevitzky.

The details of the relationship of the text copied out in Prokofieva's notebook, the various versions of the incantation published by Balmont (in 1908, 1910, 1915, and 1923), and the text printed in the first and second editions of the musical setting (in 1922 and 1933) are complex to unravel.[92] The section of the incantation copied out in the notebook (twenty-one lines) reproduces with a few variations the first twenty-five lines of Balmont's second version of the incantation, published in his booklet of 1915.[93] Prokofieva may have copied this text after Balmont gave a copy of the booklet to her son, in November 1916, or when he recited the incantation to both of them at their dacha in Kislovodsk in August 1917. The text subsequently published in the two editions of the musical setting is also largely based on the second version, with the addition of a few lines from the first version of

1908.[94] Although the two manuscripts of the setting, preserved in Prokofiev's archive, carry a dedication to Balmont, it was not included in either of the printed editions.[95]

In his short autobiography, written for a Soviet audience in 1941, Prokofiev represented *Seven, They Are Seven* as the result of a desire to compose something on a grand, cosmic scale in response to the revolutionary events rocking Russia.[96] This retrospective gloss does not quite tally with the evidence, however. Most of the entries in his diary at the time suggest that his work on the cantata resulted from a conscious decision to *detach* himself from (rather than respond to) contemporary upheavals. This was a lesson he had learned from Schopenhauer—an association clearly reflected in the juxtaposition of the aphorisms and the text of the incantation in his mother's notebook. In his diary entry of August 1917 he wonders briefly why the ancient Accadian incantation came to light after thousands of years "to resound once more, and perhaps still more threateningly than ever" at this particular time, but does not pursue this line of thought.[97] Although he may have sensed the possible connection between the evil spirits ruling the world, described in Balmont's incantation, and the destructive forces unleashed during the First World War and the revolutions of 1917, he did not make this link explicit anywhere in his comments on the cantata.

The incantation is followed by a short, humorous poem of two quatrains in trochaic tetrameter, penned by Prokofiev in Kislovodsk on the last day of 1917. This is the closing entry of the notebook and the only one written in the composer's own hand. Prokofiev spent New Year's Eve first with his mother, in whose company he evidently composed the poem and inscribed it in her notebook, and then with his Italian friend, Lina Collini, discussing her suggestion that he move to America. In late December 1917, while working on the final stages of *Seven, They Are Seven*, he became increasingly enthusiastic about the idea of this move: "Going to America! Of course! Here—everything is turning sour, there—life is bubbling away, here—butchery and savagery, there—cultural life. . . . No hesitations. I'm going in the spring. . . . And so under this flag I saw in the New Year. Surely it will not destroy my wishes?"[98] In the first entry of his diary for January 1918 he described his New Year's Eve celebrations in a similar vein: "Interesting company, shooting, lots of fun. America is getting stronger and becoming firmly established—and probably not in the spring, but the sooner the better."[99]

Prokofiev's poem responds to the turbulent backdrop; although light and amusing in tone, it contains thinly veiled allusions to political upheavals. In his self-imposed exile in the Caucasus, far from the capital, he imagines arranging an alternative "parade" and ascending Mount Ararat to celebrate the New Year. As the highest mountain in the area and traditional resting place of Noah's Ark after the deluge (Gen. 8:4), Ararat was a fitting symbol for a safe haven in which to begin the New Year or a new life, following the "liquidation" of the old order. In the Bible Ararat is also known as one of the righteous kingdoms, called upon by the prophet Jeremiah to rise up with other nations to defend Zion against corrupt and powerful Babylon (Jer. 51:27).

Biblical and apocalyptic imagery of this sort was frequently invoked by writers during the revolutions; Prokofiev's lighthearted parody goes hand in hand with an underlying strain of serious intent. We know from the diary entries written in Kislovodsk that he saw his new home as a place of refuge from the turmoil that was sweeping through his adopted hometown of Petrograd and the rest of Russia. At first the Caucasus seemed to be out of reach from the distant upheavals, a blessed sanctuary where he could achieve "spiritual equilibrium" by reading Schopenhauer and working on *Seven, They Are Seven.* By the end of November 1917, however, he was clearly worried that the fast approaching tidal wave of Bolshevik forces would submerge his beloved Kislovodsk and destroy his peace.[100] A few months later, still planning his escape to America, he compared the Caucasus to an island surrounded by a raging sea.[101]

In the second verse of his poem Prokofiev extends an invitation to "our Semyon" to come and join him in his refuge. Although Semyon is not identified, the name may be a private reference to Balmont, whom Prokofiev linked with the number seven (*sem'*) as the author of the incantation "Seven, They Are Seven."[102] The poet asks whether Semyon is "among friends or among the beasts," evidently alluding to the different factions dividing Russia. Prokofiev was not one to take sides in politics; as he noted in his diary in August 1917, "I am not a counterrevolutionary and not a revolutionary and I do not stand on one side or the other."[103] Nevertheless, he heartily disliked all forms of coercion and instinctively resisted the pressure to conform. In 1917 orthography became a political issue; to the builders of the new regime, the new spelling visibly denoted the shining world of the future, marking the break with the old on paper. We know from Prokofiev's conversation with Balmont in Kislovodsk in August 1917 that he strongly opposed the orthography reforms introduced by the Bolsheviks in the summer and even published an "indignant" newspaper article attacking them.[104] In his poem he demonstrates an oblique resistance to the demands of the new regime by deliberately confusing the old spelling rules with the new ones and introducing an entirely new rule of his own invention.[105]

Prokofiev's New Year poem serves as a fitting end to this remarkable notebook; it leaves the reader with a vivid sense of the young composer, bursting with humor and creative energy, poised on the verge of leaving his old world for a new one. As a whole, the notebook offers valuable insight into Mariya Prokofieva's close involvement in the varied literary, philosophical and musical interests that shaped her son's world at the time of the Revolution—a tangible demonstration of her abiding loyalty to Taneyev's injunction to look after his talents.

NOTES TO THE INTRODUCTION

I am indebted to Noëlle Mann for asking me to undertake research on the notebook and for her constant guidance and support, to Serge Prokofiev Jr. for his helpful advice, and to Olga Kuznetsova for her kind assistance in St. Petersburg. I am also grateful to the School of Slavonic and East European Studies, University College London, for granting me one term's sabbatical leave from September to December 2006 to work on this project.

1. For a detailed account of the papers brought to Prokofiev by his mother in 1920, see Sergey Prokof'yev, *Dnevnik 1907–1933*, ed. Svyatoslav Prokof'yev, 2 vols. (Paris: Serge Prokofiev Estate, 2002), 2:113, 607.

2. For Prokofiev's description of his mother's handwriting, see Prokof'yev, "Avtobiografiya," in *S. S. Prokof'yev: Materialï, dokumentï, vospominaniya*, ed. S. I. Shlifshteyn (Moscow: Gosudarstvennoye muzïkal'noye izdatel'stvo, 1961), 19. The handwriting in the notebook was identified as Mariya Prokofieva's on the basis of comparison with other examples of her writing: letters from her, held by the Prokofiev Estate, and two pages from another notebook kept by her (listing addresses as well as birthdays, name days, and wedding dates falling in April), were kindly supplied by Serge Prokofiev Jr.

3. Prokof'yev, "Avtobiografiya," 16–17.

4. Ibid., 18–19.

5. Ibid., 24. See also R. Glier, "Vospominaniya o S. S. Prokof'yeve," in *S. S. Prokof'yev: Materialï, dokumentï, vospominaniya*, 351.

6. Glier, "Vospominaniya," 354.

7. Prokof'yev, "Avtobiografiya," 25–26.

8. Ibid., 24.

9. Ibid., 53.

10. Prokof'yev, *Dnevnik*, 1:127 (entry of August 10, 1910).

11. Prokof'yev, "Avtobiografiya," 26, 53.

12. M. G. Prokof'yeva, "Vospominaniya o detstve i yunosti Sergeya Prokof'yeva," in *S. S. Prokof'yev: Materialï, dokumentï, vospominaniya*, 331–33; Prokof'yev, "Avtobiografiya," 36, 38, 62.

13. Prokof'yev, "Avtobiografiya," 46.

14. M. K. Morolyova, "Vospominaniya o S. S. Prokof'yeve i yego roditelyakh," in *S. S. Prokof'yev: Materialï, dokumentï, vospominaniya*, 347.

15. Prokof'yeva, "Vospominaniya," 333, 338–39; Prokof'yev, "Avtobiografiya," 28.

16. Prokof'yev, "Avtobiografiya," 78.

17. Prokof'yev, "Avtobiografiya," 69; Prokof'yeva, "Vospominaniya," 335–36; Glier, "Vospominaniya," 350–51.

18. Prokof'yev, "Avtobiografiya," 135–36.

19. Morolyova, "Vospominaniya," 349.

20. Prokof'yev, *Dnevnik*, 1:127 (entry of August 10, 1910).

21. Morolyova, "Vospominaniya," 349.

22. Glier, "Vospominaniya," 351.

23. Ibid., 356.

24. Prokof'yev, "Avtobiografiya," 79.

25. Prokof'yeva, "Vospominaniya," 336; Prokof'yev, "Avtobiografiya," 65, repeated on 133.

26. Prokof'yev, *Avtobiografiya*, ed. Miral'da Kozlova (Moscow: Klassika-XXI, 2007), 6.

27. Prokofiev contrasted the intimate simplicity of his setting of Akhmatova's poems with the multilayered complexities of op. 23, which contained his setting of another poem by Gippius from the same cycle. Prokof'yev, *Dnevnik*, 1:623 (entry of November 3, 1916).

28. Harlow Robinson, *Sergey Prokofiev: A Biography* (London: Robert Hale, 1987), 116.

29. "Iz rannikh pisem S. S. Prokof'yeva," in *Sergey Prokof'yev: Stat'i i materialï*, ed. I. V. Nest'yev and G. Ya. Edel'man (Moscow: Izdatel'stvo "Muzïka," 1965), 323.

30. On March 14, 1916, the singer Ivan Alchevsky visited Prokofiev to hear the romances he was going to perform. Prokofiev records that Alchevsky did not like the first two songs of the cycle, including Gippius's "The Gray Dress," and referred to them as "socialist romances." Prokof'yev, *Dnevnik*, 1:597.

31. On the widespread influence of theosophy in Russia, see Maria Carlson, *"No Religion Higher Than Truth": A History of the Theosophical Movement in Russia, 1875–1922* (Princeton: Princeton University Press, 1993).

32. See Eduard Shiure, *Rikhard Vagner i yego muzïkal'naya drama*, trans. from French by Baroness N. M. Rozen, ed. with an introductory essay by A. F. Kal' (St. Petersburg and Moscow: M. O. Vol'f, [1909]); Shiure, *Drama Rikharda Vagnera "Tristan i Izol'da" (Ocherk)*, trans. and preface by Viktor Kolomiytsov (Moscow and St. Petersburg: Yurgenson, 1909). This booklet was a recycled chapter from Schuré's 1886 book *Le Drame musical*.

33. See Rosamund Bartlett, *Wagner and Russia* (Cambridge: Cambridge University Press, 1995).

34. Prokof'yev, *Dnevnik*, 1:46 (entry of April 3, 1908).

35. Ibid., 1:509, 531 (entries of October 8 and November 30, 1914).

36. Ibid., 1:575 (entry of January 2, 1916).

37. Ibid., 1:583 (entry of January 26, 1916).

38. Ibid., 1:598 (entry of March 15, 1916).

39. Ibid., 1:619 (entry of October 3, 1916).

40. Ibid., 1:615 (entry of July 1916).

41. Ibid., 1:619 (entry of October 3, 1916).

42. Ibid., 2:207 (entry of February 25–November 23, 1922).

43. The four introductory lines are composed in amphibrachic tetrameter with dactylic and feminine rhymes, and the remaining forty-six lines are written in iambic tetrameter with feminine rhymes throughout.

44. Prokof'yev, *Dnevnik*, 1:615 (entry of July 1916). Prokofiev was evidently used to splashing his friend with cold water to wake him up; he recorded a similar episode in June 1916 (1:614).

45. Ibid., 1:615 (entry of July 1916).

46. Ibid., 1:617 (entry of August 1916).

47. Ibid., 1:621 (entry of October 23, 1916).

48. E. I. Ignat'yev, *V tsarstve zvyozd i svetil. Nablyudatel'naya astronomiya dlya vsekh* (Petrograd: Izdaniye T-va A. S. Suvorina "Novoye vremya," 1916).

49. Prokof'yev, *Dnevnik*, 1:639.

50. Ibid., 1:650–51.

51. Letter of May 4, 1917, in *Selected Letters of Sergei Prokofiev*, trans., ed., and introduction by Harlow Robinson (Boston: Northeastern University Press, 1998), 247.

52. See the references in Prokof'yev, *Dnevnik*, 1:521–23, 527 (entries of November 5, 9, and 20, 1914). As the only son of a widow Prokofiev managed to avoid conscription, unlike his friend Nikolay Myaskovsky.

53. See Sigrid Maurer, "Schopenhauer in Russia: His Influence on Turgenev, Fet and Tolstoy" (PhD diss., University of California at Berkeley, 1966); Joachim T. Baer, *Arthur Schopenhauer und die russische Literatur des späten 19. und frühen 20. Jahrhunderts* (Munich: Otto Sagner, 1980).

54. Prokof'yev, *Dnevnik*, 1:260 (entry of April 11, 1913).

55. Ibid., 1:654 (entry of May 1917).

56. Ibid., 1:270 (entry of April 27, 1913).

57. Ibid., 1:618 (entry of September 1916).

58. Ibid., 2:213 (entry of December 17, 1922).

59. Ibid., 1:639.

Pamela Davidson

60. Ibid., 1:648 (entry of April 1917, referring to April 22).
61. Ibid., 1:652 (entry of May 1917). *Aphorisms on the Wisdom of Life (Aphorismen zur Lebensweisheit)* is the sixth and last book of the first volume of *Parerga and Paralipomena* (1851), a two-volume collection of essays, dialogues, and aphorisms.
62. Ibid., 1:654 (entry of May 1917). The essays "On Judgement, Criticism, Approbation, and Fame," "On Physiognomy," and "On Women" are all in the second volume of *Parerga and Paralipomena.*
63. Ibid., 1:654.
64. Ibid., 1:677.
65. Ibid., 1:657 (entry of June 1917).
66. Ibid., 1:712 (entry of June 10/23, 1918).
67. Ibid., 1:716 (entry of July 1/14, 1918).
68. I. V. Nest'yev, *Prokof'yev* (Moscow: Gosudarstvennoye muzïkal'noye izdatel'stvo, 1957), 157.
69. Prokof'yev, *Dnevnik*, 1:671.
70. Ibid., 1:654.
71. A copy of the original postcard, held in the archive of the Glinka Museum in Moscow, was kindly faxed by Irina Medvedeva to Noëlle Mann. The text of the postcard is partly published (without the full text of the postscript) in *Selected Letters of Sergei Prokofiev*, 32.
72. Prokof'yev, *Dnevnik*, 1:674 (entry of October 1917).
73. Ibid., 1:648.
74. Ibid., 1:677.
75. Ibid., 2:213 (entry of December 17, 1922).
76. Ibid., 1:516, 667 (entries of October 22, 1914, and August 1917).
77. Ibid., 1:586 (entry of February 5, 1916).
78. Ibid., 1:622 (entry of October 28, 1916).
79. "Volshebniku zvukov S. S. Prokof'yevu, v vïsokiy dar kotorogo ya veryu" (ibid., 1:623).
80. Ibid., 1:637–38.
81. Ibid., 1:665, 2:213 (entries of August 1917 and December 16, 1922).
82. Ibid., 1:648.
83. Ibid., 1:646 (entry of April 1917).
84. Ibid., 1:665. The phrase occurs at the end of lines 6, 7, 8 of the text of the incantation copied out in the notebook and is frequently repeated in the published editions of the musical setting (1922, 1925, 1933).
85. Ibid., 1:666–67.
86. Ibid., 1:668.
87. Ibid., 1:670.
88. Ibid., 1:672.
89. Ibid., 1:677.
90. Ibid., 1:677–78.
91. Ibid., 1:681.
92. Balmont created two different Russian versions of the incantation and included them in four of his books, published between 1908 and 1923. In 1908 he published his first version (43 lines), "Akkadiyskaya nadpis'" (Akkadian inscription), in a poetic anthology of ancient texts. K. D. Bal'mont, *Zovï drevnosti: Gimnï, pesni i zamïslï drevnikh* [Calls of antiquity: Hymns, songs, and projects of the ancients] (St. Petersburg: Panteon, 1908), 73–74. In 1910 he republished the opening part (36 lines) of this first version under the same title in his essay, "Chuvstvo rasï v tvorchestve" (The feeling of race in art), dated November 1907. Bal'mont, *Morskoye svecheniye* (St. Petersburg and Moscow: Izdaniye T-va M.O. Vol'f, [1910]), 6–7. This second published text omits seven lines (31, 35, 39–43) from the first version of 1908 and changes the position of one line but does not introduce any new material. In 1915 Balmont published a second, untitled version (42 lines, beginning "Semero ikh! Semero ikh!" [Seven, they are seven! Seven, they are seven!]) in his treatise on the links between poetry, magic, and music. Bal'mont, *Poeziya kak volshebstvo* (Moscow: Skorpion, 1915), 73–74. Approximately 19 lines of this second version are taken from the first version of 1908; the remaining lines are all new. In 1923 Balmont republished both versions under the titles "Akkadiyskoye zaklinaniye. Raznochteniye pervoye" (Akkadian incantation. First delivery), 43 lines, and "Raznochteniye vtoroye" (Second delivery), 42 lines, in an expanded

edition of *Zovï drevnosti: Gimnï, pesni i zamïslï drevnikh* (Berlin: Knigoizdatel'stvo "Slovo," 1923), 115–18. In his preface to the expanded edition, dated spring 1922, Balmont drew attention to the addition of new material, including the second version of the incantation, "incorporated, as the theme, into the magnificent symphony [*sic*] of S. S. Prokofiev, published by S. A. Kusevitskiy." The score was first published by the State Music Publisher in 1922, reprinted by Gutheil in 1925, and reissued in a second revised edition by Édition Russe de Musique in 1933.

93. Five and a half lines are omitted, one line is split into two lines, and two breaks in the layout of the text absent from other editions are included.

94. In this respect the description of the work given on the title page of the first edition of 1922 is misleading, since it only cites *Zovï drevnosti*, the source of Balmont's first version, published in 1908: "Semero ikh (K. Bal'mont: Zovï drevnosti). Kantata dlya dramaticheskogo tenora, smeshannogo khora i bol'shogo orkestra. 1918 g." When Prokofiev came to prepare the second edition of 1933, he marked up and corrected the original title page of 1922, crossing out the word *cantata*, replacing it with "Incantation. Invocation," and writing opposite "Akkadian invocation for dramatic tenor, chorus and large orchestra. Text by K. Balmont (according to an etching on the walls of an Akkadian temple). Composed in 1917, revised in 1933." (Serge Prokofiev Archive). This amended text, together with parallel translations in French and English, appeared on the title page of the second revised edition of 1933; the deletion of the earlier reference to *Zovï drevnosti* reflects Prokofiev drawing more on Balmont's second version of 1915, part of which was copied in his mother's notebook, than on the first version of 1908. The text published in the editions of the musical setting includes all 21 lines of the 1915 text copied in the notebook; four lines taken from the comments in prose which Balmont wrote immediately after the text of the incantation in his 1915 booklet; 22 lines drawn from the remaining 17 lines of the incantation in the 1915 booklet, with some omissions, additions, and repetitions; and a further seven lines taken from the first version, published in 1908 in *Zovï drevnosti*, which were not included in the second version of 1915. The editions of the musical setting also include a new feature, absent from Balmont's two versions: an opening invocation by the choir to "Tetal," evidently a misprint for "Telal," one of the seven evil spirits later addressed by the tenor and choir.

95. Serge Prokofiev Archive, Reels 2 and 5.

96. Prokof'yev, "Avtobiografiya," 159.

97. Prokof'yev, *Dnevnik*, 1:667.

98. Ibid., 1:678 (entry of December 1917).

99. Ibid., 1:681.

100. Ibid.,1:677 (entry of November 1917).

101. Ibid., 1:685 (entry of February 7/20, 1918).

102. On April 2/15, 1918, Prokofiev gave a concert at which he played *Visions fugitives*, inspired by a poem by Balmont. In the dressing room afterward the crowd included a person referred to in Prokofiev's diary as "sam sem' ('Semero ikh')" ("seven himself ['Seven, They Are Seven']")—evidently Balmont (ibid., 1:695).

103. Ibid., 1:669.

104. Ibid., 1:665.

105. For details, see the note to the poem in the transcript of the notebook.

Mariya Prokofieva's literary notebook was begun in 1913 or 1914 and completed on December 31, 1917, the date of the last entry. All the pages are in her handwriting, apart from the last entry, written in Prokofiev's hand.

The notebook is bound in reinforced black calico and measures 8.5 cm x 13.8 cm. It comprises 116 unnumbered pages (i.e., 58 sheets, recto and verso); only pages 1–43 were used, pages 44–116 are blank. In the transcript of the notebook's contents that follows, published with permission from the Serge Prokofiev Estate, each page of the original is identified by a number in square brackets, placed immediately before the text that appears on that page. The inside front cover is not included in this pagination, which starts with the first right-hand page at [1]. Square brackets are also used to indicate material added by the editor, such as letters or punctuation omitted in the original.

The transcript is accompanied by an English translation, and followed by notes on the source of the entries and their relation to Prokofiev's interests and creative work at the time.

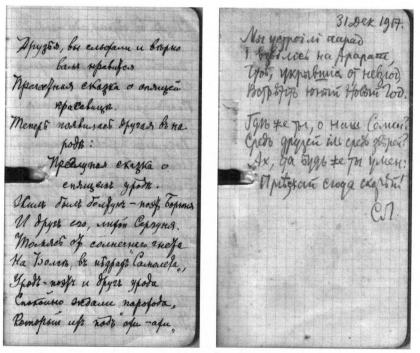

Figure 1. Facsimile of pages 23 and 43 of the notebook, showing Mariya Prokofieva's handwriting (left) and that of her son (right).

Tenir un carnet de dépenses.[1]

[1]

Книги

Saffray. Leçons de choses. 2 vol.

Livre du maître contenant 44 leçons méthodiques avec questionnaires.
1 f.50.

Livre de l'élève contenant le résumé de 44 leçons avec questionnaires.
341 gravures   1 f.50.[3]

Goffmann[4]

Quatrelles. Le parfait causeur.[5]

[2]

[3]

Сергея Рафаловича

Чувство бытия.   Письма женщин

Он унаследовал от отца живой, горячий темперамент, редкую
жизнерадостность и сильно развитое *чувство бытия*. Чувство бытия
– самое драгоценное, самое отрадное, самое прекрасное из всех
наших чувств ... Его менее всего знают, менее всего ищут, менее

Keep a notebook of expenses.[1]

[Photograph of Sergey Alekseyevich Prokofiev][2]

[1]

Books

Saffray. Object Lessons. 2 vols.

Teacher's book containing 44 systematic lessons with questionnaires.

1 f.50.

Pupil's book containing the summary of 44 lessons with questionnaires.
341 engravings 1 f.50.[3]

Goffmann[4]

Quatrelles. The perfect conversationalist.[5]

[Photograph of Mariya Grigoryevna Prokofieva][6]

[2]

[3]

<table>
<tr><td></td><td align="right">Sergey Rafalovich</td></tr>
<tr><td>*The sense of being*</td><td align="right">Women's Letters</td></tr>
</table>

He inherited from his father a lively, hot temperament, a rare joy in life, and a strongly developed *sense of being*. The sense of being is the most valuable, most gratifying, most wonderful of all our feelings . . . It is least known, least sought after, least valued. And you . . . And I . . .

всего ценят. И ты ... И я ... прежде. Прекрасна только жизнь ... и прекраснее жизни ничего нет .. И назначение наше, первое и главное – жить ... наше назначение и наша обязанность ... И отречение от жизни грех .... [4] грех против нее и против себя ... и все то, во имя чего мы отрекаемся от жизни, – и честность, и порядочность, и уважение других – все это только ложь, та же ложь[,] к[ото]рая лежит в основе несбыточных мечтаний, оскорбительных для правды жизни и порочащих ее красоту. [7]

———

Вы все всегда знали, но знали по-своему[,] а не по-моему. В этом все несчастие людей ... проклятие всякой близости между людьми ... каждый знает другого только по-своему. [8]

———

Право и любовь. К[а]к будто любовь не [5] есть отрицание всяких прав, к[а]к будто право не есть отрицание любви. [9]

———

Даже неразумный человек имеет разумные минуты. [10]

———

Жизнь именно в могучих переживаниях, хотя бы мгновенных, а не в длительности процесса бытия.
Das Leben ist die Fülle, nicht die Zeit. – Und noch der letzte Augenblick ist weit. [11]

———

Одинок не тот[,] кто один, а тот[,] кто чувствует свое одиночество. Можно быть одиноким[,] даже если вырастешь у родителей, выйдешь замуж за любимого ч[е]л[о]в[е]ка и имеешь от него [6] любимых детей. Чувство одиночества сильнее фактов, к[а]к всякое основное чувство в человеке. – Оно беспричинно, недоказуемо, непоколебимо[,] к[а]к вера, к[а]к боязливость, к[а]к подозрительность. –[12]

[7]
Любовь – мечта, любовь – мгновенье,
Звезда, блеснувшая вдали;
Любовь – волшебное виденье
Тоской, измученной земли.
  Любовь – восторг пред ярким светом,
  Луч рая в сумраке могил.
  Лишь тот был счастлив в мире этом,
  Кто был любим и кто любил.
                    Ратрауз. [13]

before. Only life is wonderful . . . and there is nothing more wonderful than life . . . And our mission, first and foremost, is to live . . . our mission and our duty . . . And the denial of life is a sin . . . [4] a sin against life and against the self . . . and everything in the name of which we deny life – honesty, and decency, and respect for others – all this is only a lie, the same lie which is at the root of impossible reveries, insulting to the truth of life and sullying its beauty.[7]

———

You always knew everything, but you knew it in your own way, not in my way. In this lies all the unhappiness of people . . . the curse of every closeness between people . . . each person knows another only in his own way.[8]

———

Right and love. As if love is not the denial of all rights, as if right is not [5] the denial of love.[9]

———

Even an unreasonable person has reasonable moments.[10]

———

Life is precisely in powerful experiences, even if fleeting ones, and not in the duration of the process of being.
Life is fullness, not time. – And even the final moment is far away.[11]

———

Lonely is not he who is alone, but he who feels his loneliness. It is possible to be lonely, even if you grow up with your parents, marry a person you love, and have [6] beloved children with him. The feeling of loneliness is stronger than facts, like every basic human feeling. – It is irrational, unprovable, unshakable, like faith, like fearfulness, like suspiciousness. –[12]

[7]
Love is a dream, love is an instant,
A star, shining in the distance;
Love is the magic vision
Of Earth, tormented by longing.
　　Love is the delight before a bright light,
　　A ray of paradise in the gloom of the grave.
　　Happy in this world is only he
　　Who was loved and who loved.
　　　　　　　　　　　　　　Ratrauz.[13]

[8]

Секта ионнитов имеет сходство с сектою хлыстовцев: ионниты отвергают церков.[ный] брак, и замен.[яют] его духовным сожительством; детей от такого сожительства след.[ует] уничтожать!! Духовных сожительниц может быть сколько угодно. Пить водку и курить табак можно, п.[отому] ч.[то] в устах ионнитов первая превращается в св.[ятую] воду, а второй в фимиам. [14]

[9]
      Напрасно
Я и услышу, и пойму –
    А все-таки молчи.
Будь верен сердцу своему,
    Храни его ключи.
       *
Я пониманьем – оскорблю
    Не оттого, что не люблю,
А оттого, что скорбь твоя,
    А я не ты, и ты не я.
       *
И пусть другой не перейдет
    Невидимый порог.
Душа раскрытая – умрет,
    Как сорванный цветок.
       *
[10] Мы два различных бытия.
    Мы зеркала – и ты, и я.
Я все возьму и углублю,
    Но, отражая, – преломлю.
       *
Твоя душа... Не оттого-ль
    Даю так много ей,
Что, все равно, чужая боль –
    Не может стать моей?
       *
Достойней плакать одному.
Пусть я жалею и пойму –
Любви и жалости не верь,
Не открывай святую дверь,
Храни, храни ее ключи,
И задыхайся – и молчи.
          Зин. Гиппиус[15]

[8]
The sect of the Johannites bears a resemblance to the sect of the *khlïstï*:
the Johannites reject church marriage and replace it with spiritual
cohabitation; the children from such cohabitation should be destroyed!!
One can cohabit with as many spiritual partners as one likes. Drinking
vodka and smoking tobacco are allowed, because in the mouths of the
Johannites the first turns into holy water and the second into incense.[14]

[9]
　　In Vain
I will both hear and understand –
　But all the same be silent.
Be true to your heart,
　Guard its keys.
　　　*
With understanding I will offend,
　Not because I do not love,
But because the grief is yours,
　And I am not you, and you are not I.
　　　*
And let no other person cross
　The invisible threshold.
An opened soul will die,
　Like a plucked flower.
　　　*
[10] We are two distinct beings.
　We are mirrors – both you and I.
I will take everything and deepen it,
　But in reflecting it, I will refract it.
　　　*
Your soul. . . Is it not because
　I give it so much
That, even so, another's pain
　Cannot become mine?
　　　*
It is more fitting to cry on one's own.
Although I may have pity and will understand –
Do not believe in love and pity,
Do not open the sacred portal,
Guard, guard its keys,
And gasp for breath – and be silent.
　　　　　　　Zin. Gippius[15]

[11]

Заветная *тайна* творчества – способность подойти к предмету своеобразно и увидеть в нем то, чего не замечали другие. [16]

———

По мере накопления богатства опустошается душа. [17]

———

Английские писатели говорят: мы всегда стремились к материализации духа, Россия-же наоборот, посвящала свои силы одухотворению материи. [18]

———

[12]

Секта «каинитов» была права, когда утверждала в «евангелии от Иуды», что совершенство просвещенного человека не может выразиться иначе, к[а]к только бестрепетным исполнением самых высших жестокостей. [19]

———

[13]

Эдуард Шюрэ
Великие Посвященные.
Очерк эзотеризма религий. [20]
М. Окорович
О мысленном внушении. [21]

———

Великие посвященны[е] – представители мировых религий. [22]

———

Начало цивилизации возник 50 тыс.[яч] лет тому назад. [23]

———

Способность страстно чувствовать вызвала у мужчины привязанность к одной определенной женщине – отсюда наклонность этой расы к **[14]** единоженству.[24]

———

Тот, кто находит в себе самом свое счастье, свою радость и в себе самом находит свет, тот в единении с Богом. Учение Кришна.[25]

[15]

Серое платьице
Девочка в сереньком платьице.
Косы к[а]к-будто из ваты.
Девочка, девочка, чья ты?
«Мамина или ничья... .
Хочешь – буду твоя.»
Девочка в сереньком платьице...

[11]

The secret *mystery* of artistic creation is the ability to approach an object in one's own way and to see in it what others have not noticed.[16]

As wealth accumulates, so the soul becomes empty.[17]

English writers say: we always strove to make spirit material, Russia, by contrast, devoted its energies to making the material spiritual.[18]

---

[12]

The sect of the "Cainites" was right when it claimed in the "Gospel of Judas" that the perfection of an enlightened person cannot express itself in any other way than in the dauntless execution of the most extreme acts of cruelty.[19]

---

[13]

Edouard Schuré
The Great Initiates.
A Survey of the Esoteric Content of Religions.[20]
M. Okorovich
On Mental Suggestion.[21]

The great initiates are the representatives of world religions.[22]

The beginning of civilization arose 50 thousand years ago.[23]

The ability to feel passionately aroused in man the attachment to one particular woman – this is the source of this race's tendency to **[14]** monogamy.[24]

He who finds his happiness, his joy within himself and finds light within himself, such a person is united with God. A teaching of Krishna.[25]

[15]

The Gray Dress
Little girl in a grayish dress.
Plaits like cotton wadding.
Little girl, little girl, whose are you?
"Mama's or nobody's. . . .
If you like – I'll be yours."
Little girl in a grayish dress . . .

Веришь-ли, девочка, ласке?
Милая, где твои глазки?
«Вот они, глазки пустые.
У мамочки точно такие.»
Девочка в сереньком платьице...
А чем это ты играешь?
Что от меня закрываешь?
«Время играть мне! Что ты!
Много спешной работы:
[16] То у бусинок нить раскушу,
То первый росток подсушу,
Вырезаю из книг странички,
Ломаю крылья у птички.»
Девочка в сереньком платьице,
Девочка с глазами пустыми,
Скажи мне, как твое имя?
«А по своему зовет меня всяк:
Хочешь эдак, а хочешь так.
Один зовет разделеньем,
А то враждою,
Зовут и сомненьем или тоскою.
Иной зовет скукою,
Иной мукою...
А мама-Смерть – разлукою,
Девочку в сереньком платьице . . .»

               Зин. Гиппиус.[26]

[17]

Боль, к[ото]рую мы наносим своему ближнему, следует за нами также, к[а]к тень следует за нашим телом. *Дела*, в основе к[ото]рых лежит любовь к ближним, должны быть предметом искания для праведного, ибо такие дела весят на чаше божественных весов более всего. Если ты будешь искать общения с добрыми, твой пример не принесет пользы; не бойся жить среди злых и стремись обратить их к добру. Праведный человек [18] подобен огромному дереву, благодетельная тень которого поддерживает в окружающих растениях свежесть жизни.

Подобно тому, к[а]к земля питает тех, к[ото]рые топчат ее ногами и, вспахивая ниву, разрывают ее грудь, т[а]к и мы должны отдавать добром за зло.[27]

               ———

Один Бог может понимать Бога. Бесконечное одно может понимать бесконечное.[28]

Do you believe, little girl, in affection?
Dear one, where are your eyes?
"Here they are, empty eyes.
Mama has just the same ones."
Little girl in a grayish dress . . .
What is that you are playing with?
What are you hiding from me?
"Do I have time to play! What do you mean!
There is much urgent work:
[16] Sometimes I bite through the thread of beads,
Sometimes I wither the first shoot,
I cut pages out of books,
I break the wings of a bird."
Little girl in a grayish dress,
Little girl with empty eyes,
Tell me, what is your name?
"Each person calls me as he likes:
By this name or that.
One person calls me division,
Or enmity,
Some call me doubt or depression.
Another calls me boredom,
Another – torment . . .
But mama-Death calls me separation,
The little girl in the grayish dress."
Zin. Gippius.[26]

[17]
The *pain* that we cause our neighbor follows us in the same way as our shadow follows our body. *Deeds* at the root of which lies the love of neighbors should be sought after by a righteous man, for such deeds carry the most weight on the scales of divine judgment. If you seek out the society of good people, your example will not serve any useful purpose; do not be afraid to live among evil people and try to convert them to good. A righteous man [18] is like an enormous tree, whose beneficent shade sustains the freshness of life in the plants that surround it. Just as the earth nourishes those who trample it with their feet and, when ploughing a furrow, tear open its bosom, so also should we return good for evil.[27]

———

Only God can understand God. Only the infinite can understand the infinite.[28]

[19]

История *одной* религии будет всегда и узкой, и суеверной и ограниченной; истинной может быть лишь история общечеловеческой религии.[29]

———

О Господи! я жил могучим и одиноким,
Дай-же мне уснуть сном всей земли. [30]

———

Все могучие души познали одиночество, к[ото]р[ое] создается истинным величием. [31]

———

Люди прощают пороки и все виды неверия, но они не прощают тем, которые **[20]** срывают с них маску. [32]

———

Я бы желал быть небом, усеянным очами, чтобы непрестанно смотреть на тебя. (Платон) [33]

———

Почему Платон был т[а]к очарован Сократом и т[а]к подчинился ему? Он через него понял превосходство добра над красотою. Ибо красота осуществляет истину в искусстве, тогда к[а]к добро осуществляет ее в глубине души.
Редкое и могучее очарование, ибо оно действует помимо **[21]** физических чувств.
Впечатление от *истинно-справедливого* человека заставило побледнеть в душе Платона все ослепительное великолепие видимой красоты.[34]

———

Платон основал школу на пятидесятом году своей жизни и умер семидесяти лет, невозможно представить себе его иначе, к[а]к молодым, ибо вечная молодость есть удел душ, у к[ото]рых к глубине мысли присоединяется и чистота сердца.[35]

———

[22]

Диалоги Платона содержат эзотерическую доктрину, но она по условиям времени, замаскирована, смягчена, нагружена диалектикой, к[а]к посторонней тяжестью, а самая суть ее преображена в легенду, в миф, в притчу.[36]

[23]

Друзья, вы слыхали и верно вам нравится
Прелестная сказка о спящей красавице.
Теперь появилась другая в народе:

[19]
The history of *one* religion will always be narrow, and superstitious, and limited; only the history of the religion of all mankind can be true.[29]

———

O Lord! I have lived, powerful and lonely,
Let me fall asleep with the sleep of all earth.[30]

———

All powerful souls have known loneliness, which springs from true greatness.[31]

———

People forgive vices and all forms of unbelief, but they do not forgive those who **[20]** tear the mask off them.[32]

———

I would like to be heaven, studded with eyes, so as to gaze upon you incessantly. (Plato)[33]

———

Why was Plato so enchanted by Socrates and why was he so submissive to him? Through him he came to understand the superiority of good over beauty. For beauty realizes truth in art, whereas good realizes truth in the depth of the soul.
A rare and powerful enchantment, for it operates independently **[21]** of physical feelings.
The impression made by the *truly just* person caused the dazzling majesty of visible beauty to fade in Plato's soul.[34]

———

Plato founded a school in the fiftieth year of his life and died at the age of seventy; it is impossible to imagine him other than young, for eternal youth is the lot of souls, who combine depth of thought with purity of heart.[35]

———

[22]
Plato's Dialogues contain esoteric teaching but, in keeping with the conventions of the time, it is masked, weakened, burdened with dialectics, as if with extraneous weight, while the actual essence is transformed into legend, myth, and parable.[36]

[23]
Friends, you have heard and probably like
The charming tale of the sleeping beauty.
Now another tale has appeared among the people:

Преглупая сказка о спящем уроде.[37]
Жил был болтун – поэт Борюня[38]
И друг его, лихой Сергуня.[39]
Томясь от солнечного гнета
На Волге, в недрах «Самолета»[40]
Урод-поэт и друг урода
Спокойно ждали парохода,
Который их под «охи-ахи»
[24] Свезет в страну, где правят шахи. [41]
Далекий путь лежал Борюне.
И вот, ложася накануне,
Пообещался он Сергушке
Подняться рано от подушки.
Покушав Гурьевской кашицы, [42]
Испивши Ланинской водицы,[43]
Закрыл поэт глаза и ротик
И задремал. Как вдруг животик
У поэтиного созданья
Почуял острые страданья.
Он пухнул… ширился… вздымался…
И с адским грохотом взрывался.
По утру, точный до минуты,
[25] Вошел Сергуня внутрь каюты,
Где распростерся труп Борюни.
А труп сопел, пуская слюни.
От происшедшего-ли взрыва,
Иль от душевного надрыва,
Но спал Борюня беспробудно,
Сопя противно, сочно, нудно.
Ни уговоры, ни упреки,
Ни злые шутки, ни намеки,
Ни призрак скорого ухода
В далекий Каспий парохода
Не разогнали сна поэта,
Сего рекламного аскета.
И гнев великий благородный
Объял Сергунин дух свободный.
Он, длань простря на умывальник,
[26] Взопил: «прими-же, жалкий спальник,
Вкруг поэтического стана
Воды холодной полстакана.»
Струя блеснула, окатила –
И двух друзей разъединила.[44]

The most foolish tale of a sleeping monster.[37]
Once upon a time there lived a chatterbox poet Boryunya[38]
And his friend, the dashing Sergunya.[39]
Languishing from the sun's oppressive heat
On the Volga, in the depths of the *Samolyot*[40]
The monster-poet and the monster's friend
Were calmly waiting for a ship
Which to the sound of "ohs" and "ahs"
[24] Would take them to a land ruled by shahs.[41]
A long journey lay before Boryunya.
And so, as he settled down the day before,
He gave a promise to Sergushka
That he would rise early from his pillow.
After eating some Gurev pudding[42]
And drinking some Lanin's beverage,[43]
The poet shut his eyes and mouth
And dozed off. But suddenly the tummy
Of this poetic creature
Felt sharp pangs.
It swelled . . . expanded . . . rose . . .
And with an infernal rumble erupted.
In the morning, punctual to the minute,
[25] Sergunya stepped inside the cabin
Where the body of Boryunya lay prostrate.
Yet the body breathed heavily, dribbling spittle.
Whether from the earlier eruption
Or from emotional strain,
Boryunya sure was fast asleep,
Breathing heavily, repulsively, juicily, tediously.
Neither entreaties nor reproaches,
Neither nasty jokes nor hints,
Nor the vision of the imminent departure
Of the ship for the distant Caspian
Were able to dispel the sleep of the poet,
This self-advertising ascetic.
And a great and noble fury
Seized Sergunya's free soul.
Raising his palm to the wash-basin,
[26] He cried out: "Please receive, oh wretched sleeper,
Around your poetic torso
Half a glass of cold water."
The water sparkled, poured over –
And parted the two friends.[44]

Уплыл Сергуня в знойный Каспий
Искать и настий и ненастий.[45]
А Боря – в сказке-ли, в легенде-ль,
Поныне спит, свернувшись в крендель.

С. П.

18/VII-916 г.[46]

[27]
Лейб-Гвардии 1-ый Стрелковый Его Величества полк[.]
Подпоручику А. А. Яблонск[ому.][47]

[28]

[29]
Венера – чудная вечерняя или утренняя звезда, к[ото]р.[ая]
загорается на западн.[ом] небосклоне во время солнечн.[ого] заката
или пред его восходом на востоке. После Солнца и Луны это самое
яркое светило неба. Астрономический знак Венеры изображает
зеркало с рукояткой (♀), к[а]к принадлежн.[ость] богини Венеры.
Яркость Венеры зависит от близости ее к Солнцу[.] Расстояние
Венеры от земли изменяется. Во время своего верхнего
соединения Венера **[30]** бывает в 6 раз удаленнее от Земли
сравнительно с нижним соединением. Свой оборот вокруг Солнца
она делает в 225 суток. Год Венеры на 140 суток менее земного. А
вращение Венеры вокруг своей оси около 24 часов.
Венера весьма близко подходит к Земле не только по величине,
объему, плотности[, но] и потому,[48] что в состав ее плотной
атмосферы входят водяные пары, [что] дает возможность
предположить жизнь на ней.
[31] Вследствие близости к Солнцу средняя t° должна быть гораздо
выше земной, ее принимают в 65° по Цельсию, с максимумом в 187° [.][49]

———

Учение Архимеда о динамике тел (движении, падении) *18 столетий*
не подвигалось вперед, пока родился гений Галилей, к[ото]р.[ый]
понял истину учения и пошел дальше Архимеда.
Архимед жил за 300 лет до Р[ождества] Х[ристова] Галилей в 16 веке.[50]

[32]
Ни простить, ни забыть нельзя немцам – это[й] обманутой веры в
культуру целого народа. У них неколебимое расовое высокомерие,
соединенное с презрением ко всему чужому, с неумением его не
только оценить, но и понять.[51]

Sergunya sailed off for the sultry Caspian
To seek out good and bad times.[45]
As for Borya – whether in the tale or legend,
To this day he is asleep, curled up like a pretzel.

S. P.

July 18, 1916.[46]

[27]
The Life-Guards 1st Rifles Regiment of His Highness. For Second
Lieutenant A. A. Yablonsk[y][47]

[28]

[29]
Venus is a wonderful evening or morning star, which burns brightly on
the western horizon during sunset or before sunrise in the East. After
the Sun and the Moon it is the brightest luminary in the sky. The astronomical sign of Venus shows a mirror with a handle (♀), an attribute of
the goddess Venus. The brightness of Venus depends on its proximity to
the Sun. The distance of Venus from earth fluctuates. At the time of its
upper conjunction Venus **[30]** can be 6 times farther from Earth than at
its lower conjunction. It takes 225 days to complete its orbit around the
Sun. A Venus year is 140 days less than an earth year. The revolution
period of Venus around its own axis is about 24 hours.
Venus is extremely similar to Earth not only in size, volume, and density,
but also because[48] the dense atmosphere is partly composed of water
vapors, which makes it possible to envisage life on it.
[31] As a result of its proximity to the Sun the average temperature
must be much higher than the Earth's; it is considered to be 65° Celsius,
with a maximum of 187°.[49]

———

The teaching of Archimedes about the dynamics of bodies (movement,
falling) did not advance for *18 centuries*, until the genius Galileo was
born, who understood the truth of the teaching and went further than
Archimedes.
Archimedes lived 300 years B.C. Galileo in the 16th century.[50]

[32]
It is impossible either to forgive or to forget the Germans – for this false
faith in the culture of a whole nation. They possess an unshakable racial
arrogance, combined with contempt for everything foreign, with an
inability not only to value but also to comprehend anything foreign.[51]

[33]

Шопенгауер. Афоризмы и мысли для усвоения житейской мудрости.—[52]

Зависть к личным преимуществам самая непримиримая и тщательнее всего скрывается. [53]

Чем больше человек имеет в самом себе, тем меньше нужно ему извне и тем меньше для него могут значить другие. Потому-что возвышенность духа ведет к необщительности.[54]

———

[34]

Красота есть открытое рекомендательное письмо, заранее располагающее сердца в нашу пользу.[55]

———

Филистер есть человек без духовных потребностей. Его существование не оживляется никаким стремлением к познанию и *прозрению.*[56]

———

Гордость есть уже прочно установившееся убеждение о собственном превосходстве в каком либо отношении.

[35]

Тщеславие, напротив, есть желание вселить такое убеждение в других. Гордость делает человека молчаливым, тщеславие – болтливым.[57]

———

Ранг есть условная ценность, придуманная, притворная. *Ордена* есть векселя на общественное мнение.[58]

———

Разумный гонится за тем, что избавляет от страданий, а не за тем, что приятно.
[36] Всякое наслаждение и счастье – отрицательны, негативны, а страдание, напротив, положительно, позитивно.
Вольтер говорит:
Le bonheur n'est qu'un rêve, la douleur est réelle.[59]

———

Если к безболезненному и беспечальному состоянию присоединится еще отсутствие скуки, то земное счастье в существенном достигнуто, ибо остальное – химера.[60]

———

[37]

Чтобы сохранить в себе спокойствие духа, нужно помнить, что нынешний день наступает только раз и никогда не возвращается.[61]

———

Quand le bon ton arrive le bon sens se retire.[62]

———

[33]

Schopenhauer. Aphorisms and thoughts for the attainment of practical wisdom.–[52]

The envy of personal qualities is the most implacable [form of envy] and the one that is most carefully concealed.[53]

The more a person has within himself, the less he needs from without and the less significance others can have for him. Because elevation of spirit leads to unsociability.[54]

———

[34]

Beauty is an open letter of recommendation that predisposes hearts in our favor.[55]

———

The *Philistine* is a person without spiritual needs. His existence is not animated by any striving for knowledge and *insight*.[56]

———

Pride is the already firmly established conviction of one's own superiority in some respect.

[35]

Vanity, by contrast, is the desire to instill such a conviction in others. Pride makes a person taciturn, vanity makes him talkative.[57]

———

Rank is a conventional value, imagined and sham.
Orders are bills of exchange drawn on public opinion.[58]

———

The prudent man seeks not that which is agreeable, but that which gives freedom from suffering. **[36]** Every pleasure and happiness is bad, negative, while suffering, by contrast, is favorable, positive.
Voltaire says:
Happiness is only a dream, pain is real.[59]

———

If the absence of boredom is joined to a painless and carefree state, then earthly happiness has in its essence been attained, for all else is a chimera.[60]

———

[37]

To preserve one's peace of mind, it is necessary to remember that today comes but once and never returns.[61]

———

When good form arrives, common sense departs.[62]

———

Табель о рангах общественный обыкновенно диаметрально противуположен табелю о рангах природному.[63]

———

Я люблю «ум сердца», искренность многих чувств и переживаний, п.[отому] ч.[то] в этом есть [38] нечто от тайны искусства, от откровения, от абсолютной истины.[64]

[39]
Семеро их! Семеро их!
В глубине Океана семеро их!
В высотах Небесных семеро их!
В горах Заката рождаются, семеро.
В горах Востока выростают, семеро.
Сидят на престолах в глубинах Земли они.
Заставляют свой голос греметь на высотах Земли они [.]
Раскинулись станом в пространствах Небес и Земли они.
Семеро их! Семеро их!
                    *
Они не мужчины, не женщины [,]
К[а]к ветер бродячий они.
К[а]к сети они простираются, тянутся.
[40] Нет у них жен, не родят они сына.
Благословенья не знают они [,]
Молитв не услышат,
Нет слуха у них к мольбам.
Злые они! Злые они!
                    *
Семеро их! Семеро их!
Дважды семеро их!
Дух Небес, ты закляни их!
Дух Земли, ты закляни их![65]

[41–42]

[43]
                31 дек. 1917.
Мы устроили парад
И взвились на Арарат,
Чтоб, укрывшись от невзгод,
Встретить юный Новый Год.

Где же ты, о наш Семен?
Средь друзей иль средь зверей?
Ах, да будь же ты умен:
Приезжай сюда скорей!
                        С. П.[66]

The social table of ranks is usually diametrically opposed to the natural table of ranks.[63]

———

I love the "mind of the heart," the sincerity of many feelings and experiences, because in this there is **[38]** something of the mystery of art, of revelation, of absolute truth.[64]

[39]
Seven they are! Seven they are!
In the depth of the Ocean, seven they are!
In the heights of the Heavens, seven they are!
In the mountains of the Sunset they are born, seven.
In the mountains of the East they grow, seven.
They sit on thrones in the depths of the Earth.
They cause their voice to thunder on the heights of the Earth.
They have spread out like a camp in the spaces of Heaven and Earth.
Seven they are! Seven they are!
                    *
They are not men, not women,
Like the wandering wind they are.
Like nets they extend, stretch.
[40] They have no wives, they bear no sons.
They know no blessing,
They will not hear any prayers,
They have no ear for entreaties.
Evil they are! Evil they are!
                    *
Seven they are! Seven they are!
Twice seven they are!
Spirit of the Heavens, exorcise them!
Spirit of the Earth, exorcise them![65]

[41–42]

[43]
                    Dec. 31, 1917.
We organized a parade
And flew up the Ararat,
In order, sheltered from hard times,
To greet the young New Year.

Where are you, o our Semyon?
Among friends or among the beasts?
Ah, do be clever now:
Come here as quick as you can!
                    S. P.[66]

NOTES ON THE LITERARY NOTEBOOK

1. Entry in pencil. The opening entry in French ("Keep a notebook of expenses") suggests that Mariya Prokofieva may have intended to keep a record of her expenses during her trip with Prokofiev to France and Switzerland in the summer of 1913 and perhaps started the notebook for this purpose. Prokofiev arrived in Paris with his mother on June 2, 1913, visited London June 9–13, returned to Paris on June 14, moved to Royat on June 17 for three weeks, traveled to Geneva on July 9, and finally returned to St. Petersburg on July 19, 1913.

2. Sepia photograph of Sergey Alekseyevich Prokofiev (1846–1910), the composer's father, shown with a white beard, wearing glasses, suit and tie, standing against a rural background with a tree and wooden fence. The picture may have been taken at Sontsovka, Prokofiev's childhood home in the Ukraine, not long before his father's death in July 1910. The photograph has been glued to the inside of the front cover.

3. Entry in pencil. A classic textbook for use in schools, based on observation of the natural world, published in several editions; see, for example, [Charles] Saffray, *Leçons de choses. Cours méthodique comprenant les matières des programmes officiels. Livre du maître* (Paris: Librairie Hachette, 1880). The textbook comprises forty-four chapters, covering topics as diverse as Earth and the planets, the elements, materials, textiles, gas, food, drink, books, the human body, and the senses; each chapter is rounded off with a questionnaire. The companion volume, *Livre de l'élève*, covers the same topics but in less detail.

4. Entry in pencil. In line with the previous entry listing Saffray's books on aspects of the natural world, this might be a reference to an edition of Julius Hoffmann's popular guide to alpine flora for amateur botanists. Prokofiev's lifelong interest in botany dated back to his childhood at Sontsovka and was encouraged by both his parents. In the earliest and longest section of his autobiography, "Detstvo" (Childhood, 1939), he recalls how his father, an agronomist, taught him in 1903 how to identify and classify plants using the system devised by the Russian botanist Pyotr Mayevsky. Many years later, in 1923, he wrote to Vladimir Derzhanovsky from Ettal, asking him to send him a book on plants and mentioning Mayevsky's work as the best he knew; he was delighted when his friend sent him a fine edition of this work (*S. S. Prokof'yev: Materialï, dokumentï, vospominaniya*, 92–93, 628). In her memoirs his first wife, Lina Prokofieva, describes their walks in the Bavarian Alps near Ettal, collecting flowers and plants, identified and sorted with the help of Prokofiev's "large book on botany." Lina Prokof'yeva, "Iz vospominaniy," in *Sergey Prokof'yev: Stat'i i materialï*, 181.

5. Entry in black ink. A satirical collection of dialogues and stories, covering a range of everyday social situations (at the sea, travel, hiring a servant, renting an apartment, political life, education), published in several editions; see, for example, Quattrelles (pseudonym of Ernest L'Épine), *Le Parfait Causeur. Petit manuel rédigé en langue parisienne suivi de six nouvelles nouvelles* (Paris: J. Hetzel, 1879). As in the case of the previous books by Saffray, Prokofieva's interest in this work may have arisen during her visit to France and Switzerland with her son in the summer of 1913.

6. Sepia photograph of Mariya Grigoryevna Prokofieva, the composer's mother, wearing glasses, white top and dark trousers, seated on a wooden bench with an open book on her lap, against a background of water and houses. The appearance of the bench suggests that the picture may have been taken in France, possibly in June 1913 at the French spa resort of Royat, where Prokofiev and his mother spent three weeks, staying at the Grand Hôtel des Sources. The photograph has been stuck onto the first page of the notebook, opposite the photograph of Prokofiev's father inside the front cover.

7. Entry in black ink, apart from the author's name and book's title, added in pencil at the top of the page. Sergey Rafalovich was a minor Symbolist. After completing his studies at the Faculty of History and Philology of St. Petersburg University, he played an active role in Russian literary circles, contributing to the journals *Vesï* and *Apollon* and publishing several works in Russian and French. Prokofieva has cited the book's title incorrectly; she is referring to *Zhenskiye pis'ma* (Women's letters) (St. Petersburg: Izdaniye "Sodruzhestva," 1906). This collection, one of Rafalovich's earliest works, comprises fifteen fictive prose letters from a variety of women, dealing with the problems and moral dilemmas posed by love. Prokofieva has copied out three extracts from the first two letters, "Tyotya Mar'ya" (9–19) and "Odinokaya" (23–27). The first extract covers two passages from "Tyotya Mar'ya" (13–14, 17), cited with some omissions and minor differences of

punctuation. The elderly narrator, Aunt Marya, is writing to Tanya, a young woman in love, recounting her past error (sacrificing the freedom of personal happiness in love to social morals) and exhorting Tanya not to repeat her mistake. She cites the views of her favorite nephew, Pavel, a character gifted with *chuvstvo bïtiya* (a sense of being), who was the first person to reveal to her the emptiness of her "moral" denial of life. The first passage (up until "Prekrasna") is drawn from Marya's description of Pavel to her correspondent; the second passage consists of her quotation of Pavel's impassioned speech to her, promoting the superiority of life over morals.

8. Entry in black ink. This statement is not found in Rafalovich's book, although it expresses sentiments in tune with many of the letters in his collection.

9. Entry in black ink. This statement is not found in Rafalovich's book, but appears to be a commentary on the second letter in his collection, "Odinokaya," quoted in n. 12 below, which deals with the conflict between free love and individual rights.

10. Entry in pencil. Unidentified source.

11. Entry in pencil. The lines in German (a rhyming couplet in iambic pentameter) are an almost exact quotation of the closing couplet from Arthur Schnitzler's historical drama, set in sixteenth-century Bologna, *Der Schleier der Beatrice*: "Das Leben ist die Fülle, nicht die Zeit, / Und noch der nächste Augenblick ist weit!" (Life is fullness, not time, / And even the next moment is far away!) *Die Theaterstücke von Arthur Schnitzler*, 5 vols. (Berlin: S. Fischer, 1912–22), 2:323. These lines are spoken by the Duke of Bologna as he stands over the corpses of both his bride and his friend at the very end of the tragedy. I am grateful to Petra Rau, University of Portsmouth, and Martin Swales, University College London, for their kind help in identifying the source of this quotation. The idea of life being found in the fullness of experience rather than in time is a leit-motif in Schnitzler's work; it is loosely related to the immediately preceding statement in the notebook and also echoes the praise of *chuvstvo bïtiya* in "Tyotya Mar'ya" in Rafalovich's collection.

Schnitzler, a leading Austrian modernist playwright and novella writer (as well as a competent amateur pianist), was well known in Russia in the 1900s. A multivolume edition of his works in Russian translation was published in Moscow by Sablin in 1903–5 and reviewed by Alexander Blok in 1906. His plays were produced in Russia by Vsevolod Meyerhold and Alexander Tairov. Prokofiev came into direct contact with his work on November 29, 1913. Prokof'yev, *Dnevnik*, 1:383.

12. Entry in pencil. An adapted passage from "Odinokaya," the second letter in Rafalovich, *Zhenskiye pis'ma*, 25. In the original text the second sentence is narrated in the first person and reads as follows: "Ya bïla bï, veroyatno, odinoka, dazhe yesli bï vïrosla u roditeley, vïshla za lyu-bimogo cheloveka, imela ot nego lyubimïkh detey." (I would probably be lonely, even if I had grown up with my parents, married a person I loved, and had beloved children with him.) In this letter a "lonely woman," as per the title, accuses her rejected lover of double standards and attacks his belief that their former liaison, formed solely for the purpose of pleasure, gives him any rights over her.

13. Entry in black ink. Prokofieva has mistakenly written Ratrauz instead of Ratgauz. Daniil Ratgauz was an undistinguished but popular poet, the author of several collections of verse on sorrowful love and longing, published in Russia and, after his emigration in 1922, in Berlin and Prague. The poem, written in iambic tetrameter with alternating feminine and masculine rhymes, portrays love as a dream or fleeting vision, illuminating suffering and death, and providing the only source of happiness in this world. Ratgauz included it in several collections of his verse. In *Polnoye sobraniye stikhotvoreniy D. Ratgauza*, 3 vols. (St. Petersburg and Moscow: Izdaniye T-va M.O. Vol'f, [1907]), 2:64, it appears under the title "Lyubov'" (Love), set out as two quatrains; line 2 ends with a period (not a semicolon, as in the notebook) and there is no comma after "toskoy" in line 4 (a punctuation error on Prokofieva's part). In D. Ratgauz, *Izbrannïye stikhotvoreniya* (Petrograd: Akts. obshch. tipogr. dela v PGR, [1915]), 12, the poem is printed under the title "Lyubov'" as in the earlier edition, with two further differences of punctuation (line 6 ends with an ellipsis, line 8 with an exclamation mark).

Ratgauz's lyrics were frequently set to music; this poem was arranged as a song by several Russian composers, including Vasiliy Vrangel (1899), Iosif Bleikhman (1900), and Reinhold Glier (1905), Prokofiev's first music tutor, who instructed his young pupil in song form. Although Prokofiev did not set Ratgauz's poem to music, it is possible that he considered doing so, as was the case with two poems that appear later in the notebook, Gippius's "Seroye plat'itse" and Balmont's "Semero ikh! Semero ikh!.."

14. Entry in pencil. Prokofieva has evidently made a spelling mistake and means *ioannitï* rather than *ionnitï*, since the former, unlike the latter, were closely associated with the "khlïstï," a Russian religious sect founded in the seventeenth century by a peasant; I am grateful to Aleksandr Etkind, University of Cambridge, for this suggestion. Whereas the *ionnitï* (Johannites) were an ancient Gnostic heretical sect—named after John the Baptist, whom they venerated as their true savior rather than Jesus Christ—the *ioannitï* were a contemporary sect, named after the Russian Orthodox priest Ioann Kronshtadtsky (Father John of Kronstadt, 1829–1908, canonized in 1990), whom they venerated alongside Jesus Christ as a miracle worker. Following the name of one of their leaders, Matrena Kiseleva (d. 1905), they were also known as *kiselevtsï, khlïstï-kiselevtsï,* and *khristoverï-kisolevtsï.* They lived in small communities, sharing property, food, and clothing, held eschatological beliefs, regarded church marriage as a sin, and practiced "dukhovnoye sozhitel'stvo" (spiritual marriage). Their popularity spread throughout Russia in the late nineteenth and early twentieth centuries as a result of their association with Father John of Kronstadt (who did not recognize them as his true disciples) and of their effective propaganda (including the journal *Kronshtadtskiy mayak,* first published in 1906). In 1883 they split from the Russian Orthodox Church, and in 1912, due to the dangerous spread of their influence, their activities were forbidden by the Holy Synod. See http://religion.babr.ru/chr/east/prav/rpc/kat/ioann.htm (accessed January 26, 2007).

The source of the information recorded in the notebook about the "ioannitï" is unknown. The comparison of them to the *khlïstï* was well founded; knowledge of this sect may have come from Vasiliy Rozanov's recently published account of his visit to a community of *khlïstï,* including discussion of their practice of spiritual marriage and a reference to the killing of children. See the sections "Poyezdka k khlïstam" and "Materialï o khlïstakh," in Rozanov, *Apokalipsicheskaya sekta (Khlïstï i skoptsï)* (St. Petersburg: Tipografiya F. Vaisberga i P. Gershunina, 1914). For recent studies of the *khlïstï* and other Russian mystic sects, see Aleksandr Etkind, *Khlïst: sektï, literatura i revolyutsiya* (Moscow: Novoye literaturnoye obozreniye, 1998); A. A. Panchenko, *Khristovshchina i skopchestvo: fol'klor i traditsionnaya kul'tura russkikh misticheskikh sekt* (Moscow: Ob"yedinennoye gumanitarnoye izdatel'stvo, 2002).

15. Entry in black ink. "Naprasno" (In vain, 1913), from Gippius's cycle *Molchaniya* (Silences), comprising fourteen poems dated 1911 to 1914, was published in the almanac *Sirin: Sbornik tretiy* (St. Petersburg: Sirin, 1914), [xxvi–xxvii]. This collection includes poems and prose works by Symbolist authors; it opens with Gippius's cycle, followed by poems by Ivanov, Valeriy Bryusov, and Blok, and closes with prose works by Belïy (the end of his novel *Petersburg*), Fyodor Sologub, and Aleksey Remizov. Prokofieva evidently copied the poem from *Sirin,* as the text in the notebook exactly reproduces this first publication (a slightly revised version of the poem was later included in Gippius's collection *Stikhi. Dnevnik 1911–1921* [Berlin: Slovo, 1922]). "Naprasno" consists of five quatrains and a sestet, written in iambic meter; in stanzas 1, 3, and 5, iambic tetrameters alternate with iambic trimeters; stanzas 2, 4, and 6 are in iambic tetrameter throughout. All the rhymes are masculine, as in Tyutchev's poem "Silentium," clearly echoed by Gippius. Prokofiev may well have been considering setting this poem to music, as was the case with two other poems copied later in the notebook, Gippius's "Seroye plat'itse" and Balmont's "Semero ikh! Semero ikh!.."

16. Entry in black ink. Unidentified source.

17. Entry in black ink. Unidentified source.

18. Entry in black ink. Unidentified source. Although the statement is attributed to English writers, the view expressed is more likely to have originated among Russian writers keen to buttress the traditional image of Russia as a spirit-bearing nation. See, for example, the extensive use of terms relating to the materialization of spirit and the spiritualization of matter in Vladimir Solovyov's "Obshchiy smïsl iskusstva" (General meaning of art, 1890), or the pithy characterization of the Russian mentality in Ivanov's poem "Russkiy um" (Russian mind, 1890): "On zdravo mïslit o zemle, / V misticheskoy kupayas' mgle" (He thinks sensibly about the earth, / While bathing in a mystic gloom). Similar cultural stereotypes are invoked by Anton Chekhov in his short story "Ariadne" (1895), which opens with the hero's reflections on the differences between German or English and Russian styles of conversation: whereas the Germans or English talk about

Pamela Davidson

material matters, Russians only discuss women or sublime truths and approach all topics, however trivial, from a lofty point of view.

Prokofieva's comment on English writers may have been related to her son's growing interest in the English language, which he began to study on June 13, 1913; his diary for 1914 includes frequent references to the English lessons he took with Miss Isaacs, a governess in the family of his close friend Nina Meshcherskaya.

19. Entry in black ink. Unidentified source. In his classic account of the Cainites' Gnostic doctrines, *Adversus omnes Haereses* (Against heresies), Irenaeus mentions their association with Esau, Korah, and the Sodomites, their approval of Judas's betrayal, the fictitious Gospel of Judas, and the sanctioning of various abominable actions in the name of angels, but he does not make any specific reference to their cult of cruelty (I.xxxi.1–2). No references to a Russian community using the name of the Cainites have been traced.

20. Entry in pencil. The theosophist Edouard Schuré published widely on esoteric religion and music, and also wrote his own mystery dramas and novels. Prokofieva cites (and subsequently quotes several extracts from) the Russian translation of his main work, *Les Grands Initiés. Esquisse de l'histoire secrète des religions. Rama—Krishna—Hermès—Moïse—Orphée—Pythagore—Platon—Jésus* (Paris: Perrin, 1889). It first appeared in Russian in 1908 and 1909 as an appendix to several issues of the journal *Vestnik teosofii* under the title *Velikiye posvyashchennïye. Ocherk ezoterizma religiy Eduarda Shiure*, translated from the third French edition by E. P[isareva] (St. Petersburg: Gorodskaya tipografiya, 1908). This was followed by two book editions in 1910 and 1914: Eduard Shiure, *Velikiye posvyashchennïye. Ocherk ezoterizma religiy*, trans. from French by E. P[isareva] (St. Petersburg: N. V. Pisarev, 1910); Shiure, *Velikiye posvyashchennïye. Ocherk ezoterizma religiy*, trans. from French by E. Pisareva, 2nd rev. ed. (Kaluga: Lotos, 1914; repr. in Moscow by Kniga in 1990, with a print run of 300,000!)

The next fourteen entries in the notebook (apart from Gippius's poem) are all taken from *Velikiye posvyashchennïye*. Prokofiev's diary reveals that he was reading this book in July 1916 during a boat trip on the Volga (Prokof'yev, *Dnevnik*, 1:615). He and his mother are most likely to have read the second edition of 1914 (hereafter cited in all references to this work).

21. Entry in pencil. A reference to the work of J. Ochorowicz, *De la suggestion mentale*, with a preface by Charles Richet (Paris: Octave Doin, 1887), published in English as J. Ochorowicz, *Mental Suggestion*, with a preface by Charles Richet, trans. J. Fitzgerald (New York: Humboldt, ca. 1891). No Russian translation of this work has been found. The fact that J. Ochorowicz is referred to as M. Okorovich rather than Yu[lian] Okhorovich (the usual Russian spelling of his name) suggests that the reference to this work was copied from the Russian edition of Schuré's book, where it is cited in the same incorrect form in the introduction. Ochorowicz's study explores the phenomena of mental suggestion (hypnosis, hallucinations, telepathy, psychic action) by examining the connections between physiology and psychology; in his conclusion he claims that his experimental scientific approach to the subject does not favor occultism; Schuré cites his study as evidence of his belief in the compatibility of modern science and ancient esoteric beliefs.

Julian Ochorowicz (1850–1917), a Polish scholar and inventor, was prominent in many different fields, including the humanities (psychology, philosophy, literature, history), medical biology (physiology, psychotherapy), and electrotechnology (physics, electronic acoustics, optics). In 1913 he published a five-volume study of mediumistic phenomena. His work on mental suggestion influenced the Russian school of mental hypnosis. See A. V. Moroz and E. S. Poltashevskaya, "Nauchnïy vklad Yu. L. Okhorovicha v psikhologiyu," http://www.voppsy.ru/issues/1991/912/912113.htm (accessed April 6, 2005). He was also known for his work on the telephone and sound, which led to the first broadcast of opera in 1886 in St. Petersburg.

22. Entry in pencil. This phrase is lifted from a sentence in the last section of the introduction to Schuré's work, "Tsel' etoy knigi" (The aim of this book), in which he declares his intention to give an account of the gradual development of esoteric teachings as revealed by "velikimi Posvyashchennïmi, predstavitelyami mirovïkh religiy, kotorïye sodeystvovali ustroyeniyu chelovechestva" (the great Initiates, the representatives of world religions, who contributed to the formation of mankind). Shiure, *Velikiye posvyashchennïye*, 13.

23. Entry in pencil. A close paraphrase of part of a sentence from "Kniga pervaya. Rama (Ariyskiy tsikl): I. Chelovecheskiye rasï i proiskhozhdeniye religiy" (Book one. Rama [the Arian

• 53 •

cycle]: I. The races of mankind and the origin of religions), in Shiure, *Velikiye posvyashchennïye*, 20: "Po bramanicheskim traditsiyam, tsivilizatsiya nachalas' na nashey zemle pyat'desyat tïsyach let tomu nazad na yuzhnom kontinente, gde obitala *krasnaya* rasa togda, kogda vsya Yevropa i chast' Azii nakhodilis' yeshcho pod vodoyu" (According to Brahmanic traditions, civilization in our world began fifty thousand years ago on the southern continent, which was inhabited by the *red* race at a time when all of Europe and part of Asia were still underwater).

24. Entry in black ink. Exact quotation from "Kniga pervaya. Rama (Ariyskiy tsikl)," in Shiure, *Velikiye posvyashchennïye*, 23. The comment is made in the context of a discussion of the "white race" and its predisposition to monogamy, marriage, family life, and the cult of ancestors.

25. Entry in black ink. The main sentence is an exact quotation from "Kniga vtoraya. Krishna (Indiya i bramanicheskoye posvyashcheniye): Glava VI. Ucheniye Posvyashchennïkh" (Book two. Krishna [India and Brahmanic initiation]: Chapter 6. The teachings of the initiates), in Shiure, *Velikiye posvyashchennïye*, 79. Prokofieva has added the comment "Ucheniye Krishna"—which should be "Ucheniye Krishnï" (The teachings of Krishna), the phrase used elsewhere in the Russian translation of Book two—to clarify that Schuré is quoting the words of Krishna, the Hindu god in human form.

26. Entry in black ink; missing punctuation and letters restored. "Seroye plat'itse" (The gray dress, 1913), from Gippius's *Molchaniya*, was published in *Sirin: Sbornik tretiy*, [xxii–xxiv]. The poem is written in accentual verse (tending toward dactylic meter) and consists mainly of masculine and feminine rhyming couplets. In *Sirin*, the poem is set out in a series of irregular stanzas of one, two, three, or four lines; in the notebook the poem is not divided into separate stanzas. There are several other changes of layout and punctuation between the texts in *Sirin* and the notebook. In *Sirin*, line 27 in the notebook, "Zovut i somnen'yem ili toskoyu" (Some call me doubt or depression) is set out as two separate lines: "Zovut i somnen'yem / Ili toskoyu" (Some call me doubt / Or depression); the published version is clearly correct, as it preserves the alternate *abab* rhyming scheme used only in this particular section. The most significant difference concerns the line repeated five times in *Sirin:* "Devochka v serom plat'itse" (Girl in a gray dress); in the notebook an extra syllable is introduced each time, changing this line to regular dactylic meter: "Devochka v seren'kom plat'itse" (Girl in a grayish dress).

In 1915 Prokofiev turned "Seroye plat'itse" into a song. Apart from a few minor differences of punctuation, the text of Gippius's poem reproduced in the editions of the musical setting is identical to the text copied out in the notebook. See Serge Prokofieff, *Cinq poésies. Op. 23. Voice and piano*. Boosey & Hawkes (B.& H. 20577), 24–31, based on the Gutheil edition of 1926.

27. Entry in black ink. Exact quotation (apart from the italicizing of the two words *pain* and *deeds*) of two adjacent passages from "Kniga vtoraya. Krishna (Indiya i bramanicheskoye posvyashcheniye): Glava VII. Torzhestvo i Smert'" (Chapter 7. Triumph and death), in Shiure, *Velikiye posvyashchennïye*, 81. Schuré is quoting the words of Krishna; Prokofieva copied these out, omitting one linking sentence of comment by Schuré before the last sentence beginning "Podobno tomu" (Just as [the earth]). For Russian readers, the last sentence may have evoked an association with the popular Russian cult of Mother Earth, absorbing sin and absolving humans from its stain.

28. Entry in black ink. Loose quotation from "Kniga vtoraya. Krishna (Indiya i bramanicheskoye posvyashcheniye)," in Shiure, *Velikiye posvyashchennïye*, 82. Schuré is quoting the words of Krishna. Prokofieva has reversed the order of the two sentences from the original, and omitted the word "lish'" from the phrase "odin lish' Bog."

29. Entry in black ink. This view is expressed at greater length by Schuré in the introduction to his book; it underpins the syncretic approach to the esoteric content of world religions adopted by him throughout his study.

30. Entry in black ink. Exact quotation from "Kniga chetvyortaya. Moisey (Missiya Izrailya): Glava VI. Smert' Moiseya" (Book four. Moses [The mission of Israel]: Chapter 6. The death of Moses), in Shiure, *Velikiye posvyashchennïye*, 171. These lines are a translation from Alfred de Vigny's poem "Moïse" (1822): "O Seigneur! J'ai vécu puissant et solitaire, / Laissez-moi m'endormir du sommeil de la terre!" (O Lord! I have lived, powerful and lonely, / Let me fall asleep with the sleep of earth!). Variations of this couplet appear three times earlier in the poem, which explores the link between spiritual greatness and the profound solitude experienced by Moses. Schuré praises these lines, claiming that they offer more insight into the state of Moses's soul before his

death than the commentaries of hundreds of theologians. For Russian readers, the translation of De Vigny's lines may have evoked an association with Lermontov's well-known poem "Vïkhozhu odin i na dorogu" (Lone, I walk the road, 1841), in which the narrator, conscious of his solitude, expresses a prayer to fall asleep (*zasnut'*), not with the cold sleep (*snom*) of the grave but in a natural setting, under a green oak, with life's forces still dormant within him.

31. Entry in black ink. Exact quotation (almost immediately after the previous one) from "Kniga chetvyortaya. Moisey (Missiya Izrailya)," in Shiure, *Velikiye posvyashchennïye*, 171. The comment relates to Moses and is followed by the statement that Moses experienced a particularly extreme form of loneliness because he followed the most absolute and transcendent guiding principle, his god.

32. Entry in black ink. An almost exact quotation from "Kniga sed'maya. Platon (Elevzinskaya misteriya): Glava II. Posvyashcheniye Platona i yego filosofiya" (Book seven. Plato [The mystery of Eleusis]: Chapter 2. The initiation of Plato and his philosophy), in Shiure, *Velikiye posvyashchennïye*, 318–19. Prokofieva has substituted *neveriya* (unbelief) for Schuré's *bezveriya* (non-belief). The comment is made in the context of Schuré's argument that Socrates's exposure of hypocrisy among his contemporaries was the real reason for his condemnation to death.

33. Entry in black ink. Exact quotation from "Kniga sed'maya. Platon (Elevzinskaya misteriya): Glava I. Molodost' Platona i smert' Sokrata" (Chapter 1. The youth of Plato and the death of Socrates), in Shiure, *Velikiye posvyashchennïye*, 313. Schuré cites this epigram after praising the understanding of various phases of amorous passion expressed by Plato in *Phaedra*; he also notes (incorrectly) that it is the only surviving piece of verse by Plato. For the original Greek text and an English translation ("On the stars thou gazest, my Star; would I were heaven to look at thee with many eyes"), see *Select Epigrams from the Greek Anthology*, ed. with rev. text, trans., introduction, and notes by J. W. Mackail (London: Longmans, Green, 1911), 227.

34. Entry in black ink. Almost exact quotation from "Kniga sed'maya. Platon (Elevzinskaya misteriya): Glava I," in Shiure, *Velikiye posvyashchennïye*, 315.

35. Entry in black ink. Almost exact quotation from "Kniga sed'maya. Platon (Elevzinskaya misteriya): Glava II," in Shiure, *Velikiye posvyashchennïye*, 320.

36. Entry in black ink. Almost exact quotation from ibid., 321.

37. The first of two original poems by Prokofiev in the notebook, copied out by his mother. The four introductory lines are composed in amphibrachic tetrameter with dactylic and feminine rhymes, and the remaining forty-six lines are written in iambic tetrameter with feminine rhymes throughout. The second poem by Prokofiev is the last entry in the notebook and the only one in Prokofiev's own handwriting. These two poems are the only dated entries in the notebook.

38. The entire entry is in black ink, with the occasional missing punctuation and letters added. As discussed in my introduction, Boryunya is Boris Nikolayevich Bashkirov, the son of a wealthy St. Petersburg merchant who wrote under the pseudonym Boris Verin and hosted a literary salon devoted to the discussion of philosophy, literature, and music. Prokofiev first recorded visiting Bashkirov at home in a diary entry of May 5, 1914 (Prokof'yev, *Dnevnik*, 1:457–58); he subsequently gave him piano lessons and became a good friend. He first attended Bashkirov's Monday salon on October 3, 1916 (1:619). On the participants and topics discussed at Bashkirov's salon, see Nest'yev, *Prokof'yev*, 96.

In his poem Prokofiev characterizes Bashkirov as a *boltun* (chatterbox) and poet. In his diary entry for May 1917 he also noted his friend's excessive banter: "B. Verin, bol'tlivost' kotorogo ravnosil'na ob"yavleniyu v gazetakh" (B. Verin, whose chattiness is tantamount to placing an announcement in the newspapers). Prokof'yev, *Dnevnik*, 1:650. His view of Bashkirov's poetic talent was mixed. On September 24, 1914, he recorded that Bashkirov read him some of his poetry and commented that it was not that good (1:502). Despite this reservation, in 1915 he turned Bashkirov's poem "Dover'sya mne" (Trust in me) into a song (no. 3 in op. 23), following Gippius's "Seroye plat'itse" (no. 2 in op. 23), the text of which appears a few pages earlier in this notebook [16–17]. A few years later, however, on December 20, 1922, he noted in his diary: "Nado soznat'sya, B. N. vse-taki ne poet. Skuden klyuch!" (It must be admitted, B. N. is just not a poet. The spring is dry!) (2:214).

39. Familiar form of Sergey (i.e., Prokofiev).

40. *Samolyot* (Airplane) was evidently the name of the ship on which Prokofiev and Bashkirov traveled down the river Volga in the summer of 1916. See the early twentieth-century postcard showing the ship *Samolyot* moored at Yaroslavl, at http://postcards.sgu.ru/ShowCard.php?pic ture=196 (accessed November 23, 2006). After leaving Rybinsk on July 1, the two friends sailed together to Yaroslavl, Ples, and Samara; Bashkirov stayed in Samara for a few days while Prokofiev traveled on to Astrakhan, where he was soon joined by his friend. For a detailed and amusing account of the voyage, see the entry for July 1916 in Prokof'yev, *Dnevnik*, 1:614–15.

41. Prokofiev sailed from the port of Astrakhan on July 17, 1916 (the day before this poem was composed). See his letter of July 16, 1916, to Eleonora Damskaya: "We have made a stop in Astrakhan. We are eating caviar, riding in a motor boat, lying on the roof of our ship, and walk-ing round the colorful bazaar. Tomorrow we leave for Persia." *Selected Letters of Sergei Prokofiev*, 27.

42. "Gur'yevskaya kasha" (Gurev pudding), a famous Russian national dish, made with semolina, milk, sugar, butter, eggs, and walnuts. According to most accounts of its origins, it was invented by Count D. A. Gurev (1751–1825), Tsar Alexander I's Minister of Finance, to com-memorate the Russian victory over Napoleon in 1812.

43. Laninskaya voda (Lanin's beverage) was a popular fizzy fruit drink or mineral water pro-duced by the Moscow firm of N. P. Lanin (1832–95). Lanin was also the publisher and editor of the newspaper *Russkiy kur'yer*. Chekhov, a contributor to this newspaper, incorporated a satiri-cal reference to Lanin "fizzing forth" a song as part of a program for a musical evening included in his sketch of 1882 "Komicheskiye reklamï i ob"yavleniya (soobshchil Antosha Chekhonte)" (Comic advertisements and announcements [reported by Antosha Chekhonte]).

44. See Prokofiev's account of this incident in his diary entry for July 1916: "Odnako v Astrakhane kompozitor i poet rasstalis' vtorichno: Boris Verin ne mog prosnut'sya poldevyatogo, ya yego oblival kholodnoy vodoy, on togda osvirepel i so zlosti prospal otkhod kaspiyskogo parokhoda. Ya uekhal odin." (However, in Astrakhan the composer and the poet parted for the second time: Boris Verin could not wake up at half past eight, I poured cold water over him, he then went mad and out of spite slept through the departure of the Caspian ship. I left on my own.) Prokof'yev, *Dnevnik*, 1:615. See also his letter to Eleonora Damskaya of July 19: "Boris Verin overslept the ship's departure and therefore remained in Astrakhan." *Selected Letters of Sergei Prokofiev*, 28.

45. The original spelling *nastey* has been changed to the correct form, *nastiy*. The word *nast'ye* is a play on *nenast'ye*—"bad weather" or "bad times"; the removal of the negative prefix suggests good times rather than bad times, evidently an allusion to the ups and downs Prokofiev expected to encounter on his further travels.

46. Prokofiev dated his tale in verse July 18, the day after he boarded the ship, leaving his friend behind in Astrakhan. On July 18 he disembarked from the ship at Petrovsk and caught a train to Tiflis. Later in the month he continued to compose verse. In his diary entry for July 1916 he noted that he had discovered a talent for rhymes and composed some humorous poems while traveling down the Georgian military high road from Tiflis to Vladikavkaz by post-chaise. Prokof'yev, *Dnevnik*, 1:615–16.

47. Entry in pencil. The Life-Guards 1st Rifles Regiment of His Highness was one of the Guards Infantry Regiments of the Russian Army in 1914; see http://www.armymuseum.ru (accessed April 8, 2005). The surname of Second Lieutenant A. A. Yablonsk[y] is not entirely legible or fully writ-ten out. In his diary Prokofiev frequently mentions members of the Yablonsky family, who were friends and regular guests at his home from 1910 to 1913; in February 1916 he also notes Mme Yablonskaya's numerous anxious telephone calls to him against the background of demonstra-tions taking place in Petrograd (Prokof'yev, *Dnevnik*, 1:103, 107, 141, 181, 191, 198, 201, 265, 294, 387, 639). The entry in the notebook may refer to a member of this family and the regi-ment in which he was serving. It was evidently written at some point after August 1916, when Prokofiev had returned to Petrograd from his trip on the Volga.

48. Prokofieva first wrote *to* (the fact), then crossed this out and replaced it with *potomu* (because). This change confused the syntax of the remaining part of the sentence.

49. Entry in pencil. Prokofieva evidently took these notes on the planet Venus for her son, who developed a passion for astronomy and regular observation of the stars from October 1916 to May 1917. Some of the information recorded in these notes remains correct; for example, Venus is indeed

the brightest planet in the sky after the sun and moon, its orbital period is calculated to be exactly 224.701 days, and it is similar to Earth in size, mass, volume, and density. Some other points of information were evidently considered correct at the time, but have since been superseded. When astronomers first observed Venus, they saw that the planet was covered entirely by clouds and concluded that its atmosphere contained large amounts of water vapor and an Earth-like atmosphere. It was later discovered that the planet's heavy atmosphere is composed mainly of carbon dioxide with virtually no water vapor (the clouds are composed of sulphuric acid droplets). The runaway greenhouse effect caused by the heavy atmosphere of carbon dioxide trapping heat accounts for the very high surface temperature of the planet (estimated at 462°–482° C). In the notebook a much lower maximum temperature of 187° C is given and attributed erroneously to the planet's proximity to the Sun (Venus's surface is hotter than Mercury's despite being nearly twice as far from the Sun). The possibility of life on the planet is ruled out by its high temperature and almost total absence of water vapor. See http://www.solarviews.com/eng/venus.htm and http://www.nineplanets.org/venus.htm (accessed April 11, 2005).

50. Entry in pencil. Archimedes (ca. 287–212 BC), the greatest mathematician and scientist of antiquity, initiated the fields of static mechanics, hydrostatics, and pycnometry (the measurement of the volume or density of an object); he also built a mechanical model planetarium. Galileo Galilei (1564–1642), mathematician and astronomer, wrote his first scientific book, *The Little Balance* (1586), to describe Archimedes' method of finding the relative densities of substances using a balance. Later he argued against Aristotle's view of astronomy and natural philosophy; from 1609 he made several astronomical discoveries with his telescopes, described in *The Starry Messenger* (1610). His challenge to the Church's established view of the structure of the universe led to a trial, at which he was found guilty of heresy.

51. Entry in pencil. Unidentified source. In the original *ne tol'ko* (not only) is written as one word without a gap. Anti-German opinions of this type were frequently expressed in Russia during the First World War. Prokofieva's views seemingly relate to the German advance and revolutionary uprisings in Petrograd, described in detail by Prokofiev in his diary entries for February, March, and April 1917 (Prokof'yev, *Dnevnik*, 1:639–49). They may also relate to the discussion of national pride and the Germans in chapter 4 of Arthur Schopenhauer's *Aphorisms on the Wisdom of Life* (cited three pages later in the notebook, one paragraph before a comment on the vanity of rank and orders).

52. Entry in pencil. In 1851 Schopenhauer published *Parerga and Paralipomena*, a two-volume collection of essays, dialogues, and aphorisms. The sixth and last book of the first volume, *Aphorisms on the Wisdom of Life*, is the source of the next eleven entries in the notebook, drawn from chaps. 2, 4, and 5 of a Russian translation of this work.

Prokofiev's interest in Schopenhauer is documented in his diary from September 1916 to June 1918. His regular joint readings of the *Aphorisms* with Bashkirov took place from September 1916 to April 1917. Some of his comments on Schopenhauer are directly related to the aphorisms cited in the notebook.

Several Russian translations of Schopenhauer's *Aphorisms on the Wisdom of Life* were available at this time, including versions by F. V. Chernigovets (St. Petersburg, 1886–95, and later editions), E. Levitskaya-Rogolya (St. Petersburg, 1902), S. I. Ershov (Moscow, 1904), Yu. I. Aikhenvald (Moscow, 1901–10), and N. M. Gubskiy (St. Petersburg, 1910 and 1914). The text cited in the notebook does not overlap exactly with any of the published translations consulted. In the notes that follow, the citations of Schopenhauer have been cross-referenced with the Russian translation of 1914: Artur Shopengauer, *Aforizmï zhiteyskoy mudrosti*, trans. N. M. Gubskiy (St. Petersburg: Tipografiya Akts. O-va Tip. Dela v SPb. [Gerol'd], 1914). References are also given to the standard academic English edition: Arthur Schopenhauer, *Parerga et Paralipomena. Short Philosophical Essays,* trans. E. F. J. Payne, 2 vols. (Oxford: Clarendon Press, 2000).

53. Entry in pencil. See Glava II, "O tom, chto takoye chelovek" (Chapter 2, "What a man is"), in Shopengauer, *Aforizmï*, 17.

54. Entry in pencil. See Glava II, "O tom. . . takoye," in Shopengauer, *Aforizmï*, 26.

55. Entry in pencil. See Glava II, "O tom. . . takoye," in Shopengauer, *Aforizmï*, 23.

56. Entry in pencil. Ibid., 41.

57. Entry in pencil. See Glava IV, "O tom, chto predstavlyayet soboyu chelovek" (Chapter 4, "What a person represents"), in Shopengauer, *Aforizmï*, 59.

58. Entry in pencil. Ibid., 61–62.

59. Entry in pencil. See Glava V, "Poucheniya i pravila" (Chapter 5, "Counsels and maxims"), in Shopengauer, *Aforizmï*, 113–14. The first sentence is a quotation from Aristotle's *Nicomachean Ethics*: "The prudent man seeks, not pleasure, but freedom from pain." *The Ethics of Aristotle. The Nicomachean Ethics*, trans. J. A. K. Thomson (Harmondsworth: Penguin, 1959), bk 7, chap. 11, 218. Aristotle returns to the same thought in bk 7, chap.12, 220–21. In the Russian version of the French saying attributed by Schopenhauer to Voltaire, *za tem* is written as one word without a gap, and *la douleur* replaces *le malheur*, which has been crossed out.

In his diary entry for May 1917, following a detailed analysis of the impact of Schopenhauer on his attitude to life, Prokofiev paraphrased these words of Schopenhauer very closely (Prokof'yev, *Dnevnik*, 1:654). He referred to the same passage again in September 1917 (ibid., 1:671).

60. Entry in pencil. See Glava V, "Poucheniya," in Shopengauer, *Aforizmï*, 115.

61. Entry in pencil. Ibid., 127.

62. Entry in pencil. A French maxim cited by Schopenhauer in ibid., 133.

63. Entry in pencil. See ibid., 132. Schopenhauer's comments on rank would have had particular resonance for Russian readers because of the pervasive influence of rank in Russia. In 1722 Peter the Great passed a decree introducing the Table of Ranks, which set out fourteen classes of ranks, defining the hierarchies of military, civilian, and court life. This system remained in effect with slight modifications until the October Revolution. The distorting influence of the national obsession with rank on human relations is explored in the work of many Russian writers, such as Chekhov, Dostoyevsky, Denis Fonvizin, and Gogol.

64. Entry in pencil. The phrase *um serdtsa* (mind of the heart) occurs in the correspondence of Leo Tolstoy and Afanasiy Fet. In a letter of June 28, 1867, responding to Fet's criticism of Turgenev's novel *Smoke* (*Dïm*, 1867), Tolstoy uses this phrase to characterize the way of thinking he shares with Fet; he attributes the phrase to Fet and thanks him for introducing him to the distinction between the "mind of the heart" and the "mind of the mind": "O 'Dïme' ya vam pisat' khotel davno i, razumeyetsya, to samoye, chto vï mne pishete. Ot etogo-to mï i lyubim drug druga, chto odinakovo dumayem *umom serdtsa*, kak vï nazïvayete. (Yeshcho za eto pis'mo vam spasibo bol'shoye. *Um uma i um serdtsa* – eto mne mnogoye ob"yasnilo.)" (For a long time I have wanted to write to you about *Smoke* and, of course, along the same lines as you write to me. This is the reason we love each other, because we think in the same way with the *mind of the heart*, as you call it. [Many thanks once more for this letter. The *mind of the mind* and the *mind of the heart* – this explained a great deal to me].) L. N. Tolstoy, *Perepiska s russkimi pisatelyami*, ed. S. A. Rozanova, 2 vols. (Moscow: Khudozhestvennaya literatura, 1978), 1:387. Fet included the full text of Tolstoy's letter to him in his memoirs, A. A. Fet, *Moi vospominaniya: 1848–1889* (Moscow: Tipografiya A. I. Mamontova, 1890), 120–21.

Prokofieva's entry echoes Tolstoy's and Fet's shared understanding of the "mind of the heart" as a vital element of artistic creation and essential criterion for its assessment. She may have heard the phrase from Prokofiev, who learned various "interesting things" from Bashkirov about Tolstoy's philosophical and religious views on November 16, 1914. Prokof'yev, *Dnevnik*, 1:525.

65. Entry in purple ink. Part of the text of an ancient Akkadian incantation, rendered into Russian by Konstantin Balmont in a few different versions. Prokofieva has copied the opening section of Balmont's second version of the incantation, "Semero ikh! Semero ikh!.." (They are seven! They are seven!), first published in 1915 in his treatise on the links between poetry, magic, and music. K. Bal'mont, *Poeziya kak volshebstvo* (Moscow: Skorpion, 1915), 73–74. The text in the notebook reproduces with a few variations 21 of the first 25 lines of Balmont's full version of 42 lines, omitting five and a half lines (9, 15–16, part of 17, 19–20), splitting one line into two lines, and including two breaks in the layout of the text that do not occur in any other editions. See n. 92 in my introduction for a further discussion of Balmont's various versions.

Prokofiev worked intensively on the musical setting of "Semero ikh" for tenor, choir, and large orchestra (op. 30) between September 4, 1917, and January 13/26, 1918 (Prokof'yev, *Dnevnik*, 1:670, 681). For the text of his musical setting he used most of the second version of 1915, as well as sections from the first version of 1908; he also incorporated a few lines from the prose commentary that followed the text of the incantation in the treatise of 1915.

For a detailed account of Prokofiev's relations with Balmont and the origins of this work, see Pamela Davidson, "Magic, Music and Poetry: Prokofiev's Creative Relationship with Bal'mont and the Genesis of *Seven, They Are Seven*," *New Zealand Slavonic Journal* (2002): 67–79, first published in shorter form in *Three Oranges: The Journal of the Serge Prokofiev Foundation* 2 (November 2001): 14–19. For a musical analysis of the work, see Noëlle Mann, "'Breathless With Excitement': Prokofiev's Incantation," *Three Oranges: The Journal of the Serge Prokofiev Foundation* 2 (November 2001): 20–23.

66. Entry in pencil. The last entry in the notebook and the only one in Prokofiev's own handwriting. It is the second original poem by him in the notebook, composed in trochaic tetrameter with masculine rhymes, paired in the first quatrain and alternating in the second quatrain. Ararat is the traditional resting place of Noah's Ark after the deluge (Gen. 8:4), according to most opinions located in Armenia. The identity of Semyon has not been confirmed. For a discussion of the poem's political allusions, see the introductory essay.

Prokofiev's poem is the only entry in the notebook to implement some of the principles of the spelling reform promulgated by the Provisional Government in the summer of 1917 and enforced by two further decrees of the new Soviet regime in December 1917 and 1918. Prokofiev opposed the orthographic reforms; as a form of resistance, he adopted some but not all of the suggested changes in a highly idiosyncratic manner. He dropped the hard sign *ier* in the terminal position following a consonant, but he did not replace the old *iat'* with *e*, as recommended by the advocates of the spelling reform. Most oddly, he substitutes all of the letters и with *i*. In prerevolutionary orthography и was occasionally replaced by *i* before vowels; the spelling reform of 1917–18 called for *i* to be scrapped and replaced by и. At no time was it suggested that и should be entirely scrapped and replaced by *i*. Prokofiev's only predecessor in this matter appears to have been Peter the Great, who at one time proposed substituting и with *i*, but then reinstated и. According to the memoirs of Prokofiev's first music teacher, he adopted this unusual practice in 1908. Glier, "Vospominaniya," 364. For several years after 1917 Prokofiev's orthography continued to exhibit similar eccentric variations.

The Krzhizhanovsky-Prokofiev

Collaboration on *Eugene Onegin*, 1936

(A Lesser-Known Casualty of the Pushkin Death Jubilee)

INTRODUCTORY ESSAY, COMMENTARY, AND
TRANSLATION BY CARYL EMERSON

The 1937 centennial of Pushkin's death was the most ambitious literary canonization mounted in the Stalinist state. It bore some resemblance to the only other Soviet-era literary centennial that can compete, that of Leo Tolstoy's birth, celebrated in 1928. There was the same flooding of the country with his books, the same ubiquitously advertised image on billboards and candy wrappers, the same amnesia about the writer's mature value system when it conflicted with a Soviet-friendly image: aristocratism in Pushkin's case, Christian anarchism in Tolstoy's. Both centennials displayed the same tendency toward repressive revisionism. Before his death in 1924, Lenin had decreed that the Jubilee Collected Works of Tolstoy were to include, uncensored, everything that the master had written, but this mandate did not prevent the launching in 1928 of organized terror against all pacifist Tolstoyan communities on Russian soil. Pushkin's politics were not the sort that inspired anti-state, spiritually suspect sects. But this restless poet who in his youth rebelled against the tsarist bureaucracy was also a libertine, a courtier, a champion of autocracy, an unrepentant owner of serfs. His image, too, required adjustment.

In the realm of Soviet culture, these two titanic jubilees stimulated different sorts of creative tribute. Tolstoy, Russia's greatest master of realist prose, distrusted poetry, considered ballet obscene, lampooned opera, abhorred Shakespeare, and had a passionate but suspicious relationship to music. His centennial emphasized his literary and moral word, not its musicalization. Only in the various versions of Prokofiev's *War and Peace* (1941–52) did the contradictions of the great novelist finally meet their match in music. The cosmopolitan Pushkin shared none of Tolstoy's phobias.

Pushkin adored the theater, worshipped Shakespeare, courted and seduced ballerinas, and loved the artifice of the lighter musical genres, whether comic opera, vaudeville, operetta, or the gypsy songs he heard in brothels. In the 1820s, he witnessed with some gratification his own lyrics being set as art songs and his longer narrative poems as staged musical events. For Pushkin, music was primarily entertainment. Its purpose was to deepen, heighten, and intensify emotional pleasure. Although the poet sought neither to write *na golos*—that is, for preexisting melodies—nor to collaborate with musicians in composing songs or operas, a vein of tolerance and even delight for the buoyantly staged or musicalized word shines through Pushkin's work.[1]

These facts help explain why Prokofiev, repatriated to Moscow in 1936, celebrated as the greatest living lyricist in Russian music and courted by Hollywood's Paramount and Disney, found himself hard at work on several ambitious projects for the Pushkin Jubilee. His commissions included a score to Mikhaíl Romm's film of *The Queen of Spades* (*Pikovaya dama*), music to a staging of the full *Boris Godunov* (twenty-five scenes) for Vsevolod Meyerhold, and incidental music to *Eugene Onegin* in an adaptation for the stage by Sigizmund Krzhizhanovsky to be produced at Alexander Tairov's Moscow Chamber Theater. Artistic commissions routinely came with a cash advance, but they were not ideological blank checks. The Pushkin Jubilee was carefully monitored from above. Guidelines changed month by month as the country's cultural establishment registered the growing impact of blacklists and capricious arrests. The first planning board for the jubilee, appointed in July 1934, was purged. Meyerhold became a member of the second "corrected and expanded" All-Union Pushkin Commission under Stalin's direct supervision.[2] In December 1935, this new commission resolved to shift the focus of the centennial from "Pushkin, victim of tsarist oppression" to a more optimistic, upbeat message emphasizing poetry, the Russian language, and a radiant future for Russian culture. Academic Pushkinists were brought in to counterbalance the Party watchdogs. It would seem that Pushkin's translucent, tuneful, lyrical aesthetics (so compatible with Prokofiev's own) could now flourish. In an interview with *Izvestiya* in 1934, the composer identified "light-serious or serious-light music" as that genre most necessary to the "new path of Soviet music."[3] Simplicity and grace were themselves Pushkinian traits.

By the end of 1936, however, Tairov, Romm, and Meyerhold had each been censured for more general "creative errors." With directorial careers in jeopardy and theaters or studios at risk, the three controversial Pushkin-Prokofiev projects fell apart. Some of Prokofiev's music found its way into the operas *Semyon Kotko*, *The Duenna*, and *War and Peace*, his ballet *Cinderella*, the Eighth Piano Sonata, and the Seventh Symphony. Krzhizhanovsky's playscript began its long, undisturbed repose in the Russian State Archive of Literature and Art (RGALI).[4] And the All-Union Pushkin Commission retreated to safer ground, turning its attention from creative projects to the size of publication runs, book distribution to schools and libraries, exhibitions, monuments, commemorative plaques, postage stamps, and the renaming of streets, factories, and collective farms in Pushkin's honor.[5] In late January–early February 1937, the specific centennial moment of the poet's duel and death, literally nothing on or by Pushkin was being performed in any Moscow theater.

The Collaboration

The early history of the *Eugene Onegin* adaptation and its music can be told through several key dates and documents.[6] On April 16, 1936, Tairov wrote to Prokofiev that he had discussed *Eugene Onegin* with Platon Kerzhentsev, chairman of the All-Union Committee on Arts Affairs, who confirmed that the composer was providing the music. On April 17, Tairov publicly announced the project. On May 25, Prokofiev signed a contract to deliver the piano score by mid-August and orchestration by October 1. On July 22 the composer informed the Soviet press that he had almost finished the forty-four musical numbers and considered the score the best of all his Pushkin Centennial music.[7] On October 15, Prokofiev enlisted Pavel Lamm to realize the orchestration. At some point in the summer of 1936, the Pushkin Commission and then Glavrepertkom (the "Main Repertory Committee" or censorship board), critiqued the score, presumably with some version of a playscript attached to it. Then on December 3, 1936, Prokofiev, while touring in Brussels, heard from his wife, Lina, that the Committee on Arts Affairs requested that work on the orchestration be halted because the project had been annulled. This collapse was not directly related to the music but appears to have been collateral damage in the wake of another troubled Tairov project, a staging of Alexander Borodin's comic opera *The Heroic Warriors* (*Bogatïri*), which that winter had fallen out of official grace. In a panic, Tairov's theater canceled all potentially problematic repertory items, including *Eugene Onegin*.

Until recently, the history of the playscript has been difficult to reconstitute. In large part this was due to the obscurity of the playwright, Sigizmund Dominikovich Krzhizhanovsky (1887–1950), a Ukrainian-born, ethnically Polish Russophone writer well known in Kiev and then Moscow circles as a lecturer, theater pedagogue, Anglophile, and Shakespeare specialist. But he was uncannily unlucky in print. After 1922 Krzhizhanovsky worked as a consultant at Tairov's Chamber Theater, introducing Russian actors and audiences to G. K. Chesterton (whose 1908 anarchist spy novel, *The Man Who Was Thursday: A Nightmare,* he adapted for the Russian stage) and to the socialist satires of George Bernard Shaw. By the late 1920s, however, his own brilliantly surreal stories, comparable to Zamyatin, Borges, Kafka, Hoffmann, and Swift, had no market. When shown a collection of Krzhizhanovsky's fiction in 1932, Maxim Gorky, head of the newly centralized Union of Soviet Writers, remarked that tales like these would "hardly find a publisher." And if they did, Gorky asked, and even managed to "dislocate a few young minds," was such writing really necessary?[8] This ungenerous judgment by the father of Socialist Realism effectively closed the door on publication during the Soviet period.

Krzhizhanovsky's 1927 autobiographical fantasy "Knizhnaya zakladka" (Bookmark) contains a scene in which an unlucky author presents an unsympathetic publisher with a collection titled *Rasskazï dlya zacherknutïkh* (Stories for the crossed-out). By the time *Eugene Onegin* collapsed in 1936, such non-personhood had long been a bitter joke for the writer himself. Beginning in the mid-1920s, Krzhizhanovsky's work had been routinely rejected. In 1924, the publishing house that had accepted his *Skazki dlya Vunderkindov* (Fairy tales for Wunderkinder) folded. Individual short stories, a screenplay, and a comic drama failed to find sponsors in 1928–29. In 1933, his "Academia" edition of Shakespeare's Collected Works was canceled. Krzhizhanovsky's beloved screenplay *Novïy Gulliver* (A new Gulliver), which

Figure 1. Krzhizhanovsky on vacation in Italy, summer 1912 (age 25).

he had worked on for years and resubmitted in several variants, was set upon by hacks and finally released without his name included in the credits. In 1934, his play *Pop i poruchik* (The priest and the lieutenant) was considered by several theaters but produced by none. That same year, censors put a stop to a collection of his stories in press with the State Publishing House. Theaters toyed with his 1937 tragifarce *Tot, tretiy* (That man, the third one) but did not stage it—and with reason: the "third" was a subversive, fugitive poet-witness.[9] His collection *Neukushennïy lokot'* (The unbitten elbow), titled after one of its most Kafka-like tales, was poised to appear together with another volume of tales in 1941, but the war intervened. Both projects were postponed and then dissolved. Krzhizhanovsky's lifelong companion Anna Bovshek (1887–1971), who stored his archive in the clothes closet of her apartment under a stretch of brocade, notes in her memoirs that when he first heard confirmation, in late 1936, that *Eugene Onegin* at the Chamber Theater had also "crashed" (*postig krakh*), he remarked: "Samson didn't wage battle against his windmill. He let his hair grow out—and perhaps also what lay beneath it: a thought."[10]

Krzhizhanovsky continued to write. But he was proud, quick-tempered, unable to curry favor, and as he watched his writer acquaintances begin to be arrested he withdrew from literary society, feeling himself (in Bovshek's words) a "played-out player, a loser, ashamed of his role but at the same time not ceasing to believe in his creative gifts and the usefulness of his work" (30). In this depressed state he began a collection of stories titled *Chem lyudi myortvï* (What men die by, or "become dead by"), in bitter counterpoint to Tolstoy's 1879 parable on the power of compassionate love, "Chem lyudi zhivï" ("What Men Live By"). And he succumbed to drink. When asked by friends what had driven him to it, Bovshek recalls him saying: "A sober relationship to reality" (30). Krzhizhanovsky died of alcoholism in 1950. Although almost wholly unpublished as a creative writer, he had belatedly been accepted into the Union of Soviet Writers in 1939 and thus qualified for official posthumous recognition (or "immortalization").[11] Between 1957 and 1959 a Commission on the Literary Legacy of S. D. Krzhizhanovsky, authorized by the presidium of the Moscow branch of the Union, generated minutes of a meeting and a publishing plan.[12] But nothing came of this initiative in the waning years of the first post-Stalinist Thaw. Only late in the glasnost era did the publication efforts of one devoted poet and scholar, Vadim Perelmuter, begin to bear fruit with the release of stories half a century old, the creation of an excellent web site, and, finally, five volumes of *Sobraniye sochinenii* (Collected works).[13] Krzhizhanovsky's name returned to public life and even experienced a modest boom. In 1990, the eminent classicist and philologist Mikhail Gasparov reviewed the maiden collection of Krzhizhanovsky's stories, *Vospominaniya o budushchem* (Memories of the future, 1989) in the journal *Oktyabr'*. "I fear," Gasparov wrote, "that readers, glancing at the name of the author, will think this is a translation from the Polish . . . they are deceived. Open the book: translations are not written in such language."[14]

For the man himself this endorsement came too late. As his first-person narrator notes in the opening line of the 1928 story "Shvï" (Stitches): "Everyone is able to forget. It's only the one who has been forgotten who cannot forget" ("Vsem dano zabït'. Odnomu ne dano—zabïtomu"). Gasparov credits two people, "the writer's widow Anna Bovshek and the poet Vadim Perelmuter," for insisting that Krzhizhanovsky's talent was an "event" and for single-handedly overcoming the inertia of his nonexistence. Gasparov's review includes this poignant detail from Bovshek's memoirs about Krzhizhanovsky's final years: "A brain spasm deprived him of the ability to read, and he had to learn the alphabet all over again. To the psychiatrist's test question, 'Do you love Pushkin?' he began to weep—for the only time in his life, according to the memory of the woman who had known him for thirty years."[15] With the exception of one slender paperback of short stories, Krzhizhanovsky still has almost no presence among an English-speaking lay readership.[16]

The paucity of people who cared about this writer and his work greatly reduced the paper trail around his partly realized creations. Published memoirs of Krzhizhanovsky are few. One, written by a woman friend twenty-four years his junior, emphasizes his odd habits and ends on disillusionment at his inebriated visits during his final years; another, more enamored, was submitted by a niece and titled "The Legend of Zigmund the First."[17] They do not mention the *Eugene Onegin* project. Those who knew about the censorship mandates—and who survived the Terror—were bound by Party discipline to cleanse their recollections or (better) not to recall at all. Politics aside, memoirs (and scholarship based on memoirs) must be read with extreme care. Constructed retroactively and conditioned by their own present, they lack the verisimilitude of diaries or of correspondence contemporary with events. In 1987 and then in 2000, the Tairov scholar N. G. Litvinenko discussed interactions among director, playwright, composer, and set designer over *Eugene Onegin*. In her earlier reconstruction of events she treats the playscript almost as an impediment to the enterprise, whereas her post-Soviet essay, written half a decade into the boom, is warmly appreciative of the playwright.[18] In commemorative tributes to the project's distinguished set and costume designer Alexander Osmyorkin (1892–1953), references to Krzhizhanovsky's work are scant, wary, and disrespectful. Osmyorkin's wife during those years, the actress E. K. Galperina, said this about the 1936 project four decades after the fact:

Today, even after the passage of so many years, it's difficult to explain why this wonderful director [Tairov] ever resolved on such a venture. The poet's greatest creation, *Eugene Onegin*—a novel in verse—was redone into a play by the writer S. D. Krzhizhanovsky. Again it's incomprehensible how that gifted, intelligent man, a brilliant translator of Mickiewicz, agreed to do a scenic adaptation of *Onegin*. Osmyorkin was struck by this "adventurism," as he called it, but he had to admit that Krzhizhanovsky, to the extent permitted by his own taste, had turned [Pushkin] into a play. For a long time he pondered over whether or not to become a participant in this unlikely enterprise. But the temptation of working on *Onegin* eventually won out. As an artist [he said], I will do everything just as Pushkin drew it. Let the actors wander about the stage and say whatever they are required to say—that's not my business. I already see mock-ups for all the scenes and I cannot refuse.[19]

Judging by ten costume sketches for *Eugene Onegin* published in 1979, Osmyorkin's own taste was anything but adventurous.[20] His blend of the lyrical and the satiric placed him well within the traditional, realist Stanislavsky school of design. The heroine Tatyana is ravishing, languid, resembling Pushkin's wife, Natalie, and the poet's own drawings of beloved women. The Name Day guests are stereotypical Gogolian caricatures: brutish face, no neck, trim potbelly tucked into white trousers, spindly legs, tiny sloping feet. There are some wonderful touches. The watercolor and graphite pencil sketch of Onegin at the duel, for example, shows the hero dressed in the hybrid style of the provinces, a visual emblem of Prokofiev's out-of-tune rural harpsichords, with a *Childe Harold* cloak billowing around his shoulders and on his feet *valenki*, Russian peasant felt boots. It appears that Osmyorkin was already familiar with Prokofiev's music by the time he began work, for he produced a sketch of the Name Day Mummers, whose visit and grotesque song are unique to the playscript (they exist nowhere in Pushkin). The art historian L. Olinskaya praises all of Osmyorkin's drawings for their "precise correspondence with the music," but she mentions Krzhizhanovsky's name only once.[21] She makes no comment on Osmyorkin's reaction to the play nor to its visually precise stage directions. Although Galperina did note that her husband grudgingly granted Tairov's actors the right to wander about the stage and "say what they were required to say" according to the script, still, the nervous quivering of Krzhizhanovsky's surreal stage space—bordering on the hallucinatory and hemmed in by walls that, once breached, open out to infinity—could not have been congenial to him as a visual artist.[22]

In the consensus of memoirists, Krzhizhanovsky's contribution to the *Eugene Onegin* project was the most dispensable. Osmyorkin appears to have drawn his inspiration straight from Pushkin (and somewhat from the composer); we do not know Krzhizhanovsky's reaction to the sketches, which were never realized onstage. Prokofiev did respond directly to the play, but there is no trace of any correspondence between him and the playwright. Tairov commissioned Krzhizhanovsky's text, but most accounts hint darkly at their disagreements. Thanks to the generosity of RGALI, a more objective, although still hypothetical, piecing together of events is now possible.[23]

In the file for Tairov's Chamber Theater, under the rubric "Unstaged Plays," *Eugene Onegin* is not mentioned. But the production had clearly been entered into repertory and was a line item in the theater's budget. On May 22, 1936, three days before Prokofiev was contracted for the music, the Chamber Theater and Osmyorkin reached an agreement stipulating "the shaping of the artistic concept: models, sketches for the layout of scenes, costumes, props, and other accessories pertinent to the production of E.O." The designer was to be paid in installments, with the final balance due "within three days after the premiere but not later than March 1, 1937," suggesting that *Eugene Onegin* was planned as a banner event early in the jubilee year.[24] Its stage run would thus coincide with the actual centennial date of the poet's death (January 27, 1837, from a bullet wound received in a duel defending his wife's honor)—eerily appropriate, given the lethal, blizzard-driven duel at the center of the play.

A half-dozen typescripts of Krzhizhanovsky's play are held at RGALI in four different personal collections. In various degrees of completion and abbreviation, they come with (and without) corrections, cross-outs, insertions, marginalia, paste-ins by Tairov and Krzhizhanovsky, which are partially traceable by different-colored pencils (black, blue, red, violet).[25] Although an intricate history of these evolving texts is beyond the scope of the present essay, a sampling of some exemplary stressful moments will suggest its dynamics. At some point in late 1935 or early 1936, Krzhizhanovsky submitted a playscript to Tairov. The two presumably revised it beginning in the winter or early spring of 1936 for a read-through involving Prokofiev. This first revision is the playscript from which the composer worked and which is translated here. It is most likely the earliest stable product of collaboration between playwright and director, still relatively free from official censorship interference. Censors entered the picture in the summer of 1936 (a textual clue in the margins helps us to determine the date), prompting a second revision, which Prokofiev refers to as the "new plan."[26] There seems to have been yet a third revision. The document translated in this volume, dated 1936, is the only one with Prokofiev's autograph markings.

There is some evidence that Krzhizhanovsky began work on his adaptation of *Eugene Onegin* as early as 1933.[27] That year Tairov produced, also

Figure 2. Princess Tatyana. Indian ink, dry brush. Petersburg salon, *Fragment 12*.

Figure 3. Onegin at the Larins' Name Day Ball. Ink wash. Name Day, *Fragment 7*.

Figure 4. Guests at the Larins' Name Day. Lead pencil, watercolor. Name Day, *Fragment 7*.

hybrid of scenes from George
…speare's *Antony and Cleopatra*,
…ovsky was probably consultant.
…ing with "classics," in which he
as *Hamlet* in twentieth-century
…motional knots" relevant to con-
…ing those values with an eye to

…tempo… institutional survival could be a … us exercise during the Stalinist period, straining the most loyal allegiances. Krzhizhanovsky and Tairov were friends of long standing. For a decade and a half, the writer had coached the Chamber Theater troupe on the "psychology of the actor" and had supported Tairov in his polemic with Meyerhold's revolutionary modernism.[30] The director, in turn, admired the writer's gift for making fantasy psychologically concrete. The two friends appear to have disagreed, however, on the precise "knots" in *Eugene Onegin* that should be foregrounded for the Soviet spectator. They did not see eye to eye on the virtues and vices of its Byronic hero. Tatyana was differently mythologized by each. And when Tairov began to feel the heat of the censors, he sought to preempt the objections of official Pushkinists (and thereby save the play) by reinserting traces of the Narrator, whose perspective unifies Pushkin's novel.

Krzhizhanovsky could only have fretted. Deleting the Narrator had originally been their highest priority. In an interview for *Krasnaya gazeta* on April 20, 1936, Tairov remarked that he "had already been working with Krzhizhanovsky on an edition of the playscript for roughly half a year . . . in general attempting to uncover those dramatic situations that were embedded in *Onegin* by Pushkin himself." The work is difficult, the director confessed, because "we immediately decided to reject the role of a reader (*chtets*/the Narrator)."[31] Other agents would be found to bind character to character and scene to scene—music being one. Tairov, who disciplined his actors to think and move synthetically by rehearsing to Beethoven and Chopin, considered it "unthinkable to realize *Eugene Onegin* on stage without the significant participation of music." For this he thanks Prokofiev. But if a new score was to work in the interests of Pushkin, it must discard existing musical associations. "The images of Onegin, Tatyana, Lensky have never found their authentic embodiment on stage, despite the magnificent music of Tchaikovsky," Tairov remarks. "I don't think opera artists have been to blame for this. It seems to me that these marvelous images can be given flesh and blood only by means of dramatic theater, the dramatic actor. This is the task that the Chamber Theater sets for itself. I understand very well that here I am taking the path of greatest resistance." Tairov was correct. Everything in Pushkin's novel seems to resist the "flesh and blood" of live theater: the distancing intricacy of the Onegin stanza, the impenetrable zone of the Narrator, and the lyric ability of Pushkin's words to leap directly from one soul into another, without having to go through bodies at all.

The literary product of this six-month collaboration between playwright and director was read aloud in Tairov's study with Prokofiev present, most likely in late spring 1936 (Prokofiev had repatriated in March). The musician was slow to react. In her 1965 *Reminiscences*, written fifteen years after the playwright's death, Bovshek recalls Prokofiev's initial reluctance to attend a read-through of the play. "He arrived gloomy, dissatisfied, sat down in an armchair in the far corner of Tairov's huge study, and listened to the first two scenes while staring at his own feet. Then, without noticing it himself, he began to move, together with the chair, on the diagonal directly toward Krzhizhanovsky. After the reading was over, [Prokofiev] joined the conversation, some argument ensued—and it ended with [the composer] agreeing to provide musical accompaniment; he was already being drawn in by some creative possibilities known to himself alone" (16). Prokofiev probably received a copy of the text soon afterward. Reading it, he jotted down his musical ideas. As we know from his newspaper interview, most of the forty-four numbers in *Eugene Onegin* were completed by the end of July, probably while Prokofiev was living at the artists' colony at Polenovo outside Moscow.

At some point between May and July came the watchdog committees. The Pushkin Commission disapproved of the play, although Sergey Bondi, a fine Pushkin scholar, and V. V. Veresayev, a montage writer himself and compiler of tales about Pushkin, were intrigued by the adaptation and spoke up for it. Bovshek notes in her memoirs that Krzhizhanovsky, always "very stubborn when it came to reworking [his texts]," generated, under duress, four versions of the play (16). After the critical Pushkin Committee verdict, Tairov pleaded with him successfully "to write a second variant." Bovshek then notes vaguely: "Matters stood far worse, however, with Glavrepertkom. He was instructed to make a third, and then a fourth, variant. These no longer afforded S. D. any pleasure. From one rewrite to the next the play became worse, it was drawing ever closer to an ordinary, standard-issue dramatic scenario" (16–17). It is unclear precisely when these changes occurred, who demanded them, how comprehensive they were, and how the stubborn Krzhizhanovsky was persuaded to go along with them. About this unpleasantness Bovshek says little: after all, she had an entire forgotten life to recall, with *Eugene Onegin* only one collapsed project among many. Two additional testimonies provide a glimpse into the progressive corrosion of the playscript—and the cost to the playwright.

The first features a familiar villain of these years, scourge of both Meyerhold and Prokofiev, the chairman of the All-Union Committee on Arts Affairs. As the theater critic Osaf Litovsky notes in his 1958 memoir *Tak i bïlo* (That's the way it was): "Tairov wasn't successful at staging Pushkin's long poem *Eugene Onegin* in the splendid scenic adaptation by Krzhizhanovsky; he wasn't successful because this venture struck the chairman of the Committee of Arts Affairs, P. M. Kerzhentsev, as formalistic. . . . A pity, because Tairov's 'venture' wasn't formalistic at all."[32] If Litovsky, a high-ranking Party watchdog who served as head of Glavrepertkom from 1930 to 1937, really did consider Krzhizhanovsky's text "splendid," he did not make this opinion public at the time and recalls the events around *Eugene Onegin* in a selective, self-serving manner.[33] Tairov himself had a different view of his allies and foes.

That view is hinted at in a series of increasingly urgent communications—two letters and a telegram—from Tairov to Krzhizhanovsky between late June and late September 1936.[34] Tairov's anxiety about *Eugene Onegin* had reached a crisis point. In a letter to Krzhizhanovsky (June 21, 1936) posted from the spa at Kislovodsk, Tairov scribbles a cautionary directive to his theater board: "Until a final confirmation of the E.O. stage adaptation, you are advised not to incur any expenses on the production." He then begs the playwright to send a new copy of his playscript "*by the most timely route*" (*samïm srochnïm obrazom*, Tairov's underscoring). "Its fate now lies in your hands." Apparently Glavrepertkom, guided by Litovsky, refused to sanction any advance publicity for the production because the playscript had not yet passed inspection. By telegraph, Tairov instructed his theater to send its members the "old text," but clearly he was nervous about circulating this much-corrected, patched, still controversial version (presumably the second revision).[35] Without proper approval, Tairov writes, Osmyorkin's set design will be held up, Prokofiev will not be paid. "It is necessary for me to have a new version either before the 22nd in Kislovodsk or before the 25th in Moscow," the director explains to Krzhizhanovsky, because possibly "I'll be going abroad for a month." And then Tairov pleads:

> *This is extremely serious.* I will *not back down* on E.O. And no Litovskys-together-with-other-so-and-so's [*nikakiye Litovskiye vkupe s drugimi imyarek*] will stop me in this work. But for this I must be well armed, that is, I must have a copy with the two companions [*s dvumya sputnikami*], overall a new *copy*, one that takes into account all those considerations that will guarantee its acceptance and the official stamp of the Repertory Committee and the Committee [on Arts Affairs]. Dear Sigizmund Dominikovich, I remember your words, that your help in this matter is unchanging. I know this to be the case, and so, with great impatience but with no less confidence, *I am waiting.*

The second letter from Tairov (undated, but later in the summer) apologizes for the earlier unrealistic deadline (apparently not met) but raises the level of reproach. "I very, very much hope that the new copy will turn out to be a weapon 'that doesn't misfire'—this is very important in today's 'situation,'" Tairov writes to Krzhizhanovsky.

> I am assuming that the "companions" [*sputniki*] will turn out to be "well disposed" and will lead us out. By the way, when speaking of "companions" I am thinking not so much of the "watchman of the Muses" as of the Muses themselves. I believe in our success. . . . So throw off your spleen and melancholy and acquire some persistence and optimism. . . . I firmly believe in your friendship, in your good faith as a comrade-in-arms—and impatiently, but confidently, continue to wait.

The "companions" and "Muses" mentioned by Tairov remain mysterious, but most likely refer to details in the Prologue and the contested Fragment 13, the mirrored opening and closing portions of the play. Symmetry was of crucial structural importance to Pushkin as well as his to twentieth-century adaptor. But Krzhizhanovsky had his own dream-inflected understanding of mirroring (and his own understanding of Pushkin), which at several points alarmed his collaborators.

In terms of its events, the plot of *Eugene Onegin* is as balanced as a lyric poem. Its eight chapters trace an arc. A St. Petersburg dandy (chapter 1) moves to the country (chapter 2) and on a single visit unwittingly infatuates a shy young maiden, Tatyana Larina, who writes him a desperate love letter (chapter 3). Onegin, not the marrying kind, gently disengages (chapter 4) but takes out his irritation on his young friend Lensky, affianced to Tatyana's frisky younger sister Olga (chapter 5). Their quarrel results in a duel in which Lensky is killed (chapter 6). Now slowly the Möbius strip turns over. In Byronic fashion, the disillusioned Onegin departs for distant lands. Tatyana is married off in Moscow to a wealthy general of princely title (chapter 7). By chapter 8, Onegin has returned to St. Petersburg, where he meets Princess Tatyana at a salon, falls hopelessly in love with her, writes her abject letters, and is definitively rejected. As we can see, the love plot repeats twice, but staggered in time—so there is no consummation, only a rising slope of lonely striving and deepening reflection. (This linear non-overlap of lovers is reproduced melodically by Prokofiev: Lensky's plaintive oboe theme that opens the score twice repeats, first in female and then, more distantly, in male *vocalise* before musical number 5.) But this spiraling love story, which circles back without overlap, does not preclude genuine moral growth. How and on what terrain this growth occurs constitutes Krzhizhanovsky's radical reading of *Eugene Onegin*. Hero and heroine mature in linear fashion, but within their own separate worlds and toward their own as yet undetermined ends. By the closing scene both Onegin and Tatyana have moved beyond their earlier, impetuous, grasping or rejecting selves, and are transposed to a slow-motion, dreamlike state. Each is reconciled and each remains alone.

In an essay written at the end of 1936, Krzhizhanovsky remarked that Pushkin "both *loved* and at the same time *did not love* Onegin," noting that the poet increasingly disparaged his hero in successive drafts: first Onegin is an imitation, then a parody, then a satirical portrait, specter, shade, caricature.[36] This ambivalence survives in the play. In Fragment 10, the heroine—aggrieved as she is—mocks Onegin's role models, grimacing comically at a bust of Napoleon on his writing table. In Fragment 12, Onegin, newly returned to the capital, is still posturing and preening before his inner mirror, congratulating himself on the return of his ability to feel ("Am I in love with her? My God, that would be marvelous"). Yet he also becomes more reflective and self-critical. Onegin tells his friend Prince Vyazemsky (a highly sympathetic double and one of Pushkin's closest friends) of his tedious travels to Crimea and Greece—bits of text that Pushkin composed but excised from the body of his novel. In the final two fragments, cast by Krzhizhanovsky in a surreal mode, Onegin emerges as a lonely, needy, absorptive figure. He has become a surrogate for the mature Pushkin, an elegiac outsider. Responsible for this deepening has been his inexplicable love for Tatyana, which affects the return of the Muse who had abandoned the disillusioned, cynical poet in the Prologue.

Krzhizhanovsky, it would appear, wished to be true to the spirit of Pushkin as well as to his contemporary culture by universalizing Onegin and turning his paralysis into a poetic statement. Tairov did not endorse this model of growth for the hero—or if he did, he considered such a personality impossible to stage (per his midsummer letter to the playwright) in "today's situation." Committed to portraying a negative, dead-ended Onegin, the director adhered to the conventional reading of the hero's triviality and "superfluity." In April 1936, Tairov brought up *Eugene Onegin* in an address to stage directors newly graduated from the Lunacharsky State Institute of Theatrical Arts.[37] Under discussion was the degree of explicitness required when portraying a classic hero in light of contemporary reality. True, in the surviving fragments of "chapter 10," Pushkin had hinted that one fate for his hero might be to join the Decembrist movement.[38] But Tairov was not eager to cast the protagonist in so progressive a light. "Does one have to turn Eugene Onegin into a Decembrist and exile him to hard labor, as some people think we must?" Tairov asked. No, that was unnecessary. What then was necessary?

It is important for me to show a young man of the nineteenth century . . . to show, let's say, that Eugene Onegin (for a whole series of

social and societal reasons, upbringing, etc.) . . . by the end of the
novel stands before us as an absolutely emptied out person [*absolyutno
opustoshonnïm chelovekom*], a person who not only could not intend to
become a Decembrist, but who was emptied out in the extreme. . . .
Without denying Onegin his charm, a charm he genuinely possesses,
to show that this gilded, brilliant external surface, this splendid
mind, endowed with an abundance of talents, still, thanks to the structure of social life and to his entire upbringing, he must inevitably be
brought to this void. And this emptiness becomes all the more vivid
because Tatyana develops on the reverse plane; Tatyana is endowed
with all those elements of the Russian woman, thanks to which she
could become (although this does not occur within the bounds of the
novel) a Decembrist's Wife, consciously and willingly following [her
husband] into exile.[39]

Tairov was, of course, alert to reigning ideological norms for representing Pushkin's fiction onstage—and to the wisdom of anticipating them. Since
tsarist times, censorship for performance had been more severe than censorship for print. In February 1936, after years of highly acclaimed tours
in Paris, Vienna, and South America, Tairov was refused permission to take
his theater to England. It was a bad sign; his *Eugene Onegin* would be closely
scrutinized. Onegin as a negative socioeconomic type was an approved topic
in Soviet criticism, but it conflicted with Krzhizhanovsky's hero, who does
not strike us as an "absolutely emptied-out person." Quite the contrary:
by the end of the play, Onegin has deepened and filled out, having absorbed
into his own person the elegiac, lyrical tones of the deleted Narrator. His
potential for growth seems more real in Fragments 12 and 13 (as it does
in Pushkin's chapter 8) than at any other point in the play. In the context
of this newly receptive hero, how could Tairov have hoped that the two
"companions," who glide up to Onegin on the Neva waterfront, might "lead
them out" of the ideological danger threatening the project?

Very likely these characters were intended to preserve in the play some
other intonations of the Narrator, specifically his ironic, distanced perspective on events. When Litvinenko examined the marginal comments on
Tairov's copy of the playscript, she concluded that Tairov was so agitated
by the cumulative effect of Krzhizhanovsky's adaptation that he did not
wait for a summons but himself solicited advice from the most authoritative Pushkinists. Having heard their complaints, he then resolved to "bring
the language of the theater closer to Pushkin's text" by preemptively restoring the Narrator's "descriptions of nature, literary quarrels, lyrical
revelations."[40] Onegin would no longer belong so wholly to himself. These
newly restored lines "should be read by the two Companions; they function

both as Companions of the main heroes, and as participants in the action." But, Litvinenko adds, "Krzhizhanovsky fulfilled this request only partially."[41]

One can see why. The Companions in Fragment 13 are verbal echoes of Pushkin's Narrator, whose lines they speak, but they function more as emanations of Onegin's autonomous fantasy and expanding realm of conscience than as speaking persons in their own right. Onegin contains and projects *them*; they do not contain and narrate *him*. In the playwright's vision, they are matured dreams: fragments of memory, regret, and hope at last coherent enough to be radiated outward. This is a familiar trajectory in Krzhizhanovsky's world. But Tairov must have sensed that the Companions could also be developed in the other direction. If sufficiently expanded, their lines could fold the hero back into someone else's third-person story. Through this portal the omniscient Narrator, that stylized carrier of Pushkin's voice, could sneak back into the play. Once that door was open, the scenic projection could be whittled down to a podium reading of Pushkin's novel, accompanied by magnificent music. As the Narrator regained his grip on the story, Krzhizhanovsky's bold revisions would fall away. Only occasionally would characters succeed in breaking free to speak their own truths.

We do not know how the playwright responded to Tairov's letter of June 21, 1936. In a maximally dark reading of events, Krzhizhanovsky saw his entire dramatic concept unraveling in the face of official pressure (from censors, Pushkinists, and finally from Tairov himself, acting as a cautious theater bureaucrat) to "return Pushkin to Pushkin" for the jubilee. When queried on this point, however, Perelmuter resisted any such dire interpretation. Krzhizhanovsky was not insulted, Perelmuter insists, just distressed at the loss of income, for he was a very poor man.[42] The relationship between playwright and director was far too durable to be undone by this single disappointment. Bovshek arrives at a similar conclusion in her memoirs, speaking of Tairov's "touching and even tender solicitude" for Sigizmund Dominikovich. "Krzhizhanovsky once found himself in a difficult situation," she notes near the beginning of her *Reminiscences*, tactfully withholding context and date. "Tairov became very upset. 'Who's your main enemy? Tell me. After all, I have connections . . . perhaps . . .' 'No, Alexander Yakovlevich, there's no perhaps, and nothing will help. My main enemy is myself. I'm like that wanderer in the wilderness who has become his own bear'" (14).

The third and final document in this summer sequence of one-way communications is a telegram from Tairov in Moscow to Krzhizhanovsky in Odessa, dated September 23, sent over a month after the second letter. "Work on *Onegin* requires your urgent presence. Request that you telegraph the day of your arrival in Moscow. Greetings. Tairov." It is not known how the playwright responded to the summons. Tairov's archive, like Krzhizhanovsky's, is silent on the matter. So, too, is Prokofiev's.

The Music

The playscript and score leave a cooler, more complete record of the summer of 1936 than this agitated exchange of letters. Fortunately for our reconstruction, the copy of the play containing Prokofiev's annotations (the first revision) and the composer's autograph score dated 1936 are precisely keyed to each other. While composing, Prokofiev entered the relevant page number of the playscript into his score before each musical number; his comments in the margins of the play are likewise easily correlated with the score.

In contrast to the successive new typescripts and cuttings-and-pastings of the play, however, the autograph score was simply "layered" with additional commentary. Prokofiev inked in his music during the summer of 1936. At some point in the autumn, responding either to his own muse or (far more likely) to the mandate of an official commission, he updated the ink autograph score in light pencil. After musical number 17, we read: "According to the new plan" (*po nov[omu] pr[o]yektu*). This penciled-in phrase in Prokofiev's telescoped script finishes with the words: "On this, O[negin] and T[atyana] exit after the explan[ation] in the garden."[43] One's heart sinks, seeing this note. For in the "old" or earlier dramatic plan, there is no scene in which Onegin explains himself to Tatyana in the garden. Together with the relocated Dream, the omission of this famous bench episode (stretching across two chapters of Pushkin's novel) is Krzhizhanovsky's most provocative departure from his source text. In the pre-censored version, Onegin's "explanation" to the heroine is not absent as a sentiment, only as a scene. His lecture is segmented and redistributed between Fragments 6 and 7. In Fragment 6, Onegin, at home alone, nervously rehearses snatches of his response to Tatyana's letter. In Fragment 7 (the Name Day), he pursues the benumbed and humiliated Tatyana around the dance floor, casting bits of patronizing advice in her direction. The ghastly embarrassment of that Name Day nightmare makes the Dream that follows hard upon it imperative for Tatyana; dream-space provides an alternate reality where she can relive these botched love events, stripped of their shame. One can only imagine the playwright's despair. If this pivotal scenic projection was forced out of his text, what was safe?

Litovsky remarked in his memoirs that the *Eugene Onegin* playscript was condemned by Kerzhentsev as "formalistic." During the 1930s, this charge could mean almost anything: too experimental, too clever, too untrue to a canonized source, or simply out of favor with a given Party authority.

The unconventional bench and dream scenes had caused discomfort. The music was not reproached for such sins but instead fell victim to peripheral, nonmusical pressures. About these matters Prokofiev was (at least in public) remarkably flexible and businesslike, the perfect client. He discussed the expectations raised by stage music in an interview for the Moscow journal *Theater and Dramaturgy*, published with the hortatory title "Study the Text, the Theater, the Orchestra."[44] When asked what place music should occupy in a dramatic spectacle, the composer answered: a modest one, nothing like its role in opera or ballet. He insisted that "going to hear an opera" was very different from "going to see a drama." Thus he was always happiest when a dramaturge or director gave him "concrete demands"—a "minute and a quarter of music," something "sad or tender"—rather than remaining silent and allowing him to evaluate the situation "solely from the point of view of a musician-specialist." Incidental music must wax and wane, reinforcing a specific emotional curve. It must never muffle the words. Terrible is the orchestra guilty of *kriklivost'*: clamoring, bawling, or shrieking in such a way that conversations on stage are lost.

Yet Prokofiev's musical practice is less self-effacing than this interview might suggest. Although music and words are not fused into a unit owned wholly by the composer—this is a major difference between incidental music and opera—stage and film music at Prokofiev's level of mastery is fastidiously constructed. It does not merely illustrate an incident. Incidents in the human domain are far too complex and occur simultaneously on too many planes; the visual and mimetic are only the most blunt. Other planes are no less real, even if they are abstract, invisible, or displaced in time or space. Alert to this complexity, Prokofiev wished his music to be integrated into the drama from the start and not mechanically applied to an already blocked-out play. He insisted on his right to attend all rehearsals. Although this commitment is difficult to document in the case of *Eugene Onegin*—where roles were never formally assigned nor rehearsals officially held—we have testimony from earlier Prokofiev-Tairov projects on Prokofiev's steady presence in the hall.[45] In the earliest phases of collaboration, reading Krzhizhanovsky's playscript, the composer not only reacted to the words but also intervened in them. While jotting down his initial musical ideas in the margins he would delete and add lines of text, substitute one dance for another, adjust details of a stage direction. He intended the sonic profile of the work to evolve alongside the scenic and the verbal.

A basic typology of stage sound will help us to grasp Prokofiev's approach to composing incidental music.[46] First comes that type of music called "diegetic" (after the Greek *diegesis*, "recounted story"), which is designed to accompany external motion on stage. As a rule, all characters on stage hear it. These sounds are produced by events occurring in visible story space: public songs, dances, the clack of trains, the cry of birds. But a musical score can also express the general mood of a scene, in which case sound emanates from beyond the visible story space. Such music is not obliged to justify its source and is not heard by the characters; it is "nondiegetic" sound, not deducible from the recounted story, and frequently a cue for the supernatural or the unconscious. There is also a third category, richly exploited by Prokofiev and a staple in film music, located somewhere between the visible-personal and invisible-impersonal realms: "meta-diegetic" sound. Most commonly, such music follows the trajectory of an internal emotion originating inside a character's head, although it can also be displaced offstage or to the past or future. Since it communicates subjective anxieties or hallucinations, this sound is not abstract but tied to a concrete consciousness. When heard by a sympathetic audience, it serves to increase the "reality component" of that character's inner psychological life. An *objective* counterpart to such internal meta-diegetic sound is also possible: a character's breathing or rhythmic heartbeat, for example, wheezed or thumped out into public space for all to hear.

In these musical amplifications of motion, emotion, and meta-commentary, opportunities for parody and disjunction are constant. The audience does not necessarily know to which realm a given stretch of music belongs. A girl might be dancing in full view of others, but to a rhythm in her own head. A dream or nightmare vision might be so real that, following the composer's prompt, everyone in the hall (onstage as well as in the audience) reacts to it as imminently threatening. This set of musical options was congenial to Krzhizhanovsky, whose stories routinely blur the boundary between waking and sleeping. In one of the most famous, "Side Branch" (1928), a train carries the hero into the land of dream-production (the conductor demands a dream-vision instead of a ticket). Eventually the creator-dreamer is obliged to compete with his own imagined creatures, surely the perfect meta-diegetic nightmare.[47] As a rule, Krzhizhanovsky calibrates fantasy more carefully than waking states. A light dream cannot hold its own against reality, he insists, for something from the outside will always wake us up. A deep or heavy (*tyazholïy*) dream, however, can easily be assimilated by authentic real life lived in the full light of day.

The playscript for *Eugene Onegin* is built out of longing, dreaming, and nonconsummation. It abounds in liminal times and spaces. Tatyana's letter to Onegin, which is easily as much about shame as about love, has the structure of a guilty fantasy, and even identifies itself as a "deep (or heavy) dream"—which Onegin, as love object, is obliged either to satisfy or to explode. Prokofiev specifies music for the first half of the letter but abruptly removes it at the depth of Tatyana's fantasy, so we can hear the sighs and rustling treetops of the nocturnal garden. Later in the play, identical monsters appear in adjacent scenes at various levels of consciousness, singing, cackling, or silent. A dreamed murder slides directly into the aftermath of a "real" duel, separated only by the sound of a horn breaking through the storm. These sequences can be experienced as diegetic or non-diegetic, produced by an outside stimulus or projected from inside a character; often they are both at once. But objective meta-diegetic sound is also present. A stage direction in Fragment 5 explains that the sound of the night watchman's wooden rattle, which Tatyana hears in the garden while composing her anguished letter, grows distant and silent "like heart-beats." In Fragment 15, taking its cue from Pushkin's line describing reveille in St. Petersburg, what begins as a regimental drum rousing the city also turns out to be a heartbeat, a distant rat-a-tat that swells to deafening pro-portions. Here the drumbeats serve as a rhythmic transition from a pensive lovesick Onegin, lingering at dawn on the waterfront with his heart pound-ing, to Princess Tatyana's boudoir on a frosty, sunny morning.

To accommodate such overlapping levels and quicksilver adjustments, Prokofiev wrote his incidental stage music in discrete units. Properly deployed, an isolated theme could become a motif, even a "theme song." Orchestration (added or withdrawn) could mark the transition between diegetic and meta-diegetic realms. Among the marvelous meta-diegetic moments in the music for *Eugene Onegin* is the "*tram-blyam* polka" at the Name Day Party (Fragment 7)—Prokofiev's attempt to create the ragtag, discordant music, banged out on harpsichords, that might have been heard at a party in the real early-nineteenth-century Russian provinces. Litovsky, in the memoir quoted earlier, recalls Prokofiev saying: "Tchaikovsky's music is magnificent, but it's not written to Pushkin's *Onegin*. Take the ball at the Larins'. Why that fashionably chic 'capital city' music for a provin-cial landowner's party? During such evenings, people danced to a piano, tinny and somewhat broken down. The Larins' ball most definitely had a *tram-blyam* polka."[48]

Prokofiev ensures that the Russian provinces do not sound like Moscow or Petersburg. But in keeping with our typology above, a simple mimetic representation of reality is never sufficient. Although the diegetic realm testifies to what externally exists, the non- and meta-diegetic realms are where people actually live, fantasize, and dream most of the time—espe-cially people passed through Krzhizhanovsky's surreal, psychologically merciless lens. Interwoven with the authentic *tram-blyam* sound is the sort of music that the Name Day guests would have *liked* to hear: the same tunes played by a classy ensemble in the big city. For example, "A Ball at the Larins" (musical numbers 25–31) opens with a tinny "Polka for two harpsichords."[49] The second number (26) begins more elegantly as a slow waltz scored for violin, viola, cello, and contrabass. Sixteen measures in, however, at the top of an ascending chromatic run, this string ensemble suddenly collapses into those two tinny harpsichords. The effect is comical, disorienting, akin to rudely waking up from a dream. For a minute or two in our imagination, we had been dancing to a string quartet in a real St. Petersburg ballroom with a polished parquet floor. But then we looked around, and our ears followed suit. The value of such music lies in its ambiguity and flexibility; it can reinforce any number of precise motions, emotions, and psychological states, on many planes, visible and invisible, conscious and unconscious.

The Music and the Playscript

From the start, the playscript was a vulnerable target. It would seem that only opera—with its long tradition of tolerating libretti that highlight vocal, not verbal, glories—is licensed to dismember a canonized literary masterpiece. Even without arbitrary censorship, huge cuts were inevitable if Pushkin's novel were to be whittled down to a play. New connecting tissue would have to be devised. And its brilliantly artificed stanzas would have to be transformed into utterances that made sense when spoken and heard in theatrical space, not only privately and silently in a book.

Krzhizhanovsky made his fundamental "verbal-musical" decision when he resolved to retain the trace and pulse of the novel's ingenious fourteen-line "verse paragraph," the Onegin stanza (*oneginskaya strofa*). The present translation does not attempt to reproduce this miraculous narrative form.[50] Indeed, Krzhizhanovsky himself declined to do so; only rarely, in "soliloquy" contexts, does he employ a full unbroken stanza, because characters in direct dialogue with one another cannot converse for long at a normal pace within its constraints. In Pushkin's novel, the Narrator provides the third-person binder necessary to fill out the poetic form—and in the drama he no longer exists. Instead, Krzhizhanovsky quotes or splices quatrains of the stanza, with patches of its intricate rhyme pattern intact. Some sense of this tightly coiled, sonnet-like structure is nevertheless important for appreciating the background intonation of the play. A flexible verse unit in iambic tetrameter, the Onegin stanza observes a regular scheme of feminine and masculine rhymes arranged in three differently rhymed quatrains (alternating, balanced, enclosed), followed by a rhyming couplet (AbAb CCdd EffE gg). The stanza has a characteristic pace or spin. The opening quatrain and ending couplet are sedate and urbane; the middle stretch is blurred, excited, often breathless. At times motions or emotions stretch and spill over the line, not unlike a Prokofiev waltz that has dancers treading on their own feet.[51] With only occasional departures for inserted genres (a berry-picking song, Tatyana's letter), over five thousand lines of these sturdy, identically structured stanzas propel the plot of *Eugene Onegin* forward with an intoxicating momentum. Krzhizhanovsky snips, grafts, and reattaches chunks of these stanzas to preserve crucial events without sacrificing the pulse or paraphrasing the words. The rhythm of the whole is preserved and the rhymes within a given quatrain remain intact. To those who were raised on Pushkin's stanza, however—the whole of the Russian literary establishment—any cutting and pasting, any adjustment of verbal person or tense, was sacrilege. Yet it is difficult to see how a play could have been created from a full-length novel without this license. Perhaps a highly visible Soviet playwright possessing impeccable authority and powerful patrons could have gotten away with it. Krzhizhanovsky could not.

More active forces were at work in the forgetting of Krzhizhanovsky, however, than the conservatives who governed the Pushkin Jubilee. According to the RGALI archival registrar, as of 2007 only a handful of persons had consulted Krzhizhanovsky's playscript since its deposit. One of those who did in the late 1960s was the Soviet musicologist Elizaveta Dattel, the first person to reassemble and edit Prokofiev's scattered, recycled stage music for the annulled jubilee events. Unfortunately, her 1973 score for *Eugene Onegin* is seriously flawed. Claiming to have been guided in her decisions by Tairov's critical marginalia, Prokofiev's second wife, Mira (whose opinion on this project is unknown), and Pushkinist Valentin Nepomnyashchiy (a purist who has championed a devout Russian Orthodox image of the poet in the post-Communist era), Dattel discredited and then dismissed Krzhizhanovsky's playscript in her editorial commentary. In the 1970s, Dattel could not publicly address the question of censorship pressure, but her own aesthetic preferences seem compatible with it. Noting that the play violates the Onegin stanza, drops Pushkin's Narrator, changes the order of episodes and omits scenes, she concludes that it "was in need of correction because of its serious contradictions with Pushkin's novel and its departures from Prokofiev's score."[52] Some of her criticisms involve changes inevitable in any stage adaptation; others are simply mystifying. (How, for example, could the playscript be "in contradiction with Prokofiev's score" when the score was conceived in response to the playscript and evolved in collaboration with it?) Out of political caution or personal taste, Dattel chose not to include Krzhizhanovsky's name on the title page. Freely borrowing from the playwright's plan when it suited her, she wedged her own selection of Onegin stanzas between the extant musical numbers. For the playwright, this treatment of his texts would have been sickeningly familiar.

The case Dattel makes against Krzhizhanovsky could easily be deployed in his defense, of course, at least for a Russian audience. So immediately recognizable is this thrilling stanza, and so many of these stanzas are known by heart, that listeners, once prompted by a line or two, would involuntarily fill in the omissions with their "mind's ear." But apparently this defense was not invoked, even by those closest to the project. Pushkin's text was both too sacred to be tampered with and (in part for that reason) too banally proverbial to be engaged seriously. Every classic is vulnerable to this double bind. Even in those places where Krzhizhanovsky changed none of Pushkin's words but merely framed a chosen stanza with a pair of stage directions, Tairov could not refrain from jotting in the margins of his playscript: "A comically familiar text!"[53] And when changes had to be made (pronouns altered, for example, so that a character could utter lines in the first person), the playwright was gently reproached for "comically coarsening the music of Pushkin's poetry."[54]

As an adapter Krzhizhanovsky was not timid. In addition to making cuts, he also boldly added. With two exceptions—an ironic portrait (perhaps self-portrait) in verse written by himself that purports to be a text by Lord Byron, and a few stanzas of a poem by Pyotr Vyazemsky recited by his fictive counterpart—Krzhizhanovsky supplemented his playscript exclusively with works by Pushkin: an early elegiac poem, a late fairy tale in verse, satiric epigrammatic verse, a youthful drinking song.[55] In several fragments, names that are merely mentioned by the Narrator appear as onstage characters, who speak their lines in their own right. The literal incarnation of an uttered name is done in the spirit of Nikolai Gogol, the greatest practitioner of this sleight of hand in Russian literature, whose grotesque aesthetic differs profoundly from Pushkin's. Whole stretches of the play, and especially those episodes set in public or social space, are dominated by a Gogolian intonation, with Gogol's trademark attention to uniforms, facial hair, and ribald quasi-absurd wordplay between caricatured cartoon figures. Gogolian doubles also turn up, among them the tipsy, leering duo Buyanov and Zaretsky at the Name Day party. Even Tatyana's future husband, so modestly concealed in Pushkin's novel and so sentimentally realized in Tchaikovsky's opera, has a touch of the Gogolian grotesque about him. It cannot surprise us that so many people had reservations about this play. But it was this text and not some vague (or even precise) recall of Pushkin's novel as a whole that served as the stimulus for the music. There is no evidence that director or composer ever wished to reduce their jubilee commission from a staged drama to a concert performance.

To date, however, the 1936 collaboration exists solely as Prokofiev's music ornamented with incidental Pushkin. The Dattel edition served as the basis for the first two recordings, in 1974 (Melodiya LP) and in 1994 (Chandos CD).[56] The more recent recording of Eugene Onegin by Michail Jurowski (2005) is heroically de-Dattelized and thus offers a bracing alternative.[57] In his liner notes, Jurowski acknowledges the existence of both the playwright and the playscript, and even admits that the play predated the music.

Prokofiev's musical numbers are linked together by Pushkin's stanzas (beautifully recited in Russian), which delineate the edges of Krzhizhanovsky's playscript where it borders on a musical number. But beyond this musical coastline we can only guess at the dramatic mainland: set design, props, interacting characters, lighting, live dialogue, the subtlety of stage directions. The play is still terra incognita. What is more, the status of Pushkin's words throughout hovers between recited novel and performed drama, with the same voice reading passages in first person (speaking *from* itself) and third person (speaking *about* itself, as Pushkin's Narrator speaks about a third party). Such conflation prevents the mind's eye from visualizing a play. The proper tribute to Pushkin, Krzhizhanovsky, and Prokofiev can be sought only in the correct music deployed as part of a fully realized, staged dramatic spectacle.

Krzhizhanovsky's "Applied Poetics": Title, Epigraph, Stage Direction

In an essay from 1936, Krzhizhanovsky announced his dissatisfaction with both branches of the twentieth-century Pushkin industry. At one extreme were the subjective critics, who analyzed their own ecstatic personal impressions after closely reading one or two works, and then offered this method to the reader as a route to the living Pushkin. The other pole had been colonized by the academic commentary–writers, who provided superficial dictionary facts and called it scholarship ("Cupid is the God of Love, and Malfilâtre, whom Pushkin quotes, was born in thus-and-thus a year and died in another").[58] In Krzhizhanovsky's view, neither the idiosyncratic depth of the one nor the "scientific" shallowness of the other was the proper way to restore a creative subject to life. In place of both he urged an "applied poetics" that would range freely through an author's output (drafts as well as finished products) and seek to identify the telltale furniture in the house of that particular creative mind. We see evidence here of Krzhizhanovsky's immense erudition and total recall that so often intimidated those who attended his lectures and workshops. For him, the life's work of any creator constituted one structure with many rooms, all of which were accessible at once. The load-bearing structures of an artwork are neither its plot nor its character types—these are usually universals in a culture—but distinctive authorial variants on formal patterns, recurring sites of moral growth, and a given author's use of a seemingly peripheral ornament or detail. What's carried by a title? An epigraph? For dramatic works, by a particular style of stage direction? Krzhizhanovsky devoted substantial essays to each of these technical parts of a work of art, which he believed contained an entire poetics.

Unlike Pushkin, Krzhizhanovsky was a theater professional. Alert to every practical aspect of the craft, he knew what Tairov's company could and could not do as well as what was possible with current stage technologies. The specialized poetics that Krzhizhanovsky worked out for three minor literary genres or "parts"—titles, epigraphs, and stage directions—are tied up with the playwright's favorite moral site, the dream. Dreams, in turn, support his "philosopheme of the theater," a three-part conceptual framework he elaborated in the early 1920s for Tairov's Chamber Theater. All dimensions of the unrealized *Eugene Onegin* are reflected in the final tier of that philosopheme, which transforms theater into an ethics and even into a mode of survival.

First, the title. In December 1939, Krzhizhanovsky delivered a casual talk on "The Play and Its Title" to the dramaturgical section of the Union of Soviet Writers.[59] At the end, he anticipated the audience's objection that to isolate the title (or any other element) from a work of art and analyze it as a genre of its own, with its own evolution and classifications, is to violate the organic whole of the artwork. The reverse is true, he insisted. Only after an act of isolation can bridges be thrown "from the title to the text"— for how can we understand any created construct if we do not dismember it? The Russian masters of stage titles (Chekhov, Ostrovsky, Tolstoy) anguished over proper labels for their work, knowing that the name was the "viewfinder of the telescope."[60] In search of the perfect lens, each obsessively tried and discarded various titles. In his entry on "Titles" for a 1925 *Dictionary of Literary Terms*, Krzhizhanovsky remarked mournfully that the seventeenth-century habit of taking twenty or thirty lines to title a philosophical treatise on, say, the history of the soul had been answered in contemporary Russian culture by the Symbolist poet Andrey Belïy, "who satisfied himself with the simple sign *I*."[61] Such a "flattening-out of the title, carried to extremes" is "manifestly an unhealthy phenomenon: books, crowding one another out on the narrow shelves of store windows, flatten out one another's letters, turn titles into *half-titles*, tease us with the insufficiently said. . . . Most often, today's title fears the predicate: it names a theme, a problem, a question. The resolution, the answer, is not noted on the cover." One title that Krzhizhanovsky considered exemplary in its predicative self-assurance was the masterpiece of the Spanish Golden Age, Pedro Calderón's 1636 drama *Life Is a Dream* (*La vida es sueño*).

Krzhizhanovsky did not comment on the title *Eugene Onegin*. His scenic projection simply imitates its source text by "naming the theme, the problem" without supplying a predicate. But when transposed, a familiar work becomes something like a palimpsest; a predicate can be teased out from the layers. For his opera, Tchaikovsky kept Pushkin's title intact while dismissing the hero as flat and foolish, refocusing on Tatyana. Tairov, too, was tugged toward the heroine as the dramatic center of interest and virtue; he explained the behavior of the eponymous hero Onegin through economics and social class. Prokofiev was morally noncommittal. Early in the score, at the end of Fragment 2, he gives Onegin a signature tune to hum, set to the words of one of Pushkin's French-language epigraphs. It marks the hero as elegant, cosmopolitan, self-confident, and condescending to the heroine. As Onegin matures, he will cease to hum it. The dramatic Onegin will eventually be justified in his title role because he does, in fact, possess a predicate: he is Tatyana's Dream.

That Onegin's signature is an epigraph exemplifies the weaving together of peripheral elements at the heart of Krzhizhanovsky's playwriting art. In his essay "The Art of the Epigraph [Pushkin]," written in October 1936, Krzhizhanovsky argues that an epigraph is not a surface ornament; like a title, it distills meaning.[62] Although lapidary and laconic, epigraphs always *speak*, even if no more than a line of that dialogue is pinned to the head of a scene, act, or entire drama. "Speaking in epigraphs" is something like speaking in proverbs; however casually or intimately uttered, the content always sounds pre-formed, "quoted," and thus somewhat detached and depersonalized. The epigraph performs important cultural work. This seemingly minor genre, especially in Pushkin's practice, is a conduit for international communication; it also preserves a nation's cultural tradition and links literary generations. In the 1820s these tasks were of great importance, since Russian literature was so young and its contribution to European culture so tenuous. Through his epigraphs, Pushkin bound his poetry to his peers and Russian literature to the larger world. So weighty and responsive is this tiny genre that Krzhizhanovsky pleads for serious research into "epigraphology."[63]

Pushkin's epigraphs fall into four categories. First are quotes from the classics or from respected predecessors (these are usually Western and often involve language puns). Then come quotes from Pushkin's poet-contemporaries (who are usually Russian and his personal friends). Folklore (for the most part stylized) constitutes the third type, and finally there is the pseudo-quote (Pushkin pretending to cite someone else, but the utterance is in fact his own invention). In *Eugene Onegin* the epigraphs are cosmopolitan, given in Russian, French, Italian, and English, and edged with wit or pathos. Five out of Pushkin's nine epigraphs (to his chapters and to his novel as a whole) turn up in the play, either as lines spoken by characters in conversation or as passages read aloud from a book.[64] Onegin's signature tune, or theme song, is the epigraph to chapter 3: "Elle était fille, elle était amoureuse" (She was a young girl, she was in love). Pushkin lifted the line from Jacques Malfilâtre's "Narcisse, ou l'île de Vénus" (1768), a work Vladimir Nabokov identifies as a "third-rate poem in four long cantos," in which the young girl is the nymph Echo, pining away for love of Narcissus, who in turn longs only for his own reflection.[65] The economy is a sterile one, and both hero and heroine (after a fashion) perish.

Their failed dialogue suits Pushkin's chapter 3. Onegin is a self-absorbed dandy who prefers his own image in the mirror to any other face. Tatyana, like the nymph Echo, is a forest creature faithful to, and fated to repeat forever, that which she has first seen and heard. Prokofiev might or might not have known the source of the epigraph, but either way he responded in Pushkin's spirit. At its first occurrence in the play, the composer wrote after the French text: *naoborot* (the other way around). It is an intriguing marginal comment. Assuming Prokofiev refers here to the words, to reverse the order ("she was in love, she was a young girl") would be appropriate for the nymph Echo, for whom causality—here only implicit—is meaningless; her experience in love is reversible and repeatable. Inverting Malfilâtre's line from "Narcisse" creates another kaleidoscope-mirror, one expressed in sound rather than space, through the repetition of Onegin's theme. "The other way around" is yet another illustration of the lovers' parallel but non-developmental fate.

Unlike titles and epigraphs, the last of our minor genres to be sampled is peculiar to drama: the stage direction (Russian *remarka*, from the French *remarque*). Krzhizhanovsky was fascinated by its role in the history of European theater. In his 1937 essay "The Theatrical Stage Direction (A Fragment)" he surveys its formal variety and function.[66] Shakespeare's directives were laconic, almost mute. But such shorthand was sufficient for a playwright-director, a man of the theater who staged his own works with his own troupe. The director's intentions are the playwright's own, transmitted directly to the company; they do not need to be fixed in print. When the director separates from the playwright, however, more elaborate guidelines are required, and the *remarka* can assume literary and narrative dimensions. These can be quite playful. In the eighteenth-century prose comedy of Denis Fonvizin, for example, a stage direction often put living people in dialogue with *things*; an object would strive to escape its imprisonment in parentheses and turn into an "almost fully-legitimate personage, perhaps still with someone else's voice but with its own thoughts" (97). And to this Krzhizhanovsky adds coyly, as if preparing the ground for his later surreal poetics: a great deal of consciousness is trapped in what looks like a thing, whether "a book, or in the visual form of a telephone receiver." Pushkin, in his stage directions for *Boris Godunov* and later for the *Little Tragedies*, returned to a Shakespearean prototype. Again the focus fell on external action: dry-eyed, laconic, a matter of verbs directing human bodies (97–98). In contrast, Chekhov, who came to playwriting after a decade of absolute mastery in the short story, introduced the "literary stage direction in its most harmonized forms" (102). Krzhizhanovsky shows in parallel columns how the opening paragraph of a Chekhov story is reproduced almost word for word in a typical Chekhovian *remarka*: the same coordination of "props," the same precise delineation of mood, lighting, and times of day (102–3).

Krzhizhanovsky does not discuss his own experience, a year before this essay appeared, of turning Pushkin's *Eugene Onegin* into a play. Stage directions were crucial to it. They function as a surrogate for the Narrator, setting characters in motion, linking clusters of stanzas, informing us of weather and props. Pushkin's own terse "Shakespearean" practice could not have been a model. Far more likely a model was the theater of Chekhov. As playwright, Krzhizhanovsky combines the impressionistic Chekhovian stage direction with a heightened sensitivity to the soundscape—pulsed, rhythmic, alert to the distant rattle or snapped string—appropriate to Tairov's musicalized chamber theater. In this as in so much else, Tatyana is the touchstone and ideal audience. More so than anyone else on stage, she "intently listens in" (*vslushivayetsya*) to the sounds surrounding her, diegetic as well as meta-diegetic: a drum, a rattle, a musical score. Together with Prokofiev's music, the stage directions in *Eugene Onegin* function as dramatic binder. Pushkin's Narrator binds up the novel with his words; the play coheres through light and rhythm.

The source, placement, and waxing or waning of light—what is illuminated or shadowed—dominate Krzhizhanovsky's *remarka*. Details of lanterns, candles, lit or dim interiors, and especially the moon permit a play of profiles versus full bodies, the shades or silhouettes of serious people versus the harshly lit, always bulky and fully fleshed-out buffoon. In early versions of the play, Krzhizhanovsky includes technical directions for a "projector" to cast light in rising and falling patterns across different parts of the stage.

Second in significance to lighting is pulse. Reading the stage directions as a single unit is akin to hearing a metronome. Acts of tapping, pacing, swaying, flapping, rocking, and chiming are fundamental. This rhythmic priority affects the playwright's choice of furniture and props, which are scant but meticulously specified. (Since Osmyorkin's surviving sketches are of costume design only, we cannot know how Krzhizhanovsky's own vision of the mise-en-scène would have been realized—or ignored.) Physical items featured in the stage directions swing on hinges or tracks (doors, windows, drapes), oscillate back and forth from a fixed point (rocking chairs, clocks with a pendulum, treetops in a night breeze), repeat in an arc or a loop (moon and sun, dawn to dusk). Thresholds between rooms are marked, because human beings can tilt to and fro across them. As with the Narcissus-Echo myth that Onegin takes as his theme song, movement in the playscript is constant but cyclical and reversible ("the other way around") and thus, in defiance of most romances, non-teleological. Relationships never arrive at a resting point and so can last forever. This is not, perhaps, a happy love story, but it cannot be called a tragic one. Like a swinging door, a pendulum, or the moon in the sky, the story is anchored and levered.

So well sculpted and paced are these stage directions that they almost constitute a serialized narrative with a plot and pulse of its own. Onegin's initial rhythm is established in Fragments 2 and 4. He is bored. He seats himself in a rocking chair that seems to start swaying of its own accord; forcibly, irritably, he halts it. Such nervous frustration is a male tension in the play, characteristic of the unkindness with which men are treated in the Romantic Byronic tradition.[67] When women are rhythmicized in this mechanical way (as is Tatyana at the end of Fragment 4, on the balcony before writing her letter, rocking in time with the breeze that sways the trees), it represents not boredom but longing. By and large, women's boredom tries to go somewhere or get out of somewhere; it is responsive and dynamic. Male boredom is existential, blocked, and thus circular, trivial, and cruel. She spirals, he repeats.

The removal of rhythm and music is always keenly felt. Prokofiev resisted any decay of precise sound into mere background noise. Near the end of Fragment 7, for example, before the Mummers arrive at the Name Day party, Krzhizhanovsky specified a tuning of instruments and "a dissonant conglomeration of sounds," to which Prokofiev responded in the margins: "Without music and without tuning-up." When, in Fragment 10, Tatyana visits Onegin's abandoned house and inspects his library, we are informed that the "familiar rocking chair" is now motionless and the wall clock's "ticking mechanism has fallen silent," its "pendulum hangs downward." Visual details all have weight—and if they do not move and create rhythmic inertia with this weight, they are felt as dead, even killed, things.

Thus does Krzhizhanovsky trap consciousness in a thing: a book, a clock, a piece of furniture. In Fragment 12, the first of the St. Petersburg scenes, we are given a stage direction where sounds and rhythms move freely on a continuum between objects and human beings. The ebb and flow of this exchange prefigures the hero's fate. Onegin has just kissed the hand of Princess Tatyana, which she calmly extends to him, but the rising strains of the music drown out their conversation. A dancer glides up to draw Tatyana out on the floor. Onegin remains alone beside her empty chair. He gives its arm a push (recalling, we are told, the movement of his own rocking chair), but "the gilded *fauteuil* stands motionless on its bent little legs." Gradually the music quiets down and fades away. Tatyana does not return to her former place. The stage direction continues: "A dozen hands punctiliously move forward a chair for her in another corner of the

hall." Like the drumbeats that double for heartbeats on the Neva embankment—our earlier example of objective meta-diegetic sound—furniture
can be a metaphor for life functions.

There is another, rarer type of stage direction in *Eugene Onegin* that
denotes the "outdoors." Examples are the brief, wintry episode of the duel
(Fragment 9) and the Neva embankment in the early morning mist
(Fragment 13). Absent here are those brightly illuminated visual details of
the indoor *remarka*: dust on the spines of books, gilt on the legs of chairs.
Instead, there are echoes, expanses, dreams, and fogs that project an
inner psychology outward. Reality is not determined by external objects
but by the responsiveness, vulnerability, porosity, and neediness of the hero.
Krzhizhanovsky began experimenting with the idea of the material world
as psychological projection in his surreal stories from the 1920s. In the
"minus-Moscow" of his story "Stitches," the starving, homeless, hallucinat-
ing narrator notes that shadows are thrown not by things but that a physical
thing is "thrown" into the outside world by its shadow. Fragment 13 of
Eugene Onegin displays a similar dynamic. Sounds have an only approximate motivation and source. The hero at dawn hears the night watchmen
calling to one another but also "the distant rattle of carriages . . . the flapping of wings of some gigantic bird, perhaps the splash of oars; a horn and
a distant, barely perceptible song."

The starting point for such stage directions is of course Chekhov's theater, but with an important difference. Whereas Chekhov's impressionism
is atmospheric, imagistic, and predominantly extra-verbal, Krzhizhanovsky
tracks the deepening consciousness of his hero along the specific trajectory of Pushkin's poetic word. The rebirth of Onegin's conscience is
mediated by verse: concrete bits of Pushkin's poetry spoken in the present trigger the memory of other bits composed in the past.[68] When
carousing students approach tipsily singing their ode to the pleasures of
wine (Prokofiev's setting of a lyric by the fifteen-year-old Pushkin), Onegin
immediately collates the words of their boisterous song with similar words,
phrases, and phonemes occurring in the novel, thereby calling up his
own melancholic memories of the shameful duel in which he killed his best
friend. Throughout this elaborate, largely subconscious verbal linkage,
stretching over years of biographical time, one spatial image remains:
Tatyana immobile at the window. Three shadowy men drift by the parapet. In the final stage direction of Fragment 13, we learn that Onegin himself
does not know whether these figures are real or merely "an illusion born
of the pre-morning St. Petersburg fog." That fog, too, was "thrown outward" from his agitated self.

We are now at the core of the problem, the pivotal moment of a scenic
projection. Krzhizhanovsky was a poet of space, not of time, and the dream

became his most respected site of testing and growth. By the time of the *Eugene Onegin* adaptation, his poetics of space and dream-space had been well worked out.[69] It has two basic parameters: *prostorno* (wide-open) and *tesno* (constricted). Mediating between these two is the *shchel'* or crack, crevice, fissure, seam. Pedestrians come across them in the city walls; residents of shabby apartments stare at them through wallpaper and decaying plaster; when we close our eyes they show up on our retina, projected against the inner lid. These crevices and seams offer a way out of the constriction, but the path is fraught. The hero of Krzhizhanovsky's 1927 story "V zrachke" (In the pupil), for example, is the tiny image of ourselves flickering in the pupil of the eye of someone who loves us. When that love wanes, this tiny image sinks deep behind the eye, slips into the sludge heap of other half-decayed, cast-off lovers, and usually fails to find a fissure through which to scramble out. Only when the Beloved again dreams of us do we escape out of her eye, down her cheek, across the pillow: one more chance to reunite with our master and again to belong to ourselves. At one point down in the sludge, the tiny, despondent little man-in-the-pupil (*zrachkovïy chelovechishko*) who tells this story—he's the Twelfth cast-off in this particular woman's eye—engages the Sixth in conversation. "Yes," says Sixth. "You see, the crack in the vault opens only for those being dreamed about and for those arrived from the outside world. But dreams won't let us go: they bar us from reality with lowered eyelids then hurl us back to the bottom when they're done."[70] Such are the psychological dynamics of this dangerous intercourse with dreams.

But Krzhizhanovsky also examined surreal space in a purely physical, even mechanical manner. His most condensed parable on this bipolar space is his 1926 story "Kvadraturin" (Quadraturin), about a mysterious ointment offered to the resident of a tiny, cage-like Moscow room. When rubbed on walls and ceilings, it expands their volume. But once applied, its results cannot be controlled. Boundaries endlessly recede. Furniture that fit snugly into the earlier "cube" suddenly rattles around in open space, revealed in all its cobwebby shabbiness. The cramped but cozy former cubbyhole becomes a wilderness or emptiness (*pustïnya*), where a feeble lightbulb "struggles to reach the dark, ever-receding corners of the vast and dead, yet empty barrack."[71] How can one possibly fill up this naked triumphant space? There is death, of course, which will return you to the cozy parameters of a cube—that is, a coffin. (Tributes to Krzhizhanovsky's forgotten life do not fail to mention that his grave has been lost.)[72] But until it is time to die, a more creative option is available for navigating unruly space: the dream that both reflects as well as generates reality, the dramatized dream.

The Dream and the Philosopheme

In 1923–24, Krzhizhanovsky composed a series of brief tributes to the Moscow Chamber Theater. He praised its repertory as "almost always *a play about a play,* which meant that it became a theater of the highest theatricality, or more precisely—theater raised to the 'theater' degree (T^T)."[73] This exponential theatricality was especially evident in Tairov's 1915 production of Calderon's *Life Is a Dream,* a drama that "divides Being into Waking and Dream, which simply exchange masks with one another." The exchange of masks lies at the heart of Krzhizhanovsky's "philosopheme of the theater," worked out in 1923 and incorporated as part of his lectures on the psychology of the stage.[74]

Krzhizhanovsky begins his discussion of this psychology with the mechanics of the eye. It is not true, he argues, that the farther away an object, the blurrier it is. Only with distance and nesting (a play within a play, a dream within a dream) does any object become distinct and thus manageable. First-level reality—that which happens directly on the skin or presents itself directly to the eye—is almost useless; second- and third-level realities, however, begin to teach us about the world. As early as 1918, Krzhizhanovsky had been working out the optimal creative relation between people, space, and things.[75] The world is divided between those who systematically root out secrets (the scientists) and those devoted to the "secrification" of things [*otayneniye veshchey*], the artists. Science strives to bring a distant thing close to the eye and the brain, to explain it with increasing precision so that "miracles can be reduced to mechanics" (3). Artistic creativity, in contrast, "is the ability to insert into the interval between the eye and the thing" a Beautiful Far-Off (4). "Distance, wound up in a spiral, lies inside every thing, no matter how small its size or how murky it might appear" (6). Routine proximity flattens an object and jettisons its space. Distance restores its depth, integrity, precision, privacy, and secrecy. An everyday object does not lose this precious spiral—but only artists can protect it. For such defamiliarization and revivification, theater is the perfect site.

Krzhizhanovsky titles the second chapter of his 1923 treatise on the philosopheme of the theater "*Bïtiye, bït, bï,*" a sequence literally but inadequately rendered "Being, everyday life, as-if." In Russian, this triad of words relies for its effectiveness on the fact that it is progressively corroded from the end: letters fall away as the series approaches the ideal representational art. *Bïtiye,* "Being," is invisible to the eye and thus by nature nontheatrical. Because it is unified, it has no need for the theater, which thrives on scattered phenomena. Because it is unchanging, its reality is immanently present and simultaneous. There are no shifts to be staged, and nothing for actors to do. As Krzhizhanovsky explains, "Theater is not necessary to Being" (53). Certain theatrical genres do serve Being, such as mystery plays and the liturgy, but these are strictly contained, ornamental, and non-developmental.

What then of *bÿt*, Being that is brought down to earth, our solid experience of everyday life? As his basic unit of daily experience, Krzhizhanovsky posits the "phenomenon that plays at being a thing" (54). Whether or not the everyday world is full of solid things we cannot know, but this world always insists that we take it seriously. It threatens us with deprivation, obstacles, irritation, traceable causes, and non-negotiable effects.[76] *Bÿt* is a link across and down to the material world, creating in us a veritable fetishism of groping, touching, seeing. "A person from everyday life does not believe in Being," nor in true fantasy, either; "he believes fervently in the reality of his three little rooms, in the body of his wife, in the official stamp that can be seen" (54). Everyday life jealously protects its hold on our sensuous perceptions and pretends that these perceptions are real. *Bÿt* is "the imaginary" (*mnimost'*) that does not want to be imaginary. For that reason it "fears the theater, which exposes [this pretension] by its very kinship with it" (54). At this point Krzhizhanovsky moves to justify theater as a moral, truth-bearing force. "Everyday life, wishing to protect itself from the danger of remembering its own imaginariness and in order to isolate and localize its own unreality, constructs among its houses a special house with the placard 'Theater' hanging on it. In doing so it naively thinks that through its windowless walls, more 'theater' will not leak out" (54–55).

The theater of "*bi*"—a Russian particle suggesting a modal, conditional "as-if" state of consciousness—is the most sophisticated state of the art. If everyday life is playing with Being, then "as-if" theater plays with *bÿt*, reconfiguring life as it is into life as it could be, or perhaps life as it eternally is. It does not compete with things but transforms and animates them. The walls of the theater remain solid. The theater of "*bi*" does not seek to dissolve the proscenium or remove the footlights but "strives to reinforce them, doubling and tripling the line that separates the world from the world, the actor from the spectator, the struggle for existence from the struggle for nonexistence" (55–56). There are obvious links between "as-if" and Symbolism, as well as suggestive parallels with magical folk theater. How interesting it would be to have Prokofiev's view on this tripartite "philosopheme of the theater" from the perspective of Christian Science. Much of the meta-diegetic, "as-if" texture of *Eugene Onegin* comes from Prokofiev's music, which permits the unimpeded flow of inside to outside to inside again with only a quiver from the solid props on stage.

With this conceptual vocabulary, we can now return to *Eugene Onegin* itself, and especially its complex use of nature mythology and dreams. One cautionary note is in order. Russian academic and artistic circles of the 1920s were well acquainted with Sigmund Freud's teachings on dream interpretation (Freud was fully translated into Russian). Many Bolshevik intellectuals, most prominently Leon Trotsky, took an active interest in the psychoanalytic movement. Although this "Western" school had been banned along with many others by the early 1930s, the concepts of condensation, dramatization, displacement, inhibition, and regression had circulated for decades. But Russian twentieth-century psychology—even its unofficial, underground branch—never canonized Freud's evocative but often arbitrary constructs in this realm, and certainly not his pan-sexualization of the human psyche. Native Russian schools of developmental psychology offered spiritualized (although still tripartite) models of the self whose explanatory power proved far more fertile and better suited to their own empirical and literary experience. Pushkin himself, for all his fascination with the workings of Eros, would never have reduced it to somatic drives. Tatyana is indeed a young girl in love, but for the Poet as well as for her own essential self, she is more importantly a Muse—a symbol and goad to creativity, both her own and another's. Art is not a surrogate or sublimation of some other thing. On the contrary, those other things serve art, which (in Pushkin's view) is the life-force that endures. We may assume that Krzhizhanovsky knew and appreciated Freud, but he was a thinker beholden to no single school, and in this project it was Pushkin's priorities that he wished most to respect. He appears to have blended Russian and non-Russian views of the subconscious and dream-fantasy in his own trademark manner.

To grasp how Krzhizhanovsky integrates "as-if" space into his theater, it might help to recall the variety of subjective inner states that can be projected onstage. Collectively they make up what we call "imagination." Simplest is mental imagery: static, realistic, a matter of concrete physical recall of an event or person in the experienced past. In the spatio-temporal realm, its metaphor is a photograph; in music, a recurring theme. One example would be Tatyana remembering what Onegin looks like—although we know from Pushkin that there is not much evidence of this in their story: they hardly glance at each other, we have no record of their first meeting, and his image, for her, is largely a composite product of all the novelistic heroes she has read about and pined for. More complex than the mental image is waking fantasy. Here, images are no longer static but dynamic and sequential. They lead somewhere—usually to a forbidden place. They grow out of a glimpse, a concrete real-life stimulus. But because this stimulus is both real and open-ended, the follow-up scene we spin out in our imagination could actually happen "as we see it." Such fantasies might be likened to watching a film and identifying with the romantic leads. In the central portion of her letter, Tatyana positions herself before Onegin in just this way, visualizing herself as a desired object. Our conscious minds and bodies can incorporate these fantasies—indeed, we can even write them out cogently to others, as Tatyana is inspired to do, although not without an immense admixture of shame.

Finally we have what Krzhizhanovsky calls the *"tyazholïy son,"* the deep (or heavy) dream, site of our most profound desires. It, too, is dynamic and sequential, but it is *un*realistic and nonrealizable as real-life experience. Our conscious mind has no control over its shapes or behaviors. It is no longer ashamed. Its metaphor, if one can be found, is a fantasy cartoon or fairy tale. Fairy-tale logic and imagery abound in Krzhizhanovsky's playscript, most prominently in Tatyana's Dream, where, in a precise replica of Pushkin's text, the heroine is pursued by a shaggy bear through a snowy forest to a hut in which monsters are tamed by the Beloved and rivals are magically dispatched. When Pushkin's Narrator relates the Dream in the novel, we recall, he does so with the self-confidence of an outsider, as Tatyana's loving protector. He relishes its picturesque, risqué details because he enjoys being a storyteller. He is also something of a voyeur. In Pushkin's novel, Tatyana—shy, unsociable, a daydreamer and reader of novels—hardly talks at all. In the play, she must be motivated to speak out this terrible, marvelous dream herself. Its events must be fused with *her* intonation. These first-person imperatives of dramatic motivation and intonation might be one reason why Krzhizhanovsky plucked the dream out of Pushkin's sequence and placed it *after* the horror of the Name Day. Had this version of *Eugene Onegin* reached the stage, and had the playwright been able to incorporate not only his verbal but also his spatial poetics into its production, Tatyana's Dream with Prokofiev's astonishing music would have been the peak of the arc, the high point of dramatic "as-if" theater. How might this dream-space have organized the episodes surrounding it? Where is space wide open (*prostorno*) and where constricted (*tesno*)? Along what fissure or seam (*shchel'*) does the humiliated Tatyana escape from unbearable real life into the Dream, and then find her way back out again to life?

The Three Central Fragments: Name Day, Dream, Duel

As presented in the play, Tatyana's Name Day party is largely the site of shame. It realizes that aspect of her letter to Onegin that we tend to underrate, so dazzled are we by its naive honesty and expressions of love. "Resolve my doubts," she writes to him, "either rouse my hopes / Or interrupt this heavy dream, / With a reproach, alas, so well deserved." Rereading her letter, Tatyana "shudders from shame and fear," but she entrusts herself to Onegin and sends it anyway. Her heavy dream, as the playwright properly sees, is fully compatible with her reality (the way a light dream could not be). Without this desired thing she will not exist; she will be compelled to change completely. Krzhizhanovsky's playscript is as Tatyana-centered as Tchaikovsky's opera, but its psychology is far less sentimental. Not romantic love (with its passionate corollaries of sacrifice or satisfaction) but something more complex and durable lies at its base. This state of mind, to which Prokofiev ascribed a *"tragizm"* or tragic element (in a marginal comment to the stage direction introducing the Dream), is powerful enough not only to save the heroine but also to resurrect the hero. We call this base value "Winter," and we will investigate it in connection with Tatyana's dual folkloric prototype. There, too, the porous dream-space of the central Fragments proves decisive.

Fragment 7, the Name Day, opens on a threshold. The front of the stage is dark, the sides are cluttered with furniture and trash. Only the rooms at the back are brilliantly lit and filled with polkas and waltzes. Onegin has cornered Tatyana and is lecturing her about the need for self-control; she clings to the doorjamb trying to repress her sobs, so inappropriate in this public party space. The next episode is an incarnated, Gogolian insert featuring two distasteful comic buffoons, Buyanov and Zaretsky, mentioned in Pushkin but now detached from his Narrator's fabric. The drunken, hiccupping Buyanov (his name means "Mr. Rowdy") heightens the heroine's terror.[77] For he is not just any provincial gentry but a simulacrum of Tatyana's future in the countryside: he had proposed marriage, after all, and her mother had not opposed the match. Tatyana's choice at this point is not between Onegin's presence or absence (that is, fulfilling her dream or fantasizing about him forever in some forested nook): her fate will be a Buyanov. This is the sinister underpinning to Prokofiev's goony, manic *tram-blyam* harpsichords. The true sound of the Russian provinces is the drunken blather of Buyanov and Zaretsky against the background of the out-of-tune polka and the "slow minuet." In her love letter to Onegin, Tatyana had remarked, again naively, that if she had not met Onegin she would, with time, have met "a soul mate" in the countryside and become "a faithful wife / And virtuous mother." This is unlikely: what we see in the countryside is a landscape populated by pure Gogol, and for the shy and sociably awkward, the suitors are all grotesque. Only girls like Olga get the poets like Lensky.

Indeed, the radiant Olga emerges at every juncture during the evening as the lovely, confident hostess who has snared the only available poet in the district, the one marriageable man who is not a buffoon. And then Onegin starts to flirt with her, to dance with her, to embrace and touch her. How can Olga have everything, Tatyana nothing? Twice in his marginalia for Fragment 5 (the Letter Scene), Prokofiev jots down "sostoyaniye

Tatyanï" (Tatyana's condition or state of mind). At the end of Fragment 7, he crosses out his initial self-directive for some music describing "Tatyana's emotion." Instead he writes in: "Very short." In a scene full of waltzes, polkas, and minuets, she is beyond mood music.

Olga's betrayal and flirtation, treated by Pushkin's debonair Narrator with such affectionate condescension, propels Tatyana to her final humiliation. In the novel we smile at Lensky and shrug off Olga because the Narrator, too, is smiling. But in the present-tense time of a play there is no distance, no buffer between reader and word. In drama we must ask: What is the trapped heroine experiencing? Her shame and degraded desire reach a crisis point in the final, startling event of the dramatized Name Day, an episode not in Pushkin, which underwent at least one textual revision to increase its grotesqueness before Prokofiev set its text to music. This is the festive arrival and singing of the masked Yuletide Mummers.[78]

The eventual text that the Mummers sing in honor of the Name Day girl is both bawdy and inappropriate, a wedding ditty informing the bridegroom "how to mount his bride." It opens on a string of similes: "He's like a pole, his head's a pestle, ears like little scissors, hands like little rakes, legs like little forks, eyes like little holes."[79] The song bears no resemblance to Monsieur Triquet's ingratiating, civilized, Frenchified couplets to Tatyana in Tchaikovsky's opera. Arguably, this Mummers' text is far more devastating to the heroine, whose private fantasies have been precisely about marriage and whose shame derives from illusions at the level of poles, pestles, rakes, and forks, not from the ballroom niceties and album verse where her sister feels so at home. The final stage direction mimics a wedding ceremony. Tatyana is brought a goblet; she bows. But before she sips, she peers across the threshold of the door into the dark room beyond. In Krzhizhanovsky's spatial vocabulary, that darkness is a dream world, both punitive and wish fulfilling, where her deepest fears and highest hopes might be successfully played out. The Name Day was unacceptable, and she must create an alternative to it. She drops the goblet—and its falling is the fissure through which Tatyana, frightened and aroused by the Mummers, can escape into the terrible, marvel-laden world of the Dream, her transition out of the Name Day humiliation into a triumph.

With this faint and fall we are catapulted into Fragment 8. Its opening stage direction presents Tatyana at dawn, her face buried in a pillow, still in her white gown, one slipper fallen to the floor. She had thrown herself there in desperation the night before. The dream she has just experienced incorporated the monstrous Mummers (their masks are copied directly from Pushkin's description of Tatyana's Dream) but was a response to their provocation, not a prefiguring of it. Tatyana mutters "Mine. Mine. Mine. Mine" (*Moyo*, in neuter gender), what the dream monsters, and then Onegin, had called out to her in the hut. This phrase is not terrible, but marvelous: it is what she *wants* to hear.[80] Her Nurse tiptoes in, then tries to leave. But Tatyana, half asleep, holds her back, for she is compelled to tell her dream. Relating it will allow her to replay elements of the shame-laden Letter Scene with her Nurse but now in folklore time, opening it up to another outcome.[81] Had she not confessed to Onegin in her impetuous letter that in her fantasy she had seen him bending over her bedstead with delight and love? Had he not ridiculed that fantasy, reprimanded her, flirted with her sister? And how much better the denouement of the dream, where all the forest monsters—crabs mounted on spiders, horned dogs, bearded witches, a crane who was half cat—instantly obey him, fall silent before him, so he can lead her to that bench in the corner and be alone with her?

The letter that Pushkin composed for Tatyana is a tissue of Romantic-era clichés, which the Narrator presents to us indirectly and with lovingly tender irony. Deprived of the Narrator's zone, Krzhizhanovsky had to solve the practical dramatic problem of externalizing a dream-space event in such a way that the untalkative Tatyana has an emotionally satisfying reason to relate it. Superstitious like her author Pushkin, Tatyana was unskilled at separating out her dreams. She was always on the border, looking out a window toward somewhere else. And why should this post–Name Day, "as-if" dream suffer in comparison with its wretched cousin, "everyday life"? At that point in her dream narration when she glimpses Onegin at the table, Tatyana begins to speak (so a stage direction informs us) "in a completely different tone." Her seasoned Nurse becomes uneasy about the unfolding story; she sees where it is leading and would like to deflect this clearly erotic narrative into something safer, a benign or distracting fairy tale. But a stage direction informs us that "her reserve of images has dried up." This is odd: a nanny's reserves are supposed to be bottomless for this sort of thing. Disapprovingly, "she glances at Tanya." The girl is not listening. Has she grown up? The fairy tale is suddenly interrupted by the intrusion of Olga and Lensky. Prokofiev's marginal comment on the playscript, to whomever it is directed, reflects the liminal moment: "Think about this." For the dream does not end on the love fantasy, happily ever after. Lensky and Olga— the intolerably satisfied happy couple, the sister who has taken her Beloved away—enter the hut, Onegin draws his knife, strikes Lensky down, and Tatyana confesses, "I woke up in terror, Nurse." She was surely terrified and awestruck. She was also (as the dream permits) gratified.

Onegin alone with Tatyana, leaning tenderly over her, had taken place in highly unstable space. The daytime fantasy of her Letter, transposed to a deep heavy dream, cracks open, and she is obliged to crawl back out into everyday life, where morality is imposed and punishment exacted. From Tatyana's snowy dream we leap directly to the blizzard of the dueling site.

If Pushkin's Narrator in chapter 6 expands on the details (and the injustice) of that botched duel of honor, Krzhizhanovsky is far too deeply sunk in his heroine's dual reality to shift domains entirely. Fragment 9, the Duel, is very brief, wedged between Dream and Library, two Fragments in which we find Tatyana essentially alone. Little music was composed for the Duel, and all of it is nondevelopmental: a three-bar motif on page 10 of the autograph score to be "repeated as often as necessary," followed by a note to recapitulate "measures 12–20" from page 5, which accompany the loneliest moment of Tatyana's Letter Scene.

The most musical stage direction is the last, after Lensky lies dead in the snow: "Both in space and in the music, the symphony of the snowstorm [*simfoniya metelya*] grows." Blizzard symbolism is common in the folklore of the Russian north as well as in Pushkin's writings. Several of his lyric poems and his 1830 Belkin tale "The Snowstorm" ("Metel'") rely on it. In its folkloric guise, a blizzard represents demonic or unclean forces that intervene to separate lovers. Lovers are tested in storms, and those who survive are transformed. These three scenes (Name Day, Dream, and Duel) contain more of the texture of folk life and fairy tale than does Pushkin's novel. To heighten this folk element, Krzhizhanovsky inserts one of Pushkin's own verse fairy tales directly into the playscript, recited and referred to by characters on stage. He employs another fairy-tale plot, more archaic and pagan, as a concealed subtext to the entire play. Both tales are associated with Tatyana's favorite season—winter—and relate intimately to solar, lunar, and seasonal cycles. To this cluster of symbols we now turn.

The Heart of Winter

Pushkin's favorite time of year was autumn. In *Eugene Onegin*, he tilts this season toward winter. Our cue comes from the Narrator's comment about the heroine in chapter 5, iv, 1–4: "Tatyana, Russian in her heart of hearts / (Herself not knowing why) / With its cold beauty / Loved the Russian winter. . . ." *Herself not knowing why:* this unconscious affinity between Tatyana and the darkest—and whitest—season sits at the core of the play. Krzhizhanovsky amplifies Pushkin's cue and moves as many events as possible to winter, when organic life and the sun's heat are in abeyance. Winter is the year's night. The dead of night (*glukhaya noch'*) is a time of obstacles and revelations: Tatyana writing her love letter, or her stumbling through snowdrifts on the way to Onegin in her dream. Nothing of significance in the play happens unimpeded in the glare of high noon.

Snow, short days, and filtered, frosty winter light are means for connecting reality, daydream, and night dream. Thus liminal times and spaces are highly marked as psychological thresholds; people loiter in doorways, dance through apertures from light into dark (the dark being downstage, closest to the audience), and gaze through windows at the rising or setting moon. The traditional concept of a dramatic scene—stirring verbal or musical closure followed by the lowering of a curtain—gives way in the Fragment to a principle akin to cinemagraphic montage: patches of action framed by a change in lighting. Overall, the temperature of the fourteen Fragments is cold. But frost and snow do not imply negativity or a drive toward death. Parallels with Northrop Frye's archetypal criticism, where the mythos of autumn as tragedy and of winter as irony and satire derives from classical Greek and Shakespearean texts, are unproductive in this play.[82] However keenly he valued those masterpieces of the Western canon, in this play Krzhizhanovsky is inspired by his native Russian climate and geography—by the darker, waning seasons and their diurnal equivalents, the edges of the day. He structured his dramatic action around them. Evidence for this is his four-page typescript signed "S. K." from 1936, titled *'Kalendar' Onegina* (A calendar for Onegin).[83]

The *Calendar* provides a glimpse into the playwright's approach to time in all its parameters: chronological, biological, cyclical, seasonal, daily, finally folkloric. In this early schema the play is still organized by scenes, of which there are eighteen. Each page contains three columns, the first labeled "Year" (*God*), the second "Time of the Year" (or season, *Vremya goda*), the third "Time of the Day" (*Vremya dnya*). The "Year" places the fictional Onegin within real Russian history, a common exercise for academic Pushkinists (Onegin was born in 1796, entered society 1812, inherited his uncle's estate 1820, and so forth). The season column includes such entries as "overcast December day," "January," "Winter, before Shrovetide." Times of the day contain meteorologically precise details, such as the desired slant of light: scene 1, for example, specifies "Morning. Sun at a 30° angle to the earth." Many scenes emphasize the descent of the solar arc: "Even closer to sunset" (scene 3), "thickening twilight" (scene 4), "the lengthening twilight of a shortened autumn day" (scene 7), "that hour when both stars and candles are lit" (scene 10), "a premonition of evening" (scene 13). From this preliminary plan, it would appear that Krzhizhanovsky visualized the stage set primarily in terms of light and shadow. Only the Prologue is exempt, a tribute to the timelessness of literary art. For "Year" we read: "All dates from all centuries crowd together on the bookshelves." And for season: "The twilight illumination of book-stacks [*knigokhranilishche*], which is identical at all times of the year." Of the eighteen scenes, two take place in spring, five in late summer, three in autumn, and eight in winter.

Krzhizhanovsky teased cold weather out of every possible Pushkinian detail. Consider, for example, the epigraph to Pushkin's chapter 1, which consists of one truncated opaque line: "And one rushes to live and hastens to feel." In his essay on Pushkin's epigraphs, Krzhizhanovsky cites its source, Prince Vyazemsky's 1819 lyric poem "Pervïy sneg" (First snow) and suggests why this wintry subtext might have won out over other candidates as the epigraphic portal to the novel (the competition included a quote by Edmund Burke and two lines from Yevgeniy Baratïnsky's influential 1816 poem, "Pirï" [Feasts]).[84] "First Snow" is a buoyant, celebratory poem. In Vyazemsky's larger poetic context, Krzhizhanovsky notes, the epigraph "has an entirely different emotional filling."[85]

During the first snowfall or first serious drop in temperature, life is more precious and more receptive to sensation. In Russia, with its huge expanse and isolated hamlets, there is also a practical engineering aspect: when roads freeze over, what was an unpaved, unpassable morass of mud during intermediate seasons of thaw again becomes a swift and efficient means of travel. In Fragment 10, while visiting Onegin's library, Tatyana recites Pushkin's homage to late November. Roads open up, horses exult and sledges speed by, tossing up powdery snow. In Fragment 11 of the play, where Vyazemsky is first brought to life as a speaking character, close attention is given to the state of Russian roads, a topic of concern both to this poet and to Pushkin, his real-life friend. Vyazemsky even recites to a spellbound Moscow salon several stanzas from his own 1829 poem "Stantsiya" (The station) on the potholes, bedbugs, and broken-down bridges that plague the Russian traveler, and on the utopian grid of highways that he predicts (with heavy irony) an "enlightened Russia" will eventually, in several centuries, construct. Unpaved roads are obstacle courses; frost and crystalline snow open up lines of communication. The cold connects people and fate, whereas spring softens the ground; the world sinks, slows down, simultaneously sprouts and decays. The dramatic *Eugene Onegin* contains few of the happy thaws or buddings that are characteristic of love stories. Everything always threatens to be "frozen out." But we cannot call this a calamity. Krzhizhanovsky associates fidelity (in friendship and in love) with this season.

Beginning with Part Two (Fragment 6), the presence of late autumn and winter becomes overwhelming. Onegin, a poor reader of the seasons and a bad regulator of his own body heat, interrupts his contemplation of Tatyana's letter with a memory of beauties he had known in St. Petersburg: "unapproachable, / Cold, pure as winter, / Unpersuadable, unbribable, / Incomprehensible." He is honestly touched by Tatyana's spontaneous flare-up and resolves to cool it down kindly, in brotherly fashion. At that point Lensky enters, shaking from his overcoat a "powdery-thin layer of the first dusting of snow." By Fragment 7 we are already deep into winter and its rituals. Krzhizhanovsky and Prokofiev add Yuletide Mummers to Tatyana's

Name Day. Fragment 8, the Dream, opens on a pursuit through snowdrifts. Here ice and snow present obstacles, not a sleek smooth road, but that is required by the Dream, which must test its inhabitants as well as reveal their deepest desire. Fragment 9, the Duel, continues this testing ground with winter at its worst, a blizzard. "The sort of weather," we read in a startling stage direction, "when one wants either to kill, or be killed, as soon as possible." A "symphony of the snowstorm" rises up to buttress the first stirrings of repentance in Onegin as he stands over the dead body of his friend.

In the novel, Pushkin does not foreground the season of Tatyana's visit to Onegin's abandoned manor house (chapter 7). It nevertheless seems to be summer: a river flows by peacefully, beetles hum, fishermen's fires light up the twilight. The equivalent scene in the play, Fragment 10, is emphatically transposed to winter. Tatyana enters in cape and mittens; the windows of the manor are "blind, piled high with snow." Her love-smitten gesture of breathing on a cool windowpane and tracing in the mist an entwined *O* and *E* (in the novel, chap. 3, xxxvii: 9–14, an event of late summer) becomes more fraught in the heightened wintry context of the play. Tatyana first etches those initials on a hoarfrost-encrusted window in Onegin's library. About to leave, she remembers them, but frost is not mere mist from a breath. She rubs at the pane: "the frozen letters won't give way." Ice, it would appear, endures. Finally a glint of the cold setting sun breaks through a thinned-out patch. Tatyana gazes out, bids farewell to her rural life, and leaves for home, her declaration of love still visibly intact on the windowpane. We next see her in Fragment 11, entering her Moscow aunt's room, bundled up against the cold and enveloped in frosty steaming air. Only after two servants proceed to "unwrap" her do the guests—Vyazemsky and an unnamed General—realize that under that shapeless cocoon of rabbitskin and furs, the slender contour of a girl is emerging. The General is captivated by the scene. He twirls his moustache, tugs on his uniform to straighten it, and by the next Fragment has become Tatyana's husband. This seasonal symbolism, so partial to winter, culminates in the final Fragment 14, when the married Princess Tatyana receives an unexpected early morning visit from Onegin. To understand this scene, however, we must consider the two wintry fairy tales that structure Tatyana's consciousness in the play.

The most lengthy of Krzhizhanovsky's additions to *Eugene Onegin* is Pushkin's "Fairy Tale of the Dead Tsarevna and the Seven Knights" ("Skazka o myortvoy tsarevne i o semi bogatïryakh"), composed by the poet in 1833. Several familiar folktale elements feed into its plot, a variant on the Grimm Brothers' "Snowdrop" or pan-European "Snow White." There is an evil stepmother, a magic mirror on the wall that knows which woman in the kingdom is the fairest of all, seven brothers/dwarfs, a poisoned apple, a sleeping beauty, and a kindly Sun, Moon, and Wind that help Tsarevich Yelisey find his bewitched bride. The "dead tsarevna" of the title is a metaphor, since the *tsarevna* (daughter of a tsar, here the romantic heroine) falls into an enchanted trance but does not in fact die. In the pre-story, however, her mother the *tsaritsa* (wife of a tsar) dies in childbirth. It is this prior, fatal maternal segment that the Nurse recites to her distraught and excited young charge in Fragment 5, the Letter Scene, in hopes of distracting her from the calamitous impact of her first love.[86] (At this point in Pushkin's novel, we recall, the Nurse relates at Tatyana's bidding not a folktale but whatever she can remember of her own courtship and marriage.) The opening 24-line stanza of Pushkin's *skazka* contains several Tatyana-like elements attached to the fairy-tale bride-mother. The tsaritsa bids farewell to her tsar, who sets out on the road. She sits down at the window and stares out at the field night and day, from morning till night. Although a raging blizzard hurts her eyes, she does not lift her gaze from the white landscape. Nine months pass. The tsaritsa gives birth to a daughter at the precise moment of her husband's return. The new mother does not survive her rapture at seeing him again, and dies.

We are expected to know the rest of Pushkin's tale. The tsar grieves, of course, but a year passes like an empty dream (*kak son pustoy*) and he remarries. The new tsaritsa is proud, jealous, beautiful, the inevitable stepmother-witch—and her dowry includes a magic mirror. Meanwhile, the orphaned tsarevna grows up and is affianced to Prince Yelisey. Hearing from her mirror that her stepdaughter (and not herself) is now the fairest in the land, the evil stepmother sends a servant into the forest with instructions to bind the young tsarevna to a tree, where she will be gnawed to death by wolves. The tsarevna successfully entreats the servant to release her. Once freed, she wanders the forest until she comes across a hut that is home to seven knights. She enters, cleans it up, and falls asleep. When the seven brothers return, they invite her to stay with them. In rapid time, of course, all seven fall in love with her, which promises some fraternal tension. The eldest asks her openly to choose one of them. The others, he promises, "will somehow reconcile themselves to it . . . / But why are you shaking your head? / Are you refusing us? / Or are the goods not to the taste of the merchant?" The tsarevna answers that for her, all seven are equally bold and intelligent, equally her dear brothers, but that she's already affianced: "I love you all sincerely / But I'm given to another / for all time." The seven brothers receive this news silently, scratch their heads, apologize for the request, quietly back out of the room, and the eight continue to live as before. The story resumes only when the evil stepmother arranges the delivery of a poisoned apple, triggering the tsarevna's death-like trance and the return of the Prince.

Caryl Emerson

The body of the fairy tale, then, produces the mandated happy ending. The maiden who is "given to another / for all time" is a transparent (although premarital) echo of Tatyana's final words to Onegin: "But I am given to another, / I shall be true to him forever." Prince Yelisey appears, albeit only as a name, at several points in the playscript, the first time uttered by Onegin himself in ironic repartee with Lensky. But ultimately it is not the returning tsarevich Yelisey who carries the wisdom of the tale. For good reason, the Nurse in Fragment 5 delivers only the pre-story of the *skazka*, those nine months before the birth of the heroine. Its somber themes are worth noting. Immobility, patient waiting, and loyalty are fertile. If and when the absent beloved actually returns, the reward is death. The cycle of love and blossoming, if it occurs at all, belongs only to the second (female) generation. These motifs provide a clue to a deeper narrative subtext governing Krzhizhanovsky's *Eugene Onegin*. Only in one phrase does the playwright allude to it directly, and several tiny details in the initial stage directions of the final Fragment reinforce this allusion. It would seem that Tatyana's fairy-tale model is not Cinderella. It is not even Prince Yelisey waking up his Sleeping Beauty. In keeping with winter, her favorite season and the setting for all major episodes in her story, Tatyana most resembles the heroine in the Russian pagan myth "Snegurochka," or "The Snow Maiden," a plot well known in dramatic and operatic repertory. One of Krzhizhanovsky's favorite playwrights, Alexander Ostrovsky, wrote a folklore fantasy-play called *Snegurochka* in 1873, which became the base for Rimsky-Korsakov's opera of the same name in 1881. That work, coincidentally, was Prokofiev's favorite out of all Rimsky-Korsakov's operas. A happy ending is not relevant to the story. Like most cosmological parables, "The Snow Maiden" serves necessity, not personal satisfaction. Here is that myth.

Grandfather Frost and Spring the Fair have a daughter. Their marriage is a difficult one, for each spouse answers for a different season and both are protective of their child. As a young girl the Snow Maiden was always icy cold and pure, but now that she is on the brink of womanhood, the Sun God Yarilo places in her heart the Fire of Love—which, if acted upon, threatens to melt her. Snegurochka knows this, but she is, after all, a young girl; she will be in love. By the final act, the Maiden, now engaged to the mortal Mizgir, awaits her mother at dawn. Spring rises from the lake, covered with flowers; this is her last day on earth, because Yarilo will usher in Summer. She counsels her daughter to hide in the forest shadows and conceal her love from Yarilo-Sun. But the impatient Mizgir rushes in and begs the Tsar's blessing on their marriage. At that moment the Sun breaks through the summer mist. When its rays fall on Snegurochka, she melts away; in despair, Mizgir throws himself into the lake. But the Sun's holiday is not dimmed by this dual sacrifice. With Snegurochka's death, Frost

• 103 •

loses its power over Spring and fertility returns to the earth. In this painful cosmic ritual, the breaking through of the winter sun's rays is a turning point.

Krzhizhanovsky provides two moments of "chilly sun rays breaking through" on Tatyana: first in Fragment 10, Onegin's Library, and then again on Princess Tatyana in Fragment 14, set (according to the *Calendar*) in a blustering, misty Petersburg April. In the first episode, Tatyana gazes out on the snowy fields. In the second, she pulls the blinds against intruding rays of the sun. The final scene of the play appears to be a hybrid of three texts: Pushkin's novel with an overlay of these two fairy tales. In this final confrontation of the would-be lovers, the poet's lines remain intact and its famous stanzas are recited in bulk. Within that familiar frame, however, Princess Tatyana, smiling, recalls the first four lines of the "fairy tale about Yelisey" with which she had prompted her Nurse in Fragment 5 (the tsarevna's lines: "But I'm given to another . . ."). After pulling the blinds, she enters folkloric time, surrounding herself—or protecting herself—with a magic circle of keepsakes linked to her life in the country. Only in this shadowy fairy-tale space can she manipulate both objects and time, turning things into rhythmic pulses and then into dreams. In the spirit of her long past girlhood, Tatyana prepares herself for the arrival of her beloved— or perhaps she conjures him up. For at just that moment Onegin himself rushes in, like Mizgir, begging her for the warmth that he knows—or needs to believe—she feels for him, and seeking in her traces of the needy girl who wrote the letter. But the Cinderella-tsarevna plot now competes with "Snegurochka," where the stakes for all parties are immeasurably higher. Support for the structural importance of this pagan folktale is found in Krzhizhanovsky's *Calendar for Onegin*, scene 17 (what will become Fragment 14 in the play, its final episode). On pages 3–4, the following detail was entered under the column "Season": "an early northern 'snow maiden' spring" (*rannyaya severnaya snegurochkina vesna*)—the sort of winter-spring transition that melts snow maidens.

Krzhizhanovsky's *Eugene Onegin* is a new fairy tale about Yelisey, a new Snow White. The abandoned tsaritsa staring out the window at the snow will die upon the return of her beloved. Prince Yelisey is the Onegin who comes back but cannot claim his bride. And as Snegurochka, Tatyana is not structured to experience passionate reciprocal love in the present. She may crave it, but her wintry heart will not survive it. Her loyalty—to her husband and also to the memory of unrequited love—is essential to her, not for her happiness but for her survival. According to this economy, Tatyana will have ultimate agency to control and remember, but not to spend.

How to End a Love Story

In Pushkin's *Eugene Onegin*, the love story ends abruptly. The Narrator cuts it off. Blessed is he, we read, who can take leave of life without having drained its cup, without having read the novel to the end, who can cut off an event before it is over, "as I with my Onegin do." Tatyana and Onegin do not touch; they do not really even converse. Tchaikovsky could not endure such a deeply unoperatic denouement. In some versions and productions of his opera, the lovers actually embrace—to the intense discomfort of the Pushkin purists. Embrace or no, the end of Tchaikovsky's opera presents us with the traditional eighteenth-century choice between love and duty. True love, the realm of fairy tale, lies with Onegin, whereas duty, the realm of necessity, lies with Tatyana.

There is more to Krzhizhanovsky's final scene, however, than a fairy tale on Tatyana's side and dashed hopes on Onegin's. The two are brought together—Onegin bursts in on his "former Tanya"—but not as Tchaikovsky brings them together, in the shared heat of a love duet. In the play, the gaps in pace and timing between Tatyana and Onegin are even exaggerated.[87] Unlike the final scene in Pushkin, Onegin speaks. But in reality he is reading. He immediately begins reciting to Tatyana his own letter, still unacknowledged: "I can predict everything." But she has seen it already from within her magic circle of keepsakes, and he is too late. Their final dialogue is not a dialogue in this world. As she speaks to him, he reads to her, in a reciprocal exchange of fateful but frozen statements. Her husband, the General, never appears and is not a factor. Amid the furniture of her noble caste, Tatyana lives out her fairy-tale ending and departs, almost floats, "stepping among the flat flowers of the ottoman meadow." There is no reason to believe that the two ever make eye contact. Onegin stands silently, head bowed. On the threshold of the door he meets the Poet, who lets him pass and then speaks the final words with his back to the audience and his face to the open door. Each dances out a different exit into a different dark space, where some form of art—for her a fairy tale, for him a written poem—is available to them out of their dreams and memories.

On the face of it, the love story is a failure. But it need not be performed in that spirit. Onegin has regained the depth and poetic inspiration that, in the Prologue, he had boasted of losing. "Why should the poet disturb the deep dream (*tyazhkiy son*) of the heart?" he had complained bitterly to the Bookseller. "He torments memory fruitlessly."[88] Now the hero, tormented by memory, has woken up to that deep and fruitful dream. Tatyana remains faithful to winter, her patron season. Each has become the necessary Muse for the other.

We recall Krzhizhanovsky's ruminations, twenty years earlier, on the "spiral of distance" trapped inside every thing, which the artist is obliged to protect. At the end of that 1918 text, he extends to the realm of the human body this same high regard for the proper unfolding of optimal distance, and even hints whimsically at a philosophy of asymmetrical love. "Human beings are complex," he writes, "they desire both distance and proximity in the beloved, both idealization and possesssion." The ancients, he said, acknowledged these twin passions through the god Eros and his opponent, Anteros (Anti-Eros), curiously the god of both mutual love and of vengeance for love spurned. Images of Anteros, like many Greek statues, "have blind eyes deprived of pupils and broken-off arms." But, Krzhizhanovsky adds, "in reconstructing these statues it is not necessary to glue back arms on marble Anteros, and for this reason: if Eros teaches us how to enclose the beloved, then Anteros teaches us about armless love, love that distances one from the beloved with an equal force."[89]

What of Prokofiev? There is no music for the end of this final Fragment. Perhaps the composer did not get to it, or perhaps he intended silence. But it is tempting to see, in the strange noncorporeal dance that unites and then gently separates Tatyana and Onegin, a hint of the ballet *Romeo and Juliet* as Prokofiev composed it in 1935 and hoped it would be produced. The romantic leads do not die; it is not a tragedy. Nor do they survive to marry in this world, for this world appears to fall away; it is not a comedy. Some other system of harmonies transcending both is at work, as the music of their youth returns. Tatyana departs in the same unearthly way. She, like Juliet, has become a young maiden again, now that the seasons have changed. "The flowers on their spiral steel stems almost do not feel the touch of her foot." Surely Prokofiev believed that such an ending is not a Dance of Death, but of Life.

NOTES

1. For an overview of these attitudes, see Boris Katz and Caryl Emerson, "Pushkin and Music," *The Pushkin Handbook*, ed. David M. Bethea (Madison: University of Wisconsin Press, 2005), 591–608, esp. 595.

2. I am indebted here and throughout this essay to Leonid Maximenkov, the most knowledgeable archival sleuth at work today on Stalinist cultural policy, who shared details from his documentary study of Soviet music history, based on research conducted at five federal archives.

3. Prokofiev introduces the phrase *legko-ser'yoznaya ili ser'yozno-lyogkaya muzïka* in "Puti sovetskoy muzïki," *Izvestiya*, November 16, 1934; repr. in *Prokof'yev o Prokof'yeve*, ed. V. P. Varunts (Moscow: Sovetskiy kompozitor, 1991), 128. In English, see the discussion in David Nice, *Prokofiev: From Russia to the West 1891–1935* (New Haven: Yale University Press, 2003), 320–22.

4. The text analyzed and translated here is most likely the first revision: RGALI f. 1929, op. 1, yed. khr. 86 ("'Yevgeniy Onegin.' Stsenicheskaya proyektsiya S. D. Krzhizhanovskogo 'Yevgeniy Onegin' [po romanu v stikhakh A. S. Pushkina] + pometï, sdelannïye na p'yese kasayushchiyesya

muzïkal'nogo oformleniya spektaklya. 1936. Avtograf i mashinopis'." 84 str.: 29 x 21).

5. For a sample of this solely "bureaucratic" activity, see Stephanie Sandler, "The 1937 Pushkin Jubilee as Epic Trauma," in *Epic Revisionism: Russian History and Literature as Stalinist Propaganda*, ed. Kevin M. Platt and David Brandenberger (Madison: University of Wisconsin Press, 2006), 196–99.

6. I thank Simon Morrison for sharing these details from chapter 3 of his *The People's Artist: Prokofiev's Soviet Years* (Oxford University Press, 2008) on the Pushkin centennial scores. In 1980, Clive Bennett wrote a brief essay on "Prokofiev and *Eugene Onegin*" for *The Musical Times* 121, no. 1646 (1980): 230–33. Beyond speculative liner notes, little else has been written on the project.

7. See the interview with Prokofiev on the *Eugene Onegin* music in *Krasnaya gazeta* and *Vechernyaya Moskva*, "Moi planï," July 22, 1936; repr. in *Prokof'yev o Prokof'yeve*, 142–43.

8. Quoted in Gleb Shul'pyakov, "Chelovek, kotorïy bïl Gulliverom," a review of Krzhizhanovsky's writings that opens with a list of all the stories summarily rejected, submitted to publishing houses that then closed, playscripts commissioned but unperformed, film scenarios highjacked. Available at http://exlibris.ng.ru/printed/izdat/2001-08-23/1_gulliver/html.

9. The plot of *Tot, tretiy* began as fragments for a novel in 1929, passed through the Tairov-Prokofiev *Egyptian Nights* collaboration in 1934, and by 1937 had been recast as a farce in fourteen scenes. In 1937, Krzhizhanovsky read the play aloud for the first and last time at a Moscow gathering in Stanislavsky's house that included among the guests the already-disgraced Vsevolod Meyerhold; the latter mournfully praised the play and predicted it would never be staged. According to Krzhizhanovsky's 1929 outline (*konspekt*), "the Third" was that anonymous poet who, in Pushkin's poem "Cleopatra" (1828), claimed the Queen's favors on the third night but then chose not to pay with his life. Instead he escaped, becoming a fugitive-at-large in the Roman Empire of Mark Antony. Antony seized on this unknown malefactor as an excuse to launch an empire-wide police investigation ("Affair #1 on the Third"). In a fit of despair, the Third turns himself in to the secret police—but then, unexpectedly, the regime changes, Octavius becomes emperor, the criminal becomes a patriot, and the Third is awarded state honors and a pension. See Krzhizhanovskiy, *"Tot, tretiy. Roman. 3 chasti,"* in "Dva fragmenta k 'Istorii nenapisannoy literaturï,'" ed. Vadim Perel'muter, *Toronto Slavic Quarterly* 20 (Spring 2007): 3–4. The editor notes that "five paragraphs of this outline were turned into four acts and fourteen dramatic scenes that were hilarious to the point of tears" (4). In the context of the 1930s, Krzhizhanovsky's unrealized novel can thus be seen as a roman-à-clef that prefigures both Kirov's (probably pre-arranged) assassination in 1934, which served Stalin as pretext and practice-ground for the purges, and Bulgakov's Imperial-Rome-and-Jerusalem novel of 1934–40, *The Master and Margarita*.

10. A. Bovshek, *Vospominaniya o Krzhizhanovskom: Glazami druga* (Reminiscences of Krzhizhanovsky: Through the eyes of a friend), http://az.lib.ru/k/ krzhizhanowskij_s_d/ text_0320.shtml, 30 (subsequent references are included in the text). The Samson allusion is crafty and bitter. What might have been the "thought" lying beneath the hair, the secret of Samson's strength? Unlike the mad Don Quixote tilting at windmills, Samson, after he is betrayed by Delilah and subsequently shaved, blinded, and imprisoned in Gaza, lets his hair grow out and then leans against the Philistines' temple. Its walls come crashing down, just as Samson had hoped—killing him together with thousands of the enemy (Judges 16:30).

11. For background on this commemorative posthumous procedure from the perspective of the Union of Soviet Composers, see Leonid Maximenkov, "Prokofiev's Immortalization," in the present volume.

12. RGALI f. 2280, op. 1, yed. khr. 117 ("Materialï Kommissii po literaturnomu naslediyu S. D. Krzhizhanovskogo: postanovleniye prezidiuma pravleniya Moskovskogo otdeleniya SSP SSSR, protokol zasedaniya komissii, plan izdaniya yego proizvedeniy, retsenzii na podgotovlenïy sbornik, zayavleniya A. G. Bovshek i dr. materialï").

13. Vadim Perelmuter, who now lives in Germany, assembled and edited the book-length publications by and about Krzhizhanovsky that have appeared since 1989, and is editor of the *Sobraniye sochinenii* (Collected works) (2001–8). He has also coordinated several forums on the writer in *Toronto Slavic Quarterly*, including three issues in 2007. All of Krzhizhanovsky's prose fiction is available in Russian online. Volume 4 of the *Collected Works* contains the critical writings on Pushkin, Shakespeare, George Bernard Shaw, Anton Chekhov, and the history of "peripheral" literary forms (titles, epigraphs, stage directions, etc.). Volume 5 is due out in 2008.

14. M. Gasparov, "Mir Sigizmunda Krzhizhanskogo," *Oktyabr'* 3 (March 1990): 201–3, esp. 201.

15. Ibid., 203.

16. Sigizmund Krzhizhanovsky, *Seven Stories*, trans. and introd. Joanne Turnbull (Glas Publishers, Moscow, distributed in North America by Northwestern University Press, 2006). In 2007, the Russian-to-English translation prize awarded annually by Academica Rossica, a British-based arts organization, was given to Joanne Turnbull for *Seven Stories*.

17. Ya. Moleva, the niece, wrote her "Legenda o Zigmunte Pervom" in July 1988; the lady friend N. [Nele] Semper her "Chelovek iz nebïtiya: Vospominaniya o S. D. Krzhizhanovskom. 1942–1949" in June 1989. Both memoirs are available online: "Vospominaniya o Krzhizhanovskom," http://az.lib.ru/k/krzhizhanowskij_s_d/text_0320.shtml, Moleva, 37–42; Semper, 42–52. Semper was scandalized that this "unfortunate man" did not recognize her when they met by chance on a staircase in the State Publishing House in March 1949; it is very possible that she did not know of his brain spasms and damaged memory.

18. N. Litvinenko, "Nesïgrannïy spektakl'," in *Rezhissyorskoye iskusstvo A. Ya. Tairova*, ed. K. L. Rudnitskiy (Moscow: Vseros. teatral'noye ob-vo, 1987), 112–30; and "Vspomnim Sigizmunda Krzhizhanovskogo—deyatelya teatra i teatral'nogo kritika," *Mnemozina*, vol. 2 (Moscow: Éditorial URSS, 2000), 350–73, esp. 358–65.

19. E. K. Gal'perina, "Predannost' Pushkinu," in *Osmyorkin: Razmïshleniya ob isskustve. Pis'ma. Kritika. Vospominaniya sovremennikov* (Moscow: Sovetskiy khudozhnik, 1981), 232–39, esp. 237–38.

20. See L. Olinskaya, "*Yevgenïy Onegin* v iskizakh A. A. Osmyorkina," *Iskusstvo* 10 (1979): 30–37.

21. Ibid., 35.

22. As a landscape artist, Osmyorkin was famous for his elegiac watercolors of "Pushkin locales" (especially Mikhailovskoye). According to his wife, he often spoke in chunks of Pushkin, with reverence or with ironic intonation: "People indifferent to Pushkin he not so much despised as pitied, the way one pities the unfortunate or deprived." Other domestic anecdotes suggest an almost talisman-like awe toward the poet. When Osmyorkin heard that part of the ceiling in his Leningrad studio had collapsed and damaged several items, he sent two urgent telegrams inquiring whether his black-and-white reproduction of Vasily Tropinin's 1827 portrait of Pushkin had been harmed; fortunately it was intact. Gal'perina, "Predannost' Pushkinu," 234–35.

23. I am grateful to Galina Zlobina, deputy director of RGALI, for transcribing relevant documents in the personal collections of Tairov, Krzhizhanovsky, Osmyorkin, and V. V. Fyodorov, a collector and repertoire consultant for the Moscow Art Theater (1935–36) and literary specialist for the Chamber Theater Museum (1937–44). Personal three-page typed communication, September 17, 2007. Zlobina also kindly provided a 22-page inventory of 121 catalogued and dated items in the Krzhizhanovsky archive, and photocopies of two variants of the full playscript: the second variant with Prokofiev's markings, and what is probably the third variant, with markings by both Tairov and Krzhizhanovsky.

24. RGALI f. 2963, op. 1, yed. khr. 163 ("Dogovor Osm. s Kamernïm teatrom ob oformlenii spektaklya E. O.," May 22, 1936).

25. In addition to the 84-page document translated in full here, the following texts are held by RGALI. In the Tairov archive, two documents: "Director's copy of Krzhizhanovsky's play, typescript with Tairov's markings," f. 2328, op. 1, yed. khr. 670, 102 pages; and "Krzhizhanovsky's play, typescript," f. 2328, op. 1, yed. khr. 671, 71 pages. In the V. V. Fyodorov archive, two documents: the earliest version, "Krzhizhanovsky. E. O. Montage for the Chamber Theater. Early variant. Without an ending. Typescript with the author's corrections and insertions," f. 2579, op. 1, yed. khr. 2053, 51 pages; and "Krzhizhanovsky. E.O. Scenic projection for Ch. Theater. Typescript with corrections by the author and markings on the musical staging of the production, made by A. Ya. Tairov," f. 2579, op. 1, yed. khr. 2054, 90 pages. The Prokofiev archive contains another copy of the 71-page version, but unmarked: "E. O. Scenic projection of Krzhizhanovsky. Typescript, without corrections," f. 1929, op. 2, yed. khr. 587.

26. On page 37 in the playscript, opposite the transitional stage direction between Name Day Fragment 7 and Dream Fragment 8, Prokofiev writes in his tiny script: *otmenit' (iyul')* (Cancel [July]). Prokofiev's note might refer to the replacement, midsummer, of the bland Mummers' text with the more colorful and threatening one that Prokofiev then set to music. More likely, however, it refers to Tatyana's behavior in that stage direction, and to the entire joint between

Caryl Emerson

Name Day and Dream. Tatyana, glancing into a dark room where Mummers in monster masks have just finished singing an obscene wedding song in her honor, drops a goblet of wine on the threshold out of fright. Perhaps she faints, or perhaps the reality of that day is simply denied; the next time we see her, she is lying facedown in bed. One of the censors, possibly, protested that in Pushkin's novel, Tatyana's Dream *precedes* the Name Day, so by what license is the order reversed? And where in Pushkin's novel does Tatyana faint from fright at masked Mummers?

27. The year 1933 appears on the title page of the earliest surviving variant of the *Eugene Onegin* playscript, but this date is corrected by hand to 1935. If we presume this changed date was not a typo but an update, it might have marked the beginning of the collaboration between playwright and director.

28. The original 1933 plans for the Tairov-Prokofiev *Egyptian Nights* (*Yegipetskiye nochi*) opened with four scenes from Shaw (Act One) and used Pushkin's poem as a transition to Shakespeare, from Antony's defeat (Act Two) to Cleopatra's death (Act Three). The production grew too long, however, and the Shaw portions were extensively cut. The play's run at the Chamber Theater in 1934–35 was a popular success. According to his essay of 1937 (pub. 1939) on "The Forgotten Shakespeare," Krzhizhanovsky considered the amalgamation a failure: "Including foreign elements in a text by Shakespeare was of course a mistake." See "Zabïtïy Shekspir," in Krzhizhanovskiy, *Sobraniye sochinenii*, ed. Vadim Perel'muter, 5 vols. (St. Petersburg: Symposium, 2001–8), 4:302–22, esp. 320. This volume is henceforth referred to in the text and footnotes as *SK:Ss* 4. In his *Autobiography*, Prokofiev agrees: "However, despite the scintillating wit of Bernard Shaw, old man Shakespeare turned out to be such a titan by comparison that the desire arose to give him as much space as possible and as little as possible to Shaw. The excised Bernard dwindled down in weight and was transformed into one brief, unimportant episode tacked on to the beginning of the production." In Sergei Prokofiev, *Autobiography. Articles. Reminiscences*, ed. S. Shlifstein, trans. Rose Prokofieva (Honolulu: University Press of the Pacific, 2000), 84. Translation adjusted.

29. A. Ya. Tairov, "Kak ya rabotayu nad klassikami," in *Zapiski rezhissyora. Stat'i. Besedï. Rechi. Pis'ma* (Moscow: Vserossiskoye teatral'noye obshchestvo, 1970), 240–42, esp. 241; orig. pub. in *Izvestiya*, July 29, 1933.

30. Meyerhold's modernist theater practiced biomechanics and the building of character "from the outside in," starting with the public gesture; Tairov's Chamber Theater was more attuned to individual psychology, building "from the inside out." In a personal communication (September 28, 2007), Perelmuter notes that this polemic between the two philosophies of performance was often carried on through sequential productions of works by the same author. In 1924, for example, Meyerhold staged Alexander Ostrovsky's *Les* (*The Forest*), and Tairov answered it with his production of Ostrovsky's *Groza* (*The Storm*). Perelmuter speculates that by the 1930s these two works by Pushkin planned for the Jubilee stage, Meyerhold's *Boris* and Tairov's *Onegin*, would have been a familiar, even an expected, theatrical dance.

31. "'Yevgenïy Onegin'—Dramaticheskïy spektakl'. Beseda s nar. art. resp. A. Ya. Tairovïm," *Krasnaya gazeta*, April 20, 1936, p. 2. A briefer interview with similar information appeared three days later in "*Yevgenïy Onegin* v drame. Beseda s nar. artistom A. Ya. Tairovïm," *Vechernyaya Moskva*, April 23, 1936, p. 3. Quotations in the text are drawn from both Russian sources.

32. O. Litovskiy, "Iz vospominaniy," in *Prokof'yev o Prokof'yeve*, 133. In his full memoir Litovsky is somewhat more critical of Kerzhentsev, and admits to his good luck in hosting a home recital where Prokofiev played the *Eugene Onegin* music (comprising, as he thought, "ten or twelve numbers," which were "accompanied by commentary" by the composer). See *Tak i bïlo* (Moscow: Sovetskiy pisatel', 1958), 244.

33. For Litovsky's role in these 1936 cancellations, see Katerina Clark and Evgeny Dobrenko with Andrei Artizov and Oleg Naumov, *Soviet Culture and Power: A History in Documents, 1917–1953* (New Haven: Yale University Press, 2007), 256–57. Fans of Mikhaíl Bulgakov's novel *The Master and Margarita* (1940) will appreciate that Litovsky is a prototype for O. Latunsky, the critic whose nasty review destroys the Master's novel about Pontius Pilate and whose apartment Margarita wrecks vengefully in chapter 22, after becoming a witch. Bulgakov's widow Yelena, deeply familiar with bureaucratic suppression of her husband's many plays, notes with some glee in her 1936 diary "the scandal in the press with Tairov and *Bogatïri*": "Litovsky didn't guess this one right: earlier he had written a toadying review praising the production." Yelena Bulgakova, *Dnevnik*,

ed. Viktor Losev and Lidiya Yanovskaya (Moscow: Knizhnaya palata, 1990), 125.

34. RGALI f. 2280, op. 1, yed. khr. 90. The two letters are June 21, 1936, from Tairov in Kislovodsk to Krzhizhanovsky in Moscow; a subsequent letter from Tairov without envelope or date, acknowledging a response from Krzhizhanovsky (not extant) and again requesting a new version of the play. Tairov's telegram of September 23, 1936, sent from Moscow to the playwright in Odessa, requests Krzhizhanovsky's immediate return to the capital for matters relating to *Eugene Onegin*.

35. The "old text" Tairov was reluctant to circulate until the playwright had incorporated their agreed-upon adjustments appears to be RGALI f. 2579, op. 1, yed. khr. 2054. If, as we assume, the copy with Prokofiev's own markings is the first revision, then this would be the second (the "new plan"). Tairov has scribbled in basic musical cues. The cynical, mercantile Prologue has been deleted. One small lyrical scene has been inserted (a new Fragment 5). The role of the companions (*sputniki*) is highlighted (66, 68), but we do not know what promises Tairov had extracted from the playwright concerning their expanded role. In the penultimate Fragment, the "Unnamed One" becomes specifically a Poet (the Narrator function), and his role as storyteller and creator of the entire drama is reconfirmed. One curious detail: between the first and second revision, a change was made in the novel's final closing couplet that is corrected in Krzhizhanovsky's hand. In the playscript, Onegin narrates his own exit (76): "[Blest is he who] can suddenly take leave of [the novel] / As I am taking leave of myself" (I vdrug umel rasstat'sya s nim, / Kak rasstayus' s soboy samim)—a collapse of third person into first "according to principle" that sounds ludicrous in this exposed position. The playwright restores Pushkin's final line to the Narrator/Poet: "As I from my Onegin do" (Kak ya s Oneginïm moim).

36. See Krzhizhanovskiy, "Lermontov chitayet *Onegina*," in *SK: Ss* 4:450–62, esp. 457 and 790. The essay was written at the end of 1936, "when it had become clear that the production of *Onegin* would not take place" (Perelmuter's note). It was first published in 2004.

37. "Iz besedï s rezhissyorami-vïpusknikami Gosudarstvennogo instituta teatral'nogo iskusstva imeni A. V. Lunacharskogo," in Tairov, *Zapiski rezhissyora*, 246–54, esp. 252–53. Subsequent references are included in the text.

38. The Decembrists were aristocratic rebels of the post-Napoleonic era, whose (easily suppressed) demonstration against Russia's absolute autocracy on Senate Square in St. Petersburg on December 14, 1825, is taken as the starting point of Russian revolutionary consciousness. Five leading Decembrist conspirators were hanged and many others exiled to Siberia and the Caucasus, including some of Pushkin's closest friends. Pushkin was in the second year of domestic exile at his family estate of Mikhailovskoye and thus not in the capital. However, he burned many personal papers when he heard the news and experienced a sort of survivor's guilt for the rest of his life. Several of the exiles' wives abandoned their lives of privilege (and their children) to follow their husbands to Siberia, an act of spousal martyrdom that became legendary in Russian literature.

39. Tairov, *Zapiski*, 252–53.

40. Litvinenko, "Vspomnim Sigizmunda Krzhizhanovskogo," 361. In the 1920s, Tairov approved a free stage adaptation of Chesterton's *The Man Who Was Thursday*, but apparently he was "significantly more strict toward Krzhizhanovsky while working on the scenario of Pushkin's novel" (Litvinenko, "Nesïgrannïy spektakl'," 116). In his copy of the *Eugene Onegin* playscript, Tairov dismissed whole scenes, crossed out stanzas, and dotted the rest with exclamation marks and questions.

41. Litvinenko, "Vspomnim," 361.

42. Personal communication from Perelmuter, October 5, 2007. Even Tairov's hostile marginalia should be taken in this gentler spirit, Perelmuter argues. He tactfully suggests that such a "trifle" (*meloch'*) as getting paid for one's work is a factor too often neglected by Western historians who study twentieth-century Russian artists. Preferring to focus on the martyred creative product, we too easily forget that these artists were part of a culture industry governed not by the market but by a carrot-and-stick combination of patronage plus terror.

43. RGALI f. 1929, op. 1, yed. khr. 86, p. 6. Musical number 17 correlates to pages 26–27 of Krzhizhanovsky's playscript.

44. Sergey Prokof'yev, "Izuchayte tekst, teatr, orkestr," *Teatr i dramaturgiya* 8 (1936): 489, in the column "Kompozitor v dramaticheskom teatre"; repr. *Prokof'yev o Prokof'yeve*, 43–44.

45. Litvinenko asserts that rehearsals for *Onegin* never began ("Nesïgrannïy spektakl'," 130).

Among the most ardent enthusiasts for the *Eugene Onegin* production (months after it had been annulled) was Tairov's wife, the theater's lead actress Alisa Koonen, who thrilled at the chance to play Tatyana. A great fan of Prokofiev, she remarks in her memoirs about the 1933 *Egyptian Nights* (where she played Cleopatra): "I don't remember a single rehearsal at which Sergey Sergeyevich was not sitting in the hall with a pad of music paper in his hand." When an actor began his monologue too early, "Prokofiev's piercing cry suddenly rang out: 'Wait, there's supposed to be trumpets here, you have to wait!'" Alisa Koonen, *Stranitsï zhizni* (Moscow: Iskusstvo, 1975), 369.

46. For one discussion, see Claudia Gorbman, *Unheard Melodies: Narrative Film Music* (Bloomington: Indiana University Press, 1987), chaps. 1–3; see also Simon Frith, "Mood Music: An Inquiry into Narrative Film," *Screen* 25, no. 3 (1984): 78–89, on diegetic and non-diegetic categories (real and associative sound).

47. "Bokovaya vetka" refers to a branch of the main train line. Krzhizhanovsky's criterion for distinguishing the dreamer-creator from the dreamt-up creature is twofold and appears to draw on the ethics of Kant, Pushkin, Dostoyevsky, and Kafka. First, only the creator (not the creature) feels a sense of honor (*chestnost'*), which is expressed in a moral imperative: we are grateful for our existence (even if we do not know to whom) and obliged to express this gratitude through art. Second, our consciousness grasps the concepts of space and time only through physically experienced pain.

48. Litovskiy, "Iz vospominaniy," 133.

49. Prokof'yev, *Yevgeniy Onegin. Muzïkal'no-dramaticheskaya kompozitsiya*, ed. E. Dattel' (Moscow: Sovetskiy kompozitor, 1973), 95–141.

50. Despite ingenious attempts, most recently by James E. Falen, it is impossible to translate Pushkin's Onegin stanza into English without awkwardness, massive paddings, and semantic imprecisions. Read to oneself, these compromises can be absorbed; they are compensated for by the pleasure of the form. But Pushkin's conversation onstage requires an English texture that is crisp, idiomatic, and free of inaccurate filler.

51. This observation was made by Sergey Eisenstein in 1947 about Prokofiev's dance music: "Its range of application is different from that of Tchaikovsky which seems to have been devised to make you move to it. Prokofiev's music is strikingly well suited to montage movement. As far as the rhythm of moving arms and legs is concerned, it is very difficult. When Prokofiev himself dances, he always treads on his partner's toes. He is so used to expanding a rhythm that he finds a normal, ordinary human rhythm difficult and his feet cannot manage it." "From Lectures on Music and Color in *Ivan the Terrible*," in *The Eisenstein Reader*, ed. Richard Taylor (London: British Film Institute, 1998), 170.

52. Dattel', "*Yevgeniy Onegin* S. S. Prokof'yeva" [commentary on the score], in Prokof'yev, *Yevgeniy Onegin*, 234–35. The harsh Dattel line against Krzhizhanovsky was repeated as late as 2007, in an essay on Prokofiev's work in the Chamber Theater. The play is assessed not on its own merits but solely according to critical comments made by Tairov in the margins of his copy of the director's script (although Tairov himself is praised for his flexibility and freedom in staging the classics), and the playwright is reproached for adding lines, straying from Pushkin, and alienating the composer. Here, the author writes, we have "the unique situation of a composer writing the music faster than the dramaturg could finish his scenic adaptation of the material"—as if the playwright was obliged to adjust to the director, set designer, and musician, carelessly forfeiting his own creative vision. See Svetlana Martïnova, "Prokof'yev v Kamernom teatre," Sergey Prokof'yev, *Pis'ma. Vospominaniya. Stat'i: Sbornik* (Moscow: Trudï Gosudarstvennogo tsentral'nogo muzeya muzïkal'noy kul'turï imeni M. I. Glinki, 2007): 288–96, esp. 295

53. Litvinenko, "Vspomnim Sigizmunda Krzhizhanovskogo," 359–60.

54. Litvinenko, "Nesïgrannïy spektakl'," 117.

55. Anna Bovshek, who came across the "portrait poem" among Krzhizhanovsky's posthumous papers, claims that this scrap of Byronic verse was a "self-portrait"; Krzhizhanovsky never identified it. The poem of his own that Vyazemsky cites, "The Station" (1829), is actually quoted by Pushkin in his footnotes to the novel.

56. The 1974 Melodiya LP recording is with Kemal Abdullaev (USSR Radio Orchestra); the 1994 Chandos CD is with Sir Edward Downes/Timothy West (BBC Radio Orchestra), using large chunks of Charles Johnston's dismal translation of *Eugene Onegin* performed by six readers.

Chandos is advertised as a "premiere complete recording," because it incorporates four pages missing from the piano score (a waltz that turned up in London at a Christie's auction circa 1980, orchestrated by Downes with Lina Prokofiev's permission).

57. The Jurowski recording (Capriccio label CD *Eugen Onegin,* Schauspielmusik Rundfunk-Sinfonie Orchester Berlin) was built from Pavel Lamm's orchestration. Lamm realized the conductor's score and parts from the piano score that Prokofiev had annotated for orchestration; the orchestrated score became available in November 1936, one month before the production was annulled, and was never used. In his recording, Jurowski makes judicious use of Prokofiev's verbal cues (that is, Pushkin's lines) written into the score to mark the opening and closing of musical numbers. There is no evidence of Jurowski having consulted the archival playscript—nor does he claim to have done so.

58. "Po strofam *Onegina*" (1936), in *SK: Ss* 4:416–49, esp. 416.

59. "P'yesa i yego zaglaviye" (1939), in *SK: Ss* 4:621–35, 814–19. Krzhizhanovsky began to research the poetics of titles and subtitles in 1931, in connection with his work on the dramaturgical equipment of his favorite playwrights (Ostrovsky, Shakespeare, and Shaw). In "The Play and Its Title" he argues that titles of plays are more "sensitive" (*chuvstvennoye*) and "sound-worthy" (*zvukovoye*) than titles of treatises or novels: they are designed to be hawked out in public squares to trumpets and drums (622). Later the title quieted down; now titles are neglected and even insulted. They are getting shorter and shorter, half-titles really, predicates with no subjects. Of the two classes of titles—the title-protagonist (the "title-who," *zaglaviye-kto*) and the title-situation (the "title-what," *zaglaviye-chto*) (624)—the title-protagonists are now in the ascendancy. These labels, he argues, are for the most part drab and empty.

60. Ibid., 623.

61. "Stat'i iz *Slovarya literaturnïkh terminov*" (1925), entry on "Zaglaviye," *SK:Ss* 4:669–73, esp. 673.

62. "Iskusstvo epigrafa [Pushkin]" (October 1936) in *SK:Ss* 4:387–415.

63. Ibid., 415.

64. An epigraph (often two) prefaces each of Pushkin's eight chapters, and a prose excerpt (in French) from a "personal letter" is epigraph to the entire novel. Of the four *not* used in the play, one is the multilingual Latin-Russian homonym (chap. 2: O rus! / *O Rus'!*); one is in French, from Necker (chap. 4: "La morale est dans la nature des choses"); one is from Vasily Zhukovsky's ballad "Svetlana" (chap. 5: "Oh, that you should not know terrifying dreams, my Svetlana"); and the fourth is a line from Byron quoted in English (chap. 8: "Fare thee well, and if for ever, / Still for ever, fare thee well").

65. Aleksandr Pushkin, *Eugene Onegin: A Novel in Verse,* trans. Vladimir Nabokov, 3 vols. (Princeton: Princeton University Press, 1964), 2:317.

66. "Teatral'naya remarka (Fragment)" (1937), in *SK:Ss* 4:89–109. Subsequent page references are included in the text.

67. Pushkin's stimuli here included Lord Byron's long narrative poems *Childe Harold's Pilgrimage* (1809–16) and *Don Juan* (1819–23), which he read in French translation. But Pushkin adds a cold, humorless quality more bitter than Byron, which comes from the French-Swiss strand of Romantic heroes created by Benjamin Constant. Constant's novel *Adolfe* (1816), the immediate source for the psychology of Onegin, features a burnt-out, cynical hero, highly gifted but the victim of too many easy conquests, too few ideals, and stifling convention. This hero is marked above all by unresponsiveness. He is full of unspecified longing and even passion, but whenever an opportunity arrives to attach himself to an idea or a person, he cannot seize it. Such freezing of emotion is due to his internal Schillerian split between a "naive" self that can feel directly, and a "sentimental" self that reflects, asks questions, interrogates, sees himself from the outside, and thus cools down every impulse before he can act on it. There is always a woman devoted to him, but he is continually asking: "Can I commit to her? Can I abandon her?" The woman gives herself to him, sacrifices herself, dies, and only then does the hero realize he loves her. The primary cause of it all is not innate cruelty or coldness, however, but passionate potential checked and braked by excessive reflection, resulting in an internal paralysis. In the Russian variant of this pan-European type, such paradoxical pressure makes the hero "superfluous" to society and to himself. In the 1860s, Dostoyevsky produced a metaphysical variant on the type, his Underground

Caryl Emerson

Man. In 1934, Gorky declared that the nineteenth-century "superfluous hero" (and especially Dostoyevsky) had been definitively discredited by the positive "man of action" celebrated in Socialist Realism.

68. The dynamics of this Fragment testify to Krzhizhanovsky's sophistication as a Pushkinist. In *Eugene Onegin*, every detail of the world passes first through a literary genre, and only subsequently through concrete images and moral consciousness. The Narrator—whose role Krzhizhanovsky exquisitely appreciated, for all that he wanted him out of his play—monitors this shift of genre, moving within a single chapter (or even within a single sequence of stanzas), from the celebratory diction of an eighteenth-century ode through an elegiac tone to the Romantic glitter of a fairy tale to the Byronic burn-out characteristic of Onegin's view of the world, never missing a beat nor distorting a jot of the Onegin stanza (see chap. 1, xvii–xxi). For Pushkin, the choice of a genre brings with it an entire world (first of styles, then of images and values).

69. Krzhizhanovsky called this backward projection a "minus-space" and considered it crucial to the reality of dreams. At the beginning of Krzhizhanovsky's return to public life (the early 1990s), the Tartu semiotician Vladimir Toporov, a specialist, together with Yuriy Lotman, on Petersburg urban semiotics, developed out of this passive and often oppressive minus-space an entire semiotics peculiar to Moscow. Working with several stories by Krzhizhanovsky (including "Bookmark," "Stitches," and "Side Branch"), Toporov extracted a theory of spatial relativity based on the walled-in experience of tiny, chaotic Moscow apartments in a sprawling, weblike, tactile metropolis (Krzhizhanovsky was addicted to walking Moscow and set himself a strict "literacy" program vis-à-vis its streets, alleys, walls, crevices). The elastic unreality of Moscow emerges as something quite distinct from the foggy unreality of the Petersburg text and the literary genius that founded it (Gogol, Dostoyevsky). See V. N. Toporov, "'Minus-prostranstvo' Sigizmunda Krzhizhanovskogo," in *Mif. Ritual. Simvol. Obraz. Issledovaniya v oblasti mifopoeticheskogo* (Moscow: Izdatel'skaya gruppa Progress/Kul'tura, 1992), 476–574.

70. Krzhizhanovsky, "In the Pupil" (1927), in *Seven Stories*, 64.

71. Krzhizhanovsky, "Quadraturin" (1926), in *Seven Stories*, 23.

72. Toporov ends his 100-page "Krzhizhanovskian" analysis of Moscow minus-space with the following tribute: "Krzhizhanovsky wrote: 'When I die, don't disturb the nettles that will grow up over me: let them sting.' And indeed, his grave is lost, although several participants in his funeral are still alive. Such breaches into the future are always sad, alas, [but] we should not be surprised: they were foreseen by the very structure of the writer's time-space. Creating it, 'playing around with it,' he himself lived in it, and it passed thickly through him, infecting him with its poisons" ("'Minus-prostranstvo' Sigizmunda Krzhizhanovskogo," 549).

73. "Stat'i, zametki, retsentsii, opublikovannïye v yezhenedel'nike 7 *dney Moskovskogo Kamernogo teatra*," in *SK:Ss* 4:643, 645. This seamless "exchange of masks" is caught perfectly by Prokofiev in his marginal note preceding Fragment 8, the Dream: "Without an Interlude."

74. "Filosofema o teatre," in *SK:Ss* 4:43–88 (subsequent references are included in the text). The essay was first published in *Toronto Slavic Quarterly*, with a lengthy, helpful contextualizing headnote by Perelmuter only partially incorporated into the *Collected Works*; see Krzhizhanovskiy, "Filosofema o teatre, publikatsiya i predisloviye Vadima Perel'mutera," *Toronto Slavic Quarterly* 4 (2003): 1–2.

75. See Krzhizhanovskiy, "Argo i Ergo" (1918), ed. and introd. Perel'muter, in *Toronto Slavic Quarterly* 21 (Summer 2007): 1–8. In this title, "Argo" is the creative route of the poet, "sailing into a land of myths" (p. 6); "Ergo" (therefore, thus) is the bringing-close of a thing with its explanation, the realm of the scientist who seeks a cause or a *because*.

76. Russian has two words for life: *zhizn'*, the generic word, and then *bït*, "everyday life as experienced," which is nuanced very negatively. *Zhizn'* implies life as it should be lived, with a spiritual and idealistic striving, whereas *bït* is the "daily grind," everyday existence, full of grim tedium, deceit, and disillusionment. The low expectations and bad reputation that surround simply "living"—or "making a living"—in the Russian context have received a good deal of attention from literary specialists and cultural anthropologists, and are considered by some to be characteristic of a dysfunctional society that overrates the salvational importance of art and clings to utopian fantasies in preference to pragmatic solutions.

77. Buyanov, carouser and devotee of brothels, was imported by Pushkin into his novel

from a famously lewd narrative poem written by his uncle, a minor poet, in 1811. See the full genealogy of Buyanov, the rakish hero of Vasily Lvovich Pushkin's *The Dangerous Neighbor* (1811), in n. 38, Notes on the Translation.

78. The ditty translated in this volume appears to be the first Mummers' variant that Prokofiev saw, an innocuous quatrain about rich peasants raking up silver with a spade, promising wealth and fame to anyone who hears the song. In his autograph score (RGALI f. 1929, op. 1, yed. khr. 86, pp. 8 verso / 9 recto), Prokofiev notes after musical number 26: "Mummers: Another text." It is unclear who initiated the change.

79. For more on the Mummers' text, taken from Pushkin's own collection of folkloric wedding songs assembled in the 1820s, see Notes on the Translation, nn. 58 and 59.

80. In his essay "Onegin, Stanza by Stanza," Krzhizhanovsky compares Tatyana's Dream with Ruslan's from Pushkin's *Ruslan and Lyudmila* (1820), which lexically and structurally it closely resembles. In the folkloric realm, Krzhizhanovsky notes, dreams of this sort are heroic and enabling as well as terror-bearing ("terrifying" [*strashnoye*] and "marvelous" [*chudnoye*] are equally key for Pushkin). Although Tatyana's dream-monsters resemble the Name Day guests who are their precise model, in the Dream these monstrous images are not lewd and aggressive, like Buyanov and Zaretsky, but static, verbless, and abjectly obedient to Onegin, "her savior." Plausibly and with a Freudian inflection, the Mummers' masks enable an unmasking of her own unconscious desires, a conclusion that Krzhizhanovsky does not draw but that his analysis would support ("Po strofam *Onegina*," in *SK:Ss* 4:438–40).

81. Revising real life through folklore when the results (usually due to complications of politics or power) were otherwise too awful to bear was a device very congenial to the mature Pushkin of *Angelo* (*Andzhelo*, his narrative-dramatic version of Shakespeare's *Measure for Measure*, 1833), *Rusalka* (his dramatic variant of the mermaid myth, 1832), and *The Captain's Daughter* (*Kapitanskaya dochka*, his historical romance in the spirit of Walter Scott set during Pugachov's rebellion, 1836).

82. See the "Theory of Myths" in Northrop Frye, *Anatomy of Criticism: Four Essays* (Princeton: Princeton University Press, 1957), esp. 206–39. Frye's examples, as do Freud's, draw heavily on the Western European and Classical canon (Shakespeare, Milton, and Greek tragedy).

83. RGALI f. 1929, op. 3. yed. khr. 253. In her work on *Eugene Onegin*, Litvinenko discusses and cites this document at length but attributes it to Tairov ("Vspomnim Sigizmunda Krzhizhanovskogo," 121–23), despite Perelmuter's several attempts to correct her.

84. "Iskusstvo epigrafa [Pushkin]," *SK:Ss* 4:393–94.

85. Ibid., 393.

86. Just how much of the story is told varies in different versions of the playscript. In the first revision translated here, only the prologue is recited; a subsequent revision includes a segment from the "mirror, mirror on the wall" episode, with lines about the tsaritsa's birthing and death crossed out; in that same revision, the proposed replacement ("God awards the tsaritsa a daughter") is also crossed out. RGALI f. 2579, op. 1, yed. khr. 2054, p. 15.

87. In an essay from 1935 on endings in Shakespeare's plays, Krzhizhanovsky makes a curious observation. Comedies tend to feature the clumsy hero who arrives too late. At the last minute, however, Shakespeare will compensate the comic hero by accelerating his learning curve and allowing him to grasp the meaning of what has passed him by. A tragic hero, on the other hand, rushes ahead of his time, impatient, and events in his life speed up as they approach their denouement: swords fly, blindings proliferate, revelation piles on revelation. Shakespeare will ultimately slow his tragic hero down, permitting those who witness his death (onstage and in the audience) sufficient time to catch up with him and learn the lessons he has to share. Throughout the Onegin story, arguably the hero has been more comic, the heroine more tragic. But neither death nor marriage consummates the plot. As romance, the plot is "hinged" to a piece of furniture and then suspended—like the other ritualistic or cyclic rhythms so prominent in the play. See "Kontsovki shekspirovskikh p'yes," in *SK: Ss* 4:85–94, esp. 291.

88. "Zachem poetu / Trevozhit' serdtsa tyazhkiy son? / Besplodno pamyat' muchit on." "Razgovor poeta s knigoprodavtsem." Lines 129–32.

89. See section VIII in Krzhizhanovskiy, "Argo i Ergo," 6–7.

SIGIZMUND KRZHIZHANOVSKY
ALEXANDER PUSHKIN

Eugene Onegin (1936)

*Except for the source key, the following translation of Krzhizhanovsky's playscript
preserves the layout of the typed archival document (RGALI f. 1929, op. 1, yed.
khr. 86) as faithfully as possible. Prokofiev's comments are reproduced in bold as
per their location in the archival document (usually in the left margin, but occasionally mid-page and even drifting to the right). When Prokofiev had second thoughts
about one of his own comments, he scribbled over it (represented here by a single
crossing-out). In one instance (beginning of Fragment 14) he deletes an entire
stanza of Krzhizhanovsky's text with a single vertical slash; elsewhere, additional
lines from Pushkin's original are inserted.*

*It appears that the typewriter had some dysfunctional keys (both the question mark
and the exclamation mark default to a period for the first two-thirds of the text);
since such departures from the punctuation of Pushkin's text are occasionally corrected by hand, they are assumed to be unintentional. Midway through the text,
brackets give way to parentheses for the stage directions; these have all been standardized to brackets. Other punctuation has not been tampered with, and details of
a mechanical nature—typos, non-Russian alphabets, etc.—are noted. Throughout
the playscript, verb tense in stage directions fluctuates: it is standardized here to present tense, except where sequencing within a sentence must be marked.*

*A key by chapter, stanza, and line to Krzhizhanovsky's sources, primarily Pushkin's
novel-in-verse* Eugene Onegin *(1823–29), coded as* EO, *has been provided to
the right of the dialogue.* Conv. *is the abbreviation for "Conversation of a Bookseller
with a Poet," a verse dialogue published by Pushkin as a preface to the first chapter
of* Eugene Onegin *published in 1825, while* OJ *refers to "Onegin's Journey," the
fragments of an unrealized chapter 9 for the novel. In addition to cutting and
splicing Pushkin's novel, Krzhizhanovsky also boldly added. With two exceptions,
these additions are all from other works by Pushkin: the early elegiac poem "I have
outlived my desires," composed on the spot by Lensky in Fragment 1; the 1833 "Fairy
Tale of the Dead Tsarevna and the Seven Knights," recited by the Nurse and selec-
tively by Tatyana throughout the playscript; a piece of polemical epigrammatic verse
(Pushkin's 1815 ditty "A troika of three gloomy singers . . . ," distributed among
three archival youths in Fragment 12); a drinking song composed by the fifteen-
year-old Pushkin in 1814 ("Carousing students," performed by a chorus of drunken
students in Fragment 13), and an obscene wedding song, "He's like a pole, his head's
like a pestle," taken from Pushkin's own folksong collection, set to music by Prokofiev,*

and given to a group of Yuletide mummers who perform in monster masks at Tatyana's Name Day. The two exceptions to this roster of supplementary Pushkin texts are, first, an ironic self-portrait in verse written (it would appear) by Krzhizhanovsky himself, masquerading as a text by Lord Byron that Tatyana reads during her visit to Onegin's deserted library; and second, two stanzas from Pyotr Vyazemsky's 1829 satire "The Station," included by Pushkin in his own footnotes to Eugene Onegin *and here brought up into Fragment 11 to be recited by Vyazemsky himself, who is given an acting role in the play.*

With the few exceptions mentioned in the notes, all spoken verse from the playscript has been newly translated. I did not attempt to reproduce the "Onegin stanza," Pushkin's flexible fourteen-line "verse paragraph" that Krzhizhanovsky retains as his basic unit of dramatic conversation (see introductory essay, pp. 80–81). Of the four most applauded translators of Eugene Onegin *into English, three respect the constraints of this stanza (Walter Arndt, Charles Johnston, and James E. Falen). Their texts are known to me and were frequently consulted and compared. On rare occasions, a line of theirs will coincide with one of mine (and the rhyming couplet that ends the play belongs to Falen; I could not devise a better rendering of those two concluding lines, the only pure echo of Pushkin's form in this translation). Nevertheless, I deemed the price of reproducing the Onegin stanza too high for this project, which aims above all at a speaking text. Even the most gifted translator who attempts to recreate Pushkin's sleek form in English is led into massive paddings, semantic inaccuracies, stylistic compromises, and awkward, literally unspeakable word order. Krzhizhanovsky began his adaptation of Pushkin's novel by eliminating the Narrator, to whom the bulk of the lines belong. Without this Narrator, whose worldview embraces and binds together the poetic whole, the fictive characters must stand and speak on their own. Their motion, pace, and personal intelligence must take precedence over any echo of formal structure.*

The fourth most widely read English translation, Vladimir Nabokov's controversial Eugene Onegin *(1964), also declines to respect the Onegin stanza. But Nabokov proved an uneasy ally: his English constructions, while generally accurate to Pushkin's meaning, are so willfully unpoetic and at times so egregiously violate the norms of accepted English usage and word order that they offer little guidance for a text designed for performance on stage. I opted for a rhythmic, literal rendering of Pushkin's images and words that imitates not the form but the mobility of Pushkin's (and Krzhizhanovsky's) text, incorporating a rhyme wherever lexically permissable.*

The notes to the translation provide cultural and historical background information, remarks on the condition of the archival document, details about minor changes made by Krzhizhanovsky to his source material, occasional differences between this version of the playscript and later, more tampered-with texts that approach a more conventional play, and interpretive commentary not incorporated into the introductory essay.

EUGENE ONEGIN

- - - - - - - - - - - - - - - - - - -

Prologue[1]

[The curtain moves aside, revealing bookshelves. At the table, his back
to the audience: the POET, bending over the scattered pages of a manuscript. The BOOKSELLER stands, leaning against the book spines.]

BOOKSELLER: The verses by this darling of the Muses and the Graces   Conv. 9–22
      We'll change to rubles in an instant,
      And we'll turn your little sheets
      Into a heap of ready cash.
      What's made you sigh so deeply,
      Might I know?

POET: I was far away:
      Remembering the day
      When, rich in hope,
      A carefree poet, I had written
      Out of inspiration, not for pay.
      Again I saw the refuge of the cliffs,
      Dark canopies of solitude,
      Where I could summon up the Muse
      To feasts of my imagination:
      The world received her with a smile;   EO 8, ii, 1–4
      What wings our first success bestowed!
      The venerable Derzhavin noticed us
      And blessed us, while descending to the grave.[2]
      And I, whose only law in life has been   8, iii, 1–12
      To give my passions unimpeded sway:
      I shared my feelings with the throng,
      And brought my playful Muse along
      Into a storm of feasts and quarrels,
      So noisy that the night patrols took notice.
      And to them, in all their rowdy partying
      She brought her gifts;
      A bacchanalian, she would frolic
      Over the punch bowl, singing for the guests.

The youth of those far distant days
Tempestuously trailed after her.
But I withdrew from those companions
Fleeing to distant parts; she followed me.
How often would this tender Muse
Sweeten my mute path
With the enchantment of a secret tale!
How often, in the Caucasus, amidst the cliffs
She raced on horseback with me,
Leonora-like, beneath the moon.[3]
Then suddenly, all this was changed.
And now she's in my garden,
With a mournful musing in her eyes,
A French book in her hands.

cuts last two lines
8, iv, 1–8

omits final 6 lines of EO 8, iv
8, v, 10–14

BOOKSELLER: It's her.

POET: She's called Tatyana . . .
For the first time shall the tender pages
Of a novel be illumined by this name.
Unsociable, and sad, and silent,
Like a fearful forest doe—
She seemed, in her own family,
A strange and alien girl.
She never learned to show affection
Toward her father or her mother;
In a crowd of children, she would not
Play games, or romp—and
Often, for whole days, she'd sit
In silence by the window.
Early on, she learned to love the novel
Which replaced all things for her;
She fell in love with its deceptions:
With the worlds of Richardson, Rousseau.

2, xxiv, 1–4

2, xxv, 5–14

2, xxix, 1–4

BOOKSELLER: And what about him?

POET: Since I had also turned my back on fashion's whirl,
Cast off society's conventions,
We became good friends around that time.
I liked his features,
His involuntary bent for dreaming,

1, xlv, 1–8

His inimitable strangeness,
And his sharp and chilly mind.
I was embittered, he was gloomy;
And how often, in the summertime 1, xlvii, 1–14
When brightly, limpidly,
The night sky over the Nevá
Did not reflect Diana's face
Across the cheerful mirror of its waters,
And remembering romances of the past,
Our previous loves,
Again, carefree and sentimental,
We silently would drink it in: the balmy fragrance
Of the breathing night.
As if a sleepy convict had been led at last
From prison to a verdant forest,
Thus were we transported, by our reveries,
Back to the start of our young lives.

BOOKSELLER: And so: by love exhausted, resume Conv. ll, 160–75
Wearied by the clack of rumor,
Early you rejected
Your inspired lyre.
Now, the noisy world abandoned,
And the Muse, and the frivolities of fashion—
What will you choose?

POET: Freedom.[4]

BOOKSELLER: Oh, excellent. Here's my advice:
Mark well this useful truth.
Ours is an age of commerce. In this iron age,
Without some money, even freedom isn't yours.
What's fame? A brightly colored patch
Upon the singer's withered rags.
What's needed here is gold, gold, gold:
So pile up gold, as many bags as possible.
But I foresee that you'll object. omits 6 lines
So let me straight out tell you: Conv. ll, 182–end
Inspiration's not for sale,
But manuscripts most surely are.
Why tarry? The impatient readers
Flock to me already,

Journalists are hanging round the shop,
Emaciated singers follow close behind them:
Some are begging food for satires,
Others for the soul, or for the pen;
And, I confess, from your sweet lyre
I know much good can come.

POET: You're absolutely right. Here's my manuscript.
          Let's agree on the terms.

PART ONE

- - - - - - - - - - - -

Fragment 1

[A church wall. A gravestone. The youthful LENSKY, standing by the
grave, cleans off the inscription with the tip of his walking stick.]

LENSKY:	*"A humble sinner, Dmitry Larin,*	EO 2, xxxvi, 12–14
	God's Servant and a brigadier,	
	Beneath this stone doth rest in peace."	

He was a simple, kindly master   2, xxxvi, 9
. . . . Poor Yorick   2, xxxvii, 6–11
How he dandled me.
How often in my childhood would I play
With his Ochakov medal![5]
And he promised Olga to me,
He would say: "Will I survive until the day? . . ."
[Lowers himself down on the edge of the grave. Thinks. Pulls
a notebook out of his pocket. Pencil slides across paper.][6]
I have outlived all my desires,
I've fallen out of love with dreams.
All that remains are cold suff . . . [crosses it out]
All that remains for me is suffering,
The fruits of my heart's emptiness;
        [Falls into thought, again crosses it out]
Wordlessly, obedient to my lot,
I don a martyr's wreath—
[He rises, having thrown the sheets down on the

stone, takes several steps, then returns to the
manuscript, writes]

    Beneath the storms of cruel fate
    My blossoming wreath has faded.
      [He continues]
    I live forgotten indifferent
      [Gnaws the pencil, crosses things out][7]
    I live sad, lonely
    I await sad . . .
      [With irritation flings down the pencil,
      then picks it up, writes]
    I live sad, lonely,
    I wait: will my end come?

ob[oe] ————————→   [The pencil slides more and more quickly]

4 b[ars]   Thus, struck by the late cold,
    The wintry whistling of a storm is heard,
    And on the branch, trembles one . . .[8]

1½ m[inutes] ⎡ ←———————————————— orchestra as above,
         ⎣   [Dims]   but louder

nature description

interlude

Fragment 2

- - - - - - - - - - - -

[A small room in ONEGIN's house. A simple unpainted floor.
In the middle, a round table. On the table some wildflowers
and a bottle of Aï.[9] Two wineglasses. The two friends sit on
either side of the table. ONEGIN is in a rocking chair; he is
wearing a motley-patterned dressing gown, unbuttoned.
LENSKY is in an armchair with a straight back. A SERVANT
changes bottles, pours wine into the glasses and, moving off
to the side, fills a pipe with tobacco.][10]

ONEGIN: Our northern summer is   EO 4, xl, 1–4
          A caricature of southern winters.
          It blinks, and then it's over. We know this
          But we can't admit it.

LENSKY: Rambling, reading, sleeping deep,   4, xxxix, 1–8
          The forest shade, the murmuring of streams . . .

ONEGIN: [finishing the utterance]
And now and then the fresh, young kiss
Of a dark-eyed, white-skinned lass.

LENSKY: A lively steed, obedient to the bridle . . .

ONEGIN: Dinner any time, on a caprice.
[makes a gesture]
A bottle of bright wine,
And solitude, and silence.
[He fills up LENSKY's glass]

LENSKY: [moving away his glass]
I'm no longer up to drinking this Aï.   4, xlvi, 5–14

ONEGIN: Aï is like a mistress,
Stunning, frivolous and frisky,
Willful, empty . . .
[pulls another bottle closer]
But Bordeaux, ah! You're a friend
Who's always ready to extend a hand
In grief or trouble, everywhere a comrade,
Or to share our quiet leisure.
Long live Bordeaux, our friend.

[They clink glasses and drink. LENSKY is slightly drunk.]

LENSKY: Pour me another half-glass . . .
That's enough, my friend . . . You know . . . I . . .
[He takes out of his pocket some crumpled sheets. He
stands up. ONEGIN, releasing a cloud of smoke from
his pipe, rocks his chair in a measured way, in time to
the young poet's reading.]

LENSKY: [reading from a manuscript][11]
At that time when, in the Lycée gardens   8, i, 1–12
Carefree, I blossomed . . .

ONEGIN: [interrupting him]
Diligently I read Prince Yelisey . . .[12]

LENSKY: Diligently I read Apuleius . . .[13]

• 122 •

But Cicero . . .

ONEGIN: . . . I cursed.[14]

LENSKY: Cicero I didn't read.
            In those days, in mysterious valleys,
            In the spring, when swans were calling
            Over waters gleaming in the silence,
            The Muse began to reveal herself to me.

mechanical   [Clock with cuckoo or bird chimes seven o'clock.
cuckoo   LENSKY continues, somewhat distracted]

theme   . . . .
            The Muse began to reveal herself to me.
            And suddenly my student cell
            Was radiant with light: the Muse
            Lit up our feasting, youthful pranks
            She sang of childish gaiety
            And . . . and—
[Takes out his Bréguet watch, pushes the spring: ringingly,
it beats seven times. LENSKY hides his manuscript in his
pocket and gestures to the SERVANT, who hands him his
walking stick, top hat, and gloves. Impatiently he fastens
the buttons of his gloves.]

ONEGIN: [with a movement of his foot stopping the
            measured, iambic rocking of the chair]
            So where're you going? Oh, these poets!   opening of 3, i, 1–10

LENSKY: [putting on his top hat]
            Farewell, Onegin, time I went.

ONEGIN: I won't keep you; but where,
            Pray tell, are all your evenings spent?

LENSKY: The Larins.
            [A pause]

ONEGIN: Oh, how marvelous.   3, i → iv, but lines
            It's up to you, of course. But isn't it hard   scrambled from
            To kill each evening there?   opening 3 stanzas

LENSKY: Not in the least.

ONEGIN: But still, how's one to understand it?
    Here's the story, it would seem:
    First (tell me if I'm right),
    A simple Russian family,
    With an eagerness for guests.   *ends at 3, i, 12*
    The ritual of refreshments: *resumes at 3, iii,*
    On the oilcloth-covered table, there's a pitcher   *5–8 but lines*
    Full of lingonberry juice;   *out of order*
    In come the little platters with the jam . . .
    A neighbor's summoned to the samovar . . .

LENSKY: [dreamily] And Olga pours out tea . . .[15]

ONEGIN: They whisper to her: "Olga, pay attention!"
    Then they bring in the guitar,
    And she begins to chirp (my God!):
    "Come to my golden chambers!"   *end of 2, xii*
    Jam, and endless talk about   *resumes w/ final 2*
    The rain, and flax, and livestock . . .   *lines of 3, i, 13–14*
    Then there's supper, then it's time to sleep.
    The guests depart.   *Inserts part of*
                                                         Larin family
                                                         history in 2,
LENSKY: [nervously] I don't see any harm in it.   *xxxiv, 13–14*
                                                         3, ii, 1–14

ONEGIN: The boredom of it, friend, that's what.

LENSKY: [tearing off his glove]
    I hate your fashionable world;
    Domestic life is much more to my taste,
    Where I . . .

ONEGIN: Again an eclogue!
    That's enough, my friend, for god's sake.
    So you're going: that's a pity.
    But now listen, Lensky: could I take
    A look at this bucolic Phyllis,[16]
    Object of your thoughts, your pen,
    Your tears and rhymes?   *omits Pushkin's et cetera*
    Introduce me.

LENSKY: You're joking.

ONEGIN: No.

LENSKY: I'd love to.

ONEGIN: When?

LENSKY: Why not right now?
            They'll welcome us with pleasure.

ONEGIN: Then let's go. [Claps his hands. The SERVANT, who   EO 3, iii, 1
            was about to disappear behind the door, again appears.
            ONEGIN stands up and with a movement of his shoulders,
            his dressing gown falls to the floor. The SERVANT grabs
            it up and, diving behind the door, immediately runs
            back into the room with high English boots, bright-
            colored trousers hanging off either side of his neck,
perhaps at   a gray top hat, a frock coat with large matte buttons and
first he hums, a whole collection of various sorts of little brushes,
then the refrain graters, boxes, scissors, and combs. LENSKY impatiently
enters, then   glances at his Bréguet. ONEGIN shoves his arms into
he sings.   the sleeves of his frock coat.]¹⁷

1/2 min   ONEGIN: [hums] . . . . *Elle était fille, elle était amoureuse*¹⁸

            . . . .
            | the other way around |

curtain
the theme
of the   **Fragment 3**
horn with   - - - - - - - - - - - -
orchestra
1 1/2 m.   [A light, extinguished from below, flickers to the left in the
            upper part of the stage cube.¹⁹ This is the upper story of the
            old wooden house of the gentry-folk Larins. A clock, wheez-
            ing like an old man, rings out eight o'clock. In the middle of
            the illuminated room, a table is set in expectation of a guest.
            Probably LENSKY. In the depths, a window, to which is
            pressed the not especially slender, but also not too rounded
            figure of a young woman. Pressing her palms to the pane of
            glass, she gazes into the fading sunset. Upstage, the old
            woman LARINA and two aging MALE NEIGHBORS. At the buf-
            fet, a FEMALE HANGER-ON, wiping the plates. LARINA, while

speaking, glances at the door that opens onto the balcony.][20]

female voice sings, but not the oboe theme

LARINA: What's to be done? Tatyana's not a child,—   EO 7, xxv, 7–13
Olenka is younger, after all.
We've got to settle her, God knows.
It's time; but what am I to do with her?
To everyone, the same retort:
I won't.

HANGER-ON: [in a patter] But always she's so sad,   end of 7, xxv, 13–14
And wanders in the woods, alone.

1st NEIGHBOR: Perhaps the girl's in love?   7, xxvi, 1–13

LARINA: With whom?
Buyanov made her a proposal.[21]

2nd NEIGHBOR: She refused.

1st NEIGHBOR: [letting out a puff of smoke]
And Petushkov, Ivan as well.

LARINA: The hussar Pykhtin called on us;
How charmed he was by Tanya!

HANGER-ON: Went to pieces over her.

LARINA: I thought: perhaps she'll do it now.
But no. Again the matter fell apart.

1st NEIGHBOR: My dear. But where's the problem?
Time to go to Moscow, to the marriage mart.

2nd NEIGHBOR: They say there's lots of vacant places.

LARINA: My good sir, I can't afford it . . .

1st NEIGHBOR: Surely for one winter, there's enough.
. . . .
[LARINA, accompanied by the HANGER-ON, exits to the
interior rooms, carrying the unnecessary dishes. Both
NEIGHBORS, their pipes drooping unattended, think it over.]

1st NEIGHBOR: It's hard to keep from joking or conjecturing,   3, vi, 7–8
A bridegroom's been predicted for Tatyana . . .

2nd NEIGHBOR: And with Lensky, long ago   3, vi, 13–14
The wedding was resolved.
A handsome fellow, in full bloom,   2, vi, 7–8
Admirer of Kant, a Poet.

1st NEIGHBOR: [finishing up his musing] Our neighbor
[gives his interlocutor a searching look]

2nd NEIGHBOR: [waves his hand] . . . he's a crackpot and a boor,   2, v, 9–14
A Freemason. He'll drink no more
Than red wine by the glass,
Declines to kiss a lady's hand;
With him it's "yes," or "no"—he doesn't say 'yes sir,'
'No sir.'

1st NEIGHBOR: Agreed; this much we all can understand.

[The light of the projector cautiously, as if it were "stealing,"
crawls to the right; there, where opened shutters indicate
doors, the outline of a balcony is clearly visible, hanging in
the air over a sleeping garden. With the help of the fading
evening twilight, the projector makes visible the slender figure of a girl, sitting by the balcony railing. She is bent over a
book, which, in the quickly encroaching darkness, moves
ever closer to the reader's eyes. Finally the sunset, like an
extinguishing lamp, definitively refuses to light up the
pages. The girl—she is TATYANA, the older sister of OLGA—
lowers the book to her knees. From behind her black hair,
the dim light from the dining room is cautiously drawn in.]

TATYANA: [reciting]
Clarissa, Julia, or Delphine,   3, x, 3
And Julia's lover Wolmar,   3, ix, 7–10
Malek-Adhel, de Linar
And Werther, restless martyr,
And the matchless Grandison . . .
Or a pensive Vampire,   3, xii, 8–11
Or Melmoth, that gloomy wanderer,
Or the Eternal Jew, or the Corsair,

Or mysterious Sbogar.[22]

[The approaching clatter of hooves is heard. At first TATYANA listens in to it, with difficulty tearing herself away from her book, then she moves away from the threshold of the door. Now her face and contours of her profile are visible in the scarcely sufficient light. OLGA tears herself away from the window, joyfully claps her hands]

OLGA: He's coming.

TATYANA: [listening intently]
            They're coming.

Fragment 4

- - - - - - - - - - - - -

[Onegin's already familiar room, at the bottom of the stage set. It is weakly lit up by the moon. Only the contours of things are visible. Voices from the outside. A SERVANT appears through an inner door, adjusting the wick of a candle, which he is cradling in his hand. Enter ONEGIN and LENSKY. ONEGIN tosses his gloves to the servant, flings his horse-whip on the table. Sits down in the rocking chair. The chair is on the verge of rocking from somewhere deep inside itself, but ONEGIN restrains it and freezes in an unmoving pose.][23]

LENSKY: Well now, Onegin. Seems you're yawning.   EO 3, iv, 5–14

ONEGIN: Habit, Lensky.

LENSKY: But you're bored
           A bit more this time, somehow.
ONEGIN: No, the same.
           What stupid places.
           By the way, that Larina's a simple sort,
           But she's a nice old woman;
           Even though I fear their lingonberry juice
           Has done me in.

[The SERVANT, half asleep, stumbling up against the table
and chairs, brings in a collection of bottles and glasses,
measures out drops from a medicine dropper. ONEGIN
yawns. LENSKY, irritated, paces from corner to corner.
ONEGIN, verifying with his eye the glass handed to him by
the SERVANT, with a movement of his hand stops the
metronome-like steps of LENSKY.]

Tatyana's theme

ONEGIN: Tell me . . .   3, v, 1–12
         [sniffs at the fluid]
         . . . Which one was Tatyana?

LENSKY: That sad one, who
         As silent as Svetlana
         Came in and sat down by the window.24

ONEGIN: [Swallows the concoction and squeamishly twitches his
         lips] Don't tell me you're in love with the younger one.

LENSKY: So?
         [Takes a step toward him, but ONEGIN, with a courteous
         gesture of his wrist, requests that he back away from
         the window and then himself looks out—in the course
         of several seconds—at the disk of the rosy-orange moon
         that has just moved inside the window frame.]

ONEGIN: And I'd have picked the other one,
         If I—as you are—were a poet.
         There's no life in Olga's features,
         Like a dull Van Dyck Madonna,
         Why, her face is round and beautiful, just like
         This stupid moon
         On this stupid horizon.

[The SERVANT understands his master in his own way,
and quickly draws the curtains over the moon.]

no music

[The light of the projector, imitating the pale light of
the moon, slides noiselessly upward: on the balcony,
TATYANA. She is leaning over the railings, her face
to the quiet gusting of nocturnal breezes that rock the
tops of the trees. Her eyes are fixed on the moon,
which has paled significantly under her gaze.]

TATYANA: One's breath dies on the lips   3, xvi, 7–12
           And noise in the ears, a brilliance in the eyes,
           Night has fallen; the moon travels
           Its distant heavenly arc,
           And in the darkness of the groves, the resonant refrain
           Of nightingales rings out.
           My soul was waiting for . . . someone.   3, vii, 14
           And was rewarded. Now my eyes are opened.   3, viii, 1
           Now, alas, all day and night,   3, viii, 3–4
           And during my hot, lonely sleep,
           Everything is full of him . . . of him: It's him.[25]   3, viii, 5, 2

Fragment 5

- - - - - - - - - - - -

[TATYANA's room. In its depths, a shabby bed curtain.
A window. Beyond the window, the dead of night. A table
pushed up against the wall. On it, in a pitcher, a bouquet of
wildflowers and ferns. An inkwell, pen and pile of paper.
To the right of the window frame, a white shelf full of the
spines of books. TATYANA sits at the table, pulls the paper
toward her, takes up the pen, then throws it down. She is
wearing a modest at-home dress. Takes up the pen again,
thinks, puts it to one side. The NURSE appears in the
doorway. The NURSE, shuffling her slippers, comes up to
TANYA, glances at the dial of the clock ticking on the wall,
and shakes her head in dissatisfaction.]

1[st couplet]
for tenors
2[nd couplet]
1[st couplet]
for tenors

Tatyana's
condition

TATYANA: I can't sleep, nurse. It's stuffy here.   EO 3, xvii, 1–9
         Open the window, come sit by me.
[The NURSE opens the window wide and, moving a low
bench toward TATYANA's chair, sits down on it.]

NURSE: So Tanya, what's the matter?

TATYANA: I'm bored.
        Let's talk about the past.

NURSE: But what about? I used to keep
        In memory a lot of fables,

Ancient fantasies and tales
Of evil spirits and of maidens.
But today . . .

TATYANA: [imitating one of her Nurse's tales]
"I love you all sincerely;
But I'm given to another
For all time. Most dear of all to me
Is Prince . . ."[26] [She draws in the air the
letters *E. O.*]

inserts into 3, xvii,
"Fairy Tale of the Dead
Tsarevna," ll, 253–56

NURSE: Yelisey.[27]
[chewing her lips and drawing her stool closer to
her precious charge, she begins the fairy tale]
The tsar said farewell to his tsaritsa
And set out on his journey.
And the tsaritsa, by the window
Sat down to wait for him.
Nine months pass.
She doesn't take her eyes off the field
And on the eve of the Epiphany, at night,
God gave the tsaritsa a daughter.
Early in the morning, the long-desired guest,
Who was now a father, the tsar
Who had been day and night awaited,
Finally returned from afar
And she gazed at him,
Sighed heavily,
Did not survive her rapture
And, toward matins, died.
But the tsarevna, young and
Blossoming, meanwhile, without a murmur,
She grew up,
And blossomed . . .

TATYANA: Ah, Nurse, I'm miserable;
It's suffocating,
And I want to cry, to weep . . .

3, xix, 3–6

NURSE: My child, you're sick,
You're in a fever . . .

here 3 lines omitted
3, xix, 10–12

TATYANA: I'm not sick.

I'm . . . Nurse, you see . . . I'm in love.

NURSE: My child, ah! God be with you,   3, xix, 9
Let me sprinkle you with holy water.

TATYANA: Leave me: I'm in love.   3, xx, 4
[Repeat: "I'm in love"]
[The NURSE, following orders, exits, casting a worried
glance at her beloved charge. TATYANA alone. She descends
a spiral staircase into the garden. Repetition: "I'm in love.
I'm in love" two to four times, to an iambic beat.]

Tatyana's condition [3]

TATYANA: [sitting on the bench in the garden—in the depth
of the stage, the window of her room gleams yellow][28]

Tatyana's letter to Onegin

I'm writing you—what else
Is there to say?
I know that now you're free to
Censure and despise me.
But if you could feel a drop of pity
For my wretched lot,
You won't abandon me.
At first I wanted to be silent . . .
You would not have known, believe me,
Of my shame, if I'd the slightest hope
Of seeing you, however rarely,
Only once a week, say, in our parts,
To hear you speak,
To say a word to you, and then
To think, to think about one thing
All day and night, until the next encounter.

music of a psycho[logical] [2] **character**

[Behind the window, in the cool of night, the
watchman's wooden rattle.[29] TATYANA listens intently,
hiding her face in her hands. The rattle grows more
distant—its beats are quiet, like heartbeats.
TATYANA raises her head.]

TATYANA: But people say that you're unsociable;
That everything in this dull spot
Is boring to you. And we're not
Illustrious in anything, although
We welcome you with open hearts.
[Nervously rearranges her knickknacks
on the table.][30]

Why did you visit us?
In this forgotten place
I never would have known you,
Never would have known this bitter torment.
Inexperienced, my hurting heart, with time,
Would have been reconciled (for who's to know?)
I would have found myself a soul mate here,
And been a faithful wife
And virtuous mother.

But . . . Another . . . No, to no one else on earth
Could I now give my heart.
It's been decreed on high . . .
The will of heaven: I am yours;
My life was nothing but a pledge of
This predestined meeting;
You were sent to me by God, I know,
As my protector, till the grave . . .

You appeared to me in dreams,
Already precious, still unseen,
Your wondrous gaze exhausted me,
Your voice resounded in my heart
Already long ago . . . No, this was not a dream.

**without
music**

[Listens intently into the thinning night. Now the
sharply etched contours of the trees become visible
in the bluish-yellow approach of dawn. As sometimes
happens before sunrise, a light burst of wind rocks the
tops of the trees, the garden sighs, precisely as if half
asleep; and then again soundlessness.]

As soon as you came in, I knew.
At once I froze, I flamed,
And in my mind, I said: It's him.
[The outlines of the landscape become clearer and clearer.]
And surely it was true. I heard you:
In the silence it was you who spoke with me
When I was giving alms,
Or when I prayed, indulging in the melancholy
Of my troubled heart.
[Sparrows have begun to chirp, somewhere in the distance
the creaking of the rim of a wheel; a chorus of wooden

rattles is heard, produced by the necks of cows being driven
out to pasture.]

> And at that very moment
> Was it not you, precious vision,
> Flickering in the transparent darkness,
> Bending quietly above my bedstead?
> Surely it was you, who with delight and love
> Whispered words of hope to me?
> Who are you: guardian angel
> Or perfidious seducer?
> Come, resolve my doubts.

1b
3b

[Returns to the house and climbs up the stairs to her
room. Goes up to the table, dips the pen in the ink and
quickly writes. During this time it has grown light
outside the window. Now TATYANA is writing, dictating
to herself.]

> Perhaps all this is nonsense,
> The deception of an inexperienced heart.
> My destiny, perhaps, is wholly different . . .
> But so be it. From now on
> My fate is in your hands,
> My tears I shed before you,
> Begging your protection . . .
> Just imagine: I am here, alone,
> Where no one understands me,
> With my reason languishing,
> I'm sure to perish here.
> I wait for you: a single glance
> From you will either rouse my hopes
> Or interrupt this heavy dream
> With a reproach, alas, so well deserved.

[She lays aside the pen. Extinguishes the candles.
Reads it over.]

> It's done. How awful to reread it,
> Shuddering from shame and fear . . .
> But let your honor be my guarantee,
> Boldly I entrust myself to it.

3 f > 1 (what?)
the peak

[On the threshold of the door, the NURSE. She carries a
tray with tea.]

**perhaps there will be a continu[ation]
of this scene, perhaps not.**

PART TWO

- - - - - - - - - - - - -

Fragment 6

[The already familiar room in Onegin's rural house. Same table, same rocker. ONEGIN sits in front of the mirror, immersed in procedures for haircutting and the cleaning and polishing of nails. Near him a HAIRDRESSER fusses around, having just placed tongs for hair-curling on a special stand in the yellow light of a candle. Jars—little jars—little powder-cases—scissors—tweezers—rough nail files—little suede pillows—little brushes, etc.][31]

perhaps this [will be the] intro[duction]?

ONEGIN: [hums under his breath] *Elle était fille, elle* . . . .

. . . .

[Tweezers, applied to his temples, interrupt the song. In the doorway, a SERVANT with mail on a tray. ONEGIN, while the BARBER polishes the nails on his left hand, with his right hand rummages through the journals, rips open a package. Having half opened one, he throws it out; does the same with another. Under the pile of foreign *Reviews* and *Spectateurs*, the letter with a pink paper seal, already familiar to the audience. At a sign from ONEGIN, the BARBER cuts the edge of the envelope with a pair of scissors and hands the letter to his master. ONEGIN reads to himself]:

"I'm writing you—what else
Is there to say?
I know that now, you're free to
Censure and despise me.
If I'd the slightest hope . . . to hear you speak . . .
Then day and night, until the next encounter . . .
But they say . . . that you . . . that everything is boring to you,
And we . . . not in anything . . . we, with open hearts

1 b
celli + sax   **Tatyana**
and below

Why did you . . . then, I'd not have known . . .
Why did you visit us."

[Pulls his left hand out from under the barber's little clippers and knives. Makes a sign for him to leave. The BARBER and the SERVANT hide behind the door in some

• 135 •

confusion. ONEGIN takes hold of the letter with both hands, turns the page and reads it silently, raising his eyebrows.]
[Goes up to the table. Opens a drawer. Pulls out a little chest. The delicate sound of a key. Rummages around in the letters, souvenirs of love, a lock of someone's hair—smiles at the reminiscences. Tatyana's letter lies right alongside the chest, ready to go inside.]

Another! No, to no one else on earth Could I now give my heart. It's been decreed on high, The will of heaven: I am yours.

I've known beauties—unapproachable,[32]   EO 3, xxii, 1–12
Cold, pure as winter,
Unpersuadable, unbribable,
Incomprehensible;
I marveled at their fashionable arrogance,
Their natural virtue.
And I confess: I ran from them,
It seemed to me I read above their brow
With horror, Hell's signpost:
Abandon hope, all ye who enter here.
For them, to inspire love is a disaster.
It's their pleasure to inspire fear.
And other charmers too I saw: 3, xxiii, 2–14
Self-centeredly indifferent
To the passionate sighs and praise
Of their obedient admirers.
And what, to my surprise, did I discover:
Having frightened off a timid love
With their severe and rigid ways,
They'd lure it back again,
And blinded by his gullibility
Yet another youthful lover   **a piece of Tatyana**
Would set off in vain pursuit.   **between the lines**

1a

And how's Tatyana more to blame?   EO 3, xxiv, 1–4
Because, in sweet simplicity
She fails to see deception
And believes her chosen dream?
Because . . .   ←———— **again T**

Tatyan.

[He wants to throw the letter into his little chest, the cemetery of his romances. But the final page of the letter restrains his hand; he rereads it.]

1 b.
celli

But so be it. From now on
My fate is in your hands,

My tears I shed before you,
Begging your protection . . .

[He abruptly pushes the chest aside. The letter continues
to lie on the table. Getting up, ONEGIN takes several steps
and then stops in indecision. Somehow he has to react to
this letter. But how? He has no doubt about the essence of
his answer. The whole question is the form he should
choose for his explanation. ONEGIN, as it were, "rehearses"
variants of his answer to TATYANA. He addresses himself to
an invisible object.]33

Onegin's
mus[ic]   ONEGIN: If ever I had wished to limit life   EO 4, xiii, 1-7
                           To hearth and home;
                           If ever . . . [changes the variant]
      the same   If ever, even for a moment, I could be
    [music] after   Enraptured by domestic happiness.
      a break   Believe you me, except for you alone, I . . .
                              [Gnaws his nails. Not right. With a sudden
                              impulse]
without   Here's my confession.   4, xii, 13-14
music   I submit it to your judgment.
                              [No—it's too blunt. He tones it down. With a
                              touch of foppishness]
new music,   I'll tell you straight, no madrigals or   4, xiii, 9-14
more foppish   Glitter: having found my past ideal
                           In you, then truly, you alone I'd choose
                           To grace my mournful days,
                           To be my measurement of beauty and of good,
                           And I'd be happy . . . If I could!
                           What could be worse   4, xv, 1-11/12
                           Than families where the wretched wife
                           Grieves over an unworthy husband
                           Day and night, alone;
                           And where the tedious husband, valuing her virtues
                           (But still prone to curse his fate),
                           Always scowling, silent,
                           Angry, coldly jealous.
                           Such am I. And such a man you sought
                           With all your ardent purity of soul,
                           When, with such innocence . . .
                           *With such intelligence you wrote to me . . .*34

[A sudden knock. ONEGIN interrupts his speech. LENSKY enters, shaking from his shoulders the powdery-thin coating of the first dusting of snow from his knee-length winter coat. He is very animated and in cheerful spirits.]³⁵

ONEGIN: So, how're our neighbor girls? Tatyana?   4, xlviii, 1–14
        [Suddenly catching himself, and remembering]
        That is, how fares your frisky *Olga*?

LENSKY: [Before answering, pours himself a glass of wine
        from the carafe and drains it in one gulp. ONEGIN
        wants to fill his glass again.]
        Pour me another half a glass.
        Enough, my friend . . . the family's

Lensky's music   Well; they send their greetings.
(either before *ah, my*   Ah, my friend, how lovely Olga's shoulders
friend **or after it)**   Have become—and what a bosom,
        What a soul . . . Sometime, let's visit
        Them together; you're obliged, my friend.
        Judge for yourself: you peek in once or twice
        And then—it's hardly nice,
        You haven't shown your face.
        But look . . . I chatter on, and here
        This very week you've been invited to their place.

ONEGIN: Who? Me?   4, xlix, 1–10

LENSKY: Indeed. Tatyana's name day,
        Coming up on Saturday. They asked me (Olenka, her mother)
        To invite you; there's no reason
        For you not to come.

1a   **Tatyana**
ONEGIN: There'll be a mass of people there
        All sorts of rabble . . .

LENSKY: Nothing of the sort, I'm certain.
        Who'll be there? Just family.
        Come, do me the favor!
        What about it?

ONEGIN: [after some hesitation] Well . . . all right.

LENSKY: How good you are.
       [A robust and lengthy handshake.]

Fragment 7

- - - - - - - - - - - - -

[The threshold of a door, wide open, divides the stage into inner and outer areas. Beyond the door a brightly illuminated hall, only a part of which is visible to the spectator. In front of the door, a small, half-dark room, three walls of which come together at oblique angles. Beyond the threshold, the parquet floor has been cleared of things but is filled with flickering figures, who are whirling around in a ~~waltz~~ **polka**. To this side of the threshold there are no people, but the space is full of all sorts of things. Here is where they've stuck the tables, piled one on top of another, together with some four-cornered desk blotters and awkward chests of drawers. In the corner, a series of potbellied jugs, woven together with straw and twigs, empty and full, water bottles and other domestic utensils.]

polka
~~waltz~~
harpsichords
offstage

[A DANCER runs in. In his haste his foot stumbles into a dish full of cold aspic. Hissing some incomprehensible word through his teeth, he alternately wipes sweat from his brow with a handkerchief and the cold jelly from the braid of his pant leg—and again dives back into the waltz.][36]

[TATYANA enters, and after her ONEGIN. The impression is that TATYANA is trying to escape from her companion's words, which are overtaking her.]

~~Onegin~~
~~speaks~~
~~offstage~~
~~orchestra,~~
~~but now the~~
~~country one~~

ONEGIN: [finishing up]   EO 4, xvi, 10–14
       It seems that heaven has fated it.
       You'll love again: but . . .
       Learn to control yourself.
       Not everyone will understand, as I did;
       Inexperience can lead to sure disaster.
       Judge for yourself, what roses . . .   4, xiv, 12
[TATYANA, leaning against the wall with one palm; her other hand pressed to her chest; with difficulty she restrains the sobbing that rises to her throat.]

ONEGIN: [glancing with irritation at a couple passing by]

You'll begin to cry: your tears   4, xiv, 9–11
Won't touch my heart,
But only drive it to a fury.
Such am I. And such a man you sought   4, xv, 9–12
With all your ardent purity of soul,
When, with such innocence
polka   With such intelligence you wrote to me?
[Having noticed the approach of outsiders, he bows and
exits into the hall.]

TATYANA: [alone] I'll perish.[37] An abyss   EO 6, iii, 9–14
Has opened up, grows black, it's howling.
But to perish by his hand is pleasant.
I do not complain. And why complain?
He cannot give me happiness.
sentimental   [Wants to return to the hall, but on the threshold,
waltz   supporting one another by the elbows: BUYANOV[38]
in strings   and ZARETSKY. Both are a little drunk.]
8 bars

continue   BUYANOV [foppishly bows to TATYANA and jokingly declaiming,
~~winds orch~~   syllable by syllable, in the Russian manner]
harpsichord
                    Réveillez-vous, belle endormie[39]
                    . . . .

OLGA   [runs in, separating the two with her hands]
        The Company commander has arrived,   5, xxviii, 4–6
        He's just come in . . . Aha, what news!
        We'll have some music from the regimental band!

immediately military music
Quadrille? Galop? If played | **1–1½ minutes**

[OLGA grabs TATYANA by the hand and pulls her back into the hall]

ZARETSKY: [pressing his companion's elbow][40]
1st polka   In duels I am a classicist, a pedant,   6, xxvi, 8–12
but military   And by temperament it's method that I love;[41]
orchestra   I won't allow a man to be dispatched
                    Just any careless way,
                    But only in strict . . .

BUYANOV: [interrupting] The pie was greasy-rich.   5, xxxii, 4

ZARETSKY: Alas, and oversalted   5, xxxii, 5–14

Ah, a bottle sealed with pitch . . .
[Notices some bottles in the corner]

BUYANOV: Behind it there's a row of long and narrow wineglasses
[Bows to the bottles, pours out some wine
into two wineglasses, clinks glasses with
Zaretsky,—and]
Similar to your slender waist
[Screws up his eyes, peers into the wineglass]
Zizi, crystal of my soul[42]
And object of my innocent verses,
Enticing phial of love,
You, from whom I'm . . .
[They clink glasses, drink, and BUYANOV staggers slightly]
. . . drunk.
[Each pours himself another drink. The clink of two glasses]
It's pleasant, with a sassy epigram[43]   6, xxxiii, 1–4
To enrage a bungling enemy
It's pleasant . . . [they drink] to see how stubbornly
He lowers his butting horns . . .

ZARETSKY: More pleasant still, in silence   6, xxxiii, 9–12
To prepare an honorable grave for him
And quietly aim at his pale forehead . . .

BUYANOV: [hiccupping] . . . at a noble distance.
How I love madcap youth: 1, xxx, 5–12
The crush, the glitter, the high spirits
And the dress of ladies, so premeditated and so neat.
[Twirls around to the sounds of the music, which are shifting
from waltz to quadrille. Snapping his fingers]
I love their little feet.[44]

ZARETSKY: But little chance
You'll find in all of Russia
Three slender pairs of women's feet.

BUYANOV: For ages I could not forget
Two little feet. Grown sad and cool . . .
Ah, precious little feet. Where are you now   1, xxxi, 3
[Distracted by the movement of the dancers and the flashing
polka   of feet, he disappears into the dance hall. ZARETSKY wants

to bow once more to the bottle, but ONEGIN appears on the
threshold, ironically fixing his lorgnette on him.]

ONEGIN: [Apparently he is seeking TATYANA, to finish
           his conversation]
           And he still flourishes today   6, iv, 5–8
           In philosophical seclusion,
           This Zaretsky, once a hothead,
           Chief among the card sharks.[45]
           [ZARETSKY politely bows and spreads his hands, as if
           begging him to speak more softly]
           Truly, from a pistol smack into an ace   6, v, 3–4

ZARETSKY: [correcting him] . . . At twenty paces I could hit the target

ONEGIN: And could quarrel cheerfully   6, vi, 9–10

ZARETSKY: [rubbing his hands]
           And cleverly and . . .

ONEGIN: . . . stupidly respond,
           And cause young friends to quarrel   6, vi, 13–14
           And to shoot point-blank[46]
           [ZARETSKY shakes his head—as if to say, those were the days]
           . . . .

ONEGIN: [abruptly turning toward the hall where people
           are dancing]
                    Who *are* these people?

a slow   ZARETSKY: With his portly spouse   5, xxvi, 1–14, minus 10–11
minuet,   That's tubby Pustyakov;
if possible   And there's Gvozdin, that model master,
                      Owner of impoverished serfs;
                      And the Skotinins, gray-haired both,
                      With children of all ages, ranging
                      From the age of thirty down to two.[47]
                      Then Petushkov, provincial fop;
                      My cousin's over there, Buyanov,
                      And Flyanov, retired counselor,
                      A heavy-duty slanderer, a rascal,
                      Glutton, bribe-taker, and . . .

ONEGIN: . . . fool.
    [At last, ZARETSKY manages to fade into the background]
    [Enter LENSKY and OLGA, without noticing ONEGIN.
without   LENSKY is carrying an open album and a pen.
music   OLGA, following him, peeks from over her fiancé's
shoulder. LENSKY jots down several lines in the album.
LENSKY reads what he has written, not yet noticing ONEGIN
to whom OLGA has already managed to nod.][48]

LENSKY: "How blessed is that modest lover   4, xxxiv, 9–14
Who can read aloud his dreams
To her who has inspired his songs, his love,
A beauty, languid, pleasing."

ONEGIN: [with a dry laugh]
Blessed . . . but perhaps she
Was attracted by some wholly other thing.

[LENSKY wants to shut the album, but ONEGIN, asking
permission from the owner of the album with a
glance, stretches out his hand toward the notebook.]

OLGA: [keeping the album in her hands for a few
seconds more][49]
Of course, how many times you've seen   4, xxviii, 1–11
The albums of provincial girls,
What all my friends have scribbled
From the back, the front, and in between.
Here . . .

ONEGIN: . . . in defiance of all spelling rules,
Verse without meter . . .

LENSKY: [heatedly]   . . . by tradition
Entered as a sign of friendship.

ONEGIN: [the album is already in his hands]
Here abbreviated, there expanded
[leafing through the pages]
On the first page you encounter
. . . . [50]

OLGA: And the signature . . . . [51]

ONEGIN: [continuing to leaf through, looking point-blank
          at LENSKY]
          Here someone's sketched some rural scenes,   4, xxvii, 5–8
          A gravestone, or the Temple of Cypris
          Or on a lyre, a dove
          Drawn lightly, with a pen and colors.
          [LENSKY blushes; he begins to get nervous]

LENSKY: And on the final page we read:

OLGA: *"Whoever loves you more and true,*

ONEGIN: [returns the album]
          Let him write further than I do."
          [OLGA's laughter is interrupted by an abrupt movement
          from LENSKY, who grabs the album at precisely the
          moment it passes to his fiancée from ONEGIN's hands;
quadrille   LENSKY then moves off to the side. OLGA is insulted. And
ritornello   when, at exactly that moment, the ~~quadrille~~ ritornello
mazurka   bursts forth, she nods in acceptance of ONEGIN's
milit. orch.   invitational bow. LENSKY, getting a grip on himself, turns
(Onegin   around: there's already nobody left in the room. LENSKY
kisses   takes a step in the direction of the brightly lit hall, but a
[her] hand   pair glides by him in the harmonious rhythm of the
               mazurka: OLGA and ONEGIN. LENSKY steps back into
harpsichord   the shadows.][52]
waltz
(perhaps the LENSKY: Monotonous and mindless,   5, xli, 1–4
same as above)   Like the whirlwind of young life
                        The noisy whirlwind of the waltz swirls
                        One pair flashing past another
               [At this point, BUYANOV leads TATYANA and OLGA up
               to ONEGIN.[53] Without hesitating, ONEGIN takes OLGA's
               hand and disappears in the dance.]

              LENSKY: Can it be possible? Scarce out of diapers,   5, xlv, 5–8
the same   And a flirt, a frivolous child.
waltz   Already knows the path to guile,
in the strings   Already she can cheat and smile!
                        Oh god—I'll be her savior,[54]   6, xvii, 5–12
                        I won't tolerate that this corruptor
                        Tempt her youthful heart

With fiery sighs and compliments;
That a despised and poisonous worm
Should gnaw this lily's stem;
Or that a flower only two morns old
Should fade, half opened.
But what of it. A pair of pistols,
And two bullets—nothing more.[55]

waltz
[~~Mazurka~~ slows its tempo and dies away; the couples
part and return to their own places; chatting gaily,
ONEGIN and OLGA pass by the door.]

OLGA: [Noticing LENSKY on the threshold of the half-
dark room]
What's the matter with you?   6, xix, 12–13

LENSKY: Nothing.[56]

OLGA: [to her cavalier, in an exhausted voice]
And this endless cotillion   6, 1, 7–8
Has worn me out, like a bad dream.[57]
[ONEGIN whispers something to her, calming her down—
and the couple passes by. Behind them, in the frame
of the door, leaning her hand against the doorjamb,
TATYANA. Her face is full of touching sympathy.]

TATYANA: What's the matter with you?

LENSKY: Nothing.
[TATYANA disappears. LENSKY makes a decisive step
toward the threshold. During this time the musicians,

~~27~~
without music
and without
tuning up

apparently preparing for a new dance, tune up their
instruments: a dissonant conglomeration of sounds.
LENSKY on the threshold collides face-to-face with
ONEGIN. Both stop and gaze at each other silently. The
sound of tuning instruments breaks off. Now something
new will begin. An auditory and visual pause.
From behind the door we see the frightened face of
TATYANA, at a loss how to respond. But then, from the
depth of the hall, cheerful guffaws, followed
by singing, whistling, barking, and stamping. ~~The stage~~

sul
ponticello

~~revolves about 60 degrees,~~ so that the wall, dividing
the half-volumed room from the hall, is now aligned

• 145 •

perpendicularly to the spectator, who can thus see both
the room and the hall. The guests, parting, make room
for the MUMMERS to pass, serfs who have come to con-
gratulate and praise their young lady on her name day:
here a half-crane and half-cat, a mask with a horned dog's
mug, a goat, two or three village musicians strumming
and maniacally banging on a tamborine.

The MUMMERS, all bowing to the waist to honor the
name-day girl, launch immediately into a peasant
dance and a ritual praise-chant.]⁵⁸

**perhaps
tamborine,
3 violins
and oboe?**

MUMMERS: [sing] There the peasants are all rich:
They rake up silver with a spade;
Whoever we sing to, that person will have riches [encore]
And glory.⁵⁹

the rest roar [[Refrain, wild animal style]

[A goblet is brought up to TATYANA; at the same time as she
bows in response and allows her hand to be kissed, she
glances fearfully at what is occurring behind her, beyond
the threshold of the dark room. The goblet, slipping from
her hands, falls.]

**cancel (July)
~~for the
concl[uding]
emotion of
Tatyana~~
ve[ry] short**

without an interlude

Fragment 8

- - - - - - - - - - - -

[Tatyana's room. The ball is already over. It is no longer
night. The second roosters are crowing. TATYANA,
exhausted by the events of the ball, sleeps, lying on the
couch. In the pre-morning light, her figure can be clearly
seen. She lies facedown on her hot pillow, still dressed in
her white ballroom gown. Only one light slipper, having
slid off her foot, lies near the couch on the floor.⁶⁰

The NURSE enters the room on tiptoe. She is carrying
a night-cape and slippers. Catching sight of TANYA fallen
asleep in her dress, she doesn't know what to do.]

**1st theme of
Tatyana
with an
admixture
of elements
of *tragizm***

TATYANA: [through her sleep] Mine—mine—mine—mine . . .   5, xix, 14, xx, 1

mus[ic] breaks off   [Suddenly she jumps up. At that instant, the visions

of the dream, in a rage, disappear under the wallpaper
and behind the pane of the window.]

[TATYANA:] I dreamed, as if . . .

NURSE: God have mercy and save you   3, xix, 7–8
              Whatever you want, just ask . . .[61]
[She wants to leave, apparently to get some water, but
TATYANA, still half-asleep, holds her back, grabbing at
her sleeve.]

TATYANA: I dreamed a wondrous dream . . .   5, xi, 1

NURSE: Oh, Tanya.

TATYANA: I dreamed, Nurse,   5, xi, 2–11
              I was walking in a snowy field
              Surrounded by a dismal fog
              In snowdrifts, dark and gray,
              A brook that winter hadn't frozen yet;
              And there, before the churning waves
              Two icy little poles were thrown
              Across the chasm,
              Like a fatally trembling bridge.
              And suddenly the snowdrift shuddered . . .   EO 5, xii, 5–14

NURSE: Who appeared from under it?[62]

TATYANA: A huge and shaggy bear.
              I almost shouted "Oh!" He howled,   5, xii, 8–14
              Stretched out a paw with its sharp claws;
              I braced myself with one unsteady hand
              And leaning against the rail,
               With frightened steps
              I made my way across the stream,[63]
              I got across—and then?

NURSE: The bear's pursuing her.[64]

TATYANA: Bellowing, the odious bear is lurching on.   5, xiii, 5–14
              Before us, forests: pine trees motionless
               In all their frowning beauty;

With their branches bending low
With clods of snow; and through the crowning heights
Of aspens, birches, naked linden trees,
The night stars gleam;
There is no path: the bushes, precipices
Covered by the storm-swept snow.
Into the snow I fell. The bear then nimbly   5, xv, 1–2
Snatched me up, and carried me.
Suddenly between the trees, a shabby hut;   5, xv, 6–12
All 'round's a wasteland; on all sides,
Sunk deeply in a wilderness of snow,
But here a little window brightly gleams;
And in the hut there's noise and shouting:
Then the bear speaks out: . . .

NURSE: [stopping TANYA, speaking the familiar formula
              of fairy tales] . . .*"My godfather lives here;*
              Come warm yourself a while at his house" . . .

TATYANA: [nodding her head in agreement]
              Warm yourself a while at his house;
              So the bear goes straight into the hall
              And on the threshold lays me down.   end of EO 5, xv, 13–14
              What do I see . . . a table   EO 5, xvi, 7–14
              And around it, monsters sitting;
              One in horns but with a dog's mug;
              Here's another with a rooster's head;
              And here, a witch who has a goatish beard,
              And then a skeleton, stuck-up and proud;
              A dwarf who has a tiny tail, and over there
              A half-crane and half-cat.
              And still more terrible, more wondrous: 5, xvii, 1–11
              A crab is riding on a spider's back,
              A skull atop a goose's neck
              Is twisting in its crimson cap;
              A windmill dances in a squatting jig
              Its wings are waving, crackling,
              Barks, guffaws and singing, claps and whistling,
              Human talk and horses' stomp.
              But what would you think, Nurse,[65]
              If you had recognized, among the guests

That very one, who . . .

mus[ic] about Oneg[in]

[She interrupts her story, but her nurse strokes her slightly trembling shoulder with her hand—so TATYANA continues, but already in a completely different tone.]

Onegin's sitting at the table;   5, xvii, 13–14
Furtively he gazes at the door.
He gives a sign: all set to clapping;   5, xviii, 1–4
Drinks: and they all drink and shout;
Breaks into laughter: everyone guffaws;
He knits his brows, and all fall silent.
Suddenly a gust of wind blew out   5, xviii, 9–13
The nighttime lanterns:
And this gang of goblins got confused,
Onegin, eyes agleam,
Arises, roaring, from the table.
Everybody rose: Yevgéniy kicked the door[66]   5, xvii, 14, xix, 5–14
And to the gaze of these infernal apparitions
I appeared, and raucous laughter
Wildly sounded forth; the eyes of all,
The hoofs, the crooked trunks,
The tufted tails, and tusks . . .

NURSE: Moustaches, bloody tongues,
And horns and bony fingers,
Everything is pointing at her . . .
[Her reserve of images dries up. She glances at TANYA]

TATYANA: Everyone is shouting: Mine! Mine![67]
Mine! Yevgéniy says, and threatening them all;   5, xx, 1–4
The whole gang disappears at once,
And only I remained, in freezing darkness . . .

NURSE: [disapprovingly] The girl remains alone with him.[68]

TATYANA: But suddenly in Olga comes, with Lensky.[69]   5, xxi, 9–10

think about this

There's a quarrel. Louder, louder: Suddenly Yevgéniy   xxi, 1–6
Grabs a knife and in an instant
Lensky is struck down; how frightening it was,
The shadows thickened: an intolerable shriek
Rang out . . . The hut all but collapsed . . .
And I, nurse, I woke up in terror . . .

→ **pause, and a horn before Onegin's words**

Fragment 9
- - - - - - - - - - - -

[A clearing in a forest. Through a thin spread of leafless trees, a dam is visible near a frozen river that skirts the edge of the forest; the wings of a windmill are lifted to the sky, plastered with snow and frozen icicles. The wind whips around clods of snow and sways the tops of the trees. Evidently a blizzard is starting up.

The opponents are already at their places. The wind rips at the edges of the frock coats and fur overcoats thrown down on the barrier—the sort of weather when one wants either to kill, or be killed, as soon as possible.[70]

ZARETSKY hands out the pistols, first to LENSKY, then to ONEGIN]

ONEGIN: It's late already; time has flown . . .
Still . . . why has that old duelist   EO 6, xi, 5–13
Interfered in this affair?[71]
He's mean, a rumormonger and a gossip . . .
Now, of course his silly words
Aren't worth a thing—
But whispers, and the giggling of stupid fools . . .
And there you have it: what the public thinks
Becomes the mainspring of our honor, and our idol!

ZARETSKY: Now, begin!
[The opponents each take four steps toward each other. ONEGIN raises his pistol. He holds it there until the fifth step. Then LENSKY, screwing up his left eye, begins to aim. ONEGIN fires.]

[LENSKY, silently lowering his pistol, falls to the ground. ZARETSKY and ONEGIN bend over the fallen man.]

ONEGIN: Well, what?   6, xxxv, 4–5

ZARETSKY: He's dead.

ONEGIN: Dead?

[Walks off to the side. At a sign from ZARETSKY, the
COACHMAN and SERVANT appear. With his help, they
carry away the corpse. GUILLOT follows after them.
ONEGIN remains alone.][72]

little
music,
more
illust[ration]
	ONEGIN: One moment back, and pulsing in this heart
	        Was inspiration, hatred,
	        Hope, and love,
	        Life played in it, and blood ran hot:
	        Now, like a house deserted,
	        Everything in it is hushed and dark,
	        Forever fallen silent.
	        Shutters tightly closed, the windows
	        Whitened now with chalk. The owner's gone,
	        Where to, God knows. No trace is left.
		6, xxxii, 5–14

[The wind sways the trunks of the trees ever more strongly.
Both in the stage space and in the music, the symphony of
the snowstorm grows.]

PART THREE
- - - - - - - - - - - - -

Fragment 10
- - - - - - - - - - - - -

[Familiar room in ONEGIN's rural house. But it faces the
spectator from another angle, so that the door, which earlier
was deep in the interior and led to the outside, is now
shown from the side, and this door, opened to the neighboring room, shows the room in perspective. The house is
abandoned. The owner is gone. This is apparent from the
already frozen state of disorder and from the dust that
covers things with a gray shroud. In the middle of the
stage is the rocking chair, already familiar to our eye. It is
motionless. Behind the door leading to the neighboring
room, the end of a billiard cue juts out, blocking the way.
On the table, among overturned jars and empty flasks,
there are two or three books; one of them is open and lies

without
music?

spine-upward.

At first the house is silent. Even the wall clock, which has lost its ticking mechanism, has fallen silent and its pendulum hangs down motionless.

After a pause, somewhere in the distance beyond the walls of the house, children's voices and laughter are heard. Then, somewhat closer, the voice of TATYANA; and then completely close by, the jangling of a bunch of keys.][73]

VOICE of TATYANA: Might I see the master's house?   EO 7, xvii, 1
    [The sound of opening doors—first one, then others.
    On the threshold, TATYANA. She is wearing a fur cape;
    on her hands, mittens. Behind her is the old caretaker,
    ANISYA, who shoos away the children poking their
    heads in through the door. TATYANA, now standing in
    the middle of the room, looks around her in leisurely
    fashion. Meeting her gaze are the blind windows,
    piled up with snow.]

TATYANA: I hesitated, full of doubt   7, xvi, 1–4
    Should I go forward, or go back?
    But he's not here. And no one knows me . . .
    I'll just glance into the house, the garden . . .

    [She runs her fingers over the spine of the book. For
    the moment she doesn't open it up. Walks up to the
    threshold of the neighboring room. Moves aside the
    billiard cue obstructing the path. For several seconds
    she disappears behind the door. Taking advantage of
    this moment, the CHILDREN burst into the room and
    gaze at the visitor with mouths agape like little birds.
    TATYANA again stands on the threshold separating
    the inner room from the outer one.]

ANISYA: Here's the fireplace,   7, xvii, 13–14
    Here the master sat, alone.
    Here, in the wintertime, our late neighbor,   7, xviii, 1–14
    Lensky, used to dine with him.
    Come this way, after me.
    And here's the master's study,
    Here's where he slept, and had his coffee,
    Listened to the steward give reports

And in the morning, where he read his books . . .
And here as well, the old master lived.
On Sunday he would put his glasses on,
And he'd be kind enough to play
A game of cards with me.
God grant his soul salvation, now he's gone.
Peace to his bones, now resting
In the grave, in damp mother earth.

Tatyana
1st theme
(1 min[ute])

[The old CARETAKER exits, ushering out the children. TATYANA is alone. Once more she does the rounds of the place. On the wall, under a net protecting it from flies, is a portrait of Byron. She examines it carefully. On the table, alongside an inkwell, a waist-high bust of Napoleon, his cast-iron arms crossed. TATYANA sits down in the armchair at the table. Falls into thought. In the distance, the weak and trembling ringing of a church bell. Probably somebody is being buried. Goes up to the window and outlines on its frosty patterns: E and O. Now and then the dried-out floor crackles. TATYANA, returning to the table, bends slightly over the spine of the book in front of her, separating its pages. Reads.]

TATYANA: *The Singer of the Giaour and Juan*[74]
[Turns the book over so the text is faceup. She reads the open page)
"I'm restrained—but sensitive to insults;
Modest—but I know my worth,
I'm changeable—but also '*semper idem*'. . . . .
Patient—but just barely patient enough,
It must be that I have—or so it seems—
Under my external skin, two or three hidden skins."[75]

[Replacing the book precisely in the same position as before, she runs the tips of her fingers across the empty flasks, having arranged them like a mute keyboard. Fingers and leafs through the books]

Here in the margins . . . there, my eye meets[76]   7, xxiii: 9–14
The marks of his pencil.
Everywhere Onegin's soul
Unwillingly expresses itself

Here with a short word, there with a cross,
Now with a question mark.

"

. . ."[77] There, beneath cloudy
And brief days, a tribe was born,
For whom it was not sad to die." *Petrarch*

[She lays aside the book. Gets up. Goes up to the fireplace.
Stirs the gray coals with the tongs. The cast-off fireplace

**maybe
simply
tremolo?**

tongs ring sharply against the grate. Goes up to the bust of
Napoleon. Suddenly TATYANA's mood changes sharply, she
makes a naughty grimace at the little cast-iron man in the
three-cornered hat, with his arms crossed on his chest,
and mimicking a pose of greatness, she crosses her arms
on her own chest, sticks out her lower lip, and gives a bow
à la Napoleon.[78]

up to the words

[Neither sadness nor joking can now be found on her face:
it is simply exhausted; between her knitted brows, some
sort of new thought. Slowly and clearly articulated:]

A sad and dangerous eccentric,   7, xxiv, 6–14
A creation of hell, or maybe of heaven,
Angel perhaps, or an arrogant demon,
What is he? Could it be he's just an imitation,
Some phantasm, empty—or perhaps
A Muscovite in Childe Harold's cloak,[79]
A glossary of others' eccentricities
A lexicon of fashionable words?
Perhaps he's just a parody?
But have I really solved the riddle?[80]   7, xxv, 1–4

**as on the
preceding page
30 sec[onds]**

Has the *word* been really found?
It's time, the hours are passing, I forgot
That they've been long expecting me at home.[81]

[On the verge of starting off toward the door, she remembers
something, walks with quick steps to the window. Taking
off her mittens, she tries to rub from the frost-encrusted
pane of glass the marks she had etched there: perhaps
"O. E." The frozen letters won't give way. TATYANA breathes
on the pane and again rubs its surface with her mitten.
A thinned-out patch of light appears, through which the

winter sun breaks through. TATYANA, pressing her hand to her forehead, gazes out at the landscape beyond the window frame. The sound of children's voices is heard and the beginning of a children's song.]

hint of a children's song

Winter! . . . The peasant, celebrating,
Opens up the road again with sledges,
And his horse, who sensed the snowfall,
Manages to break into a trot;
The little carriage swiftly flies,
With powdery furrows in its wake.
The coachman sits atop his box
In rabbit coat and crimson sash.

EO 5, ii, 1–14

unknown if we'll have it (but in any case without mus[ic])

A peasant boy runs on ahead,
His dog's been seated on the sled,
So he can be the steed.
His finger's frozen, and he finds it funny
Even as it hurts; his mother
Standing at the window, scolds him . . .

[Outside the window, children's laughter and the repetition of one of the couplets of the song. TATYANA listens, moves away from the window, and leans up against the lintel of the door. Then:]

theme of the horn but perhaps not [?] the oboe

Farewell, you peaceful valleys,
And the peaks of these familiar hills,
And you, familiar forests!
Farewell, the beauty of the sky,
Farewell, lighthearted nature!
This dear and quiet world I am exchanging
For the noisy hum of glittering vanity;
Farewell to you, my freedom!
Where am I now rushing to, and why?
What fate awaits me?

EO 7, xxviii, 5–14

end with music

[She moves toward the exit]

ENTR'ACTE

Fragment 11

- - - - - - - -

[Out of the darkness of the scenic cube, only at the top—just
barely below the theatrical flies—pre-dawn stars. The ringing
of Moscow's forty-times-forty [churches]. From the deepest
bass of the Ivan the Great [Belltower] to the fragile descants
of the bells mounted on the tiny gate-tower churches.
Barely making itself heard through all this bell-ringing is
the jangling of a coachman's bell, rattled by potholes. A
carriage, an invisible carriage, is racing through the night,
coming closer and closer.[82]

Day begins. Gradually various shapes can be distinguished: the contours of hipped [sloping] church roofs and
the outline of a columned house with a mezzanine. Then,
breaking into the night and the ringing of bells, a room at
the top of the house, in the mezzanine, blazes forth suddenly with a bright light. Near the wall on a couch, the old
PRINCESS. She is ensconced in pillows. Her thin, sunken
cheeks are wrapped in a kerchief. Near the door, on a
stool, an old servant, a KALMYK; he is dressed in a torn caftan,
wears glasses that have slipped down on his nose, and has
a stocking in his hand.[83]

A little round table has been pushed up against the
couch. On it are medicines and two cups of coffee, which
the PRINCESS is serving her guests, who have politely seated
themselves in two armchairs, also placed near the sick
woman's bed. These guests are VYAZEMSKY and the
GENERAL.][84]

VYAZEMSKY: [putting away a manuscript]
Such a rush to get to Moscow! That's to see the world!
And where's it better?

PRINCESS: Where we're not.[85]

GENERAL: Moscow, beloved daughter of Russia,
Where can one find your equal?[86]

PRINCESS: How can one not love one's native Moscow.[87]

GENERAL: The young Graces of Moscow . . .   EO 7, xlvi, 2

*music later,
when the
bells start*

VYAZEMSKY: The night has many charming stars,   7, lii, 1–5
               And Moscow, many beauties.
               But far brighter than her celestial girlfriends
               Is the moon, resplendent in the airy blue.
               But she, to whom . . .

[His speech is interrupted by a vigorous knock on the
door. The KALMYK opens it. Into the room tumble Mme
LARINA and the HANGER-ON. Behind them, timidly,
TATYANA enters. Like her traveling companions she is
wrapped up in furs on furs. Above the coat, her little
head is covered with a double fur hood. Frosty air
enters after them. Following the air, two servants,
loaded down with valises, trunks, and birdcages. The
PRINCESS, with a delighted shout, rises up in her bower.
Her Moscow guests, VYAZEMSKY and the GENERAL,
having risen from their places, move off to the side,
glancing somewhat bemusedly at the provincials.]

LARINA: Princess . . . . [88]   7, xli, 1–6

PRINCESS: . . . .

LARINA: Alina!

PRINCESS: Who'd have thought?

LARINA: How long it's been.

PRINCESS: You've come for long?

LARINA: My dear!

PRINCESS: *Cousine!*
            Sit down, how strange this is.

GENERAL: [quietly to VYAZEMSKY, slightly shrugging his
           epaulettes] My god, it's a scene out of a novel . . .[89]

LARINA: And here's my daughter, Tatyana.

[TATYANA wants to throw herself into her aunt's arms,

without taking off her fur coats. But the old woman
starts to cough. The KALMYK, with a preemptive gesture
and together with the SERVANT, takes the two winter
coats off TATYANA. Slowly, at first only approximately
and then ever more precisely, the slender contour of
a girl begins to take shape from under the fur coat,
rabbitskin coat and jacket, and from under the
thrown-back hood and unwound shawl a delicate little
face appears. As this process unfolds, the ironic gaze
of the GENERAL and to some extent of VYAZEMSKY
changes to a gaze of enchantment. The GENERAL
even twirls his moustache slightly and tugs down his
uniform to straighten it.]

PRINCESS: [deeply touched]
Ah, Tanya. Come here, closer—   7, xli, 7–10
It's as if I'm in delirium . . .

GENERAL: [into VYAZEMSKY's ear]
As if I'm in delirium . . .

PRINCESS: *Cousine*, do you remember Grandison?[90]
What Grandison? . . . ah, Grandison!

HANGER-ON: [doing inventory on the household equipment they
brought with them]
Frying pans, chairs, trunks,   7, xxxi, 7–8
Jam in jars, mattresses.

LARINA: [half closing her eyes]
Yes, I remember. Where's he now?   resumes 7, xli, 11–12

PRINCESS: In Moscow, lives at Simeón's house;

HANGER-ON: Pots, washbasins,   7, xxxi, 10

LARINA: [breaking in] . . . . [91]

KALMYK: Well, a lot of goods of every sort.   7, xxxi, 11

PRINCESS: On Christmas Eve he called on me.   7, xli, 13–14
Not long ago he married off his son.

• 158 •

[Two elderly FEMALE RELATIVES run in from the
interior doors. Embraces and exclamations.]

FIRST REL: How Tanya's grown! Was it long . . . [92]   7, xliv, 8–14

SECOND REL: How Tanya's grown.

FIRST REL: Was it so long ago
              I baptized you?

SECOND REL: And how I pulled you by the ears!

FIRST REL: And how I bore you in my arms!

PRINCESS: [drawing TANYA to her]
              And how I fed you gingerbread!

ALL THE OLD LADIES: Oh! How the years have flown!

VYAZEMSKY: [quietly, to the GENERAL]
              I can't see any change in them at all,   7, xlv, 1–14
              It's all the same old pattern.

FIRST REL: Auntie Princess Yeléna
              Has the same tulle nightcap

SECOND REL: And Lukérya Lvovna powders up—no less, no more,   .
              And Lyubóv Petróvna's telling lies, same as before,
              And Iván Petróvich: just as stupid,
              And Semyón Petróvich: just as stingy.

PRINCESS: [Tries to stop the flow of words from the SECOND
              RELATIVE]
              Pelagéya Nikolávna has
              The same old friend, Monsieur Finmouche . . .

VYAZEMSKY: [Coming closer and leading the GENERAL by the
              hand] Oh, such a model member of the Club . . .   line 12

LARINA: The same old lapdog, same old husband?   line 11

PRINCESS: [sighing] Same old lapdog, same old husband.

FIRST REL: Just as docile, just as deaf.

SECOND REL: Who eats and drinks for two.

LARINA: And that one . . . But . . .   7, xlii, 1–6, 8

PRINCESS: We'll talk about it later,
Won't we? But tomorrow we must show
Our Tanya off to all her kin.
A pity I've no energy to make the rounds.
But you're exhausted from the journey;
Oh, I've no strength left . . . and it's so hard to breathe . . .

VYAZEMSKY: [cautiously approaching her]
Our roads today are very bad,[93]   7, xxxiv, 1–4
Neglected bridges rot . . .

LARINA: [picking up the theme]
At every station, fleas and bedbugs
Keep you from a minute's sleep.

VYAZEMSKY: With time, when we have moved   7, xxxiii, 1–14
Yet closer to a prosperous enlightenment
(According to the charts and calculations
Of philosophers: about five hundred years from now)
The roads, in truth, will change immeasurably.

[Everyone from TATYANA to the KALMYK listens, as if to
a fairy tale]

Highways crisscross Russia and connect
Here to there.
Cast-iron bridges will be flung above the waters
Striding forward with an arching sweep
We'll move apart the mountains,
Burrow daring tunnels 'neath the waters.

GENERAL: And the Christian world will introduce
A pub in every station.

FIRST REL: [bending over to Tanya's left ear]
Look over there, and quickly, to the left.   7, liv: 8–9, 13–14

SECOND REL: [into the other ear]
Look over there, and quickly, to the left.

TATYANA: The left? But why? What's there to see?

FIRST REL: The one who just walked off . . . he's standing there
in profile . . .

TATYANA: [frightened] Who? Not that fat general?

PRINCESS: But you're exhausted from the journey;   7, xlvv, 6, 5, 12
And I barely drag my legs around.
Grow old, and life is so disgusting . . .

GENERAL: [sighing] Dreams, dreams. Where is your sweetness?[94]

VYAZEMSKY: [poisonously] And the eternal rhyme that follows
it: youth.

PRINCESS: [Gets up, supported by VYAZEMSKY and the
GENERAL, one hand resting on TATYANA's head;
the FEMALE RELATIVES, LARINA, and the SERVANTS
follow her: the cortege recalls partly a wedding,
partly a funeral.]

I've no strength left . . . and it's so hard to breathe . . .   7, xlii, 7–8
Let's all go rest.

[The procession slowly moves off toward the door,
whose two opened door-panels are supported by the
SERVANT-KALMYK.]

Fragment 12

- - - - - - - - - - - -

ostentatious
overture
2 m[inutes]

[Ball in a high-society Petersburg salon. Everything is bathed
in bright light. Men are dressed in frock coats and military-
dress uniforms. Ladies are in full evening wear. The dances
haven't yet started. They are waiting for someone. Guests are
gathering, dividing up into groups. To the left, avant-scene,
a group of worldly young men; to the right, an elderly ANGRY

GENTLEMAN, surrounded mostly by ladies. Lackeys distribute
fruit and cold drinks.]

**repeat last
8–16 bars,
but now
pp strings**

DECREPIT DIGNITARY: [He is hard of hearing, and therefore the
ANGRY GENTLEMAN, who is arguing with him,
almost has to shout.]
Write odes, gentlemen! EO 4, xxxii, 14
The way they wrote them in the mighty years xxxiii, 1–4
The way 'twas done in days of yore . . .

ANGRY GENTLEMAN: Only solemn odes?
Come now, my friend, isn't it all the same?

DECREPIT DIGNITARY: But all these elegies are trivial; xxxiii, 9–14
How pitiable their empty aims;
Whereas the purpose of the ode . . .

ANGRY GENTLEMAN: Here we could
Argue, but I'd rather hold my tongue.
Why cause two centuries to quarrel?

[In the depth of the hall, an already elderly guest
appears; he has a stout but short torso on long, thin
legs; he props himself up with a stick; his head,
wrapped up in a white bow, has grown deeply into his
shoulders.[95] At the sight of him, the group of archival
youths perk up.][96]

1st YOUNG MAN: A troika of gloomy singers.[97]

2nd Y. M.:   Shikhmátov.

3rd Y. M.:   Shakhovskóy.

1st Y. M.:   Shishkóv.

2nd Y. M.:   A troika of satanic foes to anything intelligent—

3rd Y. M.:   That's our Shishkov.

1st Y. M.:   Our Shakhovskoy.

2nd Y. M.:   Shikhmatov.

3rd Y. M.:   But of this banal and evil troika, who's the stupidest?

1st Y. M.:   Shishkov.

2nd Y. M.:   Shikhmatov.

3rd Y. M.:   Shakhovskoy.
[The GUEST, glancing spitefully at the archival youths,
walks by, thumping his stick.]98

1st Y. M.:   Here's one, a fan of epigrams,   EO 8, xxv, 1–8
             A gentleman who's always angry . . .

2nd Y. M.:   At the tea for being too sweet,
             At the banality of ladies, and the manners of the men . . .

3rd Y. M.:   At what that foggy novel might portend,
             And at the decorations on those maids-in-waiting . . .

4th Y. M.:   At the lies we meet in journals, at the war,
             The snow, his wife, and then . . .

1st Y. M.:   And then Prolasov, celebrated   8, xxvi, 1–4
             For the baseness of his soul,99

4th Y. M.:   And then . . . ., who's blunted
             Many a pencil in their albums.100
what   [In the depth of the hall, ONEGIN appears]
music?

1st Y. M.:   Could that be Onegin?   8, vii, 12–14

2nd Y. M.:   Yes—it's him for sure.

3rd Y. M.:   How long has he been back in town?

1st Y. M.:   Is he the same, or quieted down?   8, viii, 1–14
             Still playing the eccentric?

2nd Y. M.:   Tell me, what did he return as?
             How's he now present himself?

3rd Y. M.:   The going pose? Melmoth,[101]
              A cosmopolitan, perhaps, a patriot . . .

1st Y. M.:   *Childe-Harold*, Quaker, hypocrite,[102]
              Who knows? Perhaps some other mask . . .

VYAZEMSKY [coming up to them]
              But since you ask, could be, he's just a decent chap,
              Like you, like me, like everyone?

1st Y. M.:   That's my advice, at least:
              Give up a role, when it's outmoded.

PROLASOV [coming up to them, listening in and rubbing his
              hands] He's dirtied up the world enough.

VYAZEMSKY [to himself] Now our discussion will be livened up
              With all the salt of high-society malice.

PROLASOV: That's my advice, at least.

VYAZEMSKY [to PROLASOV] You know him?

PROLASOV [deferentially] Yes and no.

VYAZEMSKY: So why are you so rudely   8, ix, 1–14
              Sounding off about him?
              Just because we never cease to
              Pester and pass judgment on the world?
     [1st ARCHIVAL YOUTH, shrugging his shoulders, walks off]
              Because the rashness of an ardent heart
              Insults, or ridicules
              A smug, self-satisfied nonentity,
              Because our wide-ranging wit cramps us
     [2nd ARCHIVAL YOUTH also walks off]
              Or because, too often, conversations . . .

ANGRY GENTLEMAN [ironically bowing]
              We're delighted to accept in lieu of deeds . . .

VYAZEMSKY [heatedly] Because stupidity is evil and capricious,
              And because 'important people' find absurdity important,

Krzhizhanovsky/Pushkin

[Leaves the thinning group and heads for ONEGIN,
managing to shove and shoulder his way out]
And because it's only mediocrity
That suits us, and feels comfortably our own.
[Shaking ONEGIN's hand in a friendly fashion]
Returned, arrived . . .   8, xiii, 13–14

ONEGIN: Like Chatsky, from the ship directly to the ballroom.[103]

waltz | strings VYAZEMSKY: And travels . . .   8, xiii, 11–12
behind
the
scenes ONEGIN: . . . bored him
                Like all else on earth;
                And I began to wander without aim . . .[104]   xxiii, 9
                And everywhere a mercantile spirit   from OJ, ix, 13–14
                Bustles, fibs enough for two.
                How tedious!
                I saw the capricious Terek   OJ xii, 1–4
                Carving out its steep banks;
                A stag stood there, with antlers bent.

VYAZEMSKY: A mighty eagle soars before him

ONEGIN: We knew him to be very tame   fragment II from EO
                When it was not our cooks who   "chapter 10"
                Plucked the two-headed eagle
                Over Bonaparte's tent.[105]

VYAZEMSKY: And did you visit Tauris?   this line not in Pushkin
                Where Orestes argued with Pylades . . .   OJ xv, 9–10

ONEGIN: There Mithridates stabbed himself.

VYAZEMSKY: How beautiful you are, shores of the Tauris,   xvi, 1–4
                When one sees you from the ship,
                In the early-morning dawn, at Cypris,

ONEGIN: As I first saw you.
                And there's the eternal guard of wilderness   xiii, 1–9
                Compressed all around by hills,
                The sharp-peaked Beshtu,
                And the green Mashúk.

• 165 •

VYAZEMSKY: "   "
   Mashuk, the source of healing streams
   Around its magic brooks—

ONEGIN: A paling swarm of patients crowd;
   The victims of our martial honor.

VYAZEMSKY: [lowering his voice]
   Some from the Piles, some from Cypris
   How beautiful you are, shores of the Tauris . . .

ONEGIN: How come a bullet didn't wound me in the chest?   xiv, 6–8
   How come I'm not yet old, decrepit?
   How is it I've not yet felt a touch of rheumatism   xiv, 11–14
   In my shoulder?—Oh, Lord!
   I'm young, and life's robust in me;
   What's left for me to live for? Tedious! How tedious!

VYAZEMSKY: But who's not been addicted to strange dreams?[106]   EO 8, x, 5–6

ONEGIN: Who's not grown weary of the worldly mob—

VYAZEMSKY: Other days, other dreams;   OJ xvii, 10–14
   You've been subdued, the high-flown
   Fantasizing of my springtime;
   Into the poetic goblet
   I've mixed in a lot of water.

ONEGIN: But it's sad to think that youth   EO 8, xi, 1–8
   Was given us in vain,
   That we betrayed it every minute,
   That it duped us;
   That our best desires . . .

waltz

VYAZEMSKY: Our freshest dreams . . .

ONEGIN: Have rotted, and in rapid order,
   Like decaying leaves in autumn.
   At that time, I seemed to need   OJ xvii, 5–8
   The wilderness, the pearly rim of waves,[107]
   The clamor of the sea, the mounds of cliffs,
   And the ideal of a proud maiden.

[They go off to the side and sit down, back to the entrance]

minuet
slow
[From the central door, TATYANA with her husband, THE GENERAL. A murmur of admiration.]

image of
Tatyana
as given here
about 2 m(inutes)

VYAZEMSKY [turning around]

What's that? A tremor through the crowd, EO 8, xiv, 1–2
       A whisper running through the hall . . .
[ONEGIN doesn't turn around, he is sunk in his own thoughts]

begins in
full sound,
1st YOUNG MAN: Not cold, but not a chatterer. 8, xiv, 6–11

then returns
to the strings 2nd Y. M.:   With ne'er a haughty gaze for anyone.
to make
place for the 1st Y. M.:   Without pretenses to success.
conversations

2nd Y. M.:   Without those little grimaces.

3rd Y. M.:   Without those imitative tricks . . .
       Everything in her so quiet, and so simple.

1st Y. M.:   Quietly sat down and gazes around,
       Admiring the noisy throng,
       The flash of dresses. At the table 8, xvi, 9–13
       With the brilliant Nina Voronskáya,
       That Cleopatra of the north:[108]

2nd Y. M.:   You surely will agree
       That Nina, with her marble beauty
       Can't eclipse her neighbor.

[Both of his comrades bow their heads.]

DECREPIT DIGNITARY: [into the ear of the ANGRY GENTLEMAN,
       pointing to the young man who is gloomily
       leaning against the door, not taking his eyes off
       TATYANA] Some sort of mournful joker EO 7, xlix, 5–8
       Seems to find her
       [makes a gesture in TATYANA's direction]
       His ideal.

ANGRY GENTLEMAN: [also into his ear, but loudly and maliciously]

And, leaning up against the door,
Composes her an *elegy.*

VORONSKAYA: [to TATYANA, pointing to ONEGIN]
And who's that standing to the side,   EO 8, vii, 5–12
So silently, as if he's lost in fog?
He seems to everyone a stranger,
Faces flicker by him,
Like a series of tedious visions
What is it? Spleen, or martyred pride
In his expression? Why's he here?
And who is he?

TATYANA: [to herself] But could it really be Onegin?[109]

ONEGIN: [coming out of his reverie][110]
I was living then in dusty Odessa [notices TATYANA]   OJ xx, 1
And where this incoherent story's headed . . .   xxii, 1–4
I think I said: Odessa, dusty
But I could have said . . .

minuet   VYAZEMSKY: In muddy Odessa.
And truth be told, it wouldn't be a lie.

ONEGIN: But could it really be . . .

VYAZEMSKY: What's wrong, Yevgeniy?

ONEGIN: Is it really her? Precisely, yes . . . But no . . .   EO 8, xvii, 1–3
But how? From nowhere, that provincial village . . .

VYAZEMSKY: Oh, you know her?   8, xviii, 4

ONEGIN: I'm their neighbor.

VYAZEMSKY: Then let's go. There's not a word for it[111]—
Du comme il faut
. . . . (Shishkov, forgive: 8, xiv, 13–14
I don't know how to translate that.)[112]
[Takes ONEGIN by the arm, leads him to TATYANA and
her husband; ~~during this time, music sounds softly and
the moving couples are slowing down their steps.~~]
No one could find in her   8, xv, 11–14

A trace of what in highest London circles,
The all-powerful voice of fashion
Calls . . . . [113] I won't even try . . .
Defining it. Although I love the word,   8, xvi, 1–6
Translating it is hard.
The concept's still too new for us,
And scarcely could be used with style . . .

ANGRY GENTLEMAN [whom they are walking past]
But meanwhile, for an epigram, it fits.

VYAZEMSKY: [turning away from the unbidden interlocutor]
But let's go meet our lady.

repeat
waltz

[Leads ONEGIN to TATYANA and the GENERAL. ONEGIN
kisses the hand calmly held out to him, TATYANA
DMITRIEVNA's husband bows. The growing strains of
the music make their conversation inaudible. TATYANA is
completely calm. ONEGIN is at first embarrassed, then
becomes animated, but at just that moment a dancer
who had noiselessly flown up draws TATYANA into the
whirl of the dance. VYAZEMSKY goes off with the GENERAL.
ONEGIN remains alone beside TATYANA's empty easy-
chair. By a barely perceptible motion he gives a push to
the arm of the chair—perhaps it reminded him of the
"rehearsal" with the armchair-rocker—but the gilded
fauteuil stands firmly and motionless on its bent little
legs. Gradually the music quiets down and fades away.
But TATYANA does not return to her previous chair. A
dozen hands punctiliously move forward a chair for
her in another corner of the hall. Around her is a "dark
frame of men." In an unforced and calm manner she
responds to their obsequious bows and words. In the
group around TATYANA a conversation is going on,
apparently about ONEGIN.]

ANGRY GENTLEMAN: We're all looking to be Napoleons,   EO 2, xiv, 5–12
And those millions of two-legged creatures,
Are only tools for us:

1st Y. M.:   Feeling strikes us as wild and ridiculous

VYAZEMSKY: "He hastens to live, and hurries to feel."[114]
Yevgeniy was more tolerant than many,
Though, of course, he knew people well
And thus despised them;
But no rules exist without exceptions.

TATYANA: "   "[115]

VYAZEMSKY: [laughing]
Yes, pride, which forces him to confess his good
and his bad deeds with equal indifference, the
consequence . . . of a feeling of superiority . . . [116]

TATYANA: . . . perhaps imaginary.

[Laughter.]

ONEGIN: Who would have dared to seek that tender girl   EO 8, xxviii, 5–8
In this majestic, nonchalant
Lawgiver of the grand salon?
Could I have caused her heart to tremble,
Or perhaps . . .
The letter where her heart speaks out,   8, xx, 8–10
Where everything was full exposed, and offered freely,
That girl . . . or was it all a dream
"Already long ago . . . no, this was not a dream.   EO Tatyana's
As soon as you came in, I knew.   letter to Onegin
At once I froze, I flamed
And in my mind, I said: It's him."
[Wants to approach her, but at that very moment, the
1st ARCHIVAL YOUTH, to the strains of a ritornelle, quickly
flaring up and then fading away, invites her to dance.
ONEGIN returns to his previous place.]

triumphant
concluding
dance
(maybe
gliding)
but p[iano]

With what celestial pride   EO 7, lii, 9–12
She lights upon the ground.
What sensuous longing fills her breast
How languorous is her wondrous glance
She's suffocating here . . . for in her dreams,   7, liii, 7–8
She's yearning for a rural life
The twilight of the linden alleys,   7, liii, 13–14
For that place where he appeared to her.
Am I in love with her?

My God, that would be marvelous.
But stop, enough, enough.
You've paid your tribute to madness.[117]

This line not in Pushkin

7, lii, 13–14

**dance
grows up
to ff**

[Disappears in the crowd. First bars of a "Polish dance."]

Fragment 13

short pause

- - - - - - - - - - - - - - - - -

**intro
to bank
of Neva**

[The Neva embankment. A cast-iron grating. Along the bank the infrequent light of lanterns. On the far side of the river, barely visible through the fog, the contours of long houses. The first signs of dawn: the stars are already dimmed, but the lanterns are still burning. On the parapet, the black figure of a man in an overcoat. He is turned with his back to the audience. This is ONEGIN.]

ONEGIN: She doesn't notice me
No matter how I try.[118]
Freely she receives me in her home,
Elsewhere in company she'll utter a few words,
At other times, just meets me with a bow,
Sometimes she doesn't notice me at all.
And how she is surrounded
By a Twelfthtide coldness.
Where is her confusion, her compassion?
Where the stain of tears? There are none.
No answer. So I sent another letter:
And a second, and a third,
No answer.

EO 8, xxxi, 1–6

8, xxxiii, 7–8, 12–13, 1–3

[The voices of the night watchmen call out to one another; the distant rattle of carriages; through the fog, perhaps the flapping wings of some gigantic bird, perhaps the splash of oars; a horn and a distant, barely perceptible song.]

And in my silent study
I recalled the time
When cruel melancholy
Stalked me in the noisy world,
And grabbed me, took me by the collar,

8, xxxiv, 9–14

Locked me in a dismal corner.
I began to read, without discrimination.   8, xxxv, 1–4
I read Gibbon and Rousseau,
Manzoni, Herder, Chamfort
Madame de Staël, Bichat, Tisseau.[119]
And what of it? My eyes were reading   8, xxxvi, 1–14
But my thoughts were far away,
My dreams, desires, and sadness
Crowded deeply in my soul.[120]
I read between the printed lines
Other lines, with spiritual eyes. . . .   omits line 8 of Pushkin
These were the secret legends
Of the heart's dark, ancient life,
And dreams, unlinked and incoherent,
Threats, rumors, and predictions,
Or the lively nonsense of a lengthy fairy tale,
Or else a young girl's letter.

[Around the time of the final lines, a LANTERN-MAN
appears; he carries on his shoulder a stepladder, in his
hands a stick with an extinguisher. The lanterns—one
after another—are put out. From the opposite side, coming closer and closer, drunken but harmonious singing. A
group of LYCEE STUDENTS appears, apparently returning
from their all-night revels. They are walking with arms
around one another, with a step that is not entirely steady.
But their song steps firmly from bar to bar.]

SONG OF THE CAROUSING STUDENTS

**perhaps
of a somewhat
German type**

Friends, our leisure hour has come,
All is quiet, all is peaceful,
Quick: the tablecloth and goblet:
Bring the golden wine.

**perhaps
bravura-
sentimental?**

Bubble up, champagne in the carafe,
Friends, why Kant, why
Seneca or Tacitus; the table's not for that;
Book on top of book.

Under the table [with] those cold wise men,
We own the field,

> Under the table with those learned fools,
> We'll drink without them.
> Friends, our leisure hour has come . . .[121]

[The students and the song grow more distant]

ONEGIN: [Following them with his eyes, into the fog of
the river and reminiscences]
"Friends, our leisure hour has come"
Enemies, have you long been divided?[122]   EO 6, xxviii, 1
"Quick, the tablecloth and goblet"
Is it long since we, in leisure hours   6, xxviii, 3–6
At the dining table, shared in friendly ways
Our thoughts and deeds. Today, maliciously,
Resembling blood foes
Four paces we traversed,   6, xxx, 4–8
Four fatal steps.
And you, Yevgeniy, were the first,
Quietly, not ceasing your advance
To raise your pistol.
And I see: upon the melting snow   8, xxxvii, 5–14
As if he'd gone to sleep there for the night,
The youth lies motionless.
I hear a voice: What happened? Dead.
I see forgotten enemies,
Ill-wishing slanderers and cowards,
And the swarm of women who've betrayed me,
And a circle of despised acquaintants,
And then: a rural home—and by the window
She sits . . . always she . . .

Tatyana's music

[His elbows fall on the railing of the cast-iron grating.
At this time, gliding along the parapet in an absolutely
inaudible gait, the POET and TWO PEOPLE appear. They
stop in the distance.]

POET: With a heart full of regrets,   EO 1, xlviii, 1–14
Leaning against the granite wall
Yevgeniy stood, thoughtfully,
As once one Poet had described himself.[123]
Everything was quiet; only the night

Watchmen called to one another;
And the distant clatter of the carriages
Would suddenly sound forth from Million Street;
Or a boat, dipping its oars,
Floated in the drowsing river:
And from afar, a horn and rousing song
Captivated us.
But sweeter still, as nighttime reveling,
Were Tasso's octaves.[124]

1st: [as a point of information]
At first Onegin's tongue   1, xlvi, 10–14
Embarrassed me; but soon I grew accustomed to
His poisonous quarreling,
His jokes, half mixed with bile,
And to the malice of his gloomy epigrams.

POET: But was Yevgeniy happy,   1, xxxvi, 9, 12
Midst these daily pleasures?

2nd : [deferentially]
Onegin was prepared to see   1, li, 1–4
The world of foreign lands with me;
But soon fate separated us
And for a long time.

POET: [turning away sharply]   1, l, 1–14
And will the hour of my freedom ever come?[125]
It's time, it's time!—I summon it:
I wander by the seashore, wait for favorable weather,
Beckon to each passing sail.
When, battling with the storm and cresting waves
Will I begin my unencumbered flight
Upon the open crossroad of the sea?
It's time to quit this tedious shore,
The elements are hostile to me here,
And then, amid the southern waves,
Beneath the skies of Africa, my Africa,
To sigh and pine for gloomy Russia,
    [He glances at ONEGIN]
Where I suffered, where I loved,
Where I interred my heart.

music

[In the distance: the resonant, nervous rat-a-tat beating of
a drum; then the sound comes closer; and then it is utterly
up close.]

POET: [departing into the shadows]   1, xxxv, 1–4
          So what's with my Onegin?
          [His companions bow at the sound of his voice.]

1st: Half-asleep.
          He goes to bed directly from the ball:

2nd: And tireless Petersburg's   1, xxxv, 3–4
          Already woken by the drum.

ALL THREE: Already woken by the drum.
          [They disappear]

[The drum rumbles at the very edge of the stage.
A watchman with a *hallebarde* crawls out of a striped booth;
he yawns and squints, shielding his eyes with his palm
from the first rays of the sun glinting off the spire
of Peter and Paul Fortress. ONEGIN lifts his head. Was this
the dream of a character about his own author, or an
illusion born of the pre-dawn Petersburg fog? That fog
still slides along the river, and after it, as if in pursuit, a
light, rapid white sail sets out.]

**perhaps
develop**   ONEGIN: And by the window   8, xxxvii, 13–14
Tatyana's   *She* sits. Always she.
theme
and not city [The awakening of the city: in space and in the orchestra.]

Fragment 14

- - - - - - - - - - - - - - - -

[A drawing room in the house of TATYANA DMITRIEVNA's husband. TATYANA DMITRIEVNA, no, Tanya, the previous Tanya, in
simple clothes, carelessly thrown over her shoulders, sits at the
window, on a spacious ottoman placed up against the windowsill.
Close to her, lying on her knees, is a little chest, which the
spectator will perhaps remember among the few objects from

the young TATYANA's bedroom.

Although the huge Venetian window is curtained,[126] through the transparent fabric, slanting upwards, rays of the morning sun still push through. The princess moves aside the window curtain and opens the window slightly. Noises follow immediately after the sun rays.]

TATYANA: And tireless Petersburg,   EO 1, xxxv, 3–11
Already woken by the drum.
The merchant's up, the peddler's at his rounds,
pantomime   The cabbie rushes to the stock exchange,
The milkmaid hurries with her pitcher,
Under her, the morning snow crackles.
The pleasant sounds of morning have awoken,
Shutters open; pale-blue smoke in pillars
Rises up from chimneys.

music   [She turns away, covers up the window]
1 min.   switches
to   But I need other pictures: OJ xviii, 1–7
rural   Steep and sandy hills are what I love,
A hut, two mountain ash in front of it,
The fence, a broken lock,
Gray cloudlets in the sky,
The threshing hut, and piles of hay,
A pond beneath thick willows . . .
The countryside is better, our poor villagers,   EO 7, liii, 9–14
The isolated corner,
Where a limpid brook flows forth;
My flowers, and my novels,
And the shaded path of linden trees,
Where he . . .

[She rummages in her little chest; takes out medallions, a little book; TATYANA spreads her reminiscence objects over the flat flowers of the ottoman. These objects form an enchanted circle around her, as it were, which separates her from the accoutrements of her wealth and rank. Allowing herself to be drawn in to these embodied memories, shifting them around from place to place, TATYANA plays a mysterious game with them, one known only to them and to her. On her lips, a smile and a quiet refrain.]

I love you all sincerely;

But I'm given to another
For all time. Most dear of all to me
Is Prince . . .
[Suddenly ONEGIN enters, with quick steps; he is carrying
his top hat in his hands, his overcoat draped over his elbow.
At first he gazes at TATYANA silently. Coming up to the edge
of the ottoman, precisely as if his knees were broken, he
bows to her; his overcoat falls on top of the bright flowers
on the ottoman. A moment's pause.]

ONEGIN: I foresee everything: this explanation   EO 8, opening of
Of my mournful secret is an insult   Onegin's letter to
To you: and what bitter scorn   Tatyana
Your haughty glance may well express.
But so be it: I am myself   Onegin's letter, 57–60
Unable to resist it further;
All is settled: I am in your power,
My fate is in your hands.

[His glance, which rises to meet her eyes, meets in
them no disdain, only a question.]

If you could only know how terrible it is   45–52
To languish in the thirst of love,
To burn—and every moment, with one's reason
To subdue the agitation of the blood!
And to desire so madly to embrace your knees
And sobbing, at your feet,
To pour out my appeals, confessions, plaints,
All, all I could express.

TATYANA: Enough. Get up. I too owe you   EO 8, xlii, 8–14
An explanation, and an honest one.
Onegin, can you now recall
That hour in the garden, on the country path,
Where fate brought us together, and how humbly
I heard out your lecture?
Today the turn is mine.
Onegin, I was younger then,   8, xliii, 1–14
And better too, it seems.
I loved you—and what happened?
What did I discover in your heart?

What answer? Harshness only.
Certainly, for you, it was no novelty,
A humble maiden's love.
And even now—my god—my blood runs cold,
When I recall that chilly look,
That sermon . . . But I do not blame you;
In that awful hour,
You behaved in honorable fashion,
You were fully in the right before me:
And I'm grateful to the bottom of my heart . . .
Back then—you must admit—in those backwoods   8, xliv, 1–14
So far from Moscow's vanities,
You weren't attracted to me. So why now
Are you pursuing me?
And pay me such attention?
Might it be because I'm now obliged
To show myself in high society,
Because I'm wealthy and of noble rank,
Because my husband's battle wounds are prized
And for that reason we are loved at court?
Or maybe this: that my disgrace,
Which everyone would notice, would bestow on you
Seductive honor in society's eyes?

ONEGIN: How stubbornly your lips   8, xxxiii, 9–10
            Would like to check their indignation!

TATYANA: I'm weeping . . . if you've not forgotten yet   8, xlv, 1–14,
            Your Tanya, then know: skips lines 5, 8–10
            The sharpness of your keen reproach,
            That cold, stern conversation—
            All of that I would prefer to this offensive passion,
            With its letters and its tears.
            Today—what brought you
            To my feet? What pettiness of spirit!
            How could a person of your heart and mind
            Be slave to trivial feeling!

ONEGIN: I know: my days are numbered   Onegin's letter, 37–40
            But in order to prolong my life,
            I must be certain in the morning
            That I'll see you, sometime, later in the day . . .

TATYANA: For me, Onegin, all this luxury,   EO 8, xlvi, 1–14
The tinsel of a hateful life,
My triumphs in the whirlwind of society,
My fashionable home, all these soirées,
What for? I'd gladly give them up,
The whole of this bedraggled masquerade,
This glitter, noise, and fumes,
And trade it for a shelf of books, untended garden,
And our humble dwelling,
For those places where, Onegin,
First I saw you,
For the humble churchyard cemetery
Where a cross and shadowing branches
Bends today over my poor Nurse . . .

ONEGIN: . . . . In the shade of two ancient pines   EO 7, vi, 9–12
A gravestone speaks to passersby:[127]
"Here lies Vladimir Lensky
Who died the early death of the courageous,"
And then a country house, and at the window   EO 8, xxxvii, 13–14
She sits . . . always she.

TATYANA: Yet happiness had been so possible!   8, xlvii, 1–14
So close! But now my fate's
Decided. Possibly I acted rashly.
Mother begged me, with such tears, such pleading,
And for wretched Tanya,
All lots were the same . . .
I married. And you must, I beg you,
Leave me.
I am sure that in your heart
There is both pride and earnest honor.
Why should I dissemble? I love you,
But I am given to another,
And to him I shall be true forever.

[She rises and slowly walks out, stepping among the
flat flowers of the ottoman meadow. The flowers on their
spiral steel stems scarcely feel the touch of her foot.
ONEGIN stands there, silently bowed.
Near the exit, but still in the door, he runs into the

POET; the POET makes way for ONEGIN and watches him
leave, standing with his back to the footlights.]

POET: Blessed is he, who leaves the feast of life   8, li: 9–14
Early, without having drained to the bottom
His goblet of wine;
Blessed is he who did not read life's novel to the end,
But who at once, for good, withdrew
As I from my Onegin do.

- - - - - " „ " - - - - -

NOTES ON THE TRANSLATION

For poetic and scholarly aid on this annotated translation, I gratefully acknowledge my two
Princeton colleagues and fellow Pushkinists, Michael Wachtel and Olga Peters Hasty.

1. The Prologue, present in this second version of the text but already deleted from the third (RGALI
f. 2579, op. 1, yed. khr. 2054), splices together two texts. The opening comes from Pushkin's verse dialogue
in rhyming iambic pentameter, "Conversation of a Bookseller with a Poet" ("Razgovor knigoprodavtsa s poe-
tom"), written on September 6, 1824, and published as a preface to the first chapter of *Eugene Onegin* in 1825.
The opening exchange is followed by segments from *Eugene Onegin*, working backward (stanzas from chapters 8, 2, 1) and punctuated by leading questions from the Bookseller. The final portion of the Prologue picks
up the "Conversation" again with the Bookseller's riposte, and continues (with a cut of six lines) to the Poet's
final capitulation in a crassly prosaic line. The Bookseller is modeled on the influential Smirdin's Booksellers
and Publishers in St. Petersburg (A. F. Smirdin was the first Russian book trader to pay authors high fees for
their work, enabling serious writers to turn an avocation into a legitimate profession; Pushkin drove a hard
bargain and, for the era, was well compensated for his work).
2. In January 1815, when Pushkin was sixteen and in his fourth year of the lycée, he recited his
"Recollections in Tsarskoye Selo" ("Vospominaniya v Tsarskom Sele") at a school examination before the grand
old man of eighteenth-century Russian letters, Gavrila Derzhavin (1743–1816). Ilya Repin immortalized the
event as a rite of passage—for Pushkin and for Russian poetry—in an oil-on-canvas painting, *Pushkin at the
Lycée Examination*, 1911.
3. The heroine of the gothic Romantic ballad *Lenore* (1773) by the German poet Gottfried Bürger (1747–94),
which was imitated by the Russian poet Vasily Zhukovsky (1783–1852) in his ballads *Lyudmila* (1808) and
Svetlana (1812). See the long gloss on the Lenore reference in Aleksandr Pushkin, *Eugene Onegin: A Novel in
Verse*, trans. Vladimir Nabokov, paperback edition in 2 vols. (Princeton: Princeton University Press, 1975),
2:152–54. Nabokov's translation is not an aesthetic success (nor was it intended as such); the commentary,
however, remains indispensable for its droll wit and encyclopedic knowledge of European poetry. This volume is henceforth referred to in the notes as VN EO 2, followed by page number and, where relevant, Pt. 2
(vol. 3 in the original 1964 hardcover edition of Nabokov's *Eugene Onegin* project).
4. A situation rhyme answering EO 1, l, 1:"Will the hour of my freedom ever come?" (Pridyot li chas
moyey svobodï?). This Poet, a transitory embodiment of the *Eugene Onegin* Narrator, will be brought back in
Fragment 13 to confront a nostalgic, lovestruck Onegin who has unexpectedly rediscovered his Muse.
5. Dmitri Larin, of brigadier rank, must have won this medal during General Suvorov's Turkish campaign of 1788, when the small, fortified Moldavian town of Oczakow forty miles from Odessa was successfully
stormed (and three years later became Russian territory). See VN EO 2:305.
6. Lensky recites here Pushkin's own 1821 lyric "I have outlived all my desires" (Ya perezhil svoi zhe-
laniya), rather than the artificed and cliché-ridden verse for Lensky we find in EO 6, xxi ("Whither, whither are

you fled" [Kuda, kuda vï udalilis']), surely in part to avoid Tchaikovsky's famous setting of this lyric in the opera. Lensky's self-corrections in line 3 are authentically Pushkin's: the 1821 manuscript variant reads "cold sufferings" (khladnïye stradan'ya) rather than the "only sufferings" (odni stradaniya) of the 1823 published text. See Pushkin, *Polnoye sobraniye sochineniy*, ed. V. D. Bonch-Bruyevich et al., 19 vols. (1937–49; reprint, Moscow: Voskresen'ye, 1994), 2:151, for the published 1823 text and 2b:587 for the 1821 text (subtitled "An Elegy"). Henceforth this Jubilee Pushkin is referred to as P:Pss followed by volume and page.

7. This deletion accords with Pushkin's actual revisions as preserved in the earlier drafts. Line 6 of the 1821 draft reads "I live forgotten indifferent / I await sad . . ." (Zhivu zabïtïy ravnodushnïy / I zhdu pechal'nïkh dney konets [I await the end of sad days]); in the 1823 published version it reads "I live sad, lonely" (Zhivu pechal'nïy, odinokoy). The more neutral "awaiting the end of sad days" is replaced by the unambiguously minor-key "I wait: Will my end come?" See P:Pss 2b:587.

8. The final quatrain reads: "Thus, struck by the late cold / The wintry whistling of a storm is heard, / And on the naked branch / trembles one tardy leaf" (Tak, pozdnim khladom porazhennïy, / Kak buri slïshen zimniy svist, / Odin na vetke obnazhennïy / Trepeshchet zapozdalïy list).

9. Nabokov discusses this "glorious champagne" Aï and wine-drinking imagery as a metaphor for political rebellion in VN EO 2:480–84. He considers this stanza xlv and the subsequent xlvi to be "very poor, bubbling with imported platitudes" (483).

10. The setting is inspired by the final stanzas of EO 4, xliv–xlvii. Krzhizhanovsky uses the stage direction to communicate a huge amount of physical detail (furniture, weather, feelings, placement of bodies and things) that Pushkin's Narrator reveals to the reader; but of equal status in the stage direction is sentient Nature, often intensified beyond what the Narrator relates, and which tells its own mute, truthful story outdoors.

11. Lensky, in his role as the younger real-life poet Pushkin, begins to read to Onegin from a portion of *Eugene Onegin* that in 1825 had not yet been written: the beginning of EO 8, i, 1–12.

12. Here Krzhizhanovsky begins to seed the 1833 Pushkin "Fairy Tale of the Dead Tsarevna and the Seven Knights" (Skazka o myortvoy tsarevne i o semi bogatïryakh) that Tatyana will prompt her Nurse to retell during the Letter Scene (Fragment 5). Yelisey is the rescuing tsarevich.

13. Lensky stubbornly corrects Onegin *back* to Pushkin's canonical text. The name of the fairy tale "Prince Yelisey" does not turn up in the rough drafts for these lines, but there is a hint of equivalently elicit, secretive "light" reading substituting for the stern assigned classics like Cicero: "When I read Apuleius *on the sly* . . ." (Kogda *ukradkoy* Apuleya . . .). Draft from December 1829, in P:Pss 6:619.

14. Instead of "cursed" (*proklinal*), EO 8, i, 4 has "didn't read" (*ne chital*), as per Lensky's immediate correction of his friend. "Cursed" is an option in an early draft variant of this stanza; see P:Pss 6:507.

15. Here Krzhizhanovsky skips back to the introduction of Lensky, EO 2, xii, 9–12, with Olga's name substituted for Dunya's.

16. "Phyllis" (Fillida): according to Nabokov, "the beloved maiden of 'Arcadian' poetry, pastorals and the like, presupposing a bucolic space-time within which refined shepherds and shepherdesses tend immaculate flocks amid indestructible meadow flowers and make sterile love in shady bosquets near murmuring rills" (VN EO 2:322). Virgil's ten *Eclogues*, one source for this image, were immensely popular among Romantic poets.

17. The first indication in the play that Onegin's fussy, dandified Petersburg persona described in EO ch. 1, xxv (his three hours daily before the mirror; "a Venus in male attire") will be reproduced in the countryside. See also n. 31.

18. "She was a young girl, [thus] she was in love" is Pushkin's epigraph to chapter 3, taken from "Narcisse, ou l'île de Vénus" (1768) by Jacques Malfilâtre (1733–67).

19. In the third variant (page 7), this stylized, technological reference to the "scenic cube" is deleted and a more conventional, impersonal opening stage direction is written in Tairov's hand (in pencil): "The countryside. Evening. In the distance, singing and a harmonica." The later playscript exhibits a general tendency to remove Krzhizhanovsky's special intonation from the stage directions (his geometric vision as well as his trademark "animation" of chairs, metronomic rocking and pacing, etc.), returning them to a more lyrical evocation of Chekhov. At times, Krzhizhanovsky writes his details back in (in ink).

20. The following conversation is anachronistic; it occurs at the end of chapter 7 of Pushkin's *Eugene Onegin*, after Olga is already married.

21. An early first reference to the provincial squire and rejected suitor Buyanov, a fictional rake well known in Pushkin's time who will be embodied as an unpleasant proto-Gogolian figure in Fragment 7. His full genealogy is provided in n. 38.

22. Krzhizhanovsky compresses here, from two stanzas early in chapter 2, the major eighteenth-century literary influences on Tatyana, the heroines and antiheroes by whom she lives: Clarissa Harlowe from Samuel Richardson's epistolary novel *Clarissa* (1747–48); Julie from Rousseau's *Julie, ou La Nouvelle Héloïse* (1761); Delphine d'Albémar, the "21-year-old widow working her way through a love affair" in Mme de Staël's novel *Delphine* (1802); Malek-Adhel, dashing, ethnically Moslem hero of Sophie Cottin's novel *Mathilde* (1805); de Linar from Mme de Krüdener's *Valérie, ou Lettres de Gustave de Linar à Ernest de G.* (1803). Werther is the hero of Goethe's sentimental romance *Die Leiden des jungen Werthers* (1774), later a model for the Byronic hero. Grandison is the virtuous hero of Richardson's epistolary novel *Sir Charles Grandison* (1753), who rescues his beloved from abduction by a scoundrel but remains true to his own troth to another woman. The vampire could be generic, or a reference to *The Vampyre, a Tale* (1819), by Byron's physician Dr John William Polidori. The Wandering Jew was a pan-European motif, rather popular among Pushkin and his generation of poets. The diabolical Melmoth is hero of the gothic novel *Melmoth the Wanderer* (1820) by Charles Robert Maturin, widespread in Russia in French translation. Byron published his poem *The Corsair* in 1813. Sbogar is the mysterious Italian-Dalmatian brigand of the short French novel *Jean Sbogar* (1818), by Charles Nodier. See Nabokov's vastly entertaining annotation on these characters and novels, VN EO 2:338–59, where *Julie* is declared to be "total trash" (339), *Mathilde* a "completely dead novel" (342), *Delphine* "not endurable" and surely not a text Pushkin would have foisted on his Tatyana (348). Several details from this list merit noting. First, the novels are extremely long and reading them attentively could easily have filled up Tatyana's whole life. *Clarissa*, the longest novel in the English language, weighs in at one million words, and *Julie* stretches out to six volumes. Second: in most of the novels, letters exchanged between lovers play a huge role, both thematically and structurally. Tatyana's letter to Onegin is a natural outgrowth of such an education. And lastly: these heroines, for all their steamy rhetoric and exposure to seduction, ultimately remain as faithful to their respective husbands as does the married Princess Tatyana.

23. In Pushkin's *Eugene Onegin*, this conversation takes place in a carriage. Note Onegin's rocker (and in general Onegin's, and Krzhizhanovsky's, attention to the rocking, shifting, or undulating legs of chairs), whose movement will project increasingly to the audience the "pulse" of the hero's state of mind and his fluctuating ability to control it.

24. Svetlana is the heroine of Zhukovsky's *Svetlana*. Thematically and perhaps also formally, the ballad left several traces on *Eugene Onegin*, especially its silent, sad heroine by the window who divines her future and conjures up her lover. There is this crucial difference, however: Svetlana daydreams, or fantasizes, a gothic death scene (cemeteries, ghosts) which is then dispelled blissfully, almost comically, when her lover returns after a year's absence. This will not be Tatyana's fate.

25. These lines belong to the Narrator in Pushkin's *Eugene Onegin*, and some delicacy was required to create an utterance spoken by Tatyana about herself, albeit privately to the moon. Since "soul" and "eyes" in Russian require no modifying possessives, the "her" → "my" shift is automatic once the speaker changes. Otherwise Krzhizhanovsky has simply omitted phrases cast in the third person.

26. The sentiment is strikingly similar to the final line Princess Tatyana will deliver to Onegin at the end of the novel/play. This folklore text—in addition to that mass of eighteenth- and early nineteenth-century sentimental novels detailed in n. 22 above—is key to Krzhizhanovsky's understanding of Pushkin's view of fate and Tatyana's psychology. Both entail a peculiar version of fidelity: technically faithful to her husband and at the same time faithful to the unsullied *image* of her first love.

27. Recall that Onegin himself mentions reading about this folklore prince to Lensky in Fragment 2—when he should have been attending to his Cicero assignment—so now four people are aware of this fairy tale as a subtext for the drama.

28. In Krzhizhanovsky's initial version, Tatyana composes her letter on the bench in the garden, only later returning to her room to write it down. This was one means of differentiating the playscript from Tchaikovsky's most famous set pieces (such as the Letter Scene), a priority of Prokofiev's from the start.

29. In rural Russian homesteads, the night watchman did his rounds by rattling or tapping with a metal rod, an aural backdrop that became famous through the theater of Chekhov.

30. All but the first word of this stage direction is unreadably faint in this variant of the playscript. The line was deciphered with the help of a third archival variant (RGALI f. 2579, op. 1, yed. khr. 2054, p. 18): "Nervno perestavlyayet bezdelushki na stole." Tatyana rearranging tiny physical objects to express anxiety or fantasy will become an important motif in Fragment 14, and exemplifies this playwright's personification of the well-placed thing.

31. This stage direction recapitulates the mock-ironic list of equipment required for Onegin's high-society toilette in EO 1, xxiii–xxiv. That opening Petersburg chapter is not included in the playscript; Krzhizhanovsky's Fragment 1 is already in the countryside. Onegin's dandified cosmetic ritual, the "three hours at least / spent before the mirror" (EO 1, xxv, 9–10) is much emphasized by the Narrator in chapter 1, creating the Narcissus subtext, but it becomes far less prominent as Onegin (and his author) mature during the 1820s. Both the ritual and the personnel required to sustain it are out of place in a rural setting.

32. In Pushkin's *Eugene Onegin* this is the Narrator's reminiscence about his own experience, *not* Onegin's, and it comes *before* Tatyana's letter.

33. This "rehearsal" episode is one of the very few stage directions that communicate thoughts, anxieties, and in this instance even the vexed inner dialogue of a character. As a rule, Krzhizhanovsky's stage directions are limited to physical layout and the movement of objects, sounds, and light.

34. The typed playscript ends on line 11; Prokofiev writes under it Pushkin's line 12: "S takim umom ko mne pisali."

35. The November frosts, first snows, and wines featured in this Fragment are all taken from seven lyrical stanzas in EO 4, xl–xlvii that praise late autumn and early winter, Pushkin's favorite time of year.

36. Here Prokofiev forgot to correct *waltz* to *polka*.

37. Pushkin's text is altered to remove "Tatyana speaks" (Tatyana govorit).

38. Pushkin notes the arrival of this Name Day guest in EO 5, xxvi, 9: "My cousin, Buyanov" (Moy brat dvoyurodnïy, Buyanov), later (xliv) assigning to this "mischievous brother of mine, Buyanov" (Buyanov, bratets moy zadornïy) the task of leading the sisters Tatyana and Olga up to Onegin—where Onegin, fatefully, invites Olga to dance. Buyanov (Mr. Rowdy) is hero of the racy, 154-line narrative poem *The Dangerous Neighbor* (*Opasnïy sosed*) by Pushkin's paternal uncle Vasily Lvovich Pushkin (1770–1830), a very minor poet whose legacy is largely this one scandalous work. It circulated in manuscript in 1811 and became widely known by heart. In his gloss (VN EO 2:524–26), Nabokov summarizes the plot: Buyanov "invites the narrator to a bawdyhouse to sample a young whore, Varyushka, who, however, turns out to be poxy, according to an older female with whom the narrator eventually retires" (525). Nabokov, too, is impressed that this rake is allowed to seek Tatyana's hand "and to be mentioned by the mother as a possible candidate." As Fragment 7 will suggest, what for Pushkin might have been an affectionate tribute to his mediocre uncle becomes for Krzhizhanovsky's fragile, exposed Tatyana, stripped of Pushkin's protective Narrator, a far more sinister presence—and option.

39. This line is from "Triquet's Song," mentioned in EO 5, xxvii, 8, and set to music by Tchaikovsky. See Nabokov's gloss in VN EO 2:527–30: the quoted song, very popular in Russia, is "one of many imitations of *La Belle Dormeuse* (c. 1710) attributed to Charles Rivière Dufresny (1648–1724)" (527–28). Characteristic of Nabokov's disdain for the operatic *Eugene Onegin* is his comment (530): "It is typical of Chaykovsky's slapdash opera *Eugene Onegin* that *his* Triquet sings a totally different tune."

40. Zaretsky is not among the Name Day guests in chapter 5 of Pushkin's novel; he is introduced only in chapter 6.

41. The *he* of the Narrator is here replaced by an *I*, since Zaretsky is providing a capsule profile of himself. Such transfers from the Narrator's zone to the mouth of the subject, necessary for performed drama, increase the stylized, quasi-grotesque and "self-advertising" flavor of these Gogolian characters.

42. Zizi Vulf (1809–83), youngest daughter of Pushkin's closest Mikhailovskoye neighbors, the Osipovs. Nabokov claims that in 1825, the fifteen-year-old Zizi was rather plump. Pushkin's likening of her to a wine-glass is an off-color joke (VN EO 2:535).

43. These sentiments are spoken by the novel's Narrator *after* the duel.

44. These two buffoons divide up lines from the "pedal digression" in chapter 1 of Pushkin's *Eugene Onegin*.

45. The Narrator's affectionate but ironic introduction of Zaretsky to the reader in EO 6, iv is now addressed to Zaretsky face-to-face by Onegin himself—thus adding considerable irony and rudeness.

46. Missing is the end of the sentence (continuing into stanza vii, 1–2): "Or force them to be reconciled / To have breakfast together, all three" (Il' pomirit'sya zastavit', / Dabï pozavtrakat' vtroyom)—because reconciliation is precisely what Zaretsky, dueling pedant, failed to do, despite a number of procedural irregularities that could have given grounds for the duel to be canceled on a technicality, without dishonor to either party. Zaretsky's irresponsible and sinister underseam (like Buyanov's) is revealed once he is stripped of Pushkin's congenial Narrator.

47. Here Zaretsky performs the Narrator's quasi-parodic function of introducing the rural gentry at the Name Day party. These are "speaking names" in the style of eighteenth-century comic drama (Pustyakov from *pustoy*, empty; Gvozdin from *gvozd*, nail; Petushkov from *petukh*, rooster). Skotinin (Mr. Pig, Mr. Brute) is the buffoon villain uncle from Fonvizin's 1779 prose comedy *The Minor* (*Nedorosl'*) who pursues the virtuous heroine Sofya; he was notoriously fertile. Although here in the comic mode, these beastly names connect the Name Day guests with the Mummers and Tatyana's dream.

48. The following scene is adapted from EO 4, xxix–xxxiv, a lyric digression on poetic genres (the age of the ode versus the age of the madrigal), which Krzhizhanovsky was eager to see onstage. But we get only its cynical end.

49. Here Olga recites to Onegin what Pushkin's Narrator addresses to the *reader*. Together with interjections from an insulted and irritated Lensky, the "formal" debate over album verse becomes a war zone of flirtation and jealousy in the Olga/Lensky/Onegin triangle—and an active trigger for the duel.

50. The ellipses replace the French in EO 4, xxviii, 10: "Qu'écrirez-vous sur ses tablettes." Possible reasons for the omission of French lines (here and elsewhere) include: 1) Russian actors who did not or could not read foreign alphabets/languages; 2) a prohibition against non-USSR languages on the stage; 3) Krzhizhanovsky or the typist did not have access to a foreign (i.e. Latin-alphabet) typewriter and intended to write in the phrase later by hand. The third reason is by far the most likely: Latin-letter keyboards were in short supply in the 1930s.

51. The ellipses here replace Pushkin's line 11:"t. à v. Annette."

52. In Pushkin's *Eugene Onegin*, Onegin's seduction of Olga begins in chapter 5 with "The odd fellow . . . was already angry . . . he began to pout, and fuming mad / Swore he would drive Lensky into a rage / Thus avenging himself properly" (Chudak . . . uzh bïl serdit . . . Nadulsya on i negoduya, / Poklyalsya Lenskogo vzbesit' / I uzh poryadkom otomstit').

53. Precisely as Olga and Onegin glide by Lensky, the mazurka turns into Prokofiev's *tram-blyam* "harpsichord waltz." This moment marks Tatyana's ultimate humiliation and degradation, by Onegin and by her own sister.

54. In Pushkin's *Eugene Onegin*, this line begins with "He thinks" (On mïslit).

55. These lines lack Pushkin's famous concluding couplet: "And what this means, friends / Is that I'm exchanging shots with my friend" (Vsyo eto znachilo, druz'ya: / S priyatelem strelyayus' ya), which is spoken by the Narrator. In its place we have (with minor adjustment) the couplet that ends chapter 5: "And he gallops off. A pair of pistols, / two bullets—and nothing more" (I skachet. Pistoletov para. / Dve puli—bole nichego—). The play shears off a night and a day—or rather, gives the night wholly to Tatyana and her dream.

56. In Pushkin's *Eugene Onegin*, this final couplet occurs as Lensky is taking leave of a carefree Olga on the evening before the duel (the day after the Name Day fiasco). When Prokofiev recycled the *Eugene Onegin* dance music into the ball scenes of his opera *War and Peace*, he preserved its distinctive dramatic economy: a condensation of chronological time and seductive energy around a sequence of dance rhythms.

57. In Pushkin's *Eugene Onegin* these two lines are in the third person.

58. The Mummers are Prokofiev's rustic alternative to Tchaikovsky's Triquet (compare the analogous replacement of a high-society orchestra with out-of-tune harpsichords and a military band).

59. This bland text was eventually replaced by a longer, more vigorous ditty, leading directly into the grotesquerie of the dream (although on page 36 of the third archival variant the original is still in place). The new text was one that Pushkin jotted down sometime between 1825 and 1834 in a notebook of folk song verse. It roughly translates as: "He's like a pole, his head's a pestle, ears like little scissors, hands like little rakes, legs like little forks, eyes like little holes [repeat]; nightingale eyes are gazing from the tops of trees, they want porridge. The porridge was boiled up yesterday and was eaten up yesterday [repeat]; [. . .] the nose from bruises, that's the matchmaker's son." Krzhizhanovsky/Prokofiev omitted the grim penultimate couplet: "The neck is gleaming bluely / as if it had been in a noose." The text is preserved in Pyotr Kireyevsky's archive of recopied Pushkin folksongs. See A. D. Soymonov, "Pesni, sobrannïye pisatelyami. Novïye materialï iz arkhiva P. V. Kireyevskogo," in *Literaturnoye nasledstvo*, vol. 79 (Moscow: Institut literaturï Akademii nauk SSSR, 1968), 205–6.

60. The *tragizm* (tragic quality) noted by Prokofiev recalls the emotional low points of classic "happy ending" fairy tales like *Cinderella*. The model for Tatyana is not, however, Cinderella but the title character of the Russian pagan myth *The Snow Maiden* (*Snegurochka*).

61. The Nurse's responses here all come from her quasi-comic exchange with Tatyana before the writing of the letter. In Pushkin's Letter Scene, the Nurse is an enabler, instructing her grandson to deliver

messages between Tatyana and Onegin; in Krzhizhanovsky's transposition, the Nurse becomes increasingly uncomfortable with the erotic details of the dream and, by the end, disapproves of it. The play has reason to cast the Nurse and her later double Anisya (the caretaker of Onegin's house) as variants of Baba Yaga, the Russian witch and Keeper of the Door who tests the fidelity—and the stamina—of maidens during liminal moments.

62. In Pushkin's *Eugene Onegin*, this line is a question posed by the Narrator, who takes pleasure in recounting the dream. Presumably, a question mark is also required in the Nurse's delivery of this line (the typescript has a period). Krzhizhanovsky adjusts the framing lines, now spoken by Tatyana, from the third to the first person, replaces "them" with "us," and eliminates diminutives, which Tatyana would not apply to herself.

63. The fatal trembling of this little bridge, which Tatyana must cross with the bear's help, has been much discussed by writers on *Eugene Onegin*. Crossing a body of water equals marriage in Slavic folklore; bears are associated with matchmaking and wedding nights. (Pushkin knew Russian folklore well, in both its genteel and obscene variants.) For a fine bibliography and controversial interpretation, see Daniel Rancour-Laferriere, "Puškin's Still Unravished Bride: A Psychoanalytic Study of Tat'jana's Dream," *Russian Literature* 25 (1989): 215–58, esp. 219–28. The essay adopts a rigid Freudian stance, and not all will accept its hypothesis of Onegin's bisexuality, but many of its observations are extremely revealing: the bridge is sexual initiation; Onegin and his entourage "correspond to a folkloric conception of the bridegroom and his relatives as ferocious beasts"; a bride referred to in impersonal neuter-gender form is a synecdoche for a "treasure" (*sokrovishche*) that will soon be ravished.

64. It is unclear whether the Nurse's failure (here and later) to move Pushkin's third-person Narrator's voice into second person ("The bear followed *you*") is a slip on Krzhizhanovsky's part or an indication that the Nurse is "watching" Tatyana in the dream and relating what she sees to us, the audience, in an aside. Several motivations are possible for such aesthetic distancing, including compassion. Perhaps the Nurse wants to write Tatyana into a fairy tale with a happy ending.

65. Krzhizhanovsky alters Pushkin's lines: "But what did Tatyana think / When she recognized among the guests / That very one who . . . " (No chto podumala Tat'yana, / Kogda uznala mezh gostey / Togo, kto . . .) so that the Narrator's account becomes a question directly addressed to the Nurse. But he omits the end of line 12: "The very one who *was so precious and terrifying to her*" (Togo, kto *mil i strashen ey*)—in part, perhaps, to show that the Nurse is already nervous about the direction the story is taking.

66. Here Krzhizhanovsky combines two sentences: EO 5, xviii "Everybody rose:" (Vse vstali:)—xix "he goes to the door" (on k dveryam idyot).

67. Krzhizhanovsky follows Pushkin's neuter form of "Mine!" (Moyo!) referring to Tatyana. Pushkin's 1825 ballad "The Bridegroom" ("Zhenikh") involves similar motifs but to a different end: the bride Natasha reveals to her bridegroom at their wedding dinner that she had a dream in which she was lost in the forest at night, stumbled upon a hut full of gold and silver, and then suddenly heard "a shriek and horses' stomp" (krik i konskiy top)—the same sounds Tatyana hears in her dream. Natasha hides behind the stove. In come twelve men with a beautiful girl, whom they grab by the braid and whose right hand they sever. At this point Natasha's bridegroom is revealed as the leader of the intruders; he is seized and condemned to death. Folkloric wedding ritual routinely contains the potential for violence, stylized and displaced.

68. At this point Tatyana censors out—for the benefit of the disapproving Nurse? perhaps for herself, since she must hear her own story?—five lines (EO 5, xx, 5–9) with explicit sexual content, during which Onegin leads her tenderly into a corner, lays her down on a wobbly bench, and inclines his head on her shoulder. This scene, with her lover "bending over her bedpost," is a realization of one of the fantasies Tatyana describes to Onegin in the intimate middle section of her letter.

69. In her retelling, Tatyana also censors out an unkind (but understandable) line in which Onegin bawls out the "unbidden guests" (euphemisms in Russian for death): "I nezvanïkh gostey branit."

70. Tairov struck the grim penultimate line of this stage direction from his director's copy of the playscript.

71. This is a far more negative portrait of Zaretsky than in Pushkin's *Eugene Onegin*, where the thoughts about him and the morality of dueling are mediated by the Narrator the day *before* the duel. Pushkin's Onegin rather likes Zaretsky.

72. In Pushkin's *Eugene Onegin*, the second "Dead?" is repeated by the Narrator, who then records Onegin's shocked response sympathetically (EO 6, xxxv, 5–7): "Dead? . . . Struck with that terrible exclamation / Onegin with a shudder / backs off, and calls his servants." (Ubit! . . . Sim strashnïm vosklitsan'yem / Srazhen, Onegin s sodrogan'yem / otkhodit i lyudey zovet.)

73. Following directly upon the comparison of Lensky's dead body with a "house deserted by its owner," this description of Onegin's study, with its familiar props (rockers, clocks, flasks) in a newly "dead" state, condenses the Narrator's information in EO 7, xvi, 9–12.

74. The poems are Byron's *The Giaour* (1813) and the first two cantos of *Don Juan* (1819), which, according to Nabokov, were "known to Pushkin and Onegin" in a French translation of 1820 (VN EO 2:Pt. 2:94). Byron's poems are among the few books in Onegin's library that survived his "falling out of love with reading." Cf. EO 7, xxii, 1–9: "Although we know that Eugene / had long ago ceased liking to read, / Still, several creations / He excluded from the trash heap: / The Singer of the Giaour and Juan, / and together with him, two or three novels, / in which the age was reflected / and contemporary man was drawn rather truthfully / with his immoral soul, / selfish and dry . . ." (Khotya mï znayem, chto Yevgeniy / Izdavna chten'ye razlyubil, / Odnako zh neskol'ko tvoreniy / On iz opalï isklyuchil: / Pevtsa Gyaura i Zhuana, / Da s nim yeshcho dva-tri romana, / V kotorïkh otrazilsya vek / I sovremennïy chelovek / Izobrazhen dovol'no verno / s yego beznravstvennoy dushoy, / Sebyalyubivïy i sukhoy . . .).

75. According to Anna Bovshek, the page that Tatyana reads was composed by Krzhizhanovsky himself, a psychological self-portrait in verse. Bovshek reproduces it in Part VII of her 1965 memoir *Vospominaniya o Krzhizhanovskom: Glazami druga*, http://az.lib.ru/k/ krzhizhanowskij_s_d/text_0320.shtml, 9–10.

76. Pushkin's version of this line reads: "On their margins she meets" (Na ikh polyakh ona vstrechayet).

77. The space between quotation marks, which is then followed by a Russian translation, was left blank in the typescript for Petrarch's Italian phrase (translated below it) to be filled in by hand; that phrase is Pushkin's two-line epigraph to EO 6: "Là, sotto i giorni nubilosi e brevi / Nasce una gente a cui 'l morir non dole." It is identified by Nabokov as a fragmentary quotation from Petrarch's *In vita di Laura*, Canzone XXVIII (VN EO 2:Pt. 2:3), poems composed circa the 1340s and dedicated to Petrarch's idealized (and unknown) love and lifelong muse, Laura, beautiful young wife of Hugues de Sade.

78. This gestural stage direction is a psychological extension of Pushkin's oblique, trivializing reference to a bust of Napoleon in Onegin's study, EO 7, xix, 12–14: "And a little table with a cast-iron doll / Under a hat with a frowning brow, / With arms crossed over his chest." (I stolik s kukloyu chugunnoy / Pod shlyapoy s pasmurnïm chelom, / S rukami, szhatïmi krestom).

79. A reference to Byron's epic poem *Childe Harold's Pilgrimage*, whose first two books (1812–18) catapulted their author into scandalous fame.

80. Here and elsewhere, Krzhizhanovsky is aided in his transposition of third person (the Narrator speaking *about* Tatyana) to first person (Tatyana speaking to herself) by the fact that the Russian verbal past tense can do without a pronoun. No change is necessary in Pushkin's line "Uzhel' zagadku razreshila?" which can mean both "Has she really solved the riddle?" and "Have I really solved the riddle?" In terms of self-knowledge and self-presentation, the difference between the two variants is huge.

81. In addition to changing *she* to *I* and *her* to *me*, Krzhizhanovsky expands the line, adding "It's time" (*Pora*) before "hours are passing" (*chasï begut*).

82. The "Larins' carriage racing toward Moscow" is from EO 7, xxxvi–xxxviii (the "Moscow list" of landmark streets, buildings, sights as seen from a carriage jolting over potholes). Pushkin's list is largely nouns; Krzhizhanovsky's stage direction, typically, adds sound. The little provincial carriage hurtling into Moscow brings to mind the end of chapter 8 of Nikolay Gogol's *Dead Souls* (*Myortvïye dushi*, 1842), in which the landowner Korobochka lurches through the city at dawn in her strange, watermelon-shaped vehicle.

83. Details taken from the house of the Larins' old Moscow aunt, now four years ill with tuberculosis, in EO 7, xl, 8–11:"The door was opened wide for them / By a gray-haired Kalmyk, in eyeglasses, / A torn caftan, and a stocking in his hand" (Im nastezh' otvoryayet dver' / V ochkakh, v izorvannom kaftane, / S chulkom v ruke, sedoy kalmïk).

84. Pushkin was fond of writing his best friends into his works, in this case Prince Pyotr Vyazemsky (1792–1878), well-connected poet of liberal sympathies. Vyazemsky is mentioned in EO 7, xlix, 9–14: "Meeting Tatyana at her boring aunt's house, / Vyazemsky managed to sit down next to her. / And managed to divert her spirits. / And noticing her nearby, / Some old man, adjusting his wig, / Inquired about her." (U skuchnoy tyotki Tanyu vstretya, / K ney kak-to Vyazemskiy podsel / I dushu yey zanyat' uspel. / I bliz nego yeyo zametya, / Ob ney, popravya svoy parik, / Osvedomlyayetsya starik.) Nabokov cites Vyazemsky's response, in January 1828, to reading a published fragment of this chapter: he considered the description of Moscow "limp and frigid," not the poet at his best, although it contains some nice things; and "the rascal put me in, too" (VN EO 2:Pt. 2:121). For unstated reasons, Nabokov adamantly rejects the possibility that this "old man" is the Prince who will become Tatyana's husband: "The bewigged old party who is fascinated by

Vyazemski's new acquaintance is of course not Prince N., Onegin's former fellow rake, now a fat general, whom Tatiana will presently meet, but a kind of forerunner" (VN EO 2:Pt. 2:120–21). Krzhizhanovsky, with a playwright's economy of means, assumes the opposite. He creates out of Vyazemsky and the General a quasi-comic, quasi-licentious high-society equivalent to the Zaretsky-Buyanov duo in the provincial Name Day party. This General (the future husband) is first noticed by Tatiana in EO 7, liv, 14, when her aunts nudge her at a ball to look in the direction of an important personage. "Who?" says Tatiana distractedly. "That fat general?" (Kto? Tolstïy etot general?)

85. Vyazemsky and the Princess reproduce Pushkin's third epigraph (of three) to chapter 7, a famous exchange from Act 1, scene 7 of the popular verse comedy *Woe from Wit* (*Gore ot uma*), written in 1825 by the poet-diplomat Alexander Griboyedov (1795–1829).

86. The General recites Pushkin's first epigraph to chapter 7, the eulogistic lines 11–12 from the 1795 poem "The Liberation of Moscow" ("Osvobozhdeniye Moskvï") by the sentimentalist poet Ivan Dmitriev (1760–1837), a work Nabokov calls "worthless" (VN EO 2:Pt. 2:68).

87. The Princess responds with Pushkin's second epigraph to chapter 7, line 52 from the 1820 poem "Feasts" ("Pirï") by Yevgeniy Baratïnsky (1800–44). For a sympathetic account of Pushkin's loyalty to this gifted but lesser poet, see VN EO 2:380–81. According to Nabokov, "Baratïnski disliked EO and in a letter of 1832 described it as a brilliant but juvenile imitation of Byron" (381).

88. The ellipses here and in the next line (French words in Pushkin's text) were either meant to be filled in by hand or on a Latin-alphabet typewriter. EO 7, xli, 1 reads: "Princess, mon ange!—Pachette!—Alina!"

89. In Pushkin's *Eugene Onegin*, these words are spoken by the old, ill Princess as a fond reminiscence of the two friends' girlhood; in the mouth of the General, they sound slightly cynical. Pushkin says almost nothing of the General beyond the fact that he had been "wounded in battle" and that Tatiana considers him "fat." He is described as neither old nor ugly, but is usually presumed to be both. Perhaps Krzhizhanovsky's General is meant as a riposte to the saccharine Gremin of Tchaikovsky's opera.

90. Compare with n. 22 above on Grandison, virtuous hero of Richardson's *Sir Charles Grandison*. This name circulates in Pushkin's novel. The immediate reference here is to chapter 2, where the Narrator recalls Mme Larina and her "Moscow cousin Princess Alina" infatuated with a man nicknamed "Grandison"; in chapter 3, Tatiana, who has just met Onegin, is likewise revealed to be in love with Grandison—and the Narrator informs us that Onegin, "whoever our hero is, is certainly no Grandison" (No nash geroy, kto b ni bïl on, / Uzh verno bïl ne Grandison). Tatiana will foist Grandison's virtue upon Onegin in the final scene.

91. In Pushkin's *Eugene Onegin*, there is no French phrase or name at this point to motivate the ellipses.

92. In Pushkin's *Eugene Onegin*, this patter occurs later, during Tatiana's sojourn in Moscow.

93. In a note to the 1837 edition of *Eugene Onegin*, Pushkin cites as a source for his Narrator's disquisition on Russia's roads a satiric poem by Vyazemsky, "The Station" ("Stantsiya," 1829), which laments the potholes, bedbugs, fleas, nonexistent inns, and broken-down bridges that plague the traveler.

94. The General recites the first two lines of Pushkin's early lyric "The Awakening" ("Probuzhdeniye," 1817). The first four lines read: "Dreams, dreams, where is your sweetness? / Where are you, where are you, / Nocturnal joy?" (Mechtï, mechtï, / Gde vasha sladost'? / Gde tï, gde tï, / Nochnaya radost'?). Vyazemsky's "poisonous" joke invokes the third clichéd rhyme in this cluster: mladost' (youth). The General is twice or perhaps even three times Tatiana's age.

95. By this point, Krzhizhanovsky's descriptions of human bodies have become positively Gogolian.

96. These "archival youths" are described in EO 7, xlix, 1, as a group of Moscow youths who speak unfavorably of Tatiana. See Nabokov's gloss: "*arkhivnye iunoshi*" was a nickname applied to "young men of gentle stock enjoying soft jobs at the Moscow Archives (Office of Records) of the Ministry of Foreign Affairs"; for youth not wishing to go into the military, the Ministry was the only branch of the civil service "considered, in the 1820s, a fit place for a nobleman to serve" (VN EO 2:110–20, esp. 120). This group was also the focus of a scandal related to Pushkin's professional rivalries in 1830. His political enemy, the cutthroat journalist and police informer Faddei Bulgarin, wickedly caricatured the archival youths in chapter 16 of his 1829 best-selling novel *Ivan Vyzhigin* as ignoramuses, mama's boys, social parasites, skirt chasers, and fraudulent philosophers—and hinted that Pushkin's verses about them in *Eugene Onegin* were plagiarized from his own novel. See Yu. M. Lotman, *Roman A. S. Pushkina "Yevgeniy Onegin": Kommentariy* (St. Petersburg: Iskusstvo-SPb, 1997), 701.

97. "A troika of gloomy singers" (Ugryumïkh troyka yest' pevtsov) is the title of a six-line verse epigram written by Pushkin in 1815 satirizing the linguistic "archaicizers" or conservatives.

98. Typo in the document: "стча" has been corrected here to "стуча" (knocking, thumping).

99. Prolazov or Prolasov (Pushkin spells it both ways) comes from *prolaz* or *prolaza* meaning climber, crawler, and suggests a ridiculous but mischievous sycophant. See VN EO 2:Pt. 2:197.

100. For the ellipses, Pushkin's *Eugene Onegin* has the French name St. Priest. See VN EO 2:Pt. 2:197–98: Count Emmanuil Sen-Pri (Saint-Priest), 1806–28, a cartoonist, not officially published but very popular among albumists, shot himself at age twenty-two to fulfill his half of a bargain with an eccentric Englishman who agreed to pay the young man's gambling debts if he would commit suicide in his presence.

101. Maturin's *Melmoth the Wanderer*; see n. 22.

102. Quaker (Квакер) is misspelled in the document as Kvaver (Квавер).

103. A reference to the hero of Griboyedov's *Woe from Wit*.

104. What follows is from Pushkin's partially composed and then expunged "chapter 9," written in a mix of third and first person, attached by him to the 1833 and 1837 editions of *Eugene Onegin* as a supplement titled "Fragments of Onegin's Journey." It usually appears in the novel as an appendix. Krzhizhanovsky excerpts portions here, switching the order of the lines and distributing them between Onegin and Vyazemsky. In the playscript, the "Onegin's Journey" inserts follow EO 8, xiii, 9 ("And I began wandering without aim"), a mid-stanza line preceded in Pushkin by the ostensible cause for his setting off: "The bloodied shade [of Lensky] / appeared to him every day"). For a good literal rendering of the chapter 9 fragments in English, upon which I rely here, see VN EO 1:323–34.

105. Krzhizhanovsky connects here the eagle mentioned in stanza xii of "Onegin's Journey" with the second four-line stanza from Pushkin's sketches for a "chapter 10" to *Eugene Onegin*, in which the hero was supposed to become a Decembrist. See VN EO 2:314: "The MS fragments that we have of Chapter Ten, composed in the autumn of 1830 at Boldino, are represented by sets of lines belonging to eighteen consecutive stanzas. Our poet did not number these stanzas." The language is elusive, and Pushkin deliberately left out certain words of seditious flavor (Nabokov reconstitutes them).

106. At this point Krzhizhanovsky begins to combine stanzas from "Onegin's Journey"—rejected fragments that were published by Pushkin *as* fragments—with canonic *Eugene Onegin* stanzas.

107. The document reads "волн края межчужны," with the final (nonexistent) word *mezhchuzhnï* suggestive of "among foreign countries"; it has been corrected to "волн края жемчужны" (*zhemchuzhnï* = pearly).

108. Nina Voronskaya: Nabokov argues that Pushkin is not referring to an actual person but to a "stylized portrait" of a society beauty (VN EO 2:Pt. 2:175–78).

109. Pushkin's Narrator says, "Is it really *Eugene*?" (Uzhel' Yevgeniy?); Krzhizhanovsky alters the form of address when he assigns the question to Tatyana.

110. Typo in document: "дамучивость" has been corrected to "задумчивость" (reverie, thoughtful state).

111. Typo in document: "слов нет" (there are no words) has been corrected to "слова нет" (there's not a word).

112. Admiral Alexander Shishkov (1754–1841), statesman, president of the Academy of Sciences, publicist, and founder of *Beseda*, a conservative language society that aimed to protect Russian from Gallicisms and other borrowed impurities.

113. The ellipses here are for the English word *vulgar*, misspelled *volgar* in the document, probably in Krzhizhanovsky's hand.

114. Vyazemsky quotes Pushkin's epigraph to chapter 1 of *Eugene Onegin*, which comes from Vyazemsky's own 1819 lyric "First Snow" ("Pervïy sneg"). See Nabokov's summary of the poem and positive assessment of the effects of cold, VN EO 2:27–29.

115. Except for quotation marks, this line is blank in the document. Krhizhanovsky adds "in Italian" (po-ital'yanski) by hand.

116. Here Vyazemsky translates Pushkin's French epigraph to *Eugene Onegin* ("Tiré d'une lettre particulière" / taken from a personal letter) into Russian; Tatyana supplies its ironizing final words. In English, the epigraph roughly reads: "Full of vanity, he is nevertheless distinguished by that special sort of pride [*espèce*] that forces him to confess his good and bad deeds with equal indifference—the consequence of a feeling of superiority, perhaps imaginary."

117. Onegin's musings in the salon combine excerpts from several Pushkin stanzas, most delivered by the Narrator.

118. In the novel, these lines are spoken about Onegin by the Narrator in a part-compassionate, part-mocking tone (EO 8, xxxi, 1–2): "She doesn't notice him / No matter how hard he tries, even unto death." Obliged to utter these sentiments about himself, Onegin inevitably sounds more self-pitying, almost a crybaby—not at all the personality of Pushkin's hero and somewhat against Krzhizhanovsky's own model.

119. Onegin's indiscriminate reading includes famous public figures and historians who would be on the bookshelves of every European-educated Russian aristocrat: see Nabokov's extensive gloss on this list (which notes some anachronisms), VN EO 2:Pt. 2:219–23. Onegin would have read the 1793 French translation of the memoirs of Edward Gibbon (1737–94) that Pushkin had in his own library; of Rousseau (1712–78) it could be almost anything; the romantic tragedies of Alessandro Manzoni (1785–1873) would also have been read in French; Johann Gottfried von Herder (1744–1803) had not yet been translated by 1824, when the lovesick Onegin was supposed to be consoling himself through him; Sébastien Nicolas Chamfort (1741–94) would have contributed his *Maximes et pensées*, of which Pushkin had the 1812 edition; Mme de Staël (1766–1817) perhaps provided a sentimental novel, or her survey in French of German literature and culture; Marie François Xavier Bichat (1771–1802), great French physiologist and anatomist, was doubtless useful to Onegin for his *Recherches physiologiques sur la vie et la mort* (1800), especially his comments on the psychosomatic influence of passions on physical functions and the death of bodily organs; Simon Tissot (1728–97), famous Swiss doctor and author of *De la santé des gens de lettres* (1768). A certain profile—skeptical, materialistic, ameliorative—emerges from this list that fits Onegin well.

120. Typo in document: "Иеснились" has been corrected to "Теснились" (crowded).

121. Text by Pushkin, the opening 12 lines of his 1814 "Carousing Students" (Piruyushiye studentï). It exists in two versions, an earlier "To Students" ("K studentam") and then this revision, from which Krzhizhanovsky/Prokofiev obtained the title. Both variants are topical (full of personal names and insider jokes), lengthy, and irreverent. Their form parodies that of Zhukovsky's patriotic verse honoring the heroes of the 1812 War of Liberation, "A Singer in the Camp of Russian Warriors" ("Pevets vo stane russkikh voinov," 1813); see Pushkin, *Stikhotvoreniya litseiskikh let 1813–1817* (St. Petersburg: Nauka, 1994), 55–58. It is unknown whether this parodic backstory was known to Krzhizhanovsky/Prokofiev when they decided to include (and then to exclude) this drinking song from the scene.

122. This line (EO 6, xxviii, 1) is semantically awkward, because it is only half of a Pushkin sentence, reading in full (together with line 2): "Enemies! Did their thirst for blood divide them / For that long, from one another?" (Vragi! Davno li drug ot druga / Ikh zhazhda krovi otvela?) Note how Krzhizhanovsky motivates this recollection of the duel. Alone, in the fog, on a deserted embankment, Onegin gazes out at the water, stung by Tatyana's silence. His character is enriched through deprivation. The "Song of Carousing Students" triggers memories of his "childish" behavior at the duel, and provides a perfect situation rhyme, harking back to Pushkin's own youth as described in chapter 1 of *Eugene Onegin* (where Onegin and the Poet/Narrator are first introduced to the reader on the embankment).

123. Nabokov attributes these lines to a lyric by M. Muravyov (1757–1807) in which a poet spends a sleepless night leaning on granite (VN EO 1:315).

124. The "Torquato octave" is a rhyme scheme of ababacc, associated with Torquato Tasso (1544–95).

125. Another situation rhyme, answering a question posed at the beginning. Recall what the Bookseller asked the Poet: You're exhausted by love, bored, you've abandoned your lyre and Muse, what will take its place? And the Poet answers: "Freedom." The Bookseller, of course, thinks this is nonsense, and persuades the Poet to sell him his manuscript—which is, presumably, the performance we see. In these final two fragments, Onegin exchanges freedom for memory.

126. Typo in the document: "завещено" (suggesting a will and testament) has been corrected to "завешан" (from *zaveshat'*, to hang with).

127. This "dialogue that is not a dialogue" has otherworldly associations. Past images converse as surely as ideas and persons do in the present. Just as individual word images in the "Song of Carousing Students" trigger concrete images in Onegin's conscience about the duel, so Tatyana's mention of her Nurse's shady grave reminds Onegin of the two pines covering Lensky's grave, in lines that the Narrator, not Onegin, speaks compassionately. One can imagine this final confrontation being staged almost without eye contact, or as a dreamy ballet with the principles in separate time-spaces moving around each other, with attention already fixed on further things—staged as anything, in fact, but the passionate trills and physical striving to connect that fuels Tchaikovsky's final operatic scene.

Prokofiev and Atovmyan:

Correspondence, 1933–1952

INTRODUCTION AND COMMENTARY BY NELLY KRAVETZ

TRANSLATION BY SIMON MORRISON

In memory of Svetlana Levonovna Merzhanova-Atovmyan

After his permanent relocation from Paris to Moscow in 1936 and separation from his first wife in 1941, Prokofiev relied on three individuals for support: Mira Mendelson, his companion and eventual second wife; the composer Nikolay Myaskovsky, whom he had known since adolescence; and Levon Atovmyan, a major figure in the Soviet musical establishment. The nature of Prokofiev's relationship with Mendelson and Myaskovsky can be gleaned from their published letters and memoirs; his all-important relationship with Atovmyan, in contrast, remains essentially unknown.[1] Their correspondence, published for the first time in this volume, provides insight into their interactions while also furnishing new information about Soviet music before, during, and after the Second World War.

Atovmyan was born on May 25, 1901, in Ashkabad, Turkmenistan. After the early death of his parents he was raised in the family of his sister and her husband, the cellist Viktor Kubatsky (1891–1970), a member of the Bolshoy Theater orchestra and a professor at the Gnesin Institute. From 1911 to 1918 Atovmyan studied in Moscow at the School of Commerce and the music school of the Moscow Philharmonic Society, receiving cello training from Kubatsky and Anatoliy Brandukov (1856–1930), and theory lessons from Nikolay Kochetov (1864–1925). In 1921, while serving in the military, he contracted typhus; he received a long-term discharge, during which he worked for the Bolshoy Theater and the State Committee for the Preservation of Musical Instrument Collections. In 1930, Atovmyan was elected to the Presidium of the All-Russian Society of Soviet Dramatists, Composers, Film, Club, and Stage Authors (Vserosskomdram), where he chaired the division for composers; later, he chaired the

Municipal Committee (Gorkom) for composers. From 1934 to 1935 he worked as an assistant in the theaters directed respectively by Yuriy Zavadsky (1894–1977) and Vsevolod Meyerhold (1874–1940). In 1936, the Central Committee of the Communist Party dispatched him to Turkmenistan to oversee the regional Directorate on Arts Affairs and establish a curriculum at the Music Technicum. His efforts contributed to the founding of an opera theater in Turkmenistan.

Late in 1937, Atovmyan was arrested in a local bureaucratic purge and sentenced, under the treason statute of the Soviet penal code, to ten years of hard labor—felling trees in the prison camps of Irbit and Turinsk in the Northern Ural Mountains. His term, which began in January 1938, was unexpectedly commuted by Communist Party decree in July 1939 and his credentials restored. According to the decree, he had demonstrated sufficient commitment to the Soviet regime to merit rehabilitation.

At a plenary session of the Union of Soviet Composers in 1940, Atovmyan was made the director and deputy chairman of Muzfond, the financial division of the Union. He would later combine his work at Muzfond with his duties as director and chief editor of Muzgiz, the state music publisher. During the war he organized evacuations of composers and helped their families obtain essential goods. In 1947 his activities at Muzfond came under scrutiny from state auditors, and following the February 10, 1948, Central Committee resolution against formalism in music—a resolution that resulted in the removal of Prokofiev's works from the repertoire—Atovmyan lost his post at Muzfond. From 1953 to 1963 he worked as the artistic director of the State Symphony Orchestra of Cinematography. Serious illness (a brain hemorrhage that led to loss of speech and partial paralysis) forced him into retirement. Atovmyan died on January 16, 1973.

Prokofiev became acquainted with Atovmyan in Moscow during a concert tour from November 21 to December 5, 1932. During 1932–34, they developed and maintained an active correspondence; through Atovmyan, Prokofiev received composition, performance, and publication opportunities in the Soviet Union as well as regular encouragement to relocate to Moscow. Occupying a senior position in the Union of Soviet Composers from 1940, Atovmyan became Prokofiev's de facto business partner. He also served as the composer's creative and personal assistant, producing two- and four-hand reductions for piano of his symphonies, ballets, cantatas, and oratorios, arranging and realizing orchestrations, and helping him to navigate the Soviet cultural and political bureaucracy. In her memoirs Mira Mendelson recounts: "Atovmyan expressed the desire for Seryozha to dedicate one of his works to him. It seems that he completely deserves this. He attentively responds to everything that concerns

Seryozha, whether related to musical or trifling domestic affairs, which play a considerable role in life."[2] There is little doubt that, without Atovmyan's active assistance, Prokofiev could not have coped with the difficulties presented to him in Russia after eighteen years away.

In 1964 Atovmyan deposited his entire archive in the State Central Museum of Musical Culture named after Glinka (henceforth GTsMMK). The archive includes his correspondence, scores (manuscripts, transcriptions, and arrangements), and photographs. The GTsMMK staff deemed the archive insufficiently large to merit a separate listing in the catalogue, which resulted in its distribution within collections assigned to Prokofiev, Myaskovsky, and Shostakovich, as well as within the smaller holdings of Asafyev, Glier, Mosolov, and Shebalin, among others. GTsMMK possesses the letters and telegrams sent by Prokofiev to Atovmyan between September 16, 1932, and September 7, 1952, but only two letters from Atovmyan to Prokofiev, the first from the early 1930s, the second from July 12, 1943. The GTsMMK holdings also include fourteen letters sent by Prokofiev to Atovmyan between 1932 and 1934, which concern the programs of his concerts in Moscow, the dates of his visits to the Soviet Union, and performances of Soviet music in Western Europe. These fourteen letters have not been included in this gathering, since they are being prepared by GTsMMK for a separate Russian-language publication, and are thus inaccessible. In addition, the Prokofiev Archive at Goldsmiths College, London, contains forty-four pieces of correspondence between Prokofiev and Atovmyan, likewise not included here. This material, too, concerns Prokofiev's Soviet commissions and performances between 1932 and 1934, before his permanent relocation from Paris to Moscow.

What follows is the vast bulk of the correspondence between Atovmyan and Prokofiev preserved at the Russian State Archive of Literature and Art (henceforth RGALI): ninety-eight letters and telegrams presented in chronological order from December 5, 1933 to September 9, 1952. The Prokofiev correspondence is unexpurgated, with the exception of nine short notes of trivial content that are preserved in the RGALI holdings of the Committee on Arts Affairs, various theater and concert organizations, and private individuals. The correspondence is either in Prokofiev's own hand, in Mendelson's hand from his dictation, or typed. Prokofiev habitually wrote in shorthand, excluding vowels; in this English-language version of his prose, the vowels have, of necessity, been included. He was known to make copies of his letters for his records: thus there are two, and sometimes three, exemplars of each. With the exception of eight telegrams and four letters, the Prokofiev correspondence at RGALI can also be found in typed copy at GTsMMK, according to its catalogue.

In his letters, Prokofiev almost always lists his address and the date in full. On the first page of the letters from Atovmyan, he habitually indicates the date of receipt. Missing dates and grammatical interpolations have been provided here in brackets.

All of Atovmyan's letters are in his own hand, with the exception of no. 20, which is typed. This translation excludes his congratulatory and other telegrams to Prokofiev, brief notes about packages sent or received, one- or two-line requests for signatures on financial documents, and one- or two-line requests for concert tickets. The letter from March 26, 1943, excludes a detailed, somewhat redundant financial accounting; another such accounting, dated July 12, 1943, has also been omitted. Finally, an appendix to the letter from August 16, 1952—a listing of piano pieces intended for a four-volume edition—has been left out. It appears to have been appended to the letter after Prokofiev's death and contains remarks in Mendelson's hand. Atovmyan had proposed publishing a three-volume edition of Prokofiev's piano works in 1952; he and the composer subsequently worked out the contents in precise detail. The plan for a four-volume edition arose between Atovmyan and Mendelson after 1953.

The wartime correspondence (nos. 4–42) and the correspondence in 1952 is the most complete and revealing in the collection, given that both sides survive. Yet for obvious reasons, political events are not discussed in the letters: writing on February 11, 1948, a day after the Central Committee resolution against formalism, Atovmyan betrays no hint of the resolution's terrible implications for his and Prokofiev's careers. On December 29, 1947, Prokofiev willed himself to remark: "Semyon Semyonovich [Bogatïryov] tells me terrible things relating to Muzfond." Atovmyan sought always to avoid burdening Prokofiev with personal requests, and so the fact that he was forced to petition the composer for a testimonial in his defense (no. 50) speaks volumes about the graveness of the problems he faced in the wake of the resolution.

References for locating each item, and other identifying characteristics, are provided after the text of each letter. Explanatory notes furnish basic information about the works under discussion: their dates of completion, alteration, publication, and performance. Established facts about Prokofiev's career are clarified and new details from archival sources are brought to light. Basic biographical information is provided about almost every individual mentioned in the letters, including little-known musicians, Muzfond employees, and Committee on Arts Affairs officials. For purposes of concision, references to secondary sources are avoided.

Prokofiev does not devote particular attention to musical analysis, recollections of his performances, or assessments of the works of other composers. His correspondence with Atovmyan largely concerns financial and material matters: honoraria, deposits, transfers, debts, loans, material support for his first wife and their two sons, receipt of wartime rations, shortages of manuscript paper, and the procuring of adequate housing. Atovmyan obtains contracts for Prokofiev, realizes and corrects orchestrations, prepares manuscripts for printing, dispatches proof pages, and facilitates negotiations with various concert organizations. He becomes, moreover, the composer's trusted friend in hazardous, tumultuous times.[3]

From a scholarly standpoint, the significance of this correspondence resides in its elucidation of the central events in Prokofiev's later years, clarification of the chronologies of his works (both those written before and after his relocation to Moscow), and revelations about the behind-the-scenes workings of the Union of Soviet Composers.

We are indebted to Svyatoslav Prokofiev, Serge Prokofiev Jr., and Svetlana Merzhanova-Atovmyan for kindly granting permission to publish this correspondence. We are likewise grateful to the staffs of RGALI, GTsMMK, the Taneyev Library of the Moscow Conservatory, the Union of Composers Library, the Museum of the Moscow Philharmonic, and the Archive of the Ministry of Culture for their invaluable assistance.

Figure 1. The pianist Nadezhda Golubovskaya, Prokofiev, Atovmyan, the musicologist Grigoriy Shneyerson, and Mira Mendelson at a rehearsal of Prokofiev's Sixth Symphony, Leningrad, 1947.

NOTES TO THE INTRODUCTION

1. *S. S. Prokof'yev i N. Ya. Myaskovskiy: Perepiska*, ed. D. B. Kabalevskiy (Moscow: Sovetskiy kompozitor, 1977); M. A. Mendel'son-Prokof'yeva, "Vospominaniya o Sergeye Prokof'yeve. Fragment: 1946–1950," in *Sergey Prokof'yev: K 50-letiyu so dnya smerti. Vospominaniya, pis'ma, stat'i*, ed. M. P. Rakhmanova (Moscow: Gosudarstvennïy tsentral'nïy muzey muzïkal'noy kul'turï imeni M. I. Glinki, 2004), 5–226.

2. Mendel'son-Prokof'yeva, "Vospominaniya o Sergeye Prokof'yeve. Fragment: 1946–1950," 56. Seryozha was a nickname for Sergey.

3. This sentiment is confirmed by Atovmyan's memoirs, which Simon Morrison and I obtained from his recently deceased daughter, Svetlana Merzhanova-Atovmyan, and which I am in the process of editing for publication.

1. Atovmyan to Prokofiev

The first three letters predate Prokofiev's permanent relocation from Paris to Moscow, and reflect Atovmyan's effectiveness at arranging commissions and performances on the composer's behalf, part of a multi-tiered effort by Soviet officials to lure him back to his homeland.

December 5 [1933]

Sergey Sergeyevich!

I'm forwarding your account statement. Unfortunately we don't have a typewriter with a wide carriage, so we weren't able to do it in the format you requested. But the enclosed statement is clear enough: the total income is shown above, then the total expenses, and finally the amount left over. Some clarification:

1) The cost of the hotel (6 additional days in June), a total of 630 rubles, is included as an expense.[1] In order to balance this sum, 500 rubles for student lessons is included as income.[2]

2) The 2,000 rubles you received from the Leningrad Union[3] is not entered as income, because this sum, as explained, was not issued to the account for concert honoraria, but to the account for honoraria for public performances.

3) The cost of the tickets to Negoreloe (the last time) and Leningrad is included as an expense, because these trips were not part of the plan.[4] I have provisionally included them: if you find that they are incorrect, they will be written off.

4) Also, the honorarium for your public concerts is not listed as income. This money will go to your account at the Administration.[5]

Thus 12,650 rubles, 70 kopecks are in your account at the SSK.[6] I will report back regarding your accounts at the Administration (honoraria for public performances) and the savings bank. That's everything financial, it seems. Please let me know if something isn't clear.

I'll send you the six-volume Lenin edition on December 7.[7] I delayed so that the package will reach you in Paris.

I'm forwarding a letter I received for you. They came again from Tairov.[8] They insist on signing the contract as quickly as possible. I will ask about the projects at the accepted rates: if 5,000 rubles is enough, we'll sign the contract.

I'll write about the April and May concert plans in my next letter. Greetings to Lina Ivanovna.[9] How was your trip?

Atovmyan

Moscow, Tverskoy Boulevard, Building 25, Apartment 10, Union of Soviet Composers

RGALI f. 1929, op. 3, yed. khr. 142, pp. 3–4.

1. The official exchange rate between the ruble, French franc, and US dollar fluctuated wildly in the 1930s and 1940s. A November 14, 1935, Council of People's Commissars resolution placed the value of the ruble at 3 francs. Less than a year later it was revalued at 4.25 francs; 1 US dollar equaled 5.30 rubles.

2. While visiting the Soviet Union from April to June 1933, Prokofiev taught a course to recent graduates of the composition program at the Moscow Conservatory. "On April 29," he wrote in his diary, "young composers began coming to get acquainted. Sokolov is twenty-nine and Vitachek thirty. Their works are written with technique; at first glance there was nothing to say about them (I'm suddenly now teaching, but teaching what?), but slowly various abuses became apparent: ninth chords, bad Tchaikovskian combinations, parallelisms and the like. I worked with one student a day, three others looked on; I sat for two hours, getting silly near the end." Sergey Prokof'yev, *Dnevnik 1907–1933*, ed. Svyatoslav Prokof'yev, 2 vols. (Paris: Serge Prokofiev Estate, 2002), 2:827. The lessons were a success. On October 27, 1933, Prokofiev was hired as an adjunct professor for a four-year term; he lost the post on December 1, 1937, "owing to the absence of a pedagogical load." Yelena Dolinskaya, "Tema s variatsiyami-puteshestviyami (iz arkhivov Moskovskoy konservatorii)," in *Otechestvennaya muzïkal'naya kul'tura XX veka. K itogam i perspektivam: Nauchno-publitsisticheskiy sbornik*, ed. M. E. Tarakanov (Moscow: Moskovskaya gosudarstvennaya konservatoriya imeni P. I. Chaykovskogo, 1993), 75–77.

3. Leningrad Union of Soviet Composers.

4. Negoreloe is a city in northeastern Belarus. In Leningrad on April 19 and 21, Prokofiev appeared as solo pianist in two concerts of his works: the first featured his Quintet (1924), Second Piano Sonata (1912), and several short piano pieces; the second the Third Piano Concerto (1921), Third Symphony (1928), and *Scythian* Suite (1915).

5. Administration for the Protection of Authors' Rights (Copyright Agency).

6. SSK is the Union of Soviet Composers.

7. In 1932 in Paris, Prokofiev conceived a cantata based on texts by Marx, Lenin, and Stalin. He completed the Cantata for the Twentieth Anniversary of October in Moscow in 1937, although it was not premiered until 1966. For a detailed discussion of its conception and reception, see Simon Morrison and Nelly Kravetz, "The Cantata for the Twentieth Anniversary of October, or How the Specter of Communism Haunted Prokofiev," *Journal of Musicology* 23:2 (2006): 227–62.

8. Alexander Tairov (1885–1950), founder and director of the Moscow Chamber Theater. The discussion concerns the contract for the incidental music to *Egyptian Nights* (1934), Tairov's staging of scenes from George Bernard Shaw's *Caesar and Cleopatra*, a Pushkin poem, and scenes from William Shakespeare's *Antony and Cleopatra*.

9. Lina Ivanovna Prokofieva (née Carolina Codina, 1897–1989), the composer's first wife.

2. Prokofiev to Atovmyan

Paris, March 30, 1934

Levon Tadevosovich,

In reply to your letter of the 17th I can report that Defauw has confirmed his intention to perform Shebalin's symphony at the end of April or in May.[1] I asked him to let me know when this performance will take place. After that we'll send him a telegram requesting the material be returned.

I will arrive in Moscow by train from Negoreloe on the morning of April 8. Please meet me and reserve a room in a hotel—but if you can't do so, take care that Gusman does.[2] Since I'll be bringing a lot of music it would be good to notify Negoreloe customs in advance.

See you soon.

Yours, SPRKFV

RGALI f. 600, op. 2, yed. khr. 218, p. 1. Typed letter; not available at GTsMMK.

1. Prokofiev refers to the Second Symphony (1929) of Vissarion Shebalin (1902–63). The proposed performance under the direction of Désiré Defauw (1885–1960) did not occur.

2. Boris Gusman (1892–1944), repertoire programmer for the All-Union Radio Committee and, subsequently, the Committee on Arts Affairs.

3. Atovmyan to Prokofiev

This letter reached Prokofiev in Moscow during a three-month visit to the Soviet Union.

April 9 [1934]

Sergey Sergeyevich,

I've sorted out the "essentials" of your finances. The totals I show are rounded off:

1. The Composers' Union: 6,000 rubles (see the enclosed statement).
2. Your current account at the savings bank: 5,500 rubles.
3. Your royalty account at Vserosek: 6,000 rubles.[1]

The 4,000 rubles I requested have not yet been transferred to the savings bank. The 4,000 will be transferred to the savings bank on 11/IV. Then you will have 9,500 rubles at the savings bank and 2,000 rubles in the royalty account. As of today, therefore, you have 17,500 rubles at your disposal. In addition, you still haven't received:

From GABT: 718 rubles.[2]

From Lenfil[3]: 3,000 rubles.

From Radio: 3,000 rubles. SSK should receive these funds (see the enclosed statement).[4]

From Tairov to the Administration for the Protection of Authors' Rights: 2,500 rubles
The total not yet received: 3,718 rubles
_____

6,218 rubles, 26,718 rubles including
the previous sum.

These are all the "essentials." The fee for the hire of *Lieutenant Kizhe* has not yet gone to your account. It will be disbursed to you in May.[5]
You know what will be due to you after your arrival:

Ukraine: 1,500 rubles[6]
Radio: 4,000 rubles   [=]   5,500

If you have any questions, please let me know by telephone.
Greetings, Atovmyan
Forgive me for not typing. We will provide a typed accounting before you leave.

RGALI f. 1929, op. 3, yed. khr. 142, pp. 1–2.
1. Atovmyan chaired the composers' division (Sektsiya kompozitorov) of the All-Russian Society of Soviet Dramatists, Composers, Film, Club, and Stage Authors (Vserosskomdram) from 1930 to 1934. The term *Vserosek* seems to be a portmanteau of "Vsero[sskomdram]" and "Sektsiya."
2. GABT is the State Academic Bolshoy Theater. Atovmyan likely refers to the fee for a concert of Prokofiev's music at the Bolshoy Theater on October 30, 1933, which featured his Fourth Symphony (first version, 1930), Fifth Piano Concerto (1932), and *Scythian* Suite.
3. The Leningrad Philharmonic.
4. Atovmyan likely refers to the fee for a concert, broadcast by Soviet State Radio, of Prokofiev's *Divertissement for Orchestra* (1929) and the orchestral suite from his ballet *The Buffoon* (*Chout*) (1920). The rehearsal for the broadcast took place on November 2, 1933; the exact date of the broadcast is unknown.
5. Prokofiev completed the music for the film *Lieutenant Kizhe* (*Poruchik Kizhe*) in 1933.
6. Prokofiev toured in Ukraine (Odessa, Kharkiv, and Kiev) between April 24 and May 5, 1934.

4. Prokofiev to Atovmyan

Correspondence between Prokofiev and Atovmyan dwindles and then ceases between 1934 and 1941, when they were in regular face-to-face contact in Moscow. It resumes after the Nazi invasion of the Soviet Union on June 22, 1941, when Prokofiev and other major artists were evacuated to the city of Nalchik in the Northern Caucuses. Prokofiev resided there from August 11 to November 23, 1941; Atovmyan, who had arranged the evacuation as part of his official duties at the Union of Soviet Composers, stayed behind in Moscow.

Nalchik, September 1, 1941

I finished the piano score of the suite.[1] Send the honorarium general delivery to Nalchik.

Prokofiev

RGALI f. 1929 op. 2, yed. khr. 151, p. 1. In Mendelson's hand, from dictation; not available at GTsMMK.

1. According to the manuscript (RGALI f. 1929, op. 1, yed. khr. 137), Prokofiev completed the piano score of the suite *1941 god* (*The Year 1941*) on August 28 and the orchestral score on October 12. It comprises three parts: "V boyu" (At battle), "Noch'" (Night), and "Za bratstvo narodov" (For the brotherhood of the peoples).

5. Prokofiev to Atovmyan

Nalchik, September 4, 1941

Dear Levon Tadevosovich,

In keeping with my contract I finished, by September 1, detailed piano sketches for the suite that Muzfond commissioned.[1] I sent you a news flash about this. I urge you, if it's possible, to send me by general delivery the part of the honorarium that is intended for the complete piano score. If need be, the sketches can be listened to and approved right here by Myaskovsky, Kreyn, and Aleksandrov.[2] I fear that writing back and forth on this subject will absorb too much time, thus it would be better if you took me at my word. I have now begun the orchestration and turned out 60 pages of the score. Another question: in a month, when I've finished the score, I won't want to send you my only copy. But to have it copied now, at my own expense, is inconvenient. It would be good if Muzfond made this copy at its expense. If this is acceptable, please transfer 120 rubles to me and I will instruct Lamm to make the copy.[3] One other matter: before you left you promised that Muzfond would assume part of my living costs here.

I didn't telegraph you separately, since all of the composers have appealed to Muzfond from here. But nothing came from Muzfond in response to this appeal, and this greatly worries me.

I send you cordial greetings and ask you to forgive any concern caused. Yours, S. P.

RGALI f. 1929 op. 2, yed. khr. 151, p. 2. Handwritten; not available at GTsMMK.

1. The suite mentioned is *The Year 1941*. Muzfond, the musical fund of the Union of Soviet Composers, was created in 1939. In 1940 Atovmyan was named director and deputy chairman for the administration of the fund, which provided material assistance to composers, financed concerts and theatrical productions, supported the preparation and publication of scores, and subsidized the construction of composers' residences, retreats, and sanatoriums.

2. The composers Nikolay Myaskovsky (1881–1950), Alexander Kreyn (1883–1951), and Anatoliy Aleksandrov (1888–1982).

3. Musicologist Pavel Lamm (1882-1951) served as Prokofiev's principal assistant from 1935 to 1948. In a letter to the composer Dmitriy Melkikh (1885-1943) dated October 8, 1941, Lamm noted: "Prokofiev has finished the *Year 1941* orchestral suite. I have already completed the scoring for two movements." O. Lamm, "Pis'ma iz arkhiva P. A. Lamma (1941-1943)," in *Iz proshlogo sovetskoy muzïkal'noy kul'turï*, 2 vols., ed. T. N. Livanova (Moscow: Izdatel'stvo "Sovetskiy kompozitor," 1976), 2:112.

6. Prokofiev to Atovmyan

On the back of this letter Prokofiev drafted a note (also dated November 17) to his son Svyatoslav, expressing concern that he had not heard from his family. In it, Prokofiev announces his move to Tbilisi and asks Svyatoslav to write to him there.

Nalchik, November 17, 1941

Dear Levon Tadevosovich,

Having heard indirectly that you relocated to Sverdlovsk, I'm writing to you there. I've finished the *Year 1941* Suite and made a copy. Should I send it out to you?

They are soon transferring us to Tbilisi, where I'd ask you to telegraph me about the suite at the main post office, general delivery.[1] Kindly also telegraph me with what you know about my children, since I haven't heard from them or Lina Ivanovna in a long time.[2]

We, the members of MSSK,[3] have thus far not received even a single kopeck of subsidy from Muzfond, which has left all of the composers, and me in particular, in a very unpleasant situation.*

I send you cordial greetings.

Yours, SPRKFV

* I have composed two acts of the opera *War and Peace*.[4] Gayamov[5] telegrammed again in September about sending paper and 500 rubles for copying *War and Peace* for MSSK, but I received neither. If you can, please send them.

RGALI f. 1929, op. 3, yed. khr. 55, p. 1. Handwritten.
1. Prokofiev transferred to Tbilisi, the capital of Georgia, on November 24, staying there until May 29, 1942.
2. Prokofiev had two sons, Svyatoslav (b. 1924) and Oleg (1928-98). Prokofiev had separated from Lina before the war but continued to support her and the children financially.
3. Moscow Union of Soviet Composers.
4. Prokofiev refers to the first version of this opera, comprising five acts in eleven scenes.
5. Alexander Gayamov (1902-52), music critic, librettist, and dramatist.

7. Prokofiev to Atovmyan

Tbilisi, December 14, 1941
The orchestral score of the suite is finished.[1] Myaskovsky, Gauk, and Nechayev have approved it.[2] In view of my difficult material situation, I ask that you immediately telegraph the honorarium to Tbilisi, communications building, general delivery.
Greetings, PRKFV

RGALI f. 1929 op. 2, yed. khr. 151, p. 3. Handwritten; not available at GTsMMK.
1. *The Year 1941.*
2. Alexander Gauk (1893–1963), conductor, and Vasiliy Nechayev (1895–1956), composer, pianist, and teacher.

8. Prokofiev to Atovmyan

Tbilisi, March 8, 1942
Communications building, general delivery
Dear Levon Tadevosovich,
Thank you for your February 4th letter. But in actual fact, you didn't intend to answer me very quickly! I received the honorarium for *The Year 1941* Suite in full, for which I thank you. Upon arrival here Shlifshteyn collected the available copy of the orchestral score for the Committee on Arts Affairs.[1] If Muzfond also needs a copy, let me know, and I'll have another one made.*

Before leaving Moscow in August, I left Lina Ivanovna some cash and authorized her to collect my royalties at the Administration for the Protection of Authors' Rights and the Stanislavsky Theater. Since I haven't heard anything from her, I'm assuming that these sources are adequate for her needs. I'm making the arrangements with the Stanislavsky Theater; in the event she has additional financial difficulties I would ask you to provide another 3,000-ruble loan. Given that, to date, Muzfond hasn't sent me a single installment of my promised monthly subsidy, I expect I'll be able to clear this debt. I could always settle it out of the advances from the commissions you are planning to make.

In the coming days I expect to finish the piano score of *War and Peace.*[2] Lamm was copying it for the Orgkomitet,[3] but he stopped because he hasn't been paid.[4] Gayamov put it to me succinctly: the telegram requesting 500 rubles for the copying of the piano score was sent, but the actual money was not transferred. Since the composing is almost done, Lamm and I were able to determine that copying the entire score will come out to about 750 rubles. Please transfer this amount either to me or directly to P. A. Lamm, Tbilisi, 18 Artabekov St., Nikolayeva's Apt.

Best wishes to you.

Yours, SP

Enclosed application to Muzfond

* Shlifshteyn said that the Committee on Arts Affairs will commission either a symphonic work or a cantata for the 25th anniversary of October.[5] Independent of this I have begun several things—an 8th Sonata, a suite from *Semyon Kotko* and a suite from *War and Peace*.[6] I would be grateful if you gave me a commission for one or two of the aforementioned works. My thanks for authorizing the two loans (3,000 and 2,000 rubles) for Lina Ivanovna. I already knew about the first one from Shaporin:[7] I enclose an application for the second one.

RGALI f. 1929, op. 3, yed. khr. 55, p. 2. Handwritten.

1. Semyon Shlifshteyn (1903–75), musicologist. From 1939 to 1945 he served as senior consultant for music on the Committee on Arts Affairs. In February 1942 he traveled to Tbilisi to gather scores for evaluation by the Stalin Prize Committee.

2. Prokofiev completed the piano score of *War and Peace* on April 13, 1942. Of the eleven scenes in the first version of the opera, he devoted the most time to the eighth ("Shevardino Redoubt"). According to the manuscript (RGALI f. 1929, op. 1, yed. khr. 34), composition of the scene extended from January 15 to April 13.

3. Organizing Committee of the Union of Soviet Composers

4. Lamm struggled to subsist in Tbilisi and sought, like other evacuees, to return to Nalchik, where living conditions were better. Payment for copying *War and Peace* was delayed until June 1942. Lamm did not receive it from Muzfond but from Azgosopera (the Opera and Ballet Theater in Baku, Azerbaijan) which arranged a hearing of *War and Peace* on June 1.

5. Prokofiev did not receive a commission specifically related to the anniversary.

6. The *War and Peace* Suite went unrealized.

7. Yuriy (Georgiy) Shaporin (1887–1966), composer.

9. Prokofiev to Atovmyan

Prokofiev did not leave for Alma-Ata on May 18, as suggested in this letter, but on May 29.[1] He resided there until late June 1943.

Tbilisi, May 17, 1942

Dear Levon Tadevosovich,

I was very touched by your birthday telegram, although, frankly, I'm not quite sure it was intended for me.[2] Judge for yourself: "Congratulations, I am certain that great Kubinsk will long be victorious" and so on. Who is this great Kubinsk? At my birthday party, even my friends couldn't guess!

Tomorrow I am relocating from Tbilisi to Alma-Ata to work on the film *Ivan the Terrible*.[3] Address: Central Film Studio, me. Please write to me with what you've heard about *War and Peace*; that is, the impressions it made on those who heard it, the perspectives on staging it, and so on.[4]

Let me also know if *The Year 1941* Suite and the Quartet on Kabardino-Balkarian Themes are simply sitting on the shelf, or if something will be done with them.[5] And more: did Shlifshteyn pass along to you my two songs about the Kabardino-Balkarian heroes of the war? I would really like 1) these songs to be sung, 2) to be published, and 3) for the SSK to pay me the honorarium for them. I have written two more songs, which I'll send to you when the occasion arises.[6]

I await your letters in Alma-Ata. I send you and our mutual friends my cordial greetings. I much appreciated the congratulatory telegram from the Orgkomitet, which I immediately answered.

Yours, SP

P. A. Lamm has copied 8 scenes of *War and Peace* for the SSK. He would have copied the entire opera, but in light of the request from the Committee on Arts Affairs for a reworking of the people's scenes, I delayed having them copied.[7] Lamm doesn't dare send you the 8 scenes by mail; he's waiting for a courier. I would nonetheless ask you, if it's possible, to send him 561 rubles for the 8 scenes as per the enclosed invoice.

Anyhow I would remind you that citizen Gayamov telegraphed me in September 1941 about sending 500 rubles for the cost of copying *War and Peace*, but that he *did not send* the aforementioned sum. He explained this to me when he was in Tbilisi.

RGALI f. 1929, op. 2, yed. khr. 151, pp. 4–5. Handwritten. On p. 5 is a letter from Prokofiev, also dated May 17, to the Committee on Arts Affairs concerning the honorarium owed to him for his Seventh Sonata (1942)

1. See O. P. Lamm, *Stranitsï tvorcheskoy biografii Myaskovskogo* (Moscow: Sovetskiy kompozitor, 1989), 287.

2. Prokofiev was born on April 27, 1891, but he mistakenly believed April 23 to be his birth date.

3. The invitation to write the music for *Ivan the Terrible* came from the director Sergey Eisenstein (1898–1948).

4. Prokofiev refers to the official hearing of the opera at the Committee on Arts Affairs in early May 1942. Anatoliy Vedernikov (1920–93) and Svyatoslav Richter (1915–97) played a four-hand version of the score in the composer's absence. The conductor Samuil Samosud (1884–1964) recalls the work making a positive impression. See his "Vstrechi s Prokof'yevïm," in *Sergey Prokof'yev: Stat'i i materialï*, ed. I. V. Nest'yev and G. Ya. Edel'man (Moscow: Izdatel'stvo "Muzïka," 1965), 126–27. He resolved to stage the opera at the Bolshoy Theater.

5. *The Year 1941* was premiered on January 21, 1943 in Sverdlovsk (Yekaterinburg) by the All-Union Radio Orchestra under the direction of Nikolay Rabinovich (1908–72). It was first performed in Moscow on April 19, 1943 by the State Symphonic Orchestra under the direction of Natan Rakhlin (1906–79). Prokofiev composed the Quartet, a commission from the Nalchik Arts Administration, between November 2 and December 3, 1941. It was premiered by the Beethoven String Quartet on September 5, 1942 at the Moscow Conservatory.

6. Prokofiev refers to the songs "A Tankman's Oath," "The Son of Kabarda," "A Soldier's Sweetheart," and "Fritz" from his *Seven Mass Songs* for voice and piano (1942). The first and second songs were composed for the Nalchik Radio Committee for a literary and musical program about local war heroes, the third and fourth songs for the House of the Red Army in Tbilisi. RGALI f. 1929, op. 3, yed. khr. 25, pp. 16–17 (Prokof'yev-Mendel'son, *Notograficheskiy spravochnik proizvedeniy S. Prokof'yeva*, 1951–52).

7. The official request for changes to the opera came from Mikhaíl Khrapchenko (1904–86), the Chairman of the Committee on Arts Affairs, on July 16, 1942. Although he praised the lyrical sections of the score, Khrapchenko declared that the people's scenes needed to be rewritten, the domestic scenes compressed, and the patriotic scenes expanded. See Irina Medvedeva, "Istoriya prokof'yevskogo avtografa, ili GURK v deystvii," in *Sergey Prokof'yev: K 110-letiyu so dnya rozhdeniya. Pis'ma, vospominaniya, stat'i,* ed. M. P. Rakhmanova (Moscow: Gosudarstvennïy tsentral'nïy muzey muzïkal'noy kul'turï imeni M. I. Glinki, 2001), 223–25.

10. Prokofiev to Atovmyan

Alma-Ata, June 24, 1942
   Please send 100 pages of 24-stave score paper for *War and Peace*.
   Prokofiev

RGALI f. 1929, op. 2, yed. khr. 151, p. 6. Handwritten; not available at GTsMMK.

11. Prokofiev to Atovmyan

Alma-Ata, September 14, 1942
Dear Levon Tadevosovich,
   I return herewith the signed agreement for the Flute Sonata.[1] I penciled in December 1, 1942, as the tentative deadline for completion. Please pay the 1,000 ruble advance to Lina Ivanovna Prokofieva. Please send to me 1) a copy of the agreement, 2) an accountant's receipt showing the amount of tax deducted from the 1,000 rubles. It is especially important for me to have a receipt for the war tax.[2]
   Thank you for sending the 100 pages of score paper. *War and Peace* is being written on it and will take up all of it.[3] I'd be grateful for additional 24-stave score paper for *Ballad of an Unknown Boy*, and some larger paper (14- or 16-stave) for the Sonata and a cycle of piano pieces.[4]
   I'm waiting for the contract for the Eighth Piano Sonata from you.[5] I've already composed a fair amount of material for it, so I'll be able to work on it in tandem with the Flute Sonata.
   Shlifshteyn writes that my two Kabardino-Balkarian songs were lost (oh, I don't at all mean to say that you are responsible), therefore I'm sending out another copy to him. The other two songs, "A Soldier's Sweetheart" and "Fritz," were sent to you three months ago. I'm waiting for payment for these songs at the existing SSK rate. Do let me know when it will finally be made.
   Lina Ivanovna wrote that she's having difficulties getting food for herself and the children, since they are not registered with a cafeteria and don't have the proper ration cards. Is it not possible to register them at the SSK cafeteria? Perhaps the Orgkomitet and the MSSK will be able to

do this for me. I send you cordial greetings and await news from you at the address given above. It might be better to send the score paper to the local Composers' Union.

Yours

RGALI f. 1929, op. 3, yed. khr. 55, p. 5. In Mendelson's hand, from dictation.

1. Prokofiev composed the Flute Sonata over the next twelve months. It received its premiere in Moscow on December 7, 1943.

2. On December 29, 1941, the Supreme Soviet mandated the collecting of a war tax for the support of combat operations. The levy applied to all Soviet citizens over the age of eighteen with the exception of pensioners, invalids, and those others who depended on government assistance. The annual regional levies ranged from 150 to 600 rubles before 1943, but increased thereafter. The war tax was anulled on January 1, 1946.

3. According to the manuscript (RGALI f. 1929, op. 1, yed. khr. 32–36), Prokofiev began orchestrating the first version of *War and Peace* on June 3, 1942, in Baku, completing it on April 3, 1943, in Alma-Ata.

4. *Ballad of an Unknown Boy*, a cantata for soprano, tenor, chorus, and orchestra with a text by the poet Pavel Antokolsky (1896–1978), was composed in piano score between August 12 and October 15, 1942, in Alma-Ata (RGALI f. 1929, op. 1, yed. khr. 256). The piano pieces to which Prokofiev refers are his Three Pieces for Piano (1942), which includes the Grand Waltz from *War and Peace*, and the Contredanse and "Mephisto" Waltz from the film *Lermontov* (1943).

5. Prokofiev unsuccessfully sought to obtain a commission for his Eighth Piano Sonata (1944) from the Committee on Arts Affairs. After petitioning Atovmyan, he received a commission from Muzfond.

12. Atovmyan to Prokofiev

September 28, 1942
Dear Sergey Sergeyevich,

I received your letter and the signed contract. To clarify the financial statements—here's the information I received from the accountant:
Loaned:
3,000 rubles in September 1941 } (paid to Lina Ivanovna)
2,000 rubles in February 1942 }
1,000 rubles in March 1942, transferred to you in Tbilisi
Total: 6,000 rubles

I entered 536 rubles (the honorarium for the publication in collotype of the two songs, "Fritz" and "A Soldier's Sweetheart"—600 rubles minus 4 rubles and 80 kopecks income tax, 4 rubles and 20 kopecks *kul'tsbor*, and 55 rubles war tax) in partial settlement of this debt.[1] Accordingly, you have a debt of 5,464 rubles. I repeat: I'm providing this information to clarify the statements.

Besides this a one-time benefit (non-repayable) of 1,000 rubles was disbursed (also to Lina Ivanovna) in June 1942.

I can finally report for your peace of mind that Lina Ivanovna is receiving two meals a day (without vouchers) for the children in the

Composers' Union cafeteria.[2] The meals would seem a trifle but I confess that in the current conditions the matter became complicated. Complicated because the children (as well as the wives) of composers have all been refused letter-marked meals[3] and nobody uses this right. But since Lina Ivanovna is rather noisy (forgive me Sergey Sergeyevich), the "fame" of these two meals has spread. They are nonetheless being given meals, so there's no basis for your worries in this regard.

Finishing this part of the letter, the advance for the agreement (1,000 rubles) will be disbursed to Lina Ivanovna tomorrow, without retaining 25% toward the settlement of the loan (as is our practice in accordance with an Orgkomitet resolution).

The 2 songs ("Fritz" and "A Soldier's Sweetheart") have been published in collotype. Today I'll call Shlifshteyn to find out if he received the package.

Your quartet came off with enormous success. I'm keen to take measures toward its publication.[4] I'll let you know the results.

The post office won't accept the manuscript paper. I'll send it with the first available courier.

I'll send the contract for the 8th Sonata soon if Shlifshteyn doesn't do so through the Arts Committee.

I have a request. Is it not possible for you to send me the separate numbers (arias, duets, and choruses) from *War and Peace*? I would like to publish some excerpts from the opera in collotype.[5] True, the honorarium is very insignificant (300 rubles for each number), but in the first place this publication is implicit in the rights to the manuscript and doesn't stand in the way of any other publication (even a simultaneous one). In the second place it would be possible to settle part of the debt and make the next payment to Lina Ivanovna without increasing the amount owed. I await your answer to this question. I'm obtaining the piano score of *Semyon Kotko* . . . It's possible, if you're not opposed, to extract some excerpts from it.

Well, that seems to be all the questions.

Best wishes to you, with devotion,

Atovmyan

P.S. 1. There was evidently an error (so typical of Telegraph)[6] in my congratulatory telegram. The text read: "Congratulations. I'm sure that the great sorcerer will long be triumphing and gladdening with his works."

2. Kindly send me Mira Mendelson's patronymic (to my shame I don't know it).[7] For the texts of the two songs published in collotype she's owed an honorarium (alas, just 100 rubles a song, minus every possible tax). I can't transfer the money since I don't know her patronymic. (Forgive me, but I also don't know the surname given in her passport.)

3. You've evidently already received the sad news about the death of Vladimir Vladimirovich Derzhanovsky.[8] He died from a hemorrhage

on Saturday, September 19, at his dacha (in the 57th kilometer region). He was interred there on Thursday, September 24.
Greetings once more,
Atovmyan

RGALI f. 1929, op. 1, yed. khr. 446, pp. 2–3.
  1. Collotyping, a printing technique invented in the nineteenth century, involves coating a glass plate with chromate gelatin and exposing it to light under a photographic negative of an image, creating a photographic positive. *Kul'tsbor* was a supplementary income tax collected from Soviet citizens between 1931 and 1943 for residential construction as well as cultural and welfare services.
  2. This exclusive privilege allowed Prokofiev's first wife to preserve her wartime ration vouchers.
  3. Special meals offered as exclusive privileges.
  4. Prokofiev's String Quartet on Kabardino-Balkarian Themes (1942) was published by Muzgiz in 1944.
  5. Ten excerpts (arias and choruses) from *War and Peace* were published in collotype by Muzfond in 1943, in advance of the publication that same year of the complete piano score. The manuscript is preserved in GTsMMK f. 33, yed. khr. 952.
  6. The Central Telegraph Agency.
  7. Mira Abramovna (Aleksandrovna) Mendelson (1915–68) became the composer's second wife in 1948.
  8. Derzhanovsky (1881–1942), one of Prokofiev's assistants.

13. Prokofiev to Atovmyan

Alma-Ata, October 15, 1942
The director Room is traveling to Alma-Ata. Deliver 100 pages of score paper to him through the Cinema Committee.[1]
Prokofiev

RGALI f. 1929, op. 2, yed. khr. 151, p. 7. Handwritten; not available at GTsMMK.
  1. During the war the Leningrad and Moscow film studios were relocated to Alma-Ata. Film director Abram Room (1894–1976) asked Prokofiev to provide the music for his short (32-minute) film *Tonya* (1942), which was made but not released.

14. Prokofiev to Atovmyan

Alma-Ata, October 29, 1942
Dear Levon Tadevosovich,
  I'd first like to express my gratitude to the Orgkomitet and you especially for allowing my two children to take meals in the SSK cafeteria. This is a great relief to me. Yesterday I sent to you, by registered book post, ten vocal and choral numbers from *War and Peace* for collotyping. Please confirm receipt of the manuscript by telegraph. It's written in my hand, and I'm entrusting it to your care with the understanding that you won't soil or mislay it, and that you will return it to me later. Please send the hono-

rarium to Lina Ivanovna after 25% is deducted to settle my debt. I'm interested to know if you were able to choose some numbers from *Semyon Kotko* for collotyping. That would be most desirable. Kindly send me a few authorized copies of the songs that were published in collotype.[1]

I'm grateful for the notice about the taxes that are being withheld from me, but this is not what I wanted. I need an official accountant's receipt showing the total amount of war tax withheld in 1942. You see, this tax has a ceiling, so if I paid 2,700 rubles, even in different places, no more will be taken from me. So I ask you to please ensure that the accountant sends me the requested receipt and, if it's not a burden, to contact the Committee on Arts Affairs accountant, to whom I've written several times on this subject without result.

Tomorrow I will send the Seventh Sonata and the three new piano pieces to Shlifshteyn. A number of pianists have already asked me about including these in their repertoires; I've directed them to the MSSK.[2] Please, if they ask, provide them with the music. Several expressed a desire to pay for the copying.

My urgent need for score paper has now increased. The Committee on Arts Affairs is requesting a full copy of the piano score of *War and Peace*, which I've just finished reworking.

The film directors Room and Fayntsimmer will shortly be leaving Moscow for Alma-Ata. Since I'm currently working with them, they aren't likely to refuse to bring the paper. Besides them, N. Kryukov is also in Moscow.[3] If he still hasn't left for Alma-Ata, give him the paper, but impress upon him that he must bring it here intact.

Shlifshteyn did not send me a contract for the Eighth Sonata, so I await it instead from Muzfond. I'd be very pleased if you assisted in the publication of the Kabardino-Balkarian Quartet. I grasp your hand and send you best wishes.

Yours

I include with this letter 1) the copy you sent of the contract for the Flute Sonata. Read clause 1, press it to the heart of your attentive coworker, and send me a new copy. And 2) Authorization from Mira Aleksandrovna for payment of the honoraria for the songs and the texts of the *War and Peace* numbers. Since we are the co-authors of the latter we will split the honoraria in half. Kindly transfer the payments in my name to Alma-Ata.

RGALI f. 1929, op. 3, yed. khr. 55, p. 6. In Mendelson's hand, from dictation.
1. "A Tankman's Oath," "The Son of Kabarda," "A Soldier's Sweetheart," and "Fritz."
2. Richter premiered the Seventh Sonata on January 18, 1943, in Moscow.
3. Nikolay Kryukov (1908–61), composer and musical director of the Mosfilm studio complex.

15. Atovmyan to Prokofiev

November 23, 1942
Dear Sergey Sergeyevich,
    I received your letter and the excerpts from *War and Peace*. I'm grateful to you for sending them. We are publishing them in collotype in two collections, the first arias and duets, the second choruses. Within a week (before December 1) both collections will be prepared. The placement of some of the accidental signs, differing from what's done at the press, confused me. I didn't make any changes with the exception of two places where, to my mind, your pen obviously slipped. These are in Andrey's aria at Borodino

and Anatole and Natasha's duet.

    I marked those signs that, in my view, you omitted in red pencil at the very end. I refrained from making any changes elsewhere.
    It's worse with the excerpts from *Semyon Kotko*. I plan to publish the following excerpts in collotype: Mikola's song ("Early, so early") from Act 3; Frosya's song ("Rattles and drones"); the scene of Remenyuk, Mikola, and Semyon with chorus ("We honor Lenin's name"); Frosya's song in the scene of Frosya, Mikola, and Semyon ("Oh people, oh good people"); the chorus "They flew at us, they swooped down, the evil crows"; the final scene ("Over free Ukraine"); and Sonya's aria ("I had a dream").[1] In many instances the "endings" are complicated (for example, in the chorus "They flew at us," in Sonya's aria, where her phrase is cut off by her father's summons, in Frosya's song, and so on). Should resolving these issues await your arrival or will you permit them to be resolved without you? In any case I'll try to do everything without you, showing Shebalin or Myaskovsky (if he comes before then).[2] Perhaps you will be able to come before December 15. I very much want to publish these excerpts at the beginning of December.
    I will give the honorarium for the songs (and for the excerpts from *War and Peace* and *Semyon Kotko*), in keeping with your request, to Lina Ivanovna (300 rubles for each song minus taxes), but I will send the honorarium for

the texts (100 rubles each) to you. The rates for the music and the texts are unfortunately undifferentiated (standard).

I'll send the information about the withheld war tax in the coming days, including itemized statements. These statements will be done by December 1. If it turns out that you paid more taxes (combined) than were owed, we'll ask for the excess amount to be deducted.

The contract has been corrected and sent to you: I offer my apologies for the inattentiveness of my employees.

Yesterday Shlifshteyn expressed his delight about your return to Moscow on December 15. I'm truly upset that I have to leave for Sverdlovsk on 16-17/XII. I'll hasten to return in order to see you.

I send best wishes, with devotion,

Atovmyan

P.S. Return one signed copy of the contract to us.

RGALI f. 1929, op. 1, yed. khr. 446, pp. 6–7.
1. The excerpts from *Semyon Kotko* were not published in collotype.
2. Myaskovsky returned to Moscow from evacuation in Frunze on December 15, 1942.

16. Prokofiev to Atovmyan

Alma-Ata, February 12, 1943

You mistakenly gave me 30-stave score paper. Please send 24-stave score paper via Alexander Naumovich Ginzburg, without fail.[1]

Hotel Moskva, PRKFV

RGALI f. 1929, op. 2, yed. khr. 151, p. 8. Handwritten; not available at GTsMMK.
1. Alexander Ginzburg, one of the second-unit directors of *Ivan the Terrible*. Ginzburg is not credited in the film, perhaps because he was affiliated with Lenfilm rather than Mosfilm studios.

17. Prokofiev to Atovmyan

Alma-Ata, March 2, 1943

Dear Levon Tadevosovich,

Everything is pending your shipment and likewise a settlement of my agreements with Muzfond, but I still haven't received either.

First of all, allow me to express again my gratitude to you for heroically getting us to the station and onto the train. We had a wonderful journey and thought about you.[1] But although the administration of Muzfond is energetic and punctual, you wouldn't wish its staff on your worst enemy. Judge for yourself: from the very outset of my trip to Moscow I pleaded for 24-stave score paper; it was brought to me an hour before I left, wrapped in a package labeled "24-stave score paper," but when I unwrapped the package in Alma-Ata, it turned out to be 32-stave, which is no good for me because it makes my eyes blurry. Furthermore: the 800 pages (300 in 24-stave and 500 in 12-stave) that Mogilevsky sent to me, Popov, and Brusilovsky in November turned out to be addressed only to Popov, who kept all of the paper for himself.[2] Now he offers me 12-stave paper that I don't need and insists that he has already used up the orchestral paper. I'm really not interested in fighting like this over orchestral paper, especially since it isn't even 24-stave, as Muzfond said it was, but 32-stave. And so after all of my petitions at Muzfond, I find myself (thanks to the gentle pranks of its merry employees) without a single piece of paper for the score of *War and Peace*.

Sometime in February I telegraphed you asking for 24-stave paper to be sent to me through Alexander Naumovich Ginzburg, the director of *Ivan the Terrible*, who was then staying at the Hotel Moscow on a business trip and expected back soon in Alma-Ata. I also telegraphed Ginzburg with a request to contact you on this same subject.

Meanwhile, work on *War and Peace* is on hold, and since I am accustomed to fulfilling my responsibilities on time, I'd ask you to explain the cause of the delay to Samosud.[3]

Something else overlooked by Muzfond's employees: the copy you sent of the epigraph is missing 4 pages (13 to 16), which I'd ask you to provide, since as I've already said to you, I don't have another copy of the epigraph. Meanwhile I have to orchestrate it.

Returning to the issue of the paper sent through Mogilevsky. Popov maintains that he paid him 1,300 rubles for it, whereas in my understanding it should have cost a third as much. Mogilevsky says that his supervisor received the paper and paid the aforementioned amount on account to the director of Muzfond. In the end this issue doesn't concern me, but it leaves an unpleasant impression. I'm telling you about it for the common good, so to speak. I've also asked Popov to meet with Mogilevsky's supervisor (he's in Alma-Ata right now) and to write to you with his side of the story.

I include with this letter the signed contract for the Flute Sonata. Please send me a few copies of "Love of a Soldier," if it has come out, and also of "A Soldier's Sweetheart," which I didn't find among the songs you sent. But the most important thing, what worries me, is of course the 24-stave score paper. I hope that Ginzburg will bring it to me. If for some reason this does not occur, please contact the Cinema Committee and insist on getting it to those people who are coming to Alma-Ata.

Talk again also with Samosud. Perhaps the artist Vilyams or someone else will be coming here.[4] Immediately telegraph me on receipt of this letter. Mira Aleksandrovna and I send you best wishes. You forgot your belt in our train compartment; I'll send it to you with the first reliable courier, probably Kryukov, who's going to Moscow.

Yours, S. Prokofiev

1. Send me three copies of each act of the piano score of *War and Peace* as it comes out. I'll mark any mistakes I find in red pencil on the first copy and return it either to you or Samosud; I'll need the second copy to familiarize interested musicians and theaters with the opera. The third copy is for me personally.

2. Did you receive the orchestral score of *Romeo and Juliet* from the Kirov Theater?[5] Did they give it to you for copying, observing the order of the lithographed piano score that you have? How are the piano reductions of *Romeo and Juliet* and *Alexander Nevsky* coming along?[6] Shlifshteyn hasn't yet sent me the piano score of *Betrothal in a Monastery*; I need to make a number of changes to it. So work is now delayed on another opera. Oh, my Moscow friends!

3. Radin sent me a telegram saying that he hasn't yet received a single act of the piano score from you.[7] Please also send him the opera, one act at a time.

RGALI f. 1929, op. 3, yed. khr. 55, pp. 7–8. In Mendelson's hand, from dictation.

1. From the unpublished memoirs of Mira Mendelson (GTsMMK f. 33, yed. khr. 1413, p. 38): "December 2, 1942. We left for Moscow from Semipalatinsk. It was a long journey, through Novosibirsk, and we arrived in Moscow on New Year's Eve. . . . February [1943]. We left for Alma-Ata and arrived there once again on the 13th."

2. Yevgeniy Brusilovsky (1905–81), composer; David Mogilevsky (1893–1961), cellist; Gavriil Popov (1904–72), composer.

3. Samosud planned to conduct *War and Peace* in 1943, but his dismissal from the Bolshoy Theater prevented him from doing so until June 7, 1945, at which time he led the State Symphony Orchestra in a concert performance at the Moscow Conservatory.

4. Pyotr Vilyams (1902–47), set and costume designer. He was supposed to travel to Alma-Ata to discuss Samosud's proposed staging of *War and Peace*.

5. The orchestral score of *Romeo and Juliet* remained at the Kirov Theater in Leningrad following its premiere on January 11, 1940. Atovmyan retrieved the score from the theater and appears to have been its last bearer before its disappearance. Only fragments remain in the archives.

6. The reduction of *Romeo and Juliet* was published in collotype in 1944. It was republished by Muzgiz in 1946. The reduction of the *Alexander Nevsky* Cantata (1939) was also published by Muzgiz in 1946.

7. Yevgeniy Radin (1897–1944), artistic director of the Kirov Theater, which was relocated to Molotov (Perm) during the war. Rehearsals began in 1944 for the Leningrad premiere of *Betrothal in a Monastery*. It occurred, after a protracted delay, on November 3, 1946.

18. Atovmyan to Prokofiev

March 10, 1943

Dear Sergey Sergeyevich,

I haven't written because I've been awaiting receipt of the *Romeo* score from Molotov. I received a telegram from Radin (obviously "a lie") stating that he sent it by courier on 20/II. Today I sent a third telegram asking him to send the score quickly. Meanwhile I'm putting the *Kotko* excerpts in order. These will go into production in a few days.

Incidentally, the *Kotko* score (which I received from the Stanislavsky Theater) has some "vexing" errors. I'm not making any marks in it, but I'm copying out these errors on a separate page.

The phrasing in *War and Peace* has to be re-copied, since the ink (with which they copied it) turned out to be defective. Tomorrow they'll finish copying the first part; it will immediately go to press.

The money will be transferred in the coming days. I'll send a full accounting.

Life in Moscow is returning to its old self. Shostakovich arrived yesterday, recovered but weak. He's going to a sanatorium for 1/2 month.[1] Nikolay Yakovlevich looks poor but he's his usual cheerful self.[2] Shebalin is apparently "dictating" everything successfully.[3] Oborin's tragedy (a condition in the left hand, akin to paralysis) still hasn't come to an end.[4]

The Stalin Committee has finished its work.[5] We're awaiting confirmation, but the preliminary results are obviously out (you, Shebalin, Khachaturyan, Koval, Sedoy, Ashrafi, Ivanov-Radkevich).[6]

How is your Flute Sonata ("with orchestra"?!) getting on? When will we receive it? So as to send you a contract in advance—what do you propose writing after the Sonata? Will you be creating a suite from the music for the films?[7]

Greetings to your spouse. Respectfully yours,
Atovmyan

RGALI f. 1929, op. 1, yed. khr. 446, p. 11.

1. Dmitriy Shostakovich (1906–75) contracted typhus after his return to Moscow from evacuation in Kuybïshev (Samara). He convalesced at a sanatorium in Arkhangelskoye (20 kilometers from Moscow), staying there until April 5, 1943.

2. Myaskovsky. His first name and patronymic are sometimes abbreviated Nik. Yakovlevich or Nik. Yak. in the correspondence.

3. Shebalin directed the Moscow Conservatory from 1942 to 1948.

4. Lev Oborin (1907–74), pianist. In a letter of February 14, 1943, Shostakovich informed Atovmyan that "Lyova Oborin has suffered a great misfortune, even more, a tragedy. He has lost sensation in the fingers of his left hand. It's difficult for me to comment on this terrible event. If the condition is to be lifelong, then it seems to me Muzfond should consider doing something." *Dmitriy Shostakovich v pis'makh i dokumentakh*, ed. I. A. Bobïkina (Moscow: Gosudarstvennïy tsentral'nïy muzey muzïkal'noy kul'turï imeni M. I. Glinki, 2000), 260.

5. The Stalin Prize Committee for literature and art was established on December 20, 1939, Stalin's sixtieth birthday.

6. Composers Aram Khachaturyan (1903–78), Marian Koval (Kovalyov, 1907–71), Vasiliy Solovyov-Sedoy (1907–79), Mukhtar Ashrafi (1912–75), and Nikolay Ivanov-Radkevich (1904–62).

7. Of his film scores, Prokofiev extracted a suite only from *Lieutenant Kizhe*.

19. Prokofiev to Atovmyan

Alma-Ata, March 14, 1943

Dear Levon Tadevosovich,

I include with this letter your belt, which you forgot in our train compartment. I ask your forgiveness for unintentionally turning out to be the culprit who deprived you of such a crucial part of your attire.

On March 2 I sent you a long letter by registered mail. I wrote to you in detail about all of my affairs. Right now the most urgent thing is to send me the piano-vocal score of *Betrothal in a Monastery*. It can be procured from the Stanislavsky Theater and the Radio Committee library.[1] Please obtain a copy straightaway and send it to me either by mail or courier.*

I received 100 pages of 24-stave paper through Ginzburg, for which I'm grateful to you. I'm now temporarily sated. I expected to find in your parcel a few scenes from *War and Peace* in collotype, but apparently you are still to send them or did so by an alternate route.

I grasp your hand. Greetings from Mira Aleksandrovna.

Yours, SP

* I appealed both to Shlifshteyn and Samosud for it, but they don't care a straw.

RGALI f. 1929, op. 2, yed. khr. 151, p. 9. Handwritten.
   1. Prokofiev left the score of the opera at the theater following its September 19, 1940, run-through (on piano) for the artistic directors of the Stanislavsky Theater and representatives from the Radio Committee.

20. Atovmyan to Prokofiev

March 26, 1943

Dear Sergey Sergeyevich,

First, my congratulations once again.[1]

True, I have a somewhat unclean conscience (as, obviously, do most of us with awareness of your role in music): you were the first to know and the first who needed to know what was confirmed only today. Essentially, we should apologize to you for being somewhat late with our congratulations. But, as they say, the "ice has begun to crack," and what's possible and necessary now is to wait for the broad navigation appropriate to the scale of your work and to your significance in music.

Please accept again my congratulations and most sincere and best wishes. And also accept my apologies for my staff's "gentle pranks."

Concerning the score paper: apparently there's almost no 24-stave paper left in the warehouse: the head of the warehouse, who doesn't grasp "subtleties," sends out 30-stave paper all the time. We dug out 100 pages of 24-stave paper and sent it with Ginzburg. I'll obtain more and send it at the first opportunity.

800 pages (300 pages of 30-stave orchestral paper at 40 kopecks and 500 pages of piano paper at 25 kopecks) were sent with Mogilevsky and 245 rubles received from him. I summoned an employee and personally checked all of the documents, which showed, of course, that 245 rubles, not 1,350 rubles, were received for the paper. I instructed my worker to contact comrades Popov and Mogilevsky on this issue.

Concerning the publications:

"Love of a Soldier" has come out from the press; I'm sending you author's copies of "Love of a Soldier" and "A Soldier's Sweetheart." I also contacted Muzgiz. The pages of the "Epigraph" you didn't receive have been sent (I'm red-faced for my employees).

The first act of *War and Peace* is out. Scene 4 comes out the day after tomorrow. The phrasing needs to be recopied, since the collotype ink proved defective and didn't transfer. The work is under way and the publication of the piano score "is at full speed."

As you request, 3 copies of the piano score will be sent to you act by act. One copy will be sent to Radin, and 20 copies to Samosud (meanwhile I've given him 5 copies of all of the extracts).

Please send the proofread copy back to me so that I can (if need be) correct all of the other copies. I'll inform Samosud of the changes.

I haven't received the *Romeo* score, even though the people in Molotov told me three times that it was on the way. Yesterday I received a telegram from Ashkenazy saying that it will be sent with the next courier.[2] I'll try to work (upon receipt of the score) three times as fast so as not to delay the compilation of the piano score.

Now, finally, about our accounts:

Firstly, I'm sending the contract for the Sonata (the second copy). I detected another one of the staff's "gentle pranks"—not my staff this time, in truth, but the Orgkomitet staff. The amount on the contract is 4,000 rubles, but no less than 6,000 rubles should be paid for a sonata at this time. I changed the amount to 8,000 rubles. Keep hold of the copy. As soon as the Sonata is done please send it for copying and final settlement for it.

[. . .]

Of the 7,000 rubles owed to you we are deducting 3,000 to settle your debt; the remaining 4,000 is being sent to you.

In April I'll disburse the supplemental honorarium for *War and Peace* to you—for the published piano score (it will come out to about 5,000 rubles; the exact amount will be determined in the coming days). We'll deduct about 2,000 rubles and transfer the rest to you. So by May 1 you'll be left with a debt of 1,000 rubles, which will obviously be settled by the honorarium for the Flute Sonata.

Sorry for providing such detailed information on this issue, but I felt it necessary. Please let me know if you are opposed to the planned deductions.

I await your letters. Greetings to Mira Aleksandrovna.

Once more my best wishes, with devotion,

Atovmyan

I received the following telegram in your name from Ogolevets in Kuybïshev: "Congratulations on the conferment of the prize. I rejoice in the beginning of the end of the inexplicable overlooking of your creative service. Wishing you success. I kiss you. Ogolevets."[3]

RGALI f. 1929, op. 1, yed. khr. 446, pp. 12–13. This is the only one of Atovmyan's letters in this collection that is typed.

1. On March 19, 1943, Prokofiev received a Stalin Prize (Second Class) for his Seventh Piano Sonata.

2. Abram Ashkenazy (1895–1983), composer.

3. Alexey Ogolevets (1894–1967), musicologist.

21. Prokofiev to Atovmyan

Alma-Ata, April 21, 1943

I received the two transfers. Thanks. Please don't transfer the next honorarium. Details by letter.

Greetings, Prokofiev

RGALI f. 1929, op. 2, yed. khr. 151, p. 10. Handwritten; not available at GTsMMK.

22. Prokofiev to Atovmyan

Alma-Ata, April 24, 1943

Dear Levon Tadevosovich,

I confirm the receipt of two telegrams, two money transfers, two letters, and manuscript paper via Ginzburg. For all of this, first and foremost for your congratulatory telegram, I thank you. I noted that it was sent at six o'clock in the morning; I admire your industrious life. (It's obvious that you are buckling under the weight of your labors at Muzfond. You should already be on your feet at five o'clock.) I received the transfers of 3,158 and 528 rubles and telegraphed you with a request to postpone sending the next amount, for the piano score of *War and Peace*, to Alma-Ata. Please deposit this sum into my current account, No. 9718, at savings bank 5287/141. This is branch 25, at the back of the Metropole Hotel. As soon as it's deposited, telegraph me with the balance.

The letters I received from you were dated March 10 and 26. Thanks for the supplement to the contract for the Flute Sonata and the piano score of *War and Peace*. It's agreed that these amounts are to be withheld to pay off my Muzfond debt. You do liquidate my debts zealously, like a patented fire extinguisher, but what can I do: God gives, God takes away.

Two amounts aren't clear to me in your accounting: 329 rubles in accordance with the contract for *The Year 1941* Suite, and 3,600 rubles in accordance with the publishing contract. Can you kindly remind me what these amounts are for? Incidentally, it has gone clear out of my head whether we signed a contract for the publication of the orchestral score of *The Year 1941* Suite and whether I'm to receive anything for it. How in general are things getting on with the engraving of the suite?[1] Has it been performed in Moscow, and if not, have you heard the excerpts in the film *In the Ukrainian Steppe*?[2]

I'm very glad that you have begun the arrangement of the *Romeo and Juliet* ballet. And how is the arrangement of the *Alexander Nevsky* Cantata going? I would really like Muzfond to make a copy of the orchestral score of *Romeo and Juliet*, since only one exemplar currently exists. Needless to say, the copy needs to have the same sequence of numbers as the lithographed piano score I left with you.

How annoying that the piano score of *War and Peace* has to be copied anew. Work on the opera at the Bolshoy Theater must be delayed. Did you receive the piano score of the end of scene 11?[3] N. N. Kryukov brought it to Moscow at the end of March and should have given it to Samosud.

I finished the orchestration of *War and Peace* and have started the revision of *Betrothal in a Monastery*, where I'm making a series of changes. I'll finish this work in the coming days and have to send the corrected copies of the piano and orchestral scores to the Bolshoy Theater. The misfortune is that I have a clearly written orchestral score, but the draft piano score is such that nobody besides me can decipher it. Foreseeing this difficulty, I asked Shlifshteyn while I was still in Moscow to obtain the piano score for me from the Stanislavsky Theater. Shlifshteyn categorically promised to do so, but deceived me, saying he would send it later. So to this point I have neither the piano score nor even an explanation from this ill-favored youth. Please take up this matter, that is, obtain the piano score of *Betrothal* and quickly send it to me. I hope that the Bolshoy Theater is still planning to stage the opera: it would be annoying if such stupidity delayed it.[4] The Stanislavsky Theater has at a minimum five copies of the piano score, but if you find it awkward going there in connection with the staging of the opera in another theater, another piano score exists in the Radio Committee library. You might be able to take the copy without explanation, and later, when you collotype the new edition for the Bolshoy Theater, you can give them back a published copy.[5] I beseech you earnestly to take up this matter: I've made all of the corrections on scraps of paper and it's time to put them in order.

You ask what new contracts I'd like to have from Muzfond. I soon plan to finish the *Semyon Kotko* Suite, which I've already drafted, and to write my Eighth Piano Sonata, for which one movement is also now done.[6] I firmly grasp your hand and await your quick response to my numerous questions. Mira Aleksandrovna sends you cordial greetings. Radin is summoning me to the Molotov area for the summer to finish *Cinderella*.[7] It's possible that at the end of June we'll in fact move from Novosibirsk to the shores of the Kama.

Yours

RGALI f. 1929, op. 3, yed. khr. 55, pp. 9–10. In Mendelson's hand, from dictation.

1. *The Year 1941* Suite was not in fact published until 1973, twenty years after the composer's death.

2. Prokofiev refers to his reuse of sections of the Suite in his score for *Partisans in the Ukrainian Steppe* (1942), directed by Igor Savchenko (1906–50).

3. For the second version of *War and Peace*, Prokofiev extensively reworked scene 11, "The Smolensk Road."

4. The opera was not staged at the Bolshoy Theater during this period.

5. The edition was published in collotype in 1944.

6. According to the manuscript (RGALI f. 1929, op. 1, yed. khr. 135), the orchestral score of the *Semyon Kotko* Suite was completed on June 1, 1943, in Alma-Ata.

7. Prokofiev arrived in Molotov on June 29, 1943, where he resumed the work on the ballet that had been interrupted by the start of the war. The Kirov Theater planned to premiere *Cinderella* in Molotov, but it did not actually take place until after the war: first in Moscow (November 21, 1945), then in Leningrad (April 8, 1946).

23. Prokofiev to Atovmyan

Alma-Ata, May 28, 1943

In view of my son's illness please give Lina Ivanovna Prokofieva three thousand. I'll pay it off in the coming months.

Prkfv

RGALI f. 1929, op. 2, yed. khr. 151, p. 11. Handwritten; not available at GTsMMK.

24. Prokofiev to Atovmyan

Alma-Ata, June 10, 1943

Dear Levon Tadevosovich,

I've almost finished the *Semyon Kotko* Suite. Since you asked in one of your letters what commission I'd like to receive from Muzfond, I'd be grateful if you sent me a contract for the suite. The deadline for completing it can be July 1 of this year. It's turning out to be quite large, eight movements, almost 120 pages of scoring in small hand. This is so the contract won't be too meager.

In a week we're leaving for Molotov, where I'll be working on *Cinderella* with the Kirov Theater. My address: Molotov-Region, main post office, general delivery, me. So please send the contract to me at this address. I sent you a long letter on April 24 with many questions; I asked you to answer several by letter, others by telegraph. I hope to receive your answers before I leave Alma-Ata. I grasp your hand.

Yours, S. Prokofiev

RGALI f.1929, op. 3, yed. khr. 55, pp. 11–12. In Mendelson's hand, from dictation.

25. Prokofiev to Atovmyan

Molotov, July 24, 1943
Dear Levon Tadevosovich,

Thank you for your letter of July 12 and the detailed accounting of July 10. I just received a telegram to the effect that Lina Ivanovna is ill with diphtheria and has been taken to the hospital. In connection with this I telegraphed you requesting that 2,000 rubles be given to Svyatoslav. Please forgive me for besieging you and Muzfond with these personal loan requests. The fact is, to this point I haven't received my prize money and don't know what's happening. Perhaps you are aware and can write to me about it.

Besides that I'd ask you to write to me concerning the following:

1. I finished the *Semyon Kotko* Suite; a contract for it is more important than one for the Eighth Sonata, which is less than half written. (What shall we do about the orchestral score? I don't want to send the autograph manuscript. Can you enlist Ashkenazy to make a copy?)
2. At what stage is your arrangement of the ballet *Romeo and Juliet*?
3. At what stage is your arrangement of *Alexander Nevsky*?
4. Before leaving Alma-Ata I received act three of *War and Peace* (in collotype); I await the remaining acts from you here in Molotov.
5. Moreover, please tell me what you know concerning the preparation of the opera at the Bolshoy Theater and the plans for a staging.
6. I have not yet received the piano score of *Betrothal in a Monastery* and thus cannot complete work on it.
7. Are the excerpts from *Semyon Kotko* published in collotype and, if so, can you send the autograph copies here?

I'd like to receive the answers to all of these questions quickly. It's very kind that you found the means to pay for the publication in collotype of the Classical Symphony and the piano score of *War and Peace*. I'd consider, to the contrary, the 6,000 ruble honorarium for the publication of *The*

Year 1941 Suite miserly if it weren't for the generous gesture in your letter that reads "the remaining 2,400 rubles will be transferred after the
proof is signed."[1] I'm hoping that this isn't a misprint.
   Cordial greetings from Mira Aleksandrovna and me.
   Yours, S. Prokofiev

RGALI f. 1929, op. 3, yed. khr. 55, p. 13. In Mendelson's hand, from dictation.
   1. Atovmyan published the Classical Symphony (1917) in 1941.

26. Atovmyan to Prokofiev

August 4, 1943
Dear Sergey Sergeyevich,
I received your letter yesterday.

1) I didn't receive the telegrams from you about paying Svyatoslav 2,000
   rubles, so as a consequence Svyatoslav didn't receive it. Yesterday I
   called and found out that Lina Ivanovna has returned from the hospital but still isn't able to leave home. In accord with your request,
   Svyatoslav is coming today to collect 2,000 rubles.
2) Publication of the *War and Peace* piano score is finishing up. A few
   pages of scene 11 remain to be copied. I'm sending the 10 scenes that
   are finished with comrade Gorelik to the Kirov Theater.[1] Your copies
   will come to you from Alma-Ata; they will be sent upon receipt of your
   request.
3) I'm sending the piano score of *Betrothal* with comrade Gorelik. I obtained
   it from the theater with the obligation of returning it in ten days. I had to
   deceive them since otherwise you wouldn't receive the score.
4) Concerning the prizes. You've long been able to collect the money; you
   just needed to tell us where to send it. Today I'll give the Stalin Prize
   Committee your account number and ask that your (prize) money be
   transferred into it. In any case send me the following request: "To the
   Stalin Prize Committee: I request that the prize bestowed to me be transferred into such-and-such current account." Perhaps my request will
   prove superfluous, but I spoke on the phone with the secretary and
   she promised to transfer it straightaway (upon R. M. Glier's return to
   Moscow).[2] He's at a state farm right now.
5) According to a statement by S. A. Samosud (I spoke with him this
   morning) the Bolshoy Theater is undertaking preparatory work on the
   opera. Between us, I'm not entirely sure about this, more precisely
   the intensity of the preparatory work, since judging from private conversations with the GABT artists, everyone in the theater is still
   agonizing over the staging of Kabalevsky's opera *Near Moscow*. It's pre-

sumed that the staging will be off everyone's back at the end of August
... Heretical labor![3] But I'm afraid it will be fruitless. I don't believe in
that opus. True, I'm basing my judgment on the first edition of the
piano score. They say that the theater has "redone" and "remounted"
it all, but from childhood they banged it into our heads that changing
the ordering of numbers doesn't affect their total. In a word, one must
suppose that the theater will begin serious work on *War and Peace* in
the month of September.

6) The *R and J*[4] arrangement is almost finished. Two acts (37 nos.) are
almost in fair copy. I'll begin copying the third act in the next few
days. I anxiously await your arrival and critique of the work that's
been carried out. Today I received a telegram from the theater with a
request to send the orchestral score with Gorelik. But: a) the telegram
came an hour before Gorelik left, and the score is at home; b) I still
need it; and c) I will continue to need it, since it requires copying.
Please talk it over with comrade Radin and ask him to be a little more
patient. If, however, the theater needs the score for the purposes of
reviving the production—let them telegraph: I'll immediately send
the score with a courier.

7) Needless to say, the contract for *Semyon Kotko* will be completed. But
the Flute Sonata needs to be received. Could you not send the Sonata
and, while you're at it, the *Semyon Kotko* score with Gorelik or one of
the theater's other workers? They often visit Moscow. I'll arrange the
copying here.

8) The excerpts from *Semyon Kotko* are not out, owing to disputes with
Glavrepertkom (Bakhchisaraytsev).[5] They conspired to dictate what
excerpts should and should not be published. Believing that they're in
the wrong (especially as they're prohibiting most of the nos.), I began
an argument with them that has still not been resolved. I still think I'll
manage to convince them that they're making too much of it and
aren't keeping their gates.[6]

It seems these are all the issues. Alas, this is another long letter and I'll
have to postpone the information about Moscow life until the next one.
Just a couple of words: the resolution concerning your award was welcomed by everyone with great joy.[7] I'm not exaggerating—it was a festive
occasion (with much drinking), no less so than the resolution of April 23,
1932 (on the liquidation of RAPM).[8]

Heartfelt congratulations. We await you impatiently in Moscow. When
do you think you'll be here?[9]

Heartfelt greetings to Mira Aleksandrovna. I send best wishes. With
devotion,

Atovmyan

RGALI f. 1929, op. 1, yed. khr. 446, pp. 18–20.

1. Mordukh Gorelik, manager of the Kirov Theater orchestra.

2. Reinhold Moritsevich Glier (1875–1956), composer. From 1938 to 1948 he served as chairman of the Organizing Committee of the Union of Soviet Composers.

3. The premiere of the 1942 opera *V ogne: Pod Moskvoy* (*Into the Fire: Near Moscow*) by Dmitriy Kabalevsky (1904–87), occurred on September 19, 1943, at an affiliate of the Bolshoy Theater.

4. *Romeo and Juliet.*

5. Modest Bakhchisaraytsev (1903–61) worked from 1942 to 1944 as a censor for Glavrepertkom, the repertoire control division of the Committee on Arts Affairs.

6. The expression "to keep one's own gates" means "to mind one's own affairs."

7. Prokofiev received the Order of the Red Banner of Labor on July 27, 1943. The presentation ceremony, which Prokofiev did not attend, was held at the Kremlin on August 10.

8. The 1932 dissolution of RAPM (Russian Association of Proletarian Musicians) led to the establishment of the Composers' Union of Moscow and, subsequently, the Composers' Union of the USSR.

9. Prokofiev would not return to Moscow from Molotov until October 5, 1943.

27. Prokofiev to Atovmyan

Molotov, August 12, 1943

Dear Levon Tadevosovich,

I include with this letter the orchestral score of the *Semyon Kotko* Suite. This is *my only copy*: entrusting it to you, I take your word that you won't give it out to anyone and will immediately make another copy. Later on, it would be advisable for you to preserve the original (which is largely written in my hand) and to provide the copy you've made for perusal and performance.

I received your August 4 letter and the piano score of *Betrothal* and profusely thank you for them. I can now make the changes to the piano score. Let me know if you are immediately planning to publish it in collotype,* in which case I will deliver it to you after it's corrected.

I received the 9th and 10th scenes of *War and Peace*, but it would have been better had my eyes not seen "Act III," instead of "Act IV," written above scene 9.[1]

Radin has no objection to the orchestral score of *Romeo and Juliet* being with you for a while. I'm very glad that the piano score is moving forward and burn with impatience to see the results.

Needless to say, I won't ask again about the piano score of *Alexander Nevsky*.[2]

I enclose with this letter the application to the Stalin Prize Committee. Don't fail to telegraph me as soon as the evaluation concludes. Also confirm receipt of this letter, that is, of the *Semyon Kotko* Suite.

The Flute Sonata is almost finished. The reprise of the finale remains to be written up. It ended up being quite substantial: four parts, nearly 40 pages, in a word worth all 8,000 rubles.

The question of my trip to Moscow remains uncertain in view of the fact that Eisenstein expects me in Alma-Ata at the end of September to finish the music for *Ivan the Terrible* Part I.[3] By the way, I spoke in January with Mikhaíl Borisovich[4] about the possibility of obtaining an apartment. He was sympathetic. I'd like you to let me know the current possibilities on this front. I seek, of course, to obtain an apartment in the center of the city, though not in the composers' building. It would be good to settle this question during my next trip to Moscow.

We both send you cordial greetings. I grasp your hand and thank you for your concern.

Yours, S. Prokofiev

*Extremely desirable in view of the plans of a number of theaters to stage the opera.

RGALI f. 1929, op. 3, yed. khr. 55, pp. 14–15. In Mendelson's hand, from dictation.

1. The error went uncorrected in the 1943 edition of the piano score.

2. An ironic reference to the fact that Prokofiev had repeatedly requested a progress report from Atovmyan about his arrangement of the *Alexander Nevsky* Cantata.

3. Prokofiev did not travel to Alma-Ata at the end of September. On October 7, 1943, Eisenstein sent a follow-up telegram requesting the composer's presence in the Mosfilm studios, but Prokofiev was again unable to travel there, owing to work on a prospective performance of *War and Peace* in December and preparation for an orchestral concert.

4. Mikhaíl Khrapchenko, chairman of the Committee on Arts Affairs.

28. Atovmyan to Prokofiev

August 24, 1943

Dear Sergey Sergeyevich,

Yesterday I received your letter and answered by telegram. I immediately submitted the score of *Semyon Kotko* (the suite) for copying and, it goes without saying, the original will stay with me and won't be given to anyone (perhaps only to Nik. Yakovlevich). I suggest making the parts in September, so as to have the work ready for your concert. By the way: what do you advise for the program, and when are you planning on being in Moscow, since one must suppose that you'll be conducting it yourself? My own modest desire is a three-part concert:

Part 1: *Semyon Kotko* Suite
Alexander Nevsky
Part 2: Piano Concerto (any one—to be honest I'd again put on the 5th, which we seldom perform)[1]
The Year 1941 or *Zdravitsa*
Part 3: Russian Overture
War and Peace Suite (with chorus and orchestra)

For this program 2–3 months of preparation is needed (chorus, soloists) and no small number of rehearsals (about 6–7, I think).[2]

When I receive the piano score of *Betrothal* I'll immediately begin arranging permission for publication and, thereafter, submit it for collotyping. The corrections to *War and Peace* will all be done upon receipt of your proofed copy (which you promised to send). I'm afraid that you'll once again scold me for this or that error by the copyists and proofreaders. I finished the *Romeo* piano score and one of our best copyists is now almost finished with the fair copy. Before showing it to you I think I'll show it to Nik. Yakovlevich. You're a very harsh judge, you see, and it's not so easy going to you.

I'm holding on to the *Romeo* score since I want to make a copy for Moscow, rather than having to resort in the future to the Kirov Theater.[3]

I've begun the *Nevsky* arrangement. Shlifshteyn, by the way, has nothing against contracting the arrangement, but I need a letter from you (to the effect that you are asking me to do it). I'll drop the letter off to Shlifshteyn.

I sent your applications to the Stalin Prize Committee yesterday. I'll follow up and let you know the verdict.

Don't delay with the Flute Sonata, since new contracts will need arranging. I'm sending you 2 new contract forms. Please sign them (on the back) and return them to me. I'll be transferring to your account (notifying you of the date and amount of the transfer) the honorarium that is due to you, less the repayment of the 2,000 rubles recently disbursed to Lina Ivanovna and the amount of the loan payment.

Apartments in Moscow are generally tight, but if Mikh. Bor. takes on the task, then of course it's entirely possible to obtain one—what's more in the center. Shostakovich had a hard time finding an apartment but, after a fight, nonetheless succeeded in occupying an apartment on Myasnitskaya.[4]

Remind Mikh. Bor. about the apartment; I think that, from a practical standpoint, this matter awaits resolution after your arrival in Moscow.

I send you and Mira Aleksandrovna best wishes and heartfelt greetings. With devotion,

Atovmyan

RGALI f. 1929, op. 1, yed. khr. 446, pp. 21–22.
1. Prokofiev's Fifth Piano Concerto (1932) was performed in Moscow on November 25, 1932, with Prokofiev as soloist, and on March 9, 1941, with Richter as soloist and Prokofiev as conductor.
2. The concert in question did not occur. On May 20, 1944, Prokofiev conducted a concert of English and Soviet music that included two excerpts from *Alexander Nevsky* ("Arise, Russian People" and "Alexander's Entry into Pskov") and the Russian Overture (1937).
3. The Moscow premiere of *Romeo and Juliet* took place at the Bolshoy Theater on December 22, 1946, under the direction of Yuriy Fayer (1890–1971).
4. Shostakovich moved into the apartment on Myasnitskaya Street on April 20, 1943.

29. Prokofiev to Atovmyan

This letter is partly damaged; ellipses indicate the missing words.

Molotov-Region, September 3, 1943
Dear Levon Tadevosovich,

Thank you for sending me the contracts for the *Kotko* Suite and the Eighth Sonata, which I'm returning to you signed. I also enclose the request to the Music Directorate regarding *Alexander Nevsky*.[1] I'd be delighted if you started this work; I'm sure that you arranged *Romeo* successfully. A copy of the orchestral score of the ballet needs to be made, but absolutely in the same order I gave to you for the piano score.

I finished scoring *Ballad of an Unknown Boy*, a rather large and tempestuous cantata for soprano, tenor, chorus, and orchestra.[2] I've already sent the piano score to Surin, and I'll dispatch the orchestral score to him in a few days.[3] Surin asked to be sent the cantata in connection with Mravinsky's residency in Moscow.[4] Regarding your wish for me to conduct my own concert, please take into account that it's much more important for me to hear *Semyon Kotko* and *The Year 1941* from the audience so as to evaluate them and make the necessary touch-ups before publication. So I'd like someone else to conduct. Regarding your modest desire to fill at least three programs, I really don't know what to choose from your suggestions. In any case I'd like to hear *Semyon Kotko* and *The Year 1941*.*[5]

In your letter of July 12 (typed; evidently you have a copy), you reported that 1,553 rubles and 89 kopecks have been deposited into my current account [. . .]. I sent Lina Ivanovna [. . .], but received a response today [. . .] that the savings bank did not pay the funds you sent [. . .]. I have to think that I'm the victim of another prank by the merry staff of Muzfond. In any case I found it very unpleasant. Kindly clear up the matter and without fail issue Lina Ivanovna 4,000 rubles from the fee for *Semyon Kotko* and the Eighth Sonata. Let me know the standing of my accounts with Muzfond after this transfer. I estimate that I'll send you the piano score of *Betrothal in a Monastery* in ten days. I await the eleventh scene of *War and Peace* from you. We send you cordial greetings.

Yours

* I will write to you about my arrival in Moscow as soon as I find out the length of my stay in Alma-Ata, where they apparently need me for October and part of November.

RGALI f. 1929, op. 3, yed. khr. 55, pp. 16–17. In Mendelson's hand, from dictation.
1. On the back of this letter Prokofiev drafted the following letter to the Directorate for Music Organizations: "Having familiarized myself with L. T. Atovmyan's arrangement of

Shostakovich's Seventh Symphony, I would ask that the Directorate find the means to enlist L. T. Atovmyan to arrange my *Alexander Nevsky* Cantata for piano, two hands."

2. According to the manuscript (RGALI f. 1929, op. 1, yed. khr. 257), Prokofiev completed the orchestration of the cantata in Moscow on June 28, 1943.

3. Vladimir Surin (1906–94), Committee on Arts Affairs official.

4. The proposed performance by the Leningrad Philharmonic under the direction of Yevgeniy Mravinsky (1903–88) did not occur. The cantata was instead premiered by the Moscow State Symphony Orchestra under the direction of Gauk on February 21, 1944.

5. The *Semyon Kotko* Suite was performed on December 27, 1943, in Moscow in the composer's presence.

30. Prokofiev to Atovmyan

Molotov-Region, September 16, 1943

Dear Levon Tadevosovich,

The Kirov Theater has scheduled a staging of my ballet *The Buffoon*, and soon at that. Since I don't have the piano score here, and don't know where mine is, I implore you without haste to make a copy of it. It can be obtained from Nik. Yak., or perhaps from Ye. V. Derzhanovskaya[1] or the Conservatory library. The Kirov Theater will pay for the copy. Instruct the copyist to carefully write out the comments concerning the visual action, and likewise the indications for the instrumentation (fl., cl., and so forth). Second: To become familiar with the sound of *The Buffoon*, the theater wants to run through the suite in a closed rehearsal. Please send the orchestral score and parts to the theater's chairman, who will deliver them here and return them immediately after the run-through. The material is located in the SSK library and belongs to me.[2]

I confirm for you my joint telegram with Sherman on the 12th of this month, requesting that he be sent the orchestral score of my Sinfonietta, which is located in the SSK library.[3] Sherman will conduct it in Moscow around December 1 in a Radio Committee concert. I wrote to you on September 3 about the other matters. Meanwhile I asked you to pay Lina Ivanovna 4,000 rubles. I hope this has already occurred.

I received 100 pages of score paper; I'm very grateful. I finished the Flute Sonata, but let me put it aside for a while.

To this point I haven't received a telegram from you about the transfer of the prize money. I firmly grasp your hand. Cordial greetings from Mira Aleksandrovna.

Yours, S. Prokofiev

RGALI f. 1929, op. 2, yed. khr. 151, p. 13. In Mendelson's hand, from dictation.

1. Yekaterina Vasilyevna Koposova-Derzhanovskaya (1877–1959), singer.

2. Work on the reconstruction of the score of *The Buffoon* was undertaken on Prokofiev's request by the orchestrator Dmitriy Rogal-Levitsky (1898–1962). The proposed Kirov Theater staging was canceled; the unfinished reconstruction is preserved in GTsMMK f. 351, yed. khr. 139.

3. Isay Sherman (1908–72), conductor.

31. Atovmyan to Prokofiev

September 29, 1943

First: let me know if I'm to send just the score of the Sinfonietta or the parts as well. Second: there are no orchestral parts for *The Buffoon*. Where is it best to have the parts of the suite made—in Molotov or Moscow? Third: should the piano score of *The Buffoon* be copied in Moscow or a printed copy sent to the theater for temporary use?
    Atovmyan

RGALI f. 1929, op. 1, yed. khr. 446, p. 25.

32. Atovmyan to Prokofiev

Prokofiev returned to Moscow from evacuation in Molotov on October 5, 1943, after which he was in regular face-to-face contact with Atovmyan until the summer of 1944. Atovmyan evidently sent this letter from Nikolina Gora, a suburban Moscow enclave of summer homes favored by the Soviet (and post-Soviet) elite. Prokofiev received it in Ivanovo, where he stayed in the Union of Soviet Composers resort from June 9 until August 28, 1944.

July 16, 1944
Dear Sergey Sergeyevich,
    I assumed that you were coming on July 10 and thus didn't reply to you. I fulfilled your instruction (to transfer 5,000 rubles to Lina Ivanovna) with, in truth, a slight delay (on July 5 instead of July 1, since they didn't manage to receive the money before the 5th).
    If you won't be here before August 1, do you have in mind transferring another 5,000 rubles on the 1st?
    I received the score of *Betrothal* from Molotov. Since everyone at GABT is on holiday and there's nobody to send the score to, I took the occasion to submit the score for copying, so that I'll have a copy with me. I haven't yet received the score of *Cinderella* from Leningrad, though I sent a telegram. I'll remind them there. I also inquired with Leningrad as to whether I'm to send the *Romeo* score by post or wait for their courier— likewise no answer. Evidently the people there are also on holiday.
    P. A. Lamm will try to get to Nikolina Gora tomorrow—he's getting the material of the suite to me.[1] Should I keep it with me until your return or send it to you by courier?
    The *Romeo* piano score will soon be out from the press. Two acts are already printed. Just a little left. I wanted to begin *Cinderella* (the piano score), but GABT is complicating matters. They provided half of the

piano score but not the rest (they refused, saying they need it), and so I can't obtain permission from Obllit[2] to publish it. They say that Bogdanov (the librarian) is back soon—I'll try to squeeze it out of him.

I'm sending the correspondence that's addressed to you.

Regarding the apartment: of course, two rooms, what's more on Mozhayskoye Shosse, is a discomfort. However, if this proves to be the only offer from Mossovet, then you have to take the apartment, so as to exchange it for a 3-room apartment closer to the center.[3] The cost of the exchange will evidently come out to be less than the cost of waiting for other options (reckoning that you'll have to wait in a hotel). Building 11 on Mozhayskoye Shosse is located not far from a Metro station, which will facilitate the exchange. You need, importantly, to see the apartment.[4]

When are you planning on returning to Moscow? I hear that you're working a lot. I hope you're in good spirits.

Convey my greetings to Mira Aleksandrovna. I send best wishes.

Atovmyan

RGALI f. 1929, op. 1, yed. khr. 446, pp. 28–29.
 1. The Third Suite from *Romeo and Juliet*.
 2. Obllit: Oblastnoye upravleniye po delam literaturï i izdatel'stv (Regional administration on literary and publishing affairs).
 3. Mossovet (Moscow Soviet of People's Deputies), city hall.
 4. In June 1944 Prokofiev received a two-room apartment on Mozhayskoye Shosse (now Bolshaya Dorogomilovskaya Street), but did not move into it. On January 1, 1945, he received a two-and-a-half-room apartment at the same address, but lived there for less than half a year due to the noise from the neighbors (he suffered debilitating headaches) and the location. He sought without success to exchange the apartment. On November 15, 1947, he registered as a tenant in the central Moscow apartment of Mira's parents.

33. Prokofiev to Atovmyan

Ivanovo, July 17, 1944
Dear Levon Tadevosovich,
    Thank you for your July 16 letter and for the 5,000 ruble payment to Lina Ivanovna. Eisenstein is already dragging me back to Moscow, but I'd like to remain here another 2–3 weeks, since I've settled into the symphony and the work is going quite well.[1] Thus I'd ask you, if I'm delayed, to pay Lina Ivanovna another 5,000 rubles on August 1.

    There's no need to forward the suite that Lamm made from *Romeo and Juliet*, but if the orchestrated numbers from *Cinderella* are forthcoming from Karpov, immediately send them to me here by courier.[2] I'm sending you the orchestration of number 45 from *Cinderella*, requesting that you give it to Lamm for deciphering. But by a trustworthy courier, because I don't have a duplicate.

How stupid that the Bolshoy Theater is procrastinating with the *Cinderella* piano score. In any case bear in mind that I can give you the complete Act 3.

VOKS requests the violin version of the Flute Sonata from me. Since you have the violin-piano reduction, I'd ask you to send it to VOKS.[3]

It's a shame that you can't be here to admire the State Chicken Farm; it would be nice to see you gathering mushrooms and abandoning yourself to pastoral joys![4] Heartfelt greetings from Mira Aleksandrovna and me.
Yours, SP

RGALI f. 1929, op. 2, yed. khr. 151, p. 14. Handwritten.
1. He refers to his Fifth Symphony (1944).
2. Mikhaíl Karpov (1884–1960), concertmaster and conductor at the Kirov Theater, worked as Prokofiev's assistant during the composer's residency in Molotov.
3. VOKS, the All-Union Society for Cultural Ties Abroad, was established in 1925. Prokofiev refers to his Second Violin Sonata (1944), a transcription of the Flute Sonata made at the request of the violinist David Oistrakh (1908–74).
4. The Union of Soviet Composers resort was located on the grounds of a former estate. The composers-in-residence were allocated workplaces in the renovated buildings—including a former chicken hut and pig barn—that surrounded the main house.

34. Atovmyan to Prokofiev

September 13, 1944
Dear Sergey Sergeyevich,

Organizing the funerals and conversing with the widows didn't give me the chance to talk things over with you.[1]

I'm sending you the Muzfond accounting. I'll provide explanations, if necessary, when we meet. The accounting doesn't include the additional 5,000 rubles paid (with your signature) to L. I.[2] and the accounting for *Romeo*. I'm combining this accounting with that for *Cinderella* and will submit it later (bringing together, by the way, the additional expenses that I'm covering with a matching increase in the *Cinderella* honorarium).

Your financial prospects? 2–3 publication contracts (specifically the *Semyon Kotko* Suite, the Flute Sonata, and the piano pieces, if you give them to us), which will equal 25–30 thousand rubles minus taxes. Through Muzfond: the publication of *Cinderella* and the piano pieces (in collotype) which, because of the increase in the honorarium, will provide (after the calculations of the expenses for *Romeo and Juliet*) around 30,000 rubles.[3]

Expenses: taxes = x amount; L. I. for X, XI, and XII[4] = 15,000 rubles; the loan = 8,300 rubles. Perhaps part of the revenue should be transferred to 1945? I'm anticipating, though, the publication of *Semyon Kotko* in 1945 (the first edition, if you don't object) and I don't doubt that there will be new work (in the domain of opera and ballet). Finally, there's the cost of creative assistance.

So don't let yourself be anxious about material questions. Let these concerns rest with us. Now about other things:

The piano: will you be taking your instrument from Chkalovskaya when you move into the apartment or do you need a new one?[5] If the latter, then you need to let me know: a) the best maker (your preference); b) grand or upright; c) purchase (that is, an acquisition) or lease.[6] A question about furnishings: what will you need (excluding what you'll be taking from Chkalovskaya)? All of it, you see, will have to be found ahead of time at secondhand stores (so as not to have the furniture assembled from mismatched sets).

Well, we'll settle the other questions when we meet. I'd like to see you on Friday or Saturday (or next week on Wednesday or Thursday) and, if you allow it, to hear the piano pieces and the symphony.[7]

Greetings and best wishes,

Atovmyan

RGALI f. 1929, op. 1, yed. khr. 446, pp. 31–32.
1. The funerals to which Atovmyan refers are unknown.
2. Lina Ivanovna Prokofieva.
3. The *Cinderella* piano score was published in collotype in 1945.
4. October through December.
5. Chkalovskaya refers to the apartment on Chkalov Street (now Zemlyanoy Val), where Prokofiev's first wife and two sons lived.
6. Prokofiev leased a Steinway upright from Muzfond.
7. The Six Pieces for Piano from *Cinderella* (1944) and the Fifth Symphony.

35. Atovmyan to Prokofiev

January 10, 1945

Dear Sergey Sergeyevich,

Unfortunately the military commission delayed me until 1 p.m. and I wasn't able to come to the rehearsal.[1] I'm sending you 3,000 rubles in the form of a loan that will come from the amount for *Cinderella*. I'll discharge the honorarium on 15/I. These days the accountant is tortured with bookkeeping, taking inventory, and other bureaucratic tasks. But I've managed to get the small amount for the preparation of Glier's jubilee.[2] Please give the ticket for *Ivan the Terrible* to Lena Buneyeva.[3]

Today I should receive the bill from the store for the divan.

Greetings, Atovmyan

RGALI f. 1929, op. 1, yed. khr. 446, p. 33.
1. Of the Fifth Symphony.
2. Glier turned seventy on January 11, 1945.

3. *Ivan the Terrible* Part I opened at select theaters in Moscow on January 18, 1945. Several advance screenings preceded the opening.

36. Prokofiev to Atovmyan

In a diary entry dated February 2, 1945, Myaskovsky reports that Prokofiev had been suffering for almost two weeks from severe head trauma caused by a bad fall. On March 7 he was admitted to the Kremlin Hospital in Moscow. From April 9 to May 28 he recuperated at the Podlipki sanatorium in Barvikha.[1]

[April 1945]

Please, if possible, ship the things that I need here at the sanatorium. They are at the Mendelson apartment.[2]

Greetings, apologies. Prokofiev

RGALI f. 1929, op. 3, yed. khr. 55, p. 3. In Mendelson's hand, from dictation; not available at GTsMMK.

1. Lamm, *Stranitsï tvorcheskoy biografïi Myaskovskogo*, 310–12; RGALI f. 1929, op. 1, yed. khr. 446, p. 35.

2. Prokofiev refers to the communal apartment occupied by his eventual second wife, Mira, and her parents.

37. Prokofiev to Atovmyan

Prokofiev returned to Ivanovo in late June 1945, remaining there until the beginning of October.[1] *His fastidiousness about managing his income and expenses, exacerbated by the need to support his estranged wife and children, is evident on the back of the letter, which includes a draft note to the chief accountant of the All-Union Concert Society in Moscow with a request for 3,000 rubles (owed to him from a July 14, 1945 contract) to be sent to him directly or else deposited into his savings bank account.*

Ivanovo, July 15, 1945

Dear Levon Tadevosovich,

Permit me to bother you with four questions:

1. I want to have the orchestral score of the Third Suite from *Romeo and Juliet* (specifically the three last parts) to check over Lamm's work.
2. I would like to have the orchestral score of the Fifth Symphony (given to Muzgiz) and the first string parts. Berlin entered the bowings during the rehearsals. The parts were in Leningrad and should have been returned after the June 24 performance.[2]
3. If it's not too difficult, send 5,000 rubles to me here by courier.
4. Don't finalize the contracts for Malegot and the Stanislavsky to stage

my operas without first coming to an agreement with me, because I
have old accounts to square with them.[3]
As always, we expect you as our guest at the State Pig Farm and send
you cordial greetings.

RGALI f. 1929, op. 3, yed. khr. 55, p. 18. In Mendelson's hand, from dictation.
1. GTsMMK f. 33, yed. khr. 1413, pp. 103–4.
2. Anisim Berlin (1896–1961), concertmaster of the State Symphony Orchestra. Following
the Moscow premiere of the Fifth Symphony on January 13, 1945, with Prokofiev conducting,
it was performed on June 24 by the Leningrad Philharmonic with Mravinsky conducting.
3. Malegot is the Leningrad State Academic Malïy Theater of Opera and Ballet;
Stanislavsky refers to the theater of that name.

38. Atovmyan to Prokofiev

August 1, 1945
Dear Sergey Sergeyevich,
The parts for the Symphony[1] are at the Philharmonic, which is on
vacation. Entering the bowings into the score will have to wait. Soon the
librarian will return from vacation: I'll get the parts from him and send
them to you with the score. Perhaps I'll send the score earlier (I have it
now), but it's hardly worth doing so without the parts.
I'm sending the score of the 3rd Suite[2] and the contract for the
"Children's Music."[3] Please sign the contract and quickly return it to me so
that I can make the next payment to Lina Ivanovna.
I didn't sign the contract with Malegot and the Stanislavsky.
The delay in sending the money is a formality. First of all, before today
the bank was only issuing funds to demobilized soldiers. Moreover, in the
future, when you need money, I'd ask you not to write about it by letter
to me but to send a separate request, as follows, to the Muzfond administration: "Please send my royalties of . . . rubles to my account. Signature."
This is a formality, but without observing it the arrangement gets complicated. Please forgive the accountant's bureaucratic demand. Specify the
amount you need; the money will be found for you.
I evidently won't be coming to the State Pig Farm soon, since apparently I have to go to Berlin and Leipzig for scores. I'll find out soon and
let you know.
Greetings to Mira Aleksandrovna. My best wishes to you.
Atovmyan
The Album for Children is copied.[4] What should I do? Send it or await
your arrival?

RGALI f. 1929, op. 1, yed. khr. 446, p. 38.
1. The Fifth Symphony.
2. From *Romeo and Juliet*.

3. Atovmyan refers to the publishing agreement for *Summer Day* (1941), an orchestral suite based on a 1935 cycle of children's piano pieces.
4. See letter 70.

39. Prokofiev to Atovmyan

Ivanovo-Region, August 9, 1945
Dear Levon Tadevosovich,
1. I'm sending you three applications:
   a) for 1,500 rubles, which you sent to me with R. M. Glier
   b) for 3,500 rubles, which I ask you to send to me here at the first opportunity
   c) for 5,000 rubles, which I ask you to deposit in my savings bank account.
2. I return with this letter the signed contract, for which I'm grateful, for the children's music.
3. I'm returning the orchestral score of the Third Suite from *Romeo and Juliet*. Vlasov has in mind a performance at the start of the season, so please print the parts as well as making a copy of the score, because during the rehearsals I'll want to note adjustments to the sound inside of it. I placed instructions for copying the parts in the score.[1]
4. Before leaving Moscow I left you the RAYFO statement about the war tax I paid in 1945.[2] Please send a copy to the accountants at the Radio Committee (Putinkovsky Lane) and VGKO.[3] I'm owed honoraria from both of them.
5. Please send the orchestral score of the Fifth Symphony to me together with the first string parts (with Berlin's notes).
6. I enclose the list of mistakes in your edition of the Amoroso, op. 102.[4]
7. I await the proofs of the six Russian songs that I submitted to you before my departure.[5]

Mira Aleksandrovna and I are very upset that you aren't coming to our *latifundia* and wish you health and success in your affairs.[6]
Yours, SP

RGALI f. 1929, op. 2, yed. khr. 151, p. 15. In Mendelson's hand, from dictation.
   1. The prospective performance, to be conducted by Vladimir Vlasov (1903–86), was canceled. The Third Suite did not receive a premiere until March 8, 1946, under the direction of Vladimir Degtyarenko (1908–80).
   2. Rayonnïy Finansovïy Otdel (Regional Finance Division).
   3. Vserossiyskoye gastrol'no-kontsertnoye ob'yedineniye (All-Russian Concert Tour Association).
   4. From the Six Pieces for Piano from *Cinderella*.
   5. Prokofiev refers to his *Russian Folksong Arrangements* (1941). Atovmyan edited seven of these songs for their 1945 publication: "The Green Glade," "Guelder Rose on the Hill," "White Snow," "Brown Eyes," "Dunyushka," "My Beloved Is Gone," and "Sashenka."
   6. *Latifundia*: Latin for great estates.

40. Atovmyan to Prokofiev

September 17, 1945

Dear Sergey Sergeyevich,

Muzgiz, it appears, is planning to publish the piano scores of *Alexander Nevsky* and *Zdravitsa*.[1] In relation to this I'm sending you two copies (collotyped) of the *Alexander Nevsky* piano score, the *Zdravitsa* piano score, and the orchestral scores of both works in case you need to make changes.

On the subject of *Alexander Nevsky*, do you consider it worthwhile easing (simplifying) the arrangement? I'm afraid that I mistakenly attempted a "maximal" presentation. Perhaps it would be better for this reason to cut out the "third line" in several places (in particular the campanella and xylophone line in No. 7). Please give instructions. In arranging *Zdravitsa* I avoided the "third line" and unusual complexities. Please look over both piano scores, striking out those places where the arrangement is unsuitable and return, with the bearer of this letter, one of the *Alexander Nevsky* piano scores, the *Zdravitsa* piano score, and your authorization for their publication. Following the example of *Alexander Nevsky* I'm publishing a limited edition of *Zdravitsa* in collotype.

I'm also sending with the bearer of this letter the 2,000 rubles you requested. Please sign the receipt and send it to me. I'm likewise sending the knitwear: I'm not sure I chose the right things.

When are you coming to Moscow? Let me know so I can meet you.

With the bearer of this letter, please send back the music (four-hand) that I left with you. If it doesn't cause you trouble, try to look over the piano scores expeditiously so that the "envoy" can return to Moscow the next day after his arrival in Ivanovo.

Greetings to Mira Aleksandrovna. With devotion, Atovmyan

My girls send ardent greetings to you and Mira Aleksandrovna. They're charmed by her.

Continuation:

Once more now at the piano I've looked over the published piano score of *Alexander Nevsky*. I'm troubled by the difficulty of the arrangement in such places as pages 26–28 and, further on, 46–47 (Allegro).

One more question: would it be better on page 98, rehearsal number 57, and analogously on page 103, rehearsal number 60, to take out the scale (right hand) from the third line, and in the piano score to leave the theme in that guise in which it appeared at the end of page 103 and beginning of page 104?

Lastly, has the bass line (the string bass part) been left out of the first measure of page 118 (in the piano score)?

Needless to say, before the score is engraved I'll check all of the "notes" (so as to avoid as many errors as possible).

Again, I'm sending you 2,000 rubles as per your request; in addition, I'm returning the receipt for the 1,500 rubles you received on August 4, since it isn't written properly. Please destroy the receipt and sign a new one (enclosed) for 3,500 rubles. Sign, accordingly, in two places: x—just a signature; xx—indication of the amount and a signature. I await your letters. *Zdravitsa* has just now been returned from copying. I'll correct the mistakes.

Greetings to Mira Aleksandrovna. Respectfully yours, Atovmyan

P.S. I'll send out additional knitwear soon. The choice in the warehouse is dismal right now.

RGALI f. 1929, op. 1, yed. khr. 446, pp. 40–41.

1. Prokofiev composed *Zdravitsa*, a musical "toast" to Stalin's sixtieth birthday, in 1939. On January 17, 1943, Prokofiev sent Lamm a telegram reporting that Muzgiz intended to commission a piano reduction of *Zdravitsa* from him. Although he asked Lamm to do the reduction, the task instead fell to Atovmyan. Muzgiz published it in 1946.

41. Prokofiev to Atovmyan

Ivanovo, September 20, 1945

Dear Levon Tadevosovich,

I looked closely at both of your piano scores and I'm returning them with the inscription "can be engraved." The piano score of *Zdravitsa* sounds very good and I made only the most minimal of alterations. Since Muzgiz is planning to publish *Zdravitsa*, it would be good to commission straightaway an English translation from Shneyerson, who in collaboration with an American successfully coped with *Alexander Nevsky*.[1] Perhaps you can make this known at Muzfond. In both scores you need to show the instruments that are performing, as you did in *Romeo and Juliet*. There are no rehearsal numbers in some parts of *Alexander Nevsky*. The absences are annoying, since the piano score will be used to prepare the chorus. Moreover, in the piano score published in collotype the double-measure signs are again done sloppily: when will your staff finally learn to respect an author's wishes? I looked closely at your concerns, which you laid out on the page affixed to your letter, but I find that everything can be left as is.

Thanks for warming our bodies and souls by sending the pullovers: they're good things and much needed. It's not worth sending anything else here, however. With your permission, we'll stop by Muzfond on the return to Moscow.

I received the 2,000 rubles, thanks, likewise the old receipt for 1,500 rubles. In exchange I'm returning a receipt for 3,500 rubles.

I'm also sending back the signed contract for the creative help with *Ode*.[2] It would be good to see this money and that the money for Lina Ivanovna is entirely loaned. By the way, can you transfer 5,000 rubles into my current account so that there will be funds there on my arrival?

Please send a copy of the statement from RAYFO about the war tax I paid in 1945 to the accountant at Mosfilm (in Potïlikha), since Mosfilm should reimburse me.[3]

We're sending you, as an extra burden, a suitcase containing our summer things. Please lug it to M. A.'s parents or else keep it with you until we arrive.

Please accept our cordial greetings and gratitude for your concern and the promise to meet. Mira Aleksandrovna thanks your young ones for the help.

Yours

I'm sending:

Alexander Nevsky, orchestral and piano scores;

Zdravitsa, orchestral and piano scores;

The contract for *Ode;*

A receipt for the 3,500 rubles;

A receipt for the pullovers;

A parcel with your music;

Our suitcase.

RGALI f. 1929, op. 3, yed. khr. 55, p. 19. Typed letter.

1. Grigoriy Shneyerson (1901–82), musicologist, secretary of the foreign bureau of the Union of Soviet Composers, director of the music division of VOKS. The text of *Alexander Nevsky* was translated into English by Andrew Steiger.

2. *Ode to the End of the War* (1945).

3. The Mosfilm studios are located in the Moscow suburb of Potïlikha.

42. Atovmyan to Prokofiev

November 17, 1945

Dear Sergey Sergeyevich,

So as to close the accounts with Lina Ivanovna for this year, please sign the two enclosed forms. I'll cover the loan for this from the publishing honorarium. I reminded Lina Ivanovna about the books.[1] I await your response today or tomorrow.

Greetings, Atovmyan

RGALI f. 1929, op. 1, yed. khr. 446, p. 42.

1. Prokofiev had asked Atovmyan to collect some books from his former apartment.

43. Atovmyan to Prokofiev

February 4, 1946
Dear Sergey Sergeyevich,
    I'm sending my (own) copy of the Classical Symphony score and the *Romeo* piano score. Please return those nos., mistakenly sent to you, with Pogrebov's orchestration.[1] I send greetings and best wishes.
    Atovmyan

RGALI f. 1929, op. 1, yed. khr. 446, p. 46.
    1. Boris Pogrebov, Bolshoy Theater percussionist and arranger. This letter buttresses the assertion by Gennadiy Rozhdestvensky (b. 1931) that the Bolshoy Theater instructed Pogrebov to re-orchestrate parts of Prokofiev's final three ballet scores to make them more danceable. Grigoriy Pantiyelov, "Prokof'yev: Razmïshleniya, svidetel'stva, sporï. Beseda s Gennadiyem Rozhdestvenskim," *Sovetskaya muzïka* 4 (1991): 16.

44. Atovmyan to Prokofiev

February 24, 1946
Dear Sergey Sergeyevich,
    I looked over *Zdravitsa*. I corrected the few mistakes I found in the margins. Let me know when you've looked it over so that I can collect the proofs from you and submit them to Muzgiz.
    How's the Classical?[1] Will Pavel Aleksandrovich give you the work soon?[2] I send greetings and best wishes.
    Atovmyan

RGALI f. 1929, op. 1, yed. khr. 446, p. 48.
    1. The Classical Symphony.
    2. Pavel Lamm may have been working on a new edition of the Classical Symphony (with two Gavottes). See letter 88.

45. Atovmyan to Prokofiev

[Undated, received April 20, 1946]
Dear Sergey Sergeyevich,
    I'm returning "Juliet's Death." I sent the copy to Fayer at GABT. Please sign the authorization (enclosed). Lina Ivanovna still doesn't want to talk, since the children are unwell (not to mention that she's once again denying the existence of the specified books). I'll meet with her next week. Greetings, Atovmyan

RGALI f. 1929, op. 1, yed. khr. 446, p. 51.

46. Atovmyan to Prokofiev

The interruption in correspondence between the spring of 1946 and spring of 1947 can be attributed to Prokofiev's health problems, regular face-to-face contact with Atovmyan in Moscow, and secluded work on, among other scores, War and Peace.

March 28, 1947

Dear Sergey Sergeyevich,

I'm taking the opportunity to send you a note.

1. I received your promissory note for the dacha with Barsova's signature indicating that she's received the money in full.[1]

2. I received 44 pages of the score from you.[2] I'm hoping to receive the end of the first movement by return courier. No news from Lamm. Tomorrow morning I'll ask him once more.

3. I fulfilled your instruction concerning the 3,000-ruble payment to Lina Ivanovna. So for the month of March a total (together with the 3,000-ruble check received from you) of 11,000 rubles was paid out.

4. To my great sorrow Busalov is sticking to his guns and won't make any concessions.[3] Hence the only way out is to place Svyatoslav in a sanatorium (not the Kremlyovsky), once you've made sure you can get extra provisions for him close to Ivanovo, in part with the help of the market.[4] After the sanatorium he should be sent to Ivanovo for two months.

5. When are you thinking of coming to Moscow? I'm afraid that on 4/IV you'll be "cut off." They'll dismantle the bridge and you won't be able to leave. Isn't it safer for you to come earlier? Will the car you need be there? What day and time?

6. There was a misunderstanding with *Cinderella*. I left you the rough drafts and brought back what I should have given to you.

7. Gauk is beginning to worry about the 6th Symphony.[5] I haven't given him the date of your arrival.

8. On Gauk's request, Vlasov is trying to move the performance of the Waltzes to the fall.[6] Can you underscore to Vlasov that this is disgraceful and that, besides the Waltzes, a lot of your works, written and still to be written, will be premiered next year? I'll drop off your note to him.

9. I saw Semyonova. The performance was an enormous success. To me it appeared that Semyonova was the best of the three Cinderellas.[7]

10. I sent the Sonata to Muzgiz.[8]

I await your letters. Greetings to Mira Aleksandrovna. With devotion,
Atovmyan

RGALI f. 1929, op. 1, yed. khr. 446, p. 56.

1. Valeriya Barsova (Vladimirova, 1892–1967), Bolshoy Theater soprano. Prokofiev bought his dacha in Nikolina Gora from her.

2. For the Sixth Symphony.

3. The identity of Busalov is unknown.

4. The unofficial, "peasant" market, where goods unavailable in the official, state-run stores could be obtained.

5. Gauk hoped to conduct the premiere of the Sixth Symphony, but Prokofiev granted it to Mravinsky. The premiere took place in Leningrad on October 11, 1947.

6. Vlasov did not, in the end, conduct the Waltz Suite (1946). It was premiered by Mikhaíl Shteyman (1889–1949), one of Prokofiev's St. Petersburg Conservatory classmates, on May 13, 1947, in Moscow.

7. Marina Semyonova (b. 1908) danced the role of Cinderella on February 13, 1947, at the Bolshoy Theater. Subsequent performances featured Olga Lepeshinskaya (b. 1916) and Galina Ulanova (1910–98) in the role.

8. Presumably the First Violin Sonata (1946).

47. Atovmyan to Prokofiev

During the summer and fall of 1947, Prokofiev was immersed in several chamber and orchestral projects, including the Sixth Symphony, for which he traveled to Leningrad to attend rehearsals and the premiere. This letter concerns the rehearsals for the Moscow premiere of that work; Atovmyan summons Prokofiev from Nikolina Gora to attend them.

December 20, 1947

Dear Sergey Sergeyevich,

Two extraordinary developments oblige me to ask (and ask plaintively) for you to come to Moscow not on 21/XII, as we settled on, but 20/XII, that is today.

The first development: Yevgeniy Aleksandrovich[1] is having the final run-through of the 6th Symphony at 10 on 21/XII and the general rehearsal on 24/XII (the concert is on 25/XII, not 23/XII). Because of its new (different) sound—the size of the orchestra—he very much wants you to hear the complete symphony rehearsed on 20/XII.[2]

The second development: 21/XII is Election Day.[3] By order of Raykom my car has been mobilized for my electoral district (from 8 in the morning).[4] Accordingly, I can only send my car for you after everyone has voted. I doubt that this will have occurred before 4 or 5 in the afternoon. So I'm sending my car for you today and once again request that you come with Mira Aleksandrovna today, not 21/XII. Since I'm not quite sure that my entreaty will reach you, I asked Olga Alekseyevna[5] to personally convey it both from me and from Yevgeniy Aleksandrovich. To my joy, Olga Alekseyevna kindly agreed.

I send you and Mira Aleksandrovna greetings and best wishes.

Atovmyan

P.S. Boris Emanuilovich Khaykin[6] sent me a telegram inviting me to attend *The Duenna*[7] on 28/XII and travel afterward to Terioki[8] to greet the New Year. You haven't changed your plans?

By the way, if you still haven't exchanged your money, then send it to Arseniy (indicating the amount on the envelope).[9] I can't exchange it through my cashier.

RGALI f. 1929, op. 1, yed. khr. 446, p. 62.
1. The conductor Yevgeniy Mravinsky.
2. Prokofiev attended the rehearsal.
3. Atovmyan refers to the first postwar elections to Mossovet.
4. Rayonnïy komitet (District Committee).
5. The conductor Mravinsky's wife.
6. Boris Khaykin (1904–78), conductor.
7. The alternate name of *Betrothal in a Monastery*.
8. Terioki (Zelenogorsk) is a vacation area on the shore of the Gulf of Finland.
9. A Politburo resolution on December 14, 1947, resulted in a 10:1 devaluation of the ruble and the printing of new currency.

48. Prokofiev to Atovmyan

This letter was not sent, evidently in recognition of Atovmyan's troubles at the Union of Soviet Composers, the grave financial crisis that would result in his dismissal, in early 1948, from Muzfond.

December 29, 1947
Dear Levon Tadevosovich,

Khaykin is conducting my Second Violin Concerto in G Minor at the beginning of January and urgently requests the orchestral score and parts. These are with Vera Nikolayevna Kutler at the SSK library. It seems there are printed copies. Please obtain them from her and forward them to Khaykin.

What's new? Will you come by to see us on January 2, either at 1 or 3? Abram Solomonovich is coming on the 31st in the second half of the day.[1] You can leave a note with him as to: 1) the aforementioned material; 2) what's new in general. Semyon Semyonovich tells me terrible things relating to Muzfond.[2] Cordial greetings. We await you here.

Yours, SPRKFV

RGALI f. 1929, op. 2, yed. khr. 151, p. 16. Handwritten; not available at GTsMMK.
1. Abram Mendelson (1885–1968), Mira's father.
2. Semyon Bogatïryov (1890–1960), Moscow Conservatory professor. During this period Muzfond was audited and its employees, notably Atovmyan, investigated for corruption, specifically the overpayment of honoraria, the granting of long-term, no-interest loans, and the ordering of excessive print runs.

49. Atovmyan to Prokofiev

February 11, 1948

Dear Sergey Sergeyevich,

I'm sending you the "Waltz" score and the Sonata for Two Violins.[1] Please sign the following documents:

1. The advance for the trip to Leningrad (on the other side, where the amount is shown in words). Mira Aleksandrovna should also sign there.
2. Funding for the trip to Leningrad (you and Mira Aleksandrovna), two copies.[2]
3. The receipt for the Steinway piano lease (two copies).

Greetings and best wishes,

Atovmyan

RGALI f. 1929, op. 1, yed. khr. 447, p. 1.

1. The Waltz Suite and the Sonata for Two Violins (1932) were published in collotype in 1947.

2. Prokofiev twice went to Leningrad in 1947, in the first half of October and second half of November. On October 11 he attended the premiere of his Sixth Symphony (1947); a day later he heard *War and Peace* Part I at Malegot; and on November 23 and 24 he took in the Kirov Theater stagings of *Betrothal in a Monastery* and *Cinderella,* respectively.

50. Atovmyan to Prokofiev

During a gathering of Soviet composers held from February 17 to 28, 1948, Atovmyan was castigated for mismanaging Muzfond. In a futile effort to retain his job, he petitioned Myaskovsky, Prokofiev, and Shostakovich for letters in his defense. Since the three composers had themselves come under official attack in February, they could do little to help him.

August 15, 1948

Deeply respected Sergey Sergeyevich,

I read your three messages to me with great attention. I'm very grateful to everyone for the very flattering testimonials. Unfortunately, your hope "that they'll prove useful" can't be justified, for no letter of any sort can help me.

It appears Nikolay Ivanovich[1] didn't precisely convey to Nikolay Yakovlevich[2] what was needed, or else Nikolay Yakovlevich considered it necessary to change the nature of his letter, but, alas, to show the letters around with such wording would be useless at best.

You see, the contents of the letters should have been directed at the question of my so-called overpayment of honoraria (in connection with the raising of the rates), as Dmitriy Dmitriyevich did on his own initiative.[3] However, all of this is no longer so terrible. I'm sure that I'll soon be parting company with Muzfond.

Please convey to Nikolay Yakovlevich my earnest request to immediately send me (it can be by post) the copy of D. D. Shostakovich's letter that Nikolay Ivanovich absentmindedly left with him. I don't have the original, and I greatly need this one copy of it.

Please forgive me for the worry. I send you, Mira Aleksandrovna, and all of the residents in Nikolina Gora sincere greetings and very best wishes.

Atovmyan

P.S. I'm writing to your mailing address, since I think your letter-carrier delivers quickly.

RGALI f. 1929, op. 1, yed. khr. 447, p. 2.
1. Nikolay Ivanovich Peyko (1916–95), composer.
2. Myaskovsky.
3. Shostakovich.

51. Atovmyan to Prokofiev

The break in the correspondence between August 1948 and June 1949 reflects the fallout from the financial and political crisis of February 1948, which left Atovmyan unemployed and Prokofiev close to impoverished. Subsequent breaks in the correspondence attest to Prokofiev's health problems, specifically the periods in which he was hospitalized or convalescing at his dacha in Nikolina Gora or apartment in Moscow. During these periods, he was largely unable to work.

June 16, 1949
Dear Sergey Sergeyevich,

Richter[1] is leaving once again (today), and he'll be busy until June 25. For this reason I didn't take the piano score from GABT.[2] What is to be done? Either: a) wait for Richter; b) leave the piano score at GABT for Zïbtsev[3]; c) take the piano score and give it to another pianist, specifically Anatoliy Vedernikov. I await your instructions.

A certain Yuriy Konstantinovich Vinokurov greatly desires to see you on some matter (he's involved in the cinema; evidently he'll be asking you to write music for a film). Can he come to you and when? (He's in a great hurry.) I promised to call him. What should I tell Rostropovich?[4] When will you be in Moscow?[5]

I send greetings and best wishes to you and Mira Aleksandrovna.

Atovmyan

RGALI f. 1929, op. 1, yed. khr. 447, p. 3.

1. Svyatoslav Richter (1915–97), pianist.
2. Atovmyan refers to the piano score of the ballet *The Tale of the Stone Flower* (1950).
3. Alexey Zïbtsev (1908–94), pianist.
4. Mstislav Rostropovich (1927–2007), cellist and conductor.
5. On June 24, Prokofiev traveled to Moscow from Nikolina Gora for the first of several run-throughs (on piano) of *The Tale of the Stone Flower* at the Bolshoy Theater.

52. Prokofiev to Atovmyan

July 16, 1949

Dear Levon Tadevosovich,

1. Richter is a swine.[1]
2. Zïbtsev will apparently be playing. Lavrovsky[2] took it upon himself to organize the event, so it's good that the piano score is at GABT.
3. I'll have to postpone Rostropovich until the end of the month; please convey my regrets to him.[3]
4. I don't know Vinokurov, but there's no way I want to write for a film.
5. I'll obviously be in Moscow next week.[4]

I firmly grasp your hand and thank you for the prompt letter.

Yours, S. P.

Greetings to your grandsons and great-grandsons.

RGALI f. 1929, op. 3, yed. khr. 55, p. 20. Handwritten; not available at GTsMMK.
1. Prokofiev expresses his displeasure with Richter for reneging on his promise to play through the piano score of *The Tale of the Stone Flower* at the Bolshoy Theater. Richter went on tour without forewarning, forcing Prokofiev to secure Zïbtsev for the task.
2. Leonid Lavrovsky (1905–67), choreographer.
3. Prokofiev refers to his joint work with Rostropovich on a cello sonata, which serious illness forced him to put off (Prokofiev suffered a cerebral hemorrhage on July 6). He managed to complete the work in the months ahead; it was premiered on December 6, 1949, at the Moscow Conservatory during the Third Plenary Meeting of the Union of Soviet Composers.
4. For the play-through of the ballet.

53. Atovmyan to Prokofiev

September 7, 1949

Sergey Sergeyevich,

I'm sending you the contract for the Sonata. Please sign it, providing your passport number and the other information. Please return the contract by courier. I still haven't sent the music to Malegot, since Ferkelman[1] still hasn't come. If he doesn't come before the 10th, I'll send it with a different courier.

Greetings, Atovmyan

RGALI f. 1929, op. 1, yed. khr. 447, p. 4.
1. Mikhaíl (Moisey) Ferkelman (1908–77), composer.

54. Prokofiev to Atovmyan

Nikolina Gora, October 8, 1949

Dear Levon Tadevosovich,

Thank you for the contract, which I accepted as a name-day present, insofar as today is October 8. I'm returning it to you signed, but only the *single* copy that you sent. I include with my compliments 800 rubles for the *War and Peace* account.[1] I wrote in good time to Grikurov,[2] but he still hasn't answered—he's obviously waiting for Ferkelman. I send you cordial greetings. Next week, that is, the 17th, I count on being in Moscow.

Yours, SP

RGALI f. 1929, op. 3, yed. khr. 55, p. 21. Handwritten. On the next page is a letter to the administration of the Bolshoy Theater requesting a transfer of 4,768 rubles to Prokofiev's savings bank account.

1. Atovmyan was at this time preparing a new edition of the opera that included the changes Prokofiev made to it between 1946 and 1949.

2. Eduard Grikurov (1907–82), conductor.

55. Atovmyan to Prokofiev

October 10, 1949

Dear Sergey Sergeyevich,

Thanks very much for the money. Ferkelman is going to Leningrad tomorrow. I'm sending the entire piano score of *War and Peace* with him.[1]

I'm sending you the Muzgiz contract for the Violin Sonata.[2] Return it upon signing. At Muzgiz, do they know where (which savings bank) to send funds to you? If not, send them the relevant information.

I send you and Mira Aleksandrovna greetings and best wishes.

Atovmyan

RGALI f. 1929, op. 1, yed. khr. 447, p. 5.

1. Prokofiev sought to arrange a staging of a single-evening version of *War and Peace* at Malegot. The staging did not occur, however, until 1955—two years after his death.

2. Muzgiz published the First Violin Sonata in 1951.

56. Atovmyan to Prokofiev

October 22, 1949

Dear Sergey Sergeyevich,

Yesterday I was with B. V. Shmitko[1] and S. A. Balasanyan.[2] He (Balasanyan) welcomes the idea of the suites. Two suites need to be made, 3 or 4 numbers (in length), 15 minutes long. In the first suite 2–3 nos. from *Betrothal* + something else—the waltz from *Stone*; in the second suite 2 waltzes from *War*, a mazurka, a polonaise. Two small suites are more valuable than one large one.[3] I wrote a letter today to Grikurov concerning the mazurkas and polonaises. Perhaps also more waltzes? It would be good if you wrote to him so that he'd hurry. To avoid overtaxing yourself—look over the scores, annotate them, and then someone (Lamm if he's free or me) will copy them. I send greetings and best wishes.

Atovmyan

RGALI f. 1929, op. 1, yed. khr. 447, p. 6.
1. Presumably a Radio Committee employee.
2. Sergey Artemyevich Balasanyan (1902–82), composer. From 1949 to 1953 he served as vice-chairman of the Radio Committee.
3. Prokofiev did not heed Atovmyan's advice to create two suites.

57. Atovmyan to Prokofiev

October 28, 1949
Dear Sergey Sergeyevich,

Today I almost came to see you with the SSK representative Nikolay Petrovich Chaplïgin,[1] but this trip had to be put off until tomorrow the 29th. The SSK Secretariat has a pressing question—more accurately a request—for you: to present extracts from your ballet[2] in an orchestral performance at the impending end-of-November Plenary . . . You should decide whether it will be of the suite or excerpts, how many numbers, what numbers from what acts (if you in general agree to the performance).[3]

Radio agrees to acquire the suite (excerpts), if your contract with GABT allows you to sell it (them) in advance of the premiere.[4]

If this is in fact not possible, then Radio will sign a contract with you for a different suite (about which we spoke) and will pay 50% of the fee to you now, so that you can work on the suite from the ballet for the Plenary.

Consequently requested:

a. 6–7 nos. from the ballet (roughly, it appears, 2 numbers from each act). The performance at the Plenary does not deprive you of the right to sell the suite (excerpts) either now or after the premiere (depending on the GABT contract). This is for November 20.
b. The hypothetical Dance Suite No. 1, which includes the waltz that is not included in *The Stone Flower*, the mazurka, the polonaise, and something else, perhaps the waltz from the scene with the dignitary. This is for December (10–15).[5]
c. The Second Suite, which includes two or three dances from *Betrothal* and the waltz from *A Story*.[6] This is for January (15–20).[7]

I'm telling you this in advance so that you'll be briefed for the upcoming conversation with Chapligin and will have come to a decision. I'll tell you about the other things when I come (evidently the 29th or 30th).

I send greetings and best wishes to you and Mira Aleksandrovna.

Atovmyan

RGALI f. 1929, op. 1, yed. khr. 447, p. 7.
1. Nikolay Chapligin (1905–87), composer.
2. *The Tale of the Stone Flower.*
3. The Third Plenary Meeting of the Union of Soviet Composers took place from November 26 to December 11, 1949. Atovmyan refers to the plans for a concert on December 7 at the Stanislavsky Theater. Excerpts from *The Tale of the Stone Flower* were not performed at the event; excerpts from the eponymous opera by Kirill Molchanov (1922–82) took their place.
4. The Radio Committee commissioned several Prokofiev works for broadcast and recording.
5. Different numbers ended up in the Dance Suite. See letter 66, n. 1.
6. *A Story of a Real Man*, 1948 opera.
7. This suite was not composed.

58. Atovmyan to Prokofiev

Letters 58–61 concern the proofs of the Third Suite from Cinderella.

December 25, 1949

Dear Sergey Sergeyevich,

I'm sending the 1st and 2nd nos. of the Suite.[1] Please answer the three questions written in the margins of No. 2.

Don't pay attention to the missing accents (or possible slips of the pen); I'll correct and insert all the necessary accents once I receive the orchestral score from you. I had to rush to get both nos. sent to you.

Greetings and best wishes.

Atovmyan

RGALI f. 1929, op. 1, yed. khr. 447, p. 8.
1. No. 1 is the Pavane; No. 2 is the Adagio for Cinderella and the Prince.

59. Atovmyan to Prokofiev

December 28, 1949

Dear Sergey Sergeyevich,

To my chagrin I didn't manage to do No. 5[1] (there remain 30–40 measures, which I hope to finish tonight).

Severe flu prevented me from working with the required intensity. Now I'm better and making up for the neglect.

Tomorrow I'll begin pestering Radio so that the funds are in your current account before your arrival.

I send greetings and best wishes.

Atovmyan

RGALI f. 1929, op. 1, yed. khr. 447, p. 9.
1. No. 5 is the Orientalia.

60. Atovmyan to Prokofiev

January 4, 1950
Dear Sergey Sergeyevich,

I was rushed yesterday and thus didn't formulate my questions accurately.

In No. 5 you've written "like 8 measures back," but at the same time there's a sign in measures 5, 6, 7, and 8 ⊢╫╫╫┐ that designates a repeat of these four measures. How is it to be understood?

I'm sending No. 6. I'm waiting for No. 5 from you. I have Nos. 3, 7, and 8 left, which I'll try to finish in the coming days.[1]

I called Ochakovskaya.[2] She asked for everything to be handed over right away.

I'll now do No. 8 (in order to liberate No. 1) and then No. 3.

When do you plan on being in Moscow?[3] I send you and Mira greetings and very best wishes.

Atovmyan

RGALI f. 1929, op. 1, yed. khr. 447, p. 10.
1. No. 6: The Prince Finds Cinderella; No. 3: Three Oranges; No. 7: Slow Waltz; No. 8: Amoroso.
2. Olga Ochakovskaya (1914–2002), a Muzgiz editor, Gostelradio (State Television and Radio) children's division employee.
3. Prokofiev went to Moscow on January 12 for a run-through of the Cello Sonata (with Rostropovich and Richter playing) for the Radio Committee.

61. Atovmyan to Prokofiev

January 8, 1950
Dear Sergey Sergeyevich,

In fact, the funds weren't sent. The current account of the Radio Committee is temporally frozen. They promise to pay you on or around January 10. In any case, perhaps give Abram Solomonovich[1] authorization to receive the funds from the Radio Committee (in cash): I'll be there, and if on the 10th they'll be issuing payments, I'll stand in line and prepare all of the documentation so that he won't be detained in the accountant's office.

If you come on the 15–17th, I hope by then the transfer will have shown up in your current account.

I'm sending Nos. 3, 7, and 8 from the Suite. I didn't manage to write in the repeat in the waltz (pp. 35–36). I'll do this when I get the score back from you.

I have several questions:

In the waltz:

1. P. 24, 9 measures after rehearsal 16: at the 2/4 the clarinet has a C but the piano and harp a B and a D. Is there a mistake here?
2. 8 measures after rehearsal 15 and in the analogous places the cellos have a rest. Wouldn't a pizzicato be better?
3. At 3 measures after 16 and in the analogous places, shouldn't the violas and cellos be added to the second horn?
4. I wrote in the flute at rehearsal 19, measures 9–16 for naught.
5. Wouldn't the oboe playing be better at rehearsal 15, measure 1, and in the analogous places? If not, how about a rest for the oboist at the 3/4 instead of the lower B♭, so that the B♭ can be taken an octave higher?
6. Shouldn't twelve measures be written in for the harp after rehearsal 21 (as on pp. 24–25)?
7. I have the impression that p. 40 (after rehearsal 28) is missing a measure.
8. I moved rehearsals 23 and 24 a measure later (in accord with all the preceding reference points).
9. In the last measure of the violas you wrote . Thinking this is a mistake I wrote .
10. At rehearsal 27 measure 9 in the flute you wrote . I left .

In the march:

1. Rehearsal 48, measure 1: the 2nd and 3rd quarter notes have just the basses. Shouldn't something be added (bassoons, cellos in octaves)?
2. 2 measures before rehearsal 48 the cellos (the last two eighth notes) are arco, but on other occasions pizzicato.
3. At rehearsal 49 in the piano score you indicate tamborine but in the next line triangle.
4. 5 measures from the start you wrote in a left-hand piano part. Leave or delete?

I wrote the questions for No. 8 in the score. Don't pay attention to the page numbering yet. I'll add the usual numbering (I won't be able to do this without No. 6, which you have). By the way: isn't there too little percussion (especially snare drum in the waltz)?

After I receive the score from you I'll look everything over again and hand it to Ochakovskaya. When can I expect you in Moscow? I send you and Mira best wishes.

Atovmyan

RGALI f. 1929, op. 1, yed. khr. 447, pp. 11–12.
1. Abram Mendelson, Mira's father.

62. Atovmyan to Prokofiev

January 11 [1950]
Dear Sergey Sergeyevich,

I'm sending the advance copy of the Third Suite from *Romeo*. Please sign this copy (on the title page, where "for publication" is written) and return it *right back*. The signed copy has to be sent to Leipzig very quickly; only then will the edition be secured.[1] Therefore don't delay with the advance copy—sign it and send it right back.

Radio, contra expectation, deceived me: the funds weren't there on the 10th. They promise the payment on the 12th. I'll find out if the funds are there in the morning and attend to the transfer.

Greetings and best wishes,

Atovmyan

P.S. This morning Radio said that the funds were transferred (they sent the transfer to the bank). The funds will most likely appear in your account on the 17th.

RGALI f. 1929, op. 1, yed. khr. 447, p. 13.
1. The Third Suite from *Romeo and Juliet* was published in Leipzig by Edition Peters in 1973. There exists no trace of an earlier Leipzig edition.

63. Atovmyan to Prokofiev

From February 18 to April 3, 1950, Prokofiev was hospitalized for treatment of ventricular hypertrophy at the Kremlin Hospital.

March 12, 1950
Dear Sergey Sergeyevich,

Today I wasn't able to make my way to you, since there wasn't a pass in my name. If there isn't an influx on Thursday the 16th—let me know, so that they'll write out a pass for me.

I send you and Mira greetings and best wishes.

Atovmyan

RGALI f. 1929, op. 1, yed. khr. 447, p. 14.

64. Prokofiev to Atovmyan

Nikolina Gora, June 22, 1950

Dear Levon Tadevosovich,

Rostropovich sent me his edit of the Sonata. I don't doubt that his remarks are reasonable, but the copy is blurred and stained. I don't think it's possible to send it to Muzgiz in this state. Besides, none of the changes made to the cello part has been entered into the score (everything has to be entered, except the fingerings). How does the Sonata end? You know, I wanted *two* variants, i.e. *ossia*. Now: if the 1st variant is completely unsuitable, then it's not worth publishing. Let Rostropovich + Richter decide this. I gave (and entrusted to) you an altogether clean and legible copy, and you're sending Muzgiz what? You can't, for example, send it to the engraver with an "8——" (for the cellos): the part has to be written out in the treble clef (or in the bass clef, if it's low).

Unfortunately, I'm unable right now to deal with the corrections and tidying up, so I ask you, as a sufficiently experienced publisher, to put the Sonata into decent shape and send it to Muzgiz. What I hastily inscribed at the keyboard, working with Rostropovich, needs to look tidy.[1]

Cordial greetings, yours, SP

Personal: when will we finally see you?

RGALI f. 1929, op. 2, yed. khr. 151, p. 17. In Mendelson's hand, from dictation.

1 Earlier in the month Rostropovich had traveled to Nikolina Gora to assist Prokofiev with the cello part of the Sonata.

65. Atovmyan to Prokofiev

June 29, 1950

Dear Sergey Sergeyevich!

I don't understand why you attacked me. Instead of giving the Sonata to me (as I had asked him) Slava Rostropovich sent it to you in the state you found it in. But I wanted to put everything in order beforehand— then to send it to you in a final, ready-to-be-engraved state.

Things turned out differently, but absolutely through no fault of my own. I'm working these days on the Sonata—I've entered all the corrections, including the bowings—and copied the coda once again, including as a second line the second variant (*ossia*—the easier variant), and both the cello and piano parts. As proof I'm sending you the last 5 pages (so that you won't be in doubt). When I was preparing the Sonata for publication it seemed to me that the piano part was missing some phrase marks, but without your permission I didn't put them in. It can easily be done on the proofs.

The dedication wasn't clear to me. After it, was it necessary to include the Gorky quotation, the one that you have on the manuscript ("Man! The word has such a proud ring!")?[1] To be on the safe side, I entered the quote. Today I submitted the manuscript in good condition to Muzgiz. It will go to the engraver at the beginning of July. When it's ready I'll send you the contract. In general, you scolded me for nothing.

In my last letter I asked about two things: inscriptions on the two photographs that I sent to you (by the way, and not to be resentful, you were planning on giving me your extra photographs). Then I asked Mira Aleksandrovna to copy the letter about the room on Mozhayka (with its transfer on the instruction of the Arts Committee). It's very important that this be done, especially for the publishing business.[2] I'll explain in more detail when we meet.

I'll write to you about all the rest in the coming days. Sincere greetings and best wishes to you and Mira Aleksandrovna.

With devotion,
Atovmyan

RGALI f. 1929, op. 1, yed. khr. 447, p. 15.

1. The famous dictum of Satin in the play *The Lower Depths* (1902) by Maxim Gorky (1868–1936).

2. According to Atovmyan's daughter Svetlana Merzhanova (1926–2007), Prokofiev arranged for one of the rooms in his two-and-a-half-room apartment on Mozhayskoye Shosse, an apartment that had been converted into a communal dwelling, to be allocated to Atovmyan. Atovmyan's mistress Yekaterina Kartashova (1927–97) thereafter lived there with the two children that she and Atovmyan had out of wedlock: Dmitriy Atovmyan (1952–2004) and Marianna Atovmyan (b. 1956).

66. Prokofiev to Atovmyan

July 4, 1950

I'm very grateful to you for your efforts on behalf of the Sonata. Why are you asking me about the dedication? It's dedicated to you.

Will you be at the Malegot performances and meeting with Grikurov? It would be good to find out from him if *War and Peace* is part of the plan for the upcoming season (at the Arts Committee they said that it will be performed in the fall while other operas are running). If it won't be performed, try to find out the reasons. This issue worries me. Samosud related that Malegot sent a request to the Committee in the spring for permission to stage the opera. The Committee even said to me during the winter that it will be performed this fall, after several other operas are staged. If *War and Peace* is not included in the plan, I'd like to find out the reasons.

What have you heard about the performance of the Dance Suite on the radio?[1] Samosud promised to work on it. When can I count on receiving the honorarium?

I'm sending you the declaration regarding the Mozhayka living space. I hope this issue will soon be put to rest.

How's your health? Are you traveling anywhere? If convenient, come to see us next week, on Thursday or Friday. Vladimir Semyonovich will call you.[2]

RGALI f. 1929, op. 3, yed. khr. 118, pp. 6–7. In Mendelson's hand, from dictation.
1. Prokofiev began working on his Dance Suite for orchestra in 1934 to fulfill a Radio Committee commission. It comprises four movements: Polonaise, Dance, Mazurka, and a second Polonaise. The copy of the score that ended up in the Radio Committee library includes these four movements, a second Dance, a Serenade, and a Minuet (these last three from *Betrothal in a Monastery*), and a second Polonaise. Another version of the Dance Suite, comprising the Serenade, Minuet, Mazurka, a third Polonaise (from *War and Peace*), and two "Pushkin" Waltzes (1949) was broadcast on State Radio on July 11, 1950. Prokofiev included the Serenade and Minuet in his orchestral suite *Summer Night* (1950).
2. Vladimir Tabernakulov (1907–97), Prokofiev's courier and driver after 1946.

67. Atovmyan to Prokofiev

July 11, 1950
Dear Sergey Sergeyevich!
I'm using a courier: Vissarion Yakovlevich is traveling to your estate.[1] First of all a complaint: more than a week ago I sent you two photographs through Abram Solomonovich with a request for an inscription; alas, I've neither the inscription nor the photographs (never mind that you promised to supplement my album with extra copies of your photographs). I'm patiently waiting.

Today the Dance Suite with the two new numbers (the Serenade and Minuet) was finally heard. I don't know why S. A. Samosud was nervous about the instrumentation of the Serenade and Minuet. It all sounded wonderful. They performed six numbers: the Serenade, Minuet, Mazurka, Polonaise, and the 2 Pushkin Waltzes. I listened with immense pleasure. Did you hear it on the radio? What was your impression of the performance?

Now a new suite has to be done . . .[2] We'll speak on this subject when we meet.

I'm sending you the letter from S. A. Balasanyan. They (at Radio) have a bad rule—they don't issue advances before the work is submitted.[3] The first advance is provided upon submission of the work, and the final payment after the performance. True, Balasanyan intends to persuade Puzin[4] to issue you an advance, because they are very interested in your work.

I hope in the coming days to transfer to you the remaining 7,500 rubles stipulated in the contract for the Suite (with the corresponding deductions). I'll follow up on the transfer.

A final question about the Sonata, which is now at Muzgiz and will go to the engraver this month. Rostropovich wants to take it to Berlin (to perform). I'm afraid this will disrupt the publication schedule and thus I haven't retrieved it from Muzgiz. This isn't Rostropovich's final trip and he'll be able to play the Sonata in Berlin and other cities. Do you agree with my decision?

I don't know if I'll come this week to Nikolina; next week I'll certainly come and, with your permission, visit you.

I send you and Mira Aleksandrovna cordial greetings and best wishes. With devotion,

Atovmyan

RGALI f. 1929, op. 1, yed. khr. 447, p. 16.
1. The composer Vissarion Shebalin.
2. The reference is unclear.
3. Prokofiev sought an advance for his oratorio *On Guard for Peace* (1950), a setting of a libretto by Samuil Marshak (1887–1964).
4. Alexey Puzin (1904–87), Radio Committee official.

68. Atovmyan to Prokofiev

July 30, 1950
Dear Sergey Sergeyevich!

I wasn't able to send you the contract for your signature on Thursday, since the amount of the honorarium, as specified in the contract, did not suit *me*. Specifically, Muzgiz for some reason wrote a contract for 4,000 instead of the maximum 5,000 rubles. A new contract was prepared just yesterday, after a few arguments.[1]

Please sign both contracts (the Radio contract is in two copies) and send all the copies back to me. Enclose a written request to Muzgiz for the honorarium owed to you (60% of the contract total) to be transferred to such-and-such account. I'll follow up on the transfer. Concerning Radio, the question about the advance is still unresolved—more truthfully, the answer is still no, but Balasanyan has yet to brandish his weapon.

The funds for the Dance Suite were transferred to you on July 25.

I'm sending you the black folder of your children's works and a small sketchbook. I'll try to locate something else of this sort for you.

Sakva still hasn't come—thus I can't say anything about the next publication plan.[2] (By the way: in view of his absence, I sent the rent bills for Mozhayka to Abram Solomonovich, since on one occasion, as far as I understand, my effort to pay them myself displeased him . . . Besides, I regrettably don't have the proverbial means to do so right now.)

I'll find out in the near future about the publication plan and report back to you. I think we'll now put *Winter Bonfire* first in the queue. I'll borrow the score in a few days and copy it for publication.[3]

Incidentally: a request came to Moscow from France for the score of *Winter Bonfire* (for publication). Did you receive a letter from VOKS on this subject? Please send the following declaration to me:

"To VOKS:

In view of the request from a series of foreign performing and publishing organizations for my works, I submit/I request that all questions related to the distribution of my works abroad be resolved by VOKS.

If VOKS representatives consider it worthwhile to send a copy of one of my unpublished works abroad, I request that it first be given to me or, in the event of my absence from Moscow, to comrade Levon Tadevosovich Atovmyan (tel. K 44155, Nizhniy Kislovsky, bldg. 8, apt. 11) to be checked for accuracy. Signature"

The wording of the letter can of course be changed if you don't agree with it.

Regarding the edition of the 3rd Suite from *Romeo*: Muzgiz certified that 300 copies were published, so there won't be an additional honorarium.[4]

It seems this covers everything. While I was there I completely forgot to retrieve the photographs that I sent to you a month ago. If they're still intact, please send them back to me with your inscription.

How is your work progressing? I send you and Mira Aleksandrovna greetings and very best wishes.

With devotion,

Atovmyan

P.S. Did you hear the 2 movements from your Classical Symphony on July 24?

RGALI f. 1929, op. 1, yed. khr. 447, pp. 17–18.
1. Atovmyan is presumably referring to the publication contract for the Cello Sonata.
2. Konstantin Sakva (1912–96), musicologist and chief editor of Muzgiz from 1949 to 1951.
3. *Winter Bonfire* (1949) was published by Muzgiz in 1951.
4. The Third Suite was published by Muzgiz in 1949.

69. Atovmyan to Prokofiev

September 18, 1950

Dear Sergey Sergeyevich!

I intended to travel to Nikolina to consult with you on a range of issues. However getting to you "in the country" is rather complicated, so I decided to write.

1. Concerning the rental of an upright piano for Chkalovskaya. Oleg[1] called me about this. I'm not convinced that it can be done, but in order to take actual steps I'll need a written request from you on this subject (a written request addressed to the SSK Secretariat).

2. I heard that you gave the piano score of the oratorio to Samosud.[2] What are your future plans for it? When and how are you planning to present the piano score (in order to receive the advance)? Does anything need to be undertaken? What specifically?

3. The Committee is making copies of Rachmaninoff's correspondence. I recall that you once corresponded with him. Where are these letters? How might a copy be made of them?[3]

4. By the way: I also remember that you left a number of your manuscripts and letters abroad in different cities. Are you thinking of doing anything about this? Perhaps I could tentatively consult with the appropriate organizations (at least via the Arts Committee or at the Ministry of Foreign Affairs).[4]

5. Did you obtain the documents from Mezhdunarodnaya kniga (pertaining to the publication of your works in France)?[5] They ought to be signed and returned to Mezhdunarodnaya kniga. Insofar as these documents are passing through government organizations, there won't be any complications.

   By the way: I provided the Cello Sonata to Mezhdunarodnaya kniga for copying—either for America or France it seems.

6. Soon the proofs (of the Muzgiz edition) of the Cello Sonata will be done. Should the proofs be sent to you or do you trust me and Rostropovich to check them over?

7. I haven't yet had any indications regarding a telephone for Nikolina. I'll immediately let you know as soon as I find out.[6]

8. The second photograph I sent to you for an inscription (my favorite photograph: you sitting in the wicker chair at the dacha) seems to have gotten held up there. Send it if you find it.

9. In the coming days I'll begin bombarding Muzgiz on the subject of the publication plan for 1951. I'm first scheduling *Winter Bonfire* and the Violin Sonata (unison).[7]

   It seems these are all the questions.

Cinderella was very good on September 8. Struchkova danced.[8] Unfortunately, *Romeo* still hasn't been done this season.

I send you and Mira Aleksandrovna cordial greetings and very best wishes,

Atovmyan

RGALI f. 1929, op. 1, yed. khr. 447, pp. 19–20.
1. Prokofiev's younger son.
2. Samosud conducted the premiere of *On Guard for Peace* on December 19, 1950.
3. Correspondence between Prokofiev and Serge Rachmaninoff (1873–1943) has not been located.
4. For political reasons, Prokofiev decided against importing the manuscripts and letters he had left abroad.
5. Founded in 1923, Mezhdunarodnaya kniga (International Book) imports and exports printed material to and from Russia.
6. For health and professional reasons, the lack of a telephone at Nikolina Gora proved exceedingly problematic for Prokofiev. Atovmyan was obliged to handle most of the composer's business dealings with Muzfond, Muzgiz, and the Radio Committee himself.
7. The Sonata for Solo Violin or Violins in Unison (1947), a Committee on Arts Affairs commission, was intended for student musicians. Atovmyan refers to the publication contract.
8. Raisa Struchkova (1925–2005).

70. Atovmyan to Prokofiev

September 30, 1950
Dear Sergey Sergeyevich,

I was at *Romeo* yesterday. Although I obviously know all the music from the first to the last note, it seemed that I had yet to grasp the full beauty of this brilliant creation—I listened to the whole thing with such insatiability and excitement that I wasn't able to fall asleep all night.

The performance was (as always) an enormous success. The cast was wonderful: Ulanova, Ermolayev, Koren, and Gabovich.[1] True, I was a little disheartened by the orchestra in the first act, which didn't always play together, breaking the phrasing during the transitions from one instrument to another, with *pianos* that were too loud and overblown *fortes*. But in the second act—no, even in the first act (the Dance of the Knights)—the orchestra found its form and played all the rest wonderfully.

To my pleasure I saw many musicians there whom I'd seen at previous performances.

I've decided to make a new four-hand piano score in order to make it easier for amateur musicians (the reduction for solo piano is difficult for them). I'll petition Muzgiz about publishing the Album for Children (the easy transcription of excerpts from *Romeo*) and republishing your 10 Pieces.[2]

By the way, about your publications: *Winter Bonfire* will certainly be part of the plan for 1951. Will you be adding (changing) anything there?

I'll soon begin copying it for publication. A *Cinderella* suite will possibly also be part of the plan. Which suite, the 1st or the 2nd, do you prefer to begin with?[3]

I'll likewise petition for the publication of the *Cinderella* piano score[4] and the Violin Sonata (unison).

Now about performances: the concerts of new Soviet music will be taking place from December 7 to 21. *Winter Bonfire* and the oratorio *In Defense of Peace* are scheduled.[5] For this reason the oratorio needs to be presented at the Composers' Union. Does this concern you? I was bold enough to declare that Sergey Sergeyevich is not against presenting his oratorio at the Composers' Union, but only when the work is entirely complete (including the orchestral score). I await your instructions in this regard![6]

I'll receive the 1st proofs of the Cello Sonata the day after tomorrow. With your permission I'll make the corrections myself.

Well, I won't be torturing you any more for a while. If you permit me, I'll stop by to see you for a half hour in a week or two. I miss you a lot.

I send you and Mira Aleksandrovna cordial greetings and very best wishes.

With devotion,

Atovmyan

P.S. I'm still agonizing over the Mozhayka question, but a solution to the matter is a few days away.[7] Don't rebuke me for what I'm doing—it's extremely necessary.

RGALI f. 1929, op. 1, yed. khr. 447, pp. 21–22.
1. Alexey Ermolayev (1910–75), Sergey Koren (1907–69), Mikhaíl Gabovich (1905–65).
2. The two Albums for Children, containing Atovmyan's reduction of *Romeo and Juliet* for solo and four-hand piano, were published in collotype in 1947. They were not republished. The Ten Pieces from the ballet were published by Muzgiz in 1950.
3. Neither the First nor Second Suite was published during Prokofiev's lifetime. The Muzïka publishing house issued them in 1976 and 1977, respectively.
4. The piano reduction of *Cinderella* was carried out by Atovmyan with Prokofiev's approval. Muzgiz published it in 1954.
5. The concerts actually occurred from December 7–25. *Winter Bonfire* and *On Guard for Peace* were performed on the same December 19 program in the composer's presence. In a letter dated July 2, 1950, Marshak observes that the name of the oratorio changed three times during the creative process, from *Glory to Peace* (*Slava miru*) to *War for Peace* (*Voyna za mir*) to *A Word about Peace* (*Slovo o mire*). Atovmyan here adds a fourth title. See Mendel'son-Prokof'yeva, "Vospominaniya o Sergeye Prokof'yeve. Fragment: 1946–1950," 206.
6. The Union of Soviet Composers did not arrange a hearing of the oratorio until after the premiere on December 28–29, 1950. In the opinion of the assessors, the oratorio failed to represent adequately its nascent Cold War subject matter owing to its diffuse form and modernist syntax (RGALI f. 1929, op. 1, yed. khr. 986, pp. 35–45). The oratorio nonetheless received a Stalin Prize (Second Class) on March 14, 1951.
7. The apartment on Mozhayskoye Shosse.

71. Atovmyan to Prokofiev

February 3, 1951
Dear Sergey Sergeyevich,
I'm sending you:
  a. A copy of the "Lullaby" for Zara Dolukhanova.[1] Will she return this copy or do you reckon it will be gone for good?
  b. Off-prints, more accurately the proofs of the Cello Sonata
  c. The same for the Violin Sonata
  d. Your manuscript of the Cello Sonata
  e. Your manuscript of the Violin Sonata
Keep in mind that:
  a. I still haven't looked at the proofs (I did the first proofs of the Cello Sonata). I'll look at them once more after you do.
  b. No corrections can be made on the galley proofs (the typeset pages); I enclose special proof pages for this purpose.
  c. In order to answer the questions the editor inserted in the proofs I'll need a half-hour meeting with you during a convenient day and time.
  d. I immodestly direct your attention to the absence of a dedication in the Cello Sonata. The appearance of an inscription would greatly please me.
  e. I direct your attention to the fact that in your manuscript of the Cello Sonata two measures appeared where originally there was just one measure (laid out differently). This is page 4, measures 9 and 10 of the manuscript, page 8, measure 5 of the typeset copy.
  f. It would be a good idea for you to write a letter to Muzgiz. Apart from the fact that they seldom publish you, even those few works that they do publish appear not only with mediocre engraving but also (irrespective of their technical complexity) with mediocre typesetting carried out by inexperienced typesetters.
I await your call about a meeting regarding the questions in the proofs. Greetings and best wishes.
  Atovmyan
P.S. Marshak's text for *Winter Bonfire* depressed me (especially in the children's chorus).[2] I'm now searching for the old text. I reminded Ilin's secretary that he has to call you.[3]

RGALI f. 1929, op. 1, yed. khr. 447, pp. 23–24.
  1. The mezzo soprano Zara Dolukhanova (1918–2007) premiered the "Lullaby" (No. 7) from *On Guard for Peace*.
  2. Atovmyan refers to the "Pioneer Gathering" movement (No. 5). Marshak wrote the text after the music was completed.

3. Igor Ilin (1909–93), Committee on Arts Affairs and Radio Committee official.

72. Atovmyan to Prokofiev

February 15, 1951

Dear Sergey Sergeyevich!

I'm sending you the contract for the Sonata.[1] Please sign it and send it back. In a few days I'll prepare the contract for *Winter Bonfire*. I'm leaving now from Muzgiz to GABT to catch Bogdanov.[2]

Greetings, Atovmyan

RGALI f. 1929 op. 1, yed. khr. 447, p. 25.
1. The Violin Sonata.
2. Anatoliy Bogdanov, music librarian at the Bolshoy Theater.

73. Atovmyan to Prokofiev

March 4, 1951

Dear Sergey Sergeyevich,

I'm leaving the manuscript and copy of "Dovecote" with you. Please look it over and add any remarks. Incidentally: should the name "Dovecote" be kept or changed?[1]

Tomorrow or the day after tomorrow, with your permission, I'll come by for the music and, if the Radio librarian doesn't let me down, I'll bring the orchestral score of the oratorio. I send greetings and best wishes.

Atovmyan

RGALI f. 1929 op. 1, yed. khr. 447, p. 26.
1. Atovmyan refers to the sixth movement of *On Guard for Peace*, which was renamed "Dove of Peace."

74. Atovmyan to Prokofiev

[Undated]

Dear Sergey Sergeyevich!

I'm sending you the final movement of the Suite: "Khorovodnaya."[1] Two remarks:

1. Don't be confused by the fact that in a few places, in order to speed up my work, I didn't enter in the pitches. I preserved space to write out these measures and I'll fill them in later.
2. I forgot what measure 13 after 253 is, since the page showing rehearsal number 253 was left with you. I deduced that this is the fourth measure before 254.[2]

Call me when you're free in order to settle all of the questions arising from the score. I send greetings and very best wishes.

Atovmyan

RGALI f. 1929, op. 1, yed. khr. 447, p. 27.
1. Prokofiev extracted three suites from *The Tale of the Stone Flower* in 1951: the *Wedding* Suite, *Gypsy* Suite, and *Ural Rhapsody*. He considered extracting a fourth suite, "The Mistress of the Copper Mountain." Here Atovmyan refers to the round dance from the *Wedding* Suite.
2. On the left-hand side of the letter Prokofiev wrote "verified" in pencil.

75. Atovmyan to Prokofiev

May 26, 1951

Dear Sergey Sergeyevich!

I'm sending you the text for the letters.[1] If you manage to copy them, please send them with Volodya.[2] Briefly about other matters:

1. The voice parts of the Suite[3] are being copied for Radio. I hope the Suite will be performed in June.[4]
2. The proofs of the Cello Sonata (Muzgiz) have arrived. On Monday I'll look them over and, if you don't object, I'll sign off on the Sonata for printing.[5]
3. The second proofs of *Winter Bonfire* arrived at the start of the week. With your permission I'll send them out to you.
4. Today I signed off on the proofs of the schoolboy's song from "White Dove."[6] The proofs of the "Lullaby" will be done the day after tomorrow.
5. The copying of *War and Peace* is moving forward (slowly, true, but surely).[7]
6. Yarikov[8] (VOKS) doesn't have a copy of the Violin Sonata. What should be done (I don't know)? It seems all the decisions are yours.

Please forgive the brevity of the information: I still haven't recovered from my fiftieth birthday yesterday.

I don't have anything to report regarding your two instructions (the restoration of the *Betrothal* suites and the copying of the Waltzes)[9] since I haven't attended to them (I haven't forgotten).

I send you and Mira Aleksandrovna greetings and best wishes,

Atovmyan

RGALI f. 1929, op. 1, yed. khr. 447, p. 29.
1. The reference is unclear.
2. Nickname for Vladmir Tabernakulov, Prokofiev's driver/courier.
3. The *Wedding* Suite.
4. According to Mira, the *Wedding* Suite was performed in early July of 1951 by the All-Union Radio Orchestra under the direction of Samosud (RGALI f. 1929, op. 3, yed. khr. 26, p. 39).
5. In the margins of the letter Prokofiev writes in pencil "I should see what was redone."

6. Atovmyan refers to the fifth movement of *On Guard for Peace*, which Prokofiev renamed "A Lesson in the Mother Tongue" and then "We Do Not Want War." This movement was a late addition to the oratorio, composed on Samosud's initiative.

7. Atovmyan refers to the preparation for the publication of the fifth and final version of *War and Peace*, which Muzgiz issued in piano and orchestral score in 1958.

8. Fyodor Yarikov (1897–c.1978), director of the Soviet culture division of VOKS from 1949 to 1958.

9. The "Pushkin" Waltzes.

76. Atovmyan to Prokofiev

May 30, 1951

Dear Sergey Sergeyevich!

Volodya didn't come by for the letter on the 26th. He called and said he'd come by today. I enclose the text of another letter addressed to S. M. Gotgelf.[1]

Nothing has essentially changed these past few days.

I signed off on the proofs of all 3 songs from the oratorio.

A question about *Winter Bonfire*: in 2–3 days the final proofs will arrive. The maximum given for them is 10 days. I'm afraid that you won't be able to look over the 98 pages by this deadline and so perhaps you would entrust the final proofs to me on the condition that if I have serious concerns about them I'll come to you. If there aren't such concerns then I'll sign off on them for printing. I await your response.

Finally a last question: there's a minor issue with the Cello Sonata. You added 2 measures to it, as a result of which the first chord of the third measure is unclear, namely

The impression is that in the third measure (right hand) the low C disappeared owing to the fault of the engraver. Wouldn't it be better to have the first chord with a low C, which would then be written

How is it for you in the country—cold like in Moscow? Dacha dwellers are sitting tight in Moscow afraid to leave the city, even though the dachas are rented and the money already paid.

I send you and Mira Aleksandrovna greetings and best wishes.

Atovmyan

By the way: have you looked over the beginning of the transcription of the oratorio? When you've looked it over send me your comments.

RGALI f. 1929, op. 1, yed. khr. 447, p. 30.
1. Sofya Mikhaĭlovna Gotgelf (1911–94), Committee on Arts Affairs official.

77. Atovmyan to Prokofiev

June 15, 1951

Dear Sergey Sergeyevich,

About the Suite: the voice parts are now entered. Today or tomorrow there'll be a rehearsal; consequently, in the coming days the date of the broadcast will finally be decided.

I'm sending the proofs of *Winter Bonfire*—but on the condition that on Monday (the very latest Tuesday) you'll send them back. On Tuesday and Wednesday I'll have to check them over and on Thursday I have to return them to Muzgiz without fail.

I'll write to you about the rest next time, since Volodya is in a rush. I send greetings and best wishes.

Atovmyan

RGALI f. 1929, op. 1, yed. khr. 447, p. 33.

78. Atovmyan to Prokofiev

July 8, 1951

Dear Sergey Sergeyevich!

I hope that tomorrow morning (the 9th) Volodya will come by and I'll finally be able to send you this letter. Enough questions have piled up:

1. I'm sending you the manuscript of "Dumka."[1] Make a note in your journal that I've returned it to you, lest you find some occasion to blame me for losing it.

2. I'm sending Kutuzov's aria.[2] Are you keeping it with you for good or returning it? I need to know so as not to copy it a second time (or, on the contrary, to copy it a second time) for the abbreviated version of the opera. The copying is progressing, by the way.

3. I'm sending the contract and invoice for *The Stone Flower* Suite. A few important remarks:

   a) Radio insists on the name "Suite from *The Stone Flower*" rather than "Ural Suite."

   b) One movement ("Dance of the Bachelors") has not been included in the Suite.[3] It will be forwarded as a supplement (evidently on July 10th) and there will be a supplemental contract for it.

   c) The amount for the contract is not stated. Chaplïgin wasn't there and I didn't manage to reach an agreement with him. Don't let this bother you. The amount won't be less than 10,000 rubles. Sign both copies of the contract and invoice. Please quickly return *both copies* of the contract and invoice to me.

    d) Please send a written request to the accountant of the Committee for Radio Information for the transfer of the funds to the savings bank.

    e) Sign the second invoice for the advance for the "Dance of the Bachelors." However, if you're in Moscow before July 15, then it's not worth signing this invoice now.

4. I'm sending the piano score of the end of the oratorio *On Guard for Peace* along with your manuscript. Here, too, some important comments:

    a) You've looked at the first four movements, so I'm not sending them to you.

    b) I'm also not sending movements 5, 6, and 7, since they are being published separately. Only the chorus needs to be entered into them.

    c) The end of movement 8 isn't clear to me (due to the fact that music is being dropped from movement 9: "Conversation in the Ether"). On page 45 please enter the concluding measures of this movement.

    d) I didn't always manage to insert the phrase marks, accents, and other nuances. I'll do this later. I'm pressing on with the piano score in hopes of quickly putting in the actual order to Muzgiz.[4]

    e) Please sign under the words "please check against the original" on the first page.

    f) Although I didn't "add" more music to the oratorio (in any event I tried not to), I treated the harmony in several places a little impolitely (chiefly with minor seconds).

    g) What's better to write: "chorus of adults" or "mixed chorus," "chorus of boys" or "children's chorus"? Sometimes you have "chorus of adults," other times simply "chorus."

    h) It would be good if you returned the piano score (and, it stands to reason, the manuscript, in order to verify the orchestral score, where most of the errors occur) as soon as possible.

    i) Finally, I'm sending you the libretto of the ballet *Hamlet* and the two letters from its author. I confess I didn't read the libretto.[5] How should I respond to the unfamiliar Khando-Mirova? (I don't understand why she doesn't simply write Khandomirova.)

Well it seems that's everything. I'll be waiting for your reply. The texts for the cantata,[6] regrettably, aren't with Balasanyan. Did you not promise me a copy of your detailed work list?

Thanks for the Sonata.[7] I submitted it to Muzgiz. Does this establishment operate slowly enough?

How's your health? When can I expect you in Moscow?

Prepare the Second Suite in leisurely fashion, for submission in October.

I send you and Mira Aleksandrovna greetings and best wishes.

Atovmyan

RGALI f. 1929, op. 1, yed. khr. 447, pp. 34–35.
1. "Dumka," a piano piece named after a Ukrainian folk song, went unfinished.
2. Kutuzov's aria is found in scene 10 ("Fili") of the fifth version of *War and Peace*.
3. No. 2 from the *Wedding* Suite.
4. Muzgiz published the piano-vocal score of *On Guard for Peace* in 1952.
5. Prokofiev decided against setting this libretto to music.
6. Atovmyan perhaps refers to *On Guard for Peace*, which is actually an oratorio.
7. The Cello Sonata.

79. Atovmyan to Prokofiev

August 5, 1951

Dear Sergey Sergeyevich!

S. A. Balasanyan asked me to let you know that on August 19 at 10:30 the oratorio will be performed on the second program.

I'll give him the piano score of the suite on Tuesday.[1] I'm sending you the realization of the first movement of the Concerto with some questions of mine.[2]

M. Rostropovich is bringing around the 2nd movement tomorrow; I'll give him the manuscript and copy of the 1st movement.

I'm planning to travel to Nikolina Gora after August 15 and, with your permission, I'll stop by to see you.

I send you and Mira Aleksandrovna greetings and best wishes,

Atovmyan

RGALI f. 1929, op. 1, yed. khr. 447, p. 36.
1. Presumably the *Wedding* Suite.
2. Atovmyan refers to the Concerto for Cello and Orchestra in E minor, which exists in three versions. The first version was premiered in Moscow on November 26, 1938; the second version, the subject of this letter, was premiered on February 18, 1952. Prokofiev made additional revisions to the work in 1952, renaming it the Sinfonia Concertante for Cello and Orchestra. He consulted with Rostropovich throughout the year on the cello part.

80. Atovmyan to Prokofiev

August 25, 1951

Dear Sergey Sergeyevich!

I'm sending you a copy of the published score of *Winter Bonfire*. I hope in due course to receive the score back from you with an inscription.

I'm also sending the score of the oratorio *On Guard for Peace*. Please look it over and send it back to me in no later than 3–4 days so I can submit it to Muzgiz.

If, contrary to expectation, there are mistakes in the score then the editor and I will catch them during editing (not to mention, of course, the proofs).

Please attend to the following without fail:

1. Complete the orchestration of the eighth measure after rehearsal number 66. In the piano score you wrote this measure (which is now the end of the eighth movement) like this:

2. Enter the metronome markings where they haven't yet been entered.

3. On the first page (on the cover) write "please check against the original" and sign your name.

4. Check rehearsal number 77. For now I've crossed out in pencil the fl. pic. at the beginning of the measure and the cl. pic. in the middle. If I've done this right, I'll put in the appropriate correction in ink.

The delay in realizing the Cello Concerto wasn't my fault. Having begun the realization of the third sketchbook I ran across references to the first sketchbook, which Rostropovich sequestered. I finally received the first sketchbook yesterday and today I resumed work. By the way: you rightly scolded me for the superfluous annotations I made on the score. I offer you my apology for these annotations and promise henceforth not to make them, with certain exceptions (for example when a low G♭ is assigned to the violins).

Work on *War and Peace* is moving forward and I hope to finish it in the first half of September.

By the 1st or, at the latest, 4th of September Muzgiz will have finished copying the score of both suites from *The Stone Flower*. Payment will have to be made. What do you think of this?

I looked over the Cello Sonata again from start to finish. The proofs are now finally completed. Once Rostropovich resolves three small questions (differences between the cello and piano parts) it will go to press. I expect you'll receive the advance copy at the end of September or beginning of October.

The Violin Sonata will go to press right after the Cello Sonata, perhaps even at the same time.

When are you planning to give me the third movement of the Cello Concerto? I want to arrange my work schedule accordingly.

Finally, when are you coming to Moscow? I send you and Mira Aleksandrovna greetings and very best wishes.

Atovmyan

RGALI f. 1929, op. 1, yed. khr. 447, pp. 37–38.

81. Atovmyan to Prokofiev

September 4, 1951

Dear Sergey Sergeyevich!

I wanted to finish work on *War and Peace* yesterday, but it seems you haven't given me the lithographed copy of the last scenes (the 12th—A Dark Hut—and the 13th—The Smolensk Road). According to the old version these are pages 469 to the end. If they're at the dacha, please send them back with Volodya. If they happen to be in Moscow, maybe Abram Solomonovich will be able to locate them in your room.

I've already arranged things with the bookbinder so that he'll come by on Sunday; I'd like to be finished by that time.

Not much work is left. The inserts are copied: it remains to fill in the pages, add the new indications, and enter the corrections in the lithographed copy.

I'm returning the lithographed copy of the 6th and 8th scenes of the opera (if you have copies of the other scenes, perhaps we'll manage to assemble a second collection—that is, of the abbreviated version of the opera).

I'm likewise returning the piano and orchestral scores of the third act of the ballet.[1] Today I'll submit the score of both excerpts to Radio. The first excerpt I called (literally) the Gypsy Fantasy Suite, and the second the Grand Rhapsody.[2]

I'll also submit the score of *On Guard for Peace* to Muzgiz today. I've entered all of the changes (*stille* attached to *divisi*, the ordering of the percussion, and so on).

It seems that's everything. I await your reply. I send greetings and very best wishes.

Atovmyan

P.S. Volodya brought me 500 rubles, for which I'm grateful. He notified me that the second transfer from Radio hadn't come through.

Today I found out that the bank didn't in fact receive the transfer, since you didn't make a written request for it. (The first request was used for the first transfer of 12,000 rubles.) Please send either a written request for a transfer to your savings bank of the honorarium for the "Dance of the Bachelors" from the ballet *The Stone Flower*—or a signed authorization for me to receive the funds.

Volodya promised to come by for this letter on the morning of September 5; for some reason he didn't.

RGALI f. 1929, op. 1, yed. khr. 447, pp. 39–40.
1. *The Tale of the Stone Flower.*

2. In the 1956 published score the names of the excerpts are "Gypsy Dance" (Act 3, scene 7) and "Ural Rhapsody" (Act 3, scene 6).

82. Atovmyan to Prokofiev

September 17, 1951

Dear Sergey Sergeyevich!

I received the last nine pages of Movement III of the Concerto. And where's the beginning? Expecting to receive it, I naturally didn't begin work.

I checked over and submitted the orchestral score of the oratorio *On Guard for Peace* to Muzgiz. Separate questions are now being settled with the editor, after which it will be engraved.

The piano score of *War and Peace* is finished; I submitted it to the theater the day before yesterday. The minor delay came about because Muzfond didn't provide financing for the copying of the last two scenes. Everything is now in order, with the exception of the binding. I'll give it to the binder when the theater returns the piano score.

Yesterday Stasevich began rehearsing the 3rd Suite from *Romeo*.[1] It will be performed on September 25 at 22:30 on the second program. After this rehearsals will evidently begin on the Fantasy (from *The Stone*).

I send greetings and best wishes.

Atovmyan

RGALI f. 1929, op. 1, yed. khr. 447, p. 41.
1. Abram Stasevich (1907–71), conductor.

83. Atovmyan to Prokofiev

October 1, 1951

Dear Sergey Sergeyevich!

I'm sending you Movement III of the Concerto. Unfortunately Slava Rostropovich is leaving a day before my proposed deadline and so I wasn't able to check over what was written. I offer my apologies in advance for any possible mistakes.

Today Zhivtsov,[1] the chief editor at Muzgiz, called. He isn't pleased that the Cello Sonata is dedicated to me and, speaking as sympathetically as he could, asked that the dedication be removed. Well, at least he asked. His predecessor Sakva acted in simpler fashion: without either the author's or my consent, he removed the dedication to me from Nikolay Yakovlevich's Symphony no. 25.

I of course told Zhivtsov that neither I nor, I think, the author insists on this dedication being printed and that in this respect he has total freedom. However, I requested compensation and, it seems, managed to bargain for publication this year of the Sonata for Solo Violin. So let me know if there will be any changes to this opus.

I saw Shlugleyt the day before yesterday:[2] they still haven't listened to the opera.[3] They'll be listening to it in the coming days. But I'll still manage to get it bound.

Balasanyan still hasn't returned. When he's back at work I'll find out about the Fantasy Suite.[4]

The orchestral score of *On Guard for Peace* has now gone into production. The piano score will apparently go into production in November or December.

How's it going with the work list (however brief)?[5] It's certainly needed. What are you thinking about writing: an overture or suite for Knushevitsky's variety show orchestra?[6]

I send you and Mira Aleksandrovna cordial greetings and best wishes.

Atovmyan

RGALI f. 1929, op. 1, yed. khr. 447, p. 42.
1. Alexander Zhivtsov (1907–72).
2. Ilya Shlugleyt (1897–1954), assistant director of the Stanislavsky Theater.
3. *War and Peace.*
4. The *Gypsy* Suite from *The Tale of the Stone Flower.*
5. Atovmyan has in mind the first of the annotated work lists compiled by Prokofiev and Mira Mendelson in 1951–52 (RGALI f. 1929, op. 3, yed. khr. 20–27).
6. Viktor Knushevitsky (1906–74), composer and conductor. Neither work was composed for his orchestra.

84. Prokofiev to Atovmyan

Nikolina Gora, October 4, 1951
Dear Levon Tadevosovich,

I'm outraged by Zhivtsov's behavior. On the first page of the original I'll attach a little note to that fellow that he'll think about for a long time. I'm grateful to you for your noble conduct.

I'm less grateful for the quality of your work on Movement III of the concerto: there are many unclear notes, almost no dynamic markings, and so on. I'm unwell now, ordered to bed and forbidden to work. So tomorrow I'll send you Movement III to look over for three days.* **

I have little money left. What will the Gypsies earn?[1] I sketched the *Volga-Don* overture.[2] I'll write a suite for Knushevitsky. Is there hope of receiving a contract for the oratorio?[3]

I firmly grasp your hand. Yours, SP

* I owe you for the concerto; I count on receiving the honoraria from the Committee.

** It would be good to see the Sonata for Solo Violin if it doesn't delay things.

RGALI f. 1929, op. 3, yed. khr. 121. p. 1. Handwritten.
1. The *Gypsy* Suite was premiered on November 18, 1951, with Samosud conducting.
2. *The Meeting of the Volga and the Don* was commissioned through Balasanyan by the Radio Committee. Prokofiev began the orchestration on October 12 (eight days after receipt of this letter) and finished it on November 18, 1951 (RGALI f. 1929, op. 3, yed. khr. 26, p. 41).
3. A publication contract for the piano score of *On Guard for Peace*.

85. Atovmyan to Prokofiev

October 5, 1951
Dear Sergey Sergeyevich!

I'm sending you the manuscript of the Violin Sonata. After reviewing it please send it back immediately. The lithographed copy wasn't left with me. Isn't it with you? If it is, send it—this will reduce costs.

Muzgiz won't prepare the contract for the oratorio until November, since according to their plan the oratorio is to appear in 1952. I hope that the contract for the Violin Sonata (unison) will be earlier.

Today they're transferring 1,540 rubles (40% for the Cello Sonata) to your account.

Balasanyan still hasn't come. He's returning tomorrow and when he's back at work I'll hurry him along with the suite.[1]

I'm very glad that you'll be writing a suite for Knushevitsky. When do you contemplate sending the *Volga-Don* overture?

I send you and Mira Aleksandrovna cordial greetings and best wishes.
Yours, Atovmyan

RGALI f. 1929, op. 1, yed. khr. 447, p. 43.
1. The *Gypsy* Suite

86. Atovmyan to Prokofiev

June 24, 1952
Dear Sergey Sergeyevich,
1. I'm sending you the orchestral score of *On Guard for Peace* for "review." It wouldn't be a bad idea to sign the title page and, when you can, send the score back to me. I'll send you a copy for your library in a day or two.
2. I'm sending you a copy of Sonata No. 3.[1] Muzgiz intends to reprint it. If possible, please quickly return the copy with your corrections, if there are any. Take into account that the plates are intact, so don't get carried away with corrections, otherwise it will have to be newly engraved.

3. *Visions Fugitives* (republished) will soon be out from the press.[2]

4. They telephoned from Cinema. They asked you to write music for the animated film *Flight to the Moon*. Roughly 15 minutes of music is needed. It seems the honorarium will be around 15,000 (no less than 12,000) rubles. I refused at first on your behalf, but the cinema people pester all the same. Resolve the matter and let me know. At the least you could do a piano score (without an orchestral score). The deadlines, they say, won't be a worry, but this in particular can't be trusted, since cinema people are a strange sort. I await your decision.[3]

5. I'm finishing the orchestration of the excerpts from *Romeo* for small orchestra. I chose the following numbers: "Dance of the Knights," "Five Pairs' Dance," "Gavotte" (in the new edition), "The Street Awakens," "Dance of the Maidens," the "Fight" Scene and the Finale of Act 2. At the beginning of July the score will be ready and then, with your permission, I'll show it to you. I think the extracts will end up being published this year.[4]

6. The piano score of *On Guard for Peace* will evidently be printed at the end of July.

7. The Quartet of the Philharmonic (Barshay's group) recorded two excerpts for Radio from *Romeo* ("The Street Awakens," "Dance of the Maidens") and three pieces (from *Visions Fugitives*) in Barshay's reworking.[5] It turned out very nicely.

8. I won't write about the music news. I'll tell you when we meet, since writing about it is boring. Really nothing interesting.

9. How are you feeling? How's the symphony coming along?[6]

Soon fall will arrive. It's time to think about the suites. Greetings and best wishes to you and Mirochka. If you run into Valentina Yakovlevna, please convey my greetings.[7]

Atovmyan

RGALI f. 1929, op. 1, yed. khr. 447, pp. 45–46.

1. The Piano Sonata (1917) was republished in 1952.

2. The piano cycle *Visions Fugitives* (1917) was republished in 1952.

3. Prokofiev declined the proposal.

4. Atovmyan's arrangement of "Scenes and Dances" from *Romeo and Juliet* for small ensemble was published by Muzgiz in 1952.

5. The Barshay (later Borodin) String Quartet was founded in 1944 by students of the Moscow Conservatory: Rostislav Dubinsky (1923–97), first violin; Nina Barshay (1923–98), second violin; Rudolf Barshay (b. 1924), viola; and Rostropovich, cello. It was affiliated in 1952 with the Moscow Philharmonic. According to Rudolf Barshay (telephone interview with Nelly Kravetz, February 2, 2007), of the six numbers from *Visions Fugitives* he arranged for string quartet (nos. 3, 10, 13, 14, 16, and 17), four were recorded (nos. 3, 10, 14, and 16).

6. Symphony no. 7 (1952).

7. Valentina Myaskovskaya (1886–1965), Myaskovsky's second sister.

87. Prokofiev to Atovmyan

This letter attests to Prokofiev's need, in the post-1948 period, to generate income from the publication and performance of works that correctly accorded with the official aesthetic doctrine of Socialist Realism.

Nikolina Gora, July 3, 1952
Dear Levon Tadevosovich,

Thank you for the letter and scores. I'm pleased that the oratorio was properly published, but regrettably there are some irritating omissions concerning the text on pages 5 and 6. On page 6 the words "torn up" ("her forests, her fields, have been torn up, burnt up") were omitted. Page 6 excludes the phrase "where the fight for the city occurred" ("there remain piles of bricks, where the fight for the city occurred, and the necks of clay ovens, where once stood villages"). In general there's a discrepancy between the complete Marshak text, appended at the end, and the text in the orchestral score. I'm worried that these mistakes will get into the piano score of the oratorio. Perhaps you'll still be able to eliminate them.[1]

I'm sending you Sonata no. 3. I looked it over; I don't have any comments. As regards Muzgiz, I have two questions: 1. What have you heard about the op. 59 pieces—"Stroll," "Landscape," the 3rd ("Pastoral") Sonatina?[2] I personally had in mind "Landscape" and the Sonatina. 2. I'd very much like the Third Suite from the ballet *Cinderella* to be published, about which, I believe, there were discussions a long time ago now.[3] Can you not try to remind Muzgiz about the Suite? The music of *Cinderella* received a Stalin Prize, you see, and *Cinderella* was recently dubbed a Realist ballet alongside *Romeo and Juliet* in the journal *Sovetskaya muzïka*.[4]

I'm finishing the symphony, and then I'm planning to make some small changes to *The Stone Flower* in accord with a request from the Bolshoy and Kirov Theaters. They are apparently preparing to stage the ballet. In connection with this Lavrovsky and Sergeyev[5] were by. I'm redoing the Cello Concerto a little at a time.

I'm interested in your orchestration of the *Romeo* extracts. I wish you good health and hope to see you soon in Nikolina Gora. We'll arrange this in a day or two as well.

I grasp your hand. Yours

RGALI f. 1929, op. 2, yed. khr. 151, p. 18. Typed letter.
    1. Atovmyan corrected only the first of the errors in the 1952 edition of the piano score. Both errors are found in the 1973 edition.
    2. These piano pieces were previously published by Muzgiz in 1937 and 1947.
    3. This occurred in 1954.
    4. Prokofiev received a Stalin Prize (First Class) for *Cinderella* on June 27, 1946. He refers here to an article by the musicologist Tamara Tsïtovich (1907–92): *"Cinderella,* like several other

Prokofiev compositions, is a realist work, possessing at once all of the particularities and inimitably original features of the composer's style." "'Zolushka.' Balet Prokof'yeva," *Sovetskaya muzïka* 8–9 (1946): 50.

    5. Konstantin Sergeyev (1910–92), dancer and choreographer. The ballet was premiered on February 12, 1954, at the Bolshoy Theater.

88. Atovmyan to Prokofiev

July 3, 1952

Dear Sergey Sergeyevich,

    First of all I have to offer my apologies for forgetting your exact "country" address. I wasn't able to notify you in good time that Radio has arranged the funds (the advance) for the symphony (10,000 rubles, it seems).

    Surmising from the billboards at the Bolshoy Theater that you haven't been earning royalties in proper measure these past months, I should, of course, have reported to you much earlier about these funds.

    About the publications:

    I've reached an agreement with Muzgiz for the publication of the orchestral score of the Classical Symphony. It will be published in pocket format. To this end I'll provide the score in my possession (the Gutheil Edition) for copying. A question about the Gavotte: I requested on your behalf that both versions of the Gavotte be published (the first one, published by Gutheil, and the second, expanded one that you did for *Romeo*). Did I act correctly or do you disagree with this proposal? Please tell me, since the score of the Classical will soon go into production. I've all the same given both versions of the Gavotte for copying.[1]

    Incidentally, the second version of the Gavotte has some doubtful notes. The bassoon has been written , when at this point it's obviously . That is, the first note is G, not B. Then:

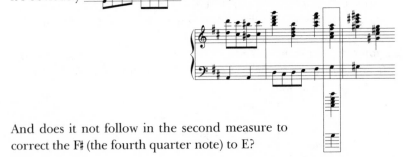

And does it not follow in the second measure to correct the F♯ (the fourth quarter note) to E?

Finally, you have written

but as far as I understand it should be

That is, the top note in the second measure is not A, but C. Since, apparently, the correcting and copying and engraving will fall to me, I'd ask you to let me know if I'm correct in making these changes.

Referring to the other publications (in particular the suites and piano score of *Cinderella*, and the orchestral scores of the dance suites that Samosud performed for Radio), I had a very cordial encounter with the chief editor of Muzgiz, Alexander Ivanovich Zhivtsov, who on his own initiative proposed something to my liking: publishing your selected piano works in three volumes in 1953.[2]

Will you yourself select the works that will go into the three volumes or leave this to Muzgiz? According to my preliminary count each volume will have about 40–50 folia, that is, three or four sonatas and no fewer than thirty named piano pieces.

I await your response to this question. I've finished the orchestration of the extracts from *Romeo* for small orchestra. I'm not sending it to you now for your approval, since I've tortured you enough with this letter.

I send you and Mirochka greetings and very best wishes.

Atovmyan

P.S. By the way, my daughter and granddaughter have rented a room in the village of Uspensky, not far from you. I intend to visit them—perhaps we'll see each other on one of the trips.

One other confusion in the Gavotte: the flute has written

Wouldn't

be better—that is, the last two notes an octave lower?

RGALI f. 1929, op. 1, yed. khr. 447, pp. 47–48.

1. The Classical Symphony was published with two versions of the Gavotte in 1953. The first version dates from 1917, as do the other three movements; the second, expanded version dates from 1935. The second Gavotte was composed for the "Departure of the Guests" scene in Act 1 of Romeo and Juliet.

2. The three volumes were published by Muzgiz in 1955–56.

89. Atovmyan to Prokofiev

July 16, 1952
Dear Sergey Sergeyevich!
    I haven't been able until now to send the letter I wrote on July 3, since there wasn't a courier. Today my daughter Svetlana is returning to her dacha (she rented a room for the summer in the village of Uspensky), and I'm sending this plus the first letter with her.
    At the same time I'm sending you the score of the extracts from *Romeo* for small orchestra. I foresee in advance that much of it will surprise you, in particular the shifting of the melody from the violas to the violins (in the "Antilles Maidens"), the doubling of the woodwinds, and the addition of the French horn or piano to the accompaniment.
    Please consider that in a small orchestra the string section comprises as a rule 4–5 first and second violins (taken together) and either 1 or in the best case two viola and two cello parts. It also needs to be borne in mind that certain instruments (in particular the 3rd French horn or even the bassoon) might be absent in a small orchestra.
    The score I'm sending will be subject to reworking. I'll do this after I receive it back from you. Don't pay attention to any possible slips of the pen, since I'll carefully correct it. It follows for you to review the orchestration in principle, taking into account that I'll be finishing up the details.
    Since this letter is long I won't touch on other issues.
    If you agree in principle with the orchestration, please sign "I approve S. Prokofiev" on the first (notated) page, and return the score as soon as possible to me (either with Svetlana or Yuriy Abramovich Levitin,[1] who lives across from you—prospekt Shmidt, bldg. 41, Tomskaya dacha—or best of all with Volodya).
    I send you and Mira Aleksandrovna greetings and best wishes.
    Atovmyan

Another proviso: the transposing instruments are not written in C in the score.[2] For small orchestras this is more convenient (more customary).

RGALI f. 1929, op. 1, yed. khr. 447, p. 49.
  1. Yuriy Levitin (1912–93), composer.
  2. Prokofiev habitually scored the transposing instruments of the orchestra in C.

90. Prokofiev to Atovmyan

Nikolina Gora, July 22, 1952
Dear Levon Tadevosovich,
    My thanks for your letters of July 3 and 16 and for the score of the

Romeo extracts, which I'm returning simultaneously with this letter.

1. I reviewed the extracts score, but unfortunately I was hampered by the absence at the dacha of the scores of either the ballet or the suite. All the same I made some minor notes.

2. My thanks for including both versions of the Gavotte in the Classical Symphony. I accept all of the corrections reported in your letter. Keep in mind that Koussevitzky had two editions of the Classical: the first, a badly ink-stamped edition, and the second edition engraved with a series of corrections. It's very good. We had a copy in Moscow, but I don't recall exactly where. It would be good to engrave with it.[1]

3. I'm very pleased about comrade A. I. Zhivtsov's intention to publish the three volumes of my piano compositions. Muzgiz had this same idea ten years ago, but unfortunately it dissipated like smoke. I would hope that this time they're serious. I'd prefer that Muzgiz proposed the list of pieces to me; I'll express my preferences independently.

4. Regarding the printing of new compositions, I think that Suite no. 3 from *Cinderella* needs to be put first in line. The score was verified and corrected by Muzgiz and its author. Besides this, the Ninth Sonata and two op. 59 pieces, "Landscape" and the Sonatina, interest me.[2] I've already written to you about them. I'd of course like for the suites conducted by Samosud to be published, but it's not entirely clear to me if you have in mind the suites from the ballet *The Stone Flower* or other ones.

5. When approximately can I count on receiving the money for the Classical, the Third Sonata, and *Visions Fugitives*? I received the advance for the Symphony from the Committee for Radio Information, but after the accountant's deductions I was given 5,700 rubles instead of 10,000 rubles. To this point they haven't paid me for the ballet score.[3] As soon as I receive the money I'll hand over what you're owed.

I'm very glad that you've settled your loved ones nearby. I hope you'll look in on us while visiting your daughter and granddaughter. It would be good if you arranged your trips with Vladimir Semyonovich.[4]

I wish you good health. SP

RGALI 1929, op. 2, yed. khr. 151, p. 20. Typed letter.

1. The orchestral score and piano reduction of the Classical Symphony were published by Gutheil in 1919 and by Édition Russe de Musique in 1925. Serge Koussevitzky (1874–1951) operated these two firms.

2. The Ninth Piano Sonata (1947) was first published in 1955.

3. *The Tale of the Stone Flower.*

4. Tabernakulov.

91. Atovmyan to Prokofiev

July 31, 1952

Dear Sergey Sergeyevich!

Yesterday, through the kindness of D. D. Shostakovich, who offered me the use of his car, I finally, for the first time this summer, made it to Uspensky (to my daughter and granddaughter's) and, afterward, to Nikolina Gora. Naturally, I desired to convey my regards to you. With this aim I drove up to your dacha, stood around for about 10 minutes and, since neither you nor Mira Aleksandrovna appeared in the garden, I drove away as fast as I could. I didn't want to risk dropping in on you unannounced since, firstly, an uninvited guest is worse than a Tatar and, secondly, Vladimir Semyonovich cautioned that you are "besieged enough" without me.

I'm hoping that my next trip will be happier (since out of spite Valentina Yakovlevna,[1] Shebalin, and Levitin were all in Moscow today).

The questions you touched on in your last letter will be resolved in the coming days at Muzgiz. I'll immediately inform you of the results.

S. A. Samosud recently performed the Capriccio and *Volga-Don* with success.[2]

The *Poem* soon needs to be published: will you look over the score in preparation?[3] The Classical Symphony (the engraved edition, not the ink-stamped) has been copied; tomorrow I'll pay for it. It will go into production in the coming days. Muzgiz would prefer to receive the engraved, not the copied, score. Can I give it to them and temporarily keep the copy (in place of the engraved score) in my library?

I'm sending you the invoice for the extracts. Please sign it (the place for the signature is marked in blue pencil) and return it to me by courier.

I send you and Mira Aleksandrovna greetings and very best wishes.

Atovmyan

RGALI f. 1929, op. 1, yed. khr. 447, p. 50.

1. Myaskovskaya.
2. The performance took place on February 22, 1952.
3. Atovmyan refers to *The Meeting of the Volga and the Don*, which was not published in orchestral score until 1958.

92. Atovmyan to Prokofiev

July 31, 1952

Dear Sergey Sergeyevich!

I intended to send the first letter with Vladimir Semyonovich, whom I specially requested as far back as July 29 to *call me without fail* today before leaving for Nikolina Gora. By the way, I wanted to send along strawberries and other berries for my granddaughter: Svetlana informed me that Mira Aleksandrovna kindly permitted the use of your car for this purpose when she makes her trip.

However, despite my urgent request, Vl. Sem. didn't call and didn't come by. I don't understand what provoked this behavior and I naturally find it unpleasant, since the berries were left at home and I didn't keep my promise to my granddaughter (not to mention the money wasted and the running around at the market).

After such behavior I won't, of course, be asking Vlad. Sem. for anything ever again. I've arranged to send future letters to you either via Yuriy Abramovich Levitin (he's a very responsible person) or Vissarion Yakovlevich, who's traveling to Nikolina Gora this evening and kindly agreed to give this letter to you. I once again send greetings and best wishes.

Atovmyan

RGALI f. 1929, op. 1, yed. khr. 447, p. 51.

93. Atovmyan to Prokofiev

August 8, 1952

Dear Sergey Sergeyevich!

I'm taking the opportunity to write you a few words. The remuneration from Muzgiz is expected no earlier than September. The reprint is in production, and according to current regulations at Muzgiz honoraria for reprints are paid in full once they are issued from the press (without any advances). Today I saw the advance copy of *Visions Fugitives*. Sales will apparently begin at the end of August; they'll then calculate the honorarium.

In a day or two I'll finish a preliminary compilation of the three-volume edition of piano compositions. Once you agree to it, this project will go to the Arts Committee for approval.

By the way, do you have any opposition to my being the compiler and editor of these collections (the three volumes)? Perhaps you'd prefer to assign this task to someone else. I conditionally told Comrade Zhivtsov that I'm willing to do the compiling and editing, cautioning him that the final choice of compiler and editor has to be determined by you.

Since this idea (the three-volume edition) hasn't fallen by the wayside, I've occupied myself for now with the compiling and negotiating. In this regard it wouldn't be a bad idea to send a letter to the chief editor at Muzgiz, Alexander Ivanovich Zhivtsov, making it clear whom you want Muzgiz to name as the compiler and editor of the three-volume edition.

Since A. I. Zhivtsov is leaving for vacation in the near future, it would be good to hasten the letter.

Svetlana is coming to Moscow on August 11. Perhaps Volodya can drop off the letter to her; she'll bring it to me.

I want to remind dear Mira Aleksandrovna that she hasn't fulfilled her promise to send me a copy of the work list. I only have the first half (more accurately the first third), ending with op. 57.

When can I get the piano score of *Cinderella* (published abroad) back from you?[1] I need this score in order to correct the new one (done by me and reviewed by you) for publication. I hope that the piano score of *Cinderella* will be published in 1953.

That's all for now; the rest in the next letter. I send heartfelt greetings and very best wishes,

Atovmyan

RGALI f. 1929, op. 1, yed. khr. 447, p. 52.
1. Atovmyan refers to the 1947 edition published by Leeds Music in New York City.

94. Atovmyan to Prokofiev

This and the next letter concern Atovmyan's efforts to prepare a collected edition of Prokofiev's piano works. Atovmyan takes pains to ensure that the collection will meet with the approval of the censors, even suggesting that Prokofiev remove a dissonant sonority from his Sixth Piano Sonata.

August 13, 1952
Dear Sergey Sergeyevich!

The approximate plan for the three-volume signed edition of select works for piano is finished and today I provisionally reached an agreement for it with A. I. Zhivtsov. Today the plan will be sent for review to the Arts Committee (N. N. Bespalov).[1] This is being done in advance of reaching an agreement with you, since Zhivtsov is leaving in 2 days for vacation and would like to settle in principle the question of the publication of the three volumes before departing. It goes without saying that you retain the right to make changes to the plan.[2]

1. Unfortunately I still can't "fit" everything in the size I'm permitted (3 volumes of 20 folia each, that is, 160 pages per volume; I arrived at approximately 25 folia each, that is, about 200 pages per volume). It falls to you, accordingly, to reduce rather than expand.

2. I laid out the volumes as follows: Volume I: Sonatas; Volume II: Piano Pieces; Volume III: Transcriptions and Arrangements. Such a layout, I think, is better than a layout by opus (in chronological order).

3. Contents:

A) *Volume I: Sonatas*: Nos. 2, 4, 6, 7, 8, and the 2 op. 54 Sonatinas (E minor, G major).

Comments on the first volume:

The volume can't accommodate a large collection of sonatas (owing to their size). Sonata no. 3 is in one movement and can be easily published separately; Sonata no. 5 will shortly be out from the press in a separate edition. They[3] aren't approving Sonata No. 9 for the three-volume edition of works for now; next year I'll see about a separate edition. But you'll need to replace the ill-fated chord (*col pugno*) in the 6th Sonata.[4] To prevent them from throwing the 6th Sonata out, I explained that it will be published in a new version.

B) *Volume II: Piano Pieces*

The op. 3–4 pieces: "Story," "Badinage," "March," and "Phantom."
The 4 op. 4 pieces: "Reminiscences," "Élan," "Despair," and "Delusion."
The op. 11 Toccata.
The 10 op. 12 pieces ("March," "Gavotte," "Rigaudon," and so forth).
Op. 17: *Sarcasms*.
Op. 22: *Visions Fugitives*.
Op. 31: *Old Grandmother's Tales*.
The 4 op. 32 pieces ("Dance," "Minuet," "Gavotte," and "Waltz").
The 3 op. 59 pieces ("Promenade," "Landscape," "Pastoral" Sonatina).
Op. 77: Gavotte no. 4.
The 3 op. 95 pieces ("Intermezzo," "Gavotte," "Slow Waltz").
Not included: the 4 op. 2 Etudes, *Things in Themselves*, *Thoughts*, the Music for Children, and others.

C) *Volume 3: Transcriptions and Arrangements*

Op. 25: The Gavotte from the Classical Symphony.
Op. 33: March and Scherzo (from *The Love for Three Oranges*).
Op. 52: Numbers from the ballet *On the Dnieper* (hypothetically included; unfortunately, I don't have the music and can't show it to Muzgiz).
Op. 75: 10 pieces from *Romeo and Juliet*.
Op. 96: 3 pieces (the *War and Peace* Waltz, the Contredanse and "Mephisto" Waltz from *Lermontov*).
Op. 97: 10 pieces from *Cinderella*.
Op. 102: 6 pieces from *Cinderella*.

I would also like to include here the Prokofiev-Schubert Waltzes for 2 pianos and, if you agree to create during the winter a "Waltz on Ice" (from *Winter Bonfire*), to include it with several pieces from *The Stone Flower*.

At present the total comes to more than 600 pages. Please let me know your opinion about all three volumes (with respect to layout and contents).

4. What's needed:

A) I need to pick up the music of all the works going into the three-volume edition. I unfortunately don't have several works, and only one copy of the others. Is it possible to do this from your library? I hope you have spare copies.

B) You should inscribe "to be checked against the original" on each work. In those cases where you'd like to change the edition or correct a misprint, you'll need to mark the pages.

C) Evidently, several works (if you decide to leave them in the three-volume edition) will have to be given to Muzfond for copying (the Schubert Waltzes, the numbers from the ballet *On the Dnieper*, and others). In this instance you'll need to send the originals and a letter to Muzfond (since, naturally, the copying will be charged to your account).

I await your letter concerning all of the subjects broached. I'll send the oratorio in the coming days.

When will I receive the continuation of the work list? At Radio everyone is delighted with your Seventh Symphony.[5]

I send you and Mira Aleksandrovna greetings and very best wishes.

Atovmyan

August 13, 1952 Supplement

Mikhaíl Ivanovich Chulaki just called.[6] He's interested in the one-evening version of *War and Peace*. He asked to be given the score for familiarization, since the question of the staging is still up in the air. Apparently he regards the idea positively. Unfortunately, you took away the copy and didn't return it. Where might I obtain it for Chulaki? Chulaki also wants to see you about a number of matters.

For him to visit you without settling the day and time in advance is hardly advisable. He's certain that you have a telephone at the dacha (is this so?). If you don't have a telephone, however, perhaps Mira Aleksandrovna can call him from somewhere there, either today before 6:30 (if you receive this letter beforehand) or tomorrow afternoon, August 14, between 12 and 1 at his office (telephone K 4-71-75).

It will be useful to meet with him: he's an extremely active and authoritative figure, able without procrastinating to settle a lot of questions (either about the staging of the opera or the publication of the three-volume edition or the performance of works at the Philharmonic, and so on). Besides, he, like many Leningraders, is a fine, trained musician and a pleasant conversationalist.

Call him without fail.

Atovmyan

RGALI f. 1929, op. 1, yed. khr. 447, pp. 53–55.

1. Nikolay Bespalov (1906–80), Chairman of the Committee on Arts Affairs.
2. The actual contents of the published three-volume edition (1955–56) do not reflect the plan devised by Atovmyan and Prokofiev.
3. The Arts Committee officials.
4. A four-note cluster in the bass clef, outlining a tritone (F–G–A–B).
5. On July 26, 1952, Vedernikov and Rostropovich performed a four-hand reduction of the Seventh Symphony at the offices of the Radio Committee.
6. Mikhaíl Chulaki (1908–89), Committee on Arts Affairs official.

95. Prokofiev to Atovmyan

Nikolina Gora, August 14, 1952

Dear Levon Tadevosovich,

Thank you for the letter and all your efforts. I hasten to express my preferences so that you can include them as quickly as possible in the preliminary plan for the three-volume edition that you are presenting to the Committee on Arts Affairs.

First Volume:

1. I'm rather confused by the inclusion in the plan of the two op. 54 Sonatinas. But if we include them, then I'd ask that you also include the op. 59, no. 3 "Pastoral" Sonatina, transferring it to the first volume from the second. It follows to keep "Landscape" in the second volume; however, please leave out "Promenade."
2. Regarding the chord in the Sixth Sonata, I'll of course replace it.

Second Volume:

1. Of the four op. 3 pieces I'd ask that you keep only one, "Story," and omit the other three.
2. Of the four op. 4 pieces I'd ask that you keep two, "Despair" and "Delusion," and omit the others.
3. Of the ten op. 12 pieces I'd ask that you keep six—"March," "Gavotte," "Rigaudon," "Prelude," "Allemande," and "Scherzo"—and omit the remaining four.
4. Concerning the op. 31 *Old Grandmother's Tales*, I'd ask that you leave the 2nd, 3rd, and 4th in the plan. Omit the 1st.
5. Of the four op. 32 pieces I'd like to keep two, "Dance" and "Gavotte," and exclude the "Minuet" and "Waltz."
6. Of the 20 op. 22 pieces I would like to keep approximately 10, which I'll specify later on.

7. The op. 95 pieces are transcriptions from the ballet *Cinderella*, so they're better placed in the Third Volume, with the first of them named not "Intermezzo" but "Pavane."

Of the pieces you haven't included I'd like to express the following preferences:

1. I'd like to include the 3rd and 4th Etudes of the 4 op. 2 Etudes.
2. I'd include the 2nd and 3rd pieces from op. 62, *Thoughts*.
3. I'd *absolutely* include 9 of the 12 pieces from the op. 65 Music for Children in the plan, namely: "Morning," "Promenade," "A Little Story," "Regret," "Waltz," "The Rain and the Rainbow," "March," "Evening," and "The Moon Strolls in the Meadow."

Volume Three:

1. The ballet *On the Dnieper* does not have numbers; it needs to be excluded from the plan.
2. Regarding op. 75, the 10 pieces from the ballet *Romeo and Juliet*, and op. 97, the 10 pieces from the ballet *Cinderella*—I'd limit each of these opuses to seven pieces.
3. I'd very much like to include in this volume No. 1 from the Divertissement, op. 43bis.
4. It's quite possibly worth including the Waltz from *Winter Bonfire* and several pieces from the ballet *The Stone Flower*. But I absolutely want *to add* the transcription of the two Pushkin Waltzes, op. 120.

In the coming days we'll try to send you the work list and look through the scores we have here. I earnestly request that you inform me how much I owe for the copying of the Classical Symphony. I send you cordial greetings and wishes for good health. I'm not against the Schubert Waltzes if there's space for them.

RGALI f. 1929, op. 2, yed. khr. 151, p. 21. Typed letter.

96. Prokofiev to Atovmyan

August 16 [1952]

I delayed sending this letter, since M. I. Chulaki visited Nikolina Gora yesterday, with favorable results:

1. They will begin rehearsing *War and Peace* in the Stanislavsky Theater at the start of the season;[1]
2. *The Stone Flower*—at the Kirov Theater;[2]
3. M. I. Ch. is not against your involvement in the compilation of the three-volume edition.

Greetings, SP

P.S. "Natasha Rostova"[3] (!) will still need the Napoleon scene.

RGALI f. 1929, op. 2, yed. khr. 151, p. 21. Handwritten.
1. The opera was first performed at this theater on November 8, 1957.
2. The ballet was first performed at this theater on April 25, 1957.
3. An alternate title for *War and Peace*, first suggested to Prokofiev in 1942.

97. Atovmyan to Prokofiev

August 25, 1952

Dear Sergey Sergeyevich!

I gave the invoice for Symphony no. 7 to the accountant with a request to rush the transfer of funds. I told G. N. Khubov[1] that you've agreed to the hearing of the symphony, but according to Vedernikov, the piano score is with you and the symphony can't be played without it. Vedernikov will clearly be coming to you for the piano score.

The hearing of *War and Peace* has seemingly been postponed until August 27.[2] Apparently the concertmaster isn't prepared.

I'm sending the full piano score of *War and Peace*. Mira Aleksandrovna should quickly edit the new text so that it can be written under the music as it is copied. There's no way that the piano score can be copied with the old text; the differences in the formulation of the prose will serve as the basis of jokes among the performers, and this is of no use. Bear in mind that the score will be copied in the near future.

I told Khubov that you aren't in a position to write the essay he requested, since you're busy with the opera, ballet, and symphony. However, he beseeches you to write a short essay for the next issue in connection with the upcoming XIX Party Congress (your thoughts and intentions, particularly as they relate to your work on the new scenes in *War and Peace*, your work on the ballet, the symphony, and so on).[3]

What should I communicate to him on this front? Did you write the letter to Muzgiz regarding the contract for the Classical Symphony?

I send greetings and very best wishes.

Atovmyan

RGALI f. 1929, op. 1, yed. khr. 447, p. 56.
1. Georgiy Khubov (1902–81), musicologist and Union of Soviet Composers administrator.
2. The hearing took place on October 17, 1952.
3. In honor of the October 5–15 Congress, Prokofiev wrote the article "Majestic Tasks." "Velichestvennïye zadachi," *Sovetskaya muzïka* 10 (1952): 4.

98. Atovmyan to Prokofiev

In the last few months of Prokofiev's life, when he resided primarily in Moscow, his correspondence was limited to short notes. Atovmyan visited him regularly.

September 9, 1952
Dear Sergey Sergeyevich,
  I received the orchestral score of the 1st scene of *W and P*; upon receipt of the piano score I'll begin the orchestration of Prince Andrey's dialogue and Natasha and Sonya's duet.
  They[1] still haven't returned the piano score, saying that it's needed "for their work." Incidentally, you've kept the complete piano score for too long (what did I send it to you for?) The Napoleon scene needs to be copied; the complete piano score, moreover, needs to be consulted for all sorts of things.
  Perhaps send it to me with Volodya along with the published piano score of *Cinderella*. As far as I recall, the changes to Kutuzov's aria have been made—I'll check when the piano score is returned to me.
  It seems to me, however, that the most pressing task, on which I'm now working, is preparing the first volume of piano works for publication. In connection with this I have a request: gradually (a little at a time) look over the pieces included in the first volume and, if you have any corrections or comments, make the appropriate notes in the margins.
  They're now pressing on with the 1st volume at Muzgiz. The matter of the honorarium for the Classical Symphony is being resolved favorably: 8,000 rather than 4,800 rubles are to be paid. I only just settled this problem when another one arose: for the 3rd Sonata reprint they paid 1,800 rubles (60% of 3,000). I protested, demanding a payment of 3,000 rubles (60% of 5,000). Evidently they'll agree: I'd rather the 4,400 rubles that Muzgiz wanted to shortchange you be allowed to settle the debt for the dacha than to be refused the funds altogether.[2]
  Tomorrow or the day after I'll be at Muromtsev's (Arts Committee) and comrade Khubov's and I'll find out everything concerning *W and P* and the upcoming Plenary.[3] I'll report back afterward.
  I send you and Mirochka greetings and best wishes.
  Atovmyan

RGALI f. 1929, op. 1, yed. khr. 447, p. 57.
  1. The Stanislavsky Theater.
  2. Atovmyan refers to the no-interest loan that Prokofiev obtained from Muzfond for the purchase of his Nikolina Gora dacha.
  3. Yuriy Muromtsev (1908–75), Committee on Arts Affairs official. The Sixth Plenary of the Union of Soviet Composers took place from January 31 to February 12, 1953. On February 6 the gathering assessed a recording of select scenes from *War and Peace*. The positive reaction paved the way for a complete staging of the opera in 1955, two years after Prokofiev's death.

Prokofiev's Immortalization

LEONID MAXIMENKOV

In January 1990, at the start of that chapter in Russian history when the authority of the Communist Party of the Soviet Union (CPSU) was crumbling and a fiscal crisis was reaching catastrophic proportions, the Central Committee's ideological department decided to endorse a lavish national project: a celebration, on April 23, 1991, of the centennial of Sergey Prokofiev's birth. The Baltic Republics were clamoring for succession, factory workers and miners had begun staging unprecedented strikes, and political protests were challenging the once supreme authority of the Communist apparatus—yet it seemed that there was no more urgent task in the realm of arts and culture than to hold festivities in Prokofiev's honor.

Despite the awkward timing, the idea bore a certain political logic. Few figures in twentieth-century Russian and Soviet culture could generate as broad a consensus among officials as the embodiment of creative genius, a source of national pride at a time of revolutionary crisis. Given Prokofiev's international stature, the marketing of his legacy could serve multiple *perestroyka* policies abroad, their aims including the promotion of shared humanitarian values.

As it turned out, Mikhaíl Gorbachev's grand ideas precipitated the collapse of the Communist regime and disintegration of the Soviet empire. When the Prokofiev anniversary arrived, the festivities altogether lacked grandeur. The Bolshoy Theater gala was a modest affair virtually ignored by the national media. No new productions of his operas and ballets were mounted, and no major publications about his life and works rolled off the presses. The failed centennial of 1991 concluded, on a sour note, the Soviet version of what is known in Russian cultural history as *uvekovecheniye pamyati*. Prokofiev's celebration was the last of its kind in the Soviet Union.

The English translation of *uvekovecheniye pamyati*, a term that denotes a central Russian political and ideological ritual, is "the immortalization of memory." There exists a subtle linguistic distinction between the Russian and English definitions of the first word. The English word derives from the Latin *mors* (death) and the semantic concept that signals its denial, *im-mors*. The Russian word either comes from Old Bulgarian or Church Slavonic, its etymology privileging life's continuation after death: *u-veko-vechen-iye*, with *vek* meaning "century" and *vechnost'* meaning "eternity"—thus *veki vechnïye*, "eternal centuries." The term is a translated borrowing from the biblical Hebrew phrase *netsakh netsakhim* (eternity of eternities).

The transfer of this concept into practice within a militantly atheistic society sometimes took bizarre forms, the most complete and eloquent example being the work of the USSR Central Executive Committee's Commission for the Immortalization of Lenin's Memory, which began right after the nominal head of the Bolshevik Party, the figurehead of the Revolution, and the founder of the Soviet State had died. The Commission not only supervised the contracting of memoirs, plays, and films, the building of monuments, the renaming of cities, factories, institutes, and schools, and the mass production of portraits, sculptures, lapel pins, and stickers—it also, importantly, completed that most sensitive and secretive of immortalization rituals, namely the mummification of Lenin's body (a special laboratory was created for this purpose). Stalin's afterlife promised to be a simulacrum of Lenin's, but the secret, anti-Stalinist speech delivered by Nikita Khrushchev at the Twentieth Congress of the CPSU in 1956 resulted in a negative reevaluation of Stalin's reputation. In the years ahead, the theory and practice of immortalization continued to be modeled on the example of Lenin, and it would be routinely applied to political and cultural figures born before the Revolution, as evidenced by the myriad of museums, academic institutes, and publications devoted to Pushkin, Tolstoy, Rimsky-Korsakov, and Tchaikovsky.

Immortalization was granted to those special Soviet citizens who occupied, at the time of their death, a leading position in the government or the CPSU. When Prokofiev died on March 5, 1953, he was considered to be a senior member of the artistic *nomenklatura*. His life, works, archive, and places of residence were entitled to a certain degree of immortalization, as was the memory of his widow, Mira (Mariya) Abramovna Mendelson-Prokofieva, who died in 1968. The fraught nature of that immortalization is the subject of this essay.

Immortalization in Practice

During the Soviet period, immortalization involved: a) fulfillment of burial procedures; b) financial and social security arrangements for the deceased's surviving family members; and c) perpetuation of the deceased's memory. The speed by which the arrangements were made, and the level at which they were initiated (government decree, executive order, Central Committee endorsement, joint Party and state decree, or decision by a republic), became important factors in defining the afterlife of Soviet luminaries. Sometimes the process of *uvekovecheniye* was short-lived, owing to a weak initial plan or absence of support; at other times, the process was reviewed, altered, and revisited long after the individual's passing.

Each of the three categories of immortalization had multiple variations. First, the news of the death had to be made public. Since Prokofiev died on the same day as Stalin, his death went unreported until March 18, thirteen days after the fact. Next came the formation of a funeral commission—although in Prokofiev's unfortunate case this step was omitted—and then the publication of a single or multiple obituaries, with or without a photograph, on the front or inside page of a national or regional newspaper. Prokofiev received just one obituary, signed by twenty-seven figures from the cultural sphere. The number and type of signature attested to the level of the person's esteem within official circles, as did the place of burial. The most important cemetery was the row of graves located directly behind Lenin's mausoleum; the second most important was inside the Kremlin wall, where urns containing the ashes of the deceased were interred. And then there was the National Pantheon, the cemetery of the Novodevichiy Monastery, which dates from the sixteenth century (the monastery itself was closed down by the Bolsheviks in 1922 and reopened in 1992). During the Soviet period, people were interred there either in coffins (more prestigious) or urns (less prestigious), with the funeral rites involving honor guards and official speeches or, as in the case of Khrushchev's burial in 1971, a low-key gathering of family members and friends. The final step involved the placement of a monument, memorial plaque, or bust at the gravesite—as specified in the original immortalization decree.

Providing support for family members was a sensitive issue in a nation that rationed food and material goods. Widows were usually allowed to remain in the apartments and summer houses (dachas) of their spouses. Instead of fully-financed funerals, family members were sometimes offered generous cash payments. The amount of the pension for the widow or widower and children (provided until they completed their higher education) reflected the deceased's position in the *nomenklatura*, his or her military rank, and/or the honorary titles he or she had received from the state (Union Republic's Merited Artist, Merited Activist in the Arts, Union Republic's People's Artist, USSR People's Artist). Over the years the number of awards varied. Three different types of Stalin Prizes were awarded between 1941 and 1952. After 1953, these were replaced by a single State Prize. Later, in 1956, the Lenin Prize was introduced—a once-in-a-lifetime award. The supreme level of artistic recognition for composers and performers was the Hero of Socialist Labor award, which came into being in 1938. Dmitriy Shostakovich was the first composer to receive it.[1]

The widows and underage children of the deceased were entitled to be treated at special government clinics, sanatoriums, and resorts either at no charge or for a minimal fee. Access to special food supplies could also be arranged (family members were allowed to visit a *stolovaya lechebnogo pitaniya*, which roughly translates as "medical diet cafeteria" but actually refers to a luxury food store in a secret location). Some family members were allowed to use a car from a government garage for up to forty hours per month in the late Soviet years. Family members also had a say in the granting of access to the deceased's archives.

Soviet immortalization rituals involved the formation, in the case of artists, of "creative heritage" commissions. These commissions, which habitually included a member of the deceased's family and a Party official, oversaw publications (select, multi-volume, or, in exceptional cases, complete works), the staging of memorial concerts, the filming of documentaries, and the mounting of exhibitions. Memorializing an artist in this fashion helped to ensure that his or her relatives would remain loyal to the regime and participate in propagandistic campaigns intended to prevent Western access to the artist's uncensored works, dubious episodes in his or her biography, and politically sensitive material. Soviet immortalization rituals were overseen, from start to finish, by an immense ideological apparatus (censorship boards, repertory agencies, the secret police, diplomatic channels, and the national media). The government and its behind-the-scenes operator—the Communist Party—determined the value of the dead, raising and lowering the price of shares in the nation's history.[2]

The apartments, houses, and dachas of the most esteemed individuals were nationalized and turned into museums. This was and continues to be the most prestigious form of immortalization in Russia. Décor, furniture, libraries, and personal effects are either preserved or restored (sometimes fabricated), and visitors to the shrines are guided, depending on their susceptibility, on nostalgic trips back in time. In exceptional cases the entire output of an artist is nationalized (the records of the patriarch of Soviet literature, Maxim Gorky, the poet Vladimir Mayakovsky, and the writer Alexey Tolstoy are preserved in this fashion), with the most sensitive items (Shostakovich's Party card, for example), classified and transported to the Presidential Archive.

In the realm of Soviet musical culture, Shostakovich received perhaps the most elaborate and expensive memorialization. His immortalization decree, which will serve as a point of reference in the upcoming discussion of Prokofiev, reads in full as follows:

On the Immortalization of the Memory of the Hero of Socialist Labor,
Composer, and USSR People's Artist D. D. Shostakovich

Taking into account the outstanding merits in the development of Soviet musical art by the Hero of Socialist Labor, Lenin and State Prize laureate, composer, and USSR People's Artist D. D. Shostakovich, the USSR Council of Ministers resolves:

1. To build a tombstone at the graveside of D. D. Shostakovich at Novodevichiy Cemetery with the expense, up to 6,000 rubles, charged to the USSR Union of Composers.
2. To establish at both the Moscow State "Tchaikovsky" Conservatory and Leningrad State "Rimsky-Korsakov" Conservatory a scholarship named for D. D. Shostakovich.
3. To award the Leningrad State Philharmonic the name D. D. Shostakovich.
4. To entrust the Ministry of the Maritime Fleet to award the name D. D. Shostakovich to one of its passenger ships.
5. To entrust the USSR Ministry of Communication to issue a postage stamp for the 70th birthday of D. D. Shostakovich.
6. For the USSR Ministry of Culture jointly with the USSR Union of Composers to establish a commission dedicated to D. D. Shostakovich's creative heritage.
7. For the State Committee on Publisher Affairs, the Printing Industry, and the Book Trade to address the matter of the publication of the collected works of D. D. Shostakovich.
8. To entrust the Commission on the establishment of personal pensions under the USSR Council of Ministers to address the question of the pension procurement for Irina Antonovna Shostakovich—D. D. Shostakovich's widow.
9. To entrust Mosgorispolkom:[3]
    a) To establish a memorial plaque on Building 8/10 (Block 2) Nezhdanov Street in the city of Moscow, where D. D. Shostakovich lived;
    b) To retain for D. D. Shostakovich's widow I. A. Shostakovich the apartment occupied by her in Building 8/10 Nezhdanov Street in the city of Moscow.
10. To preserve I. A. Shostakovich's right to access the First Polyclinic and the Hospital of the Fourth Main Directorate of the USSR Ministry of Health.
11. For expenses incurred during D. D. Shostakovich's funeral to be charged to the State account.

Chairman of the USSR Council of Ministers
(A. Kosygin)
Acting Manager of the Council of Ministers
(M. Smirtyukov)[4]

Besides Shostakovich's numerous awards, his civic duties must be taken into account when evaluating his posthumous treatment. He was a deputy of the RSFSR Supreme Soviet from 1947 to 1962 and a deputy of the USSR Supreme Soviet from 1962 to 1975. He joined the Communist Party in 1960 and served as a delegate or guest to numerous Party congresses. Shostakovich served as secretary of the USSR Union of Composers Board as well as first (general) secretary of the RSFSR Union of Composers Board and chairman of the Austria-USSR Friendship Society. These and other activities elevated him to the status of an exceedingly high-ranking public figure (*obshchestvenniy deyatel'*) and explains why the Politburo, rather than a lesser Party or government entity, placed its stamp on his immortalization decree in 1975.

Prokofiev did not partake in civic duties. The closest he came to serving as a politician in the sphere of the arts came on October 13, 1938, when Mikhaíl Khrapchenko, the acting chairman of the All-Union Committee on Arts Affairs, listed Prokofiev as a candidate member of the USSR Union of Composers Organizing Committee. At the time of his death he did not hold an official or elected position. For this reason, Prokofiev's immortalization ritual, which began portentously in the late hours of March 5, 1953, paled in comparison to that of Shostakovich.

March–June 1953

Prokofiev died on the same day as Stalin. The composer's death was sudden, whereas, according to official reports, Stalin lay in a coma for three days before expiring. The timing of Prokofiev's death could not have been more inconvenient, both in terms of arranging his funeral and planning his immortalization.

Stalin's death precipitated an enormous reshuffling of personnel within the Soviet bureaucracy. The entire Communist Party and state leadership was revamped. A new premier was designated and a nominal president installed. The Ministries of Defense, Internal Affairs (State Security), Foreign Affairs, Commerce, and Industry received new leaders, as did the trade unions. The Party Presidium (otherwise known as the Politburo) was dissolved and the number of members reduced from twenty-five to ten (overnight, fifteen Party bosses lost their privileged posts). The Central Committee Secretariat, responsible for the day-to-day work of the Party, also shed personnel.

Following this bloodless bureaucratic revolution—one that began to occur while Stalin was, technically speaking, still alive—shock waves spread to other branches of government.[5] On March 15, many of the smaller ministries were ordered combined, dissolved, or revamped. In such dire circumstances, who would dare to approach the Kremlin (the head-quarters of the Presidium and the government) or the adjacent Central Committee offices with the news of Prokofiev's death? What bureaucrat would dare to file a formal request for the composer's immortalization when the commander in chief and generalissimo had himself died? As it turned out, next to no one.

The Presidium (Politburo) entrusted Pyotr Pospelov, the newly appointed Secretary of the Central Committee, with the task of overseeing media and culture.[6] It fell to him to review the immortalization papers filed on Prokofiev's behalf. The first of these was a joint memorandum signed—on March 11, 1953—by Nikolay Bespalov, the chairman of the All-Union Committee on Arts Affairs, and Tikhon Khrennikov, the general secretary of the USSR Union of Composers.

Bespalov was a government rather than a Party bureaucrat, and thus much more ideologically tolerant than his predecessors at the helm of the Committee on Arts Affairs.[7] During his tenure as chairman there were no major crackdowns or repressions; he avoided conflict, instead devoting his energies to the difficult, arguably impossible challenge of creating a modern classic in the realm of Soviet opera. When Prokofiev's health began to deteriorate in 1952, Bespalov backed Khrennikov's proposal to grant the ailing composer a personal pension. In his appeal for approval of the proposal to Georgiy Malenkov (1902–88), a senior Party leader and Politburo member, Bespalov described Prokofiev as the nation's "most prominent composer" and a recipient of the Order of Lenin (which was actually not the case). Bespalov petitioned Malenkov to grant Prokofiev urgent financial assistance: a monthly pension of 3,000 rubles and a payment, for immediate expenses, of 25,000 rubles from Muzfond, the financial division of the Union of Composers.[8]

One month later, the chief musical expert on the Central Committee, Boris Yarustovsky, acknowledged that despite Prokofiev's previous ideological mistakes, he was a composer of international significance. He strongly disagreed, however, that Prokofiev was in dire need of financial support. As a consequence, the composer's monthly pension was reduced from 3,000 to 2,000 rubles.[9]

For Bespalov and Khrennikov, Prokofiev's poorly timed death ensured further conflict with Yarustovsky. Their March 11 letter on Prokofiev's behalf encountered more than the usual level of bureaucratic resistance. It reads in full as follows:

To CC CPSU Secretary Comrade P. N. Pospelov:

The Committee on Arts Affairs under the USSR Council of Ministers and the USSR Union of Composers advises that on March 5 of this year the outstanding Soviet Composer, RSFSR People's Artist, and Stalin Prize winner Sergey Sergeyevich Prokofiev passed away.

Taking into consideration S. S. Prokofiev's large contributions to Soviet musical art, the Committee on Arts Affairs under the USSR Council of Ministers and the USSR Union of Composers consider it prudent to approach the USSR Council of Ministers with the following proposals for the immortalization of S. S. Prokofiev's memory.

1. To arrange S. S. Prokofiev's funeral at the expense of the USSR Musical Foundation.
2. To put a memorial plaque on Building 6, Arts Theater Passage, where S. S. Prokofiev lived.
3. To erect a monument at S. S. Prokofiev's Novodevichiy Cemetery gravesite at the expense of the USSR Musical Foundation.
4. To establish a life pension for Mariya Abramovna Prokofiev, S. S. Prokofiev's wife, in the amount of 700 rubles a month.
5. To publish a collection of select works by S. S. Prokofiev.

The USSR Council of Ministers draft proposal has been attached.

The Committee on Arts Affairs and the USSR Union of Composers requests, moreover, permission to publish an article in S. S. Prokofiev's memory in *Pravda* or *Izvestiya* and to print an obituary with S. S. Prokofiev's portrait and the article "An Outstanding Soviet Composer" in the newspaper *Sovetskoye iskusstvo*.

Chairman of the Committee on Arts Affairs under the
USSR Council of Ministers
(N. Bespalov)
General Secretary of the USSR Union of Soviet Composers
(T. Khrennikov)[10]

The most provocative part of this letter concerns Bespalov and Khrennikov's request for an article about Prokofiev to be published either in *Pravda*, the Communist Party newspaper, or in *Izvestiya*, the government's official daily. To publish the obituary in one of these venues would signal official endorsement of Prokofiev's canonization. Since the composer was not a Communist Party member (unlike Khachaturyan, Khrennikov, and—later—Shostakovich), *Pravda* was ruled out as a possibility. By requesting the publication, Bespalov and Khrennikov had ventured into political territory outside of their control.

For the immortalization process to begin, the Central Committee needed to approve it. Usually the paperwork on such matters was completed and processed quickly. If, however, Bespalov and Khrennikov signed their letter to the Central Committee on March 11, having presumably worked on it since the night of March 5, why did it take until March 14 for it to reach Malenkov's office? It would seem that factions within the Central Committee apparatus wanted to postpone the authorization, to reduce the value, as it were, of Prokofiev's legacy. Yarustovsky ultimately bears the blame for the delay, though, to be sure, other factors were at work.

On March 14, 1953, the Central Committee removed Stalin's presumed successor Malenkov from the post of Central Committee secretary. Pospelov feared authorizing the decision on Prokofiev's immortalization alone and, taking into account the quarreling within the upper strata of the government, made a typical Soviet bureaucratic decision: he did nothing. Prokofiev had already been buried, but the nation had still not been officially notified of his death.

The decision to release the news was postponed beyond March 14 owing to the convening, on March 15, of the historic Fourth Session of the Supreme Soviet (the parliament), which legalized a complete overhaul of the government. The Stalinist cultural apparatus was dissolved by a simple show of hands at the Grand Kremlin Palace (Bol'shoy Kremlyovskiy Dvorets). The Ministry of Cinematography vanished, as did the Committee on Architecture, Committee on Higher Education, and Committee on Arts Affairs. These organizations and their staffs were consolidated, amalgamated into a mega-administration: the USSR Ministry of Culture.

Once Yarustovsky and his superior Vladimir Kruzhkov (1905–91) approved—seemingly with reluctance—Bespalov and Khrennikov's letter on March 14, it was forwarded to Malenkov for his signature. The archive ledger shows that the document was received by Malenkov's Central Committee office on March 14 at 3:05 p.m., and by the Government Chancellery (Upravleniye delami) at 11 p.m., by which time Malenkov had already been deposed as Central Committee secretary. Bespalov and Khrennikov's letter suddenly became moot. It was stamped null and void on March 18 at 6:05 a.m.

Despite being removed from the Central Committee, Malenkov remained a government employee. And not just any employee—the Fourth Session of the Supreme Soviet ratified his selection for the post of Soviet premier. Bespalov lost his position with the Committee on Arts Affairs, but he too remained a trusted servant of the people. He became one of the deputies to the new Minister of Culture, a hard-line military official named Panteleimon Ponomarenko (1902–84). It remains unclear if Ponomarenko had ever heard of Prokofiev, much less of his music, before the composer's death.[11] But Ponomarenko nonetheless played a significant role in Prokofiev's belated immortalization.

Bespalov and Khrennikov's original March 11 letter bore a grand title: "On the Immortalization of the Memory of the Great Activist of Soviet Musical Art, the RSFSR People's Artist and Stalin Prize Recipient Composer S. S. Prokofiev." With this description, Bespalov and Khrennikov had over-reached, since, technically speaking, only the Politburo had the authority to label an artist "great," "eminent," "famous," or merely "known." The revised version of the draft, signed on March 14 by Kruzhkov and Yarustovsky and submitted to Malenkov, had a much less inflated title: "On the Immortalization of the Memory of the RSFSR People's Artist, the Composer Prokofiev."[12] No mention was made of his greatness, his activism, or his Stalin Prizes. Prokofiev had been demoted, transformed by official-dom into just another "People's Artist."

Another draft of the resolution (*postanovleniye*) on the immortalization of Prokofiev's memory was presented to Malenkov on April 9, 1953, this time by the Minister of Culture. Ponomarenko supported an even more drastic reduction in Prokofiev's stature, one that retained just two of the five provisions in Bespalov and Khrennikov's March 11 letter: the monthly pension for Prokofiev's widow Mira (reduced from 700 to 500 rubles), and coverage of the costs of the funeral, which had already taken place. The contrast between this document and the Politburo document on the immor-talization of Shostakovich is striking.

But even Ponomarenko's stripped-down resolution languished, with no action taken on it for almost two months. The dithering represented a defeat for Prokofiev's supporters at the Union of Composers and a victory for those members of the Central Committee, specifically Yarustovsky, Pavel Apostolov,[13] and Zaven Vartanian,[14] who had participated in Prokofiev's denunciation as a formalist, anti-populist composer from 1948 to early 1949. Long after his death, there were still no graveside monuments, no memo-rial plaques, and no plans to publish either a complete or partial edition of his works.

When Malenkov finally signed the document on June 4, 1953, it had been downgraded from a resolution to an executive order (*rasporyazheniye*).[15] It differed from the April 9 document insofar as it restored the 700 ruble pension to Prokofiev's widow, Mira. She was treated, in other words, like the widow of a USSR—rather than a lesser RSFSR—People's Artist. The pension was granted, and the funeral bills finally settled by Muzfond. Though positive, this turn of events did not, however, mark the end of the problems with Prokofiev's immortalization.

Enemies Within the Central Committee Apparatus

Understanding these problems requires briefly exploring the internal workings of the Soviet regime and its core institution, the Communist Party, whose principal authority in the realm of music between August 1946 and September 1959 was Boris Yarustovsky. No sooner had he appeared on the Central Committee payroll than he began to change the course of Soviet music—its theory, practice, and international profile. An introduction to the curriculum vitae of this individual, the Tsar of Soviet Music, follows.

Born in Moscow in 1911, Yarustovsky worked as an apprentice in a factory that manufactured weights, then for a year and a half in Moscow Communal Services, and then as a laborer in a concrete and asphalt plant. This was a typical early career for someone who wanted to burnish his or her proletarian credentials for the purposes of receiving higher education. In September 1931, Yarustovsky entered the Moscow Musical College and, a year later, the prestigious Moscow Conservatory. He graduated with a diploma in historical musicology in June 1937, thereafter entering the Conservatory's graduate program. He studied for four months before taking a short-term leave of absence.

The year 1937 marked the height of the Stalinist repressions. The All-Union Committee on Arts Affairs was undergoing a top-to-bottom restructuring precipitated by the purging of its members and a string of financial audits. Yarustovsky, regarded as a competent music specialist and upstanding member of the Communist Youth League, joined the Committee as a senior inspector and manager of its concert division. In May 1939, he returned to graduate school, receiving a doctorate in musicology in June 1941.

At the beginning of the Soviet chapter of the Second World War, Yarustovsky continued to work as an inspector for the Committee, supervising musical theaters and overseeing—as a de facto censor—the activities of the State Music Publisher: Muzgiz. In September 1941, he voluntarily joined the ranks of the Red Army, initially as the conductor of one of its orchestras, later as an overseer of its musical affairs. His service, which extended until September 1946, was of crucial importance to his career, allowing him to transfer to the Central Committee as a full-time employee in its Propaganda and Agitation Department. He was neither the first nor the last professional musicologist to work for the Committee, but he was doubtless the shrewdest.[16] His only true rival in terms of musical-political acumen was Khrennikov, the longtime general secretary of the Union of Composers.

Yarustovsky's time on the Central Committee had its ups and downs. He was disciplined in January 1951, for example, for using his political influence to have his writings published, in lucrative editions, by Muzgiz. He rose spectacularly through the cultural and military ranks (the two being increasingly intertwined in the postwar period), but he found himself at odds with his apparatchik colleagues, notably Bespalov. Personal artistic frustration, prejudices (some of these instilled in him by his Conservatory instructors), and a profound inferiority complex caused him to regard the composers under his watch as undeservedly well treated.[17] Yarustovsky's opposition to the approval of Prokofiev's 3,000 ruble pension in 1952 is indicative of his antagonism toward elite Soviet artists.

However much it stemmed from Yarustovsky's personal problems, his antagonism also reflected Stalin's governing style, specifically the ruler's penchant for bureaucratic dividing and conquering. Fomenting distrust between factions inside and outside the government allowed him to increase and improve his control over them.

Cultural officials, like secret police officers, tended to work long hours in unhappy conditions. They were provided with the basics—food and clothing—but their standard of living could hardly compare to that enjoyed by the composers, writers, actors, and visual artists under their watch. Since they presumably had access to state secrets, they could neither travel nor fraternize with diplomats nor engage with the outside world. They were likewise barred from engaging in creative activities and working in areas outside their official duties. They could be summoned to their posts at any time, including the middle of the night (Stalin's sleeping habits were such that his aides tended to work from dusk to dawn). Privileged artists routinely demanded better living conditions in the city and the country, higher fees for their performances and publications, new cars and, in the case of composers, new pianos (preferably looted from East Germany rather than made in Russia); their Central Committee minders, on the other hand, were consigned to sitting and watching, noting and reporting.

To call these people inmates in their own political prisons would not be an exaggeration. The three inspectors of the film sector of the Central Committee Department of Fiction Literature and the Arts shared a single desk in a single dark and cold room. The three inspectors of the music sector were likewise crammed together. And their immediate supervisor, Yarustovsky, occupied a crowded office of just four square meters. It is therefore no surprise that he cast a jaundiced eye on Bespalov's petition to provide Prokofiev, a Stalin Prize recipient living in a large dacha in an elite area outside of Moscow, with a generous monthly pension—no matter how bad the composer's state of health.

Yarustovsky's indignation flared up again when presented with the resolution on Prokofiev's immortalization. But by this time he had been moved to a larger office, which perhaps slightly improved his mood. With his blessing, Prokofiev's obituary was finally published in *Sovetskoye iskusstvo* on March 18, 1953. It was titled, as originally proposed, "An Outstanding Soviet Composer" and signed by twenty-seven figures from the artistic—primarily musical—sphere. Bespalov headed the list, followed by Khrennikov, Reinhold Glier, Yuriy Shaporin, Shostakovich, Dmitriy Kabalevsky, Aram Khachaturyan, and others.[18] The absence of the signature of the Minister of Culture and those of musical officials on the Central Committee is striking. The symbolic date of Prokofiev's death went unmentioned. The March 18 issue of the newspaper included a second article about Prokofiev bearing the title "A Grand Creative Life."[19] Its cautious prose reflects the uncertainties precipitated by the March 15 reorganization of the government.

Both articles bear witness to the initial struggle to reinterpret Prokofiev's life and works, to present his career in a post-Stalinist light. On March 19, 1953, the April issue of the academic journal *Sovetskaya muzïka* went into print (it bore the subheading "An Agency of the USSR Union of Composers and the USSR Ministry of Culture"). The issue included a reprint of "An Outstanding Soviet Composer," but the title was changed to "In Memory of S. S. Prokofiev." It was unsigned.

The opening sentences of the original version read: "S. S. Prokofiev, an outstanding Soviet Composer, laureate of Stalin Prizes, and RSFSR People's Artist has passed away. S. S. Prokofiev's death is a great loss for Soviet music, throughout our nation. A brilliant, profound, and unique artist has left this world." The opening sentences that went into print the next day almost seem to refer to a different person: "On March 5, 1953, the gifted composer, laureate of Stalin Prizes, and RSFSR People's Artist S. S. Prokofiev passed away. A great and unique Russian artist, enormous talent, and outstanding master departed life. S. S. Prokofiev's death is a difficult loss for Soviet music, for our culture."[20] The hand of the censor is manifest in the softening of the language used to describe the composer between the two versions of the obituary. Yarustovsky's resistance to Prokofiev's immortalization had evidently been bolstered by the appointment of Ponomarenko to the Ministry of Culture.

There followed the belated staging of two of Prokofiev's final works. His ballet *The Tale of the Stone Flower* (*Skaz o kamennom tsvetke*, 1949) received a premiere at the Bolshoy Theater in Moscow in 1954; the following year, a truncated version of his opera *War and Peace* was performed at the Malïy Theater in Leningrad. Selected scores began to be published in 1955 under Kabalevsky's general editorship. Only the operas and ballets of Prokofiev's Soviet years were allowed into print at first, since the first part of his career remained under tacit prohibition. These and other events related to Prokofiev's immortalization occurred without obvious Party or government sponsorship. They were performed quietly by the Musical Theater Directorate at the Ministry of Culture and the Union of Composers.

A Memorial Plaque (1956)

The pace of Prokofiev's immortalization hastened in 1956—the year of Khrushchev's secret speech at the Twentieth Party Congress, which was also the year of civil strife in Poland, an uprising in Budapest, and the first significant signs of unrest in the Soviet cultural sphere.

Prokofiev's reputation had its ups and downs (both before and after his death), but in the year of the Twentieth Party Congress his name, works, and legacy became positive national symbols. He was both Russian and Soviet, national and international, accepted by the Stalinist regime but not compromised by it. From the government's perspective, Prokofiev could also serve to reconcile the various opposing forces in a society experiencing a profound psychological and sociopolitical crisis—all brought about by Khrushchev's denunciation of the Stalinist cult of personality. Anna Akhmatova likened the impact of that denunciation to the breaking of a spell. The "narcosis," she declared, "is lifting."[21]

In the summer of 1956, the Union of Composers, then experiencing its own form of de-Stalinization, brought the unfinished question of Prokofiev's immortalization to the attention of the Party leadership. His works were being published—a positive trend—but a crucial gesture toward his legacy had yet to be made: the mounting of a memorial plaque (*memorial'naya doska*) on Building 6, Arts Theater Passage, where, in the apartment of his in-laws, Prokofiev had lived and died. The absence of this plaque was a source of speculation for symbol-conscious Soviet citizens. Was Prokofiev one hundred percent Soviet? Would additional steps be taken toward his canonization?

The petition on Prokofiev's behalf to the government was made by the acting general secretary of the Union of Composers, Kirill Molchanov (1922–82), a dedicated opera composer who would serve in the 1970s as the director of the Bolshoy Theater.[22] On the surface, Molchanov sought clarification of the status of Prokofiev's immortalization, some hint from someone and somewhere as to his place in Russian and Soviet history. But his petition had another purpose. In 1956, the Bolshoy Theater was preparing for its first ever tour to London. Such a tour had been planned once before, in 1946, but it was scuttled both by internal politics (Andrey Zhdanov's crackdown on Soviet musical activity) and external conflict (the chill winds of the burgeoning Cold War). The central concern in 1956 was not the viability of the tour but the repertoire to be performed. Should the Bolshoy Theater mount a ballet about the French Revolution, namely Boris Asafyev's *The Flame of Paris* (*Plamya Parizha*, 1932)? What about Glier's *The Red Poppy* (*Krasniy mak*, 1927), which concerns imperialist oppression and the Chinese Revolution? How would high-brow, aristocratic Covent Garden audiences react to these works? Might not classically themed Russian and Soviet ballets be more appropriate? The answer to this last question was a resounding yes. Prokofiev's *Romeo and Juliet* was the first in line to be programmed by the Bolshoy Theater, followed by Tchaikovsky's *Swan Lake*.

A prompt reply from the upper strata of the government about Prokofiev's plaque would affirm the appropriateness of *Romeo and Juliet* for the tour. When it came, however, the reply was ambiguous. The decision-makers at the Union of Composers and Ministry of Culture were informed that permission from the government was not required for the plaque to be mounted. Yet, just two weeks before, the government had sanctioned the fixing of a plaque to the building in which Glier had lived. The turn-around suggested that the post-Stalinist liberalization of the bureaucracy had entered the realm of culture, with the task of assessing and honoring a particular composer's heritage now delegated to lower-level (city) bureau-crats. Molchanov and his colleagues were essentially given a free hand to attend to Prokofiev's immortalization.

On July 2, 1956, *Pravda* published the Central Committee Resolution "On Overcoming the Cult of Personality and Its Consequences." The front-page official document represented a step back from the circulated, for-your-eyes-only version of a report, "On the Cult of Personality and Its Consequences," presented by Khrushchev at the Twentieth Party Congress. But it served to put the recommendations of that report into practice. Prokofiev's immortalization was given new momentum by the de-Stalinization of Soviet society, but it also experienced new complications, particularly when matters turned to the settling of his estate.

In 1948, Prokofiev's first wife Lina was arrested and sentenced to twenty years in the gulag. In the summer of 1956 her sentence was commuted, allowing her to return to Moscow, where she bravely fought for a full restora-tion of her honor and civic rights. It was one thing, she discovered, to be released from the camps, but quite another to be exonerated, cleared of all charges, even if the charges in question were fabricated. Without such clearance, doubts would continue to accrue not only about her patriotism but also that of her husband, who had spent much of his career outside of Russia. Upon relocating from Paris to Moscow in 1936, Prokofiev, Lina, and their two sons had resided in a luxurious (by Soviet standards) four-room apartment. From a political standpoint, that which reflected badly on her also reflected badly on him.

The issue was complicated by the fact that Prokofiev's second wife Mira was not only alive and active, she also enjoyed, by official fiat, a monthly personal pension, royalties, and widespread recognition as the composer's heiress. In view of this, it remains an enigma why the Union of Composers—particularly its general secretary, Khrennikov—offered support to Lina following her release from the gulag. The future course of Prokofiev's immortalization suggests that cultural officials had deemed it prudent to honor his entire output: the works composed before 1918, during the "difficult" years of his estrangement from his homeland, and immediately after his repatriation. The person best able to provide substance and significance to this project was his first wife. Indeed, once Lina's reintegration into the cultural establishment was completed, Prokofiev would reach the zenith of official approbation: he would posthumously receive a Lenin Prize.

On November 3, 1956, Vyacheslav Molotov (1890–1986), a Politburo member and the First Vice-Chairman of the USSR Council of Ministers, signed a terse, single-line executive order granting Lina a personal pension of 700 rubles a month for life. The document said nothing about her tumultuous life or her relationship to Prokofiev; it merely offered her official recognition. The impetus for this recognition came from Khrennikov who, on October 17, 1956, wrote a crucially important memorandum to the Council of Ministers on Lina's behalf:

While living abroad in 1923, the RSFSR People's Artist and composer S. S. Prokofiev entered into marriage in Germany (the Bavarian Alps, location Ettal) with Citizeness Lina Ivanovna Prokofieva. This marriage produced two sons (born in 1925 and 1927).

Upon his return to the USSR in 1935 S. S. Prokofiev resided in Moscow with the above-mentioned family. L. I. Prokofieva was, moreover, a dependent of her husband.

In 1948 L. I. Prokofieva was arrested and sentenced by [Ministry of State Security] Special Assembly to 20 years in the correctional labor camps with her possessions confiscated. In June 1956 by Resolution of the Military Board of the USSR Supreme Court L. I. Prokofieva was rehabilitated and her case terminated owing to the absence of a crime in her actions. S. S. Prokofiev died in 1953.

By Resolution No. 7676-R of the USSR Council of Ministers from June 4, 1953, a lifetime personal pension of 700 rubles a month was designated for S. S. Prokofiev's second wife, M. A. Mendelson.

Taking into account the outstanding Soviet composer S. S. Prokofiev's exceptional service to Soviet art, likewise L. I. Prokofieva's age (she was born in 1897) and the state of her health, strained by a prolonged period under guard, the Secretariat of the USSR Union of Composers requests that Lina Ivanovna Prokofieva be designated a lifetime personal pension in the amount of 700 rubles a month.[23]

The period between October 17 (the date of Khrennikov's memorandum) and November 3 (Molotov's executive order) marked another crucial chapter in Soviet history: revolution broke out in the People's Republic of Hungary. The nationalist government of Imre Nagy was installed and indicated an intention to withdraw from the Warsaw Pact. The Budapest headquarters of the Hungarian Workers' Party was ransacked; secret police agents were chased down and murdered on the street.

During this period of international crisis, when Soviet officials were presumably preoccupied, Prokofiev's first wife earned her civil rights back. Lina was granted a pension in a memorandum that ignored, rather than acknowledged, her mistreatment. The head of the Culture and Arts Department of the Chancellery, V. Tepferov, approved Khrennikov's petition without a single mention of Lina's gulag prisoner status, her rehabilitation, or her health problems.

A Second Memorial Plaque and a Posthumous Lenin Prize (1957)

Lina's rehabilitation marked an unusual change in immortalization protocol. And it was followed by another one: Prokofiev's nomination for a Lenin Prize, three and a half years after his death.

Before the nomination could be completed by the Union of Composers, another matter needed to be settled: the affixing of a memorial plaque on Prokofiev's first residence in Moscow. By doing so, the government would resolve an overarching concern about the composer's career: he had spent several years abroad, wandering between capitalist nations that, in some instances, did not have a Soviet embassy or consulate. In order to confirm the official reading of his period abroad as a failure, the government needed to trumpet the time and place of his spectacular return to Russia.

The effort was once again spearheaded by Khrennikov who, in 1956, made Prokofiev's immortalization something of a personal crusade. The unwritten rules concerning the procedure specified that elite Soviet artists, like other outstanding participants in the nation's sociopolitical development, were entitled to a single memorial plaque. Usually the plaque was unveiled at the deceased's final place of residence. Depending on the artist's stature, the plaque might or might not involve bas-relief and be carved out of marble (rather than granite).

The immortalization decree specified where it was to be located. Politburo members who died in office, Red Army marshals, and scientists whose existence and activities had been declassified were entitled to plaques in multiple locations (at the schools, factories, institutes, military academies, and Red Army headquarters where they trained and worked). By the mid-1950s every place known to be associated with Lenin, even those he had visited for less than an hour, had been immortalized with a uniformly oversized plaque. The occupants of the buildings in question benefited from the designation, because it guaranteed municipal, provincial, and federal funding to preserve and maintain the building, not to mention keeping the surrounding area tidy.

Prokofiev, as noted, was to receive a plaque on the outside of the building where he lived in Moscow between sojourns at his dacha in Nikolina Gora—that is, Building 6, Arts Theater Passage. Usually the plaque marked the entranceway to the deceased's apartment. If the building had more than one entranceway, the plaque was hung over the one closest to the apartment.

For the first five years after his relocation to Moscow from Paris, Prokofiev, Lina, and their two sons had lived in a different apartment, on Zemlyanoy Val (later Chkalov) Street, part of the semicircular highway (Sadovoye kol'tso) surrounding Moscow's historical center. Prokofiev left his family in 1941, but Lina and the children continued to live in the apartment until her arrest in February 20, 1948 (the children, Svyatoslav and Oleg, vacated the premises shortly thereafter). Until the advent of semiprivate cooperative apartments in the Khrushchev era, the vast majority of residences in the Soviet Union belonged to the government, which, through its various branches (military, police, academies, institutes, and ministries) allocated desirable, centrally located apartments to Soviet citizens on a priority basis. When an apartment dweller fell out of favor or died, his or her family members were usually evicted. They were either relocated to another, smaller dwelling or, in exceptional circumstances, allowed to remain in the apartment until further notice.

Prokofiev's Zemlyanoy Val apartment belonged to the Committee on Arts Affairs. It was a historically significant dwelling, but it was tainted by Prokofiev's separation from his family and, especially, Lina's arrest. So, too, were the works that had been composed there. Lina's rehabilitation in 1956 cleansed the space of unpleasant memories and also removed the taint from the works composed before and shortly after Prokofiev's relocation to Moscow. The logic was simple: by exonerating Lina the government had sanctioned Prokofiev's life with her between 1923 and 1941. His early works could be positively reevaluated on a case-by-case basis. (This process peaked in the late 1960s and early 1970s, at which time some—not all— of Prokofiev's pre-Soviet operas and ballets received Soviet premieres.)

The essential first step toward this bright future came, as noted, in 1956, when Khrennikov facilitated Lina's unprecedentedly rapid rehabilitation. The next step came on January 29, 1957, when, during the tempestuous deliberations of the Lenin Prize Committee and the preparations for the Second Congress of the USSR Union of Composers, Khrennikov sent the following memorandum to the Council of Ministers:

> By decision of the Executive Committee of the Moscow City Council of People's Deputies (No. 40/45 of August 10, 1956) a memorial plaque is being installed at Building No. 6, Arts Theater Passage, where from 1944 to 1953 the outstanding Russian composer S. S. Prokofiev lived and died.
>
> Taking into consideration the role of S. S. Prokofiev's music in the development of Soviet musical creation and its world significance, the Secretariat of the USSR Union of Composers asks the USSR Council of Ministers to permit the installation of a second memorial plaque on Building No. 14/16, Chkalov Street, where the composer lived and worked from 1936 until 1941.
>
> Among the many works created by S. S. Prokofiev during these years and receiving distribution both in the Soviet Union and beyond the borders of our Motherland are the ballets *Romeo and Juliet* and *Cinderella*, the cantata *Alexander Nevsky*, the symphonic fairy tale *Peter and the Wolf*, the opera *The Duenna*, among other works.[24]

Permission came swiftly, a reflection of the spirit of the times, in which rules could be broken (only one plaque per artist), and lives and works could be reinterpreted. Both of Prokofiev's widows were recognized, and both periods of his post-Revolution career venerated.

The two plaques were unveiled on the same day: February 11, 1958. *Pravda* noted the solemn ceremony of "composers, writers, artists, and representatives of social organizations" that took place at the Zemlyanoy Val (Chkalov) Street apartment. The newspaper did not list the dates Prokofiev lived there. The Arts Theater Passage ceremony went altogether unreported (mention of two ceremonies for a single artist would have been too much even during Khrushchev's Thaw). *Pravda* did, however, report that Prokofiev lived at that location from 1947 to 1953.[25]

The competitive and democratic spirit of Khrushchev's Thaw was further reflected in the deliberations of the Lenin Prize Committee. In the circulated version of his secret speech Khrushchev opened a new chapter in the history of Soviet government awards with these words: "We cannot help but remember the August 14, 1925, Soviet government decision 'On the establishment of V. I. Lenin Prizes for scientific works.' This decision was promulgated in the press but until now there have not been any Lenin Prizes. This also needs to be rectified."[26] Khrushchev gave the speech at the Twentieth Party Congress in February 1956, but in November 1955 the Central Committee had already adopted a secret decision on establishing Lenin Prizes that tacitly invalidated the previous highest national prize—the First Class Stalin Prize. On November 19, 1955, it was reported to the Central Committee that over a twelve-year period the Stalin Prize had been awarded to a staggering total of 11,812 individuals. The large number of awards given every year weakened the pool of candidates and diminished the prestige associated with the prize; more than once it had been awarded in error. The memorandum also mentioned that thirty-three people had been awarded the prize four times, twenty-three had received it five times, and seven people had been awarded it six times. The last group included Prokofiev.

The new Lenin Prize would address these concerns. A candidate could receive the honor just once, and the number of arts awards was drastically reduced (by twentyfold) to a single prize in each of five categories: cinema (and/or theater), journalism, literature (fiction and/or poetry), music (composition and/or performance), and the visual arts (painting and/or sculpture). Gone, too, was the distinction between First, Second, and Third Class awards. The single prize that remained—with the new name enforcing the distinction between the Stalin and Khrushchev eras—restored prestige to the highest honor awarded by the State.

Stalin had had final say in decisions regarding the award that bore his name and effigy. He had also reserved the right to add anyone he wished to the list of laureates, including people never heard of by the selection committee. The choice of Lenin Prize winners, in contrast, was subject to public scrutiny, with the selection committee's activities reported widely in the media and amenable to public opinion. Radio and television networks were instructed to broadcast programs aimed at popularizing the candidates' works, and showings were organized in cinemas and theaters. Creative unions, cultural institutions, social organizations, and Soviet workers in general could file proposals or petitions to the selection committee.[27] Perhaps the most important development concerned the criteria for nominations. Stalin had not allowed awards to be granted posthumously and excluded old or ailing individuals as candidates; the active, tangible present was more important to him than the past. The Lenin Prize was open to all worthy nominees, living or not, allowing for the inclusion of Prokofiev as a candidate.

Both Khrennikov and Shostakovich were appointed to the selection committee as full members. This development reduced the chances of Shostakovich being chosen to receive the Lenin Prize, but by no means excluded him. (At least one other committee member, the ballerina Galina Ulanova, was a top candidate for the award as well.) With both Prokofiev and Shostakovich eligible for the award, the competition would be close and ideologically significant.

There were three rounds to the annual, post-Stalinist competition: first, the long list of candidates with their nominated works was published, along with the names of the organizations or individuals that had advanced their candidacies. Then the short list was selected. Last was the round of discussions before voting. With the appointment of the most prestigious (and therefore relatively independent) Soviet artists, intellectuals, and scientists to the selection committee, it immediately became a site of resistance to the government. Such was the atmosphere of de-Stalinization that followed the Twentieth Party Congress. The openness of the competition, quasi-democratic decision-making process, and the use of secret ballots (at least during the first five years of the competition) made the deliberations provocative and progressive.

The short list for the category of "Music, Concert, and Performing Artists" included four names: the violinist David Oistrakh for "outstanding achievements in concert and performing activity" (his candidacy was presented by the RSFSR Ministry of Culture and Moscow State Philharmonic); Shaporin for his 1953 opera *Dekabristï* (The Decembrists), advanced by the USSR Union of Composers; Shostakovich for his 1953 Tenth Symphony (Shostakovich was backed by a powerful triumvirate: two Ministries of Culture—the USSR and RSFSR—and the USSR Union of Composers); and Prokofiev (without the designation "posthumous") for his 1952 Seventh Symphony (presented by the USSR Union of Composers).

It was clear that the choice between Prokofiev and Shostakovich would be difficult. (Shaporin's *Decembrists*, which had taken him twenty-eight years to complete and finally have staged, was not a serious competitor.) Shostakovich had the implicit backing of Khrushchev and the Central Committee, but the Soviet musical community, seeking a reevaluation of the Stalinist heritage, threw its staggering support behind Prokofiev's nomination. The media conveyed this support to the public. The public, in turn, was wary of Shostakovich because of his propagandist film scores *The Fall of Berlin* (*Padeniye Berlina*), 1949, and *Nezabïvayemïy 1919-god* (The unforgettable year 1919), 1951, not to mention the two-part Great Terror blockbuster *Velikiy grazhdanin* (The great citizen), 1937–39.

The date for the competition's end, traditionally late March or early April, was a significant one. After a nine-year gap and two-year delay, the Second Congress of Soviet Composers was to be held in Moscow at the beginning of April. On the eve of the Congress, pianist Svyatoslav Richter, in a characteristically bold statement, complained that "many of the most beautiful pages of our music—Russian and especially Soviet—continue to be unknown to the listener." He singled out the damage done to *War and Peace* when, instead of being performed in its two-evening version, "Prokofiev's score was cut, compressed, and simply mutilated." Richter also called for "the true birth of Prokofiev's *Semyon Kotko* and *The Tale of the Stone Flower*."[28]

Richter was seconded by the composer Georgiy Sviridov, who asked: "Who would contest that Prokofiev's *Romeo and Juliet* is a classic achievement of Russian and Soviet ballet? But who now remembers for how long this ballet could not make it to the stage, how much routine and conservative superstition had to be broken before our art was given one of its best creations?" Sviridov also backed Richter regarding Prokofiev's hidden operatic heritage: "Is it acceptable that until now the magnificent, inspiring Prokofiev opera *War and Peace* has not been staged in Moscow? This monumental work demands a grand stage and a monumental director's solutions. But the Bolshoy 'ceded' *War and Peace* to the Stanislavsky and Nemirovich-Danchenko [Theater]." He went on: "Why isn't Prokofiev's *The Duenna* staged? It is the late composer's most appealing opera, and one of the most spirited, laughter-filled, and mischievous works in Soviet music."[29]

The campaign in favor of Prokofiev was a sign of changing times, and the Central Committee apparatus resisted vehemently. Yarustovsky and Apostolov were working for the head of the Department of Culture of the Central Committee. Their opposition to Prokofiev is evident in the unsigned editorials published in *Izvestiya* after the Second Congress had ended but before the prize winners were announced. One such editorial stressed the importance of continuing the struggle against the influences of formalism and individualism in the arts by embracing the precepts of Socialist Realism. Prokofiev's works, even his Lenin Prize–nominated Seventh Symphony, were conspicuously absent from the article. Instead, the other two nominees were hailed.[30] The preferences of the Central Committee apparatus could not have been clearer.

In February 1953 the Central Committee had reluctantly supported Prokofiev's candidacy for the Stalin Prize (Second Class) for his Seventh Symphony. Yet four years later the apparatus contested his candidacy for the Lenin Prize for the same work. On February 9, 1957, Yarustovsky and Dmitriy Polikarpov (1905–65), the head of the Department of Culture, tried to thwart the workings of the Lenin Prize Committee. In the name of the Department of Culture, the supreme authority in the field, they alerted the Central Committee to "several questionable and sometimes wrong tendencies" in the Lenin Prize Committee's methods.[31]

The first observation was relatively reasonable: it noted the tendency of each category's selection committee to include in its short lists as many works as possible. Literature had endorsed eleven candidacies, and music and theater listed four each (though cinema nominated only one). Selection for a short list was considered to be an act of endorsement, but the bureaucrats objected that "long" short lists prolonged the deliberation process. They further contended that the lists included too many performers who had been awarded multiple government and Stalin Prizes in the past. Ostensibly this complaint was directed at the ballerina Ulanova and violinist Oistrakh, but it also applied to Prokofiev, the implicit target of Yarustovsky's invective.

Ulanova had been awarded Stalin Prizes on four occasions (two fewer than Prokofiev), and half of them had been for her lead performances in Prokofiev's ballets *Romeo and Juliet* and *Cinderella*. (The other two were for Glier's *The Red Poppy* and her overall achievements in Soviet ballet.) The authors of the memorandum were particularly indignant at Ulanova's lack of modesty: as a member of the selection committee she had bluntly suggested changing her nomination for a specific role (again in a Prokofiev ballet, for her spectacular performance as Juliet in London) to a nomination for her artistry in general. The Lenin Prize Committee concurred.

Then Yarustovsky and Polikarpov articulated their principal objections:

> The CC CPSU Department of Culture considers that awarding prizes to performers may take place only in some exceptional cases. It is appropriate to evaluate performers in the fields of musical and balletic art on the basis of new concert programs and new roles, not on their old merits. On this basis G. Ulanova and D. Oistrakh can hardly at this time lay claim to the Lenin Prize. The effort to expand the awards to cover "general" merits, rather than new, ideologically and artistically vivid works is evident in other instances. S. Prokofiev is proposed for the list as a posthumous candidate for outstanding achievement in the sphere of art.[32]

Excluding new discoveries in the archives, the creation of "new, ideologically and artistically vivid" works would obviously be a problem for Prokofiev.

In writing their memorandum, Yarustovsky and Polikarpov miscalculated the pervasive mood of change, and also did not take into account one subjective factor: the Central Committee secretary in charge of ideology, arts, and culture, Dmitriy Shepilov (1905–95), was a close acquaintance of Khrennikov, whose opinion and advice were decisive. Shepilov had supreme power over subordinates like Yarustovsky and Polikarpov. Since Shostakovich certainly feared denunciations and being held accountable for his role in the promulgation of the Stalin cult (as his tongue-tied speech at the Central Committee gathering in March 1957 showed), Prokofiev became the almost unanimous choice of the artistic elite for the 1957 Lenin Prize in music. Taking into consideration that other award winners were

Ulanova in ballet and the revered Russian sculptor Sergey Konenkov (who spent almost thirty years abroad, a returned émigré like Prokofiev), it was a multifaceted victory for the departed composer.

The Failed Prokofiev Festival (1959–61)

Khrushchev's conflicting and sometimes chaotic decisions defined what Soviet historians termed the decade of *voluntarizm i sub'yektivizm* (voluntaristic and subjectivist policies). Liberal measures were followed by conservative countermeasures, then additional progressive actions, reactions, and so forth. The cultural sphere, like the political sphere, absorbed the shifts.

In the wake of the Budapest upheaval, Soviet policymakers suspected that revisionist adepts had infiltrated the cultural institutions of the other People's Democracies, particularly Poland and Czechoslovakia. Following Yarustovsky's inspection tours to the socialist capitals in the late 1940s and early 1950s, Moscow apparatchiks expressed concern that the cultural institutions in those capitals were resistant to the Sovietization of musical life. The apparatchiks wanted triumphant programmatic music with grandiloquent titles, art that was socialist in form and nationalist in content, and works saturated with Party themes (*partiynost'*) and popular nationalism (*narodnost'*) of use to the Communist regime. Ultimately, the affinity for textless, programless music (*beztekstovaya neprogrammnaya muzïka*) was viewed as anti-Soviet.

It is no surprise, then, that a 1959 festival organized in Warsaw devoted entirely to the music of Prokofiev came under suspicion in Moscow. The uncertainty hinged on which of the two Prokofievs the organizers intended to celebrate: the composer who traveled in the West far from Soviet Russia for nearly two decades, or the composer who returned to the Soviet Union, the six-time Stalin Prize winner and recipient of the Lenin Prize. In Khrushchev's Russia the only acceptable Prokofiev was, of course, the latter, but the composers and musicologists of the People's Republic of Poland did not share that view.

The festival's opening concert included the Classical Symphony, the Third Piano Concerto, and the suite from the ballet *The Buffoon* (*Chout*), an obvious selection from Prokofiev's pre-1936 music. There were three concerts of chamber, orchestral, and recorded music, a showing of two films, and a performance of *Romeo and Juliet*. The accompanying December 4–7 academic conference took place at the most prestigious location in the Polish capital, the Palace of Science and Culture—Stalin's gift to the People's Republic of Poland. This conference was an obvious wake-up call to the USSR, since no such event had ever been held in the composer's homeland. And it had powerful sponsors: the Union of Polish Composers and the University of Warsaw Musicology Institute. The Union and the Warsaw Philharmonic prepared the concerts, and the festival itself was entirely organized by Polish musicians. Several Soviet colleagues were invited, including Izraíl Nestyev, a leading Prokofiev specialist.[33] Given the relatively narrow Soviet definition of the "genuine" Prokofiev, the presentations by Polish musicologists incensed the Soviet delegates. For example, T. Zelinsky devoted only one-and-a-half pages of his fifteen-page brochure to the composer's Soviet period. Nestyev invoked official rhetoric to respond to Zelinsky, accusing him of slanderous attacks and noting the intense displeasure of the Soviet delegates.

The Union of Composers viewed the Polish conference as a sign to expect more challenges to the Soviet image of Prokofiev. They discussed ways of counteracting the expected confrontations and found the usual answer by consulting the calendar for an appropriate anniversary. The closest one was April 23, 1961, the seventieth anniversary of Prokofiev's birth. Chastened by the fact that the first "Prokofiev in memoriam" festival had been organized in Poland, the Union prepared a memorandum recommending to the Central Committee that a festival in Prokofiev's honor finally be held in his homeland.

An old decree adopted on April 10, 1941, by the Central Committee and the government stood in the way of the event. On the eve of the German invasion, Stalin himself had edited the decree, all the while mocking the bureaucratic love for jubilee bacchanalia (*vakhanaliya*).[34] It was traditional to honor high-ranking officials on the occasion of their third, fifth, tenth, fifteenth, and twentieth anniversaries of work in their profession, for their position in an institution, or for achieving a certain age. From now on, the decree ruled, awards could be given only for "serious achievements" (Stalin corrected this phrase to read "outstanding achievements") and only on the fiftieth, sixtieth, and seventy-fifth birthdays of a living honoree. For the deceased, only fiftieth and hundredth birthday recognitions were permitted.

The decree was flaunted right and left, the most ironic example being the grandiose festivities for Stalin's own seventieth birthday in 1949. In 1964 Khrushchev's seventieth birthday was celebrated, and in the 1980s Leonid Brezhnev, Yuriy Andropov, and Konstantin Chernenko seemed to treat every birthday as an apparent miracle—they had survived another year. Prokofiev, however, had been deprived of his fiftieth celebration in 1941 just after Stalin's decree, and again of his sixtieth in 1951 after the scandal surrounding the prohibition of German Zhukovsky's opera *From the Whole Heart* (*Ot vsego serdtsa*, 1950). A posthumous celebration in 1961 could not compensate for the lack of festivities during the composer's lifetime, but it would serve a purpose for the Union of Composers.

The first attempt to convince the Central Committee to allow the celebration dates from August 16, 1959. The Organizing Secretary of the Union
of Composers Board Sergey Aksyuk (a mediocre musician but shrewd
administrator and liaison to the Central Committee) submitted the following memorandum:

> April 1961 marks the seventieth birthday of the outstanding Soviet
> composer Sergey Sergeyevich Prokofiev.
> S. S. Prokofiev's art constitutes an important stage in the develop-
> ment of world musical art and has received world recognition.
> Many of S. S. Prokofiev's works are classics in our music.
> The Secretariat of the USSR Union of Composers asks to be given
> permission to hold an International S. S. Prokofiev Festival in April
> 1961 in Moscow.[35]

By Soviet rules a Central Committee draft had to be approved by its
Presidium (Politburo) in order to acquire the force of law and become
eligible for budgetary appropriation. Aksyuk's draft (the document that
accompanied his memorandum) mentioned the "outstanding merits of the
composer" and envisioned the formation of a festival committee chaired by
Shostakovich and composed of USSR Minister of Culture Nikolay Mikhaylov,[36]
Khrennikov, Kabalevsky, and First Deputy Minister of Culture Sergey
Kaftanov.[37] Finally, it proposed giving the Minister of Culture the right to
invite foreign guest musicians to participate in the festival.

Aksyuk supplied a detailed daily schedule for the festival's proposed program. It would open with a speech by Shostakovich, followed by a special report
on Prokofiev delivered by Kabalevsky. The six-day program would involve:

Day 1: the opera *War and Peace*;
Day 2: a chamber concert, a symphonic concert (the oratorio *On Guard
for Peace*, Violin Concerto no. 1, and Symphony no. 7), and, at 8
p.m., the opera *Betrothal in a Monastery* (*The Duenna*);
Day 3: Prokofiev works performed by students at institutions of
higher musical education, a symphonic concert (Violin Concerto
no. 2, the Cello Concerto, and Piano Concerto no. 3), and the
ballet *The Stone Flower*;
Day 4: fragments from the opera *A Story of a Real Man*, a symphonic
concert, and the opera *Semyon Kotko*;
Day 5: a visit to the gravesites of S. S. Prokofiev and N. Ya. Myaskovsky,
the ballet *Cinderella*, and a special concert with an introduction by
D. B. Kabalevsky titled "Myaskovsky and Prokofiev";
Day 6: Prokofiev works performed by students at institutions of
higher musical education.[38]

Yarustovsky's tenure at the Central Committee ended in August 1959, the same month that Aksyuk submitted his proposal. It is impossible to determine whether he had a say in the decision, but the Central Committee refused to approve the festival. Although the program was carefully designed to avoid any representation of pre-Soviet music, the participation of foreign guests seemed undesirable (the first Tchaikovsky competition in 1958 had not gone the way the Soviet leadership had planned, with the first prize and gold medal awarded to the American pianist Van Cliburn). In addition, during the summer and fall of 1959 the Central Committee, together with the KGB and MVD (police) had become harshly critical of deviations and failings at the Moscow Conservatory.

The Union of Composers refused to take no for an answer, and in an unprecedented move challenged the decision outright. On March 31, 1960, Kabalevsky, in his capacity as acting first secretary of the Union, wrote to the Central Committee. The date was significant: with the participation of Khrushchev and other Soviet leaders, the founding Congress of the RSFSR Union of Composers (not to be confused with the USSR Union of Composers) had been opened at the Kremlin. Politically it was the right moment to advocate the memory of Prokofiev. Kabalevsky wrote:

> April 1961 marks 70 years since the birth of Sergey Prokofiev—the most prominent Soviet composer, laureate of seven Stalin and Lenin prizes. The art of Sergey Prokofiev has long received worldwide recognition. His works belong to the highest achievements of contemporary musical art.
>
> In this respect the Secretariat and Board of the USSR Union of Composers request permission to hold in Moscow in 1961 a musical festival dedicated to the art of S. Prokofiev with the participation of outstanding foreign performers along with guest composers from foreign countries.
>
> Analogous festivals dedicated to the art of Janáček, Enescu, and other composers have taken place in Czechoslovakia, Romania, and other countries. Last year a special festival dedicated to Prokofiev took place in Poland, but the composer's art was presented at this festival in a one-sided and, as a result, distorted way. It seems to us more appropriate to organize the festival in commemoration of the jubilee of S. Prokofiev, whose art is the pride of Soviet and world progressive musical culture.[39]

Kabalevsky and his backer Khrennikov had good reason to resubmit the application. Yarustovsky had been replaced on the Central Committee by Pyotr Savintsev, an amiable gentleman of a younger generation who would in the 1970s serve as Organizing Secretary of the USSR Union of Composers

Board. Other positive signs followed at the RSFSR Congress, including the surprise election of Shostakovich as the First Secretary of the RSFSR Union of Composers Board. Khrushchev toasted the banquet with a strong endorsement of Soviet composition.

In light of these events the Central Committee released its final decision regarding the International Prokofiev Festival:

> In connection with the 70th anniversary of the birth of Soviet composer Prokofiev S. S. in April 1961 (he died in 1953) the Secretariat of the Board of the USSR Union of Composers has put forward a proposal to hold in April 1961 in the city of Moscow an International Music Festival dedicated to the art of S. S. Prokofiev, with the participation of foreign performers and composers.
>
> This issue was already considered at the CC CPSU in October 1959. The USSR Union of Composers was given permission to hold a jubilee evening dedicated to the 70th anniversary of the birth of composer Prokofiev S. S. in the Great Hall of the Moscow State Conservatory as well as concerts of his works.
>
> The celebration of an International Festival dedicated to S. S. Prokofiev and invitation of foreign artistic personalities was considered to be inexpedient.
>
> We find that there is no basis to reconsider the decision taken previously on this matter.[40]

The document was approved by Yekaterina Furtseva (1910–74), the Presidium and Secretariat member in charge of culture (who would later that year become the USSR Minister of Culture), and returned to Savintsev for communication to Aksyuk. The issue was closed and all documentation sent to the archive.

Why such a firm and final refusal? Perhaps it was fear that the presence of foreign guests at the festival would validate Prokofiev's Western heritage, leading to demands for his full and unequivocal rehabilitation. Moreover, Prokofiev's two widows, who reflected his two conflicting personas, would be at the center of media coverage and the attention of foreign embassies. Timing (the curse of Prokofiev both during and after his life) also played a role. His birthday on April 23 fell unfortunately close to Lenin's on April 22, when all programs in media outlets, cinemas, and theaters around the country were scrutinized to ensure the highest Marxist-Leninist ideological content. A congregation of foreign guests on Lenin's birthday would distract media attention and create unnecessary threats and challenges to the Party, the state bureaucracy, and secret police operatives.

The détente of 1959 was followed by an increase in Cold War tensions. Khrushchev traveled to the United States and, following his return, preparations were made for a visit to the Soviet Union by Dwight Eisenhower. But on May 1, 1960, during the spectacular May Day parade on Red Square, an American U-2 plane was shot down in Soviet territory. Eisenhower's visit would be called off indefinitely and Khrushchev would later cancel his appearance at a Paris peace summit. As the Prokofiev jubilee approached, more complications arose. On April 12, 1961 (eleven days prior to Prokofiev's seventieth anniversary), Soviet cosmonaut Yuriy Gagarin became the first person to orbit the earth. His safe return from space sparked a frenzy of national celebration. Just five days later came the failed invasion of the Bay of Pigs by American-backed anti-Castro mercenaries. This event sparked anti-American protest throughout the Soviet Union, culminating in Khrushchev's decision to support Cuba militarily. Hopes for cultural exchange faded in the climate of international distrust.

It is also worth noting how the Central Committee once again downplayed Prokofiev's status in Soviet and world music. Kabalevsky called him an "outstanding" composer, and Aksyuk went even further with "most prominent." The Central Committee officers removed these appellations, leaving just "Soviet composer," and they also—in a rather offensive fashion—placed the abbreviation of his first name and patronymic after his surname ("Prokofiev S. S." versus the polite "S. S. Prokofiev"). In Russian protocol, such lack of respect sent a subtle message that the proposal should be disregarded. No mention was made of Prokofiev's Lenin Prize and six Stalin Prizes.

In the end, the celebration was exceedingly subdued. On April 22, the newspaper *Sovetskaya kul'tura*, the mouthpiece of the USSR Ministry of Culture, published a lengthy article by musicologist Ivan Martïnov. The author repeatedly emphasized the "fifteen long years" Prokofiev spent abroad, and the "creative crises" he experienced as a result. "And yet," Martïnov proclaimed, "he chose the right path and in 1933 [*sic*] returned to the motherland."[41] The only variation in the standard rhetoric was visual: censorship rules now allowed for the occasional use of *motherland* without the capital *M*.

The gradual progression toward liberalization in music nonetheless continued following Khrushchev's removal from the Kremlin in October 1964. Minister of Culture Furtseva (appointed to her position in 1960 and retained by Brezhnev and Alexey Kosygin, who staged the coup against Khrushchev) reported to the government on January 14, 1966, about the premieres in Moscow the previous year. Newly staged operas included Benjamin Britten's *A Midsummer Night's Dream*, Francis Poulenc's *La Voix Humaine*, Gioacchino Rossini's *Il Barbiere di Siviglia*, and Mikhaïl Glinka's *Ruslan and Lyudmila*. There were three new ballets: Arif Melikov's *Legend of Love* (*Legenda o lyubvi*, 1961), Igor Stravinsky's *Le Sacre du printemps*, and Yevgeniy Krïlatov's children's ballet *Tsvetik-semistvetik* (Rainbow flower, 1965).

The list is surprising because 1965 marked the twentieth anniversary of the Soviet victory against the Nazis. The government had used the anniversary to distract the nation's attention from discussions of Stalin's crimes. The Great Terror, moreover, was being subtly redefined as a necessary precursor to the preparations for the war. Amid these ideological battles even Britten and Poulenc were better than Andrey Sakharov and Alexander Solzhenitsyn. Such repertoire at the Bolshoy Theater and Grand Kremlin Palace would have been unheard of at the height of Khrushchev's rule.

Another Memorial Plaque (Paris, May 1969)

The late 1960s were more positive for Prokofiev's memorialization. Small steps were taken toward the partial rehabilitation of works from his prerevolutionary and Western years. Pressure came again from the West: in May 1969 a second, much larger Prokofiev festival was organized, this time in Paris.

Lina Prokofiev was prevented from traveling to France to attend the festival. In an interview published in 1991, Svyatoslav Prokofiev, first son of Lina and Sergey, explicitly blamed the Union of Composers for the prohibition. Khrennikov gave his version of events in 1994 in a book of conversations with musicologist Valentina Rubtsova. These two oral versions, combined with a newly uncovered official memorandum sent to Furtseva in April 1969, elucidate yet another episode in the long struggle over Prokofiev's posthumous fate.

Svyatoslav Prokofiev recalled the situation in an interview with musicologist Nataliya Savkina:

> In May 1969 in Paris a memorial plaque was installed on the facade of the building where we lived from 1929 until 1935. Mama received a personal invitation from France's Minister of Culture. But the Union of Composers, as Lina Ivanovna would later find out, gave her a bad official recommendation [*kharakteristika*] and she could not go. Who didn't attend the ceremonial unveiling! Some choir or other was there, and a lot of bureaucrats—only the apartment's landlady was missing.[42]

It is unknown whether the French Minister of Culture did indeed send his invitation directly to the Union of Composers or whether Lina, after receiving the invitation through private channels, submitted it to the Union Secretariat for processing. To travel abroad, she, like every Soviet citizen, needed a "foreign" Soviet passport and an endless list of clearance and endorsement stamps, all of which had to be arranged by the International Commission at the Union (chaired by Nikolay Shcherbak and his deputy Nina Brodyanskaya) or by the Foreign Relations Department of the Ministry of Culture. A personal invitation from a foreign minister was not enough.

As General Secretary of the Union, Khrennikov was obligated by strict government rules to pass on the invitation from the French Ministry of Culture to the Soviet Ministry of Culture. Furtseva may or may not have requested the *kharakteristika* herself—but either way it was an important document, a voucher containing signatures and stamps without which, generally speaking, no Soviet citizen could leave Soviet territory.

Khrennikov responded to Svyatoslav's allegations in his book of conversations with Rubtsova:

Apparently some clarification must be introduced. Any more or less objective reader will understand that if the French Minister of Culture sends an invitation in somebody's name to the USSR Ministry of Culture (and the invitation was sent precisely there), then that organization, where the papers arrived, organizes the trip. It organizes it if it wishes to do so. And if it does not wish to do so, then the bureaucrat dealing with the matter can say anything his conscience can withstand. So it is easy to say that the Union of Composers gave a bad *kharakteristika*—this document is not shown to anyone, and the conversation about it is not filed away. So you see the *kharakteristika* never existed. It was not needed. What was needed was an excuse. And it was invented. That's why the Ministry with its bureaucrats exists—in order to find reasons.[43]

Khrennikov's statement likewise needs clarification. Khrennikov was not only a top-level bureaucrat appointed and then officially elected to his position of general (first) secretary of the Union of Composers, but at different stages of his career he was also a member of the Party's Central Auditing Commission (1961–76) and later a non-voting member of the Central Committee (1976–90). For over forty years he held a place on a list of the top five hundred most influential civil servants in a country with a population of nearly three hundred million people. Individuals elected to this body were entitled to receive and be briefed on top-secret issues and confidential information. Khrennikov's office on Nezhdanov Street was visited regularly by a uniformed government courier bringing him classified information in special envelopes bearing an official brown wax seal. Khrennikov also received his share of this type of information in his capacity as deputy of the USSR Supreme Soviet, a position he held from 1962 until the collapse of the Soviet Union in December 1991.

On the surface, Khrennikov correctly described the bureaucratic procedure and conflict surrounding Lina's inability to travel to Paris. But he described only the legally plausible and officially accepted face of the Soviet government, the superficial activities of the Ministry of Culture and the Union. The true powers in the decision-making process were sitting behind the walls of the Central Committee apparatus that acted on advice from the KGB. Khrennikov, most likely restrained by the oath of secrecy he had taken in January 1948 when he was named general secretary of the Union, did not discuss that aspect of the situation.

The following document unearthed at the Central Committee archive shows that, as was so often the case, the true story was not known to Prokofiev's family, the Union of Composers, or even the Ministry of Culture (implicated in Khrennikov's comments), but by shadowy figures working adjacent to the Kremlin in central Moscow. Furtseva wrote the following to the Central Committee:

The unveiling of a memorial plaque on a building where composer S. Prokofiev lived in Paris will occur on May 20 of this year. The ceremony will be part of a festival of Soviet music in Paris which is being carried out from May 17–28 with the participation of French orchestras and Soviet musicians.

The directors of the "Friends of Sergey Prokofiev" association, which include the most prominent French composers and the Minister of Culture of France A. Malraux, have invited S. Prokofiev's widow L. I. Prokofiev to travel to Paris to take part in the ceremonies dedicated to S. Prokofiev's memory.

The USSR Union of Composers and USSR Embassy in France support L. I. Prokofiev's trip to France.

The USSR Ministry of Culture requests permission for L. I. Prokofiev's trip to France in May for one week.[44]

Furtseva's memorandum was sent to the Central Committee no later than April 30, just in time for the beginning of the Labor Day national holiday. The Committee apparatus had at least two weeks to process the application.

Lina Prokofiev was an exonerated "victim of the groundless repressions that took place from the 1930s to the start of the 1950s" (this phrase being the only officially accepted way of describing Stalin's crimes) but so, too, were Solzhenitsyn and many other famous Soviet dissidents. For the first forty years of her life Lina was neither a Russian nor a Soviet citizen. She was not, nor had ever been a member of the Communist Party. Further, at the time of the petition to allow her to travel her second son, Oleg, was romantically involved with Camilla Grey, a British historian of Soviet avant-garde art (they married in 1969). There were numerous concerns about the risks of sending her with an official delegation; nobody wanted to take responsibility for the defection of a seventy-two-year-old pensioner.

On top of this, for the last fifteen years of Prokofiev's life he had been *nevïyezdnoy*, not allowed to travel outside of the Soviet Union. Although Soviet law used a lot of gimmickry to alter the personal records and official files of deceased Soviet citizens, there are no examples of someone being declared *vïyezdnoy*, allowed to travel, after his or her death. To allow Prokofiev's widow to travel to Paris would require her to be cleared by the district Party organization and, ultimately, to appear before the CC CPSU Foreign Travel Commission (vïyezdnaya komissiya TsK KPSS) which, on advice from the KGB, was responsible for the political clearance of individuals planning to travel to capitalist countries. They determined the expediency of such trips, and briefed and obtained the signature of the traveler agreeing to conform to the confidential rules and norms for a Soviet citizen's behavior abroad. Upon returning home travelers had to present a written and signed report on the trip—Khrennikov, Shostakovich, Khachaturyan, and other world-famous artists included. The materials of the Foreign Travel Commission are still classified and almost nothing is written either in Russian or English about its workings.

Taking these adverse factors into account, the second in command at the Department of Culture of the Central Committee, Zoya Tumanova, put an end to the matter: "The USSR Ministry of Culture is at this time withdrawing its proposal from CC CPSU consideration."[45] This pronouncement dates from May 19, 1969, nearly three weeks after the petition was submitted; the Prokofiev Festival in Paris was well under way.

Tumanova had the final word. As Furtseva and Khrennikov must have known, a secret Soviet law dating back to 1927 prohibited anybody, under threat of severe penalty, from disclosing whether an issue had been resolved by the Party apparatus. Consequently, the actual cause of Lina's prohibition from travel remained unknown for nearly forty years.

The Late 1960s to the Early 1980s

Throughout the 1970s Prokofiev was the most acclaimed twentieth-century composer in Soviet concert halls and theaters. His popularity reflected practical needs. Cultural activities were managed by the State as part of a command economy; Prokofiev's music was a good bet for approval by government regulators, and his widespread popularity guaranteed strong attendance at performances of his music within the Soviet Union and abroad (by Soviet artists on tour). The latter became increasingly important as the country grew desperate for foreign currency.

Prokofiev's works were of value to several government bodies: the Ministry of Culture, the State Planning Committee (Gosplan, in charge of drafting Five-Year plans for the national economy), and the Finance Ministry (in charge of budget appropriations and dispensations). The USSR did not sign the 1952 Geneva Copyright Convention until 1972. By the time it finally went into effect in May 1973, Mira Mendelson had died, Oleg had moved to the West, and Lina was about to leave the country permanently. The issue of the vast royalties due to Prokofiev's heirs was resolved by default in favor of the State. This meant that Prokofiev's music could be performed without the need to make copyright payments to the family, and as a result his works flourished in the Soviet repertoire.

Even when Prokofiev's heirs lived in the USSR, they had not financially benefited from their association with the eminent, popular composer. A report issued by the National Committee on Labor and Earning Wages in the late 1960s finds Shostakovich's earnings eclipsing those of other Soviet composers, living or dead. In 1967, when he was the dean of Soviet Music and at the height of his career as head of the RSFSR Union of Composers, Shostakovich received a staggering 40,468 rubles in royalties.[46] (The average engineer's salary was 150 rubles a month; newspapers cost 3 kopecks and a subway token 5). Khrennikov earned a modest 9,309 rubles in royalties in 1969. Prokofiev's heirs are not listed in the report as royalty recipients.

The Prokofiev biographer Daniel Jaffé claims that "Lina's existence was . . . hampered by Khrennikov, who, after realizing that foreign royalties were still accruing on Prokofiev's work, started posing as her personal friend, and, where possible, arranging for royalties to be paid care of himself."[47] This statement betrays a misunderstanding of hard currency and bank account policies in the Soviet Union before 1991. Merely the suspicion that Khrennikov, a Central Committee member, was managing foreign accounts and cashing royalties owed to Prokofiev's heirs would have brought immediate investigation by Party watchdogs (the Committee for Party Control) and the harshest penalties. It is unclear how Jaffé envisions Khrennikov succeeding with such a scheme.[48]

As the decade progressed, Prokofiev's works maintained prominence in the Soviet repertoire. In 1971 a confidential Ministry of Culture report summarized the results of a national competition the previous year, part of the lavish celebration marking the centennial of Lenin's birth. Two hundred works were presented by musical theaters in competition for the best performance; fifty-three were deemed worthy of prizes or diplomas. The best operas included Prokofiev's *Semyon Kotko* at the Bolshoy Theater in Moscow, Kabalevsky's *Colas Breugnon* (1938) at the Stanislavsky and Nemirovich-Danchenko Theater, Prokofiev's *The Gambler* in Tallinn, and Boris Lyatoshinsky's *Zolotoy obruch* (Golden ring, 1929) in Lvov. The list of the five best ballets included *Cinderella*.

Year after year, reports from the Ministry of Culture document Prokofiev's posthumous triumphs on the Soviet stage. A 1979 accounting finds the Bolshoy Theater staging George Frideric Handel's *Giulio Cesare*, Richard Wagner's *Das Rheingold*, Giuseppe Verdi's *Un Ballo in Maschera*, and Prokofiev's *Romeo and Juliet*. With the exception of *Romeo and Juliet* this repertoire could have been performed a hundred years earlier, in 1879. During a period of Soviet cultural stagnation, Prokofiev's music remained vibrant.

Khrennikov persisted in his efforts to promote Prokofiev even further, to make him the unmatched symbol of Soviet music at home and abroad. The ninetieth anniversary of Prokofiev's birth in April 1981 coincided with the First International Music Festival in Moscow. The festival was un-officially dedicated to Prokofiev and Nikolay Myaskovsky (whose one hundredth anniversary had occurred a few days before Prokofiev's nineti-eth). Khrennikov's hope for a large-scale event honoring Prokofiev, more than twenty years in the making, had finally been approved by the Central Committee. The festival coincided with Maxim Shostakovich's defection to the West, but the composer's son kept a low profile and made no overt anti-Soviet statements, and so his actions did not dampen the celebration.

In 1983 Khrennikov petitioned the Central Committee to permit the establishment of four International Gold Prizes named after Prokofiev, each intended as a kind of Soviet Nobel Prize in Music. But the Soviet regime was coming to its end. The gold needed to create the medals as well as the large monetary awards attached to them were thought to have better uses. The regime believed it had done everything it could to immortalize Prokofiev.

The Failed Centennial Celebration (1991)

In June 1989 the Congress of People's Deputies for the first time challenged the hegemony of the Communist Party. In November the Berlin Wall fell, and the ensuing velvet revolutions dismantled the puppet Communist regimes of Eastern Europe. The centennial of Prokofiev's birth was—like so many of his other anniversaries—overshadowed by unfortunate coincidence, this time the seismic changes taking place in his homeland as the Soviet Union collapsed.

His centennial was an unavoidable milestone even according to Stalin's 1941 decree concerning anniversary celebrations. The outlook for the celebration at first seemed good: the country was in dire need of a positive event to commemorate its cultural and artistic life, a "consolidating occasion" (the catchphrase at the time) that would help boost the injured mood and unite a fragmented and antagonistic society. It was hoped that such an event would bridge the abysses that had opened on several fronts: between the Communist Party apparatus and rank-and-file Communists; the Soviet government and its citizens; the Kremlin and the outside world; the Russian Federation and the other Soviet Republics, which—starting with Lithuania in March 1990—were taking steps toward secession and independence.

No cultural symbol could achieve that goal better than Prokofiev. His relatively independent life under Soviet rule, his ecumenical heritage, and his immense body of work all made him an obvious figurehead. The Ukrainian SSR would soon become an independent country; to stage some of the festivities there, where he had been born, would foster a sense of Slavic solidarity.

This view was shared by the Ministry of Culture, now headed by Nikolay Gubenko,[49] by the newly created All-Union Musical Society, headed by the leading Soviet mezzo-soprano Irina Arkhipova,[50] and by the Union of Composers, headed by the seemingly immortal Khrennikov. For Khrennikov the celebration would offer personal validation and a symbolic cap to his four decades at the helm of the Union of Composers. But the State's weakening political center became a major roadblock in the effort to mount the event; the fractured government could no longer coordinate the complicated processes of planning memorial services and mandating the appropriation of government budget funds.

According to the established validation process, the proposal needed to be scrutinized by several Central Committee departments, with individual responsibilities and the makeup of the centennial planning committee determined by the Central Committee Secretariat. After that it needed to be synchronized with the State Planning Committee and the Finance Ministry, and only then could it be approved by the Central Committee Politburo. Finally, it would be ready for submission as an order to the government, though in this case making no mention of the fact that it had already been approved at Party headquarters—the documents bore a note in pencil, "materiala net" (no incoming documents). Then the government would rubber-stamp the order and forward it to the corresponding ministries for specific measures: the Ministry of Finance to allocate funds (on advice from the State Planning Committee); the Ministry of Culture to give orders for productions by opera and ballet theaters, symphony orchestras, and television and radio stations; the Cinema Committee to make new documentaries and release pertinent old films. Lastly, the Union of Composers and its Foreign Affairs Commission would draw up lists of foreign guests for submission to the KGB and External Affairs Ministry, which would issue entry visas for them. It was a hopelessly complex process for a rapidly disintegrating country.

The economic crisis, moreover, affected the financing of fees and royalties. In 1990 the Central Committee had to pay the Bolshoy Theater to rent its premises on the occasion of Lenin's one hundred and twentieth anniversary; artists refused to take part in the most prestigious concert of the year for a miserable service fee. Moscow hotels began denying ministries and agencies rooms for their guests. Foreign artists became skittish about touring in the Soviet Union.

Despite what had at first seemed to be promising circumstances for the centennial, the January 1990 proposal could not have arrived at the Central Committee at a worse time. In only a few days the Third Congress of People's Deputies would abolish Article Six of the 1977 Soviet constitution, which institutionalized the leading role of the Communist Party in Soviet society. The Central Committee's loss of control was felt immediately in the cultural sphere. Subsidies ceased, projects halted, and the exodus of musicians and artists abroad reached proportions unseen since the triumphant Bolshevik Revolution of 1917.

The authors of the Prokofiev centennial memorandum proceeded in spite of it all. The document they addressed to the Central Committee remains the most complete record of Party and government designs for Prokofiev's legacy:

On the 100th Anniversary of S. S. Prokofiev's Birth

April 1991 marks the 100th anniversary of the birth of Sergey Sergeyevich Prokofiev, an outstanding Soviet composer, musical and social activist.

Prokofiev's art has had a tremendous influence on the development of both Soviet and world musical art and, having become the heritage of human culture in general, encompasses all musical genres. The composer created monumental frescoes in his operas and ballets, and his symphonic, chamber/instrumental and vocal compositions have become classics. Prokofiev's artistic style is unique within the multifaceted diversity of twentieth-century cultural life.

On the occasion of the composer's jubilee the USSR Ministry of Culture considers it necessary to enact the following measures:

Establishing a Jubilee Committee (the list is attached);

Holding a ceremonial gathering on April 23, 1991, at the State Academic Bolshoy Theater dedicated to the 100th anniversary of the birth of S. S. Prokofiev, followed by a concert (spectacle);

Holding in 1991 in Moscow a USSR Union of Composers theory conference with the participation of representatives from foreign countries, dedicated to S. S. Prokofiev's creativity and his contribution to Soviet and world musical art;

Directing the USSR Union of Composers to establish an All-Union competition named after Prokofiev for young composers;

Holding during the 1990–91 season an international festival dedicated to the 100th anniversary of the birth of S. S. Prokofiev, with invitations extended to outstanding foreign musicians;

Having the Ministries of Culture of the Union Republics, the State Committees on Culture together with the Republic Unions of Composers and musical societies, and the regional and local chapters of the USSR Union of Theater Activists arrange regional and local events dedicated to S. S. Prokofiev, including festivals of his operas and ballets involving major new stagings and revivals;

Having the USSR Union of Theater Activists and the Ministry of Culture of the Belorussian SSR hold in Moscow and Minsk in November 1991 an international opera and ballet festival dedicated to the 100th anniversary of the birth of S. S. Prokofiev;

Having the USSR Union of Composers hold during the summer of 1991 an All-Union competition for conservatory students for the best performances of S. S. Prokofiev's works (in the categories of piano, violin, cello, and solo voice);

Directing the Ministries of Culture of the Union Republics, the State Committees on Culture, cultural agencies, and musical societies to create Prokofiev displays in children's musical schools and colleges in 1990–91;

Directing the All-Union Musical Society together with the Ministry of Culture of the Ukrainian SSR to hold in the city of Donetsk an All-Union piano competition dedicated to the 100th anniversary of the birth of S. S. Prokofiev, and to organize during the competition an exhibition dedicated to him;

Preparing by March 15, 1991, an exhibition of photographs and documents about the life and work of S. S. Prokofiev at the Great Hall of the Moscow Conservatory;

Having the USSR Union of Composers together with the Executive Committee of Moscow City Council hold a design competition for a monument to S. S. Prokofiev, realize the monument, and erect it in a central area of Moscow;

Having the USSR Union of Composers together with the Executive Committee of Moscow City Council open an S. S. Prokofiev museum-apartment in Moscow;

Directing the Council of Ministers of the Ukrainian SSR:

To create with the USSR Union of Composers a memorial complex at S. S. Prokofiev's birthplace in the village of Krasnoye, Red Army District, Donetsk Region, Ukrainian SSR;

To review the matter of the planning, construction, and reconstruction of an S. S. Prokofiev museum complex in Krasnoye, Red Army District, Donetsk Region, Ukrainian SSR;

To review the matter of the financing of the work on the creation of an S. S. Prokofiev museum complex;

Having the Executive Committee of Moscow City Council realize with city funds the design, creation, and installation of a bust of S. S. Prokofiev in front of the musical school named for S. S. Prokofiev in Moscow (Moscow Council decision No. 2000203 from November 27, 1989);

Publishing in central newspapers and magazines materials dedicated to the memorial date, including statements from outstanding activists in Soviet art, articles on the life and work of S. S. Prokofiev, and information on jubilee events;

Reissuing in 1990–91 gramophone recordings of the best operas, symphonic, vocal, and instrumental works of S. S. Prokofiev, and recording previously unrecorded works;

Directing USSR State Radio to organize television and radio programs on the life and work of S. S. Prokofiev, show films including S. S. Prokofiev's music, and broadcast live the ceremonial gathering and concert (spectacle) at the

USSR State Academic Bolshoy Theater on April 23, 1991;

Directing USSR State Cinema to make a documentary film about the celebration of the composer's jubilee;

Directing USSR State Press to publish jubilee editions of S. S. Prokofiev's works, an album, and an illustrated wall calendar dedicated to the composer's life and work;

Directing the USSR Ministry of Communications to issue in 1991 a jubilee postage stamp dedicated to the 100th anniversary of the birth of S. S. Prokofiev;

Directing the USSR Ministry of Finance and State Bank to mint in 1991 a jubilee coin dedicated to the 100th anniversary of the birth of S. S. Prokofiev.

The USSR Ministry of Culture also considers it necessary to establish stipends named after S. S. Prokofiev for students in the composition and piano faculties of the Moscow and Leningrad State Conservatories and the Donetsk Musical Pedagogical Institute.

These proposals have been coordinated with the Directorate of Culture of the City of Moscow (comrade Bugayev I. B.), the USSR Union of Theater Activists (comrade Mikk A. A.), USSR State Cinema (comrade Fyodorin A. V.), USSR State Press (comrade Shishigin M. V.), USSR Ministry of Communications (comrade Barashenkov L. D.), USSR Ministry of Finance (comrade Sitnikov V. V.), the Executive Committee of Moscow City Council (comrade Belyakov Yu. A.), and the Council of Ministers of Ukrainian SSR (comrade Oslik M. A.).

For the realization of the tasks presented we consider it expedient to adopt a USSR Council of Ministers Resolution (the draft is attached).

USSR Minister of Culture
(N. N. Gubenko)
First Secretary of the Board of the USSR Union of Composers
(T. N. Khrennikov)
Chair of the Board of All-USSR Musical Society
(I. K. Arkhipova)[51]

Vladimir Egorov, deputy director of the CC CPSU ideological department, granted his approval in a typically Gogolian way, using the royal "we" and subjective tense as if the Party were still at the height of its power: "The CC CPSU ideological department considers it possible to support the presented proposal regarding jubilee events in connection with the 100th anniversary of the birth of S. S. Prokofiev. A draft of the Resolution is attached."[52]

The memorandum was accompanied by a list of members for the Prokofiev Jubilee Committee, to be chaired by Khrennikov.[53] Its size was unprecedented in Soviet history: seventy-eight participants in total. By comparison, Tchaikovsky's Jubilee Committee, approved by the Politburo on January 4, 1940, involved forty-seven people; Rimsky-Korsakov's Committee, approved on November 17, 1943, included forty-three names.[54]

The January 1990 list is perhaps the last and most complete record available of the "Who's Who" of Soviet musical politics as the Central Committee *nomenklatura* began to collapse. In May 1990, when a drastically abridged Prokofiev anniversary proposal was finally approved by the government, it was not accompanied by a list of Jubilee Committee members; in fact, it lacked a Committee altogether. No competition for young composers, no conferences, festivals, or museums—little of the original proposal remained.

The enormity of the abridgement is startling but understandable. The budget for arts and culture had been drastically reduced to meet demands from the police and military to deal with the problems precipitated by separatist movements, anti-Communist protests, and—most important—to implement secret and urgent measures for the forthcoming *nomenklatura* privatization of the economy.[55]

On May 11, 1990, the USSR Council of Ministers approved Resolution No. 462, "On the 100th Anniversary of the Birth of S. S. Prokofiev":

On the occasion of the 100th anniversary of the birth of S. S. Prokofiev, an outstanding Soviet composer, musical and social activist, the USSR Council of Ministers RESOLVES:

1. To accept the USSR Ministry of Culture proposal, coordinated with Moscow City Executive Committee, concerning the erecting of a monument to S. S. Prokofiev in Moscow. The USSR Ministry of Culture together with interested organizations will hold a competition in 1990 for the best monument design and realize it; Moscow City Executive Committee will facilitate the erection of the monument.

2. To direct the USSR Ministry of Culture together with the Council of Ministers of the Ukrainian SSR to review the matter of the creation of a memorial complex dedicated to S. S. Prokofiev at his birthplace in the village of Krasnoye, Red Army District, Donetsk Region.

3. To establish two stipends named after S. S. Prokofiev at the Moscow P. I. Tchaikovsky State Conservatory, the Leningrad N. A. Rimsky-Korsakov State Conservatory, and the Donetsk Musical Pedagogical Institute.

4. For the USSR State Committee on Cinematography together with the USSR Ministry of Culture to resolve the question of the creation of a documentary film about the celebration of the jubilee dedicated to the 100th anniversary of the birth of S. S. Prokofiev.

5. For the USSR State Committee on Publications to accommodate in its plans for the year 1991 jubilee editions of S. S. Prokofiev's compositions and publications dedicated to his life and work.

6. For the USSR Ministry of Communications to issue in 1991 a jubilee postage stamp dedicated to the 100th anniversary of the birth of S. S. Prokofiev.

7. For the USSR Ministry of Finance and State Bank to mint in 1991 a jubilee coin dedicated to the 100th anniversary of the birth of S. S. Prokofiev.

Chairman of the USSR Council of Ministers
(N. Rïzhkov)
Director of Affairs of the USSR Council of Ministers
(M. Shkabardnya)[56]

During the final stages of approval a final point was deleted: "For the USSR State Committee on Television and Radio Broadcasting to organize television and radio programs on the life and work of S. S. Prokofiev, show films including S. S. Prokofiev's music, and broadcast live the ceremonial gathering and concert (spectacle) at the USSR State Academic Bolshoy Theater on April 23, 1991."[57]

The original plans advocated by Gubenko, Khrennikov, and Arkhipova were abandoned, mostly for financial reasons, but not without a political message: in the absence of the Communist Party, there would be no more extravagant cultural events, festivals, competitions, scholarships, prizes, museums, state-sponsored trips, or fireworks. Once again, Prokofiev's immortalization became the conduit for scoring blunt political points. When the anniversary arrived, it was marked by little more than a modest celebration in the Ukrainian village of Sontsovka, the composer's birthplace.

The proposals retained in the resolution required little financial support. Although item 8 was crossed out, three of the films for which Prokofiev composed music (*Lieutenant Kizhe*, *Alexander Nevsky*, and *Ivan the Terrible*) could have been shown: they were readily available and not in need of restoration. Radio and television broadcasts of the Bolshoy Theater gala would not have been a problem, either, since the media remained under almost total control of the Kremlin until after the failed August 1991 coup. A jubilee coin was minted, and a stamp bearing Prokofiev's image circulated. These activities were feasible: the mint and the postal service were among the last government branches to die.

Figure 1. Coin commemorating the 100th anniversary of the birth of S. S. Prokofiev.

Figure 2. Stamp commemorating the 100th anniversary of the birth of S. S. Prokofiev.

As to the proposed publications, a handful of paperbacks appeared, a far cry from the authoritative hardcover editions envisioned. The urgent task of publishing Prokofiev's complete works remains unfinished. The 1955–67 edition does not include the operas and ballets he composed before his relocation to the Soviet Union in 1936, and yet it remains the most substantive edition available. Demands from performers, scholars, and libraries exceed what it can provide.

The film industry also endured a severe economic and artistic crisis. It desperately needed financial support, especially in the form of joint ventures with Western counterparts that would bring in foreign currency. The proposed documentary film about Prokofiev, to have included little-known newsreel footage from the Central (Russian) State Film and Photography Archive in Krasnogorsk, would suffer the same fate as the museum at the apartment where he died.

The most serious tribute came from the editorial board of *Sovetskaya muzïka*. The special April 1991 Prokofiev issue included hitherto unseen documents from the Central (Russian) State Archive of Literature and Art. The Prokofiev collection there has since become the cornerstone of Prokofiev studies, although much of it remains closed to researchers. But that was it. The deteriorating government could do nothing more, and there was no Prokofiev foundation in Russia to privatize his memorialization and assume responsibility for coordinating the anniversary.

At any given point in Soviet history, immortalization rituals reflected less the actual significance of the individuals being honored than they did their political value. Prokofiev's achievement is manifest neither in the number of plaques hung in his honor nor in the size of the festivals devoted to his memory, but by the fact that his memorialization remained such an important issue for almost fifty years. This emphasis did not come from Prokofiev institutes or societies; his case lacked even the usual impetus provided by aggressive heirs. Rather, the question of his legacy resurfaced over and over again because of a widespread recognition of his immense significance. As Apollon Grigoryev said of the greatest Russian poet, "Pushkin is our everything," or, in a more modern understanding of the axiom, "Pushkin is classless."[58] Prokofiev as well, it seems: Russian and worldly, esteemed by the left, right, and center, Westerners and Slavophiles, revolutionaries and monarchists, Soviets and anti-Soviets, Stalinists and dissidents—Prokofiev is the figure who unites them all.

NOTES

1. In order to contextualize the following discussion of the difficulties associated with Prokofiev's immortalization, it is worth itemizing Shostakovich's awards. When he died in 1975, the latter composer's collection of honorifics included Russian Soviet Federal Socialist Republic (RSFSR) Merited Activist in the Arts (1942), RSFSR People's Artist (1947), USSR People's Artist (1954), five Stalin Prizes (1941, 1942, 1946, 1950, and 1952), the once-in-a-lifetime Lenin Prize (1958), a USSR State Prize (1968), a RSFSR "Glinka" State Prize (1974), a Cavalier Gold Star Hero of Socialist Labor Award (1966), the Order of the Red Banner of Labor (1940), three Orders of Lenin (1946, 1956, and 1966), and the Order of the October Revolution (1971). This exceedingly impressive accumulation of recognitions entitled Shostakovich to the highest degree of immortalization: a joint CC CPSU and Soviet State immortalization decree.

Prokofiev's collection of awards at the time of his death was comparatively modest: RSFSR Merited Activist of the Arts (1943), RSFSR People's Artist (1947), and the Order of the Red Banner of Labor. It was more impressive than Shostakovich's collection in only one respect: the receipt of a record number of Stalin Prizes: one in 1943, three in 1946, one in 1947, and one in 1951.

2. Immortalization rituals did not have expiration dates. A 1954 decree approved a list of events in honor of the anniversary of Anton Chekhov's death. These were announced to the public as if the writer had only just died—rather than fifty years prior under a different political system. His sister Maria Pavlovna Chekhov and widow, Olga Leonardovna Knipper-Chekhov, suddenly received 20,000 rubles each from the accounts of the USSR Literary Foundation. The USSR Ministry of Culture, meantime, organized the publication of Chekhov's complete works in twelve volumes.

3. Ispolnitel'nïy Komitet Moskovskogo Gorodskogo Soveta Deputatov Trudyashchikhsya (Executive Committee of the Moscow City Soviet of Workers' Deputies).

4. State Archive of the Russian Federation (Gosudarstvennïy Arkhiv Rossiyskoy Federatsii, henceforth GARF). The document is dated December 2, 1975.

5. Prior to his death, Stalin was the supreme leader of both the Soviet government and the Communist Party. After he slipped into a coma on March 2, Georgiy Malenkov (who would replace Stalin in the Kremlin for a single week) drafted a decree that removed him from the government while still allowing him to retain the position of general secretary of the Party. The draft is preserved at the Russian State Archive of Social-Political History (Rossiyskiy Gosudarstvennïy Arkhiv Sotsial'no-Politicheskoy Istorii, henceforth RGASPI), f. 83, op. 1, d. 3, p. 2.

6. Before assuming this position, Pospelov (1898–1979) worked for eight years (1940–48) as editor in chief of *Pravda*, overseeing the publication of several policy-defining articles on Soviet music. From 1953 to 1960 he pursued a limited de-Stalinization of Soviet culture.

7. Despite his importance in Soviet cultural affairs between April 1951 and March 1953, Bespalov is virtually unknown to scholars outside of Russia. He goes altogether unmentioned, for example, in Kiril Tomoff's recent monograph *Creative Union: The Professional Organization of*

Soviet Composers, 1939–53 (Ithaca, N.Y.: Cornell University Press, 2006). Herewith, some details from his official biography:

Born in 1906 near Nizhniy Novgorod, Bespalov worked as a general laborer before joining the Bolshevik Party in 1925. He administered a provincial Youth Communist organization and managed a trade union club before finding work on the local Party committee and school-workers' union. From that local level he ascended to the top position at the regional trade union of Nizhniy Novgorod. For three years Bespalov organized cultural activities for railroad workers, after which, as a reward for his Party service, he was dispatched to Moscow to study Marxist-Leninism at the Red Professorial Institute (Institut Krasnoy Professurï). He witnessed firsthand the devastating effect of the Great Terror in the Soviet capital, which left thousands of Party and government positions vacant. Among these was the chairmanship of the Committee on Arts Affairs of the Russian Federation. In 1938, at the age of thirty-two, he assumed this position. His survival in the post through the Zhdanovite ideological campaigns of the late 1940s made him the obvious choice to succeed Polikarp Lebedev in April 1951 as the chairman of the All-Union Committee on Arts Affairs, the de facto Minister of Culture.

8. RGASPI f. 17, op. 133, d. 368, p. 28.

9. RGASPI f. 17, op. 133, d. 368, p. 30. The other signatory on the document, P. V. Lebedev (1910–?), was an employee of the Central Committee Department of Fiction Literature and the Arts in charge of cadres. From 1955 to 1958 he served as the Deputy Minister of Culture in charge of personnel. Later, he returned to the Central Committee. Such bureaucrat shuffling between the Party and the government was typical of Soviet politics.

10. GARF.

11. Ponomarenko headed the Belorussian Communist Party Central Committee from 1938 to 1947. In 1948 he moved to Moscow to supervise secret police cadres from within the USSR Central Committee headquarters. Then he headed the USSR Ministry for National Supplies. His choice for the position of Minister of Culture constitutes one of the most enigmatic and shameful personnel decisions in the history of Soviet culture. His tenure at the ministry was brief (in the late 1950s he served as the Soviet ambassador to India and Nepal) but destructive. Ponomarenko bears responsibility for removing the eminent Russian conductor Nikolay Golovanov (1891–1953) from the Bolshoy Theater for failing to produce a classic Soviet opera. This dismissal, the third in Golovanov's storm-tossed career, precipitated a fatal heart attack.

12. GARF.

13. Pavel Apostolov (1905–69) was a career military officer. He continued his service even after joining the Central Committee staff and brought it to bear on his work for the USSR Union of Composers. Tomoff somewhat misleadingly describes Apostolov as a "critic" for the USSR Union of Composers (*Creative Union*, 160); it would have been much more accurate to describe him as the musical attaché of the Ministry of Armed Forces.

14. Before joining the USSR Central Committee, Zaven Vartanian (1907–?) headed artistic affairs for the Department of Propaganda and Agitation of the Central Committee of the Armenian Communist Party. In the 1920s, at the outset of his career, he worked as a musician for the First Armenian Infantry Regiment in Yerevan. At the end of his career, in the 1950s and 1960s, he headed musical affairs for the Ministry of Culture.

15. GARF.

16. Regarding the anti-formalist campaign of 1948, Tomoff claims: "At the height of pressure from the Party, professional expertise was needed. In fact, during the brouhaha a Composers' Union member was appointed to the Central Committee apparatus *for the first time*. On 23 April 1948, Boris Iarustovskii [Yarustovsky] was named head of the *music sector of the Central Committee apparatus*." In a footnote, Tomoff clarifies that "Iarustovskii had been a consultant in the apparatus since 1946, *but this was his first full-time appointment*" (*Creative Union*, 151; emphasis added). This claim is incorrect on two fronts: first, Yarustovsky was, as noted, appointed to the Central Committee in 1946, not 1948; and second, other members of the Composers' Union were involved with the Committee before Yarustovsky, notably Georgiy Khubov (1902–81). Tomoff himself lists Khubov as a Central Committee member in 1947, which would appear to contradict his assertion about Yarustovsky's pioneering status in its ranks (103 n. 22).

17. In the 1930s Yarustovsky studied under Valentin Ferman (1895–1948) and his wife Tamara Livanova (1909–86). Both figures held arch-nationalist, rabidly anti-Semitic views.

18. "Vïdayushchiysya sovetskiy kompozitor," *Sovetskoye iskusstvo*, March 18, 1953, p. 4. The other signatories were, in order, Mikhaíl Chulaki, Marian Koval, Vladimir Zakharov, Sergey Vasilenko, Vissarion Shebalin, Nikolay Golovanov, Kirill Molchanov, Georgiy Khubov, Anatoliy Aleksandrov, Galina Ulanova, Yevgeniy Mravinsky, Svyatoslav Richter, David Oistrakh, Samuil Samosud, Leonid Lavrovsky, Alexander Sveshnikov, Vano Muradeli, Kara Karayev, Sergey Balasanyan, and Akop Arutyunyan.

19. D. Kabalevskiy, "Bol'shaya tvorcheskaya zhizn'," *Sovetskoye iskusstvo*, March 18, 1953, p. 4.

20. Unsigned, "Pamyati S. S. Prokof'yeva," *Sovetskaya muzïka* 4 (1953): 117.

21. Lidiya Korneyevna Chukovskaya, *Zapiski ob Anne Akhmatovoy*, 3 vols. (Moscow: Soglasiye, 1997), 2:190.

22. GARF.

23. Ibid.

24. Ibid.

25. Unsigned, "Pamyati vïdayushchegosya sovetskogo kompozitora," *Pravda*, February 12, 1958. Elizabeth Wilson offers two rather conflicting accounts of these events in *Shostakovich: A Life Remembered*, 2nd ed. (Princeton: Princeton University Press, 2006), 350–53. One account, by Oleg Prokofiev, correctly identifies the date of the two ceremonies as February 11, 1958; another, by the musicologist Marina Sabinina, gives the date as March 5, and should be revised accordingly.

26. N. S. Khrushchev, "O kul'te lichnosti i yevo posledstviyakh," *Izvestiya TsK KPSS* 3 (1989): 159.

27. "Ot Komiteta po Leninskim premiyam v oblasti literaturï i iskusstva pri Sovete ministrov SSSR," *Literaturnaya gazeta*, February 28, 1957, p. 3.

28. Svyatoslav Rikhter, "Probovat', dobivat'sya, ubezhdat'," *Literaturnaya gazeta*, March 28, 1957, p. 1.

29. Georgiy Sviridov, "Iskaniya i pobedï," *Literaturnaya gazeta*, March 28, 1957, p. 1.

30. Editorial, "Za ideynost' i narodnost' sovetskoy muzïki," *Izvestiya*, April 6, 1957, p. 1.

31. Russian Government Archive of Contemporary History (Rossiyskiy gosudarstvennïy arkhiv noveyshey istorii, henceforth RGANI).

32. Ibid.

33. See Izraíl Nest'yev, "Spor o Prokof'yeve (zametki o Prokof'yevskoy sessii v Varshave)," *Sovetskaya muzïka* 3 (1960): 160–68.

34. RGASPI f. 17, op. 163, d. 1309, pp. 4–5.

35. RGANI.

36. Nikolay Aleksandrovich Mikhaylov (1906–82) headed the Komsomol from 1938 to 1952, then became the Central Committee secretary in charge of ideology. He was the mastermind behind a vicious anti-Semitic campaign in the final days of Stalin's rule, after which he was demoted and sent as ambassador to Poland. Upon his return to Moscow he headed the Ministry of Culture from 1955 to 1960. He then served as Soviet ambassador to Indonesia until the bloody September 1965 coup against President Sukarno. Mikhaylov headed the Soviet Government Press Committee from 1965 to 1970.

37. Sergey Vasilyevich Kaftanov (1905–78), high-ranking bureaucrat with the Soviet higher education system, 1937–51. He became First Deputy Minister of Culture after Stalin's death. From 1959 to 1963 he headed the Soviet Radio and Television Committee.

38. RGANI.

39. Ibid.

40. Ibid.

41. I. Martïnov, "Nash sovremennik: 70 let so dnya rozhdeniya S. S. Prokof'yeva," *Sovetskaya kul'tura*, April 22, 1961, p. 4.

42. Svyatoslav Prokof'yev, "O moikh roditelyakh: Beseda sïna kompozitora (S. P.) s muzïkovedom Nataliyey Savkinoy (N. S.)," in *Sergey Prokof'yev 1891–1991: Dnevnik, pis'ma, besedï, vospominaniya*, ed. M. E. Tarakanov (Moscow: Sovetskiy kompozitor, 1991), 231–32. An abridged version of the interview not containing this passage was published under the title "Moy otets: stranitsï zhizni"

in *Muzïkal'naya zhizn'* 2 (1991): 19–21. *Muzïkal'naya zhizn'* was published by the USSR Union of Composers, so the omission of passages critical of the Union amounted to censorship. Tarakanov's book, however, was published by the All-USSR Scientific Research Institute for Arts Studies of the Ministry of Culture; in that venue criticism of the Union was welcomed.

43. Tikhon Khrennikov, *Tak eto bïlo* (Moscow: Muzïka, 1994), 174.

44. RGANI.

45. Ibid.

46. In addition to his salary of 500 rubles a month as general secretary of the RSFSR Union of Composers and his USSR Supreme Soviet salary, Shostakovich was entitled to receive numerous monthly financial supplements because of his many awards and honors. The Order of Lenin Award alone entitled him to a stipend of 50 rubles a month plus one free railway ticket a year to any destination in the Soviet Union; by October 1966 he had three Orders of Lenin.

47. Daniel Jaffé, *Sergey Prokofiev* (London: Phaidon, 1998), 213.

48. In the same paragraph Jaffé writes that Lina Prokofiev was released in 1957 (in fact it was 1956); that "she spent several years struggling for her rights as Prokofiev's widow" (her claims were sustained on November 5, 1956, soon after her release); and that "Lina was finally permitted to return to the West in 1972" (in fact it was 1974).

49. Nikolay Nikolayevich Gubenko (b. 1941), a professional actor from the once persecuted and prohibited Moscow Drama Theater directed by Yuriy Lyubimov. He was an RSFSR People's Artist, entered the Communist Party in 1987, and became a member of the Central Committee in 1990. From 1989 to 1991 he served as Minister of Culture, supporting the anti-Gorbachev coup in August 1991. He is currently the head of the Taganka Drama and Comedy Theater.

50. Irina Konstantinovna Arkhipova (b. 1925), a mezzo-soprano, USSR People's Artist, Hero of Socialist Labor, and Lenin Prize laureate, now teaches at the Moscow Conservatory. She was a member of the Communist Party until 1991. From 1956 to 1988 she performed at the Bolshoy Theater, including lead roles in Prokofiev operas.

51. GARF.

52. Ibid.

53. The membership included, but was by no means limited to, the USSR deputy minister of culture, the RSFSR deputy prime minister; the minister in charge of radio and television; the minister responsible for printed media; and the ministers of culture of the RSFSR, Ukrainian SSR, and Belorussian SSR. Also listed were the heads of the Union of Composers for each of the fifteen Soviet republics (including the Baltics, which had begun to secede from the Soviet Union), with detailed description of their honorary titles, medals, and prizes. The Moscow and Leningrad Union of Composers were represented by their heads. Other members included top bureaucrats from the Radio Committee; the directors and chief conductors of the opera houses in Moscow, Leningrad, Kiev, Donetsk, Perm, and Tbilisi; the heads of the Moscow and Leningrad Conservatories and Gnesin Institute; Ivan Martïnov and Yuriy Keldïsh, two veteran Soviet musicologists who had known Prokofiev (though Nestyev, author of the first semi-academic Prokofiev biography, was not included); Ulanova; longtime Bolshoy Theater artistic director Boris Pokrovsky (who staged most of Prokofiev's operas); the Moscow Party Secretary in charge of arts and culture; the chief editors of the official Central Committee publication *Sovetskaya kul'tura* and two specialized musicological publications (the academic journal *Sovetskaya muzïka* and popular journal *Muzïkal'naya zhizn'*), which secured media coverage of the festivities; the heads of two artist agencies (one aimed at the internal market, *Soyuzkontsert*, and the other in charge of foreign trips, *Goskontsert*), which would organize the arrival and sojourn of national and foreign musicians; the head of the State record label *Melodiya*; and the Director of the Glinka State Central Museum of Musical Culture. Svyatoslav Richter and Mstislav Rostropovich, who had premiered several Prokofiev works, were excluded from the list.

54. Shostakovich and Prokofiev participated on the Rimsky-Korsakov Committee. Their status had risen considerably in the three years since Tchaikovsky's centennial. Shostakovich had proved his loyalty by working for the NKVD Song and Dance Ensemble, and Prokofiev by providing music for the Stalin-approved film *Ivan the Terrible* Part I. Both fared well by participating in the USSR National Anthem competition in 1943.

55. The last Soviet budget of 1991 allocated 10.752 billion rubles for "social and cultural measures": 3.198 billion for health; 6 billion for sports; 1.656 billion for all media (including 1.544 billion for radio and television); and 5.431 billion for education. Arts and culture would receive 459 million, less than 5 percent of the national budget. The exchange rate in March 1991 was 25 rubles to $1, which reached 50 rubles by the end of the year. On August 4, 1991, just fifteen days prior to the failed coup, Gorbachev allocated an additional 1.5 billion rubles to keep the KGB running.

56. GARF.

57. Ibid.

58. Apollon Grigor'yev, "Vzglyad na russkuyu literaturu so smerti Pushkina," in *Iskusstvo i nravstvennost'*, ed. B. F. Egorov (Moscow: Sovremennik, 1986), 78.

PART II

ESSAYS

"I Came Too Soon":

Prokofiev's Early Career in America

STEPHEN D. PRESS

After a protracted trip from Moscow through Vladivostok, Tokyo, Honolulu, San Francisco, Vancouver, and Chicago, Sergey Prokofiev arrived in New York City for the first time on September 6, 1918, keen to establish himself as a composer and performer.[1] Ironically, he came too soon: the New York City concert season, which ran from mid-October to March, was delayed due to an epidemic of Spanish influenza. Having originally planned to spend only four months in the United States, Prokofiev was forced to prolong his stay, which would ultimately last almost two years.

The Spanish flu was but one obstacle in his path toward success in America. Ignoring counsel from friends, he resisted embracing American concert life and its demand for aggressive self-promotion while lamenting that his income fell short of his fame. Two weeks after arriving, he complained in his diary: "Every newspaper has an article about me . . . at the same time this famous composer sits with three dollars in his pocket."[2] Money worries plagued Prokofiev in America, especially as he awaited his first recital. One day he dined on stale cookies; on another, coffee and toast. In his diary, he decried his hand-to-mouth existence and fretted about his health. "To fly from the Bolsheviks to die from Spanish flu!" he fumed. "What sarcasm!" (1:739). The disease hit close to home in January 1919, when Vera Schindler, the young Russian wife of a close friend in New York, suddenly died.

Prokofiev planned to introduce himself to America with his Classical Symphony, First Piano Concerto, *Scythian* Suite, and published works for solo piano ranging from the First Sonata, op. 1 (1909), to the Fourth, op. 29 (1917). He also carried the piano score of his unperformed opera *The Gambler*, after Dostoyevsky, and a copy of the inaugural issue of Vsevolod Meyerhold's journal *The Love for Three Oranges* (*Lyubov' k tryom apel'sinam*), featuring Carlo Gozzi's fable of the same name. The latter appealed to Prokofiev with its "mixture of fairy tale, humor, and satire," and during his four-month journey from Russia he began a mental outline of an operatic treatment of it.[3] The opera defines Prokofiev's early career in the United States and thus assumes pride of place in the survey that follows.

The composer tempered disappointment with the realization that not only had he come too early for the 1918–19 season, but that America itself might not be ready for him. At the time of his arrival, new (modernist) music lacked institutional support, critics scorned it, and audiences were under-exposed to it. Such resistance and inexperience spelled trouble for his early career in America, despite attempts by loyal supporters to promote his music. Prokofiev's reputation improved markedly over the years, and by the 1930s and 1940s many of his works enjoyed regular performances and warm ovations. By then, however, he was living in Stalinist Russia, forbid-den, after 1938, from traveling to the West.

After World War I: Unknown in America

Soon after arriving in New York, Prokofiev reunited with Cyrus McCormick Jr., CEO of Chicago-based International Harvester. They had first met at the Winter Palace during the summer of 1917, when McCormick visited Petrograd (St. Petersburg) as a government emissary. The businessman was well connected in American music, serving as a guarantor of the Chicago Opera Association and a member of the board of the Chicago Orchestral Association. He and Prokofiev saw each other on September 9 and 10 while McCormick was en route to Washington, D.C. McCormick promised to introduce Prokofiev to prospective benefactors, but, being immersed in his own affairs, did not follow through. Prokofiev would later turn for help to McCormick's brother Harold.

On September 10, the composer began what he called "aggressive maneu-vers toward New York" (1:732). He visited the apartment of Kurt Schindler, a Berlin-born and trained conductor, composer, and writer whom Prokofiev had met four years earlier in Petrograd. Schindler's wife, Vera (Mikhaylovna Androchevich), was Russian, and Prokofiev quickly found himself at home with the recently married couple. Many of his early New York City contacts stemmed from Schindler. (Other notable acquaintances included the former Ballets Russes dancer Adolph Bolm, employed at the New York Metropolitan Opera, and Russian attorney Alexey Stal, whom Prokofiev knew from his stay in Japan.) Through Schindler, Prokofiev made contact with one of the Schirmers (of publishing fame), who directed him to his first manager, Adams—presumably John T. Adams, president of the Music League of America—who in turn arranged a meeting with the influential conductor of the New York Symphony, Walter Damrosch.[4] Neither Adams nor Damrosch took much interest in Prokofiev, however, compelling him to switch managers in January 1919, when he employed Haensel & Jones.

Adams advised that, to make a mark in New York, Prokofiev needed to appear as a soloist with an orchestra. That opportunity came from the conductor Modest Altschuler, who telephoned to welcome Prokofiev to the city eight days after his arrival. A medal-winning graduate in cello from the Moscow Conservatory, Altschuler emigrated to the United States in 1896; eight years later he founded the Russian Symphony Orchestra, a pickup ensemble of varying size and strength. A populist, he conducted concerts in New York's Carnegie Hall, Hippodrome, and Cooper Union, as well as outdoor stadiums, high school gymnasiums, and town halls across the nation. In 1918, at the end of his ensemble's fall tour, Altschuler led unheralded performances of Prokofiev's Classical Symphony to prepare the musicians for their upcoming rehearsal with the composer. Altshuler surprised Prokofiev at their concerts in December with a performance of the Humoresque Scherzo for Four Bassoons (1912, from the ninth of Ten Pieces for Piano, op. 12), hoping "for the establishment of good relations between the audience and [the composer]" before Prokofiev performed his First Piano Concerto (1:754). Good relations, indeed: the audience demanded an encore of the Scherzo. The reviews, however, disappointed. "After these concerts," Prokofiev recalled, "the press was unanimous in its abuse of both the orchestra and its conductor, with myself thrown in for good measure."[5] Altschuler never became an advocate of Prokofiev, as he had been of Scriabin, since (Scriabin aside) he favored conservative fare. In January, Altschuler tried unsuccessfully to program the *Scythian* Suite in a concert featuring Rachmaninoff as guest soloist, after which he largely dropped Prokofiev from his repertoire.

Far more devoted and famous conductors soon entered the composer's life. Later in the 1920s, his staunchest advocate would be Serge Koussevitzky, who assumed the podium of the Boston Symphony Orchestra in 1924. In 1918, thanks no doubt to McCormick, Prokofiev caught the attention of Frederick Stock, conductor of the Chicago Symphony Orchestra. On September 20, Prokofiev played his music for Stock and secured a booking with the orchestra. It was "the first real victory" of his American tour (1:736). At a pair of concerts on December 6 and 7, the newly appointed assistant conductor, Eric DeLamarter, led performances of the First Piano Concerto.[6] In the years ahead, Prokofiev would appear with the CSO on five occasions, most notably in December 1921 for the premiere of his Third Piano Concerto.

Three days after his audition with Stock, Prokofiev received an invitation from Leopold Stokowski to attend one of his concerts with the Philadelphia

Orchestra—"the second very pleasant event" of his sojourn, the composer reported in his diary (1:737). Stokowski, an advocate of "novelties," proved an even better backer than Stock. Although he reneged on his promise to have Prokofiev conduct the *Scythian* Suite in Philadelphia, he later, in February 1925, led the Philadelphia premiere himself. Stokowski would also conduct the first American performances of the Second Symphony in October 1929 (to some subdued hissing and hastily exiting patrons), the *American* Overture (op. 42a version) in April 1930, a staging of the ballet *Le Pas d'acier* in April 1931, and the Third Symphony in January 1932.

As word of his arrival spread, Prokofiev agreed to an extended interview with Frederick Martens for *Musical America*, published on September 28, 1918, under the splashy headline "Reports Fine Arts Flourishing in 'Red Russia.'" The column header explained: "Serge Prokofiev, Much-Discussed Ultra-Modern Russian Composer, Now in New York, Tells of Conditions Under Bolsheviki—Latter Paying Big Salaries to Noted Artists, Bringing Out New Musical and Dramatic Works in Sumptuous Style, and Regard Artists with Favor." The tone of the article was upbeat and ingratiating. "I am a natural-born traveler," Prokofiev volunteered. "I wanted to see the United States, listen with an open ear and mind to American music, and meet American musicians." American music criticism, however, held little appeal, or so he implied by comparison. "Music criticism—serious, valid critical study and analysis of new compositions—is really on a high level in Russia. Our critics in Petrograd and Moscow are scholars, *savants,* men of distinguished literary and scientific attainment who have specialized in music. . . . They lay stress on the musical, not the personal equation, in their critiques."[7] In his second interview with *Musical America*, appearing in the March 1919 issue under the banner "Criticism a More Serious Art in Russia Than Here, Says Prokofieff," he implicitly requested more elevated music criticism in America.[8]

During the first interview, Prokofiev discussed the musical and political conditions in Russia. He quipped that "the singers' salaries . . . sound better than they really are, for music paper is almost, if not more, valuable than paper currency."[9] He warned that his *Scythian* Suite met the same scandalous reception in Petrograd as had Stravinsky's *Le Sacre du printemps* in Paris, adding, "I'll be curious to know how it will be received here." The interview (or "interrogation," *dopros,* as Prokofiev humorously referred to it in his diary [1:734]) sheds light on his plans to stay "not more than a few months, but long enough, if possible, to introduce some of my own compositions—symphonic and for the piano—to American audiences." He added, "I *have* to write when the spirit moves," thus signaling that he was a composer first, a performer second. His American tour would mark the first time in his career when he needed both talents to earn a living. It took many years, and a drastic change of scene, before he could devote himself solely to composition.

On October 8, a second "Prokofiev 'Showing'" (his words, 1:740) was held at Schindler's East 52nd Street apartment for the "local ichthyosaurs," among them Madame Lanner from the Society of Friends of Music, concert pianist Harold Bauer, and Stokowski. Prokofiev's playing "won them over" (1:740). Lanner promised that her group would sponsor his first recital, but sufficient funds were unavailable. Prokofiev kept in touch with her and as a result met the Swiss-born composer Ernest Bloch. Despite Bloch's successes in the previous season, he was now "going hungry," Prokofiev anxiously recorded in his diary on November 16. Three days later he logged: "Today in my pocket are only thirty cents. In place of breakfast I drank coffee with toast. . . . No one knows about my financial crisis" (1:747). He relied on the introductions and invitations received in those first weeks to assist his search for income.

Martens (*Musical America*) had earlier told Prokofiev that publishers in America worked not for the sake of printing good music but for commerce; he reassured the composer, however, that a publisher for his music would be found. Heeding advice to write short pieces in an accessible style and thereby generate sales, Prokofiev began composing *Tales of an Old Grandmother* (*Skazki o staroy babushki*) on September 26, 1918—the day he received a Steinway piano courtesy of Schirmer. The four movements were finished within a week. When publisher Carl Fischer showed interest in *Tales of an Old Grandmother*, Prokofiev began his Four Pieces for Piano, op. 32, but the publisher balked at his exorbitant price of $1,000.

In another effort to boost his cash flow, Prokofiev on September 30 met with the director of the Aeolian Company, maker of Duo-Art piano rolls. He made a test recording the next day and was offered a paltry $50 to record four works. Prokofiev recalled telling the Duo-Art staff "if you can't pay me accordingly I'd be pleased to play them for free" (1:738). They "didn't catch my irony," Prokofiev added, and "just about rejoiced at the thought of profiting at no expense." His frustration with the day boiled over: "The American soul has the shape of a dollar." Five months later, in February 1919, Prokofiev managed to negotiate a favorable recording contract with Duo-Art for five recordings a year at $250 each.

The visit to Aeolian involved a chance encounter with Cleofante Campanini, director of the Chicago Opera. After a brief discussion, Campanini offered to stage *The Gambler*, which astounded Prokofiev: "So that's how it is! I never thought an unknown opera could be accepted in five minutes!" (1:738). Campanini later commissioned a new opera, *The Love for Three Oranges*, scheduling it for the 1919–20 season. The $1,000 advance eased the composer's financial woes and reshaped his priorities.[10] "It's my business to compose," he recorded in his diary during discussions with Campanini in Chicago, "not to rush about to concerts" (1:753). *The Love for Three Oranges* became the first of several prestigious American commissions. Prokofiev would compose the *Overture on Hebrew Themes* (op. 34 version) for the Zimro Ensemble in 1919, the *American* Overture (op. 42 version) for the Aeolian Company in 1926, the Fourth Symphony for the Boston Symphony Orchestra in 1929, and the First String Quartet for the Library of Congress in 1930.[11]

That was all to come. In the fall of 1918, before income arrived from Duo-Art and the Chicago Opera, Prokofiev was broke. On October 13, he wrote: "To sit without money, not allow myself anything, scrimp, count—it's really sickening" (1:741). Although scheduled to perform at the Fourth Liberty Loan benefit concert (Russian war relief) at Carnegie Hall on October 19 and ten days later at Metropolitan Opera stage designer Boris Anisfeld's exhibit at the Brooklyn Museum, what Prokofiev really needed was a solo recital in Manhattan—preferably soon.[12]

1918: The Manhattan Debut

A sympathetic Russian friend, Ivan Vïshnegradsky, provided $450 to secure Aeolian Hall on November 20. Prokofiev had been warned by Adams that he was too little known to expect a large crowd and reckoned that a full Aeolian Hall (capacity 1,300) would look better than a half-filled Carnegie Hall (2,800). As the concert neared, he feared a measly turnout even in the smaller hall, because no prominent pre-concert advertisement had appeared and his advice to issue invitations had not been heeded. He blamed Adams.

The program, Adams argued, needed to be all-Russian. The first notes Prokofiev ever played in concert in the United States came from his own Toccata, op. 12, for the Brooklyn Museum event. His repertoire this first season included Scriabin etudes, Rachmaninoff preludes, a Tchaikovsky sonata, and excerpts from Musorgsky's *Pictures at an Exhibition*.[13] Prokofiev opened his first recital with his Four Etudes, op. 2, and continued with the Second Sonata; after shorter works by Rachmaninoff, Scriabin, and him-self, he concluded with the *Suggestion diabolique* (*Navazhdeniye*) from Four Pieces, op. 4. On his second and third programs at Aeolian Hall, he began with the Fourth Sonata and *Visions fugitives* (on February 17) and the First Sonata and three gavottes (on March 3). At a Modern Music Society recital on January 7, he played his Second and Fourth Sonatas back-to-back.

Just before his debut, Rachmaninoff arrived unexpectedly. Although Prokofiev would come to resent Rachmaninoff's popularity and coveted his "wild success . . . raking in tens of thousands of dollars" (1:759), he welcomed his compatriot warmly amid the hubbub and revelry of Armistice Day. He treated Rachmaninoff with near-fawning respect, even though the older artist was not interested in "the thoughts of the young" and had derided Prokofiev's music for years (1:760). Dutifully preparing the works of his rival, Prokofiev neglected to invite him to the concert. Over lunch the next day, he admitted being intimidated and expressed relief that Rachmaninoff had not attended.

He recalled the event as a triumph. A capacity audience greeted him with an ovation. He had one mishap in the first piece when the tight action of his Steinway prevented a note from sounding, necessitating a skip ahead and some careful playing. He thought the Allegro of his Second Sonata was insufficiently expressive but sensed the audience's enthusiasm during the Scherzo and Finale. He took pride in his performance of Rachmaninoff's pieces, less so Scriabin's. Encores brought him back ten times during the program breaks and eight more times at the end. Afterward the audience crowded near the stage, applauding with greater enthusiasm than he had ever received in Petrograd, while acquaintances gathered in a small room offstage to offer their congratulations. "The success," Prokofiev enthused, "surpassed all expectation" (1:748).

The eleven reviews he read were mixed, however, prompting him to conclude that critics had to write something—even nonsense—to sound smart. "Even the unfavorable comment was served up in a somewhat sensational manner," he grumbled. "The best of them [Richard Aldrich of the *New York Times*] maintained that the finale of the Second Sonata made him think of a herd of mammoths charging across an Asiatic plateau. Of my playing they said that it had too little gradation, but that I had 'steel fingers, steel wrists, steel biceps and triceps.'"[14] Aldrich emphasized Prokofiev's virility at the keyboard and found his music full of "tremendous rhythmic urge" but "generally insipid" lyrical themes. Apparently it was all too much for him: "The danger in all this highly spiced music is manifest: it soon exhausts our facility of attention." Aldrich labeled Prokofiev a musical anarchist in the style of Leo Ornstein (modernist par excellence) and recoiled at "the astounding disharmonies gentle Serge extorted from his suffering pianoforte; the young man's style is orchestral, and the instruments of percussion rule in his Scythian drama." Aldrich acknowledged the "dynamic applause" from "a parterre of pianists," but concluded ambivalently. "There can be no doubt of his instant success. Whether he will last—Ah! New music for new ears. Serge Prokofieff is very startling."[15]

Other recitals ensued in January, February, and March 1919. By the end of the season Prokofiev's New York reviews were more positive. Biting comments and clever wordplay accompanied tentative or grudging recognition of his novelties and the audience's approval of them. In his review of Prokofiev's first recital, "A. H." of *Musical America* complained that in the first movement of the Second Sonata the "melody . . . is abruptly choked off and smothered under a storm of mud and steel-riveted rhythm." But then the critic added: "Immersed in the dregs of Prokofiev's trans-modernism, however, there are many vital elements. He has imagination, an astounding rhythmic sense, and he has, we are led to suspect, a certain melodic gift."[16] James Gibbons Huneker's review in the *New York Times* of the composer's First Piano Concerto (premiered at a Russian Symphony Orchestra concert in December) conformed to his acidic, curmudgeonly style. He nonetheless made some keen observations:

> The first piano concerto . . . might fairly be called an Etude in Rhythms. . . . The first descending figure—it is hardly a theme—is persistently affirmed in various nontonalities by the orchestra till the slow mood, the piano all the while shrieking, groaning, howling, fighting back, and in several instances it seemed to rear and bite the hand that chastised it. . . . But all tremendously exciting because of the verve of the pianist, and his extraordinary gift in rhythms. . . . He may be the Cossack Chopin for the next generation—this tall, calm young man. . . . The audience, a large and distinguished one, was too stunned to analyze its feelings. It was completely overcome, and when the rebound ensued, Prokofieff had scored another success.[17]

The next day, after the second concert with the Russian Symphony Orchestra, Huneker's tone softened:

> Mr. Prokofieff is a man of whims. His Piano Sonata, opus 3, is whimsical, with its saltarello rhythm and its abrupt harmonic surprises. It does not measure up in power—satanic power—to the piano concerto, which we hope to hear again. The group of little piano pieces was enjoyable, being piquant, full of the unexpected, and epigrammatic. The composer has evidently many strings to his bow, a mastery of old forms not being the most inconspicuous. . . . The audience was interested and enthusiastic.[18]

The reviews contained plenty of dross, causing Prokofiev to denounce the "asinine" incomprehension of his art (1:754). His relentless ostinati and tonally ambiguous melodic fragments defied the tuneful, harmonically transparent idioms preferred by the critics. Yet, surprisingly, Herbert F. Peyser damned the composer after his February recital for failing to uphold modernist standards:

The only trouble is that Prokofieff's bark is vastly worse than his bite
and his futurism is of the nursery variety. . . . In the particular works
exposed on Monday [the Fourth Piano Sonata and *Visions fugitives*]
he clings almost constantly to Schumann's coattails. The sonata . . .
might have been written by the composer of the "Carnival" during
his sojourn in the asylum at Bonn. The "Fugitive Visions" as well.
Fortunately they were fugitive. . . . Futurism as Ornstein and Schönberg
have exemplified the term, it was not. Merely like old familiar faces
distorted by the dreams of an uneasy night consequent upon a late
repast of lobster, truffles, champagne and kindred delicacies.[19]

Huneker countered Peyser by describing the public appeal of the February
recital. The composer "was still handing encores across to an enthusiastic
audience when we left. Serge Prokofieff is quite in the mode this season.
Luckily, he is a modest artist, else he might be spoiled."[20] Huneker pre-
sciently added: "What ballet music this young man could write!"

Prokofiev's final recital of the season, on March 30, 1919, elicited a rave
from A. Walter Kramer, who pointedly rejected the "ultra-modern" label
that Martens, among others, had applied to the composer. "Here is a musician who is positively thrilling as pianist and composer. He interested and
fascinated us—and, above all, he revealed a distinct personality that once
met cannot be forgotten. . . . There is a healthy vitality in his playing, a massive and well-nigh infallible technique and much color. . . . Of course, there
were encores at the close, when the many Prokofieff 'fans' gave him a royal
ovation. He merited every bit of it."[21] Harriette Brower, Kramer's colleague at *Musical America*, would affirm a year later that "Prokofieff . . .
performs his own music with astonishing virtuosity. The music does not sound
[as] bizarre as last season, when it assailed our ears for the first time. We
are growing accustomed to it, and other pianists are taking it up."[22]

Prokofiev was on a roll. Through the executive director of Steinway he
met Otto Kahn, president of the board of directors of the Metropolitan
Opera. Kahn hoped to stage *The Gambler* in New York, but could not convince the conservative, Italophile director, Giulio Gatti-Casazza (known as
Gatti), to produce it. Over lunch on March 26, Kahn asked Prokofiev to
outline the plot of the opera in French in an effort to capture Gatti's interest. Prokofiev imagined what a "brilliant victory" it would be if *The Gambler*
were staged at the Met while *Three Oranges* played in Chicago (2:28). The
matter went unresolved in 1919, but the possibility of a Prokofiev opera
in New York had at least been proposed. Negotiations with the Met would
resume in early 1920 during an impasse with the Chicago Opera.

In early April, the composer was felled by grave, life-threatening illness:
scarlet fever and diphtheria coupled with a throat abscess that almost

choked him to death. His Chicago engagements were postponed until the following fall and work on *Three Oranges* delayed. Upon convalescing, he divided his attention in the summer of 1919 between orchestrating the opera and enjoying the company of young ladies—one of whom, Carolina (Lina) Codina, would become his first wife in 1923. His planned four months in America had extended to almost a year. Although he kept abreast of possible performance opportunities in England and France, Prokofiev had no plans to leave. After all, the premiere of one of his operas was close at hand— or so he thought.

1918–19: Negotiations in Chicago

In the fall of 1918, Prokofiev looked ahead to concerts with the Chicago Symphony Orchestra and the promised meeting with Campanini to discuss the production of *The Gambler.* On the day he departed for Chicago, November 30, he played through the piano score and, to his dismay, found it "horrible" with "thousands of mistakes" (1:750). Worse, the vocal part needed major revision. He pondered the task of translating the libretto from Russian into French and English and the challenge of retrieving the full score from Russia. Succeeding in America, he deduced, would require writing a different opera, an action-driven farce in a more accessible style. The final minutes of *Three Oranges* turned out very "American" indeed, recalling the chase scenes that close Charlie Chaplin films.

On December 3, Prokofiev and the Russian consul general in Chicago, Anton Volkov, went to the Auditorium Theater to hear Campanini conduct *William Tell.* Prokofiev liked the décor in the hall, but did not care for that in the opera. After the performance, Campanini asked Prokofiev to call on him the next day with the score of *The Gambler.* The reality of the situation set in; as the composer recorded in his diary, "I didn't believe him before, but now, when I saw this distinct, packed theater, it seemed like quite an interesting place to stage an opera" (1:751–52).

Prokofiev played through *The Gambler* in advance of the meeting and tried to anticipate Campanini's reaction to it. Fearing the worst, he resolved to open the discussion with a description of *Three Oranges.* But Campanini showed more interest in the Russian drama than the Italian farce. (He especially liked the episode with the heroine Polina's grandmother crying out "Bravo, bravo, maestro!" [1:752]) They considered both operas but decided to postpone a final choice until after Prokofiev's concerts with the Chicago Symphony. The meeting boosted Prokofiev's spirits. He returned to his hotel certain he could write *Three Oranges* quickly and readily. The next morning, Campanini decided to produce *Three Oranges,* since *The Gambler* demanded forces (skilled Russian singers) that he did not have at his disposal.

Negotiations became adversarial as the savvy Chicago Opera brass sought to outmaneuver the composer. Prokofiev began by asking for 10 percent of the ticket sales and a guarantee of ten performances. Campanini demurred, protesting that typical earnings ranged from $2,000 to $9,000. Prokofiev asked for $6,000; Campanini countered with $4,000, then $5,000, where they finally settled. It was to be paid in installments: $1,000 at the signing of the contract, $2,000 for the presentation of the piano score, and $2,000 for the orchestral score. Campanini still needed approval from his financiers, but they settled on an October 1 deadline for the finished opera. Prokofiev departed briefly for New York and a recital in Ann Arbor, Michigan, before returning to Chicago on December 15 to confront Campanini's brusque declaration that he could pay only $3,000 for a world premiere. Prokofiev argued that the sum would hardly compensate for eight months of labor. He appealed to McCormick for help, to no avail.

Campanini came back two days later with $4,000 as the final offer, an amount Prokofiev accepted for one season with five performances. He gave the company the right to renew the contract for five more performances the following season at $200 each—a low fee that brought the grand total back to $5,000. Campanini promised a formal contract and a check for $1,000 "within days" (1:756). These arrived only on January 31, 1919, with niggling changes that caused further mistrust.

Prokofiev worked steadily on the libretto from mid-December and began composing the music on Christmas Day, noting that he had not "worked at such pace for a long time" (1:757). By New Year's Eve he had run out of libretto. Playing through what he had composed, he realized that his text-setting was too prolix. "Still nothing has happened in the plot and already twelve minutes have gone by! I have to compress and compress, otherwise . . . my famous laconism threatens to turn into endless chatter" (1:758). By January 2, he had finished the libretto of Act 1, acknowledging that his ending was "terribly abbreviated, but I don't think I'm mistaken in calculating that with the music and the décor it will turn out well" (2:13). The next day he completed the music of Act 1. "If I continue like this, then the opera will be prepared on the twentieth of February" (2:13). A few days later he wrote the libretto for Act 2 in one hour "without pausing for breath" (2:16). On February 14, Stal and his wife Vera Janacopulos offered to translate the libretto into French; Prokofiev offered $300 for the task. Although Campanini wanted *Three Oranges* to be sung in French (or Italian) at the premiere, Prokofiev felt that "it could just as easily have been translated into English as French."[23] He insisted that Stal and Janacopulos's text match the vocal lines and added extra notes as needed. The rhythmic patterns had been devised for the original Russian text, obliging Prokofiev to alter the translation, which was completed in August.

He began Act 3 in March at a slower pace, reaching the start of scene 2 (just before rehearsal number 313) by April, when he took ill. He resumed work in early June, remarking that "the third scene of the third act was easily composed" (2:32). By July 5, Anisfeld had signed the contract to design the décor of *Three Oranges*, and Bolm was on board to create the choreography. That day Prokofiev played Acts 1 to 3 for them and discussed production details. Although the run-through "tormented him to death," he reveled in his characters and plot coming to life (2:36). By the end of the month he was producing five to six pages of orchestration a day. September found him immersed in the scoring of Act 4. At 2 p.m. on the day of the deadline—October 1—Prokofiev turned out the last page, boasting how he had "calculated" everything "accurately" (2:44).

Three Oranges received little notice in press accounts of the upcoming Chicago opera season. It was, however, mentioned in the November 1 issue of *Musical America*, with a picture of the composer adorning the caption "Russian Composer-Pianist Whose Performances and Compositions Have Attracted Attention for Their Striking Originality."[24] Portentously, the quarter-page article failed to list a date for the premiere. A later issue included photographs of Prokofiev, Campanini, composer Italo Montemezzi (whose *La nave* was slated to open the Chicago Opera season), and composer-conductor Gino Marinuzzi (whose *Jacquerie* was eagerly anticipated) under the banner "Super-Season Awaits Musical Chicago."[25] In a November 1919 interview for *Musical America*, an ailing Campanini described the "novelties" of the season: "Prokofieff, the composer of 'The Love of Three Oranges,' is quite well known, and I can only add that his enthusiasm is infectious."[26] The staff conductor Louis Hasselmans and vocal coach Alexander Smallens were left to grapple with the composer's thorny music. It soon became clear that insufficient time had been allocated for the rehearsals. With Prokofiev in New York and Campanini rapidly nearing the end of his life, the 1919–20 premiere of *Three Oranges* was doomed.[27]

On November 27, Prokofiev heard rumors that his opera would be delayed owing to the late arrival of the French singers. On December 6, Bolm informed him by telegram that *Three Oranges* had been altogether dropped from the season. Bolm signed off: "I am disgusted" (2:56). Two days later a letter arrived from business comptroller Herbert M. Johnson confirming the opera's postponement for a year. Prokofiev consulted an attorney, who encouraged him to press for damages—quietly, since it would be difficult to claim would-be losses. With his checking account down to $80 and the "whole season gone to the devil" (2:58), Prokofiev brazenly demanded $15,000: $10,000 in compensation and $5,000 for a new production contract.[28]

On December 28, he arrived in Chicago for his third recital that season, and over the next two weeks failed repeatedly in his negotiations with Chicago Opera executives, primarily Johnson and Max Pam.[29] At their first meeting on December 29, Johnson reddened when Prokofiev made his demand. The price was too high, Johnson protested, and would thwart the production of the opera altogether. Prokofiev turned to Harold McCormick, who advised him to request only the $2,500 due to him for the season. But the composer dug in. The climax of the episode came at a two-and-a-half-hour meeting with Johnson and Pam on January 12. Pam, according to Prokofiev, "seethed," declaring that *Three Oranges* would be performed irrespective of the composer (2:70). Defeated, Prokofiev returned to New York, there resuming his courtship of his future wife Lina and attending the premiere of the *Overture on Hebrew Themes*.

Meantime, Campanini had succumbed to pneumonia. According to the *Herald and Examiner*, he died (on December 19) without naming his successor at the Chicago Opera.[30] But the ambitious and acclaimed Marinuzzi was soon appointed conductor, with Johnson assuming administrative duties. Marinuzzi's *Jacquerie*, like Prokofiev's *Three Oranges*, had been postponed to the fall, when they would compete for precious rehearsal time. Not surprisingly, only the former would reach the stage. By then Marinuzzi had been elevated to the position of artistic director and Johnson executive director.

While fretting over the fate of *Three Oranges*, Prokofiev began another opera, *The Fiery Angel* (*Ognennïy angel*), based on Russian Symbolist Valeriy Bryusov's novel set in sixteenth-century Cologne. It would become a frustrating labor of love (and hate), consuming much of the next decade. Prokofiev worked on the libretto during a tour to Montreal, Quebec City, and Buffalo. On January 22, 1920, he received an encouraging letter from Kahn hinting at the possibility of a production at the Met, and on February 9, Gatti finally had the meeting with Prokofiev that the composer's illness had prevented the previous spring. Unfortunately, the supportive Kahn had left for Europe, rendering the meeting unproductive. Prokofiev informed Gatti that he had three operas to pitch. Gatti reduced the field quickly, declining to discuss *Three Oranges* because it was tied to the Chicago Opera and dismissing *The Fiery Angel* as unfamiliar and unfinished. Even so, Gatti agreed to listen to the music of the two scores, promising Prokofiev a longer audience once the Met had finished its run of *Parsifal*.

That second meeting came on April 1 in New York—late to be planning the coming season. Prokofiev suspected it would be futile but nonetheless prepared *Three Oranges*. Before the meeting he also ran through *The Gambler*, again noticing its flaws. He recalled the events in his diary:

Gatti arranged a proper hearing, involving him and six conductors, though in essence it was just for show. Gatti and Bodansky [chief conductor of the German repertoire] made the decisions, and the others sat quietly. I played the scene with the Prince [Act 2, scene 1 of *Three Oranges*], having narrated it beforehand, and excerpts from *The Fiery Angel*, which made, I felt, an unfavorable impression. Gatti found it very difficult and unidiomatic for the voice. If it had been a one-act opera, they might have risked it, but five acts. . . . In the end, Gatti said that they were unable to give an immediate answer to such a serious matter. But this was tantamount to a refusal. I'm annoyed at myself, and at the Metropolitan—a good organization, but unable to stage a real opera and choking on all sorts of nonsense. For me it's highly unpleasant and a personal financial failure, so it was very nice to win $61 playing bridge in the evening (2:89).

Prokofiev continued work on *The Fiery Angel*, but by April 13 his thoughts had turned to Europe and his enthusiasm for it waned. As he wrapped up his twenty-month stay in America, Prokofiev visited Haensel & Jones and learned that he had received two concert invitations for the fall. Displeased with the terms, he lamented that he was leaving with only $800 in his pocket. Haensel & Jones offered to cable money in the summer.

On April 17, Prokofiev played through the score for Marinuzzi. Despite Marinuzzi's discouraging remarks—"it was even more difficult than he'd expected"—and his call for cuts in the second and third acts, Prokofiev remained blind to the trouble ahead (2:93). On April 27, he sailed from New York to France, his first time there since the spring of 1915. He enjoyed a tranquil summer in a spacious rented villa at Mantes-sur-Seine northwest of Paris, revising the ballet *Chout* to Diaghilev's dictates and relaxing in the company of his mother and his fiancée.

The last word from the Chicago Opera before he departed America had been unpleasant. Prokofiev received a letter from the company explaining that $100,000 had already been lost on *Three Oranges* and requesting that he quickly take legal action, "if so inclined," to spare further expense (2:92). In August, Prokofiev met with the Chicago Opera executive director Johnson, who was in Europe arranging singers' contracts. Tempers had cooled. Prokofiev offered *Three Oranges* for $6,000, which Johnson considered reasonable, though he could make no promises until he was back in Chicago. The composer returned to America hopeful.

1920–21: An Unexpected Cancellation

Prokofiev boarded the *Savoie* on October 16, 1920, bound for New York, anticipating the Chicago premiere of his opera. Bad omens failed to dampen his spirits: the crossing was rough; two passengers died; his cabinmate was sick the entire time; and one of his suitcases was stolen from his cabin. In New York, Haensel & Jones informed him that no new concerts had been booked. Johnson, moreover, reported that the Chicago Opera executives could not pay him $6,000 but worried that he would not take less.

Worse awaited him in Chicago. Arriving on October 31, Prokofiev wrote to Johnson hoping to settle their disagreement "peacefully" (2:122). The executive director responded on November 2, explaining that two weeks earlier a telegram had been sent to the composer in France with news that *Three Oranges* had been canceled permanently. "My eyes darkened as I was reading," Prokofiev despaired. "I slept poorly. I was frustrated and felt empty without the opera. . . . This is very bad. . . . Now there is nothing positive to look forward to and I have $3 in my pocket" (2:122). He realized that, for the time being, he would have to make it on concerts alone.

Why *Three Oranges* was canceled remains unclear. Likely not for financial reasons: the Chicago Opera had already spent an enormous sum on the production, and Anisfeld's pricey designs realized. Perhaps rehearsal time ran short. Although Marinuzzi and many singers were familiar with the score, the company toured until October 30 and was hard-pressed to prepare new works. Prokofiev held Marinuzzi blameless and even praised his opera *Jacquerie* (Prokofiev rarely complimented music by others). "It was better than I thought," he remarked after a rehearsal, "as an opera it was very nicely done and effective with almost no banality" (2:126). Henri Morin, conductor of French repertoire at the Chicago Opera, assured the composer that Marinuzzi was not involved and that the decision regarding *Three Oranges* had surprised them both.

Whatever the practicalities, personal tensions doubtless contributed to the cancellation. Composer John Alden Carpenter, whose ballet *Birthday of the Infanta* had been premiered by the Chicago Opera to great acclaim, spoke with Johnson and reported back to Prokofiev that the composer had "a narrow understanding of opera company pride." Prokofiev's staunch demand for $15,000 must have left a lingering bitterness. "Ah, he is stubborn quite like we will not allow," Johnson added of the composer (2:124).

Having decided that Pam was in fact the perpetrator, an acquaintance of Carpenter's wife (the writer Juliet Grant, Princess Cantacuzene) offered to intercede on Prokofiev's behalf. She asked him to write a detailed statement for presentation to the executives at lunch on November 25 along with her endorsement. Shortly before departing Chicago, he typed a four-page memorandum:

Memorandum
pertaining to the production
of the opera
"The Love for the Three Oranges"

In December, 1918, Maestro Campanini honored me by commissioning me to compose the opera "The Love for the Three Oranges." It seemed to me that the opportunity to compose an opera and to have it immediately produced by such a great company as the Chicago Opera Association was so alluring that I started work at once. Inasmuch as I was only given nine months to compose this opera, consisting of four acts and a prologue, I gave up concert work and devoted my entire time to this composition.

According to the contract, I was to receive a remuneration of $4,000, which was adequate to defray my expenses while working on this composition. I therefore did not need to worry about any possible income from concerts, and could give my undivided attention to this work. While composing this opera, I developed scarlet fever, diphtheria, and had to undergo an operation, but I continued my work, even in the hospital, and completed the opera at the time specified in the contract, i.e., October 1, 1919, and received for it $4,000.

The Chicago Opera Association ordered splendid scenery for my opera and about two hundred new costumes which were produced by the Russian artist Boris Anisfeld and for which about $80,000 were expended. The scenery which Anisfeld painted for the Metropolitan Opera House created a great sensation at the time, but he believes that the scenery for "The Love for the Three Oranges" is the best he has ever produced.

Maestro Campanini died in December 1919, and the Chicago Opera Association then informed me that the production of my opera would be postponed until the following season. This was a real catastrophe for me, for the reason that in the first place, I had neglected my concert tour while composing the opera, and in the second place the $4000, which I received in accordance with the terms of the contract, had already been spent for my living expenses during the above-mentioned time. I was therefore left without any possible means of earning a livelihood.

Furthermore, two other opera houses, the Covent Garden, through Dr. Albert Coates, and the Metropolitan, through Dr. Otto Kahn, were interested in "The Love for the Three Oranges" as well as in my other opera "The Gambler" and I was in correspondence with both gentlemen relative thereto. After the Chicago Association failed to produce my opera, the doors of the two aforementioned opera houses were also closed to me.

During a conference, I called the attention of Mr. Max Pam to the paragraph in my contract with the Chicago Opera Association, which reads as follows: "Your opera is to be produced by the Chicago Opera Association during the season of 1919–20."

Therefore, by not producing my opera in 1919–20, the Association broke the contract and if they wished to produce my opera after a delay of an entire year, I was entitled to compensation for the season during which I was deprived of earning a maintenance, through no fault of my own.

Mr. Pam inquired as to what my terms were. Inasmuch as I had lost one or two opera contracts, as well as a whole concert season, I felt that the sum of $10,000 would be reasonable. I admit it was rather difficult to arrive at a more or less exact amount of compensation to which I felt entitled, and I would have been willing to accept another fairly proportioned sum, but I could not, under any circumstances, accept the counter-offer of Mr. Pam who offered me $2,000, not as compensation, but as royalty for the following season. Although the aforementioned conversation took place in the office of the Chicago Opera Association, Mr. Max Pam, in the presence of Mr. Johnson, was very rude, raising his voice, and pounding on the table with his hands. He said that if I would not consent to have my opera produced during the following season, it would be produced without such, and if I felt dissatisfied, I could go to court.

After this conversation, I consulted my attorney, who explained to me that should the Association attempt to produce "The Love for the Three Oranges," without my consent, I could prevent them from doing so by taking out an injunction against them.

I spent the summer of 1920 in France and Mr. Johnson, while in Paris, asked me to have a conference with him. He proposed better terms, offering me $2,500 for the first five performances and $250 for each additional performance, which would make a total of about $3,000 instead of $2,000. I consented to reduce my figure to $6,000, explaining to Mr. Johnson that out of this amount I would have to pay nearly $4,000 to cover newspaper advertisements, to pay my concert manager, and my friends who maintained me during that difficult year. Until I have made a settlement with the Chicago Opera Association they would not force me to pay these sums. But as soon as an agreement is signed by me, I would be bound to pay; that is why I cannot accept his proposition of $3,000. Mr. Johnson answered that he did not believe the Association would pay me $6,000. Nevertheless, when we parted he said that he considered the state of affairs "perfectly satisfactory."

Later, in the beginning of October, Mr. Diaghilev, Director of the Russian Ballet, paid me a certain sum for the ballet which I was composing for him, and this made it possible for me to again decrease my terms, i.e. from $6,000 to $4,000. Thereupon I came to America feeling confident that everything would be settled to our mutual satisfaction.

Great was my surprise when upon my arrival in Chicago, on November 1, I was notified by Mr. Johnson that "The Love for the Three Oranges" will not be produced at all. He had cabled me to that effect in France but I sailed for America before the cable reached me. I reiterated that my terms were only $4,000, but he stated that everything is ended now. I asked Mr. Johnson whether he would use the scenery and costumes for some other opera. His reply was negative.

About ten days later my concert manager Mr. Haensel informed him that owing to some new contract engagements, I could accept the terms he made to me in Paris. Mr. Johnson replied that it is now too late, my opera requiring too many rehearsals for which they have insufficient time.

Personally, I do not see how any time has been lost; up to November 1, the opera troupe was making a tour of other cities and since then has been rehearsing "Jacquerie." The singers in the cast of my opera have learned their parts by heart, and expressed their surprise to me about losing so much time for naught. Maestro Marinuzzi has also prepared the score.

I feel very bitter and do not understand the reasons which induced the Chicago Opera Association to ruin my career in America, and at the same time to condemn to fire and destruction the $80,000 already spent on my opera.

(signed Serge Prokofieff)[31]

The memorandum reveals that Prokofiev was not above bending the truth to bolster his case and would have been well served by a third party in negotiations. As Smallens reminded him, "the most unpleasant element of theater life are the authors, for they see nothing besides their opera, and the remaining thirty-five [performers] can just go to hell" (2:174).

Defeated once again by Johnson and Pam, Prokofiev left Chicago to give a recital in Appleton, Wisconsin, thereafter traveling to the West Coast. He spent December and most of January in California, playing before small audiences and composing *Five Songs Without Words*, op. 35 (later revised for violin and piano), for the Russian soprano Nina Koshets. On January 15, 1921, he heard that Mary Garden had been appointed general director of the Chicago Opera. Returning to Chicago on January 20, Prokofiev learned more from the consul general Volkov, conductor Morin, supporter Nikolay Kucheryavïy, and a new acquaintance, Chicago insurance agent and Prokofiev aficionado Ephraim Gottlieb, compiling their accounts in his diary:

> The whole incident transpired because of the Italian music that through Marinuzzi's and Johnson's efforts crowded everything else out this year. This summoned sharp attacks from other sides. . . . Marinuzzi, both frustrated and exhausted, was the first to submit his resignation as artistic director. He thought that they would beg him [to stay] and this made him stronger, but at that time [actually one week later] Mary Garden . . . was designated director with unlimited powers; they simply suggested that Johnson retire, which he did with great regret. At present Garden is very strong, imperious, and she intends to bring all kinds of reforms to the Opera (2:146).

Garden's appointment was championed by Mrs. McCormick and engineered by her husband. Having promised to underwrite deficits beyond the guarantors' pledges for one more year, the McCormicks resolved to go out "in a blaze of glory" and, facing declining sales, "believed it would take someone with Mary's flamboyance and understanding of the public to restore the box office to its normal level."[32] Garden gained complete control over the company's artistic and financial affairs. She named her former Manhattan Opera colleague Jacques Coini stage director and put conductor Giorgio Polacco in charge of musical affairs. George M. Spangler assumed the unenviable role of business manager for a profligate boss. "Thrift had never been one of Mary Garden's virtues," Ronald Davis comments in his chronicle of opera in Chicago. "She insisted that Harold McCormick had told her the deficit for the coming season could run as high as $600,000. Therefore, when Spangler balked at an expense, Garden would turn to him and ask 'Have we reached the six hundred thousand dollar mark yet?'. . . By fall Mme. Directa had signed up the largest array of artists in Chicago's operatic history, promising them fees that were more than generous. . . . There were just about twice as many singers in each category as the company actually needed or would be able to use."[33] Garden spent freely; one report claimed the company's deficit totaled $1.1 million.[34] Unsurprisingly, her tenure ended after the 1921–22 season.

Prokofiev met with "Mme. Directa" in New York in late January or early February 1921:

I briefly told her the story of the commission and refusal, having introduced *Three Oranges* as Campanini's child, repressed by Pam and Johnson after his death and waiting for rehabilitation in the person of Mary Garden. Since she adored Campanini and hated Pam, she said, without even waiting to get to know my opera, that it would be performed with all the required number of rehearsals, with the singers I needed, not otherwise, and under my personal control and observation. She made an amazing impression on me: to this point I'd been dealing with tradesmen, now I was speaking with a true artist. I recounted the plot and her eyes burned with delight, and from the music I played just the "March," illustrating [its part in] the story. "Oh, how cute," she cried. On the business front . . . I said that I would like a guarantee of eight performances at $500 each and she answered "Oh, of course!" I felt that if instead of $4,000 I had asked for $8,000 she would have said, "Oh, of course" just as sweetly. In actual fact I requested only what was fair, since in my figures I was referring to my contract with Campanini, and Mary was doing everything that Campanini did (2:148).

"Two miracles were completed in three days" when Koshets auditioned and won the role of Fata Morgana (2:148). With this turnaround, Prokofiev quit America for Europe in February 1921, spending the spring and summer at his rental home on the Brittany coast. There he orchestrated *Chout* before attending rehearsals in Monte Carlo. On May 17, he conducted the ballet's premiere by the Ballets Russes in Paris and on June 8, in London. He also worked on *The Fiery Angel* and completed the Third Piano Concerto for its Chicago premiere.

In October 1921, Prokofiev returned to the United States on the *Aquitaine* with Garden and Polacco among his fellow passengers. On ship the composer "added to his fame" by placing first in a chess tournament involving "several skilled players."[35] Landing in New York on October 21, he found himself with little to do and moved quickly on to Chicago.

1921–22: Premieres in Chicago

Prokofiev arrived in Chicago on October 29, eagerly awaiting the premieres of his Third Piano Concerto and *Three Oranges*. The opera was in much better shape than before, and for once there was plenty of publicity. A promotional article in the November 19 issue of *Musical America* offered the first full description. Characterized as a "bristling satire," *Three Oranges* was reported to have aroused "more curiosity" than "any other operatic work for some time. Frequent postponements of the world premiere have only served to heighten this curiosity."[36] Yet author Emil Raymond perhaps unknowingly provided the very reasons it would fail to achieve unqualified success:

> Prokofieff directs keen shafts at the straight-laced purveyors of opera. He lays no claim to be a classicist. His accepted medium is in modern vein; yet his newest work takes its fling at modernism as well as at classicism, and in his treatment of the romanticists, he out-Herods Herod . . . his impudence stops at nothing; by nonsense heaped on nonsense he strips grand opera of its glamour and makes it no longer grand. He makes opera safe for democracy, and that is the justification of all great burlesque—to humanize the object of its ridicule. "The Love for Three Oranges" is great burlesque.[37]

He also noted the difficulties *Three Oranges* endured before reaching the stage, perhaps giving pause to conservative critics and audiences:

> It is laughable enough, this opera that Mary Garden has had the temerity to definitely schedule for this session. Weighty minds had contemplated the matter and had demurred. Campanini had postponed it; Johnson had relegated it to the store-house. But Miss Garden has a sense of humor; and maybe she, too, had smiled in her sleeve at swans and brimstone and flashing daggers on the stage. It is the age of airplanes, and wireless, and unnatural phenomena; why not, then, a frank discussion of a *citrous amour*?[38]

Still, he reassured readers that "the music is vivacious and somewhat blatant in parts, but powerful in the main and pleasing. . . . Dissonances are not as frequent as might be expected."[39]

By the end of October, five orchestra rehearsals had been completed under Smallens, who thought he was to conduct the premiere. Prokofiev intended to conduct it himself, however, and resolved the situation diplomatically. The composer dove into preparations, leaving Chicago only twice for concerts (in Cleveland on November 12 and Pittsburgh on November 18) and fearing while away that the opera was "frozen" (2:175). Polacco praised his efficient use of rehearsal time and conducting technique. Tensions, however, repeatedly arose between Prokofiev and Coini. At the third stage rehearsal on December 9, the stage director decided it would be more polite for the Prince to sneeze in Act 2, scene 1, instead of spitting, per the libretto. A twenty-minute shouting match ensued and ended only when Prokofiev conceded. On December 15, Coini complained about "too much music" in the final scene, carping that it would "destroy the whole performance" (2:185). Prokofiev admitted that the wings were too shallow to accommodate the madcap chase (according to the stage directions, the guards, Pantalon, Truffaldino, the Master of Ceremonies, and the courtiers pursue Smeraldina, Clarissa, and Leandro; all run off in an unspecified direction, then downstage, to the wings stage left, reemerging from the back, and disappearing stage right). There would be other flare-ups, which Garden occasionally stepped in to quell.

While in Chicago, Prokofiev attended numerous recitals and concerts, including the premiere of Carpenter's ballet *Krazy Kat* by the Chicago Symphony. He was invited by Carpenter to discuss *Three Oranges* before "a fashionable women's club" on November 25 (2:177). Facing his first address in English, Prokofiev felt anxious but rose to the occasion. "I started with an announcement that divided the ladies into two groups, those who thought I was a crazy futurist, and those who thought I was caricaturing an opera performed by the company the previous year, [Montemezzi's] *L'amour dei tre re*" (2:177). Neither group was right, he explained. The name *Love for Three Oranges* was older than Futurism or French opera, older even than Chicago itself. He spent the hour recounting Gozzi's fairy tale and received warm applause. Four days later, he took pride in seeing his picture in Chicago's *Daily News* above the caption "best-dressed man in Chicago" (2:179).

Attending a concert at Orchestra Hall on November 19, Prokofiev suddenly realized that he had not yet prepared his Third Piano Concerto. With the first orchestral rehearsal scheduled for December 5 and opera rehearsals moving to the stage the day after, Prokofiev found himself shuttling between two venues. On December 16, he premiered the concerto at a Friday matinee. He had resolved to perform it "carefully" but admitted to mistakes in the second and third movements (2:186). White-gloved ladies responded with tepid applause. Following the intermission he conducted the Chicago premiere of the *Classical Symphony* to a more favorable response. After the concert he rested at his hotel, changed, and then confronted the first rehearsal of *Three Oranges* with soloists, chorus, and orchestra. The rehearsal went well despite his exhaustion. Another Chicago Symphony concert followed the next evening. Prokofiev wrote in his diary that he "almost played for a five [that is, an A+ grade]" and achieved far greater success than he had expected (2:186). Still, the symphony received more applause than the concerto: the audience recalled him seven times.

Unhappy with the critical reception accorded the concerto, Prokofiev tried to remind himself that reviews had little value. A brief report in the *Chicago*

Tribune compared the concerto unfavorably with the symphony, a work "packed full of the sprightliest kind of tunes." The concerto, in contrast, was "greatly a matter of slewed harmony, neither conventional enough to win affections nor modernist enough to be annoying."[40] Raymond, of *Musical America*, branded it "an attenuated piece of music, complex but paltry in effect, and many opportunities for fine expression left hanging in the air." The critic then echoed a general concern about the composer's inconstant, unromantic melodic writing: "There is plenty of melody in the work, but no sooner has the composer realized that a singing, wholesome phrase has intruded into his scheme than he nullifies it by contradictory and meaningless passages." Raymond ended in the same mixed vein: "The piano part is a colossal piece of work, with much extravagant rhythm and technical demands unusually exacting. What the concerto lacks the most is continuity and climax." His comments about the symphony, however, were brief and upbeat: "There is a gratifying absence of abrupt transitions, and from the opening bars there is a steady culmination of interest to the vigorous and effective close. . . . Prokofieff has made a valuable contribution to orchestral literature." As conductor, Prokofiev cut a "commanding figure, the personification of repose and authority, and seems to invite the confidence of his men."[41]

Prokofiev overcame the reviews by plunging back into the opera. At the final stage rehearsal on December 29, he vexed Coini by repeating the prologue four times. The mood lightened, however, with Garden lauding the opera during the break after Act 1. Onlookers guffawed as Fata Morgana tripped and the Prince, recovering from his protracted bout of melancholia, laughed in endless ostinato in Act 2. Garden herself chortled at the Act 3 scene with the transvestite Cook Cleonte. Several "minor incidents" prompted Prokofiev to pause and repeat, but Coini made him rush because time was running short, assuring him that all could be fixed at the final piano rehearsal. The composer left the rehearsal, having sweated so much he was "as wet as a frog" (2:190). Late that evening, Garden telephoned Prokofiev at his hotel to praise the performance; Prokofiev graciously complimented her in turn. Last-minute intrigue put Anisfeld at odds with virtually everyone except the composer, who noted that the designer "was entirely right to confront Coini, the props people, and the electricians about nothing being done properly, and that, if they're angry at having their quiet nest disturbed, then to hell with them. Anisfeld is a true artist and the others just hired help" (2:189).

On December 30, after three years of stops and starts, the curtain rose on *The Love for Three Oranges*. From backstage the audience seemed sparse, and Prokofiev cursed the "conservative *bel canto* faction" in the media for spoiling the premiere (2:191). But when Coini gave the signal, he entered the pit and saw that the hall was occupied, with just a few loges and some seats at the front vacant. He conducted well, with only a few slip-ups, cueing Leandro, for example, a beat early in Act 1, scene 3. The prompter swiftly put the singer back on track. By the time Prokofiev ascended the stage after Act 1 to acknowledge the applause, the singers had already taken several bows. The clapping intensified as he and Anisfeld went out; the two were recalled several times. Anisfeld impetuously refused to allow Coini to join them, spoiling the stage director's mood for the rest of the evening.

The audience reveled in the Prince's antics, the March, and the décor of Act 2, but the loudest ovation came when Koshets, as Fata Morgana, pronounced the curse. This time at curtain calls, the singers dragged Coini out with them, causing Anisfeld to turn away and exit. Prokofiev took several bows. In Act 3, the audience applauded the set for Cleonte's castle and responded to the scene with the ribbon, but the luster of the performance dimmed. Backstage, one of the baritones, Georgiy Baklanov, suggested that something be cut. An ovation greeted Prokofiev's entrance into the pit for Act 4, after which there were problems: Tchelio entered a measure late in scene 1, spoiling half of his argument with Fata Morgana. In scene 2, assistant conductor Frank St. Leger began the March at the wrong tempo. Prokofiev himself set a "mad" tempo and, toward the end, noticed the staging looking "muddled" (2:191–92). He was so spent by the final curtain that he could not recall bowing, only that Garden and Harold McCormick congratulated him in his dressing room. Prohibition aside, Prokofiev "wanted to drink," and so he and his entourage went to a friend's house where he straightaway downed three cocktails. "Everyone was a little drunk," he recounted, "I more than the others, and I felt serene" (2:192).

A mild hangover and "not a single serious review" greeted him the next morning (2:192). He rang in the New Year with his companion Mariya Baranovskaya (nicknamed "Frou-Frou") at a party at Volkov's house lasting until 2:30 a.m. The year, he reflected, "had finished. It was a good year; it began well and happily in California, then there was the contract with Mary Garden, the staging of *Chout,* a wonderful summer in St. Brévin and the staging of *Oranges.* What could be better!" (2:192).

On New Year's Day, Prokofiev realized the magnitude of his success at a reception for Garden given by the company sponsors: "I hadn't for a long time heard as many excited compliments from acquaintances and strangers as today" (2:195). The next day he pondered extracting a suite from *Three Oranges*, then headed to the Auditorium Theater where he sat at the back of the parterre with his friend Gottlieb for the second performance, conducted by Smallens. From that perspective he thought the strings sounded weak, but the singers came through clearly. At first he anticipated all the difficult spots with trepidation but after a while relaxed, resolving to "let Smallens take care of it" (2:195). Prokofiev cursed Coini for the ragged appearance of the chorus in the Prologue. Evaluating the third scene of

Act 3 (in the desert with the oranges) for potential cuts, he concluded that "it only seems long for those who don't understand the music" (2:195). He saw more clearly the "mess" at the end of Act 4, again blaming the "scoundrel Coini" (2:195). Ultimately he found the performance less successful than the premiere. Yet the theater was full, and Smallens conducted well.

Prokofiev had three additional engagements before leaving Chicago for New York. The first was at Mandel Hall (University of Chicago) on January 10, 1922, followed by a benefit recital with Koshets "in the Bolshevik style" for starving Russians (2:195), and finally a benefit concert for children on a grander scale at the Auditorium. It paid nothing but Prokofiev felt he could not turn down the invitation, since it came from his friend Carpenter. The audience demanded the *Three Oranges* March as an encore. The work, he grumbled, "threatens to become as 'disagreeably modish' as Rachmaninoff's Prelude [in C-sharp Minor]" (2:196).

He departed on January 16 fully aware of the intrigues and financial problems at the Chicago Opera. Attendance that season had been excellent: only two performances had not been sold out. But financiers were already calling for a budget that could be feasibly supported by a roster of five hundred citizen-guarantors, of which only half had been found. Garden was instructed to submit the repertoire for the coming season to an oversight committee. Infighting and standoffs between her and the singers fueled rumors of an impending firing. By February 25, Garden had announced her resignation. The turmoil ended Prokofiev's hopes of another opera premiere in Chicago: "I had thought that if *Oranges* was a success, *The Fiery Angel* would enter the repertoire a year later," he wrote in his diary, "but for now it doesn't look that way" (2:196).

1922: Premieres in New York

In New York, Prokofiev prepared for the first performance of *Three Oranges* at the Metropolitan Opera on February 6 and two performances of the Third Piano Concerto with the New York Symphony under the direction of Albert Coates on January 26 and 27. Haensel & Jones also booked two solo recitals for Prokofiev at Aeolian Hall on February 14 and 17, agreeing not to take its customary fee. "We can't lose," his agent told him, "and this could help for future seasons" (2:197). When a flu outbreak confined the Prince and Truffaldino to bed, *Three Oranges* was rescheduled for February 14, just hours after Prokofiev's first piano recital and on the same evening as a Rachmaninoff concert at Carnegie Hall. Sadly, the great run on tickets for the original February 6 staging was not repeated for the later date.

Prokofiev liked playing under Coates and felt that his New York performances of the Third Piano Concerto equaled that in Chicago. The reviews,
however, were "more frivolous and ignorant" (2:197). Oscar Thompson
branded the concerto "not one to amaze or befuddle ears that have listened
to Casella, Milhaud, Schönberg, Leginska, and others of the neo-fantasts.
Chiefly rhythmical in its effects, it had its share of disharmony, yet suggested
that the composer had been looking backward rather than forward in piecing together his material, such as it was."[42] The unsigned *Musical America*
column "Mephisto's Musings" recalled an audience member complaining
about the "crash, bang, bang, crash, bang" but acknowledged that "everybody agreed that if Prokofieff's concerto was original but ear splitting, he
himself was a wonderful pianist and deserved the applause he got. . . . He
has a rare gift of melody, but I suppose he wants to attract attention by being
'different.'"[43] Aldrich's *New York Times* review was largely negative. The
concerto was "by no means unintelligible as music," he wrote, but seemed
"singularly hard and dry."[44] The third movement earned an especially
piquant critique: "[The composer] progresses further into the region of dis-
cord; and here the material seems to be more desultory, more disconnected."
Aldrich offered a damning and myopic conclusion:

> It is difficult to love Mr. Prokofieff's concerto on a first meeting. It is
> not even easy, as a whole, to endure it. Whether the stages of pity and
> of embracing would follow in the appointed course, if opportunity were
> given does not seem certain. But it does seem almost certain that the
> opportunity will not be given. It is difficult to imagine him being asked
> often to play it, or any other pianist than Mr. Prokofieff playing it.[45]

In fact, Prokofiev played the concerto in Paris under Koussevitzky and in
London under Coates in April 1922 to great success, and he would perform it again during his 1926 and 1937 American tours.

As the day of his first recital and the New York premiere of *Three Oranges*
approached, Prokofiev's chief fear was catching the flu. His solo repertoire
posed no challenge (it included arrangements of the March and Intermezzo
from the opera, a Buxtehude prelude and fugue, Schubert waltzes, and
pieces by Lyadov, Medtner, and Musorgsky), and there was no orchestral
rehearsal scheduled for the opera. He survived the marathon of playing
and conducting by drinking hot milk, taking a bath, and sleeping for two
hours in between engagements.

The new date for the opera had not been advertised, but a generous
disbursement of free tickets ensured that the hall was full on February 14.
"Mephisto's Musings" reported that "everybody who is anybody in the newspaper and musical world was there, as well as a very determined Russian

claque, whose enthusiasm, however, seemed to pale off toward the end."[46] Since it featured the Chicago cast, the performance went smoothly, although Prokofiev was not happy with the chorus. He likened the audience reception to that in Chicago, but the reviews included "brutal abuse" that "bewildered" him (2:198). "Mephisto's Musings" summarized: "While a few of the reviews in the press were kindly, the majority of them were not favorable. Most of the critics did not appear to catch the spirit of the work."[47] By late February, it was obvious that there would not be a fourth performance of *Three Oranges* that season. Nor would it, or any of Prokofiev's other operas, be staged in America during his later visits.

1921–22: Chicago and New York Opera Reviews

In both cities, reviewers of *Three Oranges* offered decidedly mixed appraisals of its music, libretto, and staging. Only Anisfeld's seven striking backdrops earned universal acclaim. As Edward Moore gushed in the *Chicago Tribune*, "never was paint applied to scene cloth any more lavishly or gorgeously."[48] Janet Fairbank likewise raved:

> No black and white reproductions can adequately portray the blaze of color as revealed on the stage. Rose and scarlet, orange and purple,

Figure 1. Boris Anisfeld's décor for *The Love for Three Oranges*, Act 1.

sapphire and gold, backdrops of wild sunset skies, foregrounds of burlesque court furnishings, deserts, mountains, and witches' caverns, all are beautiful beyond reality, and all share the happy overemphasis of the whole production. Mr. Anisfeld's imagination runs gladly along with Mr. Prokofieff's; his exaggerated settings and his gorgeously capricious costumes are the pattern to the warp of the piece. No stage sets have ever been more beautiful or more daring than these.[49]

In contrast, the discordant, unfamiliar music and complicated, foreign-language libretto provoked outright derision: "The music was enigmatic for the public of the day, a public that felt that without tunes, what was the point of opera?"[50] *Three Oranges* reuses recognizable motifs and themes including, of course, the March, but the more traditional-sounding sections (e.g., the Prince's and Linette's love duet in Act 3) are decidedly short-lived. The montage-like juxtapositions of phrases risked taxing the listener. Moore remarked:

> The music, I fear, is too much for this generation. After intensive study and close observation at rehearsal and performance, I detected the beginnings of two tunes. One is a very good march. . . . For the rest of it, Mr. Prokofieff might well have loaded up a shotgun with several thousand notes of varying lengths and discharged them against the side of a blank wall.[51]

Moore was nonetheless obliged to acknowledge the audience's enthusiastic applause at the end of each act: "But it may not be as bad as that. Last night's audience did not seem to think so."

Both in Chicago and New York, the laughter at the antics was genuine, not the defensive sort that was heard at Stokowski's Philadelphia Orchestra concerts just a few weeks before the premiere of *Three Oranges*, when Schoenberg's Five Orchestral Pieces received its first American reading.[52]

Of the New York reviewers, Aldrich was the least charitable. He condemned Prokofiev's music as

> more grotesque, more fantastic, more impossible than anything else connected with the work. The other things can beguile the eye and amuse, if they cannot stimulate the imagination. What can Mr. Prokofieff's music do for the ear? Probably, for most of the listeners, it could do little but belabor it till insensibility set in, if it did set in, and further suffering was spared. There are a few, but only a few, passages that bear recognizable kinship with what has hitherto been recognized as music. No doubt there are what pass for themes, and

there is ingenuity of some kind in manipulating them; but it seldom produces any effect but that of disagreeable noise.[53]

This was not the end of the fulmination. The New York audience, Aldrich added, found the on- and off-stage wanderings of the chorus perplexing:

The principal characters are fantastic enough in their conception and in their dramatic embodiment on the stage; but their doings are accompanied by the antics of as strange a crew of creatures as often emerge into public view. There are 'Ridicules,' 'Comiques,' 'Lyriques,' 'Tragiques,' 'Empty Heads,' devils, devilkins, doctors, 'Absurdities,' courtiers, comedians. They come and go, and sometimes are swept out by attendants with huge shovels.[54]

The question remained:

What, *in fine*, is the underlying purpose of this work? Is it satire? Is it burlesque? If so, what does it satirize; what does it burlesque? Whose withers are wrung? If it is a joke it may be a good one; but it is a long and painful one; and, on information and belief, it may be said, more painful to the Chicago Opera Company than even to listeners.[55]

Aldrich and his like-minded colleagues could only lament the cost of the staging: "$43,000 per orange."

One writer, *Chicago Daily News* columnist and socialite Ben Hecht, seemed to get the point, producing the following lines after attending a dress rehearsal:

They will never start. No they will never start. In another two min-utes Mr. Prokofieff will go mad. They should have started at eleven. It is now ten minutes after eleven. And they have not yet started. Ah, Mr. Prokofieff has gone mad.

But Mr. Prokofieff is a modernist; so nobody pays much attention. Musicians are all mad. And a modernist musician, du lieber Gott! A Russian modernist musician! . . . Music like this has never come from the orchestra pit of the Auditorium. Strange combinations of sounds that seem to come from street pianos, New Year's Eve horns, harmonicas and old-fashioned beer steins that play when you lift them up. Mr. Prokofieff waves his shirt-sleeved arms and the sounds increase.

There is nothing difficult about this music—that is, unless you are unfortunate enough to be a music critic. But to the untutored ear

Stephen D. Press

there is a charming capriciousness about the sounds from the orchestra. . . . What is it all about? Ah, Mr. Prokofieff knows and Boris
[Anisfeld] knows and maybe the actors know. But all it is necessary
for us to know is that music and color and a quaint, almost gargoylian,
caprice are tumbling around in front of our eyes and ears. . . . The
hobgoblin extravaganza Mr. Prokofieff wrote unfolds itself with
rapidity. Theater habitués eavesdropping on the rehearsal mumble
in the half-dark that there was never anything like this seen on earth
or in heaven. Mr. Anisfeld's scenery explodes like a succession of
medieval skyrockets. A phantasmagoria of sound, color and action
crowds the startled proscenium. . . .

The first act of "Three Oranges" is over. Two critics exchanging opinions glower at Mr. Prokofieff. One says: "What a shame! What a shame!
Nobody will understand it." The other agrees. But perhaps they only
mean that music critics will fail to understand it and that untutored
ones like ourselves will find in the hurdy-gurdy rhythms and contortions of Mr. Prokofieff and Mr. Anisfeld a strange delight. As if someone
had given us a musical lollypop to suck and rub in our hair.

I have an interview with Mr. Prokofieff to add. . . . Instead of quoting [him] at this time, it may be more apropos merely to say that I
would rather see and listen to his opera than to the entire repertoire
of the company put together. This is not criticism, but a prejudice in
favor of fantastic lollypops.[56]

The Chicago Opera had spent lavishly on the opera, but, assessments
like Hecht's aside, money could not guarantee critical acclaim. Had *Three
Oranges* appeared later in the 1920s, its reception would doubtless have
been different. Prokofiev had acquired loyal supporters in America, but
wizened critics, financiers, and philanthropists still had the upper hand.
When the opera premiered, jazz and so-called low art had yet to infiltrate
the orchestral repertoire, let alone the more conservative world of opera.
George Gershwin's jazz-inspired first opera, *Blue Monday*, had not been
heard; his most famous crossover work, *Rhapsody in Blue*, was two years
away. Longtime opera patrons could not countenance Prokofiev's brash,
fast-paced, fantastical score, which audaciously poked fun at the very institution they held dear. The *Chicago Tribune* even affixed the word *anarchy*
to it, a catchall dating back to Prokofiev's first recital in America.[57] It did
not help that the opera had to sell itself, owing to a dearth of advance publicity and subscription patrons.

It might have fared better set in English. As Malcolm Hamrick Brown
explains, "*Three Oranges* is one of those works that simply must be seen, heard,
and understood, if it is to be enjoyed. Visual and musical pratfalls can

• 363 •

sustain the comic intensity only so long without dialogue. Besides, Prokofiev's high jinxes result more often than not from a deliberately incongruous counterpoint between sight, sound, and text. The punch line of his jokes can come in any one of the three elements."[58] Indeed, "Mephisto's Musings" pointed out that "some of the best points were missed by the audience" because the opera was sung in French instead of English. "There is much comedy, very cleverly done by the members of the company, [and] considerable satire, most of which went for nothing."[59] Critics also groaned about the opera's length, specifically Act 3, of which Raymond reported: "The action lags badly after the drop of the second curtain, and the entire third act, despite its marvelous scenery, is not sufficient to hold the interest after the mad events of the preceding scene."[60] After acknowledging that Fata Morgana's pratfall in Act 2 "is so good and amusing that it took the audience and resulted in many curtain calls," the author decried the "scarcely unrelieved dullness" of Acts 3 and 4.[61] One peculiar solution—applying disfiguring cuts (like eliminating the three princesses) to turn the opera into an hour-long farce called *The Prince Who Couldn't Laugh*—suggests that short attention spans are not a recent phenomenon. Thompson quipped that "'The Love for Three Oranges' suggests a boy making faces." These faces might "amuse for a brief period, but not from 8:15 to 10:30."[62]

For Prokofiev, the reaction in New York, where civic pride was a factor, hurt the most:

Heavens, what a press it had the next day! It was as if a pack of dogs had been suddenly unleashed at me and were tearing my trousers to bits. If the opera had not been too well understood in Chicago at least the production, being their own, had been spared. But New York did not need to spare anything; on the contrary the rivalry of the two cities made itself felt. "You wanted to show us something we hadn't thought of producing ourselves—well here's what we think of it!"[63]

Of course, Prokofiev could not expect to be a pathbreaker and remain unscathed, especially in the conservative world of opera. Just as the reception of *Chout* in Paris and London had demonstrated months before, Prokofiev's theater music was a prime target for anti-modernist critics. His ego, understandably, sought universal approbation. But the reception was not always as bad as he perceived, especially since journal reviews tended to be kinder than those in newspapers. Surely he took some consolation from the rave in *The New Republic*:

Mr. Prokofieff's score is a masterpiece of modern descriptive music, and it is ultra-modern in orchestra treatment. It conducts the action through four acts and ten scenes of extraordinary color, with skill and humor. . . . It is true that there is nothing in the entire score which one may whistle as ones goes out; there is no contest between a flute and a soprano; there is no melting tenor solo in the spotlight, and the troglodyte who believes he may advance only by looking backward, shakes his head over Mr. Prokofieff because his work is reminiscent of nothing.[64]

He could also take solace in a sentence on the front page of the January 7, 1922, issue of *Musical America*: "Last week [Prokofiev] took his place as one of the most gifted and promising of opera composers."[65]

Two more substantial reviews of *Three Oranges* affirm that Prokofiev was rarely panned by sophisticated critics. (The distinction in the caliber of reviews, and the manner in which Western stereotypes about Russian music play into them, tends to be overlooked in discussions of Prokofiev reception.) The following thoughts on the Chicago premiere come from the *Musical Courier*:

Here is a fairy tale in strange settings and stranger music. Prokofieff, who had written not only the music for his opera, but also the words, showed unmistakable marks of genius besides a witty pen. The opera abounds with good humor, and though the novelty is not "Barber of Seville" nor a "Hansel and Gretel" nor a "Coq d'Or," it is an extremely interesting work. Prokofieff does not laugh nor even smile as would a Rossini or a Humperdinck. His laugh is coarse instead of subtle, the real humor of the Cossack, chuckling outwardly with spasms of contagious hilarity, the composer seemingly enjoying his musical jokes, which he tells over and over again. This is a grave mistake, as the best *raconteur* is the one who tells his tale, as funny as it might be, with a serious countenance, while his auditors laugh. The best numbers are a march, which no doubt will become popular, and a male chorus close to the end of the opera. The second act is the most interesting. Were the three others of the same caliber, "The Love for the Three Oranges" would be here proclaimed a huge success. . . . The music set forth by Prokofieff is extraordinary, absolutely original and fits the action to perfection. Singers will abhor the opera, as Prokofieff does not write for the voice and there are no principal roles, each of the fifteen principal characters has just about as much to sing. There are no arias, no vocal effects that will bring down the house, but circus tricks that made clowns of some of the principals. . . . The orchestra played superbly under the difficult beat of Prokofieff and columns could be written about the costumes, scenery and properties,

especially designed for this production by Boris Anisfeld, who by his
displays, put to blush all the Ziegfields of "Follies" fame, as a more
glorious panoramic production has not been seen in Chicago. A column of praise could also be written concerning the *mise en scène*,
established and staged by Jacques Coini. . . . "The Love for the Three
Oranges" will never be classed as grand opera, but even though its
music is ultra-modern and difficult, the translation of the text into
English would assure its permanency, if not in the home of grand
opera, surely in that of the comic or light opera, where it has its *raison
d'être*. A good showman who would buy from the Chicago Opera
Association its right on the production could reap a harvest touring
the country with the most amusing burlesque opera of the day.[66]

Richer yet is James Whittaker's report on the New York performance in
the *Chicago Tribune*, which takes Prokofiev's polemical Prologue as a cue and
imagines three different reactions to the opera, claiming, "The Chicagoites
attract a mysterious mixed clientele." Whittaker welcomes the arrival of
Modernism in the opera house, proclaiming *Three Oranges*

strident with a note of resolute anarchy, annoying to those who like
entertainment to be docile and a bit of a supplicant for gracious
pennies. It is gay with the fantasy of the pictorial fairy plot in which
its seething nihilisms masquerade, and brightly amusing to those who
exercise a selective instinct in the theater, taking only so much of what
the theater offers as they like. And, under its masquerades of stage
stuff, play stuff, and paint stuff, it trumpeted, to those whose ear channels do not end in their livers, a protest, keen with a generous hatred
of musty, beloved old shams of the theater. . . .
    First, those who were amused. They saw an artless and somewhat
disjointed faerie relating, with vast and kaleidoscopic paraphernalia
of Russian pantomime, a simple tale of a prince who could not smile.
. . . There is enough here of the old operatic philosophy of redemp-
tion by love and other gimcrack elements of pseudo-psychology to
satisfy the restricted intelligences. The restricted intelligences in
Manhattan were, I imagine, more nearly satisfied than any of the others. And if the restricted intelligences were somewhat puzzled by the
mysterious personages who, throughout this fable, sat in a tier of stage
boxes built up against the canvas proscenium within which the fable
was acted . . . the restricted intelligences stumbled for a moment and
then let this part of the spectacle slip out of their grasp as something
Tartar to overlook. . . . Second, those who were annoyed. These could
not quite get this last disturbing item of the spectacle out of their con-

sciousness. Nor could they quite dismiss the insistent, jeering Prokofieff music in the pit . . . and [the] Russian jazz in the orchestra. . . . Third, those who were aroused. Only these heard 'The Love for Three Oranges.' In it they heard scorn and satire. It was satire of the current theater of sentiment. It was scorn of the concoctors of the current theater of sentiment. And it was godly beautiful, with the fine, valiant wisdom of a clear-eyed youth, its composer.[67]

The entire ordeal of the opera affected Prokofiev's confidence. He struggled in his New York recitals, even though they did not pose particular technical challenges. Apprehensive about playing Beethoven's Piano Sonata in A Major, op. 101, on February 17, he faltered in the second movement and struggled to regain control. The *Musical America* reviewer "H. J." branded the rendition "perfunctory" and "almost flippant," and said the execution of Prokofiev's own Second Sonata was built on "certain restless, 'jiggly' figures and glissando effects" that were used "over and over . . . in a singularly unresourceful manner."[68] He fielded other attacks as well. Virginia-born pianist-composer John Powell used a piano roll recording of Prokofiev's *Sarcasms* alongside Charles T. Griffes's *White Peacock* to illustrate the "banal and uninteresting" music of the "ultra-modernists" at a lecture-performance titled "Americanism in Music" at Aeolian Hall.[69] Prokofiev's two New York recitals tallied a loss of $375, embarrassing his agent: "I believed in you so much, but I don't understand what's the matter with you?!" (2:198).

Clearly Prokofiev's career in America had ebbed, and for the immediate future there was more to lose than gain. He booked a departure for Germany for February 25, 1922, pinning his hopes on a favorable exchange rate for the Deutschmark. "I had to face the truth," he recalled in his 1941 autobiography,

the American season, which had begun so promisingly, fizzled out completely for me. My last hope was that Mary Garden would put on *The Fiery Angel* the following season and sing the main role, but unfortunately for me she resigned the directorship. I was left with a thousand dollars in my pocket and an aching head, to say nothing of a fervent desire to get away to some quiet place where I could work in peace.[70]

As he packed on the eve of his departure, two ladies came to express their enthusiasm for *Three Oranges*, calling it one of the most ingenious operas they had ever seen. They sought Prokofiev's support for a plan to present it in a large rented theater the following winter, and if successful, to stage it subsequently in Australia and Europe. "Now there's an offer I didn't expect!" he wrote in his diary. "If it happens I'll be a rich and world-famous person in a single stroke, but I don't really believe it—something will surely go wrong" (2:199) After talking it over they parted on the understanding that rights needed to be negotiated with the Chicago Opera and the décor rented.[71] Although Prokofiev recalled the meeting cynically, he considered it a "good farewell chord" for his stay in the United States (2:199). He would return, but he would never again see one of his operas staged there.

1926 and 1930: Prospects in New York

By the time Prokofiev returned to America in early 1926, *Three Oranges* had run successfully in Cologne and, thanks to the critical response, was to be produced in Berlin (Staatsoper) and Leningrad (State Academic Theater of Opera and Ballet). Both *The Gambler* and *The Fiery Angel*, completed in short score in 1923, awaited their premieres. But opera figured little in this profitable American tour of fourteen concerts: six with his wife, Lina, under the auspices of the Pro Musica Society and seven with Koussevitzky and the Boston Symphony Orchestra. His spare time, of which there was plenty while crisscrossing the country by train, was consumed by the orchestration of his new ballet *Ursin'ol'*, which would be premiered by Diaghilev's company in June 1927 under the choreographer Leonid Massine's title *Le Pas d'acier*. He made further recordings for Duo-Art and received a commission for an overture to be premiered at the dedication of the Aeolian Company's new headquarters at Fifth Avenue and 54th Street. Despite these successes, and growing interest in his music from more artists, Prokofiev had not satisfactorily penetrated the American music scene by 1926. In an interview with the *Boston Evening Transcript*, he responded acerbically to a question on musical developments in the United States: "You all ride in automobiles and yet you are behind in music. I would prefer that you ride in horse carriages and be more up-to-date in music."[72]

The final chapter of Prokofiev's opera career in America was written during his 1930 visit, a lengthy affair that included twelve symphony concerts and eleven chamber recitals with his wife, again for Pro Musica. Arriving on December 30, 1929, aboard the same ship as Rachmaninoff, Prokofiev traveled coast to coast for four months, also making trips to Cuba and Canada. His letters to friends and colleagues attest to his rising fame; to Nikolay Myaskovsky he wrote, "I am pleased with the trip: it seems that little by little they have come to believe in me here."[73] To Boris Asafyev he boasted, "We were well- received everywhere; America has grown up in these past four years, or maybe has simply learned my name."[74]

By this time, *The Fiery Angel* had been completely revised but not yet premiered, and Prokofiev held out hope for an American production. Performances were planned for Berlin under Bruno Walter in the autumn of 1927, but the theater used the late arrival of the full score (he completed it that summer) as an excuse to back out. Koussevitzky had conducted a concert performance of Act 2, with cuts reluctantly approved by the composer, at a Paris concert in June 1928. Prokofiev considered it a modest success, but he reflected in his diary that *The Fiery Angel* is "an old thing (in conception) . . . from which I have moved away" (2:634). That did not diminish his desire to see the entire opera, into which he had "stuffed" so much music.

His hopes were raised on January 12, 1930, when his friend Sergey Sudeykin, a stage designer at the Met (and Vera Stravinsky's first husband), telephoned to arrange a meeting with conductor Tullio Serafin and producer Ernst Lert, who had voiced interest in *The Fiery Angel*. According to Sudeykin, even Gatti was now considering a Prokofiev opera production. Despite vivid memories of his crushing defeat at the Met eight years before, Prokofiev was ecstatic, enthusing in his diary "My heart is reborn! My heart is reborn! Better later than never" (2:745). He met Serafin and Sudeykin to explain the plot and wired Paris to have the score sent to America. Suddenly, a staging in New York seemed imminent.

On January 18, Prokofiev initiated a series of meetings with Sudeykin to discuss the libretto and staging of *The Fiery Angel*. Sudeykin predicted greater success if the middle acts were reorganized as a series of tableaux, emphasizing the need for visual, not verbal, clarity. He also faulted the opera's extremely long recitatives. Prokofiev apologized, saying he had started *The Fiery Angel* a decade earlier and in the interim his operatic style had changed.

Prokofiev devised a plan to win over the more dubious Serafin and Gatti. Strategizing with Mrs. Otto Kahn, whose husband was president of the board of directors at the Met, he decided that Gatti would receive an amended libretto and Serafin a piano score. A hearing would be arranged after Prokofiev's return from California. On February 8, Prokofiev met the Russian-born tenor and opera director Vladimir Rosing, who had been appointed head of the opera department at the Eastman School of Music in 1923 and subsequently founded the American Opera Company. He, too, was interested in staging *The Fiery Angel*—if negotiations with the Met collapsed. Prokofiev offered him either *The Gambler* or *Three Oranges*, but further discussions were postponed. That same evening Walter Nuvel approached the composer with an offer to write a ballet for Serge Lifar and the Paris Opera. "Suddenly I'm in great demand," the composer exulted (2:755).

Prokofiev returned to New York in early March for a few days before journeying to Havana. In the interim, he had hoped to continue working with Sudeykin on *The Fiery Angel,* but the designer was occupied with the sketches for an upcoming Met production of *The Flying Dutchman.* Sudeykin's truncated, French-language libretto of *The Fiery Angel,* intended for Gatti, was poorly compiled, forcing Prokofiev to waste time correcting it. Serafin was out of town, so further talks with him had to be postponed until Prokofiev's return from Havana. The fate of his opera would thus be decided just days before his scheduled departure for Europe.

Back in New York on March 16, Prokofiev learned that Serafin generally liked the opera's music and that Gatti had studied the revised libretto; the two of them planned to meet the next day with Sudeykin. But the verdict came back negative, with Gatti labeling the libretto "unacceptable," thus rejecting Prokofiev "for the second time" in his career (2:763). The composer proposed *The Gambler* in place of *The Fiery Angel,* since Gatti found the plot more to his taste. The next day Prokofiev met with Rosing about *The Fiery Angel,* only to learn that his company's finances were precarious and his orchestra small (thirty-six members). Prokofiev blanched at Rosing's suggestion that he hire "one of his students" to make a reduced orchestral version of the opera under Prokofiev's supervision (2:764). It would make more sense, the composer replied, to compose a chamber opera for him.

On March 19, Prokofiev played excerpts from *The Gambler* for Serafin, including the climactic scene at the roulette wheel. Seemingly impressed, Serafin promised to forward the libretto to Gatti. Hopes of a New York staging were once again dashed when Serafin telephoned to report that although the libretto interested Gatti, the director was unable to imagine it on stage. Serafim simply advised Prokofiev to send him a copy of the piano score following its publication—in other words, don't call us, we'll call you. Feeling betrayed and insulted, Prokofiev sailed for Europe. Three more American tours lay ahead, but only after Prokofiev had begun his inexorable return to Russia, where he anticipated—inaccurately, as it turned out—greater success with his beloved genre.

After World War II: Known in America

In 1949, while the infirm Prokofiev struggled to create works acceptable to Stalinist cultural officials, the fortunes of his operas in the United States drastically improved. After twenty-seven years without it, New Yorkers fell in love with *Three Oranges.* On November 1, 1949, the New York City Opera staged Prokofiev's farce at City Center, thereafter taking it to Chicago. The demand for tickets was such that a special matinee had to be scheduled for children. *Three Oranges* remained in the company's repertoire for seven

straight years. Wisely, it was sung in English using Victor Seroff's translation. Rosing, now with the American Operatic Laboratory in Hollywood,
finally had the chance to produce a Prokofiev opera when he was summoned, three weeks before the premiere, to take over a staging of *Three
Oranges* from the deposed director Theodore Komisarjevsky. Another
Russian, Mstislav Dobjinsky, created the designs, including the commedia
dell'arte masks for the singers. Conductor Laszlo Halasz presided over the
largest orchestra ever used by the company. Rosing separated *Three Oranges*
into two acts rather than the original four and tailored the score to suit a
small performing space and budget. Minor changes in the staging were
likewise mandated: for example, in Act 4, Princess Ninetta turned into
Gozzi's pigeon instead of Prokofiev's rat. (A pigeon works for free, an actor
in rat costume does not.)

    Three Oranges was now an unqualified success. Quaintance Eaton of *Musical
America* reported: "By intermission time, it was already plain that the
evening was an occasion—one of those rare and exciting events that justify
the term 'first night' in all its dazzling connotations."[75] Viewers firmly
grasped Prokofiev's meta-theatrical intentions: "Most of all, it is a satire of
opera. The pomposity, irrelevance, and incredibility of many opera plots;
the strutting and posing of operatic actors; the denouement at any price—
all are taken off with sleek wit."[76] Another writer, Olin Downes, confirmed:
"The opera is a parody of operas, but it is also a most distinguished work
of art. . . . The orchestra is simply amazing, all the time, in its swift and
mordant commentary, its scherzo movements, which are the quintessence
of fantasy and humor, its savage accentuations of this or that piece of fool-
ery, and the hilarious march which is famous in radius much wider than
the opera itself."[77]

    There were other American successes. Prokofiev's *Peter and the Wolf* was
contracted by Walt Disney Studios for the animated compilation *Make
Mine Music,* distributed in 1946; the March from *Three Oranges* served as
the theme music for the ABC radio drama *This Is Your FBI,* which ran from
1945 to 1953. The 1949 "Annual Survey of Orchestral Repertory," which
polled the twenty-seven leading orchestras in the nation, placed Prokofiev
near the top of the modern foreign composers ranking, with eleven of his
works performed a total of sixty-two times.[78] Also in 1949 came the premiere of the Sixth Symphony by the New York Philharmonic, under
Stokowski, and with it a pointed response to Soviet musical censorship. One
of the reviewers upbraided the Central Committee of the Communist
Party for labeling the Symphony "formalist" in 1948. Rather than being
marred by "antidemocratic tendencies foreign to Soviet taste," the symphony was "the most personal, the most accessible and emotionally revealing
work of Prokofieff that has yet been played in this country."[79]

Ormandy and the Philadelphia Orchestra recorded the *Scythian* Suite for Columbia Records, as did Désiré Defauw and the Chicago Symphony Orchestra for Victor. Koussevitzky twice recorded the Classical Symphony, and the Third Piano Concerto cemented itself in the repertoire of leading pianists. In 1945, the Serge Koussevitzky Music Foundation requested a new symphonic work from Prokofiev while also extending an invitation to travel to Boston. In 1947, he received a commission from the head of the Music Division of the Library of Congress for a chamber orchestra work. For political reasons, these and other American offers could not be accepted.

Prokofiev journeyed to the United States with trepidation in 1918, but he naively trusted that his music would succeed in capturing and reflecting the nation's youthful, optimistic spirit. In his autobiography, he looked back poignantly on the days of professional uncertainty after *Three Oranges* was canceled, a period when he realized that his careerist instincts had let him down, and that he had failed in his headstrong, impetuous effort to adapt to American business practices:

> At times, as I roamed New York's Central Park and looked up at the skyscrapers facing it, I would think with cold fury of all the wonderful orchestras in America that cared nothing for my music; of the critics who never tired of uttering platitudes such as "Beethoven is a great composer" and who balked violently at anything new; of the managers who arranged long tours for artists playing the same old hackneyed program fifty times over. I had come too soon; the child (America) was not old enough to appreciate new music.[80]

Success arrived too late. After his last tour abroad in 1938, Prokofiev was confined to the Soviet sphere, unable to enjoy firsthand his triumph in America, now that the grown-up nation had adopted him as its own.

NOTES

1. On May 7, Prokofiev left Moscow on the Siberian Express, later than expected owing to delays obtaining his passport, and carrying less cash than he had hoped. His goal was to reach Buenos Aires before the end of the concert season. But the trip to Vladivostok by itself lasted sixteen days because of poor weather, heightened security, rerouting, and regional skirmishes between White and Red factions. After further delays obtaining his Japanese visa, he arrived in Tokyo on June 1. By then his remaining rubles had devalued to $535. To his alarm, he discovered he had missed by three days the last steamer to South America for two months. After some indecision, he set his sights on America, despite the prospective difficulties of obtaining a visa. He sailed from Japan on August 2 bound for Honolulu with $173 in his pocket, $100 of which had been loaned to him by acquaintances on the day of his departure. Prokofiev's financial situ-

ation remained precarious for some time. He arrived in San Francisco on August 21 but was held, along with other Russian and Chinese passengers, at Angel Island before being allowed to continue his journey. Through the generosity of newfound friends, most notably fellow *Grotius* passenger Nikolay Kucheryavïy, a Russian engineer bound for a new job in America, he finally arrived in New York. For additional information about his arrival in the United States, see my "Prokofiev's Vexing Entry into the United States," *Three Oranges: The Journal of the Serge Prokofiev Foundation* 6 (November 2003): 22–26.

2. Sergey Prokof'yev, *Dnevnik 1907–1933*, ed. Svyatoslav Prokof'yev, 2 vols. (Paris: Serge Prokofiev Estate, 2002), 1:736. Subsequent references to this publication appear in the main text and notes with volume and page.

3. Prokofiev, "Autobiography," in *Soviet Diary 1927 and Other Writings*, trans. and ed. Oleg Prokofiev (Boston: Northeastern University Press, 1991), 265.

4. Prokofiev wrote of Damrosch, "In general, this American celebrity did not sparkle with musicality" (1:735). The conductor irritated the composer by failing to follow the score of the First Piano Concerto during an audition—turning the pages either four measures early or late— and by favorably comparing the Classical Symphony to Vasiliy Kalinnikov's First Symphony (1895). One wonders what similarities he heard. Harold Schonberg claimed that Damrosch "was never taken very seriously by the critics and by his fellow musicians" in *The Great Conductors* (New York: Simon and Schuster, 1967), 345.

5. Prokofiev, "Autobiography," 265.

6. Unbeknownst to Prokofiev and the musical world at large, Stock had tendered his resignation as conductor of the Chicago Symphony Orchestra, a position he had held since 1905, effective October 1. He had neglected to obtain the necessary second papers to become an American citizen and could not join the musicians' union as an alien. Although the CSO trustees were willing to overlook the technicalities that temporarily barred Stock's citizenship, union rules stipulated that the orchestra could not play under the baton of a non-union member for more than two weeks. Stock filed for citizenship on February 7, 1919, and returned to the podium later that month—to a thunderous ovation.

7. Frederick H. Martens, "Reports Fine Arts Flourishing in 'Red Russia,'" *Musical America*, September 28, 1918, 9.

8. Harriette Brower, "Criticism a More Serious Art in Russia Than Here, Says Prokofieff," *Musical America*, March 8, 1919, 13.

9. Martens, "Reports Fine Arts Flourishing in 'Red Russia,'" 10.

10. The income Prokofiev received from concerts and recitals in America was insubstantial and further diminished by the high cost of advertising. Prokofiev's February 17, 1919, Aeolian Hall recital netted *minus* $230.

11. The Second Symphony was composed for the Boston Symphony Orchestra but actually premiered in Paris on June 6, 1925. Koussevitzky never conducted it in Boston, despite being its dedicatee.

12. Prokofiev did not want to make the Carnegie Hall benefit his American debut, but he was in no position to decline the invitation. Despite a bad head cold and fever he dragged himself to the event. To his delight, the fund-raising speeches ran longer than expected, precluding his performance. In Brooklyn, Prokofiev performed four solo piano works and accompanied Bolm as he danced to two of the composer's 1915–17 *Visions fugitives* (*Mimolyotnosti*). Opera singer Eugenie Fonariova opened the brief concert with two vocal selections. Behind his back Bolm and Schindler began asking donors for money for the composer's as yet unplanned first recital, prompting these tart words when he found out: "I don't wish to live by begging on the church porch" (1:744).

13. In his second season, he expanded his repertoire to include Bach's French Suite no. 5 in G Major, Schumann's Piano Sonata no. 1 in F-sharp Minor and *Carnaval*, and Beethoven's *Three Country Dances*.

14. Prokofiev, "Autobiography," 264.

15. [Richard Aldrich,] "Serge Prokofieff A Virile Pianist," *New York Times*, November 21, 1918.

16. A. H., "Serge Prokofieff Startles New York," *Musical America*, November 30, 1918, 16.

17. James Gibbons Huneker, "Music," *New York Times,* December 11, 1918. Since the opening phrase (mm. 2–26) is a protracted arch form, Huneker was obviously referring to the three-note figure of falling seconds (major then minor) that is worked in sequence beginning in measure 4.

18. Huneker, "Music," *New York Times,* December 12, 1918.

19. Herbert F. Peyser, "Prokofieff Appears Again in Recital," *Musical America,* February 22, 1919, 45.

20. James Gibbons Huneker, "Opera," *New York Times,* February 18, 1919.

21. A. Walter Kramer, "Prokofieff Lauded in Russian Program," *Musical America,* April 5, 1919, 25.

22. Hariette Brower, "Mission of the Piano Recital," *Musical America,* August 14, 1920, 25.

23. "Serge Prokofieff Indorses [sic] Opera in English," *Musical America,* December 17, 1921, 2.

24. "Serge Prokofieff's Achievements Win Acclaim from American Public," *Musical America,* November 1, 1919, 5.

25. Maurice Rosenfeld, "Super Season Awaits Musical Chicago," *Musical America,* November 15, 1919, 43.

26. Margie A. McLeod, "Campanini Confesses His Faith in the Art of the Musical Revolutionists," *Musical America,* November 15, 1919, 21.

27. Campanini's health had been fading for some time; the highly respected Giorgio Polacco was called in to conduct part-time during the 1918–19 season. When Campanini returned to the United States from a holiday on October 2, 1919, he was suffering from such a bad cold that he could barely speak to reporters. His doctors advised him to further restrict his conducting. On October 27, Prokofiev visited Campanini at home, finding him bedridden and looking "extremely bad" (2:54).

28. The season had not been a total waste. Prokofiev played five recitals, two each in New York's Aeolian Hall, two in Chicago's Kimball Hall, and one in Washington, D.C.; he had also secured future engagements in Chicago, New York, and Quebec.

29. The Austrian-born, Chicago-educated Pam, a corporate attorney of some renown, had helped the McCormicks organize the International Harvester Corporation in 1902. Maintaining offices in New York, Philadelphia, and Chicago, he was active in Republican Party circles and a close friend of Chief Justice William Howard Taft, even serving abroad briefly as an "unofficial observer" for President Harding. He and his fellow Chicago Opera board members were non-musical, however, as noted with dismay by W. L. Hubbard in a *Chicago Tribune* article of January 25, 1920: "Not one of these men from Mr. Pam on down . . . [is] qualified to pass in any way on musical and artistic matters. . . . They know all about their own businesses—the law, banking, real estate, dry goods, or commerce—but they know little or nothing about music." Pam had been a member of the company's board of directors since its inception as the Chicago Grand Opera in 1910. He became a guarantor at the time of the company's reorganization into the Chicago Opera Association in 1915 and was again a board member and chair of the executive committee from 1918.

30. Obituaries, *Chicago Herald and Examiner,* December 20, 1919.

31. Undated typescript generously provided by Malcolm Brown.

32. Ronald L. Davis, *Opera in Chicago* (New York: Appleton-Century, 1966), 133.

33. Ibid., 134–35.

34. Quaintance Eaton, "The Love for Three Oranges Newly Staged at City Center," *Musical America,* November 15, 1949, 1.

35. "Personalities," *Musical America,* November 12, 1921, 22.

36. Emil Raymond, "Prokofieff Tilts at Opera with Pointed Lance," *Musical America,* November 19, 1921, 3.

37. Ibid.

38. Ibid.

39. Ibid, 33.

40. "At the Orchestra," *Chicago Tribune,* December 17, 1921.

41. Emil Raymond, "Serge Prokofieff Excites Audience with Two New Orchestral Works," *Musical America,* December 24, 1921, 29.

42. Oscar Thompson, "Prokofieff Plays New Concerto," *Musical America,* February 4, 1922, 13.

Stephen D. Press

43. "Mephisto's Musings," *Musical America*, February 18, 1922, 7.
44. Richard Aldrich, "Opera," *New York Times*, January 27, 1922.
45. Ibid.
46. "Mephisto's Musings," *Musical America*, February 25, 1922, 8.
47. Ibid.
48. Edward Moore, "'Love for Three Oranges' Color Marvel, But Enigmatic Noise," *Chicago Tribune*, December 31, 1921.
49. Janet A. Fairbank, "The Love for Three Oranges," *The New Republic*, February 1, 1922, 282.
50. Edward Moore, *Forty Years of Opera in Chicago* (New York: Arno Press, 1977), 236.
51. Moore, "'Love for Three Oranges' Color Marvel, But Enigmatic Noise."
52. The reviews of Five Orchestral Pieces actually recalled those of *Three Oranges*; both works involved "multiple rhythms," a "crowding of harmonies upon unrelated neighbors," and "bizarre etching of clashing colors." F. C. B., "More Laughs for Schonberg Music," *Musical America*, December 17, 1921, 6.
53. Richard Aldrich, "Opera," *New York Times*, February 15, 1922.
54. Ibid.
55. Ibid.
56. Ben Hecht, "Fantastic Lollypops," in *1001 Afternoons in Chicago* (Chicago: University of Chicago Press, 1922), 97–100.
57. James Whittaker, "'Three Oranges' Opera in Gotham Yields Reactions for Each Orange," *Chicago Tribune*, February 19, 1922.
58. Malcolm Hamrick Brown, "*L'Amour des trois oranges*, op. 33" [review of Boosey & Hawkes edition], *Notes* 39 (December 1982): 468.
59. "Mephisto's Musings," February 25, 1922, 8.
60. Emil Raymond, "Chicago Opera Gives Prokofieff Work a Dazzling Premiere," *Musical America*, January 7, 1922, 25.
61. "Mephisto's Musings," February 25, 1922, 8.
62. Oscar Thompson, "Prokofieff's 'Love for Three Oranges' Amuses But Wearies at Its First New York Performance," *Musical America*, February 25, 1922, 6.
63. Prokofiev, "Autobiography," 272.
64. Fairbank, "The Love for Three Oranges," 282.
65. Raymond, "Chicago Opera Gives Prokofieff Work a Dazzling Premiere," 1.
66. "'The Love for Three Oranges' Produced at Last in Chicago," *Musical Courier*, January 5, 1922, 6, 16.
67. Whittaker, "'Three Oranges' Opera in Gotham Yields Reactions for Each Orange."
68. H. J., "Serge Prokofieff, Feb. 17," *Musical America*, February 25, 1922, 20.
69. D. J. T., "Powell Discusses Americanism in Music," *Musical America*, February 4, 1922, 51. Powell countered with selections from his folklore-inspired piano suites *From the South* and *At the Fair*.
70. Prokofiev, "Autobiography," 273.
71. If the two ladies actually approached the Chicago Opera they would have been disappointed. According to Moore, the *Three Oranges* décor began to fall apart after it was shipped to and from New York. He claims it was ordered destroyed (*Forty Years of Opera in Chicago*, 236–37).
72. Serge Koussevitzky Archive, box 50, folder 27, Music Division, Library of Congress.
73. Letter of February 21, 1930, in *Selected Letters of Sergei Prokofiev*, ed. and trans. Harlow Robinson (Boston: Northeastern University Press, 1998), 287.
74. Letter of March 3, 1930, in ibid., 118.
75. Eaton, "The Love for Three Oranges Newly Staged at City Center," 1.
76. Ibid., 5.
77. Olin Downes, "Prokofieff Opera at the City Center," *New York Times*, November 2, 1949.
78. By comparison, Richard Strauss had 14 pieces performed 122 times; Stravinsky, 13 pieces 53 times; Sibelius, 13 pieces 48 times; and Shostakovich, 5 pieces 33 times. Robert Sabin, "Annual Survey of Orchestral Repertory," *Musical America*, July 9, 1949, 29.
79. R. S., "Stokowski Offers Three Novelties," *Musical America*, December 15, 1949, 8.
80. Prokofiev, "Autobiography," 267.

Lieutenant Kizhe: New Media, New Means

KEVIN BARTIG

In the early months of 1930 Prokofiev visited both coasts of the United States as part of an extended concert tour. In February, while en route by train from New York to Los Angeles, the composer received a peculiar telegram from the renowned Hollywood actress Gloria Swanson (1899–1983). She inquired as to whether Prokofiev was aboard the train; the composer later joked that he was unsure if the telegram betokened a job offer or if Swanson simply hoped to arrange for a compelling photograph of him exiting his carriage in Los Angeles. Upon arrival, Prokofiev was pleased to learn that the actress wanted him to compose a score for her most recent film, the romantic comedy *What a Widow!* The prospect of such a project, Prokofiev quipped, was "splendid and smelled of money."[1] Swanson spared no pains in wooing the composer: after being whisked to Hollywood in her Rolls Royce, Prokofiev was treated to lunch and a private showing of the final edit of the movie. Evidently starstruck, the usually self-assured composer admitted to feeling timid in the actress's presence. Swanson explained that two of her financiers, dismayed at the poor quality of the planned music for *What a Widow!*, had insisted that she seek out the composer to furnish a score. Prokofiev hesitated, however, when he learned he would need to complete the music in little over a month's time, and he ultimately declined the project when the financiers refused to meet his fee.[2]

Although Prokofiev's tantalizing initial contact with Hollywood did not result in a commission, the film industry nevertheless captured his imagination. The technological marvel of film with sound in the 1930s held the potential to reach vast new audiences and carry a composer's music literally to the far corners of the earth, a detail not lost on the itinerant Prokofiev. Film attracted audiences that had radically different aesthetic and stylistic expectations than the Parisian elite and followers of chic he had become accustomed to through his work for the Ballets Russes. Musing on his experiences with Swanson and the prospect of composing film music, he wrote, "Wouldn't it be better to return to this question in my next work? . . . Is it possible to write simple music, completely accessible to the masses, and at the same time stand to put one's name under it?"[3] The self-questioning harbored an aesthetic challenge: to work in the new medium meant finding a musical language that could engage a much larger, more diverse public than Prokofiev had yet encountered. But retooling his style and syntax for the sake of easy comprehensibility ran the risk of entering the realm of what the composer termed "low-grade music."[4] Successfully negotiating the divide became, in different ways, Prokofiev's mission in the early 1930s, much as it became Aaron Copland's mission—though, to be sure, Prokofiev shared neither his American counterpart's aesthetics nor politics.[5] At least at first, Prokofiev did not attempt to advance a specific ideological agenda with his streamlined style.

Three years after his encounter with Swanson, Prokofiev confronted the Hollywood challenge with the score for the satirically anti-tsarist film *Lieutenant Kizhe (Poruchik Kizhe)*. The score now ranks among the twentieth-century's best-known compositions for the cinema, though only owing to the composer's widely performed suite based on its music. Despite the popularity of the suite, little attention has been devoted to the complete original score, which remains unpublished, or to Prokofiev's role in the film's creation.[6] The outline of the suite refers little to the earlier film score; the composer tailored the later work to fit the demands of concert performance by omitting malapropos passages (particularly those scored for percussion) and by conflating thematic material and making significant changes to the orchestration.[7] In addition to being the composer's first foray into film music, *Kizhe* was his first explicitly Soviet work. The events surrounding its creation raise the question as to how Prokofiev, an established international composer with traditional training but an iconoclastic leaning, approached a completely unknown medium. The *Kizhe* score proved to be something of an anomaly by the standards of early film music, owing to the logistics of the composer-director collaboration. It served to enhance Prokofiev's reputation within the artistic circles of Leningrad and Moscow, and shaped his conception of the function of sound on celluloid.

Cinema and New Simplicity

Before reaching the Soviet screen in 1934, *Lieutenant Kizhe* had a protracted genesis and existed in several versions and formats. The script, the work of Russian novelist and literary scholar Yuriy Tïnyanov (1894–1943), was conceived in May 1927 for a silent film. (Tïnyanov's film work, bearing traces of his Formalist writings on Gogolian parody and dynamic verbal structure, extends from 1926 to 1934, and includes the texts that evolved into the *Kizhe* script.)[8] The plot derives from an anecdote about the reign of Tsar Pavel I (1754–1801), widely rumored to be mad. A scribe's slip of the pen inadvertently adds a nonexistent lieutenant by the name of "Kizhe" to the ranks of Pavel's army, yet none of the Tsar's circle has enough courage to incur the wrath of the volatile monarch by pointing out the fictional nature of this absent lieutenant.[9] Through bureaucratic incompetence, Kizhe manages to get himself banished to Siberia, return triumphantly, marry the belle of St. Petersburg, and ultimately attain the rank of general before perishing from a mysterious illness—all, of course, absurdly engineered by members of the Tsar's court for their personal gain. Tinyanov's script is, however, much more than a trifling lampoon of an oft-told anecdote. From start to finish, the author pays conscious homage to Nikolay Gogol, freighting his text with exaggerated, carica-tured individuals who blend black comedy and the tragic. The anecdote, in the words of one critic, "developed into a gloomy phantasmagoria."[10]

The silent version, to have been directed by Sergey Yutkevich (1904–85), went unrealized for lack of studio support. Tinyanov thereafter turned his script into a successful short story that appeared in 1928 under the title *Second Lieutenant Kizhe* (*Podporuchik Kizhe*).[11] The positive reception of the short story prompted Tinyanov in 1932 to revisit the idea of a *Kizhe* film. By this point, sound cinema had appeared in Russia; Tinyanov accordingly revised his original silent scenario to include spoken dialogue.[12] The newly formed Belorussian State Film Studio (Belgoskino) agreed to produce the rewritten script at its Leningrad facility and engaged the greenish Alexander Fayntsimmer (1906–82) to direct the film under Tinyanov's close supervision.[13] The pairing was a practical one: Tinyanov lacked the tech-nical training needed to direct a sound picture and therefore assumed an advisory role, helping to shape the style and thematic content of the film. Fayntsimmer, one of the first graduates of the Moscow State Film Technicum (GTK), handled production issues.[14] According to the film's artistic con-sultant, Grigoriy Kozintsev (1905–73), Tinyanov made his presence felt advising the cast.[15] Erast Garin (1902–80), the actor who played the role of the Tsar's aide-de-camp, depended on the writer's advice:

Our work on the film alongside Tinyanov was a model of how col-laborative creation should ideally take place between a team of actors, a director, and a writer. From the very first rehearsals to the editing of the film, Yuriy Nikolayevich [Tinyanov] never failed to give us directions about the character of the figures we were play-ing and the era in which they lived.[16]

The Gogolian traits of the *Kizhe* characters, and the surrealistic world they inhabit, attest to Tinyanov's influence on Fayntsimmer, who helped transform Tinyanov's literary scenario into a usable script. So, too, did the casting: Garin's acting style, developed under the tutelage of the theater director Vsevolod Meyerhold (1874–1940), was touted for its provocative expressive aberrances.[17]

When the question of suitable music for *Lieutenant Kizhe* arose, both Tinyanov and Kozintsev insisted on seeking out Prokofiev. The Belgoskino administration expressed considerable trepidation over this choice, since they felt that the Paris-based composer's extended absences from Leningrad would hinder his ability to meet deadlines and thus disrupt the film's production schedule.[18] This was a valid concern: despite the increasing frequency of Prokofiev's visits to Leningrad and Moscow, Paris had been his home for more than a decade and his permanent return to Russia remained over three years in the future. Working with Prokofiev, however, had distinct advantages. *Kizhe* involved elaborate eighteenth-century costuming and sets (Leningrad's actual neoclassical architecture graces the outdoor scenes), and the score would need to preserve and enhance the time and place suggested by these staging efforts. Prokofiev's neoclassical syntax, emblematized by his Classical Symphony (1917), greatly appealed to Tinyanov and Kozintsev. But the real draw was his international profile, which lent prestige to a film other-wise created at a minor new studio by a virtually unknown director and little-known actors. One critic later commented: "Speaking frankly, I attended because of Prokofiev's music."[19]

When Prokofiev's third Soviet tour in late 1932 brought him to Leningrad, Tinyanov and his associates dispatched the Belgoskino employee Boris Gusman (1892–1944) to negotiate a contract for the film. *Kizhe* was the first of several commissions that Gusman facilitated for Prokofiev; in this regard he abetted the composer's transition to permanent residence in Soviet Russia.[20] On December 3, Prokofiev signed a tentative contract for the film during a meeting with Fayntsimmer and Tinyanov.[21]

From his journal entries we know that Prokofiev found the *Kizhe* subject matter appealing (the film's grating satire resonated with the composer's own sardonic sense of humor); his interest peaked when Gusman told him that the film would likely be distributed abroad.[22] This last detail was not unimportant to Prokofiev's career, for despite express-ing interest in working and perhaps even relocating to the Soviet Union, he had not taken practical steps beyond securing a Soviet passport. At this point, furthering his career in Western Europe (he possessed a French *certificat d'identité*) and America remained priorities. The film's exact musical requisites were unknown at this early stage in the production, and Fayntsimmer issued no explicit requests for the score beyond leit-motifs (hardly surprising, considering the prevalence of leitmotifs in film scores of the period). Fayntsimmer further assured Prokofiev that the film required only a modest amount of music—positive news for a peripatetic artist confronting an unfamiliar genre and an ambitious per-forming and composing schedule.[23]

Perhaps most pertinent to his prospects for the coming decade, the Belgoskino contract allowed Prokofiev the opportunity to realize his afore-mentioned interest in penning accessible music for the general public, an interest he had begun to articulate even before his 1930 visit to Hollywood. In 1929 in Paris, Prokofiev mused to his colleagues about enhancing the popular appeal of serious music. "We shall use simpler means of instru-mentation, write less fully, but still retain the best, the most potent and most poignant and most expressive of modern harmonization. . . . Thus I have grown simpler in form, less complex in counterpoint and more melodic in my musical evolution, which I call a new simplicity."[24] Articles for the Soviet and French press in the early 1930s further evince Prokofiev's efforts to connect with the masses.[25] Accessible music, he argued, was extremely difficult to compose, since it should be as uncomplicated and unprepos-sessing as possible without resorting to the "repetition of conventional formulas."[26] Exploration of this realm of music, including his score for *Kizhe* as well as his incidental music for the Shaw- and Shakespeare-based drama *Egyptian Nights* (*Yegipetskiye nochi*, 1934), supplemented Prokofiev's labor on "more serious symphonic compositions, designed for the more refined tastes of experienced musicians."[27]

From the perspective of Prokofiev's relocation to Russia in the spring of 1936, we might interpret this statement as blatant pandering to Soviet musical aesthetics. When he signed the *Kizhe* contract, however, he had by no means resolved to live in Moscow. Moreover, the anti-modernist shockwaves of the Stalinist cultural repressions had yet to be felt. Prokofiev's "new simplicity" is perhaps better understood in the general aesthetic context of Les Six and the populism—however acerbic and poli-tically charged—of Copland, Marc Blitzstein, and Kurt Weill.

The absence of any obvious interest in the *Kizhe* project on the part of Soviet cultural agencies will become increasingly apparent as its history unfolds below. The film was realized in a sociopolitical environment that drastically differed from that of Prokofiev's later film work. The official practice of defining the amount, subject, and ideological orientation of the films to be made in a given year became standard only in 1934, and arguably the first organized and effective display of the regime's control of the medium did not occur until 1935, when the nation's leading film directors were forced to denounce their past "mistakes."[28] As Peter Kenez argues, in the early 1930s official energies were directed at tempering, rather than eradicating, the Formalist methods of Sergey Eisenstein (1898–1948), Vsevolod Pudovkin (1893–1953), and Alexander Dovzhenko (1894–1956).[29]

Following a master class with composition students at the Moscow Conservatory in early May 1933, Prokofiev opened his journal and wrote almost prophetically that the meeting "gave me the idea of what I must now do: [compose music] for the masses that would at the same time remain good music. My previous work on melody and the search for a 'new simplicity' have prepared me considerably for this."[30] In the following weeks, Prokofiev busied himself with work on *Kizhe*, and with the question that had taken form years before in Hollywood.

Outlines

Work on the score began during Prokofiev's tour in the Soviet Union in spring 1933 (his most extensive to date, including Moscow and excursions to Georgia and Armenia), when he renewed contact with Gusman and Fayntsimmer in Leningrad. Among the composer's initial concerns was the mood of each of the pieces he would compose, a subject addressed in earnest at these meetings.[31] Belgoskino invited the composer to visit the set in late April, an experience that, to Fayntsimmer and Tïnyanov's presumed consternation, disappointed him. Prokofiev found the costuming uninspired and the acting sub par; the after-work party, he grumbled in his journal, was the lone positive of his visit.[32] Yet his initial displeasure with the state of the production could not have been too acute, for he began work on the score almost immediately. While still in the Soviet Union, he composed two short songs, "Stonet sizïy golubochek" (The little gray dove is moaning) and "Oh, ma belle demoiselle," which Fayntsimmer intended as diegetic (visual point of origin) music.[33] On pieces of scrap paper, Prokofiev also sketched several short pieces for military-style percussion that underlined the centrality of the imperial army in the plot, while also mocking, with clocklike rhythms, the un-clocklike vagaries of life under Pavel.[34] Prokofiev finished this group of pieces in just under two weeks; Fayntsimmer appeared pleased with the result.[35]

In late May, Prokofiev returned to Belgoskino, this time actively participating in the filmmaking process. Fayntsimmer showed the composer a rehearsal of a scene that included "Stonet sizïy golubochek," which was originally conceived as a brief duet between Pavel, played by actor Mikhaíl Yanshin (1902–76) and the female lead, Princess Gagarina, played by actress Nina Shaternikova (1902–82). Yanshin's musicianship did not rise to the task—Prokofiev scoffed that he had "the ears of a bear"—which necessitated reconceiving the music on the spot.[36] Fayntsimmer encouraged Prokofiev to sing the song himself while Yanshin mouthed the words, but the composer insisted on having his wife Lina, a trained soprano, perform the song. Fayntsimmer consented to this arrangement, but not without some trepidation, for it necessitated restructuring the scene to accommodate a solo female voice.[37] In the updated configuration, Pavel and Princess Gagarina play a game of cards as the latter's lady-in-waiting performs the song. Although no evidence survives to indicate whose voice was ultimately used in the film's sound-track, it may well be Lina's, making it the only recording of her voice known to exist. The more technically challenging "Oh ma belle demoi-selle" (No. 12) required a similar adjustment: the script called for a member of the Tsar's inner circle to entertain the guests with the song at Kizhe's wedding party, but Fayntsimmer amended the scene so that the song would be heard from a distance, outside the visual frame. Prokofiev later imported a traditional *chastushka* (a satirical Russian limerick) for Yanshin (No. 9) that he knew from Nikolay Rimsky-Korsakov's 1876 folk-song collection; it accommodated the actor's limited singing skills while underscoring Pavel's perceived imbecility. The text and the six-measure tune play over and over again, with only the slightest of variations:[38]

Yol' - nik moy yol' - nik, Cha - stïy moy ber - yoz - nik.

Example 1. No. 9: "Pesnya Pavla" (Pavel's song), mm. 1–6. The text reads "Little pine tree, my little pine tree, thick is my little birch tree."

Prokofiev no sooner arrived in Leningrad than he departed; his visits to Belgoskino were a luxury he could not indulge. At the end of May, four days after his second visit to the set, he returned to Paris. For the next four months—until the recording of the *Kizhe* score in October—Fayntsimmer's letters served as the composer's only line of contact with the studio. Composing and filming occurred simultaneously but independently, in separate corners of Europe. When Prokofiev left Leningrad, most of *Kizhe* had yet to be shot (Fayntsimmer remained on the set as late as September), and the composer himself had completed only three of the score's eventual seventeen numbers (nos. 2, 3, and 11).[39] He composed almost the entire score for images he had not seen, relying solely on verbal descriptions of the scenes in question and, in a few instances, the specific timings of those scenes. There exist other early films whose music was composed before the shooting, but the practice was unusual.[40] Shostakovich, for example, did not begin to compose his score for the 1929 film *The New Babylon* (*Novïy Vavilon*) until he viewed the edited footage with stopwatch in hand.[41]

Prokofiev sent the score from Paris to Leningrad in installments over the course of the summer. In the first group of pieces, couriered on July 13, he included precise metronome indications, which, taking into account the tempo indications, time signatures, and measure counts, permitted Fayntsimmer to calculate the exact length of the number in advance of its recording. Although the director's specific requests for Prokofiev do not survive, the available evidence suggests that he specified the lengths of several of the numbers.[42] Prokofiev voiced concern that the music for shot 19 of the film (No. 3) ran too long—21 seconds—which confirms that the director had given him the timing in advance (the composer adds that it would be a "pity" to abbreviate an attractive piece to accommodate the stopwatch). Prokofiev likewise quotes an exact duration of 60 seconds for the music that accompanies shot 359 (No. 10) in a letter dated July 13.[43] In these instances, he proved competent at composing to order, one of the obligatory tasks of the film composer—fulfilling Fayntsimmer's requests to the second.[44]

Prokofiev wrote at least four numbers, however, for scenes without precise timings, an obstacle he resourcefully navigated. The music that accompanies the opening episode (No. 1) lasts 88 seconds if performed as written, but it is designed to be lengthened or shortened in two-second increments as needed through the addition or subtraction of certain measures.[45] The conductor could reduce the four repeated measures preceding rehearsal number 2 to two measures (a passage for solo percussion, see Example 2) or alternately expand them to anywhere from 5 to 8 measures. The length of the number varied by 12 seconds.

Later in the same number Prokofiev duplicates these four measures, indicating the same option to repeat or omit, effectively increasing the amount it could be varied from 12 to 24 seconds. An analogous example exists in the music for the "Rozhdeniye Kizhe" (Birth of Kizhe) sequence (No. 5), in which the composer provided an optional four-measure episode in brackets.[46] Prokofiev thus made it possible for Fayntsimmer to experiment with different durations, contingent on how the scene had been edited: 33 seconds if the cut is taken, 42 seconds if not. While efficient, Prokofiev's method underscored the fact that, beyond the question of duration, his music did not directly engage with the images. The audio and visual tracks were, from a narrative standpoint, neither synchronic nor asynchronic—they merely coexisted. In solving the logistical challenge of composing away from the set, Prokofiev conceived an eerily lonely soundtrack.

Example 2. "Nachal'nïy boy barabanov" (The initial roll of the drums); four measures before rehearsal number 2.

He did manage to include a passing allusion (or tribute) to gestural music, otherwise known as "Mickey Mousing."[47] The director filmed the opening episode (following the unaccompanied title shots) through a kaleidoscopic lens, presenting the viewer with fragmented, surrealistic images of the imperial army marching in various slowly shifting geometric patterns. The episode foregrounds the doubles, overlays, and parallels of Tïnyanov's Gogolian plotline. This is the only section of the film in which music and image align: the soldiers' footsteps—floating oddly in the optical space—precisely match the pacing of Prokofiev's fife-and-drum accompaniment (No. 1). The audiovisual pairing invites the viewer to perceive the music meta-diegetically, as one of the character's dreams or hallucinations. (Tïnyanov's script did not actually call for this sequence: it was clearly added by Fayntsimmer.) The synchronization of sight and sound in the film thereafter ceases: with the exception of the aforementioned song (No. 11), there is no further alignment.[48] The scene depicting Pavel's ludicrous inspection of the clumsily assembled imperial army ranks offers a parallel to the opening episode. This time, however, there are no special visual effects, and the rhythm of the marching falls out of sync with the music—even though the score serves a function identical to that of the opening episode. For the roll call, Fayntsimmer and Prokofiev appear to have exchanged surrealism for caricature.

As the filming progressed, Fayntsimmer found that he could further manipulate Prokofiev's score by taking advantage of its obvious sectionalization. During Kizhe's wedding party the director fills almost an entire scene with a single excerpt from Prokofiev's score (No. 14; see Example

3), repeating different passages in different groupings. The orchestra intones the introduction over and over again to accommodate a visual sequence lasting nearly three minutes with only sparse dialog. The entire

Example 3. No. 14: "Kizhe zhenitsya" (Kizhe marries), mm. 1–8.

number is thereafter twice repeated, first with the introduction and then without it.

In this fashion, approximately 68 seconds of music accompany more than five minutes of the action. Fayntsimmer extended and expanded the score without the composer's input, and without concern for audio-visual coordination.

At the end of the summer, difficulties arose on the *Kizhe* set. Fayntsimmer's working script, derived from Tïnyanov's intricate literary scenario, proved to be cumbersome and impractical. Sensing that he and other members of the creative team had been too ambitious, the director streamlined the plot of the film in mid-production, trimming extraneous dialogue and deleting superfluous subplots.[49] His tinkering earned him the ire of at least one critic, who claimed that the transfer of Tïnyanov's scenario to the screen had reduced it to "vaudeville."[50] The alterations likewise disconcerted Prokofiev; he was putting finishing touches on the orchestration (most of the score was completed two months earlier), when an urgent letter arrived from Fayntsimmer (dated September 13) apprising him of the changes and requesting his immediate presence in Leningrad to assist with "decisions regarding the music"—the alterations had adversely affected the musical design.[51] Prokofiev later complained in his autobiography that the script suffered multiple revisions, resulting in a mediocre final product. Clearly, he found Fayntsimmer's eleventh-hour alterations exasperating.[52] The same critic (Nikolay Otten) who had trivialized the film for its vaudeville-isms agreed: the repeated abuse of the script had, from the standpoint of character development, rendered it inconsistent.[53]

The flexible, adaptable score was, however, wholly spared the cutting-room floor. Fayntsimmer merely shifted the positions of several of the score's shorter numbers to accommodate the script's revisions. It emerges that the treatment of the score by the director and composer reflected a conception of audiovisual relationships at odds with 1930s trends toward audiovisual symphonism. The disconnectedness of the seventeen numbers precluded the fashioning of a soundtrack that, in Tatiana Egorova's words, "plays an important role in the development of the action . . . , reminding the audience of past events, or anticipating those that were still to happen, and passing emotional judgment on what was shown on the screen."[54]

Prokofiev's tour of Russia in the fall of 1933 (to Leningrad, Moscow, and Voronezh) allowed him another visit to the Belgoskino facilities, where he assisted Fayntsimmer in devising an updated musical plan.[55] Their adjustments were innocuous: they transferred what was originally the sixth number of the score to the end, where it accompanies the Tsar's concluding monologue. They also extended the Tsar's *chastushka*. When the Tsar finishes singing and clapping the ditty, a brass band takes it up and carries it into the next scene, where it graces a textless visual sequence. Prokofiev evidently composed the extension while on the set; the passage for brass band does not appear in the various extant versions of the score. Further tasks included infusing Kizhe's wedding scene with traditional Russian Orthodox choral music. This music is likewise absent from the extant scores; it seems to have been taken from a preexisting recording.

In the end, Prokofiev fashioned a score with an unavoidably incidental relationship to the visual images. His early involvement in the filming process resulted in changes to the visuals in deference to the music, however, as the adjustments to "Stonet sizïy golubochek" demonstrate. Although *Kizhe* effectively shuns audiovisual coordination, the editing process was, ironically, much more symbiotic than typical in cinema.

Music for an Absent Hero

In a brief memoir, the assistant (cast) director of *Lieutenant Kizhe* reconstructed a conversation between Prokofiev and the Belgoskino team in which the composer explained his conception of the soundtrack. After cautioning the team not to expect "illustration" from his score, Prokofiev reportedly emphasized the importance of musically conveying the time and place of the action and the essence of Tinyanov's characters.[56] The composer vaguely outlined how he intended his score to function within Tinyanov's and Fayntsimmer's Gogolian world while also describing his creative method. The soundtrack, he indicated, both accorded with and deviated from standard cinematic practices of the time.

Even with Fayntsimmer's embellishments, most of the 87-minute film unfolds without musical underlay, and only four of the seventeen numbers last more than a minute. In this respect *Kizhe* differs markedly from the noise-filled "silent" films to which most Russian filmgoers were accustomed.[57] The economical score affronted the practices of other studio composers, who produced soundtracks that mimicked through-composed symphonic structures (see, for example, Shostakovich's thick scores for *Zlatniye gori* (Golden mountains), 1931, and *Lyubov' i nenavist'* (Love and hatred), 1934.[58] The *Kizhe* score behaves like the invisible lieutenant himself: it exists as an "absent" presence, a reference point in the plotline rather than an actual character.

Referring to his incidental music for *Egyptian Nights*—a theatrical conception that Prokofiev deemed the sibling of *Kizhe*—the composer wrote that "in the art of composing for the stage the following rule may be observed: music is justified if its presence in a scene reinforces the scene's dramatic or lyrical nature; in that case it occupies a rightful place."[59] The miniaturized, discontinuous numbers that characterize *Kizhe* and *Egyptian Nights* show that the composer understood his task as bolstering the emotional and psychological underpinning of select moments in select episodes. He determined that sporadic passages of nondevelopmental background music afforded a more arresting, more engaging means of enhancing and enriching the visuals than continuous developmental music.

Continuous background scoring, or what Claudia Gorbman calls "the bath of affect" that infuses most sound films, "lessens spatial and temporal discontinuities . . . , and draws the spectator further into the fantasy-illusion suggested by filmic narration."[60] The music remains outside the viewer's sphere of perception because of, rather than in spite of, its constant presence. The *Kizhe* score engages the audience through opposing means: the "bath of affect" is supplanted by punctuating shards of sound. Extended silences place the entrances of the seventeen numbers into sharp relief; as a result, the viewer becomes more cognizant of their existence. The dialogue in *Kizhe* tends to be terse, stressing the intonations of individual words, individual syllables, over complete sentences; periods of musical silence hauntingly correspond to periods of verbal silence.

The occasional intrusion of the music into the viewer's perception is perhaps best illustrated by the thirteen-note motif that comes to represent the absent protagonist:

Example 4. The Kizhe motif.

Prokofiev's reliance on this motif is neither innovative nor progressive; he, like other film composers of the period, heeded the requests of their directors for nondevelopmental recollection themes.[61] Its creation numbered among Tïnyanov's and Fayntsimmer's first requests to Prokofiev, and he fulfilled the request with typical precision.[62] Almost all of the score's numbers—the exceptions being the numbers scored for solo percussion and the diegetic songs—have the Kizhe motive at their basis. The integration of the motif into the soundtrack is noteworthy in several respects. First, the brevity and relative simplicity of the motif (it falls within the range of a perfect fourth and comprises just four pitches) illustrates the appealing directness of Prokofiev's "new simplicity." Second, because the motif lacks development, and because it persists in the soundtrack (in contradistinction to the other musical numbers)—it lingers in the ear, sounding even when it is silent.[63] The motif's chromatic displacement, finally, symbolizes Kizhe's physical displacement. For the grimmer episodes in the plotline—the imaginary lieutenant's flogging before his exile to Siberia (No. 7), and his somber funeral procession (No. 15)—Prokofiev enhances the chromaticism while ensuring that the motif remains recognizable:

Example 5a. No. 7: "Kizhe sekut" (Kizhe is flogged), mm. 10–13.

Example 5b. No. 15: "Kizhe umer" (Kizhe dies), mm. 7–11.

Throughout the film, Fayntsimmer makes comic reference to Kizhe's nonexistence, to the fact that he is, as the other characters (who at least exist on celluloid) whisper to each other, "a secret figure, without form." At Kizhe's wedding, the priest holds a crown (a traditional marriage symbol in Russian Orthodox ceremonies) over the absent head of the absent groom. Later, Kizhe's empty boots are spotted beneath his chair, drawing attention to his missing feet and legs; following the hero's death a retinue bearing an empty coffin processes through the streets of St. Petersburg. In each episode, Kizhe's motif becomes the lieutenant's aural embodiment. Herein is a reference of sorts to the ontology of music, which, despite being written down, only truly exists in performance. Prokofiev's ephemeral, apparitional score is in this regard the perfect emblem of the film's protagonist. The viewer hears rather than sees Kizhe's "appearances" at pivotal moments in the plot, from his birth at the scribe's desk to his banishment, brilliant marriage, and bathetic demise. Prokofiev also deploys the motif when Pavel muses on the greatness of the lieutenant whom he has never met (Nos. 6 and 10).

In his July 13, 1933 letter to Fayntsimmer, Prokofiev announced that he had composed "a very beautiful fanfare" that he wanted heard when a title card sets the scene in the year 1800:[64]

Example 6. No. 4: "Izdali slïshna truba" (A trumpet sounds from afar), complete.

Somewhere in the course of shooting it was decided to reprise the fanfare at the end of the film; Fayntsimmer subsequently used it a third time, in the middle, to accompany a scene showing St. Petersburg asleep at night.[65] At the beginning and ending of the film we see Pavel in the same state: slumbering in the uneasy quiet of the Imperial palace. Prokofiev's fanfare thus comes to represent both the poorly governed aristocratic city and its poorly behaved, decadent ruler, whose waking becomes the inadvertent cause of Kizhe's exile to Siberia.

Fayntsimmer and Tïnyanov entrusted Prokofiev to provide the *couleur locale* of Kizhe's exploits, a task he dutifully fulfilled. To quote one reviewer, "It is precisely [his] music that more than anything gives the film the color of the epoch."[66] Prokofiev builds his depiction of imperial St. Petersburg on a traditional tonal foundation, a late eighteenth-century patina of common practice conventions. He was loathe, however, to merely appropriate Haydnesque language for the sake of authenticity, instead maintaining a consciously modern tonal palette that more often parodies tonal practice than imitates it (note the jarringly dissonant tritone harmony in Example 3, measure 7), an approach in keeping with Tïnyanov's parodic stylizations.[67]

In addition to employing common practice allusions in the numbers coinciding with events at the Tsar's court, Prokofiev highlights the importance of the imperial army to St. Petersburg life with four numbers (2, 3, 8, and a significant portion of 1) scored for percussion. He intended each number to be repeated as needed, and Fayntsimmer took full advantage of the options. The persistent rat-a-tatting (all but absent in the familiar *Lieutenant Kizhe* Suite) at times imbues the period setting with bellicose splendor, at other times renders it surreal. "The rhythm of the drums," one critic remarked, "continues throughout the film—during the wedding, during the funeral, during Pavel's amorous scenes—giving it an extraordinarily coarse, grotesque underlining."[68] Another critic focused on the inclusion of percussion in the wedding scene: here the clattering is juxtaposed with stylized Russian Orthodox singing, imparting a "grotesque coloring to the entire wedding ceremony, which is perceived by the listener as sarcasm."[69]

The entire score's stylistic break with symphonic convention, its sparse texture, and its terseness find parallels in the soundtracks of Copland and Virgil Thomson, whose efforts in the genre reflect modernist musical

Figure 1. The wedding ceremony.

practice even while drawing upon American folk idioms.[70] These traits did not, however, strike the reviewers of *Lieutenant Kizhe* as particularly significant; their attention remained on the script, specifically Tïnyanov's strangely incongruous attention to period setting and language. During the semi-official assessment of the film that followed its completion (but preceded its general release) in early 1934, Boris Brodyansky (1902–45), a conservative Belgoskino scriptwriter, crudely and harshly attacked the film for its eclecticism and abstraction, while also branding Tïnyanov a "cheat" who had compromised the honor of the studio. Another Belgoskino employee, A. Nekrashevich, concurred, declaring the production of *Kizhe* a strategic mistake. Tïnyanov blanched at the criticism and terminated his relationship with the studio.[71] The film's detractors further decried Fayntsimmer's penchant for abstraction, asserting that it would alienate unsophisticated audiences—an ironic state of affairs considering Prokofiev's attempt to fashion an accessible, audience-friendly soundtrack. Fortunately, at least for the sake of the composer's nascent Soviet career, the post-release reviews of the film were less contentious than those of the Belgoskino ideologues.

Celluloid Sound

The sheer number of composers who tried their hand at film music in the early twentieth century attests not only to the novelty of the medium but also to its compelling, progressive manipulation of technology. Even the Moscow critic who accused Fayntsimmer of purveying vaudeville admitted that, despite the film's drawbacks, *Kizhe* marked an impressive technological advance for Belgoskino and cinema culture in general.[72] What Jennifer Doctor dubs "ultra-modern music" reached larger, more diverse audiences as the concert hall ceded to the recording studio.[73] Beyond exploring a new aesthetic paradigm in *Kizhe*, Prokofiev had to contend with such logistical challenges as composing for the microphone.[74] He discovered in the process that technology not only provided access to a larger audience, it allowed him to manipulate sound in hitherto inconceivable ways.

On June 26, 1932, Prokofiev traveled to London to perform and record his Third Piano Concerto (1921) with Pierre Coppola and the London Symphony Orchestra—one of his first experiences in a well-equipped recording studio.[75] During the two-day session (the novelty of which elicited an impromptu visit by H.R.H. Prince George, the future Duke of Kent) the process of working at the microphone alternately intrigued and exhausted the composer:

We began to record a test disc. If there are wrong notes, no matter; what matters is to know the relationship between the piano and the orchestra and that between the orchestral instruments. We played the test disc and found that the piano was a bit weak and that the second violins, bassoons, and oboes were not heard in the orchestra. Then the bassoons and oboes rushed the tempo, and the second violins got mixed up with the first. We played the second test.

This sounded so good that it's quite a shame we spoiled it (playing an unfinished disc destroys it). My playing sounded good in places, energetic, but in other places—those with a little uncertainty or artificiality—it was mannered. In general, the most insignificant of mannerisms, those that go unnoticed in a typical performance, are sufficient, since the gramophone immediately amplifies them.

We began to record the first real take. Emotion, of course, and I played with much tension, not entirely steady. The first disc nonetheless came out well except for the second clarinet playing wrong notes. We repeated it; the clarinet played correctly, but I played worse. Three hours thus passed. I worked with great interest, but I was glad when it was over since I was tired of concentrating.[76]

Like most of the composers and performers who made recordings in the 1920s and 1930s, Prokofiev found the process unsettling and unforgiving. Following the session with the Third Piano Concerto, he bemoaned the challenge of playing with complete precision for four-minute stretches (the length of one side of a gramophone record). In a letter to his Moscow-based colleague Nikolay Myaskovsky dated June 11, 1932, he joked, "Just think—I can't sneeze or miss any notes!"[77] Calculating balance among instruments, returning to correct missed notes, not to mention the opportunity to judge the technical plusses and minuses of each test disc—all taken for granted in the digital age—nonetheless captured Prokofiev's imagination while also fueling his obsessions with detail and organization.

Scholars habitually associate Prokofiev's interest in recording technology with his collaboration with Sergey Eisenstein on the 1938 film *Alexander Nevsky*. The association stems from an article about *Nevsky* written by the composer, in which he describes placing microphones close to the brass to generate repellant distortion—an obvious musical symbol of the repellant Teutonic knights.[78] Prokofiev explored similar effects in *Kizhe*. The electronic transfer of the unusually prominent percussion in the film was one of his first concerns when he began working with Fayntsimmer on the score. In May 1933 he sketched out a few drum patterns in order to assess the amount of distortion produced by the Belgoskino equipment.[79] These "exercises" evidently proved satisfactory, since he included them in the finished score.[80] Prokofiev often referred to the recording process in his dispatches to Fayntsimmer from Paris; his remarks attest to his anxieties about how his scoring would fare on disc. For "Kizhe's return" (No. 13) he wanted the violins to "play loudly and significantly, but with mutes." He clarified, however, that if the mutes made for a "poor recording," he did not oppose excluding them.[81] It is entirely possible that the composer knew that the strings reproduced weakly on disc, which would account for the prominence of wind and brass instruments in his orchestration.[82]

Prokofiev found that in the recording studio balance was less dictated by the conductor and ensemble than by the placement of the microphone. For "Kizhe's birth" (No. 5), he deduced that the trumpets could crescendo without distortion if they played away from the microphone.[83] In his draft score, he likewise noted that the horns in "Kizhe's funeral" (No. 16) needed to be placed before the microphone in order to be heard. He later added in pencil that the bassoon should join them, obviously fearing that its part would be submerged in the relatively thick orchestration.[84] Prokofiev iterated these instructions to Fayntsimmer, noting that everything except the horns and bassoon must sound "as if from a distance."[85]

In the first decade of sound film, and as exemplified by the 1927 classic *The Jazz Singer*, sound technology served as a dramatic device. This technology reached the Soviet Union later than Western Europe and North America: when *Kizhe* went into production, only 300 of the nation's 32,000 projectors were equipped for sound.[86] The complex audiovisual dialogue in the film's opening minutes doubtless struck Soviet audiences as extremely modern—Prokofiev and Fayntsimmer's technical wizardry, in short, enriched the film's surrealistic atmosphere.

Other Opportunities

In the midst of his work with Fayntsimmer, Prokofiev considered composing a score for an animated film, one that replicated the aesthetic, logistical, and technical concerns of *Lieutenant Kizhe*. The offer of a contract for this second project hardly surprised the composer; in prewar Russia cartoons accounted for a significant percentage of the films released. Of the thirty-five Soviet films that appeared in theaters during 1934, no fewer than eight were animated.[87] Films intended for younger audiences—animated versions of traditional fairy tales (*skazki*), for example—served both political and nonpolitical educational purposes.

On June 6, 1933, the last day of his tour of Russia (and following his initial encounters with Belgoskino), Prokofiev received a visit from a group he humorously referred to as "cartoon people." They showed him a working version of a new animated film called *Skazka o tsare Durandaye* (The tale of Tsar Durandai).[88] Directed by Ivan Ivanov-Vano (1900–1987), it adapted the plotline of a traditional satire about the plights of Tsar Durandai (meaning "old fool") and his covertly wicked fiancée Tyotka (old dear). The plot is suitably uncomplicated and, like that of *Lieutenant Kizhe*, transparently anti-tsarist: Tyotka, not wanting to wed the Tsar, poisons him and his faithful servant Sila (force); ultimately, she perishes as punishment for her wrongdoings. Prokofiev took to the film and immediately (perhaps owing to his imminent departure for Paris) signed the contract to compose the "accompanying music" for it.[89]

As outlined in the contract, Prokofiev's responsibilities included the composition of three dances (one for each of the principal characters in the tale) in piano score by the end of the same month, a rather tight deadline. He would need to complete the remainder of the music in short score by October 1, four months away, and to orchestrate it no later than November 1; the contract included the special provision that Prokofiev would participate directly in the film-editing process whenever he might be in Moscow. For his labors, Prokofiev was promised a commission equal to that agreed upon for *Kizhe*: 10,000 rubles.[90]

However, when *The Tale of Tsar Durandai* opened on March 2, 1934, the soundtrack comprised music by Anatoliy Aleksandrov (1888–1982), not Prokofiev.[91] Why or at what point Prokofiev ceased his involvement in the film's production remains unclear, but the absence of documents pertaining to the film in his archival holdings (beyond the unfulfilled contract) suggests that he never began work on the score. It likewise remains unclear whether he or the studio broke the contract.[92] Prokofiev perhaps thought better of committing to the project after returning to Paris, where he faced the task of completing the score for *Kizhe* as well as attending to other compositional projects, notably his *Symphonic Song* and the sketches for what would become his Cello Concerto in E Minor.

Although Prokofiev did not write the music for *The Tale of Tsar Durandai*, his interest in doing so reveals that, as in the case of *Kizhe*, he had few qualms about composing film music "to order" and even fewer qualms about working without direct contact with the studio or the director. Ivanov-Vano's film, with its streamlined, easy-to-grasp plot, would have likewise offered him a diversion from heavier creative labors.

Kozintsev

Ironically, the harshest critique of the music of *Lieutenant Kizhe* came from Grigoriy Kozintsev, who, together with Tïnyanov, had originally insisted that Prokofiev be awarded the commission for it. On the eve of the film's general release in the Soviet Union, he expressed his displeasure with the music:

> If the studio had paid more attention [to Prokofiev], he would have written remarkable music. Instead he produced merely good music. . . . Details were insufficiently explained to him, which in turn produced flawed results. This is not Prokofiev's fault. He is a first-rate European and Soviet artist who would bring honor to any studio in which he worked. But there is a need to guide him a bit more attentively in order to receive the maximum from him.[93]

Taking into account Prokofiev's subsequent successful collaboration with Eisenstein on *Alexander Nevsky* and *Ivan the Terrible* (1942–46), a collaboration that involved frequent meetings and regular contact under trying conditions, Kozintsev's remarks would seem to have merit. Producing the compact and succinct *Kizhe* score nonetheless proved beneficial both for Prokofiev's mutating technique and his nascent populist aesthetic.

Despite a long, convoluted path to the screen, *Lieutenant Kizhe* enjoyed success: following an elaborate advertising campaign in (among other Soviet newspapers) *Vechernyaya Moskva* (Evening Moscow), the film opened at no fewer than six Moscow theaters on March 7, 1934.[94] Summarizing the general public response, E. Koltsova lauded Fayntsimmer for demonstrating command and control in his first sound film, but critiqued his emphasis on the grotesque.[95] Later in 1934, the film premiered in France as *Lieutenant Nantes* and in the United States as *The Czar Wants to Sleep.*[96] Four years later, the original version still remained in the repertoire of regional Soviet theaters.[97] The relative success of the project came at a crucial juncture in Prokofiev's career, a point when he was exploring the potentials of a stripped-down style while maintaining a reputation for innovative harmonic, rhythmic, and orchestral effects. *Kizhe* opened the door for new commissions with new collaborators, increased the composer's reputation in Soviet artistic circles, and encouraged him, for better and worse, toward a permanent return to his homeland.

NOTES

I am indebted to the staffs of the Serge Prokofiev Archive, the Russian State Archive of Literature and Art, and the Russian State Film Archive (Gosfil'mofond) for their assistance with my research. Special thanks are due to Annegret Fauser and Jon Finson for their advice on early drafts. Funding was provided by the Andrew W. Mellon Foundation.

1. Sergey Prokof'yev, *Dnevnik 1907–1933*, ed. Svyatoslav Prokof'yev, 2 vols. (Paris: Serge Prokofiev Estate, 2002), 2:755 (entry of February 12, 1930).

2. Prokofiev requested $5,000 (roughly equivalent to $60,000 in today's currency), which, had he received it, would have made the project more lucrative than his performing engagements. The film's backers determined that American audiences were insufficiently familiar with Prokofiev to merit the fee. Ibid., 2:756–57 (entry of February 14, 1930).

3. Ibid., 2:756 (entry of February 13, 1930).

4. Ibid.

5. See, for example, Elizabeth Crist's discussion of the sociopolitical underpinnings of Copland's works in *Music for the Common Man: Aaron Copland During the Depression and War* (New York: Oxford University Press, 2005).

6. The suite is very different in construction than the film score, which does not appear in Prokofiev's *Sobraniye sochineniy* (Collected works), ed. N. P. Anosov, 20 vols. (Moscow: Gosudarstvennoye muzïkal'noye izdatel'stvo, 1955–67). The film score exists in two versions in the Russian State Archive of Literature and Art (henceforth RGALI). The first is a short score in Prokofiev's hand containing thirteen numbers (RGALI f. 1929, op. 1, yed. khr. 92). The second is a full score in a copyist's hand with some notes in the composer's hand (RGALI f. 1929, op. 1, yed. khr. 91). The full score is missing the four pages that contain "Kizhe dies" and "Kizhe marries"; it is otherwise complete.

7. Despite claims to the contrary, Prokofiev found that he had to extend the amount of musical material he had composed for the film when he created the *Lieutenant Kizhe* Suite. See my "Creating the *Lieutenant Kizhe* Suite," *Three Oranges: The Journal of the Serge Prokofiev Foundation* 13 (2007): 22–26.

8. Jerry T. Heil, "*Poruchik Kizhe*: A Discussion," *California Slavic Studies* 14 (1992): 174. Tïnyanov wrote scripts for *The Overcoat* (1926), *SVD* (1927), *The Monkey and the Bell* (1932), and *Lieutenant Kizhe* (1927, 1934). For an overview of his film work, see Heil, "The Russian Literary Avant-Garde and the Cinema (1920s and 1930s): The Film-Work of Isaak Babel and Jurij Tynjanov" (PhD diss., University of California at Berkeley, 1984). The creative evolution of *Lieutenant Kizhe* is further traced by Yevgeniy Toddes, "Poslesloviye," in *Podporuchik Kizhe* (Moscow: Kniga, 1981), 164–200; and by Inna Sepman, "Tïnyanov-stsenarist," in *Iz istorii Lenfil'ma: Stat'i, vospominaniya, dokumentï*, ed. N. S. Gornitskaya, 4 vols. (Leningrad: Iskusstvo, 1968–75), 3:74–76.

9. The Tsar's scribe errs by accidentally entering "Poruchik Kizhe" (Lieutenant Kizhe), rather than the intended "Poruchiki zhe" (and the Lieutenants) on a list of soldiers to be added to the Preobrazhensky regiment. Before he can correct his mistake, the Tsar's assistant enters and demands the list for the Tsar's approval. Upon examining the list, Pavel immediately notices the name "Kizhe" because his title "Poruchik" is lacking the necessary hard sign (a diacritical used in nineteenth-century Russian in masculine nominative nouns). The Tsar adds this mark himself, thus facilitating Kizhe's "birth."

10. N[ikolay] Otten, "Poruchik Kizhe," *Kino*, January 10, 1934, p. 3.

11. According to Dmitriy Moldavskiy, the film was not produced because Tïnyanov and Yutkevich did not obtain backing from Sovkino; *V. Mayakovskiy v teatre i kino: Kniga o S. Yutkeviche* (Moscow: VTO, 1975), 88. On the silent version, see Yutkevich, *O kinoiskusstve* (Moscow: Iskusstvo, 1962), 42. The short story appeared in 1928 in the journal *Krasnaya Nov'*.

Kevin Bartig

12. Tïnyanov submitted a copy of this version to the Union of Soviet Writers for evaluation. See RGALI f. 631, op. 3, yed. khr. 48.

13. Belgoskino was established in Leningrad by Sergey Kirov (1886–1934) and Anatoliy Lunacharsky (1875–1933) at the request of the Belorussian government. Although the studio began producing films as early as 1928, logistical problems prevented it from moving to its permanent home in Minsk until 1939. See P. Shamshur, "Belïye nochi Belgoskino," in *Kino Sovetskoy Belorussii*, ed. E. L. Bondareva (Moscow: Iskusstvo, 1975), 113–14. Fayntsimmer directed two films prior to *Kizhe*: *Otel' Savoy* (1930) and *Schast'ye* (1932), both silent. Although he enjoyed a long career (his last film was made two years before his death in 1982), he remained somewhat obscure. See the brief entry in *Kino: Entsiklopedicheskiy slovar'*, ed. S. I. Yutkevich (Moscow: Sovetskaya entsiklopediya, 1986), 442.

14. Jay Leyda, *Kino: A History of the Russian and Soviet Film* (Princeton: Princeton University Press, 1983), 233.

15. Grigoriy Kozintsev, "O fil'me 'Poruchike Kizhe,'" in *Sobraniye sochineniy*, 5 vols. (Leningrad: Iskusstvo, 1982–86), 2:28.

16. E[rast] Garin, "Obogashcheniye literaturï," *Literaturnaya gazeta*, January 15, 1935, as quoted in Mikhail Iampolski, *The Memory of Tiresias: Intertextuality and Film*, trans. Harsha Ram (Berkeley: University of California Press, 1998), 194. Garin, who made his screen debut in *Kizhe*, was the only member of the cast to achieve fame.

17. Julia Listengarten, *Russian Tragifarce: Its Cultural and Political Roots* (Selinsgrove, Penn.: Susquehanna University Press, 2000), 137.

18. I. Rummel', "Iz istorii Poruchika Kizhe," *Sovetskaya muzïka* 11 (1964): 69. This author's account dates from thirty years after the film was made, and may not be accurate. In a television broadcast, Garin confirmed that Tïnyanov and Kosintsev were behind the decision to approach Prokofiev. See RGALI f. 2979, op. 1, yed. khr. 224.

19. L[ev] Nikulin, "Zhizn' pod baraban," *Literaturnaya gazeta*, February 4, 1934. Clipping in RGALI f. 2979, op.1, yed. khr. 667.

20. In his early career Gusman worked for the newspaper *Pravda*, the film production unit Mezhrabpom-Rus, the Association of Revolutionary Cinematography, and, as assistant director, the Bolshoy Theater. In 1929, he lobbied for a Bolshoy Theater staging of Prokofiev's *Le Pas d'acier*. Besides the contracts for the *Kizhe* film score and suite, Gusman helped Prokofiev secure contracts for *Romeo and Juliet* (1935) and, in his later capacity as repertoire programmer for the All-Union Radio Committee, the *Cantata for the Twentieth Anniversary of October* (1937).

21. "Preliminary agreement between Prokofiev and kino-fabrika 'Sovetskaya Belorus,'" December 3, 1932," Serge Prokofiev Archive, Goldsmiths College, London (henceforth SPA), XXXII/II/03.12.1932. Rummel' relates that Prokofiev at first doubted his ability to finish the project, citing a busy schedule and the fact that he had no practical experience composing film music ("Iz istorii Poruchika Kizhe," 69). However, his journal entries for the period show no sign of hesitation. Prokofiev signed the formal contract with Belgoskino on March 16, 1933 (RGALI f. 1929, op. 1, yed. khr. 804, p.1).

22. Prokof'yev, *Dnevnik*, 2:816 (entry of December 2, 1932).

23. Ibid, 2:817 (entry of December 3, 1932). Prokofiev anticipated that the task would not overtax him ("nemnogo rabotï"). After the film had been vetted in Moscow and Leningrad in February 1934, Fayntsimmer informed Prokofiev that it had received positive reviews. He added that "the music was wonderfully received; it's a shame that there's so little of it." Letter of February 17, 1934, SPA XXXVI/222/17.02.1934.

24. "Prokofiev Hopes for the Arrival of a Period of 'New Simplicity' in Music," *Los Angeles Evening Express*, February 19, 1929, as quoted in Ludmilla Petchenina and Gérard Abensour, "*Egyptian Nights*: In Search of the 'New Simplicity,'" *Three Oranges: The Journal of the Serge Prokofiev Foundation* 7 (2004): 14.

25. See the composer's 1934 articles "Sovetskiy slushatel' i moye muzïkal'noye tvorchestvo," and "Puti sovetskoy muzïki," in *Prokof'yev o Prokof'yeve*, ed. V. P. Varunts (Moscow: Sovetskiy kompozitor, 1991), 126–28.

26. "Sovetskiy slushatel' i moye muzïkal'noye tvorchestvo," 126.

27. Ibid. This "serious" category included the composer's *Symphonic Song* (1933) and Cello Concerto in E Minor (1938). The score for Alexander Tairov's *Egyptian Nights* followed on the heels of Prokofiev's collaboration with Fayntsimmer. Prokofiev thereafter composed incidental music for two Pushkin dramas, *Boris Godunov* (1936) and *Eugene Onegin* (1936), and for Shakespeare's *Hamlet* (1938).

28. Peter Kenez, *Cinema and Soviet Society* (New York: I. B. Tauris, 2001), 117 and 121.

29. Ibid., 121.

30. Prokof'yev, *Dnevnik*, 2:829 (entry of May 2–5, 1933).

31. The first meeting took place on the evening of April 18. The composer writes that Gusman and Fayntsimmer were disappointed to learn about his other commitments. Prokof'yev, *Dnevnik*, 2:825 (entry of April 18, 1933).

32. Prokof'yev, *Dnevnik*, 2:826 (entry of April 22, 1933).

33. "Stonet sizïy golubochek" became No. 11 ("Pesnya Gagarinoy") in the final score. For this song, Prokofiev used a text by Fyodor Dubyansky (1760–96): "The little gray dove is moaning, moaning night and day, his dear little friend has long since flown away, long since flown away." Robert Kenneth Evans, "The Early Songs of Sergei Prokofiev and Their Relation to the Synthesis of the Arts in Russia" (PhD diss., Ohio State University, 1974), 54–55.

34. RGALI f. 1929, op. 1, yed. khr. 92, pp. 7–10. The fold marks and wear on these pages suggest that the composer kept them in his pocket when not working on them.

35. Prokof'yev, *Dnevnik*, 2:828 (entry of May 2–5, 1933).

36. According to Rummel', the filmmakers originally wanted to use guitar accompaniment for this song, but Prokofiev insisted on a harp, lest the piece sound like a "sentimental romance" ("Iz istorii Poruchika Kizhe," 69–70). On Yanshin's voice, see Prokof'yev, *Dnevnik*, 2:835 (entry of May 27, 1933).

37. Lina Prokofiev's voice was "tested" for inclusion in the film on May 29, 1933 (Prokof'yev, *Dnevnik*, 2:835–36).

38. The song is no. 27 in Rimsky-Korsakov's collection. In the later manuscript score, Prokofiev indicates that the song, which comprises a single phrase, can be repeated up to four times. In the film, Fayntsimmer repeats it an enervating ten times.

39. Prokofiev also sketched part of the solo percussion introduction to No. 1 while in Russia.

40. A notable exception is the classic Soviet comedy, *Vesyolïye rebyata* (1934, screened in the West as *Moscow Laughs*), which was fitted to an ersatz score by Isaak Dunayevsky (1900–1955). Thomas Lahusen discusses the audiovisual synchronization in "Ot nesinkhronizirovannogo smekha k post-sinkhronizirovannoy komedii, ili kak Stalinskiy myuzikl dognal i peregnal Gollivud," in *Sovetskoye bogatstvo: Stat'i o kul'ture, literatura i kino*, ed. Marina Balina (St. Petersburg: Akademicheskiy proyekt, 2002), 346. It merits adding that Ralph Vaughan Williams finished his score for *Scott of the Antarctic* (1948) six weeks before the filming had been completed. He worked with the script alone, without the aid of a chronometer. See John Huntley, "Music in Films," *The Musical Times* 98 (1957): 662.

41. Shostakovich's early film efforts had different stylistic and aesthetic aims than Prokofiev's. See John Riley, *Dmitri Shostakovich: A Life in Film* (London: I. B. Tauris, 2005), 7.

42. Both Rummel' ("Iz istorii Poruchika Kizhe," 69) and Garin suggest that Prokofiev had at least some exact timings; they even assert that he argued with Fayntsimmer about the duration of the numbers. RGALI f. 2979, op. 1, yed. khr. 224.

43. SPA XXXIV/210-11/13.07.1933.

44. Prokofiev was not entirely new to the task—the plans for his Parisian ballets often contained projected timings. See Stephen D. Press, *Prokofiev's Ballets for Diaghilev* (Burlington, VT: Ashgate, 2006), 210.

45. SPA XXXIV/210-11/13.07.1933.

46. Ibid.

47. On the practice of "Mickey Mousing," see Barbara White, "'As if they didn't hear the music,' Or: How I Learned to Stop Worrying and Love Mickey Mouse," *Opera Quarterly* 22, no. 1 (2007): 65–89.

Kevin Bartig

48. Of the three diegetic songs, No.11 is the only one in which the viewer *sees* any audio-visual coordination. In No. 9, the singing Tsar performs at a distance from the camera (it is unclear if his mouth is moving); in No. 12 the singing is partly unseen.

49. Here I am comparing Fayntsimmer's "rezhissyorskiy stsenariy" (reproduced in Heil, "Russian Literary Avant-Garde and the Cinema," 353–422) with my own viewing of the film. In the early 1930s it was still common for directors to prepare their own scripts from a literary scenario. Beginning in 1934, the journal *Sovetskoye kino* published scenarios for public discussion. Kenez, *Cinema and Soviet Society*, 128–29.

50. Otten, "Poruchik Kizhe," 3.

51. SPA XXXV/47/13.09.1933. In his September 27 reply, Prokofiev reports that he had completed the music for "Kizhe's funeral" and the "Return of Kizhe." All that remained was to orchestrate the former. SPA XXXV/90/27.09.1933.

52. Prokofiev wrote that the changes "muddled and confused" the film. "Avtobiografiya," in *S. S. Prokof'yev: Materialï, dokumentï, vospominaniya*, ed. S. I. Shlifshteyn (Moscow: Gosudarstvennoye muzïkal'noye izdatel'stvo, 1961), 191.

53. Otten, "Poruchik Kizhe," 3.

54. Tatiana Egorova, *Soviet Film Music: An Historical Survey* (Amsterdam: Harwood Academic Publishers, 1997), 25.

55. Prokofiev's journal unfortunately ceases before the fall of 1933; the composer briefly mentions being present for the recording in his autobiography, which was written in 1941 at the request of the editor of *Sovetskaya muzïka*. The Leningrad State Academic Orchestra recorded the score under Dunayevsky's direction on October 21, 1933.

56. Rummel', "Iz istorii Poruchika Kizhe," 69.

57. The switch to sound film in the Soviet Union was a protracted process. As late as 1938, silent film projectors still outnumbered sound film projectors. Kenez, *Cinema and Soviet Society*, 123–24.

58. Prokofiev saw *Golden Mountains* at the Théâtre Pigalle in Paris on June 26, 1932. Prokof'yev, *Dnevnik*, 2:805.

59. Petchenina and Abensour, "*Egyptian Nights*: In Search of the 'New Simplicity,'" 11.

60. Claudia Gorbman, *Unheard Melodies: Narrative Film Music* (Bloomington: Indiana University Press, 1987), 6.

61. The serious "operatic" practice of using recollection themes in film scores is given extensive attention in Soviet film studies. See, for example, I. Ioffe, *Muzïka sovetskogo kino* (Leningrad: Gosudarstvennïy muzïkal'nïy nauchno-issledovatel'skiy institut, 1938), 24–26.

62. See Prokof'yev, *Dnevnik*, 2:817.

63. After seeing *Golden Mountains* in 1932, Prokofiev remarked in his journal that Shostakovich's score was based primarily on popular urban songs that lacked development—an attempt to make the music understandable to the "simple public." Prokof'yev, *Dnevnik*, 2:805.

64. SPA XXXIV/210-211/13.07.1933.

65. In the earlier manuscript version of the score, Prokofiev jotted down in pencil "takzhe dlya kontsa" (the same for the ending) beside this number.

66. V. Tarov, "Poruchik Kizhe," *Gudok*, March 6, 1934. Clipping in RGALI f. 2979, op. 1, yed. khr. 667.

67. Prokofiev likewise eschewed the Oriental lushness suggested by the setting of *Egyptian Nights* in favor of an "exoticism by means of techniques appropriate to a modern style." Petchenina and Abensour, "Egyptian Nights: In Search of the 'New Simplicity,'" 13.

68. Nikulin, "Zhizn' pod baraban."

69. A[leksandr] Ostretsov, "Rol' muzïki v zvukovom fil'me," unpublished manuscript, RGALI f. 652, op. 4, yed. khr. 78, p. 51.

70. Neil Lerner, "Copland's Music of Wide Open Spaces: Surveying the Pastoral Trope in Hollywood," *Musical Quarterly* 85:3 (2001): 477–515.

71. A-va, "Skromnitsï iz Belgoskino," *Kino*, February 10, 1934, p. 2.

72. Otten, "Poruchik Kizhe," 3.

73. Jennifer Doctor, *The BBC and Ultra-Modern Music, 1922–1936: Shaping a Nation's Tastes* (Cambridge: Cambridge University Press, 1999).

74. Sound recording technology arrived late in the Soviet Union. Pavel Tager (1903–71) working in Moscow, and Aleksandr Shorin (1890–1941), working in Leningrad, began using sound-on-film systems in 1929 (Leyda, *Kino: A History of the Russian and Soviet Film*, 278–79). Although the Shorin method adopted by Belgoskino was reliable, the poor quality of the microphones increased distortion. *Ocherki istorii sovetskogo kino*, ed. Yu. Kalashnikov, 3 vols. (Moscow: Iskusstvo, 1956–61), 1:266.

75. Prokofiev recorded a sizable amount of piano music during his lifetime (most of it his own); notable among his early recordings are the piano rolls he produced in New York in 1926 for Duo-Art. See Prokof'yev, *Dnevnik*, 2:365–66 (entry of January 2–3, 1926). His 1932 sessions in London appear to be his first contact with a well-equipped studio.

76. Prokof'yev, *Dnevnik*, 2:806 (entry of June 27–28, 1932).

77. *S. S. Prokof'yev i N. Ya. Myaskovskiy: Perepiska*, ed. D. B. Kabalevskiy (Moscow: Izdatel'stvo "Sovetskiy kompozitor," 1977), 384.

78. Prokof'yev, "Muzïka v fil'me *Aleksandr Nevskiy*," in *Sovetskiy istoricheskiy fil'm: Sbornik statey* (Moscow: Goskinoizdat, 1939), 26–29, esp. 27.

79. Prokof'yev, *Dnevnik*, 2:828–29 (entry of May 2–5, 1933).

80. The exercises were added by Prokofiev to the earlier version of the score (RGALI f. 1929, op. 1, yed. khr. 92, pp. 9–12). The number titled "Tambours de l'Empereur Paul I" (pp. 9–10) was not used in the film.

81. SPA XXXIV/210–211/13.07.1933.

82. The choice of instrumentation could also, of course, reflect a desire to enhance the militaristic tone of the score. Prokofiev enhanced the string sound in the *Lieutenant Kizhe* Suite.

83. SPA XXXIV/210-211/13.07.1933.

84. RGALI f. 1929, op.1, yed. khr. 92, p. 28.

85. SPA XXXV/123/03.10.1933.

86. Kenez, *Cinema and Soviet Society*, 123.

87. These figures, which concern only completed and released films, come from *Sovetskiye khudozhestvennïye fil'mï*, ed. Aleksandr Macheret (Moscow: Iskusstvo, 1961), 487–503.

88. Prokof'yev, *Dnevnik*, 2:836 (entry of June 1–6, 1933).

89. Prokofiev noted in his journal that Ivanov-Vano's most recent film was "better"; the composer obviously knew the director's work. Prokof'yev, *Dnevnik*, 2:836 (entry of May 31, 1933). The contract, which was issued by Mezhrabpom-Rus, is preserved in RGALI f. 1929, op. 1, yed. khr. 804, p. 2.

90. RGALI f. 1929, op. 1, yed. khr. 804, p. 2.

91. These details come from *Sovetskiye khudozhestvennïye fil'mï*, 57–58.

92. Prokofiev made his final journal entry on June 6, 1933, barely a week after he signed the contract for *The Tale of Tsar Durandai*.

93. From a discussion of the film at the Russian Association of Workers of Revolutionary Cinematography (ROSARRK) on February 16, 1934, as recounted by Kozintsev, "O fil'me 'Poruchike Kizhe,'" 2:28.

94. The advertisements appeared daily on page 4 of *Vechernyaya Moskva* from February 20 to the end of March 1934 (smaller advertisements appeared sporadically in April). *Kizhe* opened in Moscow at the Udarnik, Pervïy khudozhestvennïy, Ars, Forum, Taganskiy, and Shtorm theaters. On the reception of the film, see Fayntsimmer's letter of February 17, 1934, SPA XXXVI/222/17.02.1934.

95. E. Kol'tsova, "Poruchik Kizhe," *Komsomol'skaya Pravda*, March 16, 1934, p. 4.

96. On the French opening, see David Nice, *Prokofiev: From Russia to the West, 1891–1935* (New Haven: Yale University Press, 2003), 308. The film opened in the United States on December 9, 1934; a review appeared on December 10 in the *New York Times*.

97. According to Prokofiev's collection of newspaper clippings (RGALI f. 1929, op. 2, yed. khr. 629), Kizhe was shown in no fewer than thirty-two Soviet cities in 1937 and 1938.

Observations on Prokofiev's Sketchbooks

MARK ARANOVSKY

TRANSLATION BY JASON STRUDLER

A sketch is the essence of a score. Pondering a scrap of paper upon which pitches have been hastily jotted down, we witness the birth of music. It is as though our sense of time bifurcates, allowing the illusion of our co-presence in the creative process to become manifest. We can imagine how the composer's pen or pencil moved, tracing the gesture that arose in his or her ear, and deduce why it moved as it did and not otherwise. Sketches and—further—manuscripts lead us simultaneously into the composer's thought processes and through the genesis of his or her work.

For Prokofiev, inventing abstract melodies and preserving them in sketchbooks was a normal part of his routine. The sketchbooks housed in Moscow at the Russian State Archive of Literature and Art (RGALI) are crucial to the understanding of his creative methods. They contain, in different states of completion, the thematic material of an enormous body of work, both finished and unfinished, from the late 1920s to the early 1950s. They also reflect the range of Prokofiev's methods and his creative psychology overall.

This essay is devoted to two interrelated issues. The first centers on Prokofiev's creative process, which we will explore with reference to his accretive technique, whereby his works grow in size through external addition. His sketches, outlines, and rough drafts document this procedure. The second issue relates to his stylistic change during the period in question, and ultimately illustrates both the positives and negatives of using sketches to trace it.

The musical syntax of a composer is never static, with both personal and cultural context governing its mutation. Style is another issue. Long-standing, recognizable styles, like those of the so-called Baroque or Classical periods, have endured; in those times, a composer's personal evolution centered on the perfection of craft, as evinced by the famous expression of the French naturalist George-Louis Leclerc de Buffon (1707–88): "The style is the man himself." Modern styles, in contrast, came and went like objects seen through the window of a speeding train. The early twentieth century witnessed Schoenberg's emancipation of dissonance, Stravinsky's return to Pergolesi, and Satie's furniture music, along with other long- and short-lived revolutions in musical practice. The relationship between psychology, personality, and style became the subject of cerebral operations, mental games. Early twentieth-century music preserved, however, a phenomenon of the period that came before it, one in which the evolution of style reflected events in the composer's life. The scores of Rachmaninoff and Shostakovich offer cases in point.

Prokofiev's example is rather unique. He combined elements of traditionalism together with a shift of attention toward different forms and modes of musical expression. The mutations were not abstract, but corresponded to the demands of the librettos and scenarios he set. Prokofiev was first and foremost a composer of the theater. Moreover, he stood apart from other early twentieth-century innovators insofar as he experienced an aesthetic and creative breakthrough exactly halfway through his career. Prokofiev labeled this breakthrough "new simplicity," but the term hardly captures the seriousness of the shift and the significance of its spiritual underpinnings.

During the Soviet era, according to a carefully cultivated legend, Prokofiev's stylistic change resulted from the beneficial influence of the composer's relocation to Moscow from Paris. The story relates specifically to the compositions that he completed during and after the relocation, including the ballet *Romeo and Juliet* (1935), the Second Violin Concerto (1935), and the Fifth and Sixth Symphonies (1944 and 1947), not to mention the opera *War and Peace* (1952). The genesis of each of these works—the specific nature of their conception—is obscure, a detail that affirms the tendentiousness of the official explanation of the composer's stylistic change. Even before the end of the Soviet era, it was clear that his relocation did not precipitate it. Thanks to the publication of new biographical documents, especially the composer's 1907–33 *Diary* (*Dnevnik*), the reasons for the stylistic change have begun to come to light. These documents elucidate the change in sound brought about by Prokofiev's indoctrination into Christian Science. His temporary decision in 1926 to terminate work on the quasi-Symbolist opera *The Fiery Angel*, which contains a handsome dose of mysticism and devilry, speaks to the strength of his beliefs. He overcame the crisis to complete what is perhaps his finest opera.[1]

Of course, the finished text of a work is capable not only of revealing but also of concealing a composer's intentions. It obscures the work's history, the composer's path toward the finished product. To understand those intentions, we must explore the documents that preserve the initial points of inspiration, the concepts that initiate creation. Sketches, like outlines and rough drafts, serve as the starting point for the perception of stylistic change. At present, eleven sketchbooks covering twenty-five years of Prokofiev's career are known to exist at RGALI.[2] The following remarks will be confined to those that attest to the composer's "new simplicity." These are Sketchbooks nos. 4 and 5, which date from the early 1930s, plus another from the same time that lacks a number that we will refer to as no. 6.[3] These sketchbooks played essentially the same role in Prokofiev's creative process as did those of Beethoven, Tchaikovsky, and Rimsky-Korsakov: they were tools for the instantaneous preservation of thematic material and, later on, catalogs from which to draw on this material. They were also musical diaries, texts that Prokofiev regularly labored on, inscribing within them the workings of his imagination.

With some composers, the creative process begins with the devising of a concept of the whole (sometimes, as Glinka reveals, with an instantaneous vision of that whole, an image of the completed score). In such cases, the final product drives the search for thematic material and the technical challenges of its assemblage. For other composers, thematic material is borne of its own accord, without an a priori plan, as an independent musical phenomenon. Such was Prokofiev's craftsmanship. He was first and foremost an inventor of abstract musical material, a composer in the literal etymological meaning of the term. He formed worlds from accumulated islands of sound. Admonishing the young Aram Khachaturyan at one point, Prokofiev said:

> It is very easy to write a concerto—but one absolutely needs to be inventive. I advise you to write out all of the textural devices without waiting for the maturation of the entire plan. It is not necessary to write out separate passages or interesting segments in succession. You may put together the whole from these bricks later.[4]

Prokofiev himself worked in this manner, even when he had to fulfill a specific proposal or commission and the final shape of the material was essentially predetermined. His working method evinced his talent for melodic invention, cultivated since childhood and adolescence when he composed simple pieces nicknamed "ditties" (*pesenki*) and "pooches" (*sobachki*). The practice he described to Khachaturyan had both positive and negative results. On the one hand, he was able to freight his scores with a superabundance of affective melodic material; on the other, he became accustomed to viewing their wholes as little more than sums of parts, as blocklike formations.

Even in his late years, Prokofiev always carried a sketchbook with him, recognizing that a new melodic, harmonic, or rhythm motif, complete melody, or even a cluster of complete melodies might suddenly crystallize in his imagination. In an interview on January 19, 1930, with the *New York Times* journalist Olin Downes, Prokofiev posited that "melody and substance are the most important things that I work with when composing music; however, I have noticed that melody—if it is a genuine melody, i.e., a new melodic design—has the most difficult time sinking in."[5] Prokofiev's diary, however, contradicts this claim, revealing that, far from "sinking in," his melodic writing was oftentimes spontaneous, inspired by periods of reflection (either while traveling or immersed in reading). "Composed a very successful theme," he randomly inserted into a February 14, 1930, entry. "My head began to ache from the three-day bustle [on an American concert tour]; but, upon awaking, I nonetheless composed the main part for the Quartet; switched on the electricity and transcribed it" (February 20, 1930). "Developed yesterday's theme a little. I see another—for a secondary section composed earlier in New York" (February 21, 1930). "The theme from the train is not bad for the Quartet's scherzo" (May 20–26, 1930).[6] Later references include "Read on Christian Science and reflected somewhat on that line of thought; composed several themes" (July 7, 1932). "Thought awhile; composed a theme and several motifs" (May 2–5, 1933).[7]

He took systematic care when transplanting sketchbook material into actual works. The most striking fact about the melodies, beyond their diversity and richness, is the absence of revision: Prokofiev usually imported them into his scores intact without alteration. He seems to have considered them complete the moment he wrote them out. But as in the case of Rimsky-Korsakov, Prokofiev subjected the sketchbook material to development, in the form of variations, repetitions, transpositions, and backtracking. Prokofiev's inspiration exceeded Rimsky-Korsakov's insofar as he composed melodies that he did not need in the here and now, depositing them in his sketchbooks for safekeeping, for an unknown future composition. But even material that languished for years found a home, Prokofiev being a highly economical composer.

Prokofiev's belief in the potential polyvalence of a theme informed his treatment of form. He did not interpret theme and form as codependent entities, having a deterministic cause-and-effect relationship. Rather, he demonstrated that a melodic, harmonic, or rhythmic idea could, when transplanted from one score to another, serve multiple contexts, and that it could traverse the borders of genre. A theme could have dual or even triple citizenship. Melodic material from Prokofiev's incidental music to *Eugene Onegin* (1936, composed for Alexander Tairov's Moscow Chamber Theater) later recurred in different guise in the opera *War and Peace*, among other scores. Prokofiev's approach to recycling is evident in the Third Symphony (1928), which, to the composer's chagrin, was interpreted at the time of its composition as a mere arrangement of music from *The Fiery Angel*.[8] The composer dismissed this assumption, noting that some of the music had originated in the instrumental realm (as an unfinished String Quartet) before being transformed into an opera. Thus the material had been returned to the instrumental realm from which it came. The argument might seem specious, but it enabled Prokofiev to defend the autonomy of the Third Symphony. It includes recycled music, but this music is recontextualized. The leitmotifs in *The Fiery Angel* are specific to the dramatis personae, defining their experiences and personalities. Relocated to the Third Symphony, they lose their human associations, instead becoming symbols of abstract spiritual concepts. Through recontextualization, the music acquires new expressive properties.

For Prokofiev, thematic invention was a spontaneous, unconscious process. His sketches nonetheless suggest an a priori stylistic context. How did this context arise? Sometimes it was provided by a preexisting text (the libretto of the 1919 opera *The Love for Three Oranges*, for example, or the scenario of the 1930 ballet *On the Dnieper*). At other times there is neither a subject-based nor a generic impetus for the creative act; the music either came into being in response to an unknown design or stemmed from an isolated creative impulse, one that might itself have a stylistic motivation. One example of the latter is recorded in his diary on May 11, 1933, en route by train to Tbilisi: "Composed a good theme on the platform—in the style of [music for] the masses."[9] The remark suggests an attempt to comply with Soviet aesthetic demands, even though the conception of the theme itself was spontaneous, unconscious. Prokofiev similarly describes the creation of melodic material for *Semyon Kotko* (1940) and *War and Peace*.

A theme might come into being in the abstract, but it always possesses distinct features. Hector Berlioz recalled a symphonic idea spontaneously coming to him one evening and, owing to unfavorable circumstances, making a conscious effort to put it out of his mind.[10] Perhaps we were deprived of a masterpiece. But how did Berlioz decide that the theme belonged specifically to a symphony? Evidently, it bore the traits of the genre, the features of a familiar stylistic paradigm. Whatever the impulse behind its creation—mood, surroundings, or an unexpected turn of events—it had an independent motivation.

The autonomous work of the imagination is evidenced in Berlioz's sketches, outlines, and rough drafts, but also those of Beethoven, Tchaikovsky, and, of course, Prokofiev. Some of the entries in his sketchbooks preserve the musical language of the 1920s, with its severity, tendency toward atonality, capricious admixture of chromaticism and diatonicism, predominance of dissonance, and driving rhythmic formulae.

These sketches derive from Prokofiev's creative past. Other entries, showing the path to the future, find him gravitating toward cantilena, diatonicism, and formal-functional harmony. Different style periods coexist, and in some cases interact, in the sketchbooks from the beginning of the 1930s.

Sketchbooks nos. 4, 5, and what we are calling no. 6 were completed roughly between 1931 and 1933. Nos. 4 and 6 bear a start date—November 28, 1931, and January 1933, respectively—but it is impossible to determine the date of the material contained therein, since Prokofiev used the sketchbooks over wide spans of time and sometimes made simultaneous entries in more than one of them or—puzzlingly—transferred entries between them. Not infrequently, he recomposed individual entries or even entire pages of the sketchbooks from scratch. Stylistic factors and the time gaps between the inscriptions of the sketches and their practical use further complicate the assignment of dates to them. Neither *The Fiery Angel* nor *The Prodigal Son* is represented in the sketches, which signals that the material does not predate 1930. The upper chronological limits of the sketches cannot be readily fixed because they inform works that would not be completed for many years to come, including *Romeo and Juliet* (1935), the Second Violin Concerto (1935), *Semyon Kotko*, the Sixth Piano Sonata (1940), the Fifth Symphony (1944), and *War and Peace*. Overall, the sketches evince two interrelated trends: anticipatory realization, within which the idea precedes its implementation into a score, and simultaneous realization, within which the idea arises in tandem with the plan for a score. Virtually everything had a purpose.

The three sketchbooks witness one of the most productive periods in Prokofiev's career. The composer completed more than twenty works during the 1930s, including, besides the aforementioned scores, the Sinfonietta (1929), Fourth Symphony (1930), First String Quartet (1930), the Fourth and Fifth Piano Concertos (1931 and 1932), the Sonata for Two Violins (1932), the incidental music for *Egyptian Nights* (1934), the score for *Lieutenant Kizhe* (1934), and the First Violin Sonata (1946), together with several shorter piano pieces. The existence of sketches for works completed only in the 1940s and 1950s suggest that the stylistic tendencies of his later works had origins much earlier than hitherto thought.

Some of the inscriptions in the sketchbooks permit dating and identification only with great effort, insofar as they evince the collision between the composer's two styles of the period (the fixed style of the 1920s and the as yet undefined manner of later years). The first style finds greater representation in the sketchbooks than the second one, but it is sometimes a challenge to distinguish them, since the latter grows out of the former, fighting its way, as it were, through the material. Another challenge in dating and identifying the materials concerns their distribution. Prokofiev created multiple versions of his melodies and deployed them as needed in his works. The same themes recur varied in different works, serving on occasion as filler material.

As a sketch worked its way into the body of a composition, it could be subject to different degrees of amendment and refinement, which poses a third problem for dating and identification. The fourth and greatest problem, however, concerns the inversion of certain lexical clichés in the sketches. Prokofiev's stylistic markers included driving toccata patterns with marcato articulations and an array of percussive gestures derived from the piano but extending far beyond it (Prokofiev's first instrument was, of course, the piano, and its dominance in his creative thinking can be heard even in his orchestration). Other qualities include brittle and severe boldness, an absence of sentimentalism, and a penchant for the grotesque. The external prevails over the internal, the prosaic over the lyrical, kinetic energy over contemplation. Rhythm, fairly simplified rhythm at that, exercises almost complete control over the music. Prokofiev's preferred meter of 4/8—interspersed with measures in 1/4, 2/8, and 2/4—forms what might be called a "temporal diatonic."

To temper the primal rhythms, Prokofiev refined his melodic writing, filtering the phrases through different modes. Perhaps he had wearied of his own sound, or feared it becoming hackneyed. But by the early 1930s, he had reached a decisive turning point. Toccata rhythms, abrupt leaps, scherzo-like motion, and acrobatic pianistic technique ceded to "new simplicity." Unemotional and somewhat estranged in the composer's early period, Prokofiev's melodic writing becomes increasingly full-blooded, impassioned. His newfound, serious interest in religion evidently humanized his creative outlook. He did not abandon his former manner but reshaped it within a harmonious system of spiritual values. The composer created musical worlds divided between positive and negative forces, calibrating his scores to ensure the ultimate triumph of good over evil.

Sketchbook no. 4 dates, as noted, from November 28, 1931, and after. The following sketchbook, no. 5, has no date, and the archival description is only approximate: "the beginning of the 1930s." Sketches from no. 4 recur in no. 5 in expanded and enriched form, signaling that both sketchbooks were compiled at near the same time. Both of Prokofiev's styles are evident in no. 4, sometimes in the same entry.

The sketches for the Fifth Piano Concerto and other works of the period come to life on the first pages of no. 4. From pages 1 to 9 (recto and the unnumbered verso sides), ideas for the Concerto, originally planned as "music for piano and orchestra," pour forth like a great flood, attesting to the deluge-like character of Prokofiev's creative method. The Concerto begins to be composed on the pages, although the sketches themselves are haphazard. On page 1 recto, we find materials for movement two, and on page 1 verso the themes and texture of movement five (rehearsal numbers 80, 83–84, and 85). As Prokofiev wrote them out, the sketches changed character, which makes identification problematic. Aside from the aforementioned passages, we can discern material for rehearsal numbers 36, 38, 86, 88, 93, 96, 97, and 108.

The inscriptions might be haphazard, but they are not random: they follow the logical order of Prokofiev's thoughts. The similarities between the melodic writing in the Concerto and elsewhere suggest that it served as a laboratory of sorts for an entire series of works dated between 1931 and 1932, most specifically the E-minor and G-major sonatinas. The sketches for these two latter works appear alongside the sketches for the Concerto, a typical habit of Prokofiev. The similarities between the third movement of the G-Major Sonatina and the fourth movement of the Concerto suggest, in fact, that melodic material traveled between the two works. The music of a third "Pastoral" Sonatina, from Prokofiev's Three Pieces for Piano of 1934, likewise has its origins in the sketches for the Concerto, indicating that it came into being from surplus material. Essentially, the music of all of these works derived from a single creative source, the lyrical impulse of the late 1920s and early 1930s, which sounds detached, removed from the world.

No. 4 helps us to understand the zigzags in Prokofiev's stylistic change. The theme in Example 1a, from page 8, unites several compositions, namely the second movement of the G-Major Sonatina (Example 1b), the Sonata for Two Violins (Examples 1c and 1d), the opening adagio penseroso from the 1934 piano cycle *Pensées* (Example 1e), and the fourth movement of the Fifth Piano Concerto (Example 1f). These excerpts have the same acoustic form, with their dynamics, tempos, and textures determined by their individual contexts. The più largamente section of the fourth movement increased from forte to fortissimo and consequently came to possess a different dynamic profile than those of the other examples; nonetheless, the intonational resemblances are clear-cut.

The G-Major Sonatina sketch resembles the theme of the Sonata for Two Violins transcribed on page 17. The sketch from the Sonata given in Example 1c is extremely close to its final version, Example 1d, which excludes the second violin (the Sonata opens with the first violin solo). The subsequent dialogue between the two violins imparts a cantilena "double coefficient" to the musical texture.

The music discussed above privileges smooth, rounded phrases, as do the sketches for the third movement of the G-Major Sonatina (page 9 verso). From this large block of material, we will focus on the sketch of

Example 1a. Sketchbook no. 4. p. 8 (recto).

Example 1b. Sonatina no. 2, second movement, mm. 1–5.

Example 1c. Sketchbook no. 4, p. 17 (recto).

Example 1d. Sonata for Two Violins, first movement, mm. 1–3.

Example 1e. *Pensées*, no. 1, mm. 46–50.

Example 1f. Piano Concerto no. 5, fourth movement, mm. 68–73.

the beginning of the right-hand part and the parallel excerpt from the final published score:

Example 2a. Sketchbook no. 4, p. 9 (verso).

Example 2b. Sonatina no. 2, third movement, mm. 29–35.

This passage was transposed from C major to B-flat major as it was realized, but otherwise little changed. The material essentially came into being in final form. It boasts the softer, gentler intonations associated with Prokofiev's ballet heroines Juliet and Cinderella.

Generally speaking, all three of Prokofiev's sonatinas (the first two comprising op. 54, the third concluding the Three Pieces for Piano, op. 59) belong to a phase in Prokofiev's career of revived conventional diatonicism. Their syntax remains complicated, involving major- and minor-key phrases on the one hand and chromatic alterations on the other. The music begins with simple consonant steps before wandering into dissonance. We also detect the origins of the cantilena style of Prokofiev's later works, at this point more in the pacing than in the gestural content. This style involves grand ascents and dramatic climaxes; since Prokofiev shuns repetition, his melodies tend to sound too brief (especially compared to those of Tchaikovsky, Rachmaninoff, and Shostakovich), but they nonetheless create an impression of breadth. They neither flow through space nor unfurl like a path through the fields but rise with great physical effort, gaining emotional weight at each step.

Tracing the origins of this new lyricism leads us to a bundle of sketches with a connection to Romeo's ecstatic love theme from *Romeo and Juliet* (one might also call it the theme of passion or rapture). It is one of Prokofiev's most delightful and inspired creations:

Example 3. *Romeo and Juliet,* Act 3, "Farewell Before Parting," mm. 5–9.

The prototypes for this theme turn up in Sketchbook no. 4, that is, in the early 1930s, long before conversations concerning the composition of a ballet on a Shakespearean subject began (various other subjects were considered). To be sure, the sketches reveal not the theme itself but that which anticipated it—a certain type of line. The following sketch for the Sonata for Two Violins illustrates how these thematic precursors varied according to context:

Example 4a. Sketchbook no. 4 [n.p.].

The melodic fabric of the Sonata abounds in formulations of this sort. For example:

Example 4b. Sonata for Two Violins, first movement, mm. 17–23.

The following sketch is reproduced almost exactly at the beginning of the first movement of the Sonata for Two Violins:

Example 5. Sketchbook no. 4, p. 17 (recto).

One of the sketches for the Second (G-major) Sonatina:

Example 6. Sketchbook no. 4 [n.p.].

Some of the entries in Sketchbook no. 4 match that quoted in Example 3 closely enough as to be tentative variations of it:

Example 7a. Sketchbook no. 4, p. 13 (verso).

Prokofiev wrote out a variant, almost a double, of this theme directly beneath it (Example 7b). Why? The persistent, reaffirming act of laying out this theme (among others) perhaps belied a more concrete intention, a bigger plan that required an expanded and altered repetition. Prokofiev deliberately reproduced these entries almost verbatim in Sketchbook no. 5. He may have filled the pages (at least partially) while contemplating the ballet, if not actually writing it, and it is possible that he recalled materials from Sketchbook no. 4 as candidates for the love theme. The

Example 7b. Sketchbook no. 4, p. 13 (verso).

sketches quoted above indeed befit the figure of the passionate Romeo very well. But the love theme possesses certain distinguishing qualities: it is acoustically richer and emotionally grander, with powerfully etched lines.

Whatever the exact sequence of events, the material from these sketches indicates that in 1931 and 1932, Prokofiev began to conceive lyrical melodies grounded in major keys. The search provided him with the source material for his Shakespearean masterpiece. Indeed, the model for one of Juliet's most delightful themes can be found alongside the previous example, further illustrating Prokofiev's stylistic approach to the ballet:

Example 8. Sketchbook no. 4, p. 13 (verso).

This passage becomes the third theme in the C-major episode from Act 1 of the ballet titled "Juliet as a Young Girl." The sketch found its way into *Romeo and Juliet* without substantial changes. The rhythmic design underwent some alteration: in the ballet the melody is written in quarter notes rather than eighths, an adjustment that lends it a meditative, self-absorbed character. At this moment in the scenario, Juliet interrupts her game-playing to listen, as it were, to herself, to her own inner voice. Certain details of the bass line (assigned to the cellos) in the sketch were likewise changed to increase the feeling of pensiveness.

In Sketchbook no. 4 this theme is like an oasis of refined lyricism within an ocean of polysemic chromatic restlessness. There is nothing like it in Prokofiev's previous sketches.[11] The transparent, largely unsullied C major reminds us of the affective power of tonal harmony. By the end of the 1940s, melodic writing such as this is unsurprising; here, however, it stands out as a harbinger of stylistic change.

Traditional diatonicism recurs elsewhere in the sketchbook, drawing attention to itself in the manner that it does in Prokofiev's Classical Symphony of 1917. There are other sporadic allusions to the common practice period in his early works, notably the Fifth Piano Sonata of 1923, but in Sketchbook no. 4 there is something more at work, a sense that the composer had wearied of tonal indecision. Traditional diatonicism provided the foundation for an exploration of melodic gestures that depended for effect on the power of the leading tone and modulations to distant tonal domains.

A sketch on page 16 verso provides another example of "new simplicity":

Example 9. Sketchbook no. 4, p. 16 (verso).

This type of multivoiced cantilena is characteristic of passages in the First String Quartet, *The Prodigal Son,* and *On the Dnieper,* the "Madrigal" from Act 1 of *Romeo and Juliet,* and the andante passage in the Finale of the Sixth Piano Sonata. The lyricism suggests a confluence of historical genres and styles: sixteenth-century madrigal, seventeenth-century (Bachian) chorale, and eighteenth-century string quartet. Characterized by a slowly rising upper voice accompanied by middle and lower voices in parallel and oblique motion, the sketch offers the impression of thickened, "multiplied" melodic writing.

Prokofiev's stylistic adjustments extend beyond the sphere of the lyrical. Within Sketchbook no. 4 one is surprised to discover the theme of the second movement Scherzo of the Sixth Piano Sonata:

Example 10. Sketchbook no. 4, p. 18 (verso).

As the Sonata was being written, the Scherzo was transposed to E major, harmonized in fourths in 2/2 meter, and embellished with a formal-functional bass line. The kinesthetic lightness of the sound suggests a theme running on the tips of its toes. The crowd scenes in *Romeo and Juliet* include music of similar content, allowing one to speculate that the sketch might have first been earmarked for the ballet.

The stylistic changes evident in Sketchbook no. 4 are not systematic; certain passages involve enhanced lyricism, others involve a return to traditional diatonicism, and still others show both processes working together. The contents are heterogeneous, merely the beginning of a transition, with the old and the new jostling for supremacy.

Sketchbook no. 5 continues no. 4, as evidenced by the migration of materials from the former to the latter. On page 16 of no. 5, Prokofiev completely rewrote Juliet's C-major theme (Example 8), either to tailor it for the future ballet or simply to improve valuable melodic material. Apart from the First String Quartet, there is no other context into which the material in question (two voices moving in thirds in the upper register with a lower voice in counterpoint) could have been included and, by this approximate time, the Quartet had already been finished. The "thirds" section of the C major theme appears on the first and second staves of page 16, the theme itself on the fourth and fifth staves. A brief sketch of Juliet's most charming and graceful melody lies in between. It is also cast in C major and, as in the ballet, appears in the upper register:

Example 11. Sketchbook no. 5, p. 16 (recto).

The sketch only approximates the final version, but its distinguishing characteristics are readily apparent.

Sketchbook no. 5 includes other themes destined for *Romeo and Juliet*. Prokofiev briefly described the conception of the ballet in his 1941 autobiography:

> At the end of 1934, discussions about a ballet arose with the Kirov Theatre in Leningrad. The lyrical subject interested me. We happened upon Shakespeare's *Romeo and Juliet*. But the theater backpedaled, and I signed a contract with the Bolshoy Theater in Moscow instead. During the spring of 1935, Radlov and I worked out a scenario, consulting thoroughly with the ballet master on all

technical matters.[12] The music was written over the course of the summer, but the Bolshoy Theater found it undanceable and broke the contract.[13]

There is an obvious discrepancy between the approximate date of the sketchbook and the 1934–35 conception of the ballet, allowing one to speculate that Prokofiev either completed the sketchbook four or five years later than presumed or, more likely, that material familiar to us from the ballet came into being independent of it.

But consider another hypothesis. In a cluster of sketches potentially belonging to the ballet, Prokofiev provided a brace joining several staves, which, as far as we can tell, he often used when drafting piano music. It follows, then, that Prokofiev originally conceived these sketches for a piano piece. Of course, the presence of the brace alone is insufficient to support this hypothesis, but Prokofiev did tend to be consistent in his notational habits.

The remaining entries in Sketchbook no. 5 illustrate a comparable transformation in Prokofiev's style as the sketches associated with *Romeo and Juliet*. Page 24 verso includes a slow contemplative tune within a polyphonic texture redolent of Example 9. It is in fact a melody for the central episode of the Andante of the Second Violin Concerto, which would be completed only in 1935:

Example 12. Sketchbook no. 5, p. 24 (verso).

The texture of this sketch changes when imported into the Second Violin Concerto: it is assigned to the clarinet with a string accompaniment whose most striking feature is a running alto part. Variants of the sketch, also used by Prokofiev in the Second Violin Concerto, appear alongside it. The sketchbook also contains a melody similar to that used in the third movement of his First Cello Concerto of 1938 (later reworked by the composer for the Sinfonia Concertante of 1952). Given that Prokofiev began the First Cello Concerto in 1933, it stands to reason that at least part of Sketchbook no. 5 dates from that year.

Example 13. Sketchbook no. 5, p. 22 (recto).

Sketchbook no. 6 continues no. 5 much as no. 5 continues no. 4. Within it, Prokofiev rewrites the sketch that would ultimately enter the third movement of the Sinfonia Concertante. It hardly differs from its first incarnation, except that Prokofiev abbreviates it with the mnemonic "etcetera." The material might, however, have been conceived for the violin rather than the cello. Page 16 features music idiomatic to the violin. The wide leaps and asymmetrical accentuations are characteristic of the Second Violin Concerto (see, for example, rehearsal numbers 60–63).

Example 14. Sketchbook no. 6, p. 16 (recto).

Example 14 turns up amid a cluster of sketches intended for Prokofiev's Symphonic Song (1933), including the following:

Example 15. Sketchbook no. 6 [n.p.].

Material for the central episode of the Andante of the Second Violin Concerto continues to be developed in this sketchbook, with new variations. Prokofiev also worked further on the First Cello Concerto, along with the music that would appear in *Romeo and Juliet*. There also exists material related to the First String Quartet.

Page 7 verso includes a sketch evocative of the opening melody of the Second Violin Concerto, although the latter excludes the rocking eighth-note accompaniment—which links the sketch to several episodes from

Romeo and Juliet (the "Arrival of the Guests" from Act I, for example). Either the overlap of the two works in the sketch is a coincidence or else Prokofiev was working out ideas for both at the same time.

Example 16a. Sketchbook no. 6, p. 7 (verso).

Example 16b. Violin Concerto no. 2, first movement, mm. 1–9 (solo part).

On page 13 verso, the initial drafts of another theme for the Second Violin Concerto appear alongside additional sketches destined for the ballet:

Example 17a. Sketchbook no. 6, p. 13 (verso).

Here we find Prokofiev experimenting with variations. Although the melody is distinct, it lacks expressiveness. Recognizing its inadequacy, Prokofiev continued to manipulate it, subjecting individual phrases, rather than the entire complex, to manipulation. The process ended with the writing of the melody found on page 27 verso:

Example 17b. Sketchbook no. 6, p. 27 (verso).

Even before conceiving this passage, Prokofiev had on page 22 verso devised the opening melody of the Adagio of the Second Violin Concerto, along with the sketch whose middle pitches are shown in Example 14. Prokofiev subsequently combined these materials in a protracted cantilena. At this point, however, he had completed only the exquisite beginning of the movement:

Example 18. Sketchbook no. 6, p. 22 (verso).

Interest in the singing timbre of the violin informed the formation of the cantilena style. The melodic writing of the Second Violin Concerto approximates that of *Romeo and Juliet* throughout. Sketches for both works appear on adjacent pages of Sketchbook no. 6, suggesting that Prokofiev composed them in parallel with the same aesthetic outlook. The Concerto might also have been a by-product of work on the ballet, with the composer saving the most songlike music for the central Adagio. The formation of the cantilena style, defined by melodic and harmonic balance, fought for a place in the sun in Prokofiev's works of the 1930s, supplanting the modernist harshness and terseness of those of the 1920s.

The entries noted above appear at the start of Sketchbook no. 6, indicating that they were composed in 1933, which is over two years before the completion of the Concerto and the ballet—further evidence that the sketchbooks constituted reservoirs of melodic material intended for future use. Prokofiev's Fifth Symphony was composed only in 1944, but some of its contents can also be traced back to the sketchbooks. Sketches for the Scherzo movement of the Symphony can be found in the pages of no. 6; they were first intended for *Romeo and Juliet*, specifically the abandoned "happy" ending, before being reallocated, nine years later, to the Symphony. Sketches for the Fifth Symphony Finale, moreover, appear alongside those for the Scherzo. This example from page 17 of no. 6, a lyrical bass melody, appears in almost the same form as in the Symphony:

Example 19. Sketchbook no. 6, p. 17 (recto).

Another fragment from the Finale is recorded on the same page:

Example 20. Sketchbook no. 6, p. 17 (recto).

And a variant of a theme from the Scherzo, performed in the Symphony by strings con sordini, occurs on page 17 verso:

Example 21. Sketchbook no. 6, p. 17 (verso).

Finally, and perhaps most surprisingly, we find melodies that anticipate choruses from *War and Peace*. The reverse side of page 14 features two adjacent sketches for them:

Example 22a. Sketchbook no. 6, p. 14 (verso).

Example 22b. Sketchbook no. 6, p. 14 (verso).

Compare them with the following excerpt from the opera:

Example 23. *War and Peace*, Scene 8, rehearsal number 304, mm. 4–8.

Although they are not exactly the same, the ear perceives the kinship between the sketches and the choruses. It remains unclear why Prokofiev conceived this music so far in advance of the opera. Perhaps the sketches stemmed from his attempts to compose music in the style of the masses, which became, in the late 1940s and early 1950s, suitable for the choruses in the fifth and final version of *War and Peace*.

We have not touched on all the inscriptions, of course, and not all lend themselves to being deciphered. Some possess a clearly experimental, intermediate character, indicating the direction of a search rather than its result. Some sketches met a dead end, the inevitable by-product of a creative process that reserved material for later use. And some of the inscriptions comprise musical clichés, with the general overshadowing the particular. Defying easy placement, these examples could have any number of "homes."

The three sketchbooks document Prokofiev's stylistic evolution at the start of the 1930s, with no. 6 finding the composer replacing the poly-semic chromatic texture characteristic of the works of the 1920s with an expanded major-minor tonal system. Prokofiev was not a theoretician, and he did not work with concrete theoretical paradigms. He was instead an empiricist, someone who depended on experience and perception in generating his ideas. Throughout his career, moreover, he remained in essence a composer for the theater, even when composing instrumental music. His commitment to dramaturgy explains the stylistic richness of his music.

The sketchbooks contain, by definition, inchoate material, but not all of the entries can be so labeled. Some of the sketches are approximate and unfinished (geared toward solving specific compositional problems), others evince the composer's variation technique, and still others appear on the page in what will prove to be finished form. The superabundance of material attests to the power of Prokofiev's imagination and inspiration, as well as to the centrality of his work to his life.

NOTES

1. See Sergey Prokof'yev, *Dnevnik 1907–1933*, ed. Svyatoslav Prokof'yev, 2 vols. (Paris: Serge Prokofiev Estate, 2002), 2:425 and 439 (entries of July 30 and September 28, 1930).

2. Inventory List (*Opis'*) no. 4 of the Prokofiev holdings at RGALI remains inaccessible.

3. RGALI f. 1929, op. 1, yed. khr. 284–86.

4. A. Khachaturyan, "Neskol'ko mïsley o Prokof'yev," in *S. S. Prokof'yev: Materialï, dokumentï, vospominaniya*, ed. S. I. Shlifshteyn (Moscow: Gosudarstvennoye muzïkal'noye izdatel'stvo, 1961), 402.

5. The composer recorded the comment to Downes in his diary. Prokof'yev, *Dnevnik 1907–1933*, 2:748–49.

6. Prokof'yev, *Dnevnik 1907–1933*, 2:756, 758–59, 773.

7. Ibid., 2:810, 829.

8. See Natal'ya Zeyfas, "Simfoniya 'Ognennogo angela,'" *Sovetskaya muzïka* 4 (1991): 35–41, esp. 36.

9. Prokof'yev, *Dnevnik 1907–1933*, 2:830. It is unclear what theme Prokofiev is referring to and likewise how it was realized.

10. Hector Berlioz, *The Memoirs of Hector Berlioz*, trans. and ed. David Cairns (London: Victor Gollanz, 1969), 470–71.

11. There are, however, other sketches in Sketchbook no. 4 that anticipate *Romeo and Juliet*. These are discussed along with the genesis of the ballet in general in S. A. Petukhova, "Pervaya avtorskaya redaktsiya baleta Prokof'yeva 'Romeo i Dzhul'yetta.' Istochnikovedcheskiye problemï izucheniya" (PhD diss., MGK im. P. I. Chaykovskogo, 1997).

12. Radlov is the director Sergey Radlov; the ballet master mentioned is Rostislav Zakharov.

13. Prokof'yev, "Avtobiografiya," in *S. S. Prokof'yev: Materialï, dokumentï, vospominaniya*, 193–94.

Prokofiev on the Los Angeles Limited

ELIZABETH BERGMAN

On January 6, 1937, Sergey Prokofiev departed Paris for New York, where he would begin his seventh tour of the United States.[1] Leaving Lina in Paris and their two sons in Moscow, he arrived on January 13, his schedule of concerts having already been announced in the *New York Times* just a few days prior to his sailing.[2] The brief news item listed engagements with orchestras in Chicago, St. Louis, and Boston; the date of his New York recital was reportedly "still pending," and there were no plans for him to appear with the New York Philharmonic-Symphony Orchestra.[3] Apparently America's cultural capital took little note of Prokofiev's presence, being perhaps too occupied by another prominent visitor: Igor Stravinsky was in town for two weeks conducting programs that prominently featured his own music as well as works by various Russian composers, Prokofiev not among them. By contrast, Prokofiev's only New York booking appears to have been a January 16 radio spot on the "Modern Masters" series broadcast nationwide by Columbia Radio. He performed a selection of his piano works, including the Andante, op. 29; *Visions fugitives*, op. 22; three pieces from *Music for Children*, op. 65; Etude, op. 52; and *Suggestion diabolique*, op. 4. The next evening, Columbia broadcast Stravinsky's concert with the Philharmonic.[4] Just as during his first trip to New York City in the fall of 1918, when Prokofiev had competed with Serge Rachmaninoff for recognition as a pianist and composer, so too in the winter of 1937 he found himself second to Stravinsky as composer and conductor, having been likewise overshadowed years before in Paris.[5]

That Prokofiev found himself with so little to do in New York during his penultimate visit to the United States in January–February 1937, and likewise during his final trip in February–March 1938, is but one curiosity of these two last American tours. The bookings are unusual, insofar as the Midwest unexpectedly takes pride of place on his schedule. And instead of the established orchestras in New York and Los Angeles, where Stravinsky was lauded, Prokofiev appeared with second-tier ensembles in St. Louis and Denver, railing memorably against the latter. The logistics are puzzling, especially considering that Prokofiev's activities were monitored—and his ability to travel determined—by Soviet officials. Irrespective of the surveillance, he seems to have been free to stay in private homes and pricey hotels, even enter into negotiations with Paramount Pictures and Walt Disney. Moreover, the schedule seems oddly fluid. Although major engagements had to have been arranged well in advance, his travel dates were not altogether set in stone. Nor were Lina's; for the most part she traveled separately from her husband in 1938. And documentation of Prokofiev's activities is sometimes slim, particularly with regard to his long stay in (and flirtation with) Hollywood.

But perhaps most striking of all is that these final two tours were never intended to be so. The 1937 and 1938 trips are bookended by aborted plans—ghost tours that never came to be because of insufficient engagements (in 1936) and political strictures (after 1938). Even in the midst of World War II, Prokofiev clearly expected to return year after year, with each projected tour to follow the pattern set by those in 1937 and 1938: he would arrive in New York in January or February, appear with orchestras in Boston and Chicago, then head west. His hopes were unrealistic, however, and ultimately unrealized. After 1938 the Soviet government refused to provide the necessary external travel passport, and the most determined efforts of his American supporters, most notably the Chicago insurance executive Ephraim Gottlieb and émigré conductor Serge Koussevitzky, could not extricate the composer from the Soviet Union. Prokofiev's trip to the United States in 1938 was, unbeknownst to all at the time, his last outside Russia.

Not all of these curiosities can be fully explained, but published press accounts and archival sources make it possible to establish firm dates for his American appearances and thus to correct minor inaccuracies in his biography. Feature articles and concert reviews of his performances describe the quality of his work as a pianist, composer, and conductor as well as his stylistic development in the context of cultural politics at a time when interest in the Soviet Union was high, particularly among progressive American artists and intellectuals. Knowing the Soviet side of the story—what the composer truly faced in Stalin's Russia—reveals these accounts in the American press to be naive at best, and much of the reporting is frankly unreliable on the facts. News of his latest compositions, whether works for the Pushkin centenary or the *Cantata for the Twentieth Anniversary of October* in 1937, is often riddled with errors, and his dalliance with Hollywood exaggerated.[6] Nevertheless, we may move closer to answering a seemingly simple but surprisingly complex question: What exactly happened during Prokofiev's tours of the United States in 1937 and 1938?

Mid-January to Early February, 1937

Returning to Paris from three months in Russia during the fall of 1934, Prokofiev wrote to his friend and unofficial United States representative Ephraim Gottlieb on February 13, 1935, with plans for future travel.[7] According to Prokofiev, conductors Serge Koussevitzky of the Boston Symphony Orchestra, Frederick Stock of the Chicago Symphony, and Bruno Walter, frequent guest conductor of the New York Philharmonic, had each promised engagements in the 1935–36 concert season. Prokofiev tried to rouse "sleepy Haensel" into making arrangements, a reference to artists' agency Haensel & Jones in New York, part of Columbia Concerts Corporation since 1930 and a predecessor of Columbia Artists Management.[8] Although an invitation from the Chicago Symphony arrived that summer, Prokofiev lamented to Gottlieb on July 28 that "perspectives for America are not very good and Hanesel [is] asleep as always."[9] By September plans had fallen through, partly because Bruno Walter had failed to sign a contract with the New York Philharmonic.[10] The fate of the tour was sealed, Prokofiev explained to Gottlieb, because of "unsufficient [*sic*] number and bad disposition of the dates." He trusted that "next year things will arrange themselves better."[11]

Some six months later, in May 1936, arrangements had indeed been made for a visit to the United States in the winter of 1937. Having recently settled in Moscow, Prokofiev apparently expected to continue his international career without interruption. He wrote to Gottlieb with the details, such as they stood, for the coming season:

> [Horace J.] Parmelee of Haensel & Jones informs me by indifferent and lazy letters that he has some concerts for me for January 1937: Chicago, Boston, St. Louis, perhaps Philadelphia. It is not too much and fees are meager. Let us hope that by and by something will come in addition between these dates. I expect to arrive to the States in the first days of January and stay one month so as to be back to Moscow about February 10 or 15, to be present at the above mentioned centenary [of Pushkin's death].[12]

The only concerts added to this calendar were the radio performance in New York on January 16 and a recital at the Soviet embassy in Washington, D.C., on February 8. Nothing was booked in Philadelphia.

After a few days in New York, presumably visiting with friend, composer, and compatriot Vernon Duke (Vladimir Dukelsky), Prokofiev traveled to Chicago. He arrived on Tuesday, January 19, and checked in to the

Auditorium Hotel on Michigan Avenue, an elegant and imposing landmark designed by Louis Sullivan where he had stayed in 1921 for the premiere of *The Love for Three Oranges*, op. 33, taking the same room as before. That first day found him at a luncheon counter eating apple pie with Edward Barry of the *Chicago Daily Tribune* and discussing a range of topics "as wide as the world—trains, tempos, composers, conductors, American scenery, hobbies, theories of music."[13] Little of substance, however, made it into Barry's piece, although he at least related Prokofiev's thoughts about musical style. The composer explained that his most recent works, especially *Romeo and Juliet*, op. 64 (1935), displayed a "new melodic line," which, Barry deduced, had something to do with "new curves to the line of melody." The reporter admitted to being "a bit hazy" on the details. Talk of a new style was part of the publicity for the 1937 tour. A press bulletin mailed to music critics in the cities on Prokofiev's itinerary, purportedly authorized by the composer himself, describes his having had a change of heart. Instead of the "smart" style of his youthful works, the latest plumbed "into the deeper realms of music."[14]

The haze surrounding the "new melodic line" never cleared for the benighted Barry, even after the American premiere of the First Suite from *Romeo and Juliet*, op. 64bis (1936). Reviewing the first of Prokofiev's two concerts with the Chicago Symphony on Thursday evening, January 21, he concluded that the composer's "melodies are good, they are real, the lighter ones among them profit by the peculiar piquancy which has always been a delectable feature of his style. But if there is anything radically different about their structure only close study or repeated hearings can discover it."[15] Fellow critic Eugene Stinson of the *Chicago Daily News* was similarly unmoved: "Mr. Prokofieff, writing in an unfeeling age, writes unfeelingly."[16] And the unnamed reviewer for *Time* magazine found the Suite to be "a sly, elusive projection of its subject, more lyric than Prokofieff's early works have been credited with being, but less so than the composer's talk of curves had suggested."[17] Only Claudia Cassidy of the *Journal of Commerce* detected "tunes" in the Suite, along with "just enough tongue in cheek to suggest that Trudi Schoop may be dancing Juliet."[18]

In addition to the First Suite, which the composer himself conducted, the program included Prokofiev at the keyboard performing his "glittering" Third Piano Concerto, op. 26, which Barry found to be "a great deal more 'modern' than the 'Romeo and Juliet' suite." As a pianist Prokofiev was "magnificent," wrote Stinson, and his performance "brought the plaudits and numerous recalls," Herman Devries reported in the *Chicago American*.[19] Barry described the concerto as having received "a cordial ovation," and likewise the reviewer for *Time* characterized the audience as "cordial but not unrestrained."[20] As a conductor Prokofiev had a "precise beat with knees that wobbled curiously but in accurate rhythm," according to Barry.[21] And to Cassidy he looked "engagingly like Henry of the cartoons," the nearly mute, bald boy of the comic strip then circulating in Hearst papers and featured in a 1935 Paramount animated short with Betty Boop (*Betty Boop with Henry, the Funniest Living American*).[22] Also on the program were Honegger's *Pastorale d'été* (1920) and William Grant Still's *Afro-American* Symphony (1930), led by associate conductor Hans Lange. Like the excerpts from Prokofiev's ballet, Still's score was novel for Chicago, and on the whole the program was notably skewed to the contemporary and non-Germanic.

Following the Thursday evening concert, Prokofiev was feted by high society at a supper reception hosted by Mr. and Mrs. Walter S. Brewster at their home on Lake View Avenue.[23] The Brewsters had met Prokofiev during a previous visit to Chicago and had since reunited with him in Paris.[24] The swank soirée was among the "highlights of the week," according to a vivid, if unlettered, fluff piece: "Serge Prokofieff, tall, humorous, extremely likeable, drinking a glass of champagne and eating hot shrimps at the Walter S. Brewsters' after his evening concert, and probably hoping somebody would ask him to play chess, which he loves passionately."[25] Both the concert Thursday evening and the one on the following afternoon were successes, with the high spirits spilling over into the Antiquarian Society reception at the Chicago Art Institute on Friday following the afternoon performance. The Society "never has had a more exciting at home than the one they had yesterday," wrote columnist India Moffett in the *Tribune*:

> And the reason it was so exciting had nothing to do with the delightful party itself or the exquisite laces that were exhibited.
>
> The atmosphere of excitement had been created at the symphony concert in Orchestra Hall, which the guests at the tea had attended, and all were thrilled over Serge Prokofieff and his music. A Friday afternoon audience so enthusiastic that cries of "Bravo" are heard is an unusual occurrence. That happened yesterday when the Russian composer appeared as piano soloist with the orchestra in one of his concertos, and as guest conductor of his ballet music, "Romeo and Juliet."[26]

Talk of Prokofiev drew attention away from the display of antique laces, which became but "a fitting and pleasant antidote to the excitement created at the concert."

Prokofiev found himself distracted in a different way that same evening. Leaving Orchestra Hall, he and Lange found themselves stuck in traffic resulting from a strike by city electrical workers. The two men considered "the strike very interesting," according to a report in the *Tribune*, and were not at all perturbed. Idling in a cab on the La Salle Street bridge, the pair marveled (in good Soviet style) at the industrial workings of the modern metropolis. "'We don't think it's necessarily inconvenient,' they said, smiling serenely. 'We're observing the dependence of a great city upon electrical power—and the men who use the power.'"[27] Prokofiev himself wrote to Duke that "Chicago has given me a pleasant reception. The orchestra was attentive and played well, and even during a daytime concert [on the 22nd] the old ladies applauded heartily, risking their white gloves." He also took pride in having bested Henry Voegli, manager of the Chicago Symphony, in a game of chess.[28]

From Chicago, Prokofiev traveled to St. Louis, arriving on Tuesday evening, January 26, for two concerts with the St. Louis Symphony on Friday afternoon, January 29, and Saturday evening, January 30. While in St. Louis he stayed at the fashionable Coronado Hotel on Lindell Boulevard, about two and a half miles east of the Municipal Auditorium, where the St. Louis Symphony performed under the direction of Vladimir Golschmann. As in Chicago, the program featured Prokofiev playing his own Third Piano Concerto, but in place of the First Suite from *Romeo and Juliet* audiences in St. Louis heard the Suite from *The Love for Three Oranges*, op. 33bis. Likewise the program included novelties—albeit of a different sort than in Chicago and of a decidedly local bent. Opening the evening were an overture by Telemann arranged by Louis Victor Saar, a hometown composer-pianist, and a chorale by Chicago composer Wesley la Violette, later a noted figure on the West Coast jazz scene in the 1950s. These works, as well as Prokofiev's Third Concerto, received their St. Louis premieres. There was also one piece of standard symphonic fare: Beethoven's Symphony no. 2.

In this weirdly varied context, the perceived modernist idiom of Prokofiev's Concerto and Suite was at issue for reviewers and likely for audiences as well. One critic pulled no punches: "Prokofieff has been ruthlessly experimental and has contributed valuable data for future composers, but his own work has suffered for it."[29] The technical innovation and "formal novelty" (an unintentional echo of the anti-modernist Soviet catchword Formalism) "obviates the possibility of warmer emotion."[30] But another, Harry Burke of the *Globe Democrat*, tried to cajole wary audiences in his review of the first concert, dismissing the view of Prokofiev as an "enfant terrible" in favor of the image of an "incurable romantic" who "is concerned with the projection of his own emotion and with arousing a correlative among his hearers."[31] His music "is eternally bursting out in a romantic lyricism," Burke added in his second article, "which suddenly freezes up as he determines to make fun of that mood even though it is his own."[32] Reed Hynds of the *St. Louis Star-Times* also defended the Concerto against its imagined detractors. "The first and last movements may seem to have that somewhat nauseating post-war experimental sound," he conceded, "but from the standpoint of music as science they are above reproach." Even so, he concluded that "from the standpoint of music as art, the verdict may be different."[33]

The performance earned more praise than the programming. Prokofiev's prowess at the piano brought accolades and "a bouquet of curtain calls," although "his turn at the podium got less applause than it deserved."[34] He was recalled to the stage some six times after the Concerto, "for each of which recalls he made two nice little 'ducky' bobs of appreciation."[35] Reviewers were as struck by his modest demeanor as his virtuosic pianism. He "approached the piano with curt dispatch and no ceremony," Hynds observed, and tellingly eschewed an artist's bench for "an ordinary straight-backed chair."[36] Burke found Prokofiev "very self-effacing" as a pianist but commanding as a conductor. "Somewhat bald, looking on the world through his glasses, Prokofieff seemed to be only concerned with personal virtuosity as it might be a means of bringing forth the color of tone which would express his precise emotion."[37] On the podium, however, he showed "an entirely different personality" and "was dynamic energy personified." He led excerpts from *The Love for Three Oranges* "with such bodily gusto" that Hynds "expected it to turn into a ballet any moment," adding that "no jazz leader ever gave a more convincing demonstration that he was 'hot.'"[38] Another critic compared Prokofiev's appearance to "that of a bald business man" and his conducting to the "abrupt" motions "of a mechanical tin tapdancer," which elicited from the orchestra a "brisk, exact, almost electric reaction."[39]

Although it was reported that Prokofiev would attend a chamber concert given Sunday evening, January 31, by the St. Louis Chamber Music Society at the Women's Club (located a mile west on the same boulevard as the Coronado Hotel), he in fact left that morning for New York.[40] Skipping out was a good choice, given the trouncing his music received by the critics. On the program was Prokofiev's String Quartet, op. 50, as well as two hoary classics: Haydn's op. 33, no. 3, and Schubert's D-Minor Quartet, "Death and the Maiden," D. 810. The reviewer for the *Post-Dispatch* felt that, compared to late Schubert, the Haydn "seemed a little light," while the Prokofiev came across as "involuntarily—and dolefully—heavy," as well as melodically "barren." Lacking too were "the wit and the impish ease which St. Louisans had come to expect from Mr. Prokofieff's recent collaboration with the Symphony Orchestra."[41] Hynds reported the remarks of one disaffected concert-goer who felt that "hearing Prokofieff two nights running is more than the human system can bear." Other listeners apparently amused themselves by inventing titles for the quartet, among them "Berceuse for an Idiotic Child" and "Fifteen Minutes Among the Lions and Moneys at the Zoo."[42] Even Burke, who had embraced Prokofiev's Suite from *The Love for Three Oranges* and professed admiration for the Classical Symphony, threw himself in with the hoi-polloi for whom "the string quartet is caviar." He parsed the first movement in colorful, if not flattering, terms:

The opening Allegro presents an introduction of lyric character with acrid harmonies and short energetic rhythms not too effectually disguising its romantic mood. Follows a groaning lament above which the first violin shrills to cello rumblings. There is a return of the choppy rhythm, more wailing of the violin with punctuations of plucked cello strings. Then a sudden and ejaculative discussion, an abusive argument in cacophonous squeals.[43]

The subtitle of the review said it all: "Quartet Does Its Best But Reviewer Regrets That It Was Ever Written." Burke allowed the composer the excuse of simply trying to get the piece "out of his system."

Whatever Prokofiev thought of St. Louis, its orchestra, or the concerts, he seems to have kept to himself—no firsthand accounts of his time in St. Louis survive. On February 1, he returned to New York and stayed a few days before moving on to Boston. There he put down the baton to appear as a soloist with the Boston Symphony Orchestra in two concerts on Friday afternoon, February 5, and Saturday evening, February 6. Accompanying him on the trip was Vernon Duke, who contrived for Prokofiev and Koussevitzky to meet the object of his affection, Polly Turnbull, at the Ritz before the Friday concert. "'Not for you,' was the consensus," Duke recalled.[44]

On the Boston programs, besides the Third Concerto, were the March and Scherzo from *The Love for Three Oranges* and the *Scythian* Suite, op. 20, with Mozart's "Prague" Symphony as opener. Koussevitzky had a (heavy) hand in choosing the oddly outmoded repertoire. Outmoded insofar as Chicago had been awarded the honor of hearing the American premiere of Prokofiev's First Suite from *Romeo and Juliet,* a very recent work whose style remained a topic of discussion in press reports and reviews, whereas Boston audiences heard only older works of long acquaintance. This fact was not lost on L. A. Sloper of the *Christian Science Monitor.* "All the compositions by which he is represented on this week's program are familiar to us," he complained. "Moreover, they are all early works. We do not wish to seem too exacting, but would it not have been more stimulating to hear something new? . . . How about music he has composed since he went back to live in Soviet Russia?" Sloper had in mind the vocal and orchestral music Prokofiev had written for the Pushkin centenary, especially *Eugene Onegin* and *Boris Godunov,* two compositions highlighted in the program booklet. "The centenary date is next Monday," Sloper noted. "Surely the work must be done. Might we not have heard something of all this?"[45]

Elizabeth Bergman

Despite such objections, the concert was warmly received by the Boston critics. Like his counterpart Harry Burke in St. Louis, Redfern Mason of the *Boston Evening Transcript* conflated romantic and modern sensibilities in describing the composer as "a sort of Russian Alfred de Musset who lives in a world of fantasy and is now uplifted Heaven high on dreams of a new and happier world, then sinks deep in the dregs of despair."[46] Once again critics praised Prokofiev the pianist. His "virtuosity is unsurpassed," wrote Ruth Marsters in her review for the *Boston American*. "Luminous clarity and precision are ever a part of his performance."[47] The "capacity audience" rewarded Prokofiev's playing with "an enthusiastic reception," according to Alexander Williams of the *Herald*.[48] All of these accolades were incorporated into the press kit Haensel & Jones put together for Prokofiev's subsequent American tour in 1938, a tour with more engagements, cities, and concerts than this one. For his part, Prokofiev "tired" of returning to the stage for the ovations.[49] Following the Friday afternoon concert came a reception at the Turnbulls, where Boston society women gushed over him; Prokofiev found them (like the city) to be very Victorian.[50]

Also on Friday afternoon, while backstage at Symphony Hall he met members of an unlikely organization: the Prokofieff Society at Dartmouth College, led by Merrell E. Condit as president and Wyman R. Vaughan as secretary. Three members, these two officers presumably among them, had traveled to Boston to attend the February 6 concert. Afterward they went backstage to meet the composer and conductor, both of whom obligingly autographed their programs even as they considered the society to be "an amiable joke," in Prokofiev's own words.[51] In fact, "we are very much in earnest," Condit assured Prokofiev and Koussevitsky in later letters. He summarized the society's simple brief: "The Society is in no way a commercial organization, its main purpose being the extension of a knowledge and appreciation of Serge Prokofieff's works and incidentally of music in general. We hope to accomplish this as informally as possible and without annoying publicity."[52] To Koussevitzky they proffered—or, as the letter has it, "beg you to accept"—honorary membership, and Prokofiev was invited to be honorary president. Each agreed.[53] Prokofiev's reply of April 2, 1937, sent from his Moscow apartment at 14 Zemlyanoy Val, reads in part:

You are right, then, on the 6th of February, I took your explanations as an amiable joke, but after your letter I am compelled to recognize the existence of the Prokofieff Society as a solid fact and beg you to accept my best thanks for the honors extended to me.

I should love to send you some other records to enlarge the phonograph repertoire of the Society, but unfortunately they cannot be found in U.S.S.R., and therefore I am obliged to limit myself by telling you the titles. They are: "Chout," suite of the ballet, Polydor 516583/4, and "Le Pas d'Acier," His Master's Voice D.C. 1680/81, fairly good as recording, though worse than the Classical Symphony. In the near future His Master's Voice will publish four records of my piano pieces I did myself. Some of them are good, others medium.

He pledged to send "several of my compositions for children" soon to be published in Moscow, referring to the *Three Children's Songs*, op. 68 (1936). "Not as a hint to the age of the Prokofieff Society," he added, "but because this will be my last novelty published and because some of the texts are in English."[54]

The final event of the 1937 tour came close on the heels of the Boston concerts. On Sunday, February 8, Prokofiev performed at an "evening musicale" hosted by Ambassador Alexander Troyanovsky and his wife (who was too ill to attend) in the ballroom of the Soviet embassy in Washington. Presumably the event was arranged by the All-Union Society for Cultural Ties Abroad (Vsesoyuznoye obshchestvo kul'turnïkh svyazey s zagranitsey), known even in English by its Russian acronym, VOKS. On this occasion Prokofiev nearly duplicated the program for the radio concert that had inaugurated his American tour except that for the Etude, op. 52, he substituted the Etude, op. 2, no. 4, and added three gavottes from opp. 12, 25 (misreported in the press as being op. 23, but surely the Gavotte from the Classical Symphony, op. 25), and 32. He also performed excerpts from *Romeo and Juliet*. One account had him playing from the orchestral score with conductor Hans Kindler of the National Symphony turning pages; this seems improbable given that a piano arrangement of ten numbers from the ballet was in Prokofiev's repertoire. As an encore, he performed the "Harp" Prelude in C Major from Ten Pieces, op. 12. The audience included diplomats from around the world (Ireland, Siam [Thailand], Czechoslovakia, Romania, South Africa, Ecuador, the Dominican Republic) and members of the Roosevelt administration (among them Secretary of Agriculture Henry Wallace and his wife).[55] A lavish buffet ensued, with a five-foot sturgeon as centerpiece on a table laden with Russian specialties. It was a stylish send-off. Precisely when Prokofiev sailed for Europe is not clear, but he arrived back in Paris by mid-February.[56] He and Lina returned to the Soviet Union on April 16, 1937.

The subject of their return—not merely from abroad but their permanent move to Moscow—had come up at some point early in Prokofiev's stay in the United States, perhaps soon after his arrival in January. He spent the day with Duke and his mother in New York. Duke's account of their conversation captures the bitter irony of a Soviet composer traveling freely while utterly bound.

"Sergei Sergeivitch," Duke's mother asked, "do you mean to tell me that the Communists let you out—just like that?" . . . "Just like that, Anna Alexevna," Prokofiev assured her, slapping his thighs. . . . "Here I am all in one piece, as you see." "And Lina Ivanovana?" Mother persisted. "She will come back to the States with me in October—I have enough engagements to warrant a speedy return." "What about your boys?" At this, Prokofiev changed the subject abruptly. I later learned that the Soviet authorities would not let them travel with their parents; in other words, that they were forcibly left behind in Russia, as hostages.[57]

The uncomfortable exchange inadvertently presaged the difficulties Prokofiev would confront in planning his next American tour. Duke found it "interesting to note that Prokofiev," now not only a citizen but also a permanent resident of the Soviet Union, "was permitted to travel continuously and extensively."[58] He would be so permitted one last time.

February 3 – March 30, 1938

In the summer of 1937, Prokofiev met with Richard Burgin, concertmaster of the Boston Symphony Orchestra, who while visiting Russia assured the composer that concerts during the coming season were "still 'on.'"[59] Prokofiev was also in touch with his representative at Haensel & Jones about booking concerts in the United States for the winter of 1938. He had accepted dates in Europe through January 20 and was expected to arrive in New York around February 1. Having received this news by cable from Russia, Parmelee wrote to Koussevitzky on August 2, 1937, to schedule dates in Boston, noting that an engagement with the Detroit Symphony had already been set for February 11. The tour was to take Prokofiev "west as far as Denver" then to Chicago for a recital originally planned for February 23 but eventually moved up to February 15. Concerts in Boston were arranged for March 25 and 26.[60]

The 1938 tour plans seemed to be coming together nicely; however, in January they suddenly began to unravel. "Friends Await Russian News of Prokofieff" read the headline of a brief article in the *Chicago Daily Tribune* published January 5. Officers and directors of the Renaissance Society, under whose auspices Prokofiev was to perform on February 15, were hampered in their efforts to publicize the recital because "they have not heard recently from the artist who is to give the concert . . . and there is fear in some quarters that he may have been delayed in leaving Russia."[61] Ephraim Gottlieb, Prokofiev's earnest American backer, wrote to the composer for an update, but the terse reply did nothing to clarify matters. Some ten days later it was again reported that the Society "has not heard definitely whether the artist, Serge Prokofieff, will be here. His friend, Ephraim Gottlieb has had a cable in answer to one he had sent to Moscow which said enigmatically 'Available date next season.'"[62] Prokofiev was having trouble securing an external travel passport. It came—late, but in sufficient time for him to make all of his dates in the United States.[63]

In addition to the recital in Chicago, these included performances with orchestras in Detroit, Denver, and Boston, a chamber concert in Denver, recitals in Boulder, Colorado Springs, and New York (one hosted by the League of Composers at the Cosmopolitan Club and a second by the American Russian Institute at the Astor Hotel) as well as an evening musicale at the Soviet embassy in Washington. Although Haensel & Jones had originally indicated the tour would swing no farther west than Colorado, Prokofiev and Lina ended up journeying across the country to Hollywood, where they stayed for nearly three weeks. There were no concerts in California but impressive social events, important meetings, and tempting opportunities that might have changed their lives.

Arriving in New York on February 3 aboard the *Normandie* bound from Southampton, Prokofiev and Lina reunited with Vernon Duke. Lina was "magnificent in sables and covered with glittering jewels," Duke remembered of their meeting, but when she "burst into tears at the sight of me," Prokofiev parked her with Duke's mother so the two men could talk shop at a bar.[64] Prokofiev's first engagement was as the guest of honor at a concert and reception put on by the League of Composers at the Cosmopolitan Club on East 66th Street.[65] The event, held Sunday afternoon, February 6, featured an unusual program of his music: the Sonata for Two Violins, op. 56; Fata Morgana's aria from *The Love for Three Oranges*, op. 33; "Mélodie" from Five Songs Without Words, op. 35; "The Butterfly" and "Remember Me" from Five Poems of Konstantin Balmont, op. 36, for soprano voice and piano. The solo piano works *Sarcasms*, op. 17, "Paysage," op. 59, and the Etude, op. 2, were originally scheduled to be performed by Nadia Reisenberg, but because she somehow injured a finger, Henry Harris stepped in with the Fourth Piano Sonata, op. 29. Prokofiev himself played a selection from *Romeo and Juliet* and the antepenultimate March from *Music for Children*.[66] The "little auditorium" of the club was filled to capacity with fellow composers and musicians.

An article appearing that same day in the *New York Times* reported that Prokofiev was in the United States for a three-week tour (the Los Angeles sojourn would extend it to nearly eight) and purported to offer readers a glimpse into the musical life of Soviet Russia.[67] The short feature reveals the degree to which the American press transmitted Soviet cultural propaganda quite uncritically. Despite serious difficulties in the Soviet Union, where his music came in for official criticism and coerced revision, per-formances were frequently canceled for political reasons, and financial transactions were convoluted, Prokofiev parroted the Party line, trumpet-ing the Union of Soviet Composers as a "most successful" organization that provided generous financial support to composers and valuable perform-ance opportunities. He struck the unnamed author of the article as an "industrial executive rather than the creator of music" and "an embodi-ment of a new social attitude toward the arts and the artist," presumably as a well-paid cultural laborer. Prokofiev claimed that in Russia composers enjoyed "four sources of income" thanks to the beneficence of Stalin's cul-tural apparatus. "First," he explained, "they have 'author's rights,'" which generate fees from performances. "Since the government is encouraging the growth of orchestras and a native repertory, a single good composi-tion can bring in a tidy sum through the many performances throughout the Soviet." Second, composers earned income by publishing their works with the Musical State Edition (Muzgiz); third, from commissions for opera, film, and theater. (Indeed, Prokofiev had finished such a project, composing music for a production of *Hamlet* en route to America and orches-trating it while crisscrossing the country on trains; he sent back pages of an annotated short score to his amanuensis Pavel Lamm in Moscow.) Finally, the Union of Soviet Composers evaluated and performed works of "merit," providing "financial aid" to composers "engaged on a projected work." Prokofiev continued: "If the completed work has merit, it will be published and performed under governmental auspices, and what fees will accrue go to the composer." Surely this last comment stuck in Prokofiev's throat, given the disparagement of his own music—notably *Romeo and Juliet*—by cultural bureaucrats. "Thus," he concluded, "with these recog-nized sources of income, the composer takes his proper place in a society to which he contributes his services." At a time when the United States gov-ernment had lately (and controversially) supported the arts through the relief programs of the Works Progress Administration, the Soviet system must have been compelling as a potential model and, accordingly, the reporter willing to relay these remarks unquestioningly.

Prokofiev's comments about the relationship between the contemporary composer and his audience surely resonated with similar sentiments expressed by politically progressive American composers, especially those connected to the Composers Collective (itself affiliated with the American Communist Party) like Aaron Copland. Meeting William G. King of the *New York Sun* for an interview in his hotel room, Prokofiev opined that "in all western Europe . . . composers are screaming about the rupture between the trend of music and the interest of the general public. Often, their works are of interest only to a small circle. That gives one to think—shall a composer write for the few, or for the great masses? In Russia, the question has been asked in a most urgent way."[68] As did Copland and other like-minded American composers, Prokofiev maintained that reconciling the desire for musical accessibility and demands of artistic integrity was not easy. "It is not enough to write merely what will please the listeners," he explained, "as many composers are content to do. I assure you, it is very difficult to find the language which will convey the new musical thought to the people, in terms they will understand, but I find the problem an inspiring one." Their common attitude derives, of course, from a common source: Communist cultural doctrine.

Following the League of Composers concert, Prokofiev traveled to Detroit while Lina remained in New York; they would not see each other again for a month. On Friday evening, February 11, he performed with the Detroit Symphony Orchestra under the direction of Victor Kolar, the program being a strange hybrid: a "concert-recital" that featured Prokofiev as solo pianist on the first half and, on the second, as soloist with the orchestra. The recital opened with Sonata no. 2, op. 14, succeeded by *Visions fugitives* ("whose value was at least debatable," thought critic Russell McLauchlin), the "Danse des jeunes Antillaises" from the original (1935) version of *Romeo and Juliet* (possessed of a "frosty charm"), and finally the "very well known" *Suggestion diabolique*.[69] The orchestra then took the stage to perform the Classical Symphony and the First Concerto, op. 10. One reviewer found Prokofiev to be "strangely lackadaisical" but for flashes of "mighty intensity" in his playing.[70] Another regarded him as standoffish, "a man of serious mien, given to jerky bowing from the hips in the face of the heartiest sort of enthusiasm from the seats."[71] Clearly, Prokofiev and his music made a harsh impression: whereas previous listeners had fashioned the composer as businessman, here he was imagined to be in a laboratory. "As a composer he sounds almost scientific," McLauchlin wrote, comparing the virtue of Prokofiev's music to the "cold, hard, and satisfying virtue" of geometry. "He seems eternally set to prove something memorable about the square of the hypotenuse."

The next day (February 12) Prokofiev was in Chicago, likely staying at the Auditorium Hotel. That evening he attended a dinner in his honor hosted by Mrs. Inez Stark, president of the Renaissance Society of the University of Chicago, which sponsored his recital on Tuesday evening, February 15, in Mandel Hall, an impressive venue (seating 1,000) on the campus. The audience was small but "enthusiastic."[72] Despite a breathless report of Lina's anticipated arrival ("Those who are planning to entertain for Serge Prokofieff when he is in Chicago are delighted to hear that his wife is going to accompany him"), she did not come to Chicago, disappointing those who "remember her as an attractive person and an addition to any social gathering."[73] There were many such social gatherings; despite being in town for but a single concert, Prokofiev had a busy schedule. Dinner on Saturday at Mrs. Stark's "charming and unusual home" at 1430 Lake Shore Drive was followed by supper on Sunday at the Brewsters', where Prokofiev had enjoyed champagne and shrimp the year before; Monday involved afternoon tea at the Arts Club in the south tower of Chicago's famed Wrigley Building.[74] Monday evening was kept open at the composer's request so he could see Helen Hayes as Queen Victoria in the wildly successful play *Victoria Regina*.

After spending the better part of a week in Chicago, Prokofiev traveled on to Denver, arriving Thursday, February 17, for appearances with the Denver Symphony as guest conductor as well as piano soloist on Friday, February 18, and as pianist with the Denver String Quartet at a chamber concert on Sunday, February 20. The latter concert, which was sponsored by Pro Musica, a local branch of the Franco-American Musical Society (founded in New York in 1921), had originally been scheduled for February 19, but at a board meeting on February 7, 1938, the date was moved to the twentieth.[75] Along with a lecture on Prokofiev's music, given Thursday, February 17 by Canon Winfred Douglas, the two Denver concerts were billed as a Prokofiev festival. Notes from Pro Musica meetings suggest that at some point a recital had been proposed with Prokofiev and his wife performing together on a program of songs by Musorgsky, Rimsky-Korsakov, Myaskovsky, and Prokofiev. This did not come to pass, and Lina was never in Denver.[76] Perhaps these various changes hindered publicity: on February 20, Prokofiev appeared before a half-empty house, facing an audience of 399 people in the Colorado Consistory, which seats 850.

The afternoon chamber recital featured Prokofiev with the Denver String Quartet and clarinetist Val P. Henrich on a program that included the String Quartet, Second Piano Sonata, four of the *Five Songs Without Words* for Violin and Piano, op. 35bis, the Gavotte from Four Pieces, op. 32, transcribed for violin and piano by Jascha Heifetz, three of the twelve pieces in *Music for Children* (the antepenultimate March, "Soir," and "Sur les prés la lune se promène"), *Suggestion diabolique*, and the *Overture on Hebrew Themes*, op. 34. As an encore, Prokofiev performed, inevitably, the March from *The Love for Three Oranges*. The program was well received and reviewed, but Prokofiev perhaps cared little about the response, having recently and publicly dismissed American critics as being "the second most insolent in the world"—behind the British.[77]

With the Denver Symphony, Prokofiev served as soloist in his First Piano Concerto, op. 10, then led the orchestra in a performance of the Classical Symphony. (This was one of two occasions in 1938 that he picked up a baton.) All did not go well. The title of one review succinctly stated the problem: "Prokofiev, at Piano, Moves Too Fast for Symphony Musicians." Although apparently the Classical Symphony had demonstrated "the mettle of [the musicians'] talent to be sound," Prokofiev's virtuosity in the Concerto proved too much for them. They simply "could not keep pace" even with conductor Horace E. Tureman working "like a Volga boatman" to drag everyone along.[78]

The poor performance cast a pall over Prokofiev's visit. While in Colorado, Prokofiev stayed at the home of Mr. and Mrs. George Cranmer, a Renaissance palace on the prairie at 200 Cherry Street, for a "difficult" ten days. Jean Cranmer, a driving force behind the founding of the Denver Symphony in 1934, lamented in a much later interview that the orchestral performance had been "very unfortunate," blaming the troubles on logistics.[79] "The music didn't arrive until the day he did," she recalled, "and the orchestra had no chance to rehearse." Moreover, the score and parts were printed on "terrible Russian paper," the notes obscured by fingerings, erasures, and re-fingerings. "Half the men in the orchestra didn't know what notes they were playing." Seemingly more upsetting than the performance was Prokofiev's demeanor. He was, she thought, "a grouch" who "hardly spoke to anyone," although of course the composer spoke perfect English. "He'd sit through a meal just not saying a word. Nobody could get anything out of him." What he did say, following a reception on February 18, was that "he didn't like anybody who was there." Determined to win over her unhappy houseguest, Cranmer took him to see *Snow White and the Seven Dwarfs*, which he enjoyed so much that he asked to go back the next day.

Still, Prokofiev was dissatisfied with the orchestra and said as much. Cranmer took offense, and in the wake of his departure, penned a reproof. Her letter does not seem to survive, but his response does, drafted on leftover stationery from the California Limited train and the Ritz-Carlton Hotel in Boston while he waited to sail from New York to Paris on May 30, 1938. Straining to be civil, he offered a dispassionate assessment of his experience in Denver and the shortcomings of the symphony. Cranmer had defended her orchestra and Prokofiev the integrity of the symphonic repertoire. His letter reads in full:

> I had such a pleasant stay at your house that it was a real disappointment to receive your letter which you found necessary to word in such an unexpected manner. But inasmuch as a glove is thrown, it must be picked up, and here I am. Let me again reassert, dear Mrs. Cranmer, that your orchestra is full of good musicians but it is not a very strong one, and its conductor, while accompanying my concerto manifested the following shortcomings: he had no grip over the

orchestra; the motions of his hands were not precise nor varied; he did not transmit to the orchestra the indications which are in the score; he did not follow the soloist.

At first I intended to take the stand, which according to your letter would have met with your approval. I thought: why should I speak against an orchestra which I perhaps will never meet again or against a conductor who did not mean to cause me any harm? But then it dawned on me that an orchestra does not exist to provide a conductor with a living, nor is it created for the personal pleasure of its board of directors. It exists in order to make the public know and love good music. Therefore, the only guide for my behavior should be the interests of the music lovers and not of the president or conductor of the orchestra. Accordingly, I explained my viewpoint to you then and to others. Incidentally it seems you were almost the only person who did not approve my stand.

It is highly praiseworthy that in your letter you are moved by a desire to defend your orchestra. But it would be still better if, instead of yielding to false pride, you would carefully listen to one who has a right to speak about music. Not all presidents of orchestras have an adequate education in music, and if they will not listen to specialists, there is a danger that, in spite of all the time and money they sacrificed for this purpose, the orchestra will not be directed in a proper way. When a music lover hears a bad performance he gets a wrong impression of symphonic music, despises it and turns always to jazz which is fairly competently played. In this case your intentions may be good but the result unfortunate [*catastrophic* is crossed out here].

I certainly appreciate the effort Colorado has made in order to engage me. On the other hand an inadequate performance is always detrimental to a composer, and don't you think that a less scrupulous one might have insisted on an increased fee for such tampering with his music?

Please believe me that it pains me to have to tell you all this. I had such a pleasant and restful sojourn under your roof. My criticism is meant to be constructive and sympathetic in spite of your rebuke.[80]

From Denver, Prokofiev traveled the seventy miles south to Colorado Springs (pop. 35,789 in 1940), where he gave a piano recital at the Colorado Springs Fine Arts Center on Monday, February 21, and thirty miles north to Boulder (pop. 12,958), for a performance on Wednesday, February 23, at Macky Auditorium on the University of Colorado campus.[81] Audiences in these towns heard a full program comprising the Andante, *Visions fugitives*, Second Sonata, *Music for Children*, "Danse des jeunes Antillaises," the Prelude and Gavotte of op. 12, Etude, op. 52, the Gavotte from the Classical Symphony, and *Suggestion diabolique*. Prokofiev was applauded in Colorado Springs by "one of the most enthusiastic audiences in recent local musical history," and despite much talk of his modernist proclivities, Boulder concert-goers—consisting mostly of students—greeted him "with warm applause" and demanded an encore.[82] "Boy, can he play!" one student exclaimed. The events had the air of the exotic in places underexposed to contemporary concerts. In Boulder, Prokofiev was amused that those in attendance were not sure when his pieces had actually ended. At a post-concert reception, he claimed to have purposely elected to play simpler works for an untutored audience, but in fact the program was no different than those he had performed in Chicago, New York, and Washington.

After Boulder, Prokofiev returned to Denver for a day and then moved on. Colorado was to have been as far west as he ventured, but his plans changed. He explained the turnabout in a February 23, 1938, letter to Gottlieb.

Sorry not to have written earlier,—up to now I did not know if I was going to Hollywood or not. Even now I have no definite proposition, but they phoned twice and persuaded me to come, saying there are many possibilities. So I decided to leave Denver on the 24th and will arrive to [*sic*] Hollywood on Saturday morning [February 26].[83]

The calls might have come from Rudolph Polk, former concert violinist turned artist's agent; he was assistant musical director at Columbia Studios and in the late 1940s served as musical director for such pictures as *A Kiss for Corliss* (1949), Shirley Temple's last film.[84] At Polk's invitation, Prokofiev boarded the Los Angeles Limited to make the forty-hour trip from Colorado to California.[85] Lina came too, traveling separately from New York to meet her husband in Los Angeles; she knew perfectly well the significance of the visit and its potential to change their lives. A letter from Lawrence Creath Ammons, a Christian Science practitioner and acquaintance of the Prokofievs in Paris, hints at her hopes:

It was good to hear from you even if it did recount the exhaustion of New York life. Yes, doesn't it make all these European cities seem like small villages? But just at present they are active ones with Hitler taking possession of Europe. This week's lesson page 95 line 12 shows what it all is but we have to see that we are on the "side of Science and peace" and thus bring more of it into one personal experience.

Hollywood sounds promising and if it opens as you both hope I trust that that heaven planned place may be your quiet abode with the children for a few years. It has so much of the real Science about it there even if there is another artificial side in the movie life. Ideal American atmosphere for raising children! Page 591 line 16 tells us what Mind is and that [it] is our one and only Mind which outlines our future and present and we have only to accept the divine outline every day here we are on earth.[86]

On February 28, two days after Prokofiev had arrived and installed himself at the exclusive Roosevelt Hotel on Hollywood Avenue, Polk brought him to Walt Disney to play through *Peter and the Wolf* at the Hyperion Studio. (The scene was re-created in 1957 for the fourth-anniversary show of the series *Your Host, Walt Disney* on ABC television.) By the time of this meeting Prokofiev had an offer in hand from Paramount. On March 4, he wrote to his mother-in-law, Olga Codina, with the news.

> I've already been in Hollywood a week. There were terrible rains and flooding. But Hollywood is in the hills and so it wasn't so noticeable here. And now it's once again sunny, warm, and green.
>
> Paramount immediately approached me to do music for a film and offered a nice big sum. But for this I would need to remain here for 10 weeks. That is to return to Moscow around June 1. And this would be inconvenient. And so it had to be turned down, and now we're in negotiations about a future season. [Lina] has left New York and will be here in a few days. . . . We'll be here until March 15th and will arrive in Paris on April 4th on the *Normandie* for a short stay.[87]

The trip to Hollywood may have been precipitated by Polk, but Paramount had expressed an interest in Prokofiev well before this letter indicates. On January 29, while in London, he wrote Olga that "a representative from Paramount asked about my arrival in New York. Perhaps it's a prospective project."[88] Whatever the offer (no available documents corroborate or elaborate his letters), nothing ever came of it.

Presumably pursuing the offer, the Prokofievs visited Paramount during the second week of March. Their activities and impressions were recorded in a story that ran throughout the country in such small-market newspapers as the Zanesville (Ohio) *Times-Signal,* Lowell (Massachusetts) *Sun,* and the Ironwood (Michigan) *Daily Globe.* Writing a syndicated column for the Newspaper Enterprise Association, Paul Harrison reported that "the plush red carpets of Paramount were rolled out" for the couple, who were fascinated by a native Alaskan "orchestra" auditioning for *Spawn of the North* (1938) and entertained by songwriter Ralph Ranger and lyricist Leo Robin.[89] "The team were as bashful as little boys about playing their own stuff," Harrison recounted. "'Aw-w-w,' they blushed, 'he doesn't want to hear us!'"

But once they had been persuaded to play, "the pair finally got going, and the visitors tapped their feet and liked it." Lina understood an ersatz cowboy song from *The Texans* (1938), presumably "Silver on the Sage," to be a "cow lullaby." For his part, Prokofiev preferred "It Don't Make Sense," written for Martha Raye in *Give Me a Sailor* (1938), but had his doubts.

> The team's delight changed to embarrassment when he said of Miss Raye's swing tune, "It is not original!"
>
> "No," said Robin, "it isn't. We take a little of this and a little of that and—"
>
> "But that is not honest!" exclaimed the shocked composer.
>
> "Mister," said Robin, "if our stuff was original we'd starve to death. We tried that once. People didn't like it."
>
> Prokofieff laughed and went away to see the sound laboratory.

Escorting them around the studio that day was Russian émigré Boris Morros, a native of St. Petersburg, a cellist (who claimed to be Gregor Pyatigorsky's first teacher), and music director at Paramount from 1936 to 1940. He was also a Soviet spy. Morros, code name FROST, began working for the NKVD (Narodnïy Komissariat Vnutrennikh Del, the People's Commissariat for Internal Affairs) in 1934; he was doubled by the FBI in 1947. In exchange for the ability to travel and send packages back to his family in Russia, he helped place another agent, Vassily Zarubin (known also as Edward Herbert and Vassily Zubilin) in Paramount's newly opened Berlin office; Morros then passed payments from the NKVD to Zarubin. The Soviet strategy was to use such positions at Paramount as cover for agents working in Europe and the Far East; the United States was not, during this period, of special concern. At the time of the Prokofievs' visit, however, Morros had been out of touch with the Soviets for a year.[90]

Also while together in Hollywood, Prokofiev and Lina attended the Academy Awards at the Biltmore Hotel on March 10, 1938, and three days later, on March 13, the director Rouben Mamoulian hosted a dinner in their honor at the Victor Hugo, a finely appointed restaurant in Laguna Beach.[91] Among the guests were Mr. and Mrs. Edward G. Robinson, Myrna Loy, Marlene Dietrich, Douglas Fairbanks Jr., and Arnold Schoenberg. After dinner everyone retreated to Mamoulian's home, where Prokofiev gave an impromptu recital. Gladys Lloyd Robinson (that is, Mrs. Edward G.) described the evening in *Rob Wagner's Script*, an insider magazine for the film industry. "Myrna turned on the charm and Mr. Prokoffieff [*sic*] responded brilliantly, much to our joy," playing excerpts from *Romeo and Juliet* along with a selection of his piano works. "Then he told us all about his 'Peter the Wolf,' which he had just played to Walt Disney, with all the instruments in the orchestra playing the characters. Mme Prokoffieff confessed that she is really Lena Lluberra [*sic*], of the opera in Europe, and still concertizes with her famous husband."[92] On Tuesday, March 15, the Robinsons held a tea that Prokofiev seems to have attended without Lina.[93] This was likely the last event of their stay, and the couple must have left together on or around the fifteenth to be back on the East Coast for their next engagement in Washington.

As in 1937, Prokofiev performed at the Soviet embassy, although on this occasion—a musicale on Monday, March 21, 1938—he was joined by his wife. Ambassador Troyanovsky's counterpart in London had hosted a similar event at the embassy there on January 27, before Prokofiev and Lina departed for the United States; that concert had been arranged by VOKS and so, one must conclude, was this recital in America. Before an audience of three hundred distinguished guests (including ambassadors from Turkey, Poland, Ecuador, Spain, France, and Finland, as well as a smattering of senators, representatives, and the wife of the secretary of the navy), the Prokofievs showcased songs from various parts of Russia and his piano works. The "Shepherd's Song of Georgia" was, according to *Washington Post* society editor Hope Ridings Miller, "done to a fine turn by Mme. Lluberra," and the music from *Romeo and Juliet* was "especially well received, as were other of the pianist's compositions." A buffet supper "climaxed the evening's entertainment."[94]

From Washington Prokofiev traveled north for two concerts with the Boston Symphony Orchestra on Friday afternoon, March 25, and Saturday evening, March 26, meeting again with members of the Dartmouth College Prokofiev Society for dinner on Friday.[95] This was his second appearance as conductor on the 1938 tour, and his first ever with the Boston Symphony. Unlike the concerts in 1937, which had featured earlier works familiar to local audiences, this time Prokofiev and Koussevitzky scheduled two American premieres: the Second Suite from *Romeo and Juliet*, op. 64ter (1936) and *Peter and the Wolf*, op. 67, for which Koussevitzky possessed the only score and set of parts then in the United States. Prokofiev also led a performance of the Suite from *Chout*, op. 21bis, and played the First Piano Concerto under the direction of concertmaster Richard Burgin. Despite the inclusion of novelties on the program, Alexander Williams of the *Herald* was disappointed. "It was a mistake not to have included one of his more serious formal works on the program," he suggested, "rather than two ballet suites." The composer had thereby missed an opportunity "to have repeated the symphony which he believes was misunderstood"— namely, the ill-received Fourth Symphony, op. 47, commissioned by the BSO in celebration of its fiftieth anniversary in 1930.[96]

Romeo and Juliet itself was revealed to have been controversial, at least in the Soviet Union. The program booklet reproduced brief dispatch from the *Musical Courier* detailing the reception of the ballet and its surprisingly happy ending. "The preview of the work left the critics in dismay," V. V. Konin wrote on November 16, 1935. Although the music had been deemed "excellent" by Soviet cultural arbiters, the libretto was pronounced problematic. "The social atmosphere of the period and the natural evolution of its tragic elements have been robbed of their logical culmination and brought to the ridiculously dissonant 'happy end' of the conventional ballet." Boston audiences and critics were of course unaware of the politics surrounding *Romeo and Juliet* in the Soviet Union, but L. A. Sloper of the *Christian Science Monitor* managed to get close to a basic truth of the matter in suggesting that "Marxist ideology" had "laid a cold hand on an imagination that never was notable for warmth." It was not, however, Marx but Stalin's Committee on Arts Affairs under whose thumb the composer labored.[97]

The Suite made less of an impression than *Peter and the Wolf,* narrated by Richard Hale, then known for his work on Broadway and later as a character actor on television. Despite Prokofiev's suggestion that he was conducting the piece only to spite Boston audiences—"If the public in Boston cannot understand my serious music," the composer told *Time* magazine, "I'm going to give them simple things"—*Peter and the Wolf* was generally well received.[98] Warren Storey Smith considered the music "purposefully infantile" and "the joke . . . overlong," but Cyrus Durgin of the *Globe* deemed it as "sleek and ingenious, pointing up the story with unerring humor."[99] Williams likewise found it "amusing" as well as "charming," and Sloper judged it "easily the most successful item of the program, by the vote of popular response."[100] The duck was especially amusing and surely, he quipped, "a relative's of Donald's."[101]

Thus it seems only fitting that Prokofiev eventually received an offer from Disney for *Peter and the Wolf.* On March 27, 1938, just after the Boston concerts and just before leaving the States, Prokofiev wrote to Rudolph Polk, authorizing him "to sign the agreement for 'Peter and the Wolf'" with Disney. The composer also sent the Boston reviews (perhaps omitting Storey Smith's) and indicated that Koussevitzky would write to Disney as well, "persuading him to use it for cartoons."[102] Negotiations began in earnest in the early summer of 1940, and a contract to animate the orchestral children's tale was signed on February 4, 1941.[103]

Prokofiev's last concert of the 1938 tour was a joint recital on March 28 with Lina at the Astor Hotel in New York City. They performed under the auspices of the American Russian Institute, which defined itself as "a nonpolitical membership organization formed in 1926 for the purpose of promoting cultural relations between the peoples of the United States and the Soviet Union."[104] Two days later, they boarded the *Normandie* for Le Havre, but dense fog forced the liner to anchor in Gravesend Bay, delaying their departure by some twenty-two hours.[105]

The Ghost Tours, 1939–1941

On May 29, 1938, a notice appeared in the *Chicago Daily Tribune* of the upcoming musical arts piano series. Slated for the 1938–39 season was Sergey Prokofiev. In a second story that October, a date was announced: his recital would be February 7, 1939.[106] News of a concert with the Los Angeles Philharmonic was published in the *Los Angeles Times* on August 7. "Serge Prokofieff, whose 'Peter and the Wolf' was played at the Bowl Tuesday evening for the second time in America with Edward G. Robinson's vivifying reading, has been engaged to conduct the Philharmonic Orchestra of Los Angeles in March. He is also scheduled to write a film score at that time and has taken a house for several weeks."[107] Also on August 7, 1938, the *New York Times* reported that Prokofiev "will concertize in Europe next Fall, returning to America after the first of the year for another tour."[108] But nearly a year to the day he was to have performed in Chicago, Prokofiev wrote to Nicolas Slonimsky (on February 9, 1939) that although he had "expected to come to the States around this time," his tour had been "postponed until next season."[109] And on March 11, the composer wrote to Wyman Vaughan and the Prokofieff Society at Dartmouth College to cancel his visit there. "I have postponed my American tour until next season. This involves the same postponement of my visit to Dartmouth, which otherwise I would accept with much pleasure."[110]

Even as he was sending news of the canceled 1939 tour, Prokofiev was planning for 1940. He wrote to Haensel & Jones in February 1939 with news that he would be in the United States for the entire month of February 1940. The agency set to work booking concerts with Koussevitzky and the Boston Symphony as well as in Chicago. By July those were scheduled (seemingly by Prokofiev himself, no doubt assisted by Gottlieb, since Haensel appears not to have known the Boston dates), and Prokofiev cabled Haensel & Jones with a request to end his tour on the West Coast during the first half of March.[111] Nothing was certain, however, as Koussevitzky acknowledged to Gottlieb in a letter of October 3, 1939—a month after Britain and France had declared war on Germany. "Prokofiev is engaged to appear with us in Boston this season," he wrote, referring to the spring of 1940. "But who can foresee what may happen between now and then? We hope for the best." With Europe plunged into all-out war, Prokofiev himself must have recognized that his plans might fall through. Still, an article in the *Chicago Tribune* of January 7, 1940, previewing the rest of the symphony season, stated that Prokofiev was to be there to conduct the Chicago Symphony on February 15 and 16, 1940—a week before Stravinsky was to do the same.[112]

Three days later, however, it was announced in the *New York Times* that Prokofiev would not in fact come to America, with the war in Europe not wholly to blame. As the story notes, "Serge Prokofieff, Russian composer, will be unable to come to America this season to fulfill his engagement as guest conductor of the Philharmonic-Symphony Orchestra, it was announced yesterday. Political conditions have made it impossible for him to obtain the necessary visas."[113] The *Chicago Tribune* carried the news on February 11, 1940, stating bluntly: "Prokofieff, the distinguished Russian composer-conductor, remained in Russia on government orders."[114] In his stead, Stravinsky stepped up to the podium in New York for four concerts (April 3, 5–7), and Frederick Stock forewent his vacation to fill the unexpected vacancy in Chicago on Thursday, February 22, and Friday, February 23. In Boston, Prokofiev missed the premiere of his Cello Concerto with the virtuoso Pyatigorsky performing under Koussevitzky's direction.

To Gottlieb, Prokofiev conveyed his regrets as well as his persistent hopes. "You know probably from Parmelee that I had to cancel my American tour—and so the pleasure to come again to the States has to be postponed to some better future."[115] Prokofiev continued to make plans, or at least Koussevitzky did for him. To Polk, who inked the deal with Disney on February 4, 1941, Koussevitzky wrote in October: "It is my sincere hope that Prokofieff may come over to this country."[116] Hope was dashed on November 8, 1941, by a terse telegram from Andrei Gromyko, chargé d'affaires at the Soviet embassy in Washington. "It is regretted that it would not be safe to depend on Serge Prokofiev's coming to the United States due to war situation."[117] Prokofiev never again toured in America, nor anywhere abroad; his foreign colleagues, enthusiasts, and representatives could only speculate as to the future course of his Soviet career.

NOTES

Research for this article was made possible with the kind and able assistance of many librarians, among them Sarah Hartwell (Rauner Special Collections Library at Dartmouth College), Kevin LaVine (Music Division, Library of Congress), Mary Linneman (Hargrett Rare Book and Manuscript Library at the University of Georgia), Autumn Mather (Newberry Library, Chicago), Janice Prater (Denver Public Library), Gina Scioscia (Boulder Public Library), and Amy Ziegler (Pikes Peak Library District). I am likewise grateful to Barbara Hall, Head of Special

Collections at the Margaret Herrick Library of the Academy of Motion Picture Arts and Sciences, Malcolm Brown (who provided photocopies of many of the letters cited), and especially Simon Morrison.

1. Prokofiev supplies the date of his sailing in a letter to Nikolay Myaskovsky of January 12, 1937, written en route from Paris while approaching New York. In *Selected Letters of Sergei Prokofiev*, ed. and trans. Harlow Robinson (Boston: Northeastern University Press, 1998), 321. The previous six American visits were August 21, 1918 (arriving San Francisco on the *Grotius*)–April 27, 1920 (departing New York); October 24, 1920 (arriving New York on the *Savoie*)–February 3, 1921 (departing New York on the *Aquitaine*); October 21, 1921 (arriving New York on the *Aquitaine*)–February 25, 1922 (departing New York for France on the *Noordam*); January 1 (arriving New York on the *De Grasse*)–March 6, 1926 (departing for France on the *France*); December 31, 1929 (arriving New York on the *Berengaria*)–March 28, 1930 (departing for France on the *Île de France*); December 1932 (arriving New York on the *Europa*)–March 1933 (leaving New York on the *Conte di Savoia*).

2. "Notes Here and Afield," *New York Times*, January 3, 1937. The date of Prokofiev's arrival is confirmed by a telegram from Haensel & Jones to the Arts Club of Chicago, January 9, 1937, Arts Clubs Manuscripts, "Music 1937–1938: General Correspondence," Series 4, 63, f. 55, Newberry Library (Chicago).

3. "Notes Here and Afield."

4. "Behind the Microphone," *Christian Science Monitor*, January 9, 1937.

5. Interestingly, Prokofiev chose some of the same repertoire for the 1937 radio recital as for his New York debut concerts in 1918, which likewise featured *Visions fugitives* (in Brooklyn on October 29) and *Suggestion diabolique* (at Aeolian Hall on November 20). See David Nice, *Prokofiev: From Russia to the West* (New Haven: Yale University Press, 2003), 151.

6. Despite being mentioned in advance notices ("Prokofieff as Soloist," *Chicago Daily News*, January 16, 1937), a review in *Time* magazine ("Prokofieff's New Line," February 1, 1937), and in the program for Prokofiev's concerts with the Boston Symphony Orchestra in February 1937, the incidental music for *Boris Godunov* and *Eugene Onegin* was not performed during Prokofiev's lifetime. The protracted, unhappy tale of the *Cantata for the Twentieth Anniversary of October*, publicized unproblematically in the *New York Times* ("Opera and Concert," February 13, 1938) during Prokofiev's visit to the United States in 1938, is told in Simon Morrison and Nelly Kravetz, "The *Cantata for the Twentieth Anniversary of October*, or How the Specter of Communism Haunted Prokofiev," *Journal of Musicology* 23, no. 2 (2006): 227–62.

7. Ephraim Gottlieb was a Chicago-based insurance agent with New York Life whom Prokofiev met during his first visit to the United States; the two maintained an active and personal correspondence.

8. Prokofiev to Gottlieb, February 13, 1935, Hargrett Rare Book and Manuscript Library, University of Georgia. Unless otherwise noted, photocopies of this and other correspondence were generously provided by Malcolm Brown.

9. Prokofiev to Gottlieb, July 28, 1935.

10. Prokofiev wrote to Duke on September 29, 1935: "I had thought of going to the States this winter [1936], but, since Bruno Walter failed to sign his contract, the New York engagement was canceled." As quoted in Vernon Duke, *Passport to Paris* (Boston: Little, Brown, 1955), 313. Walter did not conduct the New York Philharmonic-Society Symphony in the 1935–36 season.

11. Prokofiev to Gottlieb, November 14, 1935.

12. "My wife and boys arrived here a fortnight ago," Prokofiev wrote of the move to Moscow, which he had made in March. "The furniture and the piano are on the way as we will take an apartment in Moscow." Prokofiev to Gottlieb, May 31, 1936.

13. Edward Barry, "Prokofieff Here to Present New Curve in Melody: Composer Eats Pie and Views Modern Trend," *Chicago Daily Tribune*, January 20, 1937.

14. The "alarming bulletin" is described in Alexander W. Williams, "Prokofieff Works at Symphony," *Boston Herald*, January 31, 1937.

15. Edward Barry, "Ovation Given Prokofieff at Concert Here," *Chicago Daily Tribune*, January 22, 1937.

16. Eugene Stinson, "Music Views: Realm of His Own," *Chicago Daily News*, January 22, 1937.

17. "Prokofieff's New Line," *Time*, February 1, 1937.

18. Trudi Schoop was a dancer often described as the female Charlie Chaplin. Claudia Cassidy, "On the Aisle: Prokofieff Appears as Pianist, Conductor, and Composer with Lange and Chicago Symphony," *Chicago Journal of Commerce and La Salle Street Journal*, January 22, 1937.

19. Stinson, "Music Views"; Herman Devries, *Chicago American*, January 22, 1937, as quoted in Haensel & Jones Press Kit (1938), Papers of the Prokofieff Society (DO-10) at Rauner Special Collections Library, Dartmouth College.

20. "Prokofieff's New Line," *Time*.

21. Barry, "Ovation Given Prokofieff at Concert Here."

22. Cassidy, "On the Aisle"; also quoted in "Prokofieff's New Line," *Time*.

23. Judith Cass, "Mrs. M'Cormick Will Display New Paintings," *Chicago Daily Tribune*, January 21, 1937.

24. Judith Cass, "Prokofieff to Bring Wife on Chicago Visit," *Chicago Daily Tribune*, February 11, 1938.

25. June Provines, "Front Views and Profiles," *Chicago Daily Tribune*, January 25, 1937.

26. India Moffett, "Famous Laces are Viewed by Antiquarians," *Chicago Daily Tribune*, January 23, 1937.

27. "End Strike Just Before J. Public Gets Dander Up," *Chicago Daily Tribune*, January 23, 1937.

28. Prokofiev to Duke, January 24, 1937, in Robinson, *Selected Letters of Sergei Prokofiev*, 154.

29. "Prokofieff Presents Program of Contrast," *St. Louis Post-Dispatch*, January 30, 1937.

30. Ibid.

31. Harry R. Burke, "Prokofieff, Master Pianist, Is Dynamic Also as Conductor," January 30, 1937.

32. Harry R. Burke, "Prokofieff Again Scores Brilliantly in Role as Soloist," *St. Louis Daily Globe Democrat*, January 31, 1937.

33. Reed Hynds, "Prokofieff at Top Form in Concert," *St. Louis Star-Times*, January 30, 1937.

34. M. P., "Prokofieff Presents Program of Contrast," *St. Louis Post-Dispatch*, January 30, 1937.

35. Burke, "Prokofieff, Master Pianist."

36. Hynds, "Prokofieff at Top Form in Concert."

37. Burke, "Prokofieff, Master Pianist."

38. Ibid.

39. M. P., "Prokofieff Presents Program of Contrast."

40. Prokofiev explained this schedule to Duke in the letter of January 24, but a brief announcement of the concert in the *Post-Dispatch* states that "Prokofieff will attend tonight's concert" ("Chamber Music Concert Tonight," *St. Louis Post-Dispatch*, Women's Sunday Magazine, January 31, 1937). The review by Reed Hynds in the *Star-Times* confirms that the composer was not in attendance ("Prokofieff's Enigmatic Music," *St. Louis Star-Times*, February 1, 1937).

41. H. E. D., "Moving Performance of Schubert Music," *St. Louis Post-Dispatch*, February 1, 1937.

42. Hynds, "Prokofieff's Enigmatic Music."

43. Harry R. Burke, "Society Presents Prokofieff Opus," *St. Louis Globe Democrat*, February 1, 1937.

44. Duke, *Passport to Paris*, 346.

45. L. A. S[loper], "What's Going on in the Arts," *Christian Science Monitor*, February 6, 1937.

46. Alfred de Musset, French Romantic poet and novelist. Redfern Mason, "Serge Prokofieff Dominates Symphony," *Boston Evening Transcript*, February 6, 1937.

47. Ruth Marsters, *Boston American*, February 6, 1937, as quoted in Haensel & Jones Press Kit (1938).

48. Alexander Williams, "Music: Symphony Concert," *Boston Herald*, February 6, 1937.

49. Quoted in Duke, *Passport to Paris*, 345.

50. Ibid., 346.

51. The autographed program is among the Papers of the Prokofieff Society.

52. Merrell E. Condit to Serge Koussevitzky (copy), April 21, 1937, Papers of the Prokofieff Society; original in Serge Koussevitzky Archive, Music Division, Library of Congress (henceforth, MDLC). The Society's entreaty to Prokofiev is not found in the Prokofieff Society papers.

53. Koussevitzky replied: "This is just a line to thank you for your kind offer of an honorary membership of [*sic*] 'The Prokofieff Society' which I accept with great pleasure." Koussevitzky to Condit, May 1, 1937, Papers of the Prokofieff Society.

54. Prokofiev to Condit, April 2, 1937, Papers of the Prokofieff Society.

55. Jessie Ash Arndt, "Soviet Envoy Entertains at Musicale in Embassy," *Washington Post,* February 9, 1937.

56. Harlow Robinson, *Sergei Prokofiev: A Biography* (New York: Viking, 1987), 333.

57. Duke, *Passport to Paris,* 344. The strange spelling of Prokofiev's prenames appears to be Duke mocking his mother's Russian accent.

58. Ibid., 314.

59. Prokofiev to Duke, June 10, 1937, quoted in *Passport to Paris,* 349; also in Robinson, *Selected Letters,* 156–57 (dated June 19).

60. Horace J. Parmelee to Serge Koussevitzky, August 2, 1937, Koussevitzky Archive, MDLC.

61. Judith Cass, "Friends Await Russian News of Prokofieff," *Chicago Daily Tribune,* January 5, 1938.

62. Judith Cass, "John Cameron and Dorothy Palmer Wed: Prokofieff Sailing Date Uncertain," *Chicago Daily Tribune,* January 14, 1938. The wedding has nothing to do with the sailing.

63. The difficulties Prokofiev experienced are detailed in Simon Morrison, *The People's Artist* (New York: Oxford University Press, 2008).

64. Duke, *Passport to Paris,* 364.

65. Their arrival is announced in "Ocean Travelers," *New York Times,* February 3, 1938; the concert in "Prokofieff as Guest," *New York Times,* January 9, 1938. Prokofiev himself supplied the dates of his travel to Duke in a letter of January 14, quoted in *Passport to Paris,* 362; see also Robinson, *Selected Letters,* 157–58.

66. "Music in Review," *New York Times,* February 7, 1938. The program for the event is found in the clippings files for Prokofiev at the New York Public Library for the Performing Arts.

67. "Prokofieff Hails Life of Artist in Soviet; With 4 Incomes, He Is Here for Concerts," *New York Times,* February 6, 1938.

68. William G. King, "Music and Musicians: Serge Prokofieff—About the Ex-'Enfant Terrible' of Russian Music," *New York Sun,* February 9, 1938.

69. Russell McLauchlin, "Modernist Prokofieff Plays With Symphony," *Detroit News,* February 12, 1938.

70. J. D. Callaghan, "Music: Prokofieff," *Detroit Free Press,* February 12, 1938.

71. McLauchlin, "Modernist Prokofieff Plays With Symphony."

72. Edward Barry, "Piano Concert Justifies Rank of Prokofieff," *Chicago Daily Tribune,* February 16, 1938.

73. Cass, "Prokofieff to Bring Wife on Chicago Visit."

74. Telegrams between Mrs. Charles B. Goodspeed of the Arts Club and Gottlieb reveal that the tea was to have been held on Tuesday, February 15. Prokofiev would thus have been the sole guest of honor rather than appearing in the company of "the slim, pretty piano donnas of the Salzburg Opera Guild" (Moffett, "Fill Arts Club for Reception to Musicians," *Chicago Daily Tribune,* February 15, 1938) as was the case on Monday afternoon. Goodspeed to Gottlieb, January 27, 1938, and Gottlieb to Goodspeed, January 27, 1938; in the Arts Clubs Manuscripts, Newberry Library.

75. Prokofiev's appearance was set for February 19 by the Executive Committee and Technical Board of Pro Musica at its meeting on Tuesday, June 22, 1937; a program for the Pro Musica concert on October 25, 1937, featuring dancer Angna Enters, advertised his chamber concert with the Denver String Quartet as being on February 19, 1938. The date was changed at a meeting of the board on February 7, 1938. Minutes of the meetings (Box 2) and program of the October 25, 1937, dance recital (Box 1) are preserved in the Pro Musica Records, Western History/Genealogy Department, Denver Public Library.

76. Manuscript notes, October 25, [1937], Pro Musica, Denver Public Library, Box 1.

77. Alberta Pike, "American Critics Upset Famous Soviet Composer Visiting Here," *Rocky Mountain News,* February 18, 1938.

78. Frances Wayne, "Prokofiev, at Piano, Moves Too Fast for Symphony Musicians," *Denver Post,* February 19, 1938.

79. Arlynn Nellhaus, "Jean Cranmer Hosted Earliest DSO Artists," *Denver Post*, February 26, 1978.

80. Prokofiev to Jean Cranmer (draft), March 30, 1938.

81. The recitals in Colorado Springs and Boulder are mistakenly placed in Denver by Robinson in *Selected Letters*, 323 n. 253.

82. Robert Gross, "Serge Prokofieff Cheered by Enthusiastic Audience After Brilliant Concert," *Colorado Springs Gazette*, February 22, 1938; and "Boulder Hears New Kind of Music at Prokofieff Concert," *Boulder Daily Camera*, February 24, 1938.

83. Prokofiev to Gottlieb, February 23, 1938.

84. "Rudolph Polk, Manager of Concert Artists, Dies," *Los Angeles Times*, June 17, 1957. He is misrepresented as a lawyer and his name misreported as "Randolph" in Russell Merritt, "Recharging *Alexander Nevsky:* Tracking the Eisenstein-Prokofiev War Horse," *Film Quarterly* 48, no. 2 (1994–95): 34–47; the source of the misinformation is Dave Smith, chief archivist at Disney.

85. Polk explained his involvement in a letter to Koussevitzky, detailing negotiations surrounding *Peter and the Wolf*, of January 4, 1941, Serge Koussevitzky Archives, MDLC.

86. Lawrence Creath Ammons to Lina Prokofiev, March 15, 1938. In "lesson" references, Ammons is citing sections of Mary Baker Eddy's *Science and Health with Key to the Scriptures,* which both Prokofiev and his wife studied in depth.

87. Prokofiev to Olga Codina, March 4, 1938. This and the next quotation translated by Simon Morrison.

88. Prokofiev to Codina, January 29, 1938.

89. Paul Harrison, "In Hollywood," *Ironwood Daily Globe*, March 26, 1938.

90. On Boris Morros, see his (melodramatically written) autobiography, *My Ten Years as a Counterspy: As Told to Charles Samuels* (New York: Viking Press, 1959); also Allen Weinstein and Alexander Vassiliev, *The Haunted Wood: Soviet Espionage in America—the Stalin Era* (New York: Random House, 1999), 110–39; information in this secondary source cannot be verified, however, since the Lubyanka archive in question has been closed again.

91. Special thanks to Barbara Hall, Head of Special Collections at the Margaret Herrick Library of the Academy of Motion Picture Arts and Sciences, for discovering that the Prokofievs were invited to the Academy Awards. On the dinner at the Victor Hugo restaurant, see Read Kendall, "Around and About in Hollywood," *Los Angeles Times*, March 17, 1938.

92. Gladys Lloyd Robinson, "'Horrible Hollywood': A Happy Toasting for Jean at the Quarter-Mark," *Rob Wagner's Script*, March 19, 1938.

93. "Robinsons Entertain," *Los Angeles Times*, March 20, 1938. Prokofiev is listed among the guests, but there is no mention of Lina.

94. Hope Ridings Miller, "Troyanovskys Present Two Soviet Musicians," *Washington Post*, March 22, 1938. The evening was also reported in the society pages of the Washington *Evening Star*, March 22, 1938.

95. Prokofiev to Wyman Vaughan, March 23, [1938], Papers of the Prokofieff Society. The telegram reads: "Accept with pleasure but will have to attend a tea between concert and dinner."

96. Alexander Williams, "Music: Symphony Concert," *Boston Herald*, March 26, 1938.

97. L. A. Sloper, "Serge Prokofieff Conducts Symphony," *Christian Science Monitor,* March 26, 1938.

98. "Young Russia," *Time*, April 4, 1938.

99. Warren Storey Smith, "Prokofieff Dominates Symphony: Entire Concert from Works by His Hand," *Boston Post*, March 25, 1938; C[yrus] W. D[urgin], "Music: Symphony Hall," *Boston Globe*, March 26, 1938.

100. Williams, "Music: Symphony Concert"; Sloper, "Serge Prokofieff Conducts Symphony."

101. Sloper, "Serge Prokofieff Conducts Symphony."

102. Prokofiev's letter of March 27, 1938, is quoted by Polk in his own letter to Koussevitzky regarding negotiations with Disney. Polk to Koussevitzky, January 4, 1940 [*sic*, 1941], Koussevitzky Archive, MDLC.

103. Information about the contract, itself inaccessible to researchers, was supplied by the archivist at Disney.

104. This description is found on the inside cover of the journal published by the Institute, *The American Quarterly on the Soviet Union* 1, no. 3 (1938).

105. "Fog Disrupts Traffic in Harbor; *Normandie* and *Bremen* Halted," *New York Times*, April 1, 1938.

106. "Current Music News," *Chicago Daily Tribune*, May 29, 1938. A second notice appeared on July 31, 1938, and the date was announced ("Notes of Music and Musicians") on October 16, 1938.

107. "Reviewer's Notebook," August 7, 1938. A second notice—less sure of the date—appeared on August 14, 1938: "Serge Prokofieff will be here in March or April."

108. "Prokofieff's Plans," *New York Times*, August 7, 1938.

109. Prokofiev to Slonimsky, February 9, 1939; quoted in Morrison, *The People's Artist*, typescript, chap. 2.

110. Prokofiev to Vaughan, March 11, 1939, Prokofieff Society Papers.

111. On February 18, Parmelee wrote to Koussevitzky, letting him know that the agency had "just received a cable from the artist from Moscow informing us that he will be in the United States during the entire month of February 1940." And on July 5, 1939, Haensel & Jones wrote to Prokofiev to confirm his cable of July 3, with its request to end his West Coast tour, and to solicit details about his appearance with the Boston Symphony. Both letters are found in the Koussevitzky Archive, MDLC.

112. Edward Barry, "The Musical Spotlight Shifts Back to Symphony," *Chicago Daily Tribune*, January 7, 1940.

113. "Prokofieff Unable to Come to America," *New York Times*, January 10, 1940.

114. "Current Music News," *Chicago Daily Tribune*, February 11, 1940.

115. Prokofiev to Gottlieb, January 19, 1940.

116. Koussevitzky to Polk, October 20, 1941, Koussevitzky Archive, MDLC.

117. Andrei Gromyko to Koussevitzky, November 8, 1941, Koussevitzky Archive, MDLC; also in Robinson, *Selected Letters*, 205.

Between Two Aesthetics: The Revision of Pilnyak's *Mahogany* and Prokofiev's Fourth Symphony

MARINA FROLOVA-WALKER

The more talented the artist, the more politically inept he is.
—Boris Pilnyak

For several decades, audiences heard only the 1947 revision of Sergey Prokofiev's Fourth Symphony (op. 112), never the original of 1930 (op. 47). The composer's later thoughts were deemed binding, and the earlier work consigned to oblivion. Soviet scholars had little reason to consider the merits of Op. 47, since the music from Prokofiev's years abroad (1918–35) was viewed with suspicion. Izraíl Nestyev counted the revised version among "the greatest achievements of Russian epic symphony in the 20th century" and declined to discuss the original in its own right.[1] Mikhaíl Tarakanov complained that Op. 47 lacked symphonic complexity, dismissively labeling it a "symphony-suite," and analyzed only the revision.[2] Sergey Slonimsky compared the two in more detail but arrived at the same conclusion: the longer and weightier revision "increased the melodic expressiveness of [the symphony's] themes and finished up the form and orchestration" to yield a "stylistically and structurally clear and unified composition based on the material of his early work."[3] Writing in the post-Soviet era and outside the Soviet sphere, Helmut Loos considered both in a study examining material shared among the ballet *The Prodigal Son* (1928–29), the concert suite based on the ballet, and the two versions of the Fourth Symphony.[4] He, too, saw a progression from the "character pieces" of Op. 47 to the universal *Weltmuster* (world model) of Op. 112—an evolution he associates, strangely, with the shift from Liszt to Mahler. Consensus decreed the revision a genuine symphony; the original was considered at best a slight prototype of academic interest, at worst a mere

concert suite on the ballet. (Prokofiev could not have agreed, having composed a suite from *The Prodigal Son* that differs greatly from the original
version of the symphony.) The conductor Neeme Järvi enabled Western
listeners to judge for themselves when he recorded his complete set of
Prokofiev's symphonies in the mid-1980s with both versions of the Fourth.
But the recording of the original was eventually deleted from the catalog,
and only recently, with Valery Gergiev's complete set, have Russian and
Western listeners been able to hear the original again. Likewise a study
score of Op. 47 was just published.

Although I do not agree with conventional wisdom, it is not my purpose to commend the original over the revision even as I seek to draw out
the merits of Op. 47 as a work in its own right, one of the high points of
Prokofiev's years abroad. Instead, I wish to examine an issue that critics
and scholars have failed to raise, but that anyone approaching the symphony afresh should find startling: Why would any composer take a lean,
twenty-three-minute neoclassical piece and transform it into a socialist realist epic? Why would an artist take a work within one aesthetic, kick it around,
and then patch it up to reflect a very different aesthetic? And note that
this second aesthetic—Socialist Realism—countered the first: Neoclassicism.
These conflicting aesthetics rub up against each other in the 1947 revision,
sparking dramatic ruptures and striking incongruities. Thus I question the
view that the revision is a grand, unified conception and bring to light
the tension within the later work between incompatible aesthetics. The following discussion does not simply elevate one version over the other, for both
document Prokofiev's struggle to meet Soviet aesthetic prescriptions.

Prokofiev was not alone in his attempt to smuggle his art across aesthetic
borders, for there is another extraordinary Soviet revision that contains
similar unresolved conflicts. The artist is Boris Pilnyak, a leading writer
of experimental prose in the early Soviet period who found himself adrift
under Stalinism. Like Prokofiev, he took a relatively brief work, his forty-
three-page novella *Krasnoye derevo* (Mahogany, 1928–29), and in 1931
expanded it into a monumental novel—some six times longer—under the
title *Volga vpadayet v Kaspiyskoye more* (The Volga falls to the Caspian Sea).
I will never forget my astonishment as I read *Volga* and recognized page
after page from the original, wrenched out of context. The novella had
nothing to do with the novel, which features vast armies of laborers sent
to construct grandiose dams; instead, *Mahogany* spoke nostalgically of
Russian furniture and household ornaments, and how the painstaking labor
of Russian artisans is known and valued through the entire world. How
could this delicate material be transported into such a different realm, which
threatens not merely to recontextualize the original, as with Prokofiev's
symphony, but to obliterate it?

In tracing these parallel artistic histories, I am not suggesting that Pilnyak and Prokofiev were united by friendship or artistic purpose. Nor do I find it particularly interesting that Prokofiev began work on his Fourth Symphony the day after Pilnyak finished *Mahogany* (January 16, 1929); the coincidence has no inherent significance. Although the original works were created in the same short span of time, early in the Stalinist era, the two artists lived in separate societies in Paris and Moscow (admittedly both moved in elite circles). The circumstances of the revisions also differed: Pilnyak's closely followed the completion of the original and occurred under duress (according to one account, with Nikolay Yezhov literally standing over the writer's shoulder).[5] Prokofiev, in contrast, revised the symphony two decades after composing the original, seemingly of his own accord.[6]

Nevertheless, concrete similarities facilitate comparison. First, Pilnyak had a propensity for collecting thoughts and observations for future use, without any particular artistic context in mind. Prokofiev likewise jotted down felicitous thematic ideas, many remaining in his notebooks for years before he decided that their time had come. For both artists, these notebook inscriptions had immanent value; for the most part, no larger purpose was initially assigned to them. Pilnyak often constructed his works by placing these *visions fugitives* (to use Prokofiev's term) side by side, with only the most tenuous of narrative threads binding them. Exposed ruptures took preference over smooth transitions, the result suggesting montage technique, as in many Prokofiev works of the 1920s (including *The Love for Three Oranges* and *Le Pas d'acier*). Some of Pilnyak's writings seem to be constructed in a quasi-musical form, drawing coherence from repetitions and reshufflings of passages, which like musical refrains or ritornelli, change their import according to context. This highly personal and boldly innovative manner distanced Pilnyak from the organic, narrative-driven novel of the Stalinist period such that it is difficult to imagine him adapting to Socialist Realism without reinventing himself completely.[7] Prokofiev also had to reassess his montage-like technique, although he had already moved in this direction before returning permanently to the Soviet Union. Even so, he was frequently criticized for failing to privilege such socialist realist virtues as thematic development.

A further connection makes for fruitful comparison: although written in Russia, *Mahogany* was first published by an émigré press in Berlin and thus regarded as a foreign work—even anti-Soviet. Prokofiev's original Fourth Symphony was also tainted by its foreign provenance and suspected of being anti-Soviet, especially because the ballet score from which it emerged was commissioned by the impresario Sergey Diaghilev (1872–1929), who stood at the center of Paris-based émigré circles. Both Prokofiev and

Pilnyak confronted the challenge of turning "bourgeois" art into Soviet art. And both were ultimately motivated by a desire to salvage past creative efforts, however high the cost of tailoring their material to a drastically different ideological and aesthetic context. They found it painful to discard good work simply because it failed to meet official requirements, and so each managed to preserve 80 percent or more of his original. Cut up and spliced to suit Socialist Realism, the old yet haunts the new.

Pilnyak: From *Mahogany* to *The Volga Falls to the Caspian Sea*

Boris Pilnyak (real surname Wogau, 1894–1938) never shrank from writing about the Revolution and its effect on Russian life. Indeed, he made the tsarist past and the post-Revolutionary present his main theme, filtered through stories about former landowners, engineers, workers, Whites and Reds, Bolsheviks and anarchists. Gritty realism, at times exhibiting a documentary-like precision, exists within fragmented narratives that move back and forth in time, switching between characters with frequent interruptions from the highly poetic and metaphorical authorial voice; his earlier works in particular are so elusive as to border on incomprehensibility. The results reward the patient reader with an epic breadth of perspective and poignant moral dilemmas.

Pilnyak's political stance was never very clear: he could perhaps be characterized as an apolitical humanist, with his portrayal of Communist characters ranging from sympathetic, bemused, and humorous to merciless. From the start of his Soviet career he was a controversial figure destined to run into trouble. As Stalin consolidated his power, Pilnyak received advice from such Left Opposition figures as Trotsky, Voronsky, and Polonsky.[8] In the following decade, when Stalin had embarked on his purges and show trials, the writer remained friends with the former Left Oppositionist Karl Radek, disregarding his own safety (a likely factor in Pilnyak's eventual downfall). Despite his choice of company, Pilnyak was able to travel freely abroad even in the early 1930s—a privilege accorded to very few favored persons at the time.

His greatest offense against Stalin came in 1926 with "Povest' nepogashennoy lunï" (Tale of an unextinguished moon). The story insinuates (plausibly) that the death of the Russian civil war hero Mikhaíl Frunze resulted from an unnecessary and unsafe abdominal operation ordered by Stalin. After it was published in the literary periodical *Novïy mir*, the entire print run was confiscated, keeping the incident out of public view and, by lucky corollary, preventing Pilnyak from being publicly associated with the scandal. In effect,

Pilnyak's transgression was so serious that it could not be discussed, thereby temporarily letting him off the hook. (Stalin was not as yet in a position to have his enemies assassinated or arbitrarily arrested.) But the publication of *Mahogany* by an émigré press in 1929 became a pretext for his literary opponents to bring him to heel. By the standards of the time, foreign publication could scarcely be regarded as a misdemeanor, since many writers indulged in the practice with impunity; it was generally regarded as a financial expedient rather than a sign of political skullduggery.[9]

Despite the various scandals, *Mahogany* cannot be described as anti-Soviet. The most that could have been said against the text was that it lacked Soviet didacticism. Its main characters are the brothers Bezdetov, traders in antique furniture, and their customers, who hope to preserve a little of their former lives and past wealth. Pilnyak seems to share their nostalgia. The most striking character in the novella is Ivan Ozhogov, a onetime Communist (expelled from the Party in 1921) who tries to remain true to his youthful ideals by forgoing personal possessions and living in a commune of tramps. The bedrock of honesty and morality underlying his alcoholic madness makes him the most sympathetic character. Ozhogov, like the Bezdetovs and their customers, belongs to an irretrievable past, but his was the heroic age of Revolution. Ozhogov's nephew, Akim, had struggled for an alternative to Stalinism, but with the defeat of Trotsky and the Oppositionists, his brief era has also expired. Even the Russian provincial town they call home is located in neither the tsarist past nor the Soviet future; it exists in a vague eternal present where nothing much happens.

This description might imply a political work, but Pilnyak's main theme owes less to contemporary politics than to his characteristic mystical musings on the Russian national character. The novella is really about the holy fools who inhabit a strand of Russian literature that long predates the Revolution:

Paupers, soothsayers, beggars, mendicant chanters, wanderers from holy place to holy place, male and female, cripples, idiots of both sexes, fools in Christ—these names, so close in meaning, of the double-ring sugar cakes of the everyday life of Holy Russia, paupers on the face of Holy Russia, wandering psalm singers, Christ's cripples, fools in Christ of Holy Russia—these sugar cakes have adorned everyday life from Russia's very beginnings, from the time of the first Tsar Ivans, the everyday life of Russia's thousand years. All Russian historians, ethnographers, and writers have dipped their quills to write about these holy fools. These madmen or frauds—beggars, bogus saints, prophets—were held to be the Church's brightest jewel, Christ's own, intercessors for the world, as they have been called in classical Russian history and literature.[10]

The litany is bewildering, both in its nuanced density and repetitiveness.

Volga is very different. It begins with an epic passage on the birth of rivers and their changing courses over thousands of years. This opening presages the monumental theme of the novel, namely the power of people—through collective labor—to control nature and even reverse the flow of rivers. The human struggle to transform the landscape in turn becomes a symbol of the changes wrought by the Revolution. The novel's closing peroration, by Professor Pimen Poletika, exemplifies the grandeur and ambition of the novel's subject:

> I have worked out the project of stopping the desert that is encroach-
> ing upon us. I have already made the maps and drawn up the plans.
> We need to block the Volga with a dam near Kamïshin, and throw
> it into the region beyond this, into the Aral and Caspian desert. . . .
> In this desert, new lakes and rivers will spring up, and thousands of
> square miles will be covered with water—but *hundreds* of thousands
> of square miles will be brought back to life, snatched away from the
> desert. Loesses, irrigated by water, a territory half the size of France,
> saturated by Volga soils, will be devoted to the sowing of cotton and
> rice. The desert will be transformed into an ancient Mesopotamia,
> with rains, lakes, and subtropical flora. Only a tenth of the Volga water
> will reach the sea (and the Volga will not descend to the Caspian at
> its present location, but into Komsomol Bay instead), while the rest
> of the water, flowing into new rivers, canals, and lakes, will evapo-
> rate into the sky; creating a curtain of vapor from the desert, the water
> will offer itself to the land in rain and storms, leaving behind soils
> for cotton and rice.[11]

This passage recalls Part II, Act 5, of Goethe's *Faust*, in which Faust becomes obsessed with constructing dykes to turn back the sea and reclaim the land. In Goethe's play, the awe of technological advance is accompanied by mis-givings and warnings. These are absent in *Volga*, since Pilnyak had to produce an optimistic epic of socialist construction, carried out by heroes. Professor Poletika, although a member of the pre-revolutionary intelli-gentsia, is such a hero: redeemed by the Revolution, he is now morally pure, ascetic, and utterly devoted to his work for the state. The last vestige of his pre-revolutionary days is his habit of studying the lives of Christian saints, but this is no more than the tolerable eccentricity of an old man, soon to delegate his work to a successor, fellow engineer Fyodor Sadïkov. Sadïkov is one of the new wave of technical experts from a working-class background, educated under the provisions of the Soviet government. Tempered in the furnace of the Revolution and the Civil War, he appears strong-willed and determined. The purity of his revolutionary morals leads (unintentionally) to the suicide of his unfaithful wife after he coolly demands that they divorce and she marry her lover. Even though Pilnyak's characterization suggests that Sadïkov's Revolutionary virtue can become a vice *in extremis*, in the end Sadïkov finds a good Communist woman (the archaeologist Lyubov, who happens to be Poletika's daughter). Poletika, too, finds happiness by returning to his former wife, Olga.

There would be no human drama, however, if the novel were inhabited only by heroes. Among the less exemplary characters is the engineer Edgar Laszlo, who is as hardworking as Sadïkov but morally weak. It was Laszlo who caused Poletika to separate from Olga fifteen years earlier, and within the time frame of the novel he embarks on an affair with Sadïkov's wife Mariya. Thus Laszlo, too, plays a part in her suicide. But at least Laszlo is on the same side as the characters we have encountered so far, determined to see through the project as a step toward the socialist future. There are much darker characters. Engineer Yevgeniy Poltorak leads a thoroughly decadent life, drinking excessively, womanizing, buying antique furniture, and hobnobbing with shady foreigners. We are hardly surprised to learn that he is a saboteur, prepared to blow up the dam on the orders of a British spy. His accomplice is the aged Yakov Skudrin, a Dostoyevskian figure of malice whose repulsive appearance indexes his bad behavior. Skudrin's background is not suspect (he's a former serf who becomes a clerk to his landlord), but he nurtures a ruthless devotion to personal gain. An oppressive patriarch who presides over his household, he comes undone with the discovery that his unmarried daughter is pregnant.

Poltorak's misdeeds catch up with him, and he becomes unbalanced. One night the equally miserable and agitated Laszlo discovers the two plotters and, knowing of their sabotage, fiercely condemns them. Poltorak and Skudrin have in fact abandoned their plot, for they are too immersed in their personal troubles to carry it out. Instead of the intended cataclysm, the dam is left intact, while each of the three characters, tormented by his personal demon, wishes to see himself dead as much as the other two. Poltorak and Laszlo allow Skudrin to shoot them, after which Skudrin turns the pistol on himself. This macabre operatic climax is alien to Pilnyak's art, but nothing suggests that he sabotaged his own novel to protest the ideological constraints placed upon him. For all his verbal mastery, Pilnyak had never apprenticed as a writer of conventional narrative fiction, and his literary aesthetic had afforded him little chance to experiment with developing characters or constructing adequate motivation for their actions. The clumsiness may best be understood as the faltering steps of an artist acquiring new skills on the job.

The moral certainties of *Volga* bring it within the orbit of the socialist realist novel but destroy the nuanced, fragile world of *Mahogany*. And yet

Pilnyak still chose to take the material of *Mahogany* and transport it into this foreign environment. His aim in writing *Volga* was obvious enough: needing to appease his critics, he resolved to produce a work that would aver his ardent support for the Five-Year Plans and the glorious socialist future (these critics were concentrated in the "proletarianist" literary organization RAPP, which had momentarily earned the backing of the state). So the motivation may be transparent enough, but the choice to revise *Mahogany* is not. If he had wanted his critics to forget the scandal generated by *Mahogany*, surely he could have more easily written a proto–socialist realist novel from scratch. Why revisit *Mahogany*?

The details of the transformation reveal a certain logic. In particular, many of the substantial monologues delivered by the saboteurs in *Volga* are lifted verbatim from the author's own interventions in *Mahogany*. Pilnyak's affectionate description of antique furniture restorers who "take pride in their craft like philosophers and love it like poets" ends up in the mouth of the debauched Poltorak. The author's own unflattering description of drunken women in *Mahogany* returns in *Volga* assigned to one of the Bezdetov brothers, now mere hawkers of decadence to those estranged from the new society. Moreover, the entire trade in antiques, presented as quirky and nostalgic in *Mahogany*, becomes in *Volga* a symbol of decadence. The greatest moment of self-betrayal, when Pilnyak spits on the deepest values of *Mahogany*, occurs when he transplants his own reflections on the wanderers, beggars, tramps, and holy fools—the spiritual center of the novella—into a conversation between Skudrin and Poltorak. Skudrin speaks the words, which do not fit within the conversation; twice Poltorak interrupts the old man, demanding, "Why are you telling me this?" Skudrin never answers the question. Poltorak's puzzlement becomes our own, and perhaps there is some quiet irony here on the author's part, an acknowledgment that he found it impossible to integrate material from *Mahogany* into *Volga* at this juncture. Now we see the message that Pilnyak hoped to send his opponents—at least those who had actually read *Mahogany*, if only to condemn it. By giving the words of his own authorial voice in *Mahogany* to the Enemies of the People in *Volga*, he signaled his personal transformation into a Soviet Man.

Was Pilnyak sincere? As with so many Soviet artists who were not mere hacks, the question is misguided. They might express detachment in certain company but were participants in the game nonetheless. The mythical secret dissident, always champing at the bit when no one is looking, seems to have had no counterpart in reality. Nor is there anything to be gained by asking whether Pilnyak's critics were convinced. Pilnyak publicly displayed loyalty to the regime, and that (together with a subsequent letter to Stalin) was enough to win him official acceptance—for a time.

In addition to the transplanted authorial interventions, many characters are absorbed into the new narrative. Here Pilnyak confronted additional problems, for even if their personalities could be preserved, their functions had to change. The intimate novella had required little or no personal development, but *Volga* propels its characters into an action-packed drama, forcing them to take sides and react to each other. Of *Mahogany*'s principals, Ozhogov alone retains his place on center stage. His much older brother, Skudrin, moves from the fringes of *Mahogany* to the heart of *Volga*; he remains an oppressive patriarch but assumes the new role of saboteur. Ozhogov also functions as a commentator, passing moral judgment on the actions of others. While Skudrin plots the destruction of the dam, Ozhogov attempts to denounce him to the GPU (the political police); he is turned away several times but is eventually taken seriously. At one point, he administers justice directly by beating up Laszlo for all the trouble he has caused. Pilnyak preserves some sense of Ozhogov as Holy Fool—a central topic in *Mahogany* that otherwise disappears from *Volga*. As a relic of the Revolution and Civil War, he now feels politically redundant, and Pilnyak gives him a romantic suicide scene in the final pages of the novel: when the dam springs into action, Ozhogov waits to be drowned by the flood waters that roar across the plain, wiped off the map along with the empty villages.

Other characters from *Mahogany* suffer a demotion. The brothers Bezdetov perform no obvious function in the plot, apart from one arbitrarily impregnating Skudrin's daughter (an event perhaps suggested to Pilnyak by their surname, meaning "childless"). Like the brothers, the subplot about antiques becomes decidedly irrelevant. An uplifting passage from *Mahogany* on the history of Russian porcelain now sits uncomfortably with the thoroughly decadent pursuits of the Bezdetovs (the sole link to *Mahogany*'s world of antiques). Moreover, many secondary characters become superfluous, serving only to encumber the action. Skudrin's sisters, for example, hover in the background until the final pages, when the reversal of their personal fortunes is rather flippantly likened to the turning back of the river. In short, the novel is overpopulated. The fleeting presences perfectly at home in *Mahogany* seem out of place in the dramatic narrative of *Volga*.

Prokofiev: From *The Prodigal Son* to the Fourth Symphony

Prokofiev too transformed a leaner work into a grand drama, although his original itself has a predecessor. As is well known, the Fourth Symphony uses material from his ballet *The Prodigal Son*, and so it is often assumed that the symphony derives from the ballet. This is not borne out by the evidence. Prokofiev's diary details the compositional history of the two works, revealing that when the composer came to the ballet's fourth number, his thematic material inspired a sonata form. The resulting structure ill suited a ballet that required simple, episodic designs. Compounding the problem, the composer possessed only the barest outline of Boris Kochno's scenario and no clear sense as to whether sonata form could accommodate the characters and stage action. After having finished about a third of the ballet's No. 4, Prokofiev determined that the material was inappropriate for the ballet and began to imagine a symphony. Henceforth, the symphony took shape simultaneously with the ballet. The sonata that had outgrown the ballet would form the first movement of the symphony, and material from the ballet's fifth number (the pas de deux) fed into the finale. Extracts from Prokofiev's diary document the process, proving that the sonata allegro was a problem from the start.

January 14, 1929: Just at the moment when a slightly Mozartean theme for No. 4 was beginning to emerge, Diaghilev called. I said to him: "I wouldn't have come to the telephone for anyone else, because I'm writing a new theme for you just now." . . .

Not one but two themes were written—in my opinion, both very good. Decided to write this number as a condensed sonata allegro.

January 15: The exposition (without a closing theme) is ready.

January 16: Composed the closing theme—nothing very significant, but it does the job of closing things. Idea: I could—get ready for it!—cook up a Fourth Symphony out of the ballet! The sonata allegro is already there, and what a slow movement could be made out of the final theme!

January 18: The development is progressing, albeit slowly (would have been good to do it all at once!)

January 28: Very quickly finished No. 4, even though it broke all my fingernails. Extremely glad, since this number cost me a lot of fuss and bother. The momentum carried me to the next number, and . . . I got some idea of how it could be written.

February 1: . . . was composing the pas de deux. The general plan has been sketched out. But I'm afraid that this is not quite what Diaghilev wants—not passionate enough.

February 5: Yesterday, it turned out, I quite unexpectedly managed to finish No. 5.

February 6: I played Nos. 4, 5, and 6, which Diaghilev hadn't heard, and, to my surprise, all three won his approval. I was pleasantly surprised, because I feared that the pas de deux would be found insufficiently amorous, and that I'd be told, regarding No. 4, that a sonata allegro doesn't belong in a ballet. Diaghilev made several useful comments about the pas de deux, such as: it needs to be taken more slowly, but since that will make it longer, it should be cut down a bit, which I promised to do. Then Kochno started inventing a plot for the unexpectedly sprawling No. 4: he had a few "brilliant ideas" but immediately withdrew them. When it turned out that inventing things was not so easy, there were complaints that this music doesn't really fit in very well, that it's not very danceable. The sticking point was the second subject, since it brings in a female topic. The Enchantress, who is already sitting on the stage, couldn't be brought in here because the whole idea for this number was to separate her two dances. But to bring in another female character would mean drawing attention away from the first one, and this would also be undesirable. Fortunately, we busied ourselves with the other numbers, and this matter was left for another time.[12]

February 7: All that remains is to finish orchestrating three of the numbers. And to recut No. 4 together with Diaghilev. I had a look at it: it can be disassembled easily and stuck together again whatever way you like. In its present shape, it'll become the Sonata Allegro for the Fourth Symphony, but for the ballet I'll do it the way Diaghilev wants it.

February 10: Since my No. 4 can easily be disassembled and reassembled as required for the purposes of the ballet, I drew a plan in a notebook so that Diaghilev could orient himself better within it, and I titled the page "A Visual Aid." Diaghilev tore it out of the notebook and stuck it in his pocket. But we didn't have any time to deal with the number. So my visual aid didn't serve any purpose—it just ended up in Diaghilev's collection.

February 14: A very good (abstract) introduction to the Fourth Symphony was written. At first I looked for material in the ballet, but when I didn't find anything suitable there, I composed new material—and all the better for that.

February 16: Composed the beginning of the Andante for the Fourth Symphony (four measures before the melody); was orchestrating Nos. 5 and 6 for the ballet, but only bit by bit, because Diaghilev hasn't given everything his approval yet.

February 17: I played the pas de deux [for Diaghilev], and he indicated where another cut could be made. This I eagerly carried out for him, since I decided to put the deleted passage into the symphony. As for No. 4, he started grumbling that it's not danceable, and that he'd thought he could make it a fight number, but that the music can't really be staged. . . .

I said: On the contrary, I always felt that there's a lot of dance music here, but I'll cut out the non-danceable parts for you.

Diaghilev said: Just because something is fast and accented doesn't mean it's danceable.

February 22: Now everything has been orchestrated apart from the controversial No. 4. But I will orchestrate that too—if not for the ballet, then for the symphony.

March 7: Thought up a new theme for the ballet's No. 4, the most controversial of all.

March 10: Around five o'clock, Diaghilev, Kochno, and Lifar appeared.[13] I played the new No. 4, hesitant and flustered because it was written on crossed-out sheets. I didn't like it myself, but Diaghilev and Co. praised it, showed me where a cut could be made and then saying: Great, now you can orchestrate it.

March 15: Worked a little on the Andante of the Fourth Symphony.

April 16: Orchestrated the first movement of the symphony.[14]

The symphonic thinking that emerged in No. 4 carried over into No. 5, the pas de deux, which develops a theme assigned to the Prodigal Son in No. 2, first heard in C major at rehearsal number P30 + 2mm. (Hereafter, rehearsal numbers in Prokofiev's scores will be indicated by a number with the letter prefix *P, S,* or *S¹*, with *P* standing for *The Prodigal Son; S* for the Fourth Symphony, op. 47; and *S¹* for the revised Fourth Symphony, op. 112.) The theme was probably composed several years earlier: in one of Prokofiev's notebooks, it precedes ideas from *Le Pas d'acier* (1925).[15] There it appears much as in No. 2 of *The Prodigal Son:* cast in C major, placed in the bass, with the same accompanying string patterns (see Figure 3). The only significant difference between sketch and score is the hint of another, dissonant layer below, which Prokofiev dropped from the ballet. The Prodigal Son theme was dynamic enough to lend itself to symphonic development, thanks to its off-tonic beginning and asymmetrical structure. As the music heads toward a C-major cadence (with a C–G–C figure), Prokofiev suddenly pulls an A-flat major fanfare out of his hat, giving the theme an open-ended quality that he put to good use in the ballet. In No. 2, a short symphonic development casts the theme in F (abridged) and G-flat. No. 5 probes this symphonic dimension more deeply: at P93, the Prodigal Son's theme appears in a new variant, whereupon it separates into two segments that are developed independently. Prokofiev focuses on the second, reducing it from four measures to two and combining it with the C–G–C cadential figure in A-flat major (the fanfare key) before restoring C major.

Figure 1. Themes for No. 4 of *The Prodigal Son*, sketched January 14, 1929.

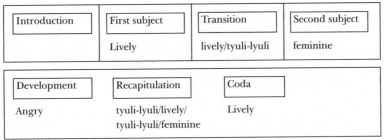

Figure 2. Schematic reconstruction of the "visual aid" for No. 4 of *The Prodigal Son*, given to Diaghilev on February 10, 1929. The *Introduction* shown above is likely not the one we know from the symphony, which was, according to the diary, written later (on February 14), but possibly the affirmative C-major theme that begins the final version of No. 4 from *The Prodigal Son*.

Throughout the pas de deux, familiar material is enriched with new textures and countermelodies. P97, for example, offers a variation on the version of the theme that had appeared at P93, now abridged and with a new fanfare figure in the bassoon. At P100, the cadential figure is deftly linked to the music of the *camarades* (as in No. 2), and the resulting figuration accompanies an expansive theme in the horns and tuba. This brass theme seems new but in fact derives from one of the Seductress's themes in No. 3. Within the context of No. 5, it combines the minor-major chromaticism of the *camarades* with the expressive legato of the Prodigal Son's theme in a symphonic synthesis. After statements of the brass theme in C and F, the variant from P97 returns in B-flat major with minor alterations. Prokofiev chose to follow his symphonic inclinations here without reference to the stage action: there is little relation between the choreographed sexual act and the dense, mutable music composed for it. The point is that Prokofiev was thinking symphonically not merely in No. 4 but elsewhere in the ballet.

Thus the notion that the Fourth Symphony comprises but a potpourri of *The Prodigal Son* is refuted by its compositional history as well as the work itself, which is a coherent neoclassical symphony. The first movement is "somewhat Mozartean," as Prokofiev says, with a pastoral second subject, but the first subject draws on Beethoven. Witness the bold first gesture, whose B–G–C motif echoes the opening of Beethoven's First Symphony (G–B–C, in the same C major). The introduction also draws from a classical topic: the minuet. The distinction between the two main themes as well as the motoric transitional passages ("tyuli-lyuli"), abundant cadences, Alberti-type basses, and scalar passages render Prokofiev's symphonic intentions unmistakable.

Figure 3. Theme used in *The Prodigal Son,* as sketched by Prokofiev.

Within a neoclassical style, Prokofiev's distinctive modernist idiom shines through in his pungent harmonies and the machine-like ostinati of the development; surprisingly, the gentle second subject is sent to work in the factory. There is also some deliberately exposed, montage-like cutting from one texture to another (in Prokofiev's words, the movement can be disassembled *po vintikam* (down to the screws).[16] At S32, for example, the cutting-room technique works hand-in-hand with classical models to truncate the exposition's transitional material when it returns in the recapitulation. In the finale, Prokofiev manipulates classical conventions, playing with expectations aroused by what is plainly a sonata allegro. He makes typical gestures only to empty them; for example, the modulations of the transition fail actually to modulate, simply returning to the C-major starting point. In the recapitulation, the second subject begins in the tonic, as in Haydn or Mozart, but then floats away on a lyrical wave to E major (in the exposition, its key is A major). In this respect, Prokofiev appears to jumble the sequence of events in Beethoven's "Waldstein" Sonata, the coda of which also throws in A-flat major, to produce a characteristically Prokofievian mix of keys a major third apart: here C, E, and A-flat.

The fourth movement, which draws material from Nos. 1, 2, 5, and 9 of the ballet, might seem inherently less symphonic than the first movement, which was conceived from the start as a sonata form. But the finale in fact rivals the opening movement in its symphonic intricacy; it is also in sonata form, and thus only superficially of the lieto fine type. The first subject unites material from two disparate sources: the fleet, toccata-like opening of the ballet, and the lyrical melody from No. 2 (at P30). Not only did Prokofiev combine these elements in one subject, he was also able to use them simultaneously, shaping the toccata-like material into an accompaniment, for example, while developing the lyrical melody. Developmental ideas from Nos. 2 and 5 are put to good use in the transition from the first to second subject and later in the development proper. A sequence of variations on the lyrical melody ushers us away from the first subject (S84–88). The modulations (which include a remote G-flat major) lead nowhere in particular, since Prokofiev appends further statements of the lyrical melody back in C major (for trombone solo, with spiky accompaniment from the toccata material), and the questioning phrases from No. 5 (P109–10) briefly return before we reach the newly composed second subject in A major.

The finale's development quotes a long sequence from No. 5 (P93–108) with the horns-and-tuba theme taking pride of place. An intricate passage from the ballet is elaborated at the beginning of the development and in the coda with the toccata-like material. The B-flat major statement of the first theme from No. 5 serves as the off-key beginning of the recapitulation, interrupted by a dramatic statement of the fanfare motif on a diminished seventh chord—a humorous nod to another classical convention. The tension is only momentary, however, and quickly relieved by the recapitulation of the second subject. And the fanfare motif, already significant in the ballet, finds its place in the symphonic argument through its dramatic transformation at S109. The minor/major material of the *camarades* is developed in the coda, which is based on material from No. 9.

Thus although the first movement has good symphonic credentials, the finale has even more to recommend it. What of the middle movements? The third movement, fine as it is, holds little interest apart from the ballet, since it runs through No. 3 with scarcely a change and takes its ending from No. 5. The slow movement is quite another matter. "What a slow movement could be made of the final theme!" writes Prokofiev in his diary, anticipating future events. The composer was especially proud of the ballet's final theme, and the diary reveals how it came to be:

November 23, 1928: The ballet's ending hasn't been devised yet.

I said: The close is conceived here as an apotheosis, but we can't have that—we need to find something rather different.

I suggested we use a theme from the second *Chose en soi* [op. 28], which I like very much. Diaghilev didn't seem to agree: It needs to be simpler, softer and tenderer, he said.

And I myself felt that the theme I had suggested, although very good, is not quite the right thing. We parted on good terms. Diaghilev left happy with the ballet. In the evening, falling asleep, I was searching for a new theme, pure and clear, and I thought that for the illustration of a Gospel parable it ought to come from above. Around one o'clock in the night, I got up and wrote down two measures.

November 24: Sat down to work in the morning on yesterday's theme, the final one in the ballet, when the father embraces the son. Worked on, continuing with the same train of thought as last night. The theme came out absolutely amazing—and after that the whole day felt like my birthday. . . . Once I returned home, I played delightedly through the theme, which I hadn't been able to remember fully on my way home. It was all the more pleasing to encounter it again!

December 1: I informed [Diaghilev] that I'd finished the last number.
    Diaghilev: How's that? Completely? Well then play it. Phew, this is scary. . . .
    This means that Diaghilev had staked all on the last number, and if I let myself down there, then the whole ballet was lost. . . . But I knew that the ending was good, and I played it quite calmly. Diaghilev was happy, and even advised me to play it slower, so that the melody could sing through properly. . . . Diaghilev left extremely pleased, and on the stairs announced that he's considering the possibility of doing without Stravinsky in the spring season. Incredible! Up to now, Stravinsky has been god-like for Diaghilev, and he clearly preferred *him* over me. Is this another sign that the god has fallen?[17]

The "amazing" theme admired by Diaghilev is used sparingly in the ballet. Prokofiev exercised iron discipline in restricting it to two statements that form a single expansive period. In the new context of the symphonic slow movement, Prokofiev could make more of the theme, but he had to create a movement worthy of it. This required something considerably graver than the first movement.
    A superficial analysis of the slow movement could demonstrate that it shares the structure of the third: a rondo with two episodes (ABACA). This is a fair summary of the third movement, but the slow movement offers something more profound in its formal subtleties and its thematic material. We come much nearer the mark if we list the sequence of themes as ABCB¹A¹DXA², with A being the "amazing" theme from the close of the ballet and X a reminiscence of the symphony's introduction. The BCB¹ component can be considered a ternary episode, but B is quite unstable, suggesting a sonata transition, while the C material, in the distant key of G-sharp minor, arrives with the weight of a sonata second subject (although

it never returns). In a purported sonata allegro scheme, the B[1] section would inaugurate the development, given its more active texture and return to the main key of C (the tonic return at this juncture was an occasional pattern in classical sonata form). The A theme is developed next, with canonic imitations in E-flat major, after which the mysterious B-major chords move to uncharted waters in section D. The music unexpectedly shifts to a storytelling mode, which I hear as the "authorial voice." Such unusual passages seem to step outside the bounds of the symphony proper, marking the composer's own subjectivity or at least a narrative presence apart from the main thrust of the music. These moments are more important in the revised version of the symphony; for now, suffice it to say that the authorial voice is characterized by a ruminative unison melody doubled in several instruments. The reappearance of the theme from the introduction to the first movement (X) assumes the air of something momentous thanks to the preparation of the D passage and dramatic scoring. These two sections (D and X) shatter the proposed sonata scheme, and in place of a recapitulation, the movement closes with a lyrical apotheosis of the A theme.

Reception and Revisions

The hopes Prokofiev pinned on Op. 47 as a prime example of his "new style" were fulfilled neither in the West nor in the Soviet Union. In April 1929, while orchestrating the first movement, he expressed confidence that (against all odds) the symphony would reverse the course of his declining reputation in Soviet Russia:

> A card from Asafyev, at last, after a long break. But this was the most pessimistic letter I've ever received from him: headaches, nerves, and his removal from office. No sign of any good cheer from his trip abroad or anything about CS.[18] And musical life in the capital is not so good: young composers have "a different orientation," and in Moscow Myaskovsky alone "is firm in relation to your (my) music." At the Academy Opera, Dranishnikov and Radlov are on their way out....[19] Then it's time for me to go to the USSR and fight for my cause, although it wouldn't go amiss to root myself deeper abroad (Gaveau? Columbia? America?). The Third and Fourth Symphonies will carry me through, but most of all—my new outlook on music![20]

The Fourth Symphony was premiered, in the composer's absence, by Serge Koussevitzky and the Boston Symphony Orchestra on November 14, 1930. In a letter to the conductor (October 11, 1930), Prokofiev insisted that the symphony was an independent work; as we can now appreciate, this was a sincere and accurate description:

I am sending you some information on the Fourth Symphony as material for the program notes. The symphony was begun in 1929 and completed on June 23, 1930. In some parts of this symphony I used the same musical material as in the ballet *The Prodigal Son*. This does not mean that the symphony is written on the material from the ballet, or that *The Prodigal Son* is written on material from the symphony; rather, in the symphony I simply had the opportunity to develop symphonically what the form of the ballet did not allow. The precedent can be found in Beethoven, with his ballet *Prometheus* and the Third Symphony.[21]

All did not go well in Boston, and Prokofiev registered his disappointment in his diary on November 28, 1930: "The criticism was moderate. The success, apparently, was also moderate. I'd counted on an instant success, as with the Divertimento and the Sinfonietta, but there you go—my latest works aren't immediately accessible. Why is this?"[22]

The symphony met a similar reception on December 18 at its European premiere under Pierre Monteux in Brussels. From Prokofiev's diary we learn that the symphony had to be rehearsed in the smaller hall, because the main Pleyel Hall was already booked for Ernest Ansermet's rehearsals of Stravinsky's *Symphony of Psalms*—a reminder of an earlier rivalry.[23] Prokofiev took this hitch in good spirit and expressed interest in Stravinsky's score, but the prospects for his own remained foremost in his mind:

December 15: First rehearsal of the festival. Monteux begins with the Overture op. 42 and puts in some serious work. The orchestra reads through it well, and the Overture is soon on its feet. . . . But I'm most interested in the Symphony. It seems that it sounds well, [although] not everything comes out in the finale. The contrabassoon and tuba in the Andante, which they wrote about in America, sound as they should—I don't know why the Boston papers were so struck [by them, although it was] probably because Koussevitzky turned them into performing sea lions.

December 18: Fourth rehearsal.

[Nikolay] Nabokov and [Pyotr] Souvtchinsky came. They are in raptures over the Fourth Symphony, especially the second movement and the second subject of the first. Monteux is working through it with care, but, in spite of the four rehearsals, he hasn't had time to finish learning the fourth movement.

In the evening—the concert. In the vast Pleyel Hall, there aren't many people, less than half, perhaps a third. At the last moment Monteux suggests switching my Second Concerto with the Fourth Symphony. I was happy with this, because it meant I could finish playing the Concerto and then listen to the Symphony in peace. But later I was told that the pianistic triumph of the Concerto killed off the Symphony, so it was only a moderate success, although Monteux brought me out to take a bow. But I'm inclined to think, nevertheless, that the Symphony would still only have enjoyed limited success [compared to the Concerto]. That's what I think now anyway, but before the performance it seemed that it ought to be accessible straightaway.

After the concert there were quite a lot of people in the green room. I'm happy when people call this Symphony my best work, but there are only a few who do so.[24]

Despite these frustrations, Prokofiev still hoped the Fourth might earn the esteem he thought it deserved at its Russian premiere. But Prokofiev's new style was no more successful in the Soviet Union than in the West; neither his closest friends nor his usually sympathetic critics made much of it. When he first perused the score of *The Prodigal Son*, Myaskovsky sent an eloquent and insightful letter to Asafyev, evaluating the accessible and challenging aspects of the work:

> Prokofiev sent me the proofs of *The Prodigal Son*. As ever, it's original and seems better than *Le Pas d'acier*, lyrical, but still there's something that I just don't get. The themes are predominantly diatonic, the layout is contrapuntal (at times descending into Glazunovisms!), and everything is very transparent, relatively simple, even consonant—it was probably the novelty of this simplicity that he himself particularly liked. Because of its diatonic character, the material is slightly dry, but thanks to its harmonic freshness (although not all the time) it acquires, as always with Seryozha, a kind of guile [*vkradchivost'*] and an ability to penetrate through the exterior shell of perception, and then it attaches itself to such parts of the memory and sensibility that one would wish to stir them again and again [*shto vsyo vremya khochetsya beredit' ikh*]. I always have trouble understanding Prokofiev's new and incomprehensible pieces, but I think I'm going to like *The Prodigal Son*.[25]

The following extract from the Prokofiev-Myaskovsky correspondence covers similar ground with reference to Prokofiev's Sonatinas, op. 52 (1931–32).

Myaskovsky: Visiting the Derzhanovskys, I discovered the Sonatinas.
. . . I seem to have arrived at an understanding of both their finales.

On the whole, both sonatinas continue to amaze me, and they don't fatigue me for a single second. Yesterday I even got K. S. Saradzhev hooked on your Second Sonatina, and he, as I noticed, has little grasp of your new style.[26]

Prokofiev: How strange that Saradzhev, once such a lively presence, is now resisting my new manner. And Asafyev, too, writes: "Over here, the lyrical tendency of your recent work is not appreciated." What is the matter? Melody is something that goes straight to the heart, and the form is as lucid as can be. . . . Explain to me the reasons for this resistance.[27]

The Russian premiere of the Fourth Symphony finally took place on October 30, 1933, at the Bolshoy Theater, on a program with the Fifth Piano Concerto (1932) and the *Scythian* Suite (1915). Myaskovsky looked over the score of the symphony two days before the performance and judged it "not at all bad" (*ves'ma nedurno*), but the premiere came and went with little interest shown in the symphony.[28]

Prokofiev persevered with the Fourth Symphony after his permanent return to Russia. He selected it for a prestigious showcase of his music: an all-Prokofiev concert (*avtorskiy kontsert*) at the *dekada* (ten-day festival) of Soviet music in 1937, a weighty event marking the twentieth anniversary of the Revolution. The concert mattered much to Prokofiev, since his *Cantata for the Twentieth Anniversary of October* had just been rejected for the festival. The concert took place on November 20 under the baton of the composer; sharing the program with the symphony was the Second Violin Concerto (1935) and Second Suite from *Romeo and Juliet* (which had not yet been staged). Viktor Tsukkerman's review in *Sovetskoye iskusstvo* discussed the Fourth Symphony, but there was little to please the composer. Tsukkerman diagnosed the symphony's "dry, business-like manner" as a symptom of the creative crisis Prokofiev must have suffered during his years abroad. The opening of the slow movement was "very expressive," Tsukkerman conceded, but the rest of the movement was "not of equal worth."[29]

At the same time, a storm was brewing at the Committee on Arts Affairs (*Komitet po delam iskusstv*), which had been responsible for programming the *dekada*. On December 9, 1938, the chairman of the committee, Platon Kerzhentsev, convened a special debriefing.[30] Prokofiev's Fourth Symphony was discussed, along with the other items on the concert. Here are the comments of Semyon Shlifshteyn, a critic who would later play an important role as a mediator between Prokofiev and the committee:

Let's take, for example, the concert of works by Prokofiev. Our press evaluated the Fourth Concerto [*sic*, Symphony] correctly: it evaluated it as a formalist concerto [*sic*]. That such an evaluation was made demonstrated that the lessons of Formalism left some trace upon our musical community, but I must say that the tone in which they spoke out showed that these lessons have not been fully understood. Even if we haven't evidence of any open defense, we do find some attempts at covert defense—[Henrich] Neuhaus's article, for instance. I will present two passages in the article by way of example, both of which are grossly wrong: "We cannot overlook the fact that this piece, as a formalist work lacking in ideological content, was not accepted by our public"—but what conclusions does he draw from this? Does he conclude that the work shouldn't have been played? [No,] he writes that "there was no rehearsal, and we will have to wait for the second performance." It is our critics who are to blame for not having found the words to persuade, for not being sufficiently principled to say that this work . . . should not have been given a place in the *dekada,* which is not supposed to be a mere showcase for everything that happens to have been written. On no account should Prokofiev's Fourth Symphony have been programmed. Turning to other matters, I think that we still failed to find the right tone and the passion to comment on his *Romeo and Juliet.* This work should have been presented as a triumph for this Soviet composer, because if the Fourth Symphony had been written by Prokofiev in 1929, when he went through the most serious and critical period in his creative life, facing the real threat of becoming disconnected from the present, then *Romeo and Juliet* was written in [the midst of] Soviet actuality.

Shlifshteyn's comments were echoed by Alexander Gauk, one of the leading Soviet conductors of the day.

I will touch upon Prokofiev's Fourth Symphony. I have conducted [it] twice, and there was a good response each time, but in musical terms I must say that I listened but quite failed to understand any of it. I had certain images and I think that had I conducted I would have conveyed these images. But the fact of the matter is that Prokofiev is not emotional, and he is illiterate.[31] I can confirm that there were enough rehearsals. The orchestra wasn't to blame, but rather Prokofiev. . . . A piece that is all technique and no imagery—this, of course, is a formalist piece. Naturally, the images of the Fourth Symphony are not related to Soviet themes.

Another critic, Georgiy Khubov, the mouthpiece of Soviet musical policy, concocted an odd defense of the concert:

I think that in the all-Prokofiev concert it was necessary to fulfil the composer's wishes if he insisted on presenting his path. We should have presented his works, analyzed them, and exposed their harmful aspects. Neuhaus, carried away by purely professional and technical issues, incorrectly assessed this work. It is a formalist work, deserving of sharp criticism. But in this concert Prokofiev offered a wonderful piece, *Romeo and Juliet*, which is great both in its symphonism and closeness to Shakespeare. We should, in truth, be able to say this. And the same goes for the Violin Concerto.

Boris Gusman, another prominent critic and a long-standing supporter of Prokofiev, shed some light on how the program had emerged:

We'd been working on the program for four months. We rejected several major works. We decided that the first *dekada* of Soviet music should be based around works accessible to the masses. We were afraid to put works that were too complex into the *dekada* program. For instance, we were afraid to include Shostakovich's Fifth Symphony, and Prokofiev's Fourth.[32] How often we had to have words with him! He wanted the Third Piano Concerto to be included. We argued with him for ages before we got him to include *Romeo*.

Kerzhentsev concluded categorically that "it was wrong that approval was given for the performance of Prokofiev's Fourth Symphony."

It remains unclear how much of this discussion was conveyed to Prokofiev, but henceforth the hapless Fourth Symphony became a symbol of the supposed "creative crisis" of the composer's time abroad. In a 1939 *Sovetskoye iskusstvo* editorial, Prokofiev's new Cello Concerto was hailed as "heroic and romantic" as opposed to the "cold contrivances" of the Fourth Symphony.[33] Yet even the Concerto soon came to be seen as un-Soviet. The ghost of the Fourth returned once more after the premiere of Prokofiev's Fifth Symphony, his first Soviet essay in the genre. The critic Arnold Alshvang, writing about the Fifth in 1945, contrasted its "full-blooded national melos" with the "linearity" of the composer's earlier (misguided) quest in the Fourth for a "new simplicity."[34] Over a decade after its completion, the Fourth was still rejected, and with Prokofiev now regarded as a genuine Soviet symphonist, it looked as if it would always be eclipsed by the monumental Fifth and Sixth symphonies. Only at this stage—in 1947— did Prokofiev begin revising the Fourth in hopes that it would finally find favor with Soviet critics.

From Neoclassicism to Socialist Realism

Mira Mendelson, Prokofiev's eventual second wife, wrote the following entry in her diary on June 16, 1947:

> Now Seryozha is working on his revision of the Fourth Symphony. He said that the third movement kept coming out wrong. He did the first, the second, and the fourth movements first, and then went back to the third: "A useful idea appeared, and I wrote it [the movement] in two days." Seryozha thought that there was a lot of good material in the symphony, but the composition of the Fifth and Sixth showed him that the Fourth Symphony could be strengthened in terms of the overall structure. He revised it to such an extent that he gave the new version a new opus number.[35]

In revising the Fourth Symphony, Prokofiev added passages of two sorts: introductory material prefiguring a theme, and contemplative unison melodies. Many sections stand virtually unaltered, although there are a few other significant revisions, as we shall see when we examine the movements separately.[36]

First Movement

The most important change to the first movement was the addition of a new theme in the introduction to precede (not replace) the existing theme of the introduction. In Op. 47, the introduction theme returned in the slow movement, following the mysterious B-major chords. It seemed to stand outside the symphony proper as an authorial intervention. The new opening theme encloses the old and likewise returns, at the end of the symphony, in a heaven-storming apotheosis that ensures the monumentality of what had been a small-scale work. The revised introduction successfully integrates new and old, but that integration proves more difficult elsewhere in the symphony.

The new introduction begins with a heroic C-major fanfare, much brighter and more confident than the original. As a student in the 1980s, I (like others of the Soviet era) considered this the symphony's "Motherland theme," owing to a myriad of associations accrued from Soviet musical culture and especially from film scores. Like Pilnyak's titanic dam, Prokofiev's new theme affirms faith in the glorious socialist future, supplying the Soviet imagery previously lacking. Yet there is nothing brash here. Shortly after the fanfare arpeggio, the theme becomes more lyrical, with softer triplet rhythms replacing the initial dotted ones. The sound world here is highly characteristic of late Prokofiev, so that we can perceive in the new opening not only a Motherland theme but a new authorial presence—since the author of the original introductory theme was Prokofiev in his pre-Soviet existence. The Sixth Symphony, which immediately preceded the revision of the Fourth, made prominent use of just such textures (particularly in the first movement, second subject), and they served to enhance its elegiac mood.

In the allegro, the character of the first subject persists, but the Beethovenian echoes are replaced by something headier and more peculiarly Prokofievian. The newly added piano and harp introduce the machine music earlier than in the original, where it appeared in the development. The transition to the second subject in Op. 47 features a new theme in Prokofiev's grotesque style; this is jettisoned in Op. 112 in favor of material from the first subject. After building momentum, the transition suddenly halts with the insertion of three mysterious measures in 3/4 marked poco meno mosso (six measures after S¹7). The lyrical melody, doubled in the oboes, floats above a three-part texture in the strings; for the moment, Prokofiev's intentions are inscrutable, but this melody will return.

The second part of the original transition ("tyuli-lyuli") remains, but whereas it had previously passed gracefully to the second subject, in the revision Prokofiev interpolates new material. Foreshadowing the second subject, a short preamble in 9/8 harkens back to the opening theme of the introduction: the texture here is again a unison line in the winds punctuated by string chords. We are immersed in the ruminations of the authorial voice—that uncertain entity that looks askance at the symphonic drama. When the melodic line shifts to the upper strings, marked espressivo (and poco meno mosso), the melancholy deepens.

The new material established a radically different context for the second subject, enclosing the theme within quotation marks and divorcing the second subject from its neoclassical surroundings. The Mozartean character now seems somehow uncanny. Just as Pilnyak distanced himself in *Volga* from his authorial persona in *Mahogany*, so too Prokofiev separates himself from his own themes through such interpolations. The authorial voice of the Soviet Prokofiev returns at the end of the exposition to supplant the assertive neoclassical cadences of the original. Classical conventions will no longer do; the unison lines so characteristic of the composer's final works articulate the form. The unison melody appears first in the violins and violas espressivo, then in the oboes and clarinets, with the same punctuating chords.

Although disassembled and assimilated in the very different project of Op. 112, the original exposition of Op. 47 remains largely intact. The development section does not survive in all its details, but two basic elements endure: the machine music and the drastic transformation of the second subject. Yet the machine music of Op. 47 no longer serves the same purpose in Op. 112; the original, with its roaring brass, was marked *zlaya*, meaning "angry" or "evil." Such malevolence had to be replaced by the music of heroic Soviet labor, so Prokofiev's new factory hums along in major keys and more lucid orchestration. Also in keeping with the monumental, socialist realist revision, Prokofiev develops the first subject material as a huge monolith, noisily affirmative and harmonically static (this section alone of the new development remains for forty-five measures on a G pedal, whereas in Op. 47 the entire development section lasted only eighty measures).

In contrast to the clatter, at S¹18 the pensive authorial-voice material returns with flutes and bassoons espressivo ma tranquillo. Prokofiev prevents the music from crystallizing into a theme until the climax of the development. After a tutti statement of the new introduction theme in canonic imitation, the graceful second subject becomes an apotheosis; the Alberti-bass accompaniment of the exposition transforms into jubilant carillons with the theme itself heard first in the horns and then, gloriously, the solo trumpet. The summit is reached at S¹27. The new introduction theme leads unexpectedly to a climactic statement of the pensive authorial-voice material in unison winds and horns (see Example 2). Now the melancholic rumination becomes a genuine theme, recalling the melody from the puzzling 3/4 insertion in the exposition's new transition and incorporating a Borodinian heroic (*bogatïrsky*) topic at S¹28. The music rises here to a higher, epic plane, but the position is precarious. Three woodblock strokes cut through the texture, invoking the darker context of similar orations in the Sixth Symphony, tempering triumph with poignancy. The tension between light and dark, triumph and despair evokes a passage in Pilnyak's novel: while dreaming of victoriously beating back the desert, Professor Poletika becomes acutely aware of his own mortality.

The new development fulfills the requirements for a monumental symphony, but the recapitulation disappoints, merely repeating the maneuvers of the exposition. Here the original neoclassical design conflicts with the progressive drama of the socialist realist revision. A return to Mozartean symmetry seems psychologically false after the dramatic events of the development. In the jargon of Soviet musicology, the material of the exposition has experienced "qualitative changes" and demands more than its repetition in the tonic. Nor does Prokofiev offer a weighty coda of the sort Beethoven used to balance (dramatically as well as formally) his complex, stormy development sections. Instead Prokofiev recycles the original retransition and ends the movement by restating the first subject. The new introduction theme and pensive authorial-voice material acquired such significance in the development that they overshadowed the themes from the original, like Pilnyak's new characters in *Volga*. But the significance fades, the gestures quickly forgotten. Although Prokofiev had achieved something

Example 1. The introduction theme in the first movement of Op. 112.

Example 1 continued

Example 2. "Authorial voice" material at the climax of the first movement development, Op. 112.

Example 2 continued

greater in the development than his Soviet contemporaries might have, the movement as a whole falls short of socialist realist ideals.

Second Movement
To take up the Soviet jargon once more, Prokofiev's changes to the Andante were "quantitative" rather than "qualitative," because this movement already exhibited the symphonic qualities of Socialist Realism. Most noticeably, Prokofiev iterates the final theme from *The Prodigal Son*, heard sparingly in both the ballet and Op. 47. In the economy of Socialist Realism, a striking melody goes to waste if heard only once; it should be repeated until every worker happily whistles it on the production line.

To match the proper scale of the socialist realist symphony, Prokofiev inflates the movement by expanding units of the original to twice their size. The four-measure introduction is extended by four measures and freighted with striking new harmonies. The eleven-measure phrase of the A theme receives an answering phrase of twelve measures in the violins with a warmer, fuller sound; this latter was originally reserved for the end of the movement, but in the inflationary economy of the revision, Prokofiev needed to make greater use of it. There are other such expansions: Prokofiev doubles the seven measures of the B theme by alternating its sub-phrases with new material of a "ticking clock" quality. And after a canonic statement of the A theme in E-flat major (retained from the original) another begins in B major. This, however, preempts the B major of the mysterious chords of the original; consequently, they are transposed to G major, and this section also doubles in size. The authorial voice reappears in a characteristic unison passage (in 3/4, with the melody in the oboes and English horn). As in Op. 47, this passage leads to a reminiscence of the original introduction theme.

After the appearance of the introduction theme, a longer preparatory passage heralds the fifth and final appearance of theme A. Finally Prokofiev awards the theme full tutti scoring and elaborate texture. But perhaps feeling that he had added enough weight to this statement and fearing the theme might overstay its welcome, he moves quickly to the original, restrained ending from *The Prodigal Son*. Concluding a large and effusive movement, the borrowed material is rendered more moving.

Third Movement
According to Mira Mendelson's diary, the revision of the third movement proved most vexing—understandably, since in the original version, this movement alone had passed down almost unchanged from *The Prodigal Son*. Granted, the music of this section of the ballet (No. 3) already had symphonic aspirations, but it nonetheless lay furthest from the goals of the

revision. After considering various solutions, Prokofiev decided to write an introduction, extend the coda, and insert material at the main points of articulation in the form. The introduction begins with a light touch, presenting motifs that anticipate the ensuing themes, but the pensive authorial-voice material returns to lend gravitas. This more serious strand returns four measures after S¹70 in the solo bassoon and muted violins marked espressivo. The newly added coda has its own seriousness that stems from a somber flat II chord and the momentary appearance of a chorale-like texture. Such passages place the original, lighter material in quotation marks and again confirm the Soviet Prokofiev's efforts to distance himself from his pre-Soviet utterances. But the resulting movement is not schizophrenic. Itself coherent, it fits into the overall symphonic plan as a pleasant diversion from the main thrust of the drama.

The Finale

What could be done with the original finale, so tightly constructed in every detail? How could this happy ending become a monumental apotheosis befitting the socialist realist symphony? True, Prokofiev managed to pull off a carnivalesque ending in the Fifth Symphony using a perceptibly Soviet "pioneer music" sound. In the Sixth, he also produced a carnival, but a weighty epilogue rises above the preceding merriment. In the revision of the Fourth, Prokofiev decided to follow the pattern set by the Sixth, except that his festivities in Op. 112 are interrupted by a more conventional apotheosis. But this solved only the least of his problems. What was he to make of the highly compressed original finale in the context of a newly expansive socialist realist symphony?

At first, and as in the other movements, Prokofiev inflates his material. A new introductory passage slows the fleet eighth notes of the original toccata theme to quarters. Yet the introduction does not make the movement more serious: on the contrary, Prokofiev adds a new grotesque element by underlining every note of the decelerated melody with the stamping of the timpani and bass drum. Rather than lifting the movement above the carnivalesque, Prokofiev grounds it. The original first subject and transition remain intact, but the transition renders the toccata theme a mechanical moto perpetuo. The original second subject is gone and the sonata form along with it.

Now Prokofiev takes drastic action. A brooding passage at S¹88 leads in an unexpected direction. The movement grinds to a halt with a disproportionately long episode in E-flat major and 6/8. Of all the interpolations in Op. 112, this sounds the most inexplicably alien. The carnivalesque might conceivably justify anything, including a procession that suspends the frantic revelry, but the contrast between the fast, dense thematic work of the original and this static one-dimensional music does not so much impel the listener to imagine an explanatory scenario as shrug in confusion. After the episode comes to an arbitrary close, we discover that it has displaced nothing: the original development section simply runs its course. Indeed, the development functions as a reprise.

One theme from the original could have suited a socialist realist aesthetic: the horns-and-tuba theme evokes Russian songs from the fairground and recalls the second theme in the *Russian* Overture (1936). In the original finale, this theme distinguished itself from the surrounding bustle. But because the episode has so drastically altered the scale of the movement, the popular ditty has no place in the revision despite its socialist realist potential. Even one of the Soviet critics who had enthusiastically commended the revision over the original thought that this theme cluttered up the movement, hinting that Prokofiev should have excised it altogether.[37]

A still more incongruous moment comes in the coda, when material resembling nothing more than a cancan (described by Prokofiev as "thievish") is interrupted by the new theme from the introduction of the symphony appearing in a blaze of glory.[38] This is a deus ex machina. In the montage aesthetic of the original, such abrupt, jarring changes might have been legitimate, but these same moves were not available to Prokofiev in the socialist realist aesthetic of the revision. The return of the opening theme is a hollow apotheosis. For it to be convincing requires dramatic preparation; to pass from the preceding cancan to the apotheosis should entail several pages of determined transition, but Prokofiev simply plunges from one to the other.

Whereas in the first three movements the revisions paid their dues to the original, preserving its coherence, the altered finale violates the musical conception of Op. 47. The small-scale work loses its integrity, just as the small-scale characters and mini-plot lines of Pilnyak's *Mahogany* are lost in the vast expanses of *Volga*. The finale of Op. 112 stands as a misshapen monument to Prokofiev's encounter with Socialist Realism.

On Prokofiev and Pilnyak

Prokofiev's conviction that the new Fourth would be a success was hardly fanciful. In June 1947, his standing in the Soviet Union was never higher: he had just received another Stalin Prize for his First Violin Sonata, and three productions of his works were also so recognized (the Bolshoy for *Romeo and Juliet*, the Kirov for *Cinderella*, and Malegot for a partial production of *War and Peace*). In September, his Sixth Symphony was well received at its premiere, and in November he received the grand honor of being named "People's Artist of the RSFSR." He was encouraged to think that his foreign works were no longer out of bounds and could point as evidence to a Moscow performance of his Third Symphony in 1945.[39] Had the idea to revise the Fourth occurred to him earlier, the symphony might have met with success. But the tide turned in January 1948.

That month the new Communist Party resolution on Muradeli's opera *The Great Friendship* darkened the skies over Soviet music. Discussing the resolution in February at the Moscow Union of Composers, Tikhon Khrennikov condemned almost all of Prokofiev's major works as "formalist."[40] Both versions of the Fourth were criticized. "Sergey Prokofiev alone received eight commissions," Khrennikov noted, "among them [a commission] to create a 'new' version of the Fourth Symphony, based on the themes from the ballet *The Prodigal Son*, which had been condemned by the Soviet public."[41] Revision could not rescue a failed work of the foreign period, he argued, but merely perpetuated the ideological errors of the original.

This stance against revision should not be surprising, because the aesthetics of Socialist Realism assumed that every scrap of musical material possessed specific content relating to the world around it; this content determined the work's ideological leanings apart from the composer's stated intentions. Thus critics could gainsay the composer when they detected and exposed vestiges of "bourgeois ideology" in a given work. The origins of the Fourth spared them the usual imaginative exercise required for exposing bourgeois ideology. (Had they compared symphony to ballet, the more enterprising would doubtless have discovered the presence of prostitution and robbery in the finale.) As one remarked of Op. 112: "[My] acquaintance with the work in piano arrangement showed that the author still did not manage to avoid the intellectualism [*umozritel'nost'*] and coldness which had been characteristic of most of his 'Paris period' works."[42] The critic is Nestyev, who would later declare the symphony a masterpiece (as quoted in the first paragraph of this essay).

After January 1948 prospects for the performance of the revised Fourth fell to none as much of Prokofiev's music was banished from concert halls and opera houses. The composer never recovered from the humiliation of 1948, and his enemies never rested until he was dead. Even his last symphony, the Seventh, intended to be as innocuous as possible, provoked a quarrel on the Stalin Prize Committee while the composer lay on his deathbed.[43] In the end, the Soviet premiere of Op. 112 came only in 1957—four years after Stalin's death, and one year after his rule was "secretly" condemned by Khrushchev at the Twentieth Party Congress. The performance occurred in Moscow under the baton of Gennady Rozhdestvensky, the Western premiere having come in 1950 on a radio broadcast by Adrian Boult and the BBC Symphony Orchestra.

Pilnyak's efforts in revising *Mahogany* proved more fruitful, at least in the short term. *Volga* was quickly passed for publication in 1930 (albeit with sixty pages cut) and was even, astonishingly, translated into six languages— including Catalan. Pilnyak cited these facts in a December 1930 letter to Stalin; this tactic evidently paid off, since the attack dogs of RAPP were brought to heel.[44] As with Prokofiev, revision was not enough to expunge the supposed offense of the original work: in 1936, *Mahogany* was used against Pilnyak once again, as if he had never troubled to write *Volga*.[45] The revision failed to protect him from his persecutors and stained his reputation. Max Eastman, for example, claimed unsympathetically in 1934 that with *Volga* Pilnyak had "violated his artist's conscience" and "prostituted himself."[46] Pilnyak's luck ran out in 1937, when he was arrested and eventually executed for reasons speciously related to his nonliterary activities.

The requirements for the new Soviet novel, as understood by Pilnyak and his (tor)mentors in 1929, nearly matched the requirements for the Soviet symphony as perceived by Prokofiev in 1947. Events were to unfold on a grand scale and be bound together by a conventional, accessible, and edifying plot (or symphonic development and musical "dramaturgy"). Flying in the face of such demands, *Mahogany* concerned human flotsam, borne on the tides of the Revolution, and the petty matter of antique collecting, which had no role to play in the grand scheme of things. Those items of mahogany furniture and dainty porcelain were little specks of chiseled and painted beauty made twice obsolete: first by the Revolution, then by the Five-Year Plan. In revising his nostalgic novella, Pilnyak found his grandeur in the image of the dam and Poletika's plans for reshaping the terrain beyond recognition. *Volga* begins in nature, with the author's ruminations on majestic rivers whose genesis is lost in the depths of time, and ends with Poletika's Faustian dreams, which place human reason as a force above nature.[47] Pilnyak fleshes out his characters by giving more information about their backgrounds, ties everyone together with a cross-generational love intrigue, adds the suspense of sabotage, and crafts a moral conclusion. Ultimately *Volga* inaugurates a socialist realist genre: the stock Soviet element of the struggle between old and new takes the new form of an industrialization novel.

Prokofiev's Op. 47 occupied the similarly narrow world of Neoclassicism, with technical considerations taking priority over the great dramas of the world. In his revisions, Prokofiev imposed a clearer plot on the symphony by bringing the cyclic element to the fore, such that the new theme of the introduction frames the work, undergoes significant transformation, and leads to a final (unpersuasive) apotheosis. As Pilnyak develops his characters from snapshots in *Mahogany* to portraits in *Volga*, so too Prokofiev enlarges and expands material from his original. Themes of the third movement are foreshadowed in the introduction, for example, while the slow movement's main theme realizes its symphonic potential. The significantly altered scoring of Op. 112 as well as the overpowering clangor of the first movement and the closing pages bring the symphony out of its narrowly artistic concerns into the wide world just as recognizably as in Pilnyak's novel.

Some old material had to be adapted radically to the new context and colored by specifically socialist realist imagery. In *Volga*, for example, Ozhogov is no longer allowed to mope about aimlessly; rather, he assumes the very topical task of denouncing the saboteurs to the GPU. In Prokofiev's symphony, the first and second subjects of the first movement solidify their roles: the first loses something of its neoclassical character to become more noisy and "industrial," while the second ascends to an exalted climax in the development. And new contexts shaped old material into acceptable form. Pilnyak places his former authorial observations in the mouths of his characters (especially his negative characters), and Prokofiev sets off several of his lighter themes with lengthy introductions, depriving them of the immediacy and directness they once possessed but endowing them with more gravity and distancing them (as well as himself) from the neoclassical character of the original.

Despite evident reluctance to abandon anything, Pilnyak and Prokofiev each discovered that some things could not be reconciled with the new aesthetic. In *Mahogany* Ozhogov's nephew Akim, the follower of Trotsky, had to be cut. Too much was invested in his position as an Oppositionist, and even if Pilnyak had purged the character of his political leanings, critics might still have searched for Trotskyism. The sinister machine music in Op. 47 had to be expunged for similar reasons: in the aesthetics of the original, Prokofiev could leave such passages unexplained as scarecrows, but if retained in Op. 112, they would introduce conflict that would have to be dramatically justified and resolved. And as with Pilnyak's Akim, retaining the machine music would have introduced an ideological problem: Just what was the import of such sinister passages? If the "glorious socialist future" depended on accelerated industrialization, as critics would have pointed out, there was no place for such things—not outside the minds of saboteurs.

Beyond structure and subject lies the question of subjectivity. In the socialist realist novel, the authorial persona controls the narrative, preventing readers from arriving at interpretations that might subvert the tale's moral values. In the earlier versions of both works the authorial voice and its musical counterpart were quite conspicuous: the author's own lyrical musings fill Pilnyak's novella, and Prokofiev's Op. 47 opens with a similarly lyrical device standing outside the argument of the first movement proper. In the revisions, such interventions shape the narrative more actively. Abandoning his earlier posture as a curious but generally nonjudgmental observer in

Mahogany, Pilnyak spells out his moral and political stance at every juncture in *Volga* (or if not *his* stance, then the stance required of him). The revision of the Fourth Symphony magnifies Prokofiev's presence, with the lyrical material of the symphony's introduction undergoing transformations at each occurrence over the course of the first three movements; these lyrical moments function as a heuristic device in the symphonic drama, knitting together the first three movements. Still more important are the many single-line interpolations that the revision shares with its immediate predecessor, the Sixth Symphony; these often anticipate lighter themes retained from Op. 47 and thereby lend them greater weight. Such prefiguring mirrors socialist realist redundancy, which painstakingly prepares and explains events in the narrative at the cost of controlling the reader or listener (the cost being a benefit in socialist realist terms).[48]

From our point of view, Pilnyak and Prokofiev are redeemed, because their interventions are not confident and ponderous, in the socialist realist manner, but lyrical and melancholy. Pilnyak does not quite end his novel with the grandiose vision of the future. The dam serves its purpose, but instead of the expected bird's-eye view of the flooding that follows, Pilnyak zooms in unexpectedly and distressingly on a single person, Ozhogov, who lies on his back awaiting his death under the approaching floodwaters; only his dog sits, uncomprehendingly, at his side, and when he finally sees the deluge his attempts to flee are futile. In socialist realist fashion, Pilnyak's authorial interventions should have foreclosed ambiguities, but they merely propagate doubt. The effect was insightfully described by Trotsky in 1923, writing in an admittedly different political and aesthetic environment:

> Pilnyak often willfully breaks the thread of his narrative with his own hands in order to tie the knots himself quickly, end to end, to explain (somehow or other), to generalize (and very badly) and to ornament lyrically (sometimes beautifully and much more often superfluously). Pilnyak tied a great number of such purposeful authors' knots. His whole work is dualistic, sometimes it is the Revolution that is the invisible axis, sometimes, very visibly, it is the author himself who is timidly rotating around the Revolution.[49]

These comments apply equally to Prokofiev, whose "authorial voice" is neither committed to the (now thoroughly mythologized) Revolution, nor to a uniquely personal outlook, which he abandons altogether in the finale. The loss of this voice in the apotheosis makes the finale the least satisfying part of the 1947 version.

But however much both artists applied their experience and ingenuity to assimilate old material in the new aesthetic, the resulting works are full of ruptures and incongruities. Linking passages written to cover cuts create new gaps far wider and more glaring. Remnants of the modest but elegant old structures remain within the grand new towering edifices; the older, intricately woven passages fought for space with rough-hewn monolithic slabs and crumpled under their weight. Reprises and symmetries, so vital for the shape of *Mahogany*, confuse the drama of *Volga*, and the neoclassical symmetry of the exposition and recapitulation in Prokofiev's first movement impedes the progress of the new development.

With hindsight we see that both artists placed themselves in an untenable position, because it proved impossible to marry Modernism and Socialist Realism. To suit the aesthetics of Stalinism, they would have had to start almost from scratch, building themselves up again as party-line devotees. Their revisions exemplify the problems that beset the finest Soviet artists. Setting aside the myth of the genius subverting political pressure, we see that like most Soviet artists, Prokofiev and Pilnyak were sincere in their attempts to adapt to their new artistic environment. But they could not give up their craft.

Let the final word fall to Alexander Voronsky, a friend of Pilnyak in the 1920s who published several of his works. Although Voronsky's comments address the writer in 1923, his assessment applies equally to the problems facing Pilnyak and Prokofiev in their revisions:

> The author's imagery splits into opposed fragments. His [work is] woven together from different, yet miraculously intertwined and contradictory moods. . . . In all this, there is something that is artistically unfinished, or not thought through, or not attributable to one world outlook. It is as if the author stands in the middle of a crossroads. If you go down that road, you will lose one thing; if you go down the other road, you will lose something else.[50]

NOTES

1. I. Nest'yev, *Zhizn' Sergeya Prokof'yeva* (Moscow: Sovetskiy kompozitor, 1973), 532.

2. M. Tarakanov, *Stil' simfoniy Prokof'yeva* (Moscow: Muzïka, 1968), 202.

3. S. Slonimskiy, *Simfonii Prokof'yeva: Opït issledovaniya* (Leningrad: Muzïka, 1964), 67.

4. Helmut Loos, "Ballett, Suite, Sinfonie: Die Fassungen des *Verlorenen Sohnes* und der vierten Sinfonie von Sergej Prokofjew," *Bericht über das Internationale Symposion "Sergej Prokofjew: Aspekte seines Werkes und der Biographie": Köln 1991*, ed. Klaus Wolfgang Niemöller (Regensburg: Gustav Bosse, 1992), 305–23.

5. Nikolay Yezhov (1895–1940) joined the Bolsheviks in 1917, fought in the Russian Civil War from 1919–21, and thereafter rose through the ranks of the Communist Party and Soviet government bureaucracy. At the time of his work with Pilnyak, he was already deputy minister of agriculture. He accessed the literary world through the activities of his second wife, Yevgeniya Feinberg, an editor and organizer of writers' gatherings frequented by Ilya Ehrenburg and Isaak

Babel. From 1936 to 1938, Yezhov headed the NKVD secret police during its most notorious period, the great purges or "Yezhovshchina." He thus presided over the arrest, trial, and execution of senior Party members, Red Army officers, scientists, and artists. Pilnyak was among those arrested by Yezhov, who accused the writer of plotting to assassinate a former collaborator. Once the Yezhovshchina had fulfilled its purposes, Stalin wished to distance himself from the events. In 1939 Yezhov was dismissed from his official duties, then arrested and, a year later, executed.

Of the revision, Victor Serge left the following account in *Memoirs of a Revolutionary*, trans. Peter Sedgwick (Iowa City: University of Iowa Press, 2002), 269:

Boris Andreyevich Pilnyak was writing *The Volga Flows into the Caspian Sea*. On his work-table I saw manuscripts under revision. It had been suggested to him that, to avoid banishment from Soviet literature, he should remodel *Forest of the Isles* [a mistranslation of *Bois des îles*, the French title for *Mahogany*], that "counter-revolutionary" tale of his, into a novel agreeable to the Central Committee. The body's Cultural Section had assigned him a co-author who, page by page, would ask him to suppress this and add that. The helpmate's name was Yezhov, and a high career awaited him, followed by a violent death: this was the successor to Yagoda as head of the GPU, shot like Yagoda in 1938 or 1939.

Pilnyak would twist his great mouth: "He has given me a list of fifty passages to change outright!" "Ah!" he would exclaim, "if only I could write freely! What I would not do!" At other times I found him in the throes of depression. "They'll end up by throwing me in jail. Don't you think so?" I gave him new heart by explaining that his fame in Europe and America safeguarded him; I was right, for a while. "There isn't a single thinking adult in this country," he said, "who has not thought that he might be shot." And he related to me details of killings which he had picked up drinking with tipsy executioners.

Realizing that *Mahogany* would cause him trouble, Pilnyak jumped to avoid being pushed. He published a letter in the August 28, 1929, issue of *Literaturnaya gazeta* before any of his critics' accusations found their way into print, claiming that he had decided, on his own initiative, to revise *Mahogany* before a word had been said against it. The implied chronology of the letter is dubious: if true, the revision must have started so soon after he completed *Mahogany* that one might reasonably ask why Pilnyak bothered to finish it in a form that must already have been unacceptable to him. See Boris Pilnyak, *"Mne vïpala gor'kaya slava…": Pis'ma, 1915–1937* (Moscow: Agraf, 2002), 333–37.

6. Prokofiev most likely solicited the commission himself from the Committee on Arts Affairs, as he had on previous occasions for other works.

7. In Pilnyak's case, this was Socialist Realism *avant le lettre*, but literature was well ahead of the other arts in working out socialist realist principles. Many works that became exemplars of socialist realist literature date from the 1920s, among them Dmitriy Furmanov's *Chapayev* (1923) and Konstantin Trenyov's play *Lyubov' Yarovaya* (1926).

8. Leon Trotsky was the leader of the Left Opposition group opposed to Stalin and author of *Literature and Revolution* as well as numerous literary essays and reviews; Alexander Voronsky was editor of the literary periodical *Krasnaya Nov'*; Vyacheslav Polonsky, a sympathizer rather than an active Oppositionist, was editor of the literary periodical *Novïy Mir*.

9. The New Economic Policy (NEP) was implemented at the end of the Civil War in 1921, when the continued requisitioning of food for the cities was no longer tolerated by the peasantry. A pragmatic measure, the NEP allowed a market economy in agricultural produce and revived small businesses in the towns. It rendered large-scale and rapid industrialization impossible, however, and Stalin finally replaced the NEP in 1929 with his first Five-Year Plan. The NEP provided limited funding for the arts, and even the most loyal artists had to earn what they could, where they could—whether at home or abroad. By the time *Mahogany* was published, NEP had officially ended, but the Soviet government had not yet begun to finance the arts.

10. Pilniak [Pilnyak], "Mahogany," in *Chinese Story and Other Tales*, trans. and with an introduction and notes by Vera T. Reck and Michael Green (Norman and London: University of Oklahoma Press, 1988), 102.

11. Pilnyak, *Volga vpadayet v Kaspiyskoye more* (1930; repr., Pullman, Mich.: Russian Language Specialties, 1973), 259–60; my translation.

12. There is more than a hint of sarcasm in Prokofiev's reference to Kochno's "brilliant ideas." Prokofiev disdained him; when writing in Russian, he used endings that highlighted the resemblance of Kochno's name to a common Russian obscenity and went so far as to excise Kochno from the credits for the ballet, a move Kochno countered with a lawsuit.

13. Lifar is the dancer and choreographer Serge Lifar.

14. Sergey Prokof'yev, *Dnevnik 1907–1933*, ed. Svyatoslav Prokof'yev, 2 vols. (Paris: Serge Prokofiev Estate, 2002), 2:667–91.

15. A copy of the notebook in question is held at the Serge Prokofiev Archive, Goldsmiths College, London, R8825/001-100/004-067. It was begun in 1919 and filled during the 1920s.

16. Prokof'yev, *Dnevnik*, 2:672 (entry of February 7, 1929).

17. Ibid., 2:648–53.

18. Asafyev is Boris Asafyev. Prokofiev introduced several of his Russian friends to Christian Science, his chosen faith, and hoped that they would convert to it. There is no evidence to suggest that this occurred.

19. Myaskovsky is the composer Nikolay Myaskovsky, Dranishnikov the conductor Vladimir Dranishnikov, and Radlov the director Sergey Radlov.

20. Prokof'yev, *Dnevnik*, 2:690–91.

21. Prokofiev to Koussevitzky, October 11, 1930, Serge Prokofiev Archive.

22. Prokof'yev, *Dnevnik*, 2:790.

23. Ibid., 2:791 (entry of December 11). Prokofiev's anxiety about Stravinsky's Neoclassicism was at this time rife as never before. *Apollon musagète* (1928) gave him food for thought, and in many ways *The Prodigal Son* was a direct response.

24. Ibid., 2:792.

25. Myaskovsky to Asafyev, May 13, 1929, Russian State Archive of Literature and Art (henceforth RGALI), f. 2658 (Asaf'yev), op. 2, yed. khr. 51.

26. Myaskovsky to Prokofiev, July 20, 1932, in O. P. Lamm, *Stranitsï tvorcheskoy biografii Myaskovskogo* (Moscow: Sovetskiy kompozitor, 1989), 216.

27. Prokofiev to Myaskovsky, July 27, 1932, in ibid.

28. Entry in Myaskovsky's diary, October 28, 1933, in ibid., 223.

29. V. Tsukkerman, "Sergey Prokof'yev," *Sovetskoye iskusstvo*, November 23, 1937.

30. The typed transcript of the meeting is in RGALI f. 962 (Komitet po delam iskusstv), op. 3, yed. khr. 314. The following quotations come from this source, in my translation.

31. The accusation of illiteracy is presumably directed at Prokofiev's conducting.

32. Shostakovich's Fifth was premiered during the *dekada* in Leningrad (not Moscow).

33. V. Berkov, "Violonchel'nïy kontsert Sergeya Prokof'yeva," *Sovetskoye iskusstvo*, November 26, 1938; K. Kuznetsov, "Zametki o violonchel'nom kontserte Prokof'yeva," *Sovetskoye iskusstvo*, February 14, 1939.

34. A. A. Al'shvang "Posle 25-letiya: O nekotorïkh sochineniyakh sovetskikh kompozitorov za 1943–44 godï," RGALI f. 2658, op. 1, yed. khr. 733. The quotation comes from the typescript of this article, included in a letter of May 29, 1945, from T. E. Tsïtovich to Asafyev.

35. M. A. Mendel'son-Prokof'yeva, "Vospominaniya o Sergeye Prokof'yeve. Fragment: 1946–1950," in *Sergey Prokof'yev: Vospominaniya, pis'ma, stat'i*, ed. M. P. Rakhmanova (Moscow: Gosudarstvennïy tsentral'nïy muzey muzïkal'noy kul'turï imeni M. I. Glinki, 2004), 58.

36. These additions, in rough score, can be found in RGALI f. 1929 (Prokof'yev), op. 1, yed. khr. 118.

37. Tarakanov, *Stil' simfoniy Prokof'yeva*, 253.

38. "Orchestrated No. 2, completed No. 9—a parody, with the stolen goods [the false friends don the Prodigal Son's clothes and imitate him after having robbed him]. Kochno wanted something contemptuous, but I rejected that—it came out merry and thievish." Prokof'yev, *Dnevnik*, 2:660 (entry of December 24–26, 1928).

39. Entry in Myaskovsky's diary, November 17, 1945, in Lamm, *Stranitsï tvorcheskoy biografii Myaskovskogo*, 314.

40. In April, following this performance, Tikhon Khrennikov was appointed General

Secretary of the Union of Soviet Composers. According to his memoirs, the speech had been written for him, and he was simply ordered to deliver it. *Tak eto bïlo: Tikhon Khrennikov o vremeni i o sebe*, ed. V. Rubtsova (Moscow: Muzïka, 1994), 130.

41. Tikhon Khrennikov, "Za tvorchestvo, dostoynoye sovetskogo naroda," speech at the meeting of Moscow composers and musicologists devoted to the discussion of the Resolution of the Central Committee of the Communist Party, February 17–26, 1948, in *Sovetskaya muzïka* 1 (1948): 54–62.

42. Nest'yev, *Prokof'yev* (Moscow: Gosudarstvennoye muzïkal'noye izdatel'stvo, 1957), 421–22. It is hard to say the extent to which his later change of heart stemmed from a new political climate and the rise in Prokofiev's posthumous status.

43. The quarrel over the Seventh Symphony was fueled by Vladimir Zakharov, who insistently claimed that the "grimacing" and the "galop" dance topic in the finale could not be considered a faithful representation of Soviet youth. RGALI f. 2073 (Komitet po Stalinskim premiyam), op. 2, yed. khr. 10, transcripts from January 8–February 4, 1953.

44. See Pilnyak, *"Mne vïpala gor'kaya slava,"* 345–48.

45. Gary Browning, *Boris Pilniak: Scythian at a Typewriter* (Ann Arbor: Ardis, 1985), 73.

46. Ibid., 47. Eastman, at the time, was aligned with the exiled Trotsky, and beyond his aesthetic reservations, he could not have warmed to a novel reflecting Stalinism. But in this period we can hardly expect aesthetic judgments upon such works to emerge from a political vacuum. Browning, however, dissents from this view. He believes that Pilnyak displayed "uncommon courage" in refusing to disown *Mahogany*. Surprisingly, Browning even considers *Volga* "a better work," in which the material from *Mahogany* finally "found its rightful place."

47. To be punctilious, Poletika's vision is recounted on the second to last page. Pilnyak robs it of some of its impact by reserving Ozhogov's suicide for the last one.

48. For a discussion of redundancy in the socialist realist novel, see Régine Robin, *Socialist Realism: An Impossible Aesthetic*, trans. Catherine Porter (Stanford: Stanford University Press, 1992), 251–52.

49. L. Trotsky, "Literatura i revolyutsiya" (1924), trans. Rose Strunsky, http://www.marxists. org/archive/trotsky/1924/lit_revo/, accessed September 20, 2007.

50. A. Voronsky, "Boris Pilnyak," *Krasnaya Nov'* (August 1922); repr. in *Art as the Cognition of Life: Selected Writings 1911–1936*, trans. and ed. Frederick S. Choate (Oak Park, Mich.: Mehring Books, 1998), 74. This essay was the first substantial critical study of Pilnyak's work.

After Prokofiev

PETER J. SCHMELZ

Consider the following two photographs and trio of personages:

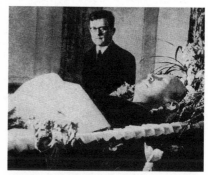

Figure 1. Stalin lying in state.

Figure 2. Prokofiev lying in state with Shostakovich standing by.

Both Stalin and Prokofiev died on March 5, 1953, a bitter irony musicologists cannot help but note. Richard Taruskin calls the coincidence of their demises a historical "trick no novelist would dare contrive."[1] Also common is the linking of Stalin and Shostakovich, owing to the reductive popular perception of the latter as a dissident.[2] Prokofiev and Shostakovich have likewise been joined, their works frequently appearing together on concert programs that foreground the plight of artists under Stalin. What these photographs capture, however, goes beyond any casual pairing; for while that day in early March seems to fix the connections each to each, in truth the significance of the relationships among the three—of the entire grouping—shifted in step with the transformations of Soviet society over the next decade. During the period that took shape under Nikita Khrushchev in the mid-1950s and 1960s, a time known as the Thaw (*ottepel'*), the revelation of Stalin's most heinous acts, the process of de-Stalinization, and the refutation of the "cult of personality" allowed greater freedom in many areas of Soviet life, including drama, literature, and music. Political and cultural liberalization affected the legacies of Stalin, Prokofiev, and Shostakovich in different but equally profound ways.

Shostakovich and Prokofiev began the 1950s severely cowed. Following the 1948 resolution of the Central Committee of the All-Union Communist Party (Bolsheviks) against the opera *Velikaya druzhba* (The great friendship), 1947 by Vano Muradeli, they were obliged to recant their perceived "formalist" tendencies and produce bland patriotic scores; Prokofiev's oratorio *Na strazhe mira* (*On Guard for Peace*), 1950 is just such a work. On September 1, 1948, Shostakovich was stripped of his teaching responsibilities at the Moscow and Leningrad Conservatories, while Prokofiev, suffering debilitating hypertrophia, became less and less visible, confined to his dacha at Nikolina Gora.[3] As a result of Prokofiev's premature death, however, Shostakovich became the leading Soviet composer in the late 1950s. Joining the Communist Party in 1960 only solidified his official reputation; by that time he was, as Laurel Fay puts it, the "mouthpiece of official Soviet aesthetic policy."[4]

Prokofiev's posthumous reputation improved to the extent that, by the early 1960s, he had officially become a Soviet "classic." As with most changes brought about by the Thaw, his transformation was in some respects immediate (justified by his permanent relocation to the Soviet Union in the spring of 1936), in other respects incremental, governed by three related trends. First, young Soviet composers, once influenced by both Prokofiev and Shostakovich, turned away from the former and looked instead to the latter, even as their knowledge of modern music expanded beyond the Soviet sphere. Second, cultural officials dubbed Prokofiev a "classic," first canonizing his post-1936 piano works, ballets, and symphonies, and then steadily expanding the repertoire list to include operas, chamber pieces, and even some of the works he composed in the West.[5] Third came the debate between conservative and reformist music critics about Prokofiev's "contemporaneity" (*sovremennost*), a term that had several contradictory meanings. By the end of the Thaw in the 1970s, the formerly shunned composer was likened to the sun by conservatives, reformers, and moderates alike.

The official co-optation of Prokofiev may be a familiar fact, but it remains an unexamined one; the process by which it occurred, its effect on young Soviet composers, and its relation to the changing cultural discourse have not yet been traced. Such an exploration illustrates, first of all, Prokofiev's difficult position in Soviet society both before and after his death. More broadly, it encapsulates the central developments of the musical Thaw, a period loosely demarcated by Prokofiev's passing in 1953 and Shostakovich's in 1975.[6] In what follows, I assess Prokofiev's posthumous reception between those years and also note Shostakovich's impact on the composers, musicians, and performers who came to prominence under Khrushchev. I argue that Prokofiev's legacy evolved in accord with the cultural policies of the Thaw, from their hesitant introduction in the 1950s to their large-scale manifestation in the 1960s and their seeming disintegration in the 1970s.[7] Ultimately, in his life after death—or as Russian musicologist Marina Nestyeva has it, his "life after life"—Prokofiev reflected the complicated, often paradoxical changes in Soviet music after Stalin.[8]

Being Eclipsed

Predictably, Stalin's funeral was an epic event, and just as predictably, Prokofiev's paled by comparison. Soviet recognition of his achievements was initially eclipsed by the extensive press coverage of the Great Leader and Teacher's passing and the resulting changes in the Kremlin. *Sovetskoye iskusstvo* published an obituary only on March 18, and *Sovetskaya muzïka* buried a brief remembrance at the back of its April issue, the bulk of which was devoted to Stalin tributes.[9] Western news outlets actually released the news of Prokofiev's passing ahead of the Soviet media: the *New York Times*, for example, ran an obituary on March 9. (This and other Western notices, however, incorrectly gave the date of his death as Wednesday, March 4.)[10]

The atmosphere following Stalin's death was memorably described by poet Yevgeny Yevtushenko in his autobiography: "A sort of general paralysis came over the country. Trained to believe that they were all in Stalin's care, people were lost and bewildered without him. All Russia wept. And so did I. We wept sincerely, tears of grief—and perhaps also tears of fear for the future."[11] Historian Elena Zubkova highlights the anxieties of the post-Stalin environment, writing that "the principal element of the atmosphere of those days was not hope of changes for the better but fears of the worst."[12] The sense of apprehension Yevtushenko and Zubkova describe was not universal, however, as evidenced by the reception of Ilya Ehrenburg's 1954 novella *The Thaw*. On the surface, the novella is a socialist realist parable about good and corrupt factory workers and their lives and loves; beneath the surface it discloses grim facts about the Stalin years, including the false arrest of prominent Jewish physicians in the so-called Doctors' Plot against Party leaders. The hint of openness in Ehrenburg's novella took hold in reality, so much so that it became a symbol of its time and place; some of the author's friends even suggested that he had written *The Thaw* "solely to inject the title into the country's vocabulary."[13]

Yet trepidation and uncertainty persisted. As Flora Litvinova recorded in a diary entry of October 27, 1956: "The novel is bad, but Ehrenburg found the right word—the Thaw. We must relish it while it lasts, as experience shows that frosts will follow, and hard ones at that."[14] Three years after Stalin's death Shostakovich still feared what the future might bring, telling composer Edison Denisov (1929–96): "Edik, the times are new, but the informers are old."[15] Sofia Gubaidulina (b. 1931) likewise recalled being scared: "It is possible that at that moment people understood the kind of wild and unhappy [*neschastnaya*] country within which they lived," she remarked, "but feared that it might get even worse than before."[16] This pervasive apprehension indicates just how thoroughly Stalin's policies had traumatized Soviet society. In her memoirs, soprano Galina Vishnevskaya mockingly assessed the implications of Stalin's demise for the new Soviet leadership: "The genius, the divinity, was gone; after him came mere mortals." Others like Zubkova noted the appearance of cracks in the official Soviet facade: "It was as if Stalin's death had conferred on him a human dimension. It was an irony of fate: Stalin as human seemed superfluous."[17] As a result, "his successors . . . also became mere mortals."[18]

Stalin's reputation among the Communist Party elite declined after his death; and so too for a time did Prokofiev's reputation within educated musical circles. Shostakovich, in contrast, remained popular. In the cloistered Soviet conservatories of the early 1950s, students came to know the music of both composers, even though some of it remained officially off-limits. Alfred Schnittke (1934–98) recalled that when he began his studies at the Moscow Conservatory in the fall of 1953, "it was impossible to hear the works of Stravinsky without special authorization, [and] the fundamental compositions of Prokofiev and Shostakovich were inaccessible."[19] Respected conservatory instructors like Vissarion Shebalin (1902–63) still taught the three composers, however, and their music, especially Shostakovich's, was featured on recitals and performances of the Scientific Student Society (Nauchnoye studencheskoye obshchestvo, or NSO).[20] Denisov remembered Shebalin sharing "forbidden" scores with his class, among them Shostakovich's still unperformed Fourth Symphony (completed in 1936, but premiered only in December 1961) and Prokofiev's ballet *Chout* (*The Buffoon*), 1921.[21]

The 1954–55 schedule for the NSO of the Moscow Conservatory (Theory and Composition Department) included meetings devoted to Prokofiev's Fourth and Sixth symphonies (both of which had unhappy histories with Soviet critics), Shostakovich's Fourth Symphony, and scores by Stravinsky.[22] Shostakovich and Prokofiev may both have been on the course of study, but the former received more attention than the latter. In the recollections of many NSO participants, Prokofiev's compositions were increasingly overshadowed by Shostakovich's (particularly his Ninth and Tenth symphonies). Schnittke found himself drawn to more exotic fare: Stravinsky's

Petrushka, *Rite of Spring*, and *Oedipus Rex*, as well as Boulez's *Marteau sans maître*—all discussed at NSO sessions.[23] Shostakovich's Eighth and Ninth symphonies were featured in November and December 1954, and the composer himself attended a meeting in the spring of 1955.

In his last years, Prokofiev had extremely limited contact with young composers. Schnittke only remembered seeing Prokofiev at performances of his own music, notably the premiere of the Symphony-Concerto for Cello and Orchestra on February 18, 1952, after which Prokofiev gingerly mounted the stage to receive applause. "I can see to this day his tall thin figure wearing dark glasses," Schnittke wrote in 1990.[24] Denisov recalled seeing Prokofiev "just one time, on the staircase in the Great Hall of the Conservatory; he asked me the shortest way to the *loges des artistes*."[25] Even the pianist Svyatoslav Richter, the dedicatee of Prokofiev's Ninth Piano Sonata (1947), seldom saw him, "I had more contact with Prokofiev's music than with the composer himself. I was never particularly close to him as a person: He intimidated me."[26]

Despite his absence from the halls of the conservatories, Prokofiev was accused—with Shostakovich—of exerting a negative influence on emerging composers by the Central Committee. The 1948 resolution advised that the "creative output of many students of our conservatories consists of blind imitation of the music of Shostakovich, Prokofiev, and others."[27] In a January meeting of composers with the hostile cultural official Andrey Zhdanov—a meeting that informed the infamous February 10 document—director of the Leningrad Conservatory Pavel Serebryakov declared that "in the finals we often see nothing but little Prokofievs or little Shostakoviches."[28] The greater threat came from Shostakovich, who found himself being chided in an April 1948 *Sovetskaya muzïka* cartoon that depicted "little Shostakoviches" (*malenkiye Shostakovichi*) issuing forth from the Moscow and Leningrad Conservatories.[29] He was in fact the only composer so targeted in *Sovetskaya muzïka* following the 1948 Resolution, and received withering criticism in a three-part essay by Marian Koval (1907–71), "a highly tendentious tract," Fay observes.[30] In the years after 1953, Shostakovich's influence on the new generation of Soviet composers caused further official anxiety. His recent compositions, particularly his Tenth Symphony (1953), were decried for the negative effects they might have on his youthful imitators.[31]

In the immediate post-Stalinist period, Prokofiev and Shostakovich both provided inspiration to students. Gubaidulina recalled that "for us the names Prokofiev and Shostakovich were our main means of support. We did not have access to information from the outside world, and those two composers presented at that time the single reality in contemporary [*sovremennaya*] music."[32] In the end, Gubaidulina assigned greater value to Shostakovich, who had encouraged her as a student to "continue on [her] own, *incorrect* path."[33] Her admiration for Shostakovich also had a spiritual dimension. He "was able to transfigure the [musical] material into a spiritual entity," she believed, "whereas Prokofiev's music lacks the contrast between terrible darkness and an ever-expanding light."[34]

The downturn in Prokofiev's reputation is illustrated by Denisov's reactions to him. Like all of Denisov's self-aggrandizing autobiographical statements, his comments about Prokofiev must be read with a degree of skepticism. They do, however, reflect the general attitude of his circle. Denisov remembered being enamored of Prokofiev's music while growing up in Tomsk, but thinking of it "a little less" after enrolling in the Moscow Conservatory in 1951.[35] He attended Prokofiev's funeral, and boasted (implausibly) that he had confronted two policemen barring his passage across a street otherwise commandeered by Stalin's mourners. "The death of 'your' Stalin does not interest me," he asserted, "I want to bid farewell to Prokofiev."[36] He also recalled spending fifteen minutes in Prokofiev's apartment standing before his corpse "because I felt obligated to bow for the last time before the great composer."[37]

Denisov's opinion changed decisively in the early 1960s while writing an essay on Prokofiev's approach to sonata form.[38] He claimed to have "literally studied all of his work . . . and sometime in that very period I also understood that Prokofiev as a composer had ended for me, that I could take nothing from him, and that my enthusiasm for him was perhaps even a serious mistake."[39] It was a mistake because "his world and the language of that world—all of it was not mine, everything was foreign to me, foreign." Denisov increasingly identified with Shostakovich's sensibilities, whereas Prokofiev interested him only as a subject for academic research.[40] He grew close to Shostakovich personally, corresponding with him throughout the 1950s. This connection inspired Denisov to compose two chamber works in Shostakovich's honor: a piano trio in 1954 and a quartet for clarinet, trombone, cello, and piano titled *DSCH* in 1969, although the latter is hardly an uncritical homage.[41]

In Denisov's revised view, Prokofiev lacked an "individual 'style of Prokofiev,'" a distinct creative persona. "After all, there was practically nothing to learn from him. Everything [in Prokofiev] had already appeared in the [works] of others."[42] Or, as he bluntly told French pianist Jean-Pierre Armengaud, "Prokofiev does not have any importance for modern music."[43] Although Denisov favored early experimental works like op. 4, no. 4, *Suggestion diabolique* (*Navazhdeniye*) and op. 17, *Sarcasms*, he scorned Prokofiev's obligatory paeans to the Soviet regime: the opera *Povest' o nastoyashchem cheloveke* (A story of a real man, 1948); the "festive" tone poem *Vstrecha Volgi s Donom* (The meeting of the Volga and the Don, 1952); and especially the cantata *Zdravitsa* (A toast! 1939), which, Denisov complained, "gives the impression that it was sincerely written to the glory of Stalin."[44]

Denisov's interests expanded in the late 1950s to include French music, chiefly the works of Debussy and Ravel (Denisov arranged the the latter's *Chanson espagnole* for voice and two guitars in 1958). He also mimicked Bartók, conceiving his 1961 String Quartet no. 2 in the Hungarian composer's manner. That Bartók "meant nothing as a composer" both to his teacher Shebalin and to Shostakovich undoubtedly heightened his appeal.[45] He also began to explore the music of the Second Viennese School. By the time his essay on Prokofiev was published in 1972 (it had a decade-long gestation), Denisov had written on Bartók's string quartets, Shostakovich's orchestration, "jazz and new music," and Webern's op. 27 Piano Variations, among other topics.[46]

Following Khrushchev's "Secret Speech" of February 1956 at the Twentieth Party Congress, in which he drew attention to the destructive effects of the Stalinist "cult of personality," the Thaw began to be felt in Soviet cultural and musical life. As the Leningrad composer Sergey Slonimsky (b. 1932) recalled, it "became easier to breathe" after this speech.[47] A greater variety of scores by Debussy, Ravel, and Bartók became available; Stravinsky's neoclassical works, meanwhile, attained a controversial foothold in conservatory curriculums. Moscow composer Andrey Volkonsky (b. 1933) wrote his suggestively titled piano piece *Musica Stricta* at precisely this time: the provocative interaction of twelve-tone techniques and neoclassical, toccata-like passages in the last movement collapses, like many works of the Thaw, the new and the old. *Musica Stricta* brings together the sounds of Schoenberg and Prokofiev (specifically the *Suggestion diabolique* and the Toccata, op. 11).[48]

The chromatic melodic descents and propulsive rhythmic motion in both Prokofiev pieces—illustrated in Examples 1b and 1c—were extended by Volkonsky into the descending sixteenth-note, twelve-tone row in the right hand of Example 1a, one of the two primary rows at work in this "double fugue" (the second row appears in the left hand at the outset). Within the context of his self-consciously new vocabulary, Volkonsky adapted other elements from Prokofiev: namely, his characteristic motivic repetitions, textures (continuous percussive eighth- or sixteenth-notes in the upper voice punctuated by fragmented lines with larger note values in the lower), and triadic constructions otherwise considered off-limits in a "strict" twelve-tone composition (Volkonsky especially favored such tonal recollections at climaxes). Yet the two Prokofiev pieces were only general models for *Musica Stricta*: Volkonsky also drew on Bartók, Stravinsky, and—as evidenced by the double fugue and the subtitle "Fantasia ricercata"—Bach.

Example 1a. Andrey Volkonsky, *Musica Stricta*, IV, mm. 1–8.

Example 1b. Sergey Prokofiev, *Suggestion diabolique*, op. 4, no. 4, mm. 46–56.

Example 1c. Prokofiev, *Toccata,* op. 11, mm. 20–37.

During the Thaw young Soviet composers tried simultaneously to comprehend and contribute to the postwar movements they had only just discovered. Because of the limitations imposed on Soviet music by the 1948 resolution, catching up meant, in part, familiarizing themselves with unknown works by Prokofiev and Shostakovich. (Schnittke's 1979 *Hommage à Igor Stravinsky, Sergey Prokofiev and Dmitry Shostakovich* for piano six hands partly recalls that period of reacquaintance.) Young Soviet composers did not imitate Prokofiev's methods as overtly as they did Shostakovich's, but many still felt the need to pay obeisance to his achievements, if in some cases only rhetorically. Dmitriy Smirnov (b. 1948) recalled his student years as follows:

> When I was young and people asked me what I wanted to be I answered, "A composer." And they responded "Like Shostakovich?" The "like Shostakovich" was understood, because Prokofiev had already died, and all the rest were of no account [*ne v schyot*]! Exactly with those two began my entry into contemporary music.[49]

As Smirnov's qualifying statement reveals, the "two titans," as he later called them, were not of equal importance.[50] "Truly," he insisted, "could you imagine music even more modern, new, and 'of the present' [*sovremennaya, novaya, 'segodnyashnyaya'*] than the music of Shostakovich?"[51] On a 1964 questionnaire he listed his early influences as Beethoven, Saint-Saëns, and Gershwin; his other early musical models included Mahler, Stravinsky, and Prokofiev, who according to theorist Yuriy Kholopov (1932–2003) became Smirnov's "idol for a long time." That is, until he encountered the music of Webern at the Moscow Conservatory, which he attended from 1967 to 1972.[52] Smirnov also found himself drawn to Boulez, Cage, Nono, Xenakis, and Stockhausen, whose works embodied the type of nonconformist iconoclasm to which he aspired.[53]

Viktor Yekimovsky (b. 1947) recalled beginning his career firmly under the influence of Prokofiev. When he started his musical studies at the Moscow Gnesin Institute in the early 1960s he was unfamiliar with the composer, even misidentifying him on a listening exam.[54] Later, after overhearing the *Suggestion diabolique*, Yekimovsky experienced a self-described "Prokofiev metamorphosis." Yekimovsky thereafter began to mimic Prokofiev—and especially that piece—in several of his own early piano works, among them his unpublished Gavotte (1963).[55] As he told the theorist Vladimir Barsky, "I began to compose at the age of thirteen, and very quickly Sergey Prokofiev became my true idol. Perhaps more than any other composer he influenced the formation of my creative personality, although already after several years I moved far away from his style in the direction of newer, more radical music."[56] Yekimovsky further detailed his early attraction to Prokofiev in a 1991 essay, in which he wrote that among students at the Gnesin Institute even in the 1960s, "new music of the twentieth century . . . remained practically unknown, and Prokofiev was virtually the only one of the authentic innovators in musical syntax that they allowed us the indulgence of hearing."[57] Yekimovsky highlighted

Prokofiev's *Suggestion diabolique* (a constant favorite of the Thaw generation), as well as his Toccata (another such favorite) and First Violin Concerto, op. 19.[58]

Yekimovsky acknowledged that his own "more radical" works began only with his appropriately titled *Composition 1* (1969). Few of his compositions from the first half of the 1960s have been published, making it difficult to determine how much his attraction to Prokofiev informed his early style. Even so, his comments—like those of Denisov and Smirnov—reveal the tensions between older and newer influences during the Thaw. The progression from Prokofiev to Shostakovich to other Western composers past (Debussy) and present (Boulez) became a common one in the schooling and self-schooling of musicians of the 1950s and 1960s. Most indicative of Prokofiev's precarious position between "classic" and "modern" modes of composition was a point made by the Leningrad composer Georgiy Sviridov (1915–98) after Stalin's death, as recounted by Sergey Slonimsky. Prokofiev, Sviridov commented, did not represent "new music"; like Shostakovich, he had "already" become a "classic." Slonimsky clarified that there was "no trace of the recent disparaging of Prokofiev and Shostakovich" in Sviridov's language. Rather, it was a sign of respect. "Yes, they are already classics, but we should write differently—in a new way."[59]

In the late 1950s, Slonimsky added, "the password [*parol'*] among progressive musicians" was the phrase "fresh [*svezhaya*] music."[60] Despite Sviridov's purported rejection of *both* Shostakovich and Prokofiev, for most composers and performers Shostakovich's music remained "fresher," and hence more potentially dangerous than Prokofiev's. For Slonimsky, "fresh" meant the same thing that "modern, new, and 'of the present'" meant to Smirnov and "radical" to Yekimovsky. These terms were sometimes associated with Shostakovich, but over time they came to refer to recent (or recently available) works by Western composers. In some quarters they also were associated with Prokofiev, though he inevitably lost some of his freshness when cultural officials decreed him classic.

Becoming Classic

The stages of Prokofiev's official co-optation are easily traced. Important landmarks include the 1956 publication of the first documentary volume dedicated to his life and works, edited by Semyon Shlifshteyn (1903–75); the official Prokofiev biography by Izraíl Nestyev (1911–93), first published in 1957; in the same year, Prokofiev's belated receipt of the Lenin Prize for his (revised) Seventh Symphony (it was given a new, more "optimistic" ending by the composer in 1952 at the suggestion of conductor Samuil

Samosud); the placement of memorial plaques on his principal Moscow residences in early 1958; and the publication of Nestyev's 1962 essay "A Classic of the Twentieth Century (Notes on Prokofiev's Role in Contemporary Musical Culture)."[61] Prokofiev's official biographer most clearly documented his canonization; in fact, one could argue that Nestyev actually initiated the process with his 1945 dissertation on the composer. Prokofiev himself may have attended Nestyev's oral defense.[62]

The first substantive posthumous overview of Prokofiev's career came in Nestyev's essay "The Path of Sergey Prokofiev," published in *Sovetskaya muzïka* a month after his death. As Nestyev rhapsodized at the end of his introduction, "It falls to us to investigate Prokofiev's legacy sensitively, to eliminate all that is false and obsolete, and gratefully to include in the treasury of Soviet music culture that which represents actual, permanent value."[63] This statement neatly anticipates Prokofiev's reception during the Thaw. Debates arose within the Union of Soviet Composers and Ministry of Culture over which of his official works were obsolete, which were relevant, and how his more suspect, modernist works should be interpreted and preserved. The dialogues about his career overlapped and conflicted with one another. As was the case with the reforms of the Thaw in general, Prokofiev's canonization was incremental, his significance determined by different competing factions within the cultural establishment.

The fraught nature of the process is evident in the chronology of the publication of Prokofiev's *Sobraniye sochineniy* (Collected works).[64] Instead of proceeding by genre, the editors emphasized "the best and most vigorous part of his enormous legacy," which included several scores from his youth. Most important, of course, were the "outstanding achievements" of his final twenty years—those that postdated Prokofiev's relocation to the Soviet Union.[65] Thus the order of the early volumes is idiosyncratic but revealing: Piano Works (vol. 1, 1955), Piano Sonatas (vol. 2, 1955), Piano Transcriptions (vol. 3, 1956), Piano Concertos (vols. 4–5, 1956 and 1957), *War and Peace* (vols. 6–7, 1958), *Romeo and Juliet* (vols. 8–9, 1960 and 1961), *Cinderella* (*Zolushka*) (vols. 10–11, 1959), *The Tale of the Stone Flower* (*Skaz o kamennom tsvetke*) (vols. 12–13, 1962), and then Symphonies (vol. 14, 1963). Prokofiev's early ballets and operas, among other major works, are missing.[66]

War and Peace was published in response to earnest demands from critics like Mattias Sokolsky (Grinberg), who in a May 1956 essay in *Sovetskaya muzïka* lamented that none of Prokofiev's operas—not even *War and Peace*— could be found in a recent Soviet edition of three hundred opera librettos. "It is possible to evaluate [*War and Peace*], the best of Prokofiev's eight operas, in different ways," he noted. "Praise it, be enraptured by it, or criticize it." But "to pretend that it does not exist" could only signal "panicked fear or excessive zeal."[67] Sokolsky likewise decried the paucity of serious academic studies of the "greatest Soviet musicians," specifically Prokofiev, Shostakovich, Aram Khachaturyan, and Yuriy Shaporin. His petition for openness approximated the tone of Khrushchev's February 1956 "Secret Speech." Precisely because Prokofiev was now safely part of the past, he played a central role in debates about the gaps, the missing elements, in Soviet music history. The Thaw allowed for these gaps at least to be discussed, if not filled.

It is significant that Prokofiev's output, specifically *War and Peace*, was the focus of Sokolsky's argument. The fifth and final version of the opera had been performed (with cuts) for the first time at the Malïy Theater in Leningrad in 1955—that is, a year before the publication of Sokolsky's essay—and it would be performed again (with fewer cuts) at the Stanislavsky Theater in Moscow in 1957. Sokolsky praised the 1955 premiere in his essay, and asserted that the opera's "turn should come" in the *Collected Works*.[68] An essentially complete performance of Prokofiev's fifth and final version (with its oft-maligned Epigraph) took place in 1959 at the Bolshoy Theater in Moscow.[69] The premiere in 1960 of a de-Stalinized version of his *A Story of a Real Man* at the Bolshoy Theater offered further evidence of the changed official attitude toward Prokofiev. In the same year *Semyon Kotko* also received its first complete staging since its 1940 premiere.[70]

As if in response to Sokolsky's demands, 1956 and 1957 witnessed the appearance of the aforementioned volumes by Shlifshteyn and Nestyev, respectively.[71] With these and other publications on Prokofiev—including Marina Sabinina's 1957 introduction to his life and works, a brief book by Ivan Martïnov released in conjunction with Prokofiev's receipt of the Lenin Prize, and a 1961 monograph by Tatyana Boganova exploring the influence of the Russian folklore traditions on his music—Prokofiev became what Nestyev called "A Classic of the Twentieth Century."[72]

Nestyev was not alone in labeling Prokofiev a classic but he was the first to politicize and nationalize the term. The unsigned April 1953 obituary in *Sovetskaya muzïka* states that Prokofiev had "continu[ed] the noble tradition of the Russian classics."[73] In the preface to the first volume of the *Collected Works*, Dmitriy Kabalevsky noted the "indubitable fact that many of Prokofiev's best compositions are not only performed alongside classic compositions, but successfully bear up to that so-promising partnering."[74] Tellingly, Nestyev declared in his 1957 biography that "it is still too early to speak of Prokofiev's works as classics; his music is too firmly rooted in the present."[75] Just two years later, however, he called Prokofiev "one of the classics of the twentieth century" in a presentation at an international conference in Warsaw dédicated to the composer (December 4–7, 1959); the phrase emphatically recurs in Nestyev's 1960 *Sovetskaya muzïka* report on the Warsaw conference.[76] The revised text of his presentation, published in 1962, has a polemical edge. And there are also nationalist undertones. Nestyev uses the term "classic" to refute those foreign (Polish) critics who privileged the innovations of Prokofiev's early, non-Soviet scores while discounting his significance for contemporary composers.[77]

Nestyev's target audience included Denisov and Volkonsky, who had followed the Polish lead and started to experiment with serialism and other advanced methods. Pushing back, Nestyev pointed out Prokofiev's rejection of Schoenbergian dodecaphony and Stravinskian Neoclassicism, or as Nestyev disparagingly called it, "pseudoclassicism" (*psevdoklassitsizm*).[78] Other Soviet writers had pointed out Prokofiev's disdain for Schoenberg, and during the Thaw, when interest in twelve-tone music expanded, the dismissal accrued more weight.[79] As Nestyev declared, "The entire makeup of Prokofiev's music, with its avid bent for living reflections of the actual phenomena of the surrounding world, decisively contradicts the withdrawn subjectivity so characteristic of many works by Schoenberg or Webern."[80] Prokofiev was a firewall against the "contemporary super-dodecaphonists and electronic music composers" (*nineshnïye superdodekafonistï i elektroniki*) who were then beginning to attract so much attention in the conservatories.[81] Nestyev appended that Prokofiev was one of few twentieth-century composers to enter the standard orchestral and theatrical repertoire and insisted that "only along this path can contemporary composers attain actual creative results and produce new art truly worthy of our great time."[82] Prokofiev's "living reflections of the actual phenomena of the surrounding world" made him, in Nestyev's opinion, an ideal model for young composers of the early 1960s.

As a composer supposedly balanced between the classic and the contemporary, Prokofiev was frequently invoked to counteract the musical practices taking root in the Soviet Union during the Thaw. Another 1962 example comes from the essay "Prokofiev and Schoenberg" by the Ukrainian composer and music critic Miroslav Skorik (b. 1938).[83] Like Nestyev, Skorik portrayed Prokofiev as an innovator of a proper sort, not a "dogmatist" like Schoenberg. The latter's music was less well known than the controversy surrounding his name, Skorik admonished, whereas the former's music was known worldwide.[84] The supposed freedom associated with Schoenberg's system was a falsehood that, in his opinion, appealed only to the untalented. Prokofiev was actually the more independent of the two composers: his music sounded "new" without being beholden to a "system." Although Prokofiev was "one of the first composers" to arrive at what Skorik termed a "twelve-step diatonic mode" (*dvenadtsatis-tupennïy diatonicheskiy lad*), he could hardly be associated with Schoenberg's "atonal school." Prokofiev's twelve-step "mode led to a strengthening of tonal thinking," whereas Schoenberg's resulted in its "disintegration."

Prokofiev, Skorik added, "did not need any kind of 'series.'" There follows a tortuous syllogism: "If he needed to, Prokofiev could without trouble have invented a harmony that the dodecaphonists would consider characteristic of their system. And yet not a single dodecaphonist, even if it were in his creative powers, would be able (they would not have the right!) to compose a single theme of Prokofiev's." Specious or no, the argument served to define Prokofiev as both classic and contemporary.

Skorik's polemic was intended for composers. Prokofiev's harmonic thinking, he instructed,

> provides that authentic freedom of composition that young composers so long to find and that, of course, the dogmatic, artificially created system of Schoenberg and his contemporary followers will never give them. So naturally, Prokofiev, not Schoenberg, is the real, authentically progressive innovator who may truly be called the father of contemporary music![85]

Here Skorik addresses a central concern of the Thaw. Acknowledging the seductiveness of Schoenbergian dodecaphony, Soviet cultural officials designated Prokofiev the "true father of contemporary music," despite his limited influence on the composers who came after him.[86]

Becoming Modern

Paradoxically, Prokofiev's official acceptance in the 1950s facilitated the more open theoretical debates that followed in the 1960s, as Kholopov observed in a 1972 essay.[87] If Nestyev, Skorik, and other conservative critics hoped to canonize Prokofiev, the younger generation of reform-minded theorists and musicologists, among them Kholopov and Mikhaíl Tarakanov (1928–96), advanced a different interpretation of his life and works. Exchanges between "conservatives" and "reformers" or "modernizers," to borrow art historian Susan Reid's useful distinction, affected many areas of Soviet life in the late 1950s and early 1960s; in the musical realm, these labels mark the limit points on a broad spectrum of responses to current trends, rather than denoting a clear-cut binary.[88] Rarely did any individual exclusively occupy either extreme, and the question of one's "contemporaneity" always loomed. As historian Iurii Gerchuk argues, this term was "the fundamental criterion of artistic quality" for conservatives and reformers alike.[89]

The Russian noun *sovremennost'* can be translated as "contemporaneity," "modernity," or "the present"; the adjective *sovremenniy* means "contemporary" or "contemporaneous," though it can also be rendered as "modern," "state-of-the-art," "up-to-date," and "present-day." Being contemporary or reflecting "contemporary reality" (*sovremennaya deystvitel'nost'*) had long been a demand of cultural officials, especially at the end of the Stalin era, when, as historian Kiril Tomoff notes, the "patriotic preoccupation with 'contemporary reality'" was essential to the campaign against cosmopolitanism.[90] During the Thaw the demand had different implications: being contemporary was a reflection of Soviet policy pronouncements and technological advances in the 1950s, specifically as they pertained to the Cold War struggle between East and West; being contemporary also characterized Soviet youth culture.[91]

Conservatives and reformers alike agreed that the new era demanded new art. What exactly this might mean had consumed Soviet aesthetics since the Revolution and was best encapsulated in Narkompros (People's Commissariat of Enlightenment) leader Anatoliy Lunacharsky's oft-noted declaration to Prokofiev in April 1918: "You are a revolutionary in music, we are revolutionaries in life. We ought to work together."[92] The conjunction of revolutionary political action and revolutionary art in the 1920s proved difficult to sustain, and eventually officials crafted the doctrine of Socialist Realism as a way to balance radical political ideals and conservative, accessible expression. This vague aesthetic hardly eased the cultural and political strains, however, and similar tensions between "tradition and innovation" (*traditsiya i novatorstvo*)—another pair of Soviet buzzwords—only increased amid the rapid technological and social developments of the Thaw.[93]

In the late 1950s and early 1960s (especially from 1961 to 1963), debates about music (form and content) were divided between reformers and conservatives. Reformers argued that theorists needed to investigate "contemporary harmony" and take the term "contemporary" beyond its conventional association with "contemporary reality." They thus returned the term to its original definition: modernism. On the other side of the debate were the views of conservatives like Nestyev, who remarked in a 1958 discussion of the "contemporary theme in music" that "there was a time when 'contemporary music' both [in the Soviet Union] and abroad was considered to be absolutely equivalent to 'modernism.'"[94] Nestyev clarified, however, that this earlier period (the 1920s) had passed, and that for cultural officials in the 1950s and 1960s, "contemporary" needed to mean something else. Boris Schwarz reports that two other conservatives—musicologist Yuriy Keldïsh (1907–95) and Union of Composers General Secretary Tikhon Khrennikov (1913–2007)—used *sovremennïy* to designate "not a modern musical *idiom*, but . . . an up-to-date *topicality* or *attitude*."[95] Since the reformers had adopted the term "modernism" as their own, the conservatives were left to associate *sovremennost'* with "contemporary reality." Such was how Keldïsh and Khrennikov defined it in their speeches at the Third All-Union Congress of Composers (held March 26–31, 1962).

Among the early reformers was the young Schnittke, who complained in a 1961 letter to the editor of *Sovetskaya muzïka* that the publication devoted too little space to theoretical investigations of "questions of contemporary musical language." He reminded the editor that "we are no longer conservatory students for whom it is well known that the content is primary and not the form."[96] Although *Sovetskaya muzïka* had featured several discussions of "music and contemporaneity" and "contemporary harmony" in the late 1950s, the debate became more focused and the respective positions of the participants more polarized in the wake of Schnittke's salvo.[97] It was followed by two reformist articles, the first by Tarakanov in the same issue of *Sovetskaya muzïka*. Taking up select works by Prokofiev and Shostakovich, Tarakanov isolated the "distinctive features of the harmonic style of contemporary Soviet and foreign music." He then deplored the absence of a "single monograph specially dedicated to questions of the musical language of *contemporary* Soviet and foreign art."[98]

For the next issue of *Sovetskaya muzïka*, Kholopov furnished an essay on twentieth-century harmony. He examined works by Bartók, Debussy, Myaskovsky, and Prokofiev while introducing ideas regarding consonance and dissonance that he would further develop, over the next decade, in writings dedicated solely to Prokofiev.[99] Beyond this work, Kholopov followed the careers of the more adventurous and provocative of the emerging composers, chief among them Denisov. His advocacy of their music earned him prestige among reformers and notoriety among conservatives. His first publications about Prokofiev stressed the deceased composer's modernism and, by extension, his continued relevance.

Kholopov first discussed Prokofiev's modernism in the 1962 essay "On the Modern Features of Prokofiev's Harmony." Here Prokofiev served as a pretext for a challenging discussion of broad theoretical topics, including the blurring in twentieth-century music of the distinction between chromaticism and diatonicism, atonality and tonality. Kholopov furthered his exploration of this issue in a 1967 monograph and 1972 essay devoted to recent theoretical writing on Prokofiev.[100] He sought in these publications to redefine "dissonant [harmonic] combinations" as "stable elements of a mode."[101]

Kholopov deemed the "problem of tonality" (*problema tonal'nosti*) the most pressing issue in Prokofiev scholarship. The best tool for tackling this problem was "the idea of twelve-step tonality," in which "every chord may be in every tonality."[102] For his first example, he turned to the final cadence of the opera *Betrothal in a Monastery* (*Obrucheniye v monastïre*, 1946), and asked rhetorically: "How does one explain the pitch C♯ in C major (it is exactly C♯ and not D♭), especially if it resolves up to E?"[103]

Example 2a. Sergey Prokofiev, *Betrothal in a Monastery*, final cadence, ninth tableau, scene 5, mm. 5–6 before end.

Kholopov explained that, in this cadence, "the chord D–F♯–A–C♯ is a variant of the supertonic II_7 in C major, whose possible independent (rather than simply altered) roots [*osnovnïye stupeni*] can include C♯ and, as analysis reveals, the remaining non-diatonic pitches and chords."[104] In other words, even if the root of this chord were C♯, it would still be a functional—not merely chromatically altered—variant of the supertonic in C major. By taking this substitution one step further, Kholopov was able to conclude that any chord from any other key might replace it, since any borrowing could be interpreted as a variant of a functional scale degree in C major. Kholopov illustrated this concept in a diagram accompanying his 1962 essay:

Example 2b. Diagram of all twelve possible chromatically altered roots in C major in the context of Kholopov's "twelve-step tonality."

Thus relying on Prokofiev's example, Kholopov proved the infinite flexibility of the newly expanded tonal system, which allows any chord to function in any key.[105]

In his 1962 essay Kholopov further defined this phenomenon as a *universal'naya khromaticheskaya sistema* (type of universal chromatic system), acting as a general modal (*ladovaya*) basis for contemporary music.[106] In his account Prokofiev did not employ traditional diatonic harmony but focused either on the "chromatic tonal system" (*khromaticheskaya tonal'naya sistema*) or "full chromatic modal system" (*polnaya khromaticheskaya ladovaya sistema*), which "fundamentally differs from dodecaphony most of all because it is a *tonal* system."[107] Despite the disclaimer, Kholopov linked Prokofiev and Schoenberg in a more positive manner than had Skorik, eliminating the pejorative comments. Kholopov also highlighted the "stability" and hence acceptability of what had previously been considered dissonant and thus something to be avoided; he implied that other systems thought to be inherently dissonant and unnatural, like Schoenberg's twelve-tone method, might instead be viewed in a more positive manner. After all, if Prokofiev's systems were but a tonal version of Schoenberg's dodecaphony, and Prokofiev's dissonances were now acceptable, then Schoenberg's dissonances and his method of articulating them should be tolerable as well. Kholopov did not explicitly make this connection in his 1962 essay, but the hierarchy he sketched ultimately encompassed tonality, atonality, and dodecaphony. At the conclusion of his 1967 Prokofiev monograph, he described the full range of the twelve-step systems in detail.[108] "Each modern tonal system represents one of the possible types of organizing twelve tones," he argued, including the "chromatic tonal-functional system," the "special modal systems," "so-called free atonality," and dodecaphony.[109] Prokofiev fit within all of these categories except the last.[110]

The idea that Prokofiev used chromatically inflected harmonic language immediately caused alarm. It was hardly radical, but it challenged the Soviet aesthetic claims about Prokofiev's traditionalism. Kholopov's favorite examples, after all, came from the innocent comic opera *Betrothal in a Monastery*, and he also turned to *Cinderella* and *Romeo and Juliet*, among other "classic" scores.

Thus the term *sovremennost'*—already associated with rebellious aspects of Soviet culture—acquired more radical connotations through the efforts of writers like Kholopov, who ascribed it to the most modern of musical trends. Rebuttals soon appeared in *Sovetskaya muzïka*, but they were not uniformly dismissive. The conservatives in the debate about "contemporary harmony" tended to be reactionary, but they sincerely grappled with the issues and entered into productive dialogue with the reformers—even accepting the premises of their arguments, albeit hesitantly and reluctantly. The Prokofiev debates were theoretical, but they also reflected the shifting politics of the Thaw.

The conservative reaction commenced with a December 1961 *Sovetskaya muzïka* essay by Abram Yusfin (1926–?), which stressed the importance of functional harmony, voice-leading, and solfege in the training of young Soviet composers. Essays by Yuzef Kon (1920–?) and Skorik "continued the discussion," in Kon's words, and indeed the argument dominated subsequent 1962 *Sovetskaya muzïka* issues, which featured lengthy contributions by Viktor Berkov (1907–75), Lev Mazel (1907–?), Boganova, Vadim Salmanov (1912–78), Lidiya Rappoport (1929–?), and Yuriy Tyulin (1893–1978).[111] Most of these conservative critics emphasized the centrality of common practice harmony and disputed the efficacy of teaching young composers "contemporary harmony," since they doubted the existence of such a uniform entity, despite Schnittke's claim to the contrary. Instead, most conservatives advocated a "wide," all-encompassing interpretation of the "contemporary" that could include current tonal approaches and not just twelve-tone or atonal examples.[112] Some condemned the reformist call for the study of "contemporary harmony" outright, because in Yusfin's words "this idea resembles the extremely hasty judgments about the contemporary style [by reformers] in literature, drama, and painting (the recommendations of minimalism, conventionality, and dynamics [*lakonizm, uslovnost', i dinamika*])."[113]

Although Shostakovich was often discussed by the conservatives, the majority invoked Prokofiev as an example of twentieth-century innovation resolutely grounded in traditional tonal thinking. They stressed the tonal basis of Prokofiev's language because they feared that Kholopov's expanded version of tonality (twelve- rather than seven-step scales) would undermine or ultimately overthrow the rules of common practice harmony taught in Soviet conservatories. The debate had substance, but rhetoric and semantics often dominated. An anecdote in Tyulin's essay, one of the last in the *Sovetskaya muzïka* series, neatly summarizes the conservative stance. Tyulin recalled Prokofiev telling him in 1934: "Whoever does not master classical harmony does not have the right to innovation."[114] (For a one-two punch Tyulin quoted a similar statement by Shostakovich: "Without a solid command of traditional harmony there cannot be craft [*masterstvo*], and without craft true innovation is unthinkable.")[115]

Resisting "contemporary harmony" involved promoting traditional professional training and "craft." The Union of Soviet Composers was intimately involved in the debates over "contemporary harmony" in the early 1960s, both in the pages of its official journal, *Sovetskaya muzïka*, and in the colloquies it convened to discuss the matter. Most prominently, the Leningrad Union of Composers held a heated "Discussion on the Harmony of Contemporary Music" on three successive Saturdays beginning February 24 and continuing on March 3 and 10, 1962, during which Kholopov's, Schnittke's, and Tarakanov's reformist views were alternately criticized and defended by Alexander Dolzhansky (1908–66), Iosif Pustïlnik (1905–?), Salmanov, and others.[116]

In this and other gatherings, Prokofiev's music was enlisted to support a conservative position. Such was also the case in the 1962 inaugural issue of the relatively liberal scholarly yearbook *Music and the Present* (*Muzïka i sovremennost'*), which led off with an essay by the musicologist Arnold Sokhor (1924–77). Sokhor opposed the formalist definition of *sovremennost'* offered by the reformers (though he did not mention them by name, he surely had Kholopov, Schnittke, and Tarakanov in mind), claiming that, in focusing on the innovative technical procedures of a given work, they completely ignored its expressive content. Sokhor's preamble gives some sense of his general stance:

> Music and the present . . . this is the problem that today finds itself at the center of attention for Soviet musicians. Life itself advances it before us. Its importance is underscored in Party calls to Soviet artists to vividly and truthfully reflect contemporary reality in their works, to be active assistants of the Party and government in the business of the Communist education of the workers, [and] to strengthen the connection of art with the life of the people. The problem of contemporaneity is thus indissolubly connected with the fundamental questions of our art: questions of Party-mindedness [*partiynost'*] and national character [*narodnost'*], and with the further developments of the method of Socialist Realism. It is therefore understandable that it stands at the center of all of the discussions occurring in the musical realm.[117]

Sokhor develops these ideas in exhaustive detail, concentrating on the compatibility of twentieth-century form and content and offering a purposely obscure definition of *sovremennost'*: "The most fruitful understanding of the contemporaneity of art occurs when its conformity to the problems of our epoch functions as the criterion."[118] Further contortions enable him to conclude that "several of the most important processes of contemporary reality began neither today nor yesterday, but have a more or less lengthy history." To represent the present, in other words, composers needed to take inspiration from historical subjects. But not any subject from any historical period would do: Sokhor has in mind subjects drawn from Soviet history, including the 1905 Revolution, the Great October Revolution, and Lenin.[119]

Like Skorik, Sokhor placed Prokofiev in the proper (that is, official conservative) camp by juxtaposing him with Shostakovich. The latter composer's music, he argued, had earned favor for its "lyrical-dramatic style, with [its] exaggerated psychological contents and sharpest internal contrasts of mood." Now, however, composers were showing greater interest in "objective themes and subjects" of an epic, heroic, and optimistic nature. Sokhor detected a move in Soviet music circles away from Shostakovich's "optimistic-tragedies" and toward Prokofiev's emblematic simplicity (*prostota*).[120] According to Sokhor, "In various genres of Soviet music the influence of works in the tradition of S. Prokofiev is felt with increasing frequency. One could say that Prokofiev has become the principal influence on young contemporary composers." Once negative—recall the 1948 resolution and the attendant fears of producing "little Prokofievs"—the composer's presence in the conservatories had suddenly become positive.[121]

Sokhor acknowledged that, in contrast to Shostakovich, Prokofiev lacked a school of followers, but he nonetheless felt that Prokofiev's "tradition" was "the strongest in contemporary creative activity."[122] The claim evinced utopian thinking, but it held some truth. As Smirnov and Yekimovsky argued, and as Moscow Conservatory instructor Kara Karayev (1918–82) corroborated, Prokofiev served as an influence for emerging composers well into the 1960s.[123] The rejection of Prokofiev was neither as quick nor as complete as Denisov (and others) suggested or encouraged. Nor was Shostakovich entirely beyond reproach.

Sokhor's problematic claims about Prokofiev's stature, buttressing the composer's official designation as a Soviet classic, altogether contravened Kholopov's attempts to advance a richer theoretical reading of Prokofiev's legacy. For Sokhor, "classic" and "contemporary" were interconnected terms; both, moreover, were rooted in the Soviet past. For Kholopov, they were unrelated. Being contemporary, in his view, meant keeping pace with advances in musical thought, the newer the better. Both stances, of course, had political dimensions, even if, as in Kholopov's case, the politics were negative (like those of the young Soviet composers who manipulated twelve-tone rows). Kholopov privileged non-referential modern form, whereas Sokhor privileged socially relevant contemporary content, as did the respective camps to which they belonged

Scholarship on Prokofiev expanded in the final years of the 1960s as more primary source materials became available, usually in the section of *Sovetskaya muzïka* titled "Toward the Study of Prokofiev's Legacy," which appeared in the April issue in conjunction with the anniversary of his birth.[124] The debate about Prokofiev's modernism ebbed as conservatives gradually accepted the reformist positions. It became less controversial to acknowledge the prominence, even dominance of chromaticism in his works. Mazel's three-part essay titled "Concerning the Paths of Development in the Language of Contemporary Music" offers a typical example of this softer stance.[125] The author openly discussed Soviet engagement with the latest compositional practices and techniques of the West, including serialism and aleatorism. In his discussion of twelve-tone methods, Mazel focused almost exclusively on Schoenberg, though he acknowledged that such "modern" figures as Prokofiev and Shostakovich introduced atonal episodes into their works as a contrast to tonality; therefore, he rather paradoxically deduced, they "are less dependent on tonality than the strict dodecaphonist Schoenberg, who is constantly forced to recall tonal-harmonic associations in order to avoid them unwaveringly."[126] Mazel hedged his claims by sympathetically reporting Kholopov's assessment of

Prokofiev's chromaticism and avoidance of standard tonalities as an alternative to Schoenberg's methods.[127] Mazel likewise recognized the existence of a middle ground between tonality and atonality. This middle ground was populated by chromatic harmonies and weakened tonal relationships.[128] Such measured conservative discussion of modernist musical language became increasingly common as the 1960s progressed.[129]

Sokhor returned to the fray with a 1965 essay titled "On the Nature and Expressive Possibilities of Diatonicism," an attempt to bolster the beleaguered diatonic system, then seemingly under attack from all sides. While moderates like Mazel advocated an expanded, more relativistic understanding of tonality, and reformers like Kholopov described dissonance as a potentially stabilizing syntactical element, Sokhor looked to Prokofiev for the "renaissance and renewal of diatonicism," seen also in the music of Stravinsky, Hindemith, Orff, and Sviridov.[130] He responded to those theorists who fixated on Prokofiev's chromatic or expanded diatonic features (notably Kholopov, Boganova, Skorik, and Slonimsky) by coining a new term: dodecatonicism (*dodekatonika*).[131] Although similar in some ways to Kholopov's (and Skorik's) understanding of Prokofiev's "chromatic tonal system," the shift in emphasis implied by Sokhor's label is important. With dodecatonicism, Sokhor created an alternative to dodecaphony that, he hoped, would absorb some of the latter term's cachet. Kholopov criticized Sokhor's neologism because it sounded like dodecaphony and hence confused the theoretical distinctions between the two systems.[132] But the power of the new term lay precisely in this confusion. Sokhor sought to portray Prokofiev as a fundamentally tonal composer whose works offered either a substitute or complement to Schoenberg's system. Thus he pulled Prokofiev from the reformist (modern) camp back into the conservative (classical) camp.

Being Prokofiev

As Mazel's 1965 essay suggested, by the late 1960s the need to be "contemporary" became less urgent, and the term itself less fraught, than had been the case in the early 1960s, the height of the Thaw. Composers, too, were changing course. Many young Soviets, foremost among them Arvo Pärt (b. 1935) and Schnittke, began to turn away from the experimental abstractions of serialism, moving instead to traditionally dramatic, "mimetic" compositional styles.[133] Modernism ceased to have the desired effect of shock and subversion, especially as more official, more senior Soviet composers like Shostakovich began using the chromatic harmonies that had previously been the domain of adventurous upstarts. Simultaneously, Soviet officials and critics became more amenable to advanced techniques, so that by the late 1960s and early 1970s even twelve-tone methods had become politically acceptable—when pragmatically, dramatically employed. By the end of the Thaw (which, in music, coincided with Shostakovich's death), the mimetic approaches adopted by Pärt, Schnittke, and others began to fulfill socialist realist musical demands for accessibility.[134] As "contemporary reality" changed, so too did the tastes of Soviet composers and their audiences.

By the end of the Thaw, Prokofiev had been canonized. In 1972 Tarakanov proclaimed Prokofiev's indubitable importance to Soviet musical composition and scholarship, observing that "the stream of articles, monographs, and collections of essays [about Prokofiev] has now achieved such a degree of intensity that perhaps soon Soviet research to a significant, if not to a decisive, measure will be represented by Prokofievology [*budet predstavlena Prokof'yevedeniyem*]."[135] Tarakanov now perceived a more harmonious Prokofiev: "His style presents an organic unity of the classical and modern, where the well-known, thoroughly mastered appears in new, occasionally extremely unexpected and paradoxical combinations."[136] Although Tarakanov discounted the notion that music advanced like science or technology, he devoted several paragraphs to Prokofiev's prospective role in the music of the future, foregrounding his connections with dance, film, and theater; his uniting of "high" and "low," "serious" (*ser'yozniy*) and "light" (*lyogkiy*) genres and styles; as well as his continued reliance on the "simple (that is, major or minor) triad."[137] Like Pärt, Schnittke, and other Soviet composers disillusioned with Western modishness, Tarakanov advocated a return to traditional dramaturgy, tonality, and popular idioms (all featured in Schnittke's First Symphony of 1972) and saw Prokofiev's innovative use of classical elements as the guiding light. For Tarakanov, as for many others, Prokofiev was the radiant, warming "sun of Russian music" (*solntse russkoy muzïki*).[138]

Kholopov similarly branded Prokofiev the "sunny genius of Russian music" (*solnechnïy geniy russkoy muzïki*) and discerned a balance of elements in his music. The twelve-step system was "neither diatonic nor chromatic," the composer "a classic of Soviet music [and of] modern music."[139] Kholopov, like Tarakanov, concluded his assessment of Prokofiev's sound world with some thoughts on the future. Assessing the "meaning of theory for the development of new music," he argued for a greater exchange between Soviet composition and theory. Rather than waiting to take the full measure of a composer's output, as they had with Prokofiev, theorists needed to address more quickly the newest musical trends. Kholopov was interested not only in Prokofiev's music and its modern techniques, but also in the acceptability of fashionable techniques for emerging composers.

The classic Prokofiev won out. By 1972 the debates had cooled, and Prokofiev had been consigned to the theoretical field awkwardly nicknamed

"Prokofievology"; young composers had moved on. As was the case in the 1950s, Prokofiev was overshadowed by Shostakovich, the indisputably dominant figure in Soviet music. The latter's reputation reached its zenith after his passing in 1975, when foreign and domestic critics alike recognized how much Soviet musical culture depended on him. That year Mazel affirmed that "Soviet music study—insofar as it concerns the study of contemporary music—developed to a significant extent through the analysis of Shostakovich's compositions, and remains indebted to his work."[140] Forgotten was Tarakanov's 1972 claim that the study of "contemporary" music in the Soviet Union emerged from Prokofiev's works.

Unlike the responses to Shostakovich's death, the reaction to Prokofiev's was not primarily musical; it was aesthetic, analytical, and documentary. After Shostakovich's passing composers wrote, and continue to write, works in his memory, often using his DSCH (D–E♭–C–B♮) musical monogram. By contrast, after Prokofiev's death several volumes of expurgated diaries, letters, memoirs, and theoretical essays appeared—most of them subsequently translated into European languages to demonstrate Soviet musical prowess during the cultural Cold War.[141] Such collections appeared in greater numbers than those commemorating Shostakovich.

Although Prokofiev did not inspire the same outpouring of memorial compositions as Shostakovich, some works were written in tribute to him in the following decades, as many by non-Russians as Russians. The best known is Francis Poulenc's Oboe Sonata (1962). Other examples are the quintet for flute, oboe, clarinet, bassoon, and horn, *To the Memory of Prokofiev* (1964) by English composer Geoffrey Bush (1920–98); and the String Quartet no. 1, *In Memory of Sergey Prokofiev,* by the Italian Alberto Colla (b. 1968). Russian offerings include the Piano Sonata, op. 4 (1953/56), by Roman Ledenyov (b. 1930); and the Third Quartet "Preludes, In Memory of Prokofiev" (1965), by Vladimir Vlasov (1903–86). The outer movements of Ledenyov's sonata capture the acerbities of the "modern" Prokofiev— its opening is a distant descendent of the March from *The Love for Three Oranges* while the tranquil middle movement reflects Prokofiev's refined lyricism:

Example 3a. Roman Ledenyov, Piano Sonata, op. 4, first movement, mm. 1–12.

Example 3b. Ledenyov, Piano Sonata, op. 4, second movement, mm. 1–8.

Vlasov's quartet mirrors these same sides of Prokofiev's musical persona. The languid first movement cedes to what musicologist Dmitriy Blagoy (1930–86) terms its "complete antipode," a "grotesquely sinister" second movement:[142]

Example 4a. Vladimir Vlasov, Third Quartet, "Preludes," first movement, mm. 1–14.

Example 4b. Vlasov, Third Quartet, second movement, mm. 1–17.

Example 4b continued

As Blagoy opined in his positive 1961 review of Vlasov's quartet, "With every year Prokofiev's music becomes closer and more familiar," and so "there is every reason to believe that the list of such 'Prokofiev' works will be expanded in the future."[143] But the list remained short, containing dutiful scores like Kabalevsky's *Rondo in Memory of Prokofiev* (1973) for cello and piano, penned for the twentieth anniversary of Prokofiev's passing. Other works, including Karayev's ballet *In the Path of Thunder* (*Tropoyu groma*, 1957), were not inspired by Prokofiev but merely dedicated to him.[144] A recent example, marking the fiftieth anniversary of his death, is Anatoliy Kisselyov's *Fantasia* (2003).

To recall my first image in this essay, on the night of October 31, 1961, Stalin's embalmed body was unceremoniously evicted from the mausoleum in Red Square it had shared with Lenin's remains since 1953. It then was interred under "several truckloads of cement," a symbolic burial of all that Stalin had produced.[145] Soon thereafter, his name and image disappeared from cities, institutions, and awards; Stalingrad, for example, was once again Volgograd. At just this time, Prokofiev was returning to prominence. His music, now thawed, inspired debate and, for conservatives and reformers alike, lived on.

NOTES

I would like to thank Simon Morrison, Elena Dubinets and her family, and Roman Ledenyov for their invaluable assistance in obtaining materials for this essay.

1. Richard Taruskin, "Art and Politics in Prokofiev," *Society* 29, no. 1 (1991): 61. By all official accounts Prokofiev died about an hour before Stalin (at 9 p.m.). The actual cause of Stalin's death—whether he died from a cerebral hemorrhage or was assassinated by his "inner circle" (Beria, Molotov, Malenkov, Khrushchev, and others)—has recently been debated by historians, with most evidence pointing to the conventional official explanation. For a summary, see David Brandenberger, "Stalin's Last Crime? Recent Scholarship on Postwar Soviet Anti-Semitism and the Doctor's Plot," *Kritika* 6, no. 1 (2005): 202–4; see also Simon Sebag Montefiore, *Stalin: The Court of the Red Tsar* (New York: Vintage, 2003), 638–50, esp. 641.

2. Solomon Volkov, *Shostakovich and Stalin: The Extraordinary Relationship Between the Great Composer and the Brutal Dictator*, trans. Antonina W. Bouis (New York: Alfred A. Knopf, 2004). Also see the film *The War Symphonies: Shostakovich Against Stalin* (1997), directed by Larry Weinstein.

3. Laurel E. Fay, *Shostakovich: A Life* (New York: Oxford University Press, 2000), 162 and 226–27. In 1961, Shostakovich went back to teaching in Leningrad but never formally returned to the Moscow Conservatory.

4. Ibid., 214.

5. The best example of this process is the resurrection of his *Cantata for the Twentieth Anniversary of October*, which was belatedly (if not wholly) premiered on April 5, 1966. See Simon Morrison and Nelly Kravetz, "The *Cantata for the Twentieth Anniversary of October*, or How the Specter of Communism Haunted Prokofiev," *Journal of Musicology* 23, no. 2 (2006): 250.

6. In other spheres of Soviet life, the Thaw is generally considered to have ended in the mid- to late 1960s, its close most vividly signaled by the Soviet Union's 1968 invasion of Czechoslovakia. For more on the changing generations in the late-Soviet period, and on the musi-

cal consequences of intergenerational conflict, see my "What Was 'Shostakovich,' and What Came Next?" *Journal of Musicology* 24, no. 3 (2007): 297–338; the consideration of Shostakovich's role in Soviet music after his death in that essay serves as a companion to the present one. See also my "From Scriabin to Pink Floyd: The ANS Synthesizer and the Politics of Soviet Music Between Thaw and Stagnation," in *Otherwise Engaged: Avant-Garde Music and the Sixties*, ed. Robert Adlington (New York: Oxford University Press, forthcoming).

7. This and other thematic points made in this essay are developed in my *Such Freedom, If Only Musical: Unofficial Soviet Music and Society During the Thaw* (New York: Oxford University Press, forthcoming).

8. Marina Nest'yeva, *Sergey Prokof'yev* (Chelyabinsk: Arkaim, 2003), 204–13.

9. "Vïdayushchiysya sovetskiy kompozitor," *Sovetskoye iskusstvo*, March 18, 1953; "Pamyati S. S. Prokof'yeva," *Sovetskaya muzïka* 4 (1953): 117. The first article bears twenty-seven signatures; the second is unsigned. For the Western reaction to their publication, see "Prokofieff Is Lauded: Leading Soviet Composers Pay Memorial Tribute to Colleague," *New York Times*, March 19, 1953.

10. "Prokofieff, Soviet Composer, Dies; In Favor After Communist Rebuke," *New York Times*, March 9, 1953 (as well as "Sergei Prokofieff," an editorial in the same issue). See also Olin Downes, "A Great Composer: Prokofieff at His Best Was a Modern Master," *New York Times*, March 15, 1953.

11. Yevgeny Yevtushenko, *A Precocious Autobiography*, trans. Andrew R. MacAndrew (New York: E. P. Dutton, 1963), 84.

12. Elena Zubkova, *Russia After the War: Hopes, Illusions, and Disappointments, 1945–1957*, trans. and ed. Hugh Ragsdale (Armonk: M. E. Sharpe, 1998), 152.

13. Joshua Rubenstein, *Tangled Loyalties: The Life and Times of Ilya Ehrenburg* (New York: Basic Books, 1996), 279. Ehrenburg and Prokofiev were well acquainted; in 1950, for example, Ehrenburg proposed that they collaborate on an oratorio. See M. A. Mendel'son-Prokof'yeva, "Vospominaniya o Sergeye Prokof'yeve. Fragment: 1946–1950," in *Sergey Prokof'yev: Vospominaniya, pis'ma, stat'i*, ed. M. P. Rakhmanova (Moscow: Gosudarstvennïy tsentral'nïy muzey muzïkal'noy kul'turï imeni M. I. Glinki, 2004), 199–201.

14. Quoted in Elizabeth Wilson, *Shostakovich: A Life Remembered*, 2nd ed. (Princeton: Princeton University Press, 2006), 312.

15. Quoted in Fay, *Shostakovich: A Life*, 184.

16. Valentina Kholopova and Enzo Restan'o, *Sofiya Gubaydulina* (Moscow: Kompozitor, 1996), 15. This book is a re-translation from the Italian of Enzo Restagno, *Gubajdulina* (Turin: E.D.T., 1991).

17. Zubkova, *Russia After the War*, 153.

18. Ibid., 154; see also Jeffrey Brooks, *Thank You, Comrade Stalin! Soviet Public Culture from Revolution to Cold War* (Princeton: Princeton University Press, 2000), 233 and 238.

19. Al'fred Shnitke and Dmitriy Shul'gin, *Godï neizvestnosti Al'freda Shnitke: Besedï s kompozitorom* (Moscow: Delovaya liga, 1993), 13.

20. Edison Denisov and Jean-Pierre Armengaud, *Entretiens avec Denisov: Un Compositeur sous le régime soviétique* (Paris: Editions Plume, 1993), 51–52; and Shnitke and Shul'gin, *Godï neizvestnosti Al'freda Shnitke*, 13–14.

21. Denisov and Armengaud, *Entretiens avec Denisov*, 52. Regarding the suppression of Shostakovich's and Prokofiev's works after the 1948 Resolution, pianist Svyatoslav Richter commented: "Of course, there was no formal ban on public performances of their music, but it was just as if there was, and certainly that's what was intended." Sviatoslav Richter, *Notebooks and Conversations*, ed. Bruno Monsaingeon, trans. Stewart Spencer (Princeton: Princeton University Press, 2001), 62–63. On the bans that Glavrepertkom (the Main Repertory Committee) did in fact enact, see "Iz arkhivov," *Sovetskaya muzïka* 4 (1991): 17; Fay, *Shostakovich: A Life*, 172; Kiril Tomoff, *Creative Union: The Professional Organization of Soviet Composers, 1939–1953* (Ithaca: Cornell University Press, 2006), 275–77; and Alla Bogdanova, *Muzïka i vlast' (poststalinskiy period)* (Moscow: Naslediye, 1995).

22. "Plan rabotï NSO teoretiko-kompozitorskogo fakul'teta [1954/55 uch. g.]." From the personal archive of the late Yuriy Kholopov. For a representative Soviet assessment of Prokofiev's

Fourth and Sixth symphonies, see Israel [Izraíl] V. Nestyev, *Prokofiev*, trans. Florence Jonas (Stanford: Stanford University Press, 1960), 235, 401–2 (Fourth), and 398–401 (Sixth).

23. Shnitke and Shul'gin, *Godï neizvestnosti Al'freda Shnitke*, 13–14; Denisov and Armengaud, *Entretiens avec Denisov*, 42.

24. Alfred Schnittke, "On Prokofiev (1990)," in *A Schnittke Reader*, ed. Alexander Ivashkin, trans. John Goodliffe (Bloomington: Indiana University Press, 2002), 65.

25. Denisov and Armengaud, *Entretiens avec Denisov*, 53.

26. Richter, *Notebooks and Conversations*, 67.

27. "Resolution of the Central Committee of the All-Union Communist Party (Bolsheviks) of 10 February 1948," in *Music Since 1900*, ed. Laura Kuhn and Nicolas Slonimsky, 6th ed. (New York: Schirmer Reference, 2001), 943. On the aftereffects of the 1948 Resolution, see Tomoff, *Creative Union*, 124 and 206–7; as well as Levon Hakobian, *Music of the Soviet Age, 1917–1987* (Stockholm: Melos Music Literature, 1998), 208–10.

28. Quoted in Alexander Werth, *Musical Uproar in Moscow* (London: Turnstile Press, 1949), 60–61. The role of the conservatories in enforcing the 1948 Resolution is discussed by A. Zhivtsov, "Sistema muzïkal'nogo obrazovaniya nuzhdayetsya v reforme," *Sovetskaya muzïka* 4 (1948): 2–64.

29. A. Kostomolotskiy, "Pedagogical Humor," repr. in Fay, *Shostakovich: A Life*, 163; and David Fanning, "Shostakovich and His Pupils," in *Shostakovich and His World*, ed. Laurel E. Fay (Princeton: Princeton University Press, 2004), 284 .

30. Fay, *Shostakovich: A Life*, 164; Marian Koval', "Tvorcheskiy put' D. Shostakovicha," *Sovetskaya muzïka* 2 (1948): 47–61; 3 (1948): 31–43; and 4 (1948): 8–19.

31. The composer Ivan Dzerzhinsky (1909–78) remarked, "There is anxiety, for example, over the highly talented Shostakovich's artistic development in the past six years, for a good many young composers are influenced by him." I. Dzerzhinskiy, "Borot'sya za realisticheskoye iskusstvo!" *Sovetskaya muzïka* 1 (1954): 48, quoted in Boris Schwarz, *Music and Musical Life in Soviet Russia: Enlarged Edition, 1917–1981* (Bloomington: Indiana University Press, 1983), 277; trans. amended.

32. Kholopova and Restan'o, *Sofiya Gubaydulina*, 15–16 and 13.

33. Quoted in Wilson, *Shostakovich: A Life Remembered*, 347; see also Kholopova and Restan'o, *Sofiya Gubaydulina*, 16. Emphasis in original.

34. Quoted in Wilson, *Shostakovich: A Life Remembered*, 348.

35. Denisov and Armengaud, *Entretiens avec Denisov*, 53.

36. Ibid. Almost four decades after Prokofiev's death, in a speech delivered at the October 1990 Prokofiev festival in Duisberg, Germany, Schnittke described the composer's funeral procession allegorically. To participate in it, he intimated, was to resist the State. Schnittke, "On Prokofiev (1990)," 65–66.

37. Denisov and Armengaud, *Entretiens avec Denisov*. Denisov's anecdote conflicts with the facts of Prokofiev's death and funeral services. Prokofiev's widow received visitors on the night of his death; his memorial occurred on March 6 and 7 in Moscow's House of Composers (he was buried on March 7). Stalin's death was not publicly announced until the morning of March 6, 1953. Thus Denisov must have been heading to the House of Composers and not Prokofiev's apartment when he had his purported encounter with the police.

38. Denisov, "Sonatnaya forma v tvorchestve S. Prokof'yeva," in *S. S. Prokof'yev: Stat'i i issledovaniya*, ed. V. Blok (Moscow: Muzïka, 1972); repr., *Sovremennaya muzïka i problemï evolyutsiy kompozitorskoy tekhniki* (Moscow: Sovetskiy kompozitor, 1986), 31–45. An unpublished draft of the essay is cited in Sergey Slonimskiy, *Simfonii Prokof'yeva: Opït issledovaniya* (Leningrad: Muzïka, 1964), 7.

39. Denisov and Shul'gin, *Priznaniye Edisona Denisova: Po materialam besed* (Moscow: Kompozitor, 1998), 21.

40. Ibid., 19–20.

41. See Schmelz, "What Was 'Shostakovich,' and What Came Next?" 305–10.

42. Denisov and Shul'gin, *Priznaniye Edisona Denisova*, 21.

43. Denisov added: "[Prokofiev] is not very Russian; his psychology is rather American." Denisov and Armengaud, *Entretiens avec Denisov*, 53–54. Denisov also took Prokofiev to task for structural problems, including a lack of "plasticity" (43, 45–46), and for the grotesque features of his early works (132). The references to Prokofiev in Denisov's diaries are likewise critical.

Peter J. Schmelz

See *Neizvestnïy Denisov: iz zapisnïkh knizhek (1980/81–1986, 1995)* (Moscow: Kompozitor, 1997), esp. 18–20 of the introduction by theorist Valeriya Tsenova.

44. Denisov and Armengaud, *Entretiens avec Denisov,* 54.

45. Denisov and Shul'gin, *Priznaniye Edisona Denisova,* 22; Denisov and Armengaud, *Entretiens avec Denisov,* 69. This was Denisov's assumption about the older composers' tastes; Shostakovich did not entirely discount Bartók. See Fay, *Shostakovich: A Life,* 176 and 258.

46. The essays in question—"Strunnïye kvartetï Belï Bartoka" (1965), "Ob orkestrovke D. Shostakovicha" (1967), "Dzhaz i novaya muzïka" (1968), and "Variatsii op. 27 dlya fortepiano A. Veberna" (1972)—appear in Denisov, *Sovremennaya muzïka.*

47. Sergey Slonimskiy, *Burleski, elegii, difirambï v prezrennoy proze* (St. Petersburg: Kompozitor, 2000), 117; see also Slonimskiy, "Zapretit' zapretï!" in *Georgiy Sviridov v vospominaniyakh sovremennikov,* ed. A. B. Vol'fov (Moscow: Molodaya gvardiya, 2006), 91.

48. Marina Sabinina also detected the influence of Prokofiev in the development section of the first movement and melodic writing of the second movement. "Fortepiannïy kvintet Andreya Volkonskogo," *Sovetskaya muzïka* 6 (1956): 22.

49. Dmitriy N. Smirnov, "Moy Shostakovich," *Muzïkal'naya akademiya* 3 (2006): 31.

50. Dmitriy N. Smirnov, "Prokofjew und Schostakowitsch," in *Schräg zur Linie des Sozialistischen Realismus? Prokofjews spätere Sonaten sowie Orchester und Bühnenwerke,* ed. Ernst Kuhn (Berlin: Ernst Kuhn, 2005), 35.

51. Smirnov, "Moy Shostakovich," 31.

52. Yuriy Kholopov, "Nashi v Anglii: I. Dmitriy Smirnov," in *Muzïka iz bïvshego SSSR,* vol. 2, ed. Valeriya Tsenova (Moscow: Kompozitor, 1996), 257.

53. Smirnov, "Moy Shostakovich," 31.

54. Viktor Yekimovskiy, *Avtomonografiya* (Moscow: Kompozitor, 1997), 12.

55. Ibid., 13 and 365.

56. Vladimir Barskiy, "Liricheskoye otstupleniye s kommentariyami ili tot samïy Yekimovskiy," in *Muzïka iz bïvshego SSSR,* vol. 1, ed. Valeriya Tsenova, (Moscow: Kompozitor, 1994), 241.

57. Yekimovskiy, *Avtomonografiya,* 354.

58. Ibid.

59. Slonimskiy, "Zapretit' zapretï!" 90 and 95. In a 1978 diary entry, Sviridov recalled that, when he was a student, "Prokofiev's music did not make any kind of impression. . . . Prokofiev thus remained a composer whom I could not love; he always seemed to me a bit toy-like (spoiled muse!), inauthentic, a clown with cranberry juice instead of blood." Here Sviridov quotes from Alexander Blok's 1906 play *Balaganchik* (*The puppet theater booth*). Georgiy Sviridov, *Muzïka kak sud'ba,* ed. Aleksandr Belonenko (Moscow: Molodaya gvardiya, 2002), 132 and 637.

60. Slonimskiy, "Zapretit' zapretï!" 91.

61. Nest'yev, "Klassik XX stoletiya (zametki o roli Prokof'yeva v muzïkal'noy kul'ture sovremennosti)," in *Sergey Prokof'yev: Stat'i i materialï,* ed. I. V. Nest'yev and G. Ya. Edel'man (Moscow: Sovetskiy kompozitor, 1962), 11–52. The author's daughter traces the stages in Prokofiev's official recognition in her biography of the composer (Nest'yeva, *Sergey Prokof'yev,* 204–13). For more on the process see S. S. *Prokof'yev: Materialï, dokumentï, vospominaniya,* ed. S. I. Shlifshteyn (Moscow: Muzgiz, 1956; rev. ed., 1961; in English, 1960; 2nd English ed., 1968; in German, 1965); I. Nest'yev, *Prokof'yev* (Moscow: Gosudarstvennoye muzïkal'noye izdatel'stvo, 1957; in English as Nestyev, *Prokofiev*); I. Martïnov, *Laureat Leninskoy premiy: Sergey Prokof'yev. Kratkiy ocherk zhizni i tvorchestva* (Moscow: Znaniye, 1958); and Wilson, *Shostakovich: A Life Remembered,* 350–53. Kholopov usefully surveys the Soviet theoretical work related to Prokofiev (most of it from after his death) in "Tvorchestvo Prokof'yeva v sovetskom teoreticheskom muzïkoznanii," in S. S. *Prokof'yev: Stat'i i issledovaniya,* 301–2. Finally, Slonimskiy gives a "short survey of the literature" on Prokofiev in *Simfonii Prokof'yeva,* 5–8.

62. An advertisement for the defense of Nestyev's dissertation, "Tvorcheskiy put' S. S. Prokof'yeva," appeared in *Vechernyaya Moskva* on May 22, 1945. My thanks to Simon Morrison for bringing it to my attention.

63. Nest'yev, "Put' Sergeya Prokof'yeva," *Sovetskaya muzïka* 5 (1953): 22 (see also 31); the essay was reprinted in *Sovetskaya simfonicheskaya muzïka: Sbornik statey,* ed. M. Grinberg (Moscow: Gosudarstvennoye muzïkal'noye izdatel'stvo, 1955), 69–88.

64. "Collected" in this context means selected, rather than complete.

65. Nest'yev, "Tvorchestvo Sergeya Prokof'yeva," in S. Prokof'yev, *Sobraniye sochineniy*, vol. 1, ed. N. Anosov et al. (Moscow: Gosudarstvennoye muzïkal'noye izdatel'stvo, 1955), xvii.

66. This list undercuts Alexander Ivashkin's claim that "even works by Prokofiev and Shostakovich were not readily available [in the 1950s]. In fact, Prokofiev's piano sonatas and piano concertos remained unpublished in Russia until the late 1960s." Alexander Ivashkin, *Alfred Schnittke* (London: Phaidon Press Limited, 1996), 56.

67. Mattias Sokol'skiy [Grinberg], "Tormozï sovetskoy muzïki," *Sovetskaya muzïka* 5 (1956): 58–59.

68. Ibid., 58.

69. This performance information from Richard Taruskin, "*War and Peace*," in *The New Grove Dictionary of Opera*, 4 vols., ed. Stanley Sadie, (London: MacMillan, 1992), 4:1101.

70. Richard Taruskin, "*Semyon Kotko*," in *The New Grove Dictionary of Opera*, 4:312–13; see also Schwarz, *Music and Musical Life in Soviet Russia*, 329.

71. Nestyev's biography was actually first published abroad under the title *Sergei Prokofiev: His Musical Life* (New York: Alfred A. Knopf, 1946). His daughter notes that the edition was denounced for its "formalist mistakes" (Nest'yeva, *Sergey Prokof'yev*, 207).

72. Sabinina, *Sergey Prokof'yev* (Moscow: Glavpoligrafprom, 1957); Martïnov, *Laureat Leninskoy premii: Sergey Prokof'yev*; Tat'yana Boganova, *National'no-Russkiye traditsii v muzïke S. Prokof'yeva* (Moscow: Sovetskiy kompozitor, 1961). *Sovetskaya muzïka* dedicated the bulk of its April 1961 issue to the seventieth anniversary of Prokofiev's birth, even though a planned festival of his music had been scrapped. The year also witnessed the release of a film about his career.

73. "Pamyati S. S. Prokof'yeva."

74. Dmitriy Kabalevskiy, "O Sergeye Prokof'yeve," in Prokof'yev, *Sobraniye sochineniy*, iv.

75. Nestyev, *Prokofiev*, 487.

76. Nest'yev, "Spor o Prokof'yeve (zametki o Prokof'yevskoy sessii v Varshave)," *Sovetskaya muzïka* 3 (1960): 167. His Warsaw paper was titled "Znacheniye tvorchestva Prokof'yeva v muzïke XX stoletiya" (The significance of Prokofiev's work for music of the twentieth century).

77. Schwarz, *Music and Musical Life in Soviet Russia*, 323–24.

78. Nest'yev, "Klassik XX stoletiya," 26–28. "Pseudoclassicism" was a favored term; Nestyev also used it in the 1960 Polish response ("Spor o Prokof'yeve," 165).

79. In his letter of reply to the 1948 resolution, Prokofiev declared: "Tonal and diatonic music lends many more possibilities than atonal and chromatic music, which is evident from the impasse reached by Schoenberg and his disciples. In some of my works in recent years there are sporadic atonal moments. Without much sympathy, I nevertheless made use of this device, mainly for the sake of contrast, in order to bring tonal passages to the fore. In the future I hope to get rid of this mannerism." "Discussion at a General Assembly of Soviet Composers, Moscow, 17–26 February 1948," in *Music Since 1900*, 950–52.

80. Nest'yev, "Klassik XX stoletiya," 27–28.

81. Ibid., 35. Nestyev likely meant Pierre Boulez and Karlheinz Stockhausen, among others.

82. Ibid., 52. Nestyev also urged young composers to model themselves on Prokofiev in "Put' Sergeya Prokof'yeva," 31.

83. M. Skorik, "Prokof'yev i Shenberg," *Sovetskaya muzïka* 1 (1962): 34–38. In 1967, Skorik completed a dissertation at Kiev University on Prokofiev's treatment of modes.

84. This and the following quotations in the paragraph from Skorik, "Prokof'yev i Shenberg," 34–38.

85. Ibid., 38

86. On the Soviet response to Schoenberg, see Schwarz, "Arnold Schoenberg in Soviet Russia," *Perspectives of New Music* 4, no. 1 (1965): 86–94; and Grigoriy Shneyerson, *O muzïke, zhivoy i myortvoy* (Moscow: Muzïka, 1964). On Shostakovich's response, see Fay, *Shostakovich: A Life*, 214–15 and 258; and Schmelz, "Shostakovich's 'Twelve-Tone' Music and the Politics and Practice of Soviet Serialism," in Fay, *Shostakovich and His World*, 303–4.

87. Kholopov, "Tvorchestvo Prokof'yeva v sovetskom teoreticheskom muzïkoznanii," 327.

88. Susan E. Reid, "The Exhibition *Art of Socialist Countries*, Moscow 1958–59, and the Con-

Peter J. Schmelz

temporary Style of Painting," in *Style and Socialism: Modernity and Material Culture in Post-War Eastern Europe*, ed. Susan E. Reid and David Crowley (New York: Berg, 2000), 102.

89. Iurii Gerchuk, "The Aesthetics of Everyday Life in the Khrushchev Thaw in the USSR (1954–64)," in Reid and Crowley, *Style and Socialism*, 90.

90. Tomoff, *Creative Union*, 153 and 184.

91. On Soviet youth culture from 1950 to 1980, see Hilary Pilkington, *Russia's Youth and Its Culture: A Nation's Constructors and Constructed* (New York: Routledge, 1994), esp. chap. 2.

92. Sergei Prokofiev, "Autobiography," in S. *Prokofiev: Autobiography, Articles, Reminiscences*, ed. S. Shlifstein, trans. Rose Prokofieva (Moscow: Foreign Languages Publishing House, n.d.), 50.

93. See M. E. Tarakanov, "Traditsii i novatorstvo v sovremennoy sovetskoy muzïke (opït postanovki problemï)," in *Problemï traditsiy i novatorstva v sovremennoy muzïke*, ed. A. M. Gol'tsman (Moscow: Sovetskiy kompozitor, 1982), 30–51.

94. Nest'yev, "Zametki o sovremennoy teme v muzïke," *Sovetskaya muzïka* 1 (1958): 12.

95. Schwarz, *Music and Musical Life in Soviet Russia*, 351 (emphasis in original).

96. Shnitke, "Razvivat' nauku o garmonii: Pis'mo v redaktsiyu," *Sovetskaya muzïka* 10 (1961): 44.

97. These earlier essays included, in sequence, S. Skrebkov, "O sovremennoy garmonii," *Sovetskaya muzïka* 6 (1957): 74–83; V. Berkov, "Yeshcho o politonal'nosti," *Sovetskaya muzïka* 10 (1957): 84–86; Skrebkov, "Otvet V. Berkovu," *Sovetskaya muzïka* 10 (1957): 87–88; Berkov, "Spor ne okonchen," *Sovetskaya muzïka* 1 (1958): 53–56; V. Blok, "Neskol'ko zamechaniy o politonal'noy garmonii," *Sovetskaya muzïka* 4 (1958): 49–52; V. Vanslov, "K voprosu o politonal'nosti," *Sovetskaya muzïka* 4 (1958): 53–55; and K. Rozenshil'd, "K sporam o sovremennoy garmonii," *Sovetskaya muzïka* 6 (1958): 100–110; and *Sovetskaya muzïka* 8 (1958): 38–50.

98. Tarakanov, "Neotlozhnïye problemï," *Sovetskaya muzïka* 10 (1961): 50 (emphasis added).

99. Yuriy Kholopov, "Nablyudeniya nad sovremennoy garmoniyey," *Sovetskaya muzïka* 11 (1961): 50–55.

100. Yuriy Kholopov, "O sovremennïkh chertakh garmonii S. Prokof'yeva," in *Chertï stilya S. Prokof'yeva: Sbornik teoreticheskikh statey*, ed. L. Berger (Moscow: Sovetskiy kompozitor, 1962), 253–311; Kholopov, *Sovremennïye chertï garmonii Prokof'yeva* (Moscow: Muzïka, 1967).

101. Kholopov, "O sovremennïkh chertakh garmonii S. Prokof'yeva," 254.

102. Yuriy Kholopov, "Tvorchestvo Prokof'yeva v sovetskom teoreticheskom muzïkoznanii," 303, 305, 328.

103. Ibid., 303–4.

104. Ibid., 304.

105. Note that the idiosyncratic marking of the degrees (i.e. ♯III for what would normally be the uninflected mediant in C major) reflects Kholopov's idea that each of these alterations have a separate meaning within the world of twelve-step tonality. In his ambiguous formulation, the "numbering of the degrees is in some respects inaccurate, since it follows the dual meaning of the intervals (major and minor intervals, etc.)." Enharmonic spellings, especially of the tritone, complicate matters for Kholopov (hence the designation ♯IV and ♭V in the example). He consequently maintained that "strictly speaking, one should set a separate indicator for each of the twelve steps, considering the tonic the first step and the leading tone the twelfth." Kholopov, "O sovremennïkh chertakh garmonii S. Prokof'yeva," 259.

106. Ibid., 257.

107. Ibid., 257 and 266; emphasis in original.

108. Kholopov, *Sovremennïye chertï garmonii Prokof'yeva*, 434–35.

109. Ibid.

110. Ibid., 326.

111. A. Yusfin, "Davayte razberyomsya!" *Sovetskaya muzïka* 12 (1961): 46–48; Yu. Kon, "Prodolzhim diskussiyu," *Sovetskaya muzïka* 1 (1962): 31–34; Berkov, "K izucheniyu sovremennoy garmonii," *Sovetskaya muzïka* 4 (1962): 39–43; L. Mazel', "K diskussii o sovremennoy garmonii," *Sovetskaya muzïka* 5 (1962): 52–61; Boganova, "V poiskakh noviznï," *Sovetskaya muzïka* 6 (1962): 68–71; V. Salmanov, "Delo slozhnoye i vazhnoye," *Sovetskaya muzïka* 7 (1962): 48–50; "Spor prodolzhayetsya (V Leningradskom soyuze kompozitorov)," *Sovetskaya muzïka* 7 (1962): 51–52; Lidiya Rappoport, "O muzïkal'nom yazïke A. Oneggera," *Sovetskaya muzïka* 8 (1962): 52–56; and Yu. Tyulin, "Mïsli o sovremennoy garmonii," *Sovetskaya muzïka* 10 (1962): 100–105. A greatly

expanded version of this last essay was published the following year under the title "Sovremennaya garmoniya i yeyo istoricheskoye proiskhozhdeniye," in *Voprosï sovremennoy muzïki*, ed. I. V. Golubovskiy (Leningrad: Muzgiz, 1963), 108–56.

112. See Skrebkov, "O sovremennoy garmonii," 74.

113. Yusfin, "Davayte raberyomsya!" 48. The author noted that these issues had been discussed in other venues. See, for example, Yuriy Nagibin, "Chto sovremenno?" *Literaturnaya gazeta*, December 3, 1960, cited in Reid, "The Exhibition *Art of Socialist Countries*, Moscow 1958–59," 103; also Gerchuk, "The Aesthetics of Everyday Life in the Khrushchev Thaw in the USSR (1954–64)," 90.

114. Tyulin, "Mïsli o sovremennoy garmonii," 104.

115. Ibid.

116. An official summary appeared in "Spor prodolzhayetsya (v Leningradskom soyuze kompozitorov)"; a transcript is preserved in the Russian State Archive of Literature and Art, f. 2077, op. 1, yed. khr. 2058 ("Stenogrammï diskussii o garmonii sovremennoy muzïki").

117. A. Sokhor, "O sovremennosti v muzïke nashikh dney," *Muzïka i sovremennost'* 1 (1962): 3.

118. Ibid., 6.

119. Ibid., 7 and 10.

120. Ibid., 41–42. The term "optimistic tragedy" was often applied to Shostakovich's music at the time (it comes from a 1933 play by Vsevolod Vishnevsky, later the basis of a 1965 opera by Alexander Kholminov). See Andrey Volkonskiy's article on Shostakovich's Tenth Symphony, "Optimisticheskaya tragediya," *Sovetskaya muzïka* 3 (1954): 25–28.

121. Sokhor, "O sovremennosti v muzïke nashikh dney," 31.

122. Ibid., 58.

123. K. Karayev, "Mïsli o Prokof'yeve," *Sovetskaya muzïka* 4 (1961): 89.

124. See for example "K izucheniyu naslediya S. S. Prokof'yeva" in *Sovetskaya muzïka* 3 (1962): 102–10; also 8 (1962): 40–51; 3 (1963): 42–56; 4 (1966): 27–50; 4 (1967): 77–99; and 4 (1968): 95–111.

125. Lev Mazel', "O putyakh razvitiya yazïka sovremennoy muzïki," *Sovetskaya muzïka* 6 (1965): 15–26; 7 (1965): 6–20; and 8 (1965): 6–20.

126. Mazel', "O putyakh," *Sovetskaya muzïka* 8 (1965): 15.

127. Ibid., 15–16.

128. Ibid.

129. See Slonimskiy, *Simfonii Prokof'yeva*, 16–17, for a moderate assessment of Prokofiev's symphonic language; see M. E. Tarakanov, *Stil' simfonii Prokof'yeva: Issledovaniye* (Moscow: Muzïka, 1968).

130. Sokhor, "O prirode i vïrazitel'nïkh vozmozhnostyakh diatoniki," in *Voprosï teorii i estetiki muzïki*, vol. 4 (Moscow: Muzïka, 1965), 160. Skrebkov likewise maintained a conservative position. In a series of Moscow Conservatory lectures on harmony he defended "the theoretical principles of harmony established by our theorists on the basis of their study of classical music [common practice tonality]." *Garmoniya v sovremennom muzïke: Ocherki* (Moscow: Muzïka, 1965), 5.

131. Sokhor, "O prirode i vïrazitel'nïkh vozmozhnostyakh diatoniki," 174–75. Sokhor also used the term twelve-step heterotonicism (*dvenadtsatistupennaya geterotonika*) to describe the presence of several different tonics in the course of a piece.

132. Kholopov also worried that the new coinage implied twelve separate tonics, when the "necessary term should presume a single tonic" ("Tvorchestvo Prokof'yeva v sovetskom teoreticheskom muzïkoznanii," 309). Khrushchev touted the popular misunderstanding of dodecaphony by declaring in a March 8, 1963, speech that "apparently it means the same as the word 'cacophony.'" Quoted in Priscilla Johnson [McMillan], *Khrushchev and the Arts: The Politics of Soviet Culture, 1962–1964* (Cambridge, Mass.: MIT Press, 1965), 175.

133. I borrow this terminology from Karol Berger, *A Theory of Art* (New York: Oxford University Press, 2000).

134. Schnittke's renewed respect for tradition is evinced in a 1972 essay on Prokofiev's piano sonatas, in which he declared: "In [Prokofiev's] works classicalness, strictness and rational structures are organically combined with striking innovation in musical language." Schnittke also discussed the theatrical elements in Prokofiev's instrumental compositions—a reflection of his

own growing interest in mimetic composition. "O nekotorïkh chertakh novatorstva v fortepi-annïkh sonatnïkh tsiklakh Prokof'yeva," in *S. S. Prokof'yev: Stat'i i issledovaniya*, 185 and 214–15.
135. M. E. Tarakanov, "Prokof'yev i nekotorïye voprosï sovremennogo muzïkal'nogo yazïka," in *S. S. Prokof'yev: Stat'i i issledovaniya*, 7.
136. Ibid., 9.
137. Ibid., 30–36.
138. Ibid., 36. For more metaphors of Prokofiev as the sun, see "Chto vï dumayete o solntse?" (What do you think about the sun?) in the Prokofiev centennial issue of *Sovetskaya muzïka* 4 (1991): 2–7, 50–54, and 89–95. During his childhood, the composer posed this question to friends, recording their responses in a notebook. Arthur Rubinstein told him, "You, my dear Prokofiev, might say: 'I am the sun! [*solntse—eto ya!*].'" Ibid., 2.
139. Kholopov, "Tvorchestvo Prokof'yeva v sovetskom teoreticheskom muzïkoznanii," 326 ("sunny genius"); 309 ("neither diatonic nor chromatic"); and 325 ("classic" and "modern").
140. Mazel', "Razdum'ya ob istoricheskom meste tvorchestva Shostakovicha," *Sovetskaya muzïka* 9 (1975): 8.
141. The most significant publications were *S. S. Prokof'yev: Materialï, dokumentï, vospominaniya* and *Sergey Prokof'yev: Stat'i i materialï*.
142. D. Blagoy, "Kvartet 'pamyati Prokof'yeva,'" *Sovetskaya muzïka* 4 (1961): 42. K. Kondakhchan paraphrased Blagoy's description of the second movement in his introduction to the published score. See V. Vlasov, *Tretiy kvartet, Prelyudii dlya dvukh skripok, al'ta i violoncheli* (Moscow: Muzïka, 1965), 2.
143. Blagoy, "Kvartet 'pamyati Prokof'yeva,'" 44.
144. See Karayev, "Mïsli o Prokof'yeve," 89. Poems were also written in his memory; see Vadim Semernin, "S. S. Prokof'yev," in *Den' poeziy, 1965* (Moscow: Sovetskiy pisatel', 1965), 68.
145. William Taubman, *Khrushchev: The Man and His Era* (New York: W. W. Norton, 2003), 514–15; and Roy A. Medvedev and Zhores A. Medvedev, *Khrushchev: The Years in Power*, trans. Andrew R. Durkin (New York: W. W. Norton, 1978), 147.

Beyond Death and Evil: Prokofiev's Spirituality and Christian Science

LEON BOTSTEIN

The long shadow cast by the nineteenth century's undue fascination with the biography of great composers is hard to escape. As a musical culture tied to concert life and domestic amateurism spread to an ever larger literate urban public, the tradition already well established in the visual arts, associated with Giorgio Vasari, found its imitators in music journalism. Biography held the key to the mystery of inspiration and genius. The early discovery and declaration of exceptional genius, as well as the inevitable struggle for realization and recognition, became routine hallmarks of composers' biographies.[1] Through biography, amateurs and connoisseurs learned, at one and the same time, about musical genius and their own ordinariness. The popular genre of biographical storytelling about composers thrived alongside scholarship and criticism. Consider, for example, Otto Jahn's biography of Mozart and, later, Max Kalbeck's massive account of the life of Johannes Brahms. Equally important were often hagiographical accounts of famous composers by close contemporaries, including Anton Schindler's on Beethoven, Liszt's book on Chopin, and Modest Tchaikovsky's biography of his brother.

The cult of the genius became a self-justifying ideology. The great composer was so extraordinary and deviant that he was doomed to suffer, making his life hardly the object of envy. But the embrace of his work was an ennobling experience, a visible sign to the ordinary listener of refinement and depth of feeling. Biography in the nineteenth century, notably those by La Mara (Marie Lipsius), provided comfort and mitigated envy. Once the price paid by genius was recognized, conventional happiness on the part of the average music lover appeared the object of gratitude. Extreme individuality and routine conformism were reconciled. A reader repeatedly confronted by accounts of the alienation and loneliness experienced by great composers could feel more at home with being ordinary.

Envy was supplanted and sustained by a mix of compassion, condescension, and adoration.

Prokofiev was born in 1891, a high-water mark for these late-Romantic attitudes, a time in which such cultural prejudices were made all the more plausible by Richard Wagner's construct of himself and his vision of music history, particularly the career of Beethoven.[2] Sergey's talent was first noticed by his mother, to whom he remained particularly devoted. She cherished hope that her only surviving child and son should turn out to possess exceptional talent. She, like Abraham Mendelssohn, Adam Liszt, and countless parents in succeeding generations, sought confirmation of her suspicion of incipient greatness. She consulted great musicians. Glier and Glazunov would be to Prokofiev what Cherubini had been to Mendelssohn and, in legend, Beethoven to Liszt. Prokofiev's lifelong pose of arrogance and self-confidence were by-products of the extent to which he saw himself as vindicating in his career the premises disseminated by popular biography. He had demonstrated striking precocity, early anointment by authority, and in his conservatory years sufficient rebellious notoriety.

The nineteenth century's cult of personality led as well to a market for autobiography by musicians, the most fanciful and distinguished of which was penned by Berlioz. The most notorious example was Wagner's elaborate effort to control the account of his life and career in his mendacious *Mein Leben*. Twentieth-century figures in the history of music were equally eager to tell their stories, though they were more circumspect and cautious, reflecting some ambivalence toward Romantic conceits about inspiration and the making of art. Prokofiev was no exception. Like Wagner, he published his own autobiography. It primarily covered his childhood and education. He suppressed the meticulous diaries he kept until 1933, just prior to his move back to the Soviet Union.[3]

Nevertheless, despite his early success and visible career, first in Russia and then in America and Europe, Prokofiev has remained an opaque and poorly understood figure. Until recently it has not been clear that biography has been particularly helpful in understanding the origin and character of his art.[4] He was known to be vain and self-assured, an only child devoted to his mother, with a formal and distant relationship to his father.[5] He was, among other things, a brilliant chess player and later an avid bridge enthusiast. Until the recent publication of his voluminous diaries, however, much of the private Prokofiev remained hidden from view. In fact, Prokofiev has escaped the sort of psycho-biographical foray we encounter in writings on Mahler, Brahms, and Ives, and, more controversially, Mozart, Beethoven, and Schubert.[6] Yet Prokofiev's life was marked by sharp turns that call out for explanation. Indeed, Prokofiev is one case where biographical insight could be useful in understanding his music.[7] What drew him repeatedly to and from America? Why did he settle in France, where he was plagued by the shadow cast by his somewhat older rival and fellow Russian, Stravinsky? Most important, why did he declare a new aesthetic agenda in the early 1930s and in the mid-1930s return to Stalinist Russia and the Soviet Union? (Note that, regarding his relationship to Stalinism, nothing akin to the controversy that has erupted around Shostakovich's intentions has been suggested for Prokofiev.)

Prokofiev said that if he had not been a musician, he would have been a writer. In truth, apart from a few published short stories, the literary material he published about himself and music (childhood reminiscences notwithstanding) pales in comparison to that written by Schumann, Berlioz, Wagner, Bartók, Copland, and Stravinsky (even with ghostwriters).

The historical context of Prokofiev's career offers some clues about his life as a composer. Prokofiev's engagement with language, for example, reveals the implicit debt his compositional strategy owes to the discourse regarding art and life that dominated St. Petersburg in the decade before his departure to America in 1918.[8] Prokofiev's pride in his status as an enfant terrible, particularly in his employment of "wrong notes" within recognizable patterns, jarring rhythms, and sardonic rhetorical moves, may stem from an appropriation into music of contemporary ideologies and "devices" isolated by Russian literary formalists, of which the most famous was *ostraneniye* ("making strange"). The new needed to rescue the familiar from banality and convention, to strip forms from too evident a dependence on history. Prokofiev would not follow Scriabin's foray into Symbolism and textured mysticism (although the young composer admired Scriabin and emulated him in some early works). Rather, by the time he left the United States in early 1922, Prokofiev had pioneered an aggressive, modern-sounding distortion of anticipated pitch relations in melody, tonality, and rhythm in repetition and variation.

Given the new evidence provided by the diaries, what is to be made of the recurring if reductive appeal to Prokofiev's "Russianness"? One of the most succinct accounts of the impression Prokofiev made on his contemporaries, particularly in the Paris years of the 1920s, belongs to Arthur Rubinstein: "Over the long years of my life, I came to consider Prokofiev the most important Russian composer. Stravinsky became a cosmopolitan and this is expressed in his music. As to the other composers, one misses in them the authenticity of the Russian musical idiom that is in the works Prokofiev left us."[9]

Prokofiev's status as a Russian patriot—the manner in which he considered himself distinctly Russian—is confirmed and clarified by the diaries. Unlike Stravinsky and Rachmaninoff, he never subscribed to the mix of virulent anticommunism that consumed so many Russians in Paris and New York. There is no evidence of leftist sympathies, either. Unlike the writer Maxim Gorky or Prokofiev's mentor the director Vsevolod Meyerhold, Prokofiev engaged in no serious flirtation with Marxism, though he apparently did go to the trouble of reading *Das Kapital* and, later, select speeches and essays by Lenin and Stalin.[10]

At the same time, Prokofiev possessed his own enormous nostalgia for pre-1917 St. Petersburg and a concomitant sense of Russia's imperial destiny and grandeur.[11] In his trips to Russia in 1927 and 1929, Prokofiev responded more to the continuities than to the changes. He felt overwhelmingly attached to the Russian urban landscape and the mores of his contemporaries in the intelligentsia. This is most poignantly expressed in his long and close relationships with his best musical friend, Nikolay Myaskovsky, and with composer, scholar, and critic Boris Asafyev (though his relationship with the latter eventually soured). Although he returned to Revolutionary Russia, Prokofiev, as has been often argued, was no "revolutionary," even in art. Rather he sought to extend tradition into modernity or bring modernity into tradition, with invention, wit, and even sarcasm. It was not difficult for him to accept both populism and nationalism as the Soviet artist's ideological imperative.[12] He never felt comfortable or secure as an elite artist in exile.[13]

Prokofiev's cultural chauvinism (notably vis-à-vis America and France) overwhelmed his rather apolitical distaste for the autocratic nature of the new Soviet regime. This dynamic did not apply to such contemporary émigrés as Stravinsky, Rachmaninoff (or the writer Vladimir Nabokov), or to Prokofiev's friend, the younger émigré composer Vladimir Dukelsky (Vernon Duke), no matter how much each of them felt the pain of exile.[14] Nor was it true for the Russian-Jewish contemporaries who overlapped with Prokofiev at the St. Petersburg Conservatory and later emigrated—Joseph Achron, Lazare Saminsky, and the violinist Michel Piastro; not to speak of other more famous Russian-Jewish musicians, including Jascha Heifetz, Nathan Milstein, and the cellist Gregor Pyatigorsky. Despite his attachment to things Russian, Prokofiev, in his music before the 1930s, did not exploit easily recognizable markers of Russian identity, such as allusions to folk music as it was construed in the work of the Mighty Five and the polemics of Vladimir Stasov. Appropriations of the distinctive sound of Russian church music were rare. Evocations exist of what Marina Frolova-Walker has termed the "tragic soul" and the exotic (from a Western perspective), but they are subordinated to Prokofiev's (and Myaskovsky's) foregrounding of musical craftsmanship defined by established techniques in the formation and elaboration of melody, and in the use of harmony to generate form and structure across musical time.[15]

A new and revelatory clue to understanding Prokofiev's life and personality emerges from the diaries, as well as recent research. It has nothing to
do with Russia. Rather, it rests in his interest in and adherence to Christian
Science. Many composers have been religious. One thinks of Haydn and
Dvořák. But few have dabbled in extensive theological reading and speculation. Prokofiev, however, from the early 1920s on, embraced in an
idiosyncratic yet quite orthodox way one of the most distinctly American
modern theological movements, which was also one of the only Christian
sects to be founded by a woman. Indeed, the trajectory of Prokofiev's aesthetic ambitions was shaped by his construct of Christian Science. Christian
Science also played a role in his decision to return to the Soviet Union and
accommodate the aesthetic requirements of the regime.

The roots of Prokofiev's enthusiasm for Christian Science were biographical and psychological. His conversion coincided with his courtship of
and marriage to Spanish-born singer Carolina (Lina) Codina and the
birth of their first child, Svyatoslav. The theology of Christian Science, as
Prokofiev understood it, provided him with a way to come to terms with
his prior relationships with women and his marriage. His personal journey to Christian Science also led him to an outlook on life that could
justify the most controversial and momentous decision of his life, his move
to Moscow in the mid-1930s.

Prokofiev's adherence to Christian Science has been acknowledged and
documented. More often than not it has been passed over as a minor if
not eccentric characteristic of his life. In the process, the tenets of Christian
Science have been misrepresented.[16] The basic facts are that sometime around
the summer of 1924 Prokofiev discovered Christian Science—not in
America but in Paris, where he returned from Germany.[17] Lina was not
the driving force behind his interest in Christian Science. After the birth
of her son, she attended church regularly, but it was Prokofiev who engaged
in concentrated reading and rumination on Christian Science. He even
lamented Lina's periodic doubts about the healing power of the faith.[18]
Before attempting an interpretation of the origins and consequences of
Prokofiev's adherence to Christian Science, though, we require an analysis of Christian Science and Prokofiev's version of it.

I. The Theology of Christian Science

By the early twentieth century, Christian Science, which had been founded
in 1879 by Mary Baker Eddy, possessed a constituency that was far more
female than male. In 1926 there were slightly over 200,000 members in
the United States, organized in over 1,900 congregations, the single largest

being the mother church in Boston, with over 62,000 registered members. Although the movement, frequently deemed a cult, had been founded in the Northeast, by the 1920s the bulk of the membership was in the Midwest and Far West.[19] Eddy's inspiration was distinct but not new. During the nineteenth century in America, a variety of new forms of Protestantism had taken hold whose beliefs centered on the unity of the divine, the priority of the metaphysical realm over physical reality, and the possibility of healing through faith.[20] Indeed, Eddy was plagued by claims that she had stolen her ideas from others, a charge made most popular by Mark Twain, one of Christian Science's most vociferous opponents. Prokofiev's allegiance to Christian Science was itself a contradiction of the claim made by many of its critics, including Twain, that its appeal (and danger to society) rested on its power of attraction for the uneducated, ignorant, and naive masses.[21]

Prokofiev owned and read closely Eddy's central work, *Science and Health with Key to the Scriptures*. He also possessed and read a widely known primer on Christian Science by prominent disciple, practitioner, and teacher Edward A. Kimball. Prokofiev's annotated copy of Kimball's book (largely a collection of public lectures) is preserved in the Glinka Museum in Moscow.[22]

The fundamental claim underlying Eddy's theology is the singularity and unity of the divine mind as the exclusive constituent of reality. Eddy takes the strategy used by Descartes in the *Meditations on First Philosophy* to a counterintuitive result. Sleep and dreams are illusions only in the sense that they seem "less" real. There is in fact no duality of the metaphysical and the physical, of the physical phenomena that constitute so-called external reality and the imaginary or spirit world (or soul or mind). Believing that "in reality there is no other existence" than "spiritual existence," Eddy concluded that "life cannot be united to its unlikeness, mortality." Reality, in its exclusive spiritual existence, was immortal, eternal, constant, and timeless.[23]

According to Eddy, the presumption of a real material world that included space and time was mythical, a reflection of man's self-imposed limited understanding of truth and reality. Therefore our sense perception of having bodies in a real temporal world is a cognitive error generated by fear and insufficient understanding of the unity, power, and perfection of spiritual reality. This epistemologically radical claim—that real "being" was exclusively and purely spiritual—is precisely what made Eddy's argument assume the status of "science." Furthermore this science was divine, and therefore holy and good. Despite all surface differentiation—the seemingly empirically demonstrable phenomena in biological life and in the human community—the divinity and unity of spirit remained undisturbed. The divine spirit was perfect, permanent, and implicit in all living beings.

Granting sensory experience the status of knowledge or truth was a mental illusion. Since space and time were ultimately illusory, so too was mortality. The spirit, whose existence was "the one fact," was incapable of imperfection, of a beginning or an end. Death therefore does not exist, since we all partake of the divine spirit who created us.

Eddy's epistemology demanded no Kantian concession regarding the perspective of the subjective seeker of truth and the independent existence of external reality. Indeed, Prokofiev's attraction to Eddy's thought rested in part in her neo-Cartesian resolution of Kant's analysis of the possibility of knowledge of the external world. Prokofiev's limited foray into reading philosophy prior to reading Eddy centered on the classic texts of German idealism, particularly the work of Kant and Schopenhauer.[24] But Prokofiev misread Kant, believing that Kant's positing of a priori truths and his awareness of the contingency of the perceiver was a claim, as Prokofiev put it, "that the world around us is only representation and probably fallacious." For Prokofiev, Kant had undermined the truth content of the a posteriori world, making reasonable Eddy's notion that material reality and therefore empirical science (on which medicine was based) were illusions.[25]

Eddy considered her views to have the characteristics of science. Her truth was consistent, universal, harmonious, and logical in the sense that it required no exception and would survive logical analysis and so-called empirical scrutiny, so long as one conceded that our perception of the external world was not so much imperfect as delusional.[26] In Eddy's view, humans had employed for far too long a false dichotomy (whether between the mental and the material, the observer and observed, or the subject and object) that gave materiality legitimacy as reality, even if, as in Plato, in a subordinate status. Eddy therefore rejected Kant's framework of a distinction between a priori and a posteriori truths. There was only one truth and one reality: that of God and the Spirit. Christ's birth and resurrection proved the point, and the Bible could be read as underscoring that simple truth.

For Eddy, therefore, the common imperfect grasp of the immortality and unity of spirit as the sole dimension of reality resulted in scientific error. Chief among these errors was the distinction between mind and matter. Eddy made the optimistic assumption that all individuals are made of spirit, and that this spiritual individuality of all humans was theoretically incapable of error, and therefore "never wrong." All that was needed to grasp the essential truth was the disciplined training of the mind, the "science of mind." All humans were made in the divine image and therefore partook of the unity and truth of being. All individuals were capable of finding "the indissoluble spiritual link which establishes man forever in the divine likeness, inseparable from his creator."[27]

The most salient consequence of the subordination of space, time, causality, and all external material reality as imperfect mental constructs was her rejection of the reality of death. Eddy denies the existence of death with persuasive perfection, highlighting the singular appeal of her radical epistemology. For her, merely conceding matter to be a valid dimension of reality, as opposed to an illusion, would require a notion of death. The cardinal false belief in all other forms of Christianity, she claimed, was the epistemological concession of human mortality and death. "In reality man never dies," Eddy wrote, "the belief that he dies will not establish his scientific harmony. Death is not the result of Truth but of error and one error will not correct another." Death was "an illusion."[28]

With this one startling and radical notion, that in death there is nothing to deny and therefore nothing to fear, Eddy broke the common thread of denial—the denial of death, which, if Ernest Becker was correct, constitutes the central focus of the development of human thought, in particular theology and psychology.[29] That man "dies" is mere belief. It is not true: "The great spiritual fact must be brought out that man is, not shall be, perfect and immortal." Since death is "nothingness," Eddy concluded that "mortals waken from the dream of death with bodies unseen by those who think that they bury the body."[30]

The rejection of death as a dimension of truth placed Eddy at odds with traditional Christianity. With her rejection of man's mortality, she generated another deviation from Christian doctrine on the question of the nature and origin of evil. In the commonplace view, the consequence of the Fall of Man, as described in Genesis 3, was the twin loss of divine grace and the gift of immortality. With the advent of human consciousness or knowledge that followed came the commencement of human time, the cycle of life, the pain of childbirth, moral responsibility for one's actions, and the inevitability of aging and death. The theologies surrounding Christian accounts of the relationship between God and man include notions of original sin and God's plan regarding the gift and burden of having been created in God's image. These in turn helped define free will, duty, choice, and the prospect of damnation or salvation. All such notions assumed a reality in time, material existence, and the body. They also claimed a conventional mind-body duality involving spirit and matter, body and soul. Death, then, was mitigated through the idea of eternal life and the immortality of the soul.

Here Eddy was at her most radical. According to her, the soul, as part of the immortal unified spirit, was never born and never died in the material sense, but was eternal. Individuals continued to live and develop as individuals after so-called death. The consciousness of our individuality was a divine gift. But true faith and understanding required a complete absence of fear regarding any loss of material life, which never possessed truth-value anyway. Our primary sin, and only sin, was to believe that we existed in the material sense at all. Furthermore, the "soul" could never sin, since it was divine and perfect. Sin, evil, and imperfection all derived from an inadequate human mental strategy—the assumption that the material world was true and subject to the Second Law of Thermodynamics, to entropy, rendering life finite and making decay and death in the biological so-called real world true.

Eddy's radical spiritual epistemological monotheism led her to deny the reality of evil. It only appeared real because it was the consequence of mortal error correctable by proper understanding, not mere faith. The singularity and perfection of mind permitted Eddy and her followers, notably Kimball, to circumvent conventional notions of sin and the flawed moral nature of man. Man was the creation of God and partook in the divine perfect spirit, which, for Eddy, was love. Therefore, in this form of immortality, the soul— the real man—could not be imperfect. And perfection was divine and in the most extreme Platonic sense, good. God, for Eddy, was "good." Since man's "reality" was his spiritual being and represented the gift of God, it was illogical to believe that God "made man capable of sin." In other words, "Evil is an illusion, and it has no real basis. Evil is a false belief."[31]

Eddy abolished the Kantian distinction between ontology ("is" propositions) and ethics ("ought" propositions, imperatives dependent on human freedom and choice). The good was real and unitary in the same sense as the spiritual was the only truth. Sin was "an error" and therefore scientifically "unreal."[32] The notion of evil derived from false reasoning on man's part: evil was in fact a man-made illusion. Man, not God, created evil through insufficient understanding of reality and an undisciplined acceptance of sense perception and observation as the basis of knowledge.

All notions of pain and pleasure, indeed all sense perceptions, were likewise derived from the conventional belief in the reality of the material world. Man could realize his goodness, since his reality was good, but "man has adulterated the meaning of the word soul" by making it "resident in matter."[33] By understanding that matter is an illusion and the individual soul is nothing more than God in the individual, man could realize the possibility of goodness, removing the experience of bodily pain and psychological guilt.

God could never be the author of evil or suffering. The Christian Scientist need no longer "be afraid of God," as Kimball put it.[34] But most important, man could overcome evil and pain through mental discipline. The overriding human obstacle to this was fear. The failure to understand or to maintain the understanding of truth lent the material world a false sense of power and importance that in turn led men to be fearful and therefore to do and sense evil, suffer pain, and fear death. Prayer through reading, and the vigilant, disciplined, daily reflection on Christian Science were the means to conquer the fear that generated sin and evil and that in turn derived from the allure of the legitimacy the world defined as material reality.

Eddy's fame as a theologian derived as much from the manner in which she solved the problem of evil in the world as it did from the form of healing she taught. If God was all-knowing, loving, and perfect, why then did he create evil and suffering? The usual pattern of reasoning concerning the creation of the world and of man led to the paradox most eloquently presented in the Book of Job. Eddy believed she had solved the central question of man as God's creation in his own image and that elaborate explanations regarding the painful consequences of man's rejection of God's grace and use of his gift of freedom were no longer needed. Human imperfection, the fall from grace, mortality, autonomy, and the free capacity to create evil were all required to reconcile the presence of evil in the world with the perfection of an all-knowing and all-powerful loving God.

Eddy believed she had resolved the paradox of evil by making belief in time, history, and materiality the central obstacle to man's faith. Man was, rather, "incapable of sin, sickness and death."[35] But man was capable of disciplined understanding—not blind faith—sufficient to recognize his own divine nature and perfection as part of God. With such a grasp of science, man could realize that all evil and pain, including the idea of death, were seductions fueled by the materiality of the body. To refute these demanded constant vigilance on the part of each individual. Eddy wrote that the Christian Scientist must "expose and denounce the claims of evil and disease in all their forms, but recognize no reality in them. The sinner is not reformed merely by assuring him that he cannot be a sinner because there is no sin. To put down the claim of sin, you must detect it, remove the mask, point out the illusion, and thus, by proving sin's unreality, gain victory over it. The sick are not healed by merely declaring there is no sickness, but by knowing there is none."[36]

Humans were capable of using their own freedom to achieve divine perfection. Human reason—rational cognition through language and argument—not an intuitive or miraculous leap of faith was required of the Christian Scientist to grasp the divine truth and make it the basis of conduct. Mental discipline was essential.[37] The fact that man was not inherently evil but inherently good placed a powerful burden on the individual to realize man's divine spiritual goodness. It also raised the prospect that one could live eternally without a sense of guilt, sin, evil, pain, and suffering.

But Christian Science generated its own paradox. If all evil in the world was unreal, and all pain an illusion, moral and ethical judgment about the evil and suffering in the material world could easily be devalued, and even considered unnecessary. Were poverty, torture, and illness mere illusions since they were unreal and contingent on real time and the material world? Were all personal actions and ethical commitments—promises and loyalties as well as little lies and large crimes—irrelevant? One might be led through Christian Science to dismiss or devalue social evils and personal suffering as illusory, just like illness and death. If the denial of death led to the rejection of medical science and the disregard of physical pain and the elimination of sorrow and grief within bodily existence, then the denial of evil could have parallel consequences with respect to ethics and politics.

For Eddy, life on earth was a pilgrimage that allowed one to experience joy and goodness, all without suffering. One only had to grasp the monopoly on the truth of mind and spirit and to reject the reality of matter. In this context the individual artist, particularly the musician, could be seen as furthering the primacy of the mind, of the spiritual. After all, the musician's medium was purely imaginative. Music possessed no correspondence to external reality, it was not representational. It was audible in the imagination without material sound—a closed system or a mental game of sorts, akin to mathematics. Just as ethical truth mirrored the scientific truth of mind in Eddy's theology, so could a parallel singular notion of beauty as truth be suggested: aesthetic creations of individuals had the potential to reflect spiritual harmony. Eddy placed little emphasis on the aesthetic, but her inference was clear. Each individual's immortality was both distinct and part of the unified divine spirit. Therefore the creations of the individual could bolster the sense of the reality of the divine spirit within the human community.

The making of art could be reconciled with the propagation of the truth of Christian Science. As Eddy argued, the Christian Scientist and the opponent of Christian Science could be understood as two artists, one who saw his or her art as the "true light and loveliness" and the manifestation of "spiritual ideals, indestructible and glorious"—and the other for whom art was a function of selfishness, materiality, sense perception, personal pleasure, and "not so shockingly transcendental."[38] (The irony for Prokofiev was that the music used in Christian Science services was unusually awful.)[39]

Eddy's total attack on the material world and its reality lent the Christian Science movement its appeal and power. She defied the claims of contemporary American pragmatism, using the strategy of principled criticism of empiricism to lend her ideas the prestige of science, without conceding that the external material world was significant or reflective of true reality. Theology became an accessible, simple science, not a system of beliefs based either on revelation or authority. Adherence by each person depended on arguments about the true reality—the existence of a unified spiritual realm, that of God.[40] Since God was a God of Love, whose existence made human evil and suffering for all a "moral impossibility," each individual could access God's grace.[41] Christian Science was radically democratic. Eddy's dismissal of medicine and science as reflections of error and human arrogance rested on her conviction that modern culture had lost its understanding of the loving power of the divine. Furthermore, it emancipated individuals from a growing dependence on education and on superior human authority in the form of priests, professionals, and scientists. Christian Science made every believer a scientist, giving all humans renewed power over their own lives, in a manner characteristically individualistic, Christian, and egalitarian in the American sense.[42]

II. Overcoming Guilt: The Personal Roots of Prokofiev's Religious Adherence

What drew a brilliant, self-assured, well-educated, and successful Russian composer in his early thirties to this idiosyncratic American theology? The key rests in what Kimball eloquently identified as the impact of Christian Science on one's mood and personal behavior. Prokofiev marked the sections of Kimball's book that deal with how Christian Science teaches one to reject anger, fear, envy, and guilt about interactions with others.[43] Part of Christian Science's intent is to persuade the individual to take responsibility for all that is bad by rejecting its existence and not blaming God. One need not be resigned to the notion that the individual is a powerless cog in an existential framework that contains both good and evil. The assumption of responsibility asked of the believer may require constant work, but it is work worth undertaking because God and man are both good and potentially perfect. Christian Science is not therefore a religion of resignation, but of optimism, a route to sustained self-confidence and happiness. As Kimball put it:

> It will make him happier under any and all circumstances than he otherwise would be. It will make him a better man, a better friend, a better citizen. It will improve him morally and physically. It equips him with a dominant control over circumstances and conditions that he never before possessed. It purifies his individual and social status. It enables him to cope more successfully with pain, disease, fear, grief, sorrow, and other desolating emotions and conditions of human experience. It rationally and satisfactorily reconciles him to abandonment of evil.[44]

Prokofiev was from his adolescent years sufficiently aware of his own self-confidence and conceits. The way in which he juggled girlfriends, understood his own superiority over others (in music and chess), and reveled in winning the 1914 Conservatory competition comes through in the first volume of his diaries, as does an unusual capacity to observe himself with critical candor. But his behavior troubled him, particularly his relationship to peers, with the exception of the significantly older Myaskovsky. The attraction to Christian Science seems to have been part of Prokofiev's struggle to control anger and depression.[45] In the undated list of twenty points of a personal religious credo articulated by the composer to describe the nature of his commitment to Christian Science, the framing preamble to all the points reads as follows: "Depression is a lie of the mortal mind. Consequently it cannot have power over me, for I am the expression of Life, i.e., of divine activity."[46] This statement illuminates why the composer asserted in a succinct letter dated 1933 and addressed to one of his favorite Christian Science teachers, a "Miss Crane," that "Christian Science is helping me enormously in my music. To say more exactly, I do not see any more my work outside of science."[47]

Christian Science provided Prokofiev with the mental discipline to control a variety of reactions to daily events.[48] From a healing point of view, what ailed the composer most were headaches, toothaches, and heart palpitations. The use of Christian Science seemed helpful in combating these ailments. Beyond this was depression. For Prokofiev, Christian Science was "a ray of light" that prevented the human spirit from descending into "dark dungeons," including Marcel Proust's "lost time" and Nikolay Nekrasov's "lack of faith."[49] Christian Science also counteracted his envy (particularly of Stravinsky), anger at his wife, and anxiety about his own work.

In the end, the tempering of Prokofiev's quite off-putting manner, most astonishingly evident in his treatment of his contemporary George Balanchine and his periodic loss of temper with Serge Koussevitzky, was finally achieved by the 1940s. Prokofiev's assistant Pavel Lamm and his wife were astonished to discover during the first years of the war how changed he was.[50] Whether this was the result of years of practicing the mental discipline of Christian Science or the process of aging, not to speak of the terrors and uncertainty of daily life under Stalin, is not clear.

Given Prokofiev's narcissism, it is also not surprising that on the question of aging and death he found solace in Christian Science.[51] As he observed in 1925 in his diary:

I am 34 years old. Before I used to exclaim, "What, already 25? Already 30? I'm so old!" But now, with Christian Science, years have somehow lost their significance. Years, and time in general, are made for finite life; in eternal life there can be no conception of time. It's silly to try to divide infinity into several parts![52]

But of all the personal motivations behind Prokofiev's fascination with Christian Science it is perhaps guilt that played the most powerful role. Prokofiev's turn to Christian Science took place around the birth of his first son. That event was not entirely uncomplicated. It appears from his diary that Lina suffered not only in childbirth but also from something that might well have been severe postpartum depression.[53] This is not an unreasonable assumption. Prokofiev's marriage to Lina in 1923, which took place in Ettal, Germany, may have been the result of an unplanned pregnancy. In the two years before the marriage, during their courtship, Prokofiev had an on-and-off but intense and sustained affair with Stella Adler, then a beautiful, high-strung, and brilliant young actress, which began in New York in 1919 (Figure 1). She was twenty and part of a family theatrical company in the Yiddish theater.[54] She left for London in late 1919, after meeting Prokofiev, for an extended theatrical run with her family during which time Prokofiev's relationship with Lina deepened.

But the affair that had begun in 1919 picked up when Adler returned to New York in early 1920, and she and Prokofiev began to see each other

Figure 1. Stella Adler

again even though he was already involved with Lina.[55] On one memorable occasion, he accompanied a close mutual friend of Adler's to a performance of hers in New York's Yiddish theater but had to leave before the end because he had made a date with Lina the same evening. Prokofiev remarked, "It was terrifying to shift from one world to an entirely different one, but besides, there was Linette, sweet, shy, timid, and after all, so full of ardor."[56] Indeed the contrast was stark. Stella was not only beautiful and brilliant, but outspoken and ambitious. The diaries confirm that no woman had previously fascinated and attracted him quite so completely, nor would one subsequently (with the possible exception of his second wife, Mira Mendelson, much later).[57]

Had Lina not become pregnant, perhaps the trajectory of Prokofiev's career might have been different. This is not to suggest he was not also in love with Lina, although the ambivalence he felt was undeniable.[58] What recommended Lina to him in large measure was her devotion and persistence, threats and complaints on her part notwithstanding. She was not Adler's equal in terms of talent, something Prokofiev knew from the start.[59] There is no evidence that after 1922 he and Adler had any contact during his travels in America or Europe.[60] Prokofiev's relationship to Christian Science was bound up with Lina, but not in the way it has been most often described.[61] The religion provided the composer with a framework in which he could exercise the mental discipline to maintain a connection to Lina and to control his anger toward her.[62]

In 1927 Prokofiev confided in his diary that "memory is a godly creation, created for the gradual removal of bad memories (the unreal)—on the same principle on which the divine world was created by God."[63] Christian Science provided Prokofiev the means by which an individual could come to grips with bad memories, residues of pain, regrets, and bad deeds by rejecting them as illusory and insignificant. Christian Science taught that the individual was, as Prokofiev put it, "the expression of Life . . . Love . . . Mind, the effect of one Great Cause, the expression of perfection, and this leads me to the perfect use of my time." Christian Science, if practiced with intensity and regularity, was a route to "good" thoughts that in turn were like a light that "warms the human soul."[64]

Prokofiev was particularly attracted to Eddy's notion of God's universal love, as well as the idea that each individual could express God's spirit and perfection in life, without death. From his close reading of Kimball's primer, notably the last chapter, "Love as an Absolute Essential," Prokofiev appears to have embraced Kimball's argument that "Love is the animus, the Principle of Life, and throw aside everything we will, we must learn to delineate Life, substance and the attitude of Love."[65] Love, after all, was the expression of God's spirit, reality, and power.

The challenge was to pursue the spiritually real, not the shadows of reality in the material world. Man, for Prokofiev, was a privileged creation, the "reflection of God" and therefore ought not to be afraid of "the human bark, directed at the materialistic 'I,' appearing as the weak shadow of the real person, the reflection of God."[66] Therefore "sin (mistakes) is also not real because God is all-embracing and can only create what is good. For this reason, only what is good is real while mistakes and the material world are not real." Memory as an attribute of immortality contained its own protective but justified device, the positive power of selection, the holding on to good memories and the erasing of bad ones.[67] This was a useful way by which the composer could discard sources of guilt in his own behavior, either by forgetting them or denying their significance. Prokofiev developed his own epistemological logic to justify the idea that bad memories, and therefore guilt, were insignificant and could be forgotten—indeed, had never happened on the plane of reality.

Christian Science inspired Prokofiev to reconsider the essential nature of time. For a musician, this subject was naturally compelling. Music recalibrates the experience of time for both performer and listener. In Prokofiev's view, as influenced by Christian Science, time was not linear or unidirectional. Time was multidimensional, permitting movement back and forth. Time measured by clocks was a construct of materialism. It had to be transcended to understand eternity and immortality, the reality of the spirit. Sequences of events, although necessary for our comprehension of them, were illusions. Memory is the human instrument that proves man's participation in the eternal spirit, since memory can manipulate time in the imagination in ways that defy the one-dimensional forward march of time experienced and measured in the material world.[68] Memory legitimated the belief in the unreality of past and present, and therefore the immortality of the human being.

Only two temporal experiences at the extremes of ordinary time were of significance to Christian Science: the moment and the timeless. Consciousness in the present was always a relevant consideration. Beyond the moment, there was only memory and eternity, where the category of ordinary time was no longer relevant. For Prokofiev, given the individual's control over memory and the essential nonreality of events measured in ordinary time, Christian Science was a religion directed at present action. The struggle was to effect good deeds in the moment of self-actualization, deeds that demonstrated the potential of the individual as the instrument of God's perfection.[69] The consequences of this in conventional terms of moral judgment were to minimize guilt vis-à-vis the past and the sense of lingering responsibility that might be sustained by memory.

For Prokofiev, as for all Christian Scientists, the religion offered an antidote to the fear of illness and death.[70] "According to Christian Science, there should be no fear," Prokofiev wrote in his diary.[71] He was persistently concerned about his heart and plagued by headaches. In early 1925, he experienced, after some failures, the first true success using Christian Science to cure a headache. At the same time he noted that Christian Science was having a "noticeable effect in softening my character, smoothing out—and doing away completely with unnecessary arguments."[72] The connection between guilt over his behavior and his symptoms of physical illness became clear to Prokofiev. The banishment of "sinful thoughts," guilt, and thoughts about illness, fortified by Christian Science, helped with toothaches and stage fright.[73] That recognition required of him more careful and systematic reading of Christian Science, particularly with regard to his perceived "heart" condition, where short-term relief, as he confessed in 1927, did not lead to long-term healing. By thinking over every word in Eddy's *Science and Health*, every definition, the grandeur of his own being would become more apparent, namely his status as the "reflection of God." This required controlling "what moves the heart (motives)."[74]

After the mid-1920s, Christian Science became the vehicle by which Prokofiev could control his hypochondria and come to grips with its roots in his behavior. Christian Science dominated his dialogue with himself about his behavior with others. The ultimate reward for Prokofiev came in the ability to overcome not only the fear of his own death but any guilt of having failed those who had died. Prokofiev admitted to having had little remorse at the death of his father.[75] He also exhibited disregard for his elders, notably his teachers, except for Glier and Nikolay Tcherepnin.[76] Christian Science allowed him to come to terms with the memory of unresolved relationships left behind by death. He was consoled by the idea that he did not have to visit the grave of his mother since "the dead continue to grow as people in the afterlife," making irrelevant any sense of unfinished business and remorse about one's relationship to those who had died.[77] Christian Science taught that fear was unnecessary and wrong, particularly about death and one's relationship to it. The only true fear was being afraid, which the composer defined in the terms of Christian Science as the "fear of not being in the likeness of God."[78]

The depth of the power of Christian Science over the composer's psychological engagement with death and his sense of guilt are perhaps most eloquently revealed in a dream he detailed in September 1924. The dream took place in a theater foyer where Prokofiev encountered Jacques Hébertot, a theater impresario to whom he was hostile.[79] Hébertot told him there would be no new production for him. After Hébertot left, with Prokofiev following, he saw Nikolay Rimsky-Korsakov walk in, looking even younger than when Prokofiev had been a student. In the dream Prokofiev realized that this could not be real, knowing that more than a decade had passed since Rimsky's death. As Prokofiev neared Rimsky to touch him, he disappeared only to reappear in a bigger room, a hotel dining room. Prokofiev went up to him and grasped his hand, which was warm and real. He kissed it. Rimsky looked away but did not move away and smiled a bit. Prokofiev then kissed Rimsky's beard and put his hands on the elder composer's face, turned it toward him, and kissed him on the lips several times. Then, in the dream, he thought momentarily about Christian Science. Rimsky disappeared and Prokofiev wanted to leave but realized he had forgotten his hat, which he thought had some connection to Rimsky's sudden departure. He could not find the hat. Looking around him, he wondered why others nearby were not surprised at his behavior and what had happened. But they seemed not to notice, being engaged in their own conversations, which he could hear in fragments. He then woke up.[80]

An obvious Freudian reading of this dream would be to identify Prokofiev's desire to resolve guilt regarding perceived wrongdoing in relationship to his father and father figures, such as teachers and mentors (and perhaps older rivals including Stravinsky and even Myaskovsky). The dream suggests repressed guilt. Wish fulfillment dreams can express infantile feelings of wishing the death of others and the more commonplace adult ambition to supplant and eclipse the parental generation. Another plausible Freudian interpretation would be to point to Prokofiev's anxiety about having felt humiliated by authority and his failure to win approval even when he tried to show signs of affection. Prokofiev is left symbolically castrated by those in power; the opening discovery of the absence of a new commission is mirrored by the rejection by Rimsky and the loss of his hat.[81] The inability to find his hat, the concern about what people might have thought, and the absence of response from others (e.g., Rimsky) suggest the intensity of Prokofiev's internal struggle concerning his own self-worth. Prokofiev became engaged with Christian Science as a means of coming to terms with the truly terrifying possibility of personal and professional defeat (even though, as solace, Rimsky's handshake was warm and real). But as the dream reveals, the idea of death as an illusion had been internalized through Christian Science, and had entered his unconscious as a redeeming idea and source of hope. Rimsky vanished at the thought of Christian Science.[82]

III. Spirituality and the Problem of Evil: The Accommodation with Stalinist Russia

Beyond its usefulness as a tool for what is admittedly speculative psychobiography, Christian Science held a central place in Prokofiev's adult life as a credo, defining such issues as the existence of God and the character of human evil. Prokofiev did not grow up in a religious household. He possessed little nostalgia for Russian Orthodoxy, as is revealed by his comments on a 1928 trip to an Orthodox service celebrating the thirty-fifth anniversary of Tchaikovsky's death.[83] As Prokofiev explained to his friend Pierre Souvtchinsky, the Orthodox Church celebrated man's sin and suffering, whereas in Christian Science man becomes deserving of happiness. He had learned that in contrast to traditional Christianity, where "repentance and self-flagellation for transgressions were good and necessary . . . such self-denigration was incompatible with the likeness of God, that it did not move us forward."[84] By defining all of reality as spiritual, Christian Science solved the issue of meaning and purpose in the world since nature itself became conscious—it, too, is the reflection of mind and spirit. The duality of the material and the spiritual was erased by the unity of the spiritual.[85]

But this doctrine of the unity, perfection, and dominance of God as Spirit forced Prokofiev to muse on its troubling consequences. Why was man created in the first place? And since man is the manifestation of perfection and God's spirit and love, why did there seem to be evil, both in the form of personal life experience (e.g., lying, envy, hate) and in terms of suffering, violence, and poverty?[86] Prokofiev's answer rested in the notion that God's gift to man was free will, which "in some instances leads to mistakes. These materialized mistakes are the material world that is not real because it is false."[87] The overwhelming share of such "unreal" mistakes was bound up in the undisciplined exercise of freedom and individuality. For Prokofiev, individuality was a God-given gift to all humans. But it led easily to selfishness and competition. Love of neighbor, in the conventional Christian sense, offered no solution because it compelled the dissolution of the individual.[88] It suggested conformism that erased, suppressed, or diminished the individual. For Prokofiev, the evil created by individuality was ultimately temporary. Sufficient strength in one's sense of individuality needed to be developed—a nondestructive positive celebration of oneself. Prokofiev concluded, "Man's turn to goodness and rejection of evil is a symptom of maturation of his individuality."[89]

The fundamental challenge Prokofiev encountered as his connection to Christian Science deepened was the rational atheism not uncommon in his generation and prevalent within his circle in Paris in the 1920s.[90] Having little attachment to Russian Orthodoxy and coming of age without any significant religious conviction beyond secularized ideas of sin, guilt, and repentance, Prokofiev, whose mental habits would have made him an ideal candidate for a Spinoza-like skepticism or agnosticism, flirted with atheism.[91] He was intuitively a rationalist, skilled at chess, as evidenced by his tournament victories, and mathematics, later defending the survival of melody in an argument based on statistical calculations regarding melodic possibilities.[92] Indeed, the turn to Christian Science had much to do with Christian Science's pretense to the elegant simplicity characteristic of great scientific hypotheses and mathematical proofs.[93] The notion that evil was a lie, as taught by Christian Science, was defended by Prokofiev by analogy to the theory of positive and negative numbers, and the power of the procedures represented by the equal sign.[94]

What troubled Prokofiev was the existence of man. If man is a reflection of God's perfection, his goodness, and his eternity, what was there before his existence? Why were time and humanity created? Prokofiev posited the notion of the gift of free will, the spiritual power of creation characteristic of the divine Spirit. Free will in turn led each individual through a personal journey (mirrored by the species) to overcome the mistakes that derive from freedom, including false reliance on the material world and the experience of time as real. The key to the purpose behind the creation of man was that the gift of life was a sign of God's love.

Prokofiev never resolved the question of why human spirituality needed to experience, even as illusory, the material and temporal world. But the discovery by Christian Science that they were subordinate rendered nature and the entire material universe by definition a reflection of the divine, the work of a conscious creator. Materiality, although an illusion, gave man the hint that God existed.[95] Therefore atheism for Prokofiev was implausible, because of the inherent consciousness resident in everything. Atheism, Prokofiev declared to Souvtchinsky, was a sign of the decline of philosophy.[96] The absence of God robs all existence of meaning, including material forms and the physical elements of the world. It also leaves us without the most important of all human experiences, that of creativity.[97] Creativity cannot be automatic or mechanical. The entire material world immanently revealed the existence of truth, of the divine mind, that the free human needed to discover. The struggle that man experienced in the exercise of free will was a peculiar amalgam of the need to develop freedom and creativity into true individuality and reconcile that individuality with an understanding and expression of God-like perfection.

Having established the existence of God as a unitarian, all-powerful, perfect entity of love, Prokofiev pursued, with characteristically systematic logic, the question of evil. He devised a theory of historical evolution that permitted him to subordinate as transitory and irrelevant evil of all kinds, personal as well as political. Given that time itself was as much an illusion as illness, there was, in the end, no real evil of which humans were capable. The denial of the existence of evil rested in the ephemeral character of experience.[98] God's love permitted the individual to perfect his soul and thus to forget bad memories, pain, suffering, and his or her own mistakes.

This denial of evil in the context of the exclusive, purposeful reality of God's love constitutes the ethical and psychological framework that allowed Prokofiev to contemplate a return to Stalin's Russia from the mid-1920s through the early 1930s. As the composer observed in 1929, musing on Lina's loss of faith, "If one is certain of the idea that the world is made up spiritually, and that everything terrible in it is spiritual as well, then what is the point of feeling unsettled and rolling around in circles and on your side. I am writing this for myself: remember this, remember, remember."[99]

The only person living in Russia whom Prokofiev appears to have made a strong effort to convert to Christian Science was his friend Boris Asafyev.[100] After Myaskovsky, Asafyev was Prokofiev's closest colleague in Russia from his Conservatory days. Unlike Myaskovsky, Asafyev was a shrewd politician who adapted himself with relative ease to the shifting requirements of the Soviet regime. He was at one and the same time politically competent and frightened—a dubious and fragile figure in the eyes of Shostakovich biographers.[101] It seems that Prokofiev understood his friend well. His efforts to persuade Asafyev of the merits of Christian Science, particularly in 1928, was part of his attempt to receive confirmation from a respected intellectual of the theoretical justification for conducting one's professional and personal life in collaboration with a regime that in the eyes of the émigrés in Paris was viewed with moral disdain if not horror. Prokofiev, it seems, was trying to convince Asafyev that evil did not exist because God was incapable of evil, and that man, partaking in God's perfection, could not lend evil the status of reality. In the end, even with free will, all that was viewed as evil was, in the sea of eternity, unreal and false. Asafyev would have been a worthy fellow traveler in Christian Science. Prokofiev, sensing his friend's compromised status, may have sought to provide him with a more honorable and principled basis for collaboration.[102]

However much Prokofiev sought to use his reasoning and the discipline of Christian Science to believe that personal and political evil were illusory and false, he struggled with doubts. In a conversation in 1932 with Nina Rubinstein, the idea of writing music for a scenario about the building of the Temple of Solomon came up. Prokofiev confessed in his diary on June 1: "It worries me how I reconcile the construction of the Temple of Solomon with that of Soviet Russia. Even the reconciliation of the two is unacceptable."[103] To help him think through the problem of representing an Old Testament story of the building of the temple to God by a wise but flawed king in the context of Stalin's regime, Prokofiev resolved to consult a Christian Science practitioner then in Paris, Thomas Graham.

Ultimately, Prokofiev minimized the evil with which, for the sake of his own career, he had decided to work. In the context of eternity and the perfection of a loving, divine spirit Stalin's evil was just another lie, a forgettable mistake. Prokofiev could tolerate it because of his construct of what he, as an artist capable of perfecting his individuality, could do: realize and communicate through music the recognition of the harmony and goodness of the only truly scientific reality, the timeless world of the spirit.

IV. Simplicity and Populism: The Aesthetic Consequences of Prokofiev's Christian Science

From the earliest days of his involvement with Christian Science Prokofiev struggled with the problem of the individual. How could an individual have meaning if material existence was subordinate, if there was no birth and death and we are immortal? Although Christian Science was optimistic, it was not obvious how it might make a place for the individuality of human existence, human perception, and the experience of time.[104]

Prokofiev's answer, predictably, lay in the creation of art. In 1932, a Christian Science practitioner told the story of a singer who, like Lina, hedged his bets and consulted both a doctor and went to church. This man, it was said, was only supporting an unreality, creating an object of fear, a "demigod." Prokofiev drew the following conclusion: "Art is not something to be considered personal; art is a depiction through God. Moreover it is very important to learn how to differentiate that man is an individual being, but not necessarily a personal being. To put aside one's 'persona,' and all of its cares—does not mean the loss of individuality. Rather it cleanses the 'persona' and turns it into a better reflection of God."[105]

If "every good deed" testifies to the presence of God, not as an abstract concept but as "a principle of goodness," making us "the reflection of the Father" and not "distant" from perfection, then we can comprehend Prokofiev's well-documented struggle with and eventual loss of interest in *The Fiery Angel* during its composition. The plot was "inimical to Christian Science." Apart from its pseudo-sixteenth-century elements, including devil worship and mystic practices, or the vague moral of the tale, the plot was based on the assumption that evil and death exist in the world and the contrast between the world of experience and a spiritual realm of heaven and hell is genuine. Prokofiev compared himself to Gogol, who on religious grounds (in Prokofiev's words, the need to "destroy values that were abhorrent") burned the second part of *Dead Souls*. But music was, by its nature, not representational and possessed of specific meaning. Therefore he could continue to write and "cut" himself off from the plot, and work only on the music. He did not need to "reach the heights of Gogol's insanity."[106]

Simon Morrison suggests that Prokofiev's interest in the libretto stems from 1919, which would put it before his encounter with Christian Science. However, the composition of *The Fiery Angel* took place as Prokofiev's attachment to Christian Science deepened. It also overlapped with two momentous shifts in the composer's life and work: the formulation of a new aesthetic and his decision-making process with regard to Russia. There is a connection between Prokofiev's flirtation with Scriabin-like mystic notions of music as "theurgy" (as articulated by Andrey Belïy) and the end point of Prokofiev's theological musings on Christian Science.[107] Both Christian and pagan notions of theurgy share with Christian Science the notion that man can produce through art a mediation of the divine. Prokofiev accepted Christian Science's claim of a rational conception of the divine and a process of human mediation through art. Prokofiev resisted the idea that the aesthetic is privileged, accessible only to a few and therefore a sort of secret code. However, Christian Science as well as fin-de-siècle theurgy shared the claim that the aesthetic realm of human activity, particularly music, mirrored the divine and was universal.

It is often said that in contrast to Shostakovich's music much of Prokofiev's, for all its striking refinement and craft, is less evidently personal or confessional. Indeed, Prokofiev was aware from the start that music was a complex game with a nearly objective logic at which he was particularly good. He therefore valued the tradition of craft characteristic of Classicism and was uncomfortable with the ethos of Romanticism, the cult of the artist as hero. Much as he admired Rachmaninoff, he remained aloof from his highly subjective pathos and overt emotionalism. He admired Stravinsky's *Les Noces*, a work that outraged Rachmaninoff.[108] Unlike Rachmaninoff, Prokofiev insisted on an evident modernity in music, music of the present that he found lacking in Rachmaninoff. But he was equally suspicious of the sort of nostalgic Neoclassicism that Stravinsky and his imitators supported in the 1920s.

These prejudices are coherent and consistent with Prokofiev's internalization of Christian Science beliefs. In the first instance, art had to be of the moment, objective, transparent, and not mystical, thereby properly reflective of the rational truth of God's perfection. Art also had to be accessible, reflective of God's egalitarian, universal love. A composer's art needed to be individualistic and therefore distinctive and original, without being self-indulgent. It must not become an excessive display of subjectivity, opaque to the listener, inaccessible, arcane, and overly personalized. Radical subjectivity, particularly in the use of time, worked against the capacity to enter the listener's memory. This cut against the proper task of art: to further the good by evoking in listeners the sense of the spiritual immortality and universality of God.

If one takes away the metaphorical scaffolding of Christian Science theology, one ends up with an aesthetic credo that accurately describes what Prokofiev espoused during the last phase of his career, from the late 1930s onward. As his 1936 review of Myaskovsky's Sixteenth Symphony suggests, mere craftsmanship is not enough. A "clever" scherzo, the attempt to curry favor with the public or strive for external effects, including saccharine naiveté or acrobatics, cannot characterize the kind of art demanded of the individual.[109] What was needed was something Prokofiev blandly termed "great music." Greatness as a category, however, needed to be recognizable by more than a "handful of aesthetes." By the mid-1930s Prokofiev sought to write music that would reach a mass audience without being insincere, pandering, or vulgar. The key to doing this rested in the inexhaustible possibility for good new melodies that could withstand the test of time and were more than cheap or trivial tunes.[110]

Already in 1918 Prokofiev, in an effort to define his own voice, had highlighted the idea of clarity and a certain kind of restraint and economy of expression associated with the nineteenth-century image of Sparta. The use of the term *laconic,* the English word used in the Russian retranslation of Prokofiev's 1918 *Musical Observer* interview, derives from an eighteenth-century distinction between Athens and Sparta.[111] Athens as celebrated in Pericles' "Funeral Oration" suggested what by the late eighteenth century could be understood as individualism. In contrast, the Spartan ideal, particularly for Jean-Jacques Rousseau (who emulated Plato in this respect), highlighted an admirable internal discipline by all on behalf of a community and shared ideals. The restraint in expression and the implication of discipline associated with the laconic and the Spartan suggest an absence of selfishness, narcissism, and the undisciplined cult of the subjective.

The internal discipline, clarity, and restraint in Prokofiev's music described in 1918 reappear in the last two decades of his life. In 1951 he published statements arguing against the "ivory tower" self-image of the artist. The composer should not "circumscribe the circle of his creativity with subjective emotions." The purpose of the artist was to "help the people live a better and more interesting life." Prokofiev asked, "But can the true artist stand aloof from life and confine his art within the limits of subjective emotions or should he be where he is needed most to help people lead a better, finer life?"[112] Although these statements can be dismissed as boilerplate designed to conform to ideological strictures, it is more likely that this credo comes from Prokofiev himself and for reasons that derive from his lifelong struggle to achieve a sense of purpose and discipline in the face of demons of hidden self-doubt, aggravated health problems, and visible fears. An abiding sense of isolation and detachment surrounds the composer's life. Yet Christian Science helped him define his ultimate aesthetic ideals.

Prokofiev articulated his final mature aesthetic credo, which has been described as the aesthetics of a "new simplicity," in a statement written in 1934 after having resolved his conflict with *The Fiery Angel*. He was essentially committed to return to Russia. He construed the role of the artist in theological terms. By definition, the harmony and goodness of God needed to be accessible through art, and art was a medium of the transmission of that sensibility. Soviet ideology after 1932 seemed compatible with this credo. The embrace of Socialist Realism in music during the 1930s was not oppressive for Prokofiev; rather, the Spartan-like, dictatorial uniformity was liberating.[113] Indeed, as Prokofiev pointed out, the Soviet composer had to address "millions of people who formally had little or no contact with music." This type of music needed to be "light-serious" or "serious-light." Prokofiev followed the oft-cited remark by Brahms that the hardest thing in music was to write a good melody. Imitating the old (something he accused the neoclassicists of doing) was wrong because by definition it created distance between the listener and composer through a self-conscious surface of nostalgic anti-modernity. Trivial and commercial music of the kind Dukelsky wrote may have been modern but it lacked the fingerprints of an individual. It was too formulaic and mechanical. The "new kind of simplicity" could be achieved only by a composer who had gone through the experience of writing music that was not simple, music within the classical and late-Romantic traditions.[114]

It was as if Prokofiev in 1934 was describing an aesthetic journey that paralleled his own progress from a nominal atheism to a flirtation with mysticism and passive agnosticism. That journey would eventually result in a devout adherence to Christian Science. The artist, in service to the ideals of Christian Science, needed to acquire "the technique of expressing himself in simple yet original terms."[115] In Prokofiev's case it is therefore unnecessary to speculate whether his embrace of Stalin and Soviet Russia in the 1930s was devoid of political commitments or cynical, the result of the composer's recognition that his career in the West was uncertain and his reputation in decline. Nor is it sufficient to posit some overwhelming nostalgia for his homeland.

In the same vein, it becomes unnecessary to embark on an elaborate search for hints of irony, anger, and resistance to the insecure, oppressive, and dangerous context in the Soviet Union during the last period of the composer's life, such as abound in the literature on Shostakovich. There may be some truth to these claims in the case of Prokofiev. But the core explanation for Prokofiev's life and music from the mid-1920s on can be found in his profound engagement with Christian Science. There is considerable irony in the suggestive symmetry between a highly democratized American theology defined by resistance to materialism and positivism and

Leon Botstein

the terrifying but successful Stalinist amalgam of nationalism and communism. That symmetry between Stalinism and Christian Science rests in the
shared populist conception of art and beauty and of the role of the artist.
On the surface these two movements had distinctly opposite goals. Christian
Science was about the celebration of the individual as freely capable of
reflecting God's goodness and perfection and living a life without fear, suffering, and evil. Stalinism was all about fear, the suppression of the
individual, suffering, and evil. Perhaps only in Prokofiev's version of
Christian Science, in which the horrors of Stalin's Russia in the end possessed no reality, could an artist of his stature work and produce art in good
conscience that, as Prokofiev wished, has withstood the test of time, fulfilling Gorky's admonition to the composer that his music should be
"vigorous and optimistic" as well as "warm and tender."[116]

NOTES

I wish to thank Jane Smith for her help and Simon Morrison for guiding me
through Prokofiev scholarship and sources. I am also grateful to my colleagues
Christopher Gibbs, Irene Zedlacher, and particularly Gennady Shkliarevsky,
Jennifer Day, and Peter Karpushin, who assisted with the translations, although
the responsibility for them is mine alone. Additional thanks go to Paul De Angelis
and Lynne Meloccaro.

1. See Ernst Kris and Otto Kurz, *Die Legende vom Künstler: Ein geschichtlicher Versuch* (Vienna: Krystall Verlag, 1934). An English translation, *Legend, Myth, and Magic in the Image of the Artist: A Historical Experiment*, was published by Yale University Press in 1979.
2. See Richard Wagner, "Beethoven," trans. William Ashton Ellis, in *Richard Wagner's Complete Prose Works*, 8 vols. (London: K. Paul, Trench, Trubner, 1896; repr., New York: Broude Brothers, 1966), 5:59–126; Teodor de Wyzewa, *Beethoven et Wagner, essais d'histoire et de critique musicales* (Paris: Perrin et Cie, 1914); and K. M. Knittel, "Wagner, Deafness, and the Reception of Beethoven's Late Style," *Journal of the American Musicological Society* 51/1 (Spring 1998): 49–82. On the recep-tion of Wagner in Russia, see Rosamund Bartlett, *Wagner and Russia* (New York: Cambridge University Press, 1995).
3. See Simon Morrison's review of Sergey Prokof'yev, *Dnevnik 1907–1933*, ed. Svyatoslav Prokof'yev, 2 vols. (Paris: Serge Prokofiev Estate, 2002), in *Journal of the American Musicological Society* 58/1 (Spring 2005): 233–43.
4. See Neil Minturn, *The Music of Sergei Prokofiev* (New Haven: Yale University Press, 1997), 3–11. Among the best biographies of Prokofiev are David Nice, *Prokofiev: From Russia to the West, 1891–1935* (New Haven: Yale University Press, 2003); Harlow Robinson, *Sergei Prokofiev: A Biography* (New York: Viking, 1987); Daniel Jaffé, *Sergey Prokofiev* (London: Phaidon, 1998); Lawrence Hanson and Elisabeth M. Hanson, *Prokofiev: A Biography in Three Movements* (New York: Random House, 1964); Claude Samuel, *Prokofiev* (New York: Grossman Publishers, 1971); Friedbert Streller, *Sergej Prokofjew und seine Zeit* (Laaber: Laaber-Verlag, 2003); and Suzanne Moisson-Franckhauser, *Serge Prokofiev et les courants esthétiques de son temps: 1891–1953* (Paris: Publications Orientalistes de France, 1974).
5. See, for example, Galina Vishnevskaya's description of Prokofiev's fondness for perfume and neckties in her autobiography, *Galina: A Russian Story* (San Diego: Harcourt Brace Jovanovich, 1984), 154.

6. See, for example, Stuart Feder, *Gustav Mahler: A Life in Crisis* (New Haven: Yale University Press, 2004); and *Charles Ives: "My Father's Song": A Psychoanalytic Biography* (New Haven: Yale University Press, 1992); Robert Haven Schauffler, *The Unknown Brahms: His Life, Character and Works* (New York: Dodd, Mead, 1933); and Maynard Solomon's two books, *Mozart: A Life* (New York: HarperCollins, 1995) and *Beethoven* (New York: Schirmer Books, 1977), as well as his article "Franz Schubert and the Peacocks of Benvenuto Cellini," *19th-Century Music* 12/3 (Spring 1989): 193–206.

7. On the question of Prokofiev's attitude to mysticism, an interesting marginal note in a November 4, 1976, interview with Lina Prokofiev asserts that "the Prokofievs were different from most Russians in that they did not have the mystical strain peculiar to the Russians." Interview by Lee Z. Johnson, archivist of the Mother Church, and Charlotte Saikowski, writer and former Moscow bureau chief of the *Christian Science Monitor*. A transcript of the interview can be found at the Mary Baker Eddy Library, Boston.

8. I refer to the debates and ideas surrounding the avant-garde in pre-Revolutionary St. Petersburg, particularly the language theories of Mikhaíl Bakhtin and Viktor Shklovsky. See Katerina Clark, *Petersburg: Crucible of Cultural Revolution* (Cambridge, Mass.: Harvard University Press: 1995), 31–35.

9. Arthur Rubinstein, *My Many Years* (New York: Alfred A. Knopf, 1980), 48.

10. Prokof'yev, *Dnevnik 1907–1933*, May 2, 1932, 2:797.

11. See the entry of March 13, 1924, in ibid., 2:245, an ironic critical commentary on the French endorsement of the Romanian annexation of Bessarabia, one of the few diary entries on politics.

12. See "'The Russian Style' Returns to Russia," a discussion of musical nationalism in Stalinist Russia, in Marina Frolova-Walker, *Russian Music and Nationalism: From Glinka to Stalin* (New Haven: Yale University Press, 2007), 338–55.

13. See Richard Taruskin, *Defining Russia Musically: Historical and Hermeneutical Essays* (Princeton: Princeton University Press, 1997), 52, 85–98; and Prokofiev, "The Path of Soviet Music" (1934), in S. I. Shlifshtein, *S. Prokofiev: Autobiography, Articles, Reminiscences*, trans. Rose Prokofieva (Moscow: Foreign Languages Publishing House, n.d.), 99–100.

14. On Rachmaninoff, see Victor Ilyitch Seroff, *Rachmaninoff* (New York: Simon and Schuster, 1950), 239; and Ewald Reder, *Sergej Rachmaninoff: Leben und Werk 1873–1943* (Gelnhausen: Triga, 2001), 360–61, 395–415, 425–26, 439–41. On Stravinsky's return to Russia in 1962, see Stephen Walsh, *Stravinsky: The Second Exile: France and America 1934–1971* (New York: Alfred A. Knopf, 2006); and Robert Craft, *Stravinsky: Chronicle of a Friendship 1948–1971* (New York: Alfred A. Knopf, 1972).

15. See Marina Frolova-Walker, "Music of the Soul," in *National Identity in Russian Culture: An Introduction*, ed. Simon Franklin and Emma Widdis (New York: Cambridge University Press, 2004), 121–31; and Francis Maes, *A History of Russian Music: From Kamarinskaya to Babi Yar* (Berkeley: University of California Press, 2002), 318–42. Interestingly, Gerald Abraham made a similar argument after the composer's death that led to the conclusion that Prokofiev was clearly a superior composer to Shostakovich. Abraham pointed out the extent to which Prokofiev, his advocacy of "new simplicity" notwithstanding, held on to high standards of formal compositional strategies in his final Soviet phase. In this ironic sense, the 1948 Zhdanov attack on Formalism was particularly apt for Prokofiev and his closest musical friend, Myaskovsky. See Abraham, *Serge Prokofieff*, Musik der Zeit 5 (Bonn: Boosey and Hawkes, 1953), 39–40.

16. See, for example, the account, among the most extensive, in Moisson-Franckhauser, *Serge Prokofiev*, 150–51. The most recent discussion in a biography can be found in Nice, *Prokofiev*, 206–7. See also Peter J. Hodgson's letter to the editor, dated March 9, 2006, in *Three Oranges: The Journal of the Serge Prokofiev Foundation* 11 (May 2006), http://www.sprkfv.net/journal/three11/summary11.html, correcting claims made in Natalia Savkina, "The Significance of Christian Science in Prokofiev's Life and Work," *Three Oranges: The Journal of the Serge Prokofiev Foundation* 10 (November 2005), http://www.sprkfv.net/journal/three10/summary10.html.

17. See Prokof'yev, *Dnevnik 1907–1933*, from 2:263; also Sarah A. Paden, "Belief and Consequence: Prokofiev and Christian Science" (unpublished manuscript).

18. See the entries for February 4 and October 5, 1929, in Prokof'yev, *Dnevnik 1907–1933*, 2:670–71 and 725. See also Sugi Sorensen's December 24, 2000, interview, "Q & A with Sviatoslav

Prokofiev," *Three Oranges: The Journal of the Serge Prokofiev Foundation* 1 (January 2001), http://www.sprkfv.net/journal/three01/summary1.html; and Noëlle Mann, "Georgii Gorchakov and the Story of an Unknown Prokofiev Biography," *Three Oranges: The Journal of the Serge Prokofiev Foundation* 11 (May 2006), http://www.sprkfv.net/ journal/three11/summary11.html. Gorchakov, Prokofiev's secretary, was also a Christian Scientist.

19. The movement remained throughout Prokofiev's lifetime distinctly American. All the practitioners with whom Prokofiev came into contact, even in France, were Americans. See Rodney Stark, W. S. Bainbridge, and Lori Kent, "Cult Membership in the Roaring Twenties," *Sociological Analysis* 42 (1981): 137–62, esp. 141.

20. See Edith Talbot, "The 'New' American Religion," *The Biblical World* 47/2 (February 1916): 99–107; and Catherine L. Albanese, "Physic and Metaphysic in Nineteenth-Century America: Medical Sectarians and Religious Healing," *Church History* 55/4 (December 1986): 489–502.

21. Mark Twain helped popularize the widespread idea that Eddy, a mediocrity, had taken her ideas from others (e.g., Phineas Quimby) and that she was an ignorant but shrewd quack, unwilling and unable to confront the progress of modern science. It should be remembered, however, that even in the 1920s, medicine—despite advances from Pasteur's time on in hygiene, diagnosis, vaccines, and surgery—was yet to experience the breakthroughs of the midcentury, starting with penicillin. As Stephen Gottschalk argues, the assault Christian Science made on scientism, the embrace of materialism and positivism vis-à-vis the aches and pains (literally) of daily life, seemed relatively reasonable. Gottschalk also has an insightful account of Twain's obsession with Eddy and Christian Science. See Twain, *Christian Science* (1907; repr. New York: Oxford University Press, 1996); and Gottschalk, *Rolling Away the Stone: Mary Baker Eddy's Challenge to Materialism* (Bloomington: Indiana University Press, 2005), 44–87.

22. Marina Rakhmanova, "Prokof'yev i Christian Science," in *Sergey Prokof'yev: K 110-letiyu so dnya rozhdeniya. Pis'ma, vospominaniya, stat'i* (Moscow: Gosudarstvennïy tsentral'nïy muzey muzïkal'noy kul'turï im. M. I. Glinki, 2006), 258–67. On Edward Kimball, a leader in the Christian Science movement, see Gillian Gill, *Mary Baker Eddy* (Cambridge, Mass.: Perseus Books, 1998), 410–11, 467.

23. Mary Baker Eddy, *Science and Health with Key to the Scriptures* (Gloucester, UK: Dodo Press, 2007), 472.

24. Curiously, Paden in "Belief and Consequence" follows Prokofiev's uncritical assumption of a connection between the claims of Christian Science and Kantian epistemology.

25. See Prokof'yev, *Dnevnik 1907–1933*, July 30, 1924, 2:275; and Prokofiev, *Diaries 1907–1914: Prodigious Youth*, trans. and annotated by Anthony Phillips (Ithaca, N.Y.: Cornell University Press, 2007), xiv.

26. See Edward A. Kimball's summary of this claim in his *Lectures and Articles on Christian Science* (Valparaiso, Ind.: H. H. Wait, 1921), 459–63.

27. Ibid.

28. Eddy, *Science and Health*, 281, 467.

29. Ernest Becker, *The Denial of Death* (New York: Free Press, 1973), 13–24, 203–5.

30. Eddy, *Science and Health*, 337, 414. The latter passage suggests why Prokofiev insisted on an ending in which the protagonists in his ballet *Romeo and Juliet* do not die. For a Christian Scientist, they in fact did not. The inconsistencies and contradictions and even possible absurdities in Christian Science theology, notably concerning its view of death and reality, are not at issue here, but they are perhaps most evident in Eddy's own personal struggle with illness and death, including her resort to medication, pain relief, and the suggestion of the existence of "Malicious Animal Magnetism." See Gill, *Mary Baker Eddy*, 528–32, 544–47.

31. Eddy, *Science and Health*, 463; Kimball, *Lectures and Articles*, 215–17.

32. Eddy, *Science and Health*, 444.

33. Ibid., 463.

34. Kimball, *Lectures and Articles*, 157.

35. Eddy, *Science and Health*, 457.

36. Ibid., 431.

37. The marginalia in Prokofiev's copy of Kimball's *Lectures and Articles on Christian Science*, 284, confirms the composer's focus on this argument. See Rakhmanova, "Prokof'yev i Christian Science," 259.

38. Eddy, *Science and Health*, 349.

39. See, for example, Prokof'yev, *Dnevnik 1907–1933*, December 19, 1926, 2:450, and October 25, 1927, 2:600.

40. See Raymond J. Cunningham, "The Impact of Christian Science on American Churches 1880–1910," *American Historical Review* 72/3 (1967): 885–905.

41. See the best and most sophisticated exposition of Eddy's thought, Gottschalk's *Rolling Away the Stone*.

42. See Nathan O. Hatch, *The Democratization of American Christianity* (New Haven: Yale University Press, 1989), 27–30.

43. Marginalia in Prokofiev's copy of Kimball's *Lectures and Articles on Christian Science* are collected and described in Rakhmanova, "Prokof'yev i Christian Science," 258–67.

44. Kimball, *Lectures and Articles*, 31.

45. Ibid., 201; and marginalia in Prokofiev's copy of Kimball's book in Rakhmanova, "Prokof'yev i Christian Science," 259.

46. The text is reproduced in Samuel, *Prokofiev*, 128–29.

47. Series SF, Folder ID Prokofiev, Mary Baker Eddy Library.

48. Kimball, *Lectures and Articles*, 463; and marginalia in Prokofiev's copy of Kimball's book in Rakhmanova, "Prokof'yev i Christian Science," 260.

49. Prokof'yev, *Dnevnik 1907–1933*, December 13, 1927, 2:612.

50. Robinson, *Sergei Prokofiev*, 392–93.

51. Kimball, *Lectures and Articles*, 471. Prokofiev marked the passage where Kimball discusses the so-called raising of the dead by claiming, "I know that the dead have been raised," and since there is no death, "it matters not." See Rakhmanova, "Prokof'yev i Christian Science," 260.

52. Prokof'yev, *Dnevnik 1907–1933*, April 23, 1925, 2:316.

53. Prokof'yev, *Dnevnik 1907–1933*, June 8, 1924, 2:263.

54. The affair is referenced in Stephen D. Press, *Prokofiev's Ballets for Diaghilev* (Aldershot, UK: Ashgate, 2006), 105 n. 40, but not in Nice's *Prokofiev* or previous biographies. Adler was the daughter of Sarah and Jacob Adler, who were among the finest actors in the American Yiddish theater. She made her first stage appearance at the age of four and in 1919, at age eighteen, she made her debut at the Pavilion in London as Naomi in *Elisa Ben Avia*, a role she performed for a year. After hundreds of performances all over the world as a leading lady to the most famous leading men of the Yiddish theater, she made her Broadway debut in *The World We Live In* and subsequently worked with émigré veterans of the Moscow Art Theater. Her second husband was Harold Clurman, whom she met in the mid-1920s. (Clurman, incidentally, was Aaron Copland's cousin, with whom the composer first went to Paris.) In 1934 Adler went to Moscow, where she studied with Konstantin Stanislavsky, and seems never to have crossed paths with Prokofiev again. Although Adler had a distinguished stage career (from which she retired in 1961) and worked as a producer for MGM, she is best remembered as a teacher whose pupils included Marlon Brando, Robert De Niro, Warren Beatty, and Candice Bergen. She died in 1992. Although official records state her birth year to be 1901, the consensus is that she was two years older than she admitted.

55. Shortly after her return in early March 1920, Stella confessed to a relationship in London that "bordered on love." The composer noted that he was "stung" by this revelation, but became "mollified" by recalling Lina. Prokof'yev, *Dnevnik 1907–1933*, March 1, 1920, 2:83.

56. Prokof'yev, *Dnevnik 1907–1933*, March 10, 1920, 2:85.

57. Prokofiev's conceit regarding his attractiveness to women, a quite constant refrain in his self-regard, remained undiminished through 1921, Lina and Stella notwithstanding, as testified to in diary accounts of several flirtations and conquests on the West Coast, particularly with Dagmar Godowskaya, Leopold Godowsky's daughter. The relationships with Adler and, decades later, with Mira Mendelson, both of Jewish descent, raise the issue of Prokofiev's attitude toward Jews. Anti-Semitism was a commonplace in the culture in which Prokofiev grew up, and he periodically noted in the diaries which of his acquaintances were Jews. In America he was repeatedly

amused when individuals treated him as if he were Jewish. A striking scene in the diaries describes Adler's accusation that Prokofiev represented Russian Orthodox nationalist anti-Semitism and was thus metaphorically responsible for the pogroms. See Prokof'yev, *Dnevnik 1907–1933*, August 4, 1919, 2:40. However, Prokofiev exhibited little of the virulent prejudice exhibited by Stravinsky and tended to behave in a manner reminiscent of Shostakovich, who was quite free of prejudice. At the same time, particularly in Adler's case, the exotic temperamental personality routinely stigmatized by the term "Jewish American Princess" may have attracted Prokofiev, if he understood it as an ethnic reality at all.

58. For example, Prokofiev went to Europe in the spring of 1921 and traveled there with Lina before returning to America in the fall. When he saw Adler again, he remarked that she had gotten even prettier, that she dazzled him every time he saw her. Prokofiev's relationship with Lina, with whom he corresponded during the fall, became strained. Adler was still on his mind in early 1922. Prokof'yev, *Dnevnik 1907–1933*, January 17–February 25, 2:197.

59. Lina, who used the stage name Lina Llubera, performed with Prokofiev. She had formal training and a bit of operatic experience but after marrying restricted herself to recital work. The diaries testify to Prokofiev's doubts about Lina's talents and to the nearly endless anxiety and self-doubt she expressed regarding her concert appearances. See Nice, *Prokofiev*, 153–54.

60. This pattern has a suggestive analogue in the biography of another composer, Richard Strauss, famed for a complicated but seemingly happy and productive married life with Pauline de Ahna. Strauss had an intense earlier relationship with Dora Weis (a pianist of Jewish descent once married to the Czech cellist Hans Wihan), disapproved of by his parents, whose opposition hastened the relationship's end and precipitated what some have regarded as a nervous breakdown. The evidence of that relationship seems to have been destroyed, and no mention of it was ever made afterward as Strauss embarked on his very visible and stable marital life. See Bryan Gilliam, *The Life of Richard Strauss* (Cambridge: Cambridge University Press, 1999), 21.

61. There is a tragic irony in the connection between Lina and Christian Science. The most recent research, bolstered by Lina's interviews after her move to the West, long after Prokofiev's death in 1953, indicates that she was arrested in 1948 in part perhaps on suspicion of religious proselytizing. Lina, who remained an active Christian Scientist despite earlier doubts, may have been denounced by Mira Mendelson, a committed Communist. Lina's arrest file remains sealed. Prokofiev's relationship with Mendelson was seen by some, including Lina, as motivated on the composer's part by a search for security, given Mendelson's connections through her parents, both active Party workers. See Lina Prokofiev, interview.

62. Prokof'yev, *Dnevnik 1907–1933*, May 14, 1926, 2:402; and December 5, 1927, 2:609–10.

63. Ibid., July 4, 1927, 2:571.

64. Samuel, *Prokofiev*, 128; and Prokof'yev, *Dnevnik 1907–1933*, November 6, 1927, 2:603.

65. Kimball, *Lectures and Articles*, 468; on Prokofiev's marginalia, see also Rakhmanova, "Prokof'yev i Christian Science," 260.

66. Prokof'yev, *Dnevnik 1907–1933*, January 29, 1929, 2:669–70.

67. Ibid., August 13, 1924, 2:277.

68. Ibid., July 2, 1925, 2:336; and December 18, 1926, 2:450.

69. Ibid., August 4, 1926, 2:426–27.

70. See also Kimball, *Articles and Lectures*, 436; and the marginalia in Prokofiev's copy of Kimball's book in Rakhmanova, "Prokof'yev i Christian Science," 260.

71. Prokof'yev, *Dnevnik 1907–1933*, May 5, 1926, 2:397.

72. Ibid., February 3, 1925, 2:305.

73. Ibid., February 15, 1926, 2:379; October 25, 1927, 2:600; November 1, 1927, 2:602.

74. Ibid., January 3 and November 6–12, 1927, 2:457–58. See also Kimball, *Articles and Lectures*, 224.

75. Prokofiev, *Diaries: Prodigious Youth*, 168.

76. See Ludmila Korabelnikova, *Alexander Tcherepnin: The Saga of a Russian Emigré Composer*, ed. Sue-Ellen Hershman-Tcherepnin, trans. Anna Winestein (Bloomington: Indiana University Press, 2008), 8–9. For the composer's characteristically shifting but favorable attitude, see *Prokofiev by Prokofiev: A Composer's Memoir*, ed. David H. Appel, trans. Guy Daniels (Garden City, N.Y.:

Doubleday, 1979), 217; and *Diaries: Prodigious Youth*, 156, 586, and 626. For Prokofiev on Glier, see "My Teacher," in *S. Prokofiev Autobiography, Articles, Reminiscences*, 120.

77. Prokof'yev, *Dnevnik 1907–1933*, January 3, 1927, 2:457.

78. Prokof'yev, *Dnevnik 1907–1933*, September 24, 1927, 2:593–94. See also Kimball, *Lectures and Articles*, 200–202, 254–57; for marginalia in Prokofiev's copy, see Rakhmanova, "Prokof'yev i Christian Science," 259.

79. So was Stravinsky. See Stephen Walsh, *Stravinsky, A Creative Spring: Russia and France, 1882–1934* (Berkeley: University of California Press, 1999), 387.

80. Prokof'yev, *Dnevnik 1907–1933*, September 21, 1924, 2:281–82. Simon Morrison reports that this was not the only dream Prokofiev had about Rimsky. A late notebook describes a dream about a socialist realist version of one of Rimsky's operas.

81. See Sigmund Freud, *The Interpretation of Dreams*, ed. and trans. James Strachey (1900; New York: Avon Books, 1965), 385–97; and "A Connection Between a Symbol and a Symptom" (1916), in *Collected Papers*, vol. 2, ed. Joan Riviere (New York: Basic Books, 1959), 162–63. The use of Freud in this context has utility apart from normative claims on behalf of Freudian psychoanalytic theory. Freud's interpretations of dreams and the psyche, particularly with respect to generational dynamics (e.g., the Oedipal dynamic) and symbols in the unconscious, date from the same historical era. They come from a context very much like Prokofiev's in terms of class and culture: Central and Eastern Europe in the first two decades of the twentieth century.

82. See Sigmund Freud, *Introductory Lectures on Psychoanalysis*, ed. and trans. James Strachey (1917; New York: W. W. Norton, 1966), 210–12, 330–34. There is a musical dimension to the dream as well. Prokofiev—for all his early reputation as a "modernist" and his pride in offending the conservative Glazunov, Rimsky's successor as head of the St. Petersburg Conservatory (and in this context perhaps the real object of the dream)—knew that he was in some sense well within a traditional Russian musical aesthetic framework. The dream can also be interpreted as a wish fulfillment to gain the approval of an establishment he had overtly challenged in his youth. Prokofiev eventually sought and achieved that approval by returning to Russia three years later, in 1927, and then permanently in the 1930s, armed with a clear agenda regarding his own compositional practice. The other possible musical-psychological reading derives from a hypothesis that Rimsky is a replacement symbol for Prokofiev's rivalry with and envy of Stravinsky, who was also in Paris and had worked with Hébertot on *L'Histoire du soldat*. See Walsh, *Stravinsky, A Creative Spring*, 341. Stravinsky was widely regarded as Rimsky's true heir. On Prokofiev's relationship to Rimsky, see Robinson, *Sergei Prokofiev*, 47–49.

83. Prokof'yev, *Dnevnik 1907–1933*, November 11, 1928, 2:647. The following discussion takes a different view from that articulated by Natalia Savkina in *Prokofiev*, trans. Catherine Young (Neptune City, N.J.: Paganiniana, 1984).

84. Prokof'yev, *Dnevnik 1907–1933*, December 16, 1926, 2:449–50.

85. Prokof'yev, *Dnevnik 1907–1933*, February 4, 1929, 2:670–71. See Kimball, *Articles and Lectures*, 263; for marginalia in Prokofiev's copy, see Rakhmanova, "Prokof'yev i Christian Science," 259.

86. See Kimball's discussion of these issues in *Lectures and Articles*, 190–92, 261–67; also see the marginalia in Prokofiev's copy, in Rakhmanova, "Prokof'yev i Christian Science," 259.

87. Prokof'yev, *Dnevnik 1907–1933*, August 13, 1924, 2:277. Prokofiev highlighted similar ideas articulated by Kimball in *Lectures and Articles*, 458, with marginalia in his copy of the book. See Rakhmanova, "Prokof'yev i Christian Science," 260.

88. Kimball, *Lectures and Articles*, 468–71. See Rakhmanova, "Prokof'yev i Christian Science," 260, for Prokofiev's marginalia in his copy of Kimball's book.

89. Prokof'yev, *Dnevnik 1907–1933*, February 6, 1926, 2:377.

90. Prokofiev noted the rationality of Christian Science in the margin of his copy of Kimball, *Lectures and Articles*, 283. See Rakhmanova, "Prokof'yev i Christian Science," 259.

91. Robinson, *Sergei Prokofiev*, 38–39. In his memoir, Prokofiev described both his parents as atheists and unconcerned, particularly with his father, with death. For Prokofiev, it seems that conquering the fear of death was a way of emulating his father. He felt the need to gain his approval, something his father's early death, in July 1910, made impossible. The death of his father and

the composer's early desire to have a "life free from pain and trouble" are linked. See *Prokofiev by Prokofiev*, 268; and his *Diaries: Prodigious Youth*, 167–68, 177, 190.

92. Prokofiev "Can There Be an End to Melody?" in Shlifshtein, *Prokofiev*, 115–17

93. Prokof'yev, *Dnevnik 1907–1933*, February 3, 1925, 2:305.

94. Ibid.

95. Ibid., February 4, 1932, 2:670. See also Kimball, *Lectures and Articles*, 260–61, 435–38; for the marginalia in Prokofiev's copy, see Rakhmanova, "Prokof'yev i Christian Science," 260.

96. Prokof'yev, *Dnevnik 1907–1933*, August 1929, 2:722–23.

97. Ibid., August 11, 1927, 2:580.

98. See Kimball's eloquent version in his *Lectures and Articles*, 215.

99. Prokof'yev, *Dnevnik 1907–1933*, October 5, 1929, 2:725.

100. Marina Frolova-Walker, "From Modernism to Socialist Realism in Four Years: Myaskovsky and Asafyev," *Musicology* (Journal of the Institute of Musicology of the Serbian Academy of Sciences and Arts) 3 (2003): 199–217. Prokofiev apparently also sought to persuade Boris Demchinsky, whom he had consulted on the libretto of *The Fiery Angel*, but to no avail. I thank Simon Morrison for pointing this out.

101. Laurel E. Fay, *Shostakovich: A Life* (New York: Oxford University Press, 2000), 30, 91.

102. On Asafyev's potential to help Prokofiev adjust to the Soviet Union, see Streller, *Sergej Prokofjew*, 200, 227.

103. Prokof'yev, *Dnevnik 1907–1933*, June 1, 1932, 2:800; see also May 18, 1932, 2:798. For a different reading of this episode, see Savkina, *Prokofiev*, 21–22.

104. Prokof'yev, *Dnevnik 1907–1933*, August 22, 1924, 2:278.

105. Ibid., May 18, 1932, 2:798.

106. Ibid., February 15 and September 28, 1926, 2:379 and 439. Early in his engagement with Christian Science Prokofiev mused on the purpose of so-called talent, a "God-given gift," and on "human perfection." Ibid., June 11, 1925, 2:326. On *The Fiery Angel* and Prokofiev's struggle with it (he reused musical material in the Third Symphony), see Simon Morrison, *Russian Opera and the Symbolist Movement* (Berkeley: University of California Press, 2002), 242–99. As early as May 5, 1926, the composer acknowledged that the Third Symphony, built on material from *The Fiery Angel*, "will be bright," bringing to an end his "dark" period (marked by the Second Symphony), revealing how Christian Science helped him overcome fear and embrace optimism. But the process took longer and extended to the end of 1926. See Prokof'yev, *Dnevnik 1907–1933*, 2:397.

107. Morrison, *Russian Opera*, 7–8.

108. Prokof'yev, *Dnevnik 1907–1933*, February 13, 1926, 2:379.

109. Prokofiev, "A New Soviet Symphony," in Shlifshtein, *Prokofiev*, 104.

110. Prokofiev, "The Masses Want Great Music" and "Can There Be an End to Melody," in Shlifshtein, *Prokofiev*, 106 and 115.

111. Prokofiev, "Clarity and Laconism," trans. Andrew Markow, in *Sergei Prokofiev: Materials, Articles, Interviews*, comp. Vladimir Blok (Moscow: Progress Publishers, 1978), 27.

112. Prokofiev, "I adhere to the conviction . . . ," in *Sergei Prokofiev: Materials, Articles, Interviews*, 52; and "Music and Life," in Shlifshtein, *Prokofiev*, 135.

113. See Marina Frolova-Walker, "Stalin and the Art of Boredom," *Twentieth-Century Music* 1 (2004): 101–24, esp., 122–23.

114. Prokofiev, "The Path of Soviet Music," in Shlifshtein, *Prokofiev*, 99–100.

115. Ibid.

116. Prokofiev, "On Gorky," in Shlifshtein, *Prokofiev*, 102. On Gorky's career and relationship to Soviet Russia, perhaps the best source is Orlando Figes, *A People's Tragedy: A History of the Russian Revolution* (New York: Viking, 1997), passim; and Maxim Gorky, *Untimely Thoughts: Essays on Revolution, Culture and the Bolsheviks 1917–1918* (1968; New Haven: Yale University Press, 1995).

Permissions and Credits

Boosey & Hawkes has graciously given permission to reprint musical excerpts from the following copyrighted works by Sergey Prokofiev: *Suggestion diabolique*, op. 4; *Toccata*, op. 11; Sonatina no. 2, op. 54; Piano Concerto no. 5, op. 55; Sonata for Two Violins, op. 56; *Pensées* no. 1, op. 62; Violin Concerto no. 2, op. 63; and Symphony no. 4, op. 112.

G. Schirmer, Associated Music Publishers, Inc., has graciously given permission to reprint musical excerpts from the following copyrighted works by Sergey Prokofiev: *Romeo and Juliet*, op. 64; and *War and Peace*, op. 91.

The following copyright holders have graciously granted permission to reprint or reproduce the following copyrighted material:

The Serge Prokofiev Estate, Paris, for the literary notebook of Mariya Prokofieva.

The Russian State Archive of Literature and Art, for: the playscript of *Eugene Onegin* by Sigizmund Krzhizhanovsky and Alexander Pushkin (1936), as well as the photograph of Krzhizhanovsky; the correspondence between Sergey Prokofiev and Levon Atovmyan; also, the photograph of Nadezhda Golubovskaya, Prokofiev, Atovmyan, Grigoriy Shneyerson, and Mira Mendelson; excerpts of the music by Prokofiev composed for *Lieutenant Kizhe*; examples from Prokofiev's sketchbooks in the essay by Mark Aranovsky.

Gosfilmofund, Moscow, for the still photograph of the wedding ceremony from *Lieutenant Kizhe*, in the essay by Kevin Bartig.

The Serge Prokofiev Archive, Goldsmiths College, London, for the schematic reconstruction of the "visual aid" for No. 4 of *The Prodigal Son*; and for a page from Prokofiev's sketchbook; both in the essay by Marina Frolova-Walker.

Roman Ledenyov, for an excerpt from his piano sonata in the essay by Peter Schmelz.

Muzïka, Moscow, for an excerpt from Vladimir Vlasov's Third Quartet in the essay by Peter Schmelz.

Ellen Adler, for the photo of Stella Adler in the essay by Leon Botstein.

We would also like to credit:

Alexander Osmyorkin and *Iskusstvo* for the three drawings from the unrealized 1936 production of *Eugene Onegin*, reproduced from L. Oginskaya, "'Yevgeniy Onegin' v eskizakh A. A. Osmyorkina," *Iskusstvo* 10 (1979): 31–33.

Rare Books and Special Collections, Northern Illinois University, for the photograph of Boris Anisfeld's stage set for *The Love for Three Oranges*.

Pravda, for the photograph of Stalin lying in state from page 1 of its March 7, 1953 issue; and S. Khentova and Sovetskiy kompozitor for the photograph of Prokofiev and Shostakovich, reproduced from S. Khentova, *Shostakovich: Zhizn' i tvorchestvo*, 2 vols. (Leningrad: Sovetskiy kompozitor, 1985–86), 2: 288–89.

Yuriy Kholopov and Muzïka for the *Betrothal in a Monastery* example, from Yuriy Kholopov, "Tvorchestvo Prokof'yeva v Sovetskom teoreticheskom muzïkoznanii," in *S. S. Prokof'yev: Stat'i i issledovaniya*, ed. V. Blok (Moscow: Muzïka, 1972).

Yuriy Kholopov and Sovetskiy kompozitor for the diagram from Kholopov's essay, "O sovremennïkh chertakh garmonii S. Prokof'yeva," in *Chertï stilya S. Prokof'yeva: Sbornik teoreticheskikh statey*, ed. L. Berger (Moscow: Sovetskiy kompozitor, 1962), 259.

Grateful acknowledgment is also made to Furthermore, a program of the J. M. Kaplan Fund, for a grant underwriting the publication of this volume.

Index

Subject and Name Index

Congress of People's Deputies, 319, 321
Constant, Benjamin, *Adolfe*, 112n67
Copland, Aaron, 377, 380, 390, 435,
   436, 532, 558n54
Coppola, Pierre, 391
Council of Ministers, 289, 290, 300,
   324–26
Cranmer, Jean, 438–39
Cuba, Bay of Pigs invasion of, 313
Culture, Soviet Ministry of, 293, 299,
   305, 313–25, 328n2, 329n14,
   330n36, 504; Foreign Relations
   Department, 315; Musical Theater
   Directorate, 298

Damrosch, Walter, 336, 373n4
Damskaya, Eleanora, 19, 20
Dartmouth College Prokofieff Society,
   431, 443, 445
Dattel, Elizaveta, 81, 82, 111n52
Davidson, Pamela, 2–59
Davis, Ronald, 352
Debussy, Claude, 499, 503, 509
Decembrist movement, 73–74, 110n38
Defauw, Désiré, 197, 372
Defense, Soviet Ministry of, 290
DeLamarter, Eric, 336
Denisov, Edison, 496–99, 503, 506, 509,
   514, 524n37, n43; String Quartet
   no. 2, 499
Denver String Quartet, 437, 449n75
Denver Symphony, 437–38
Derzhanovsky, Vladimir, 11, 50n4,
   206–7, 471
Derzhanovskaya, Yekaterina, 226
Descartes, René, 535
Detroit Symphony Orchestra, 433, 436
Devries, Herman, 426
Diaghilev, Serge, 347, 351, 368, 454,
   461–63, 463, 467–68
Diederichs, Andrey, 20
Dietrich, Marlene, 442
Disney, Walt, 61, 371, 424, 441, 442,
   444, 446
Dobjinsky, Mstislav, 371
Doctors' Plot, 495
Dohnányi, Ernö, 8
Dolukhanova, Zara, 258
Dolzhansky, Alexander, 512
Donetsk Musical Pedagogical Institute,
   324, 325
Dostoyevsky, Fyodor, 58n63, 111n47,

112n67, 113n69, 334
Douglas, Canon Winfred, 437
Dovzhenko, Alexander, 381
Downes, Olin, 371, 404
Drashnikov, Vladimir, 469
Duke, Anna, 432–33
Duke, Vernon (Vladimir Dukelsky), 425,
   428, 430, 432–34, 447n10, 448n40,
   554
Duo-Art, 338, 339, 368, 400n75
Durgin, Cyrus, 444
Dvořák, Antonin, 534

Eastman, Max, 486, 492n46
Eastman School of Music, 369
Eaton, Quaintance, 371
Eddy, Mary Baker, 450n86, 534–41, 544,
   557n21; *Science and Health*, 535, 546,
   557n30
Egorov, Vladimir, 324
Egorova, Tatiana, 386
Ehrenburg, Ilya, 489n5; *The Thaw*, 495
Eisenhower, Dwight D., 313
Eisenstein, Sergey, 111n51, 203n3, 223,
   228, 381, 392, 395
Emerson, Caryl, 60–114
Ermolayev, Alexey, 256

Fairbank, Janet, 360–61
Fairbanks, Douglas, Jr., 442
fairy tales, 101–5, 184n60
Falen, James E., 111n40, 116
Fay, Laurel, 494
Fayer, Yuriy, 224n3, 237
Fayntsimmer, Alexander, 208, 378–93,
   395, 397n13, n23, 398n31, n38,
   n43, 399n49
Ferkelman, Mikhaíl, 243, 244
Fet, Afanasiy, 17, 58n64
Finance Ministry, Soviet, 318, 320–21,
   324, 326
Fischer, Carl, 338
Five-Year Plans, 459, 486, 490
Flight to the Moon, 270
Fonvizin, Denis, 58n63, 86; *The Minor*,
   184n47
Foreign Affairs, Soviet Ministry of,
   187n96, 255, 290
Formalism, 377, 380, 428, 485, 556n15
Freud, Sigmund, 93, 114n82, 547,
   560n81
Frolova-Walker, Marina, 452–92

Index

Frunze, Mikhaíl, 455
Frye, Northrop, 99, 114n82
Furtseva, Yekaterina, 312–15, 317
Futurism, 7, 342, 355

Gabovich, Mikhaíl, 256
Gagarin, Yuriy, 313
Galileo Galilei, 15, 45, 57n50
Galperina, E. K., 65–66
Garden, Mary, 352–57, 367
Garin, Erast, 378–79, 397n16, n18, 398n42
Gasparov, Mikhaíl, 64–65
Gatti-Casazza, Giulio, 342, 346–47, 369, 370
Gauk, Alexander, 201, 224n4, 238, 239n5, 473
Gayamov, Alexander, 200, 201, 203
Geneva Copyright Convention, 318
George, Prince (Duke of Kent), 391
Gerchuk, Iurii, 507
Gergiev, Valery, 453
Gershwin, George, 502; *Blue Monday*, 363; *Rhapsody in Blue*, 363
Ginzburg, Alexander, 210, 211, 214, 215, 216
Gippius, Zinaida, 2, 9, 26n27, 35, 52n13, 55n38; *Silences*, 9–12, 37–39, 52n15, 53n20, 54n26
Glazunov, Alexander, 4, 531, 560n82
Glier, Reinhold, 4–5, 8, 51n13, 192, 220, 222n2, 230, 233, 297, 531, 546; *The Red Poppy*, 299, 307
Glinka, Mikhaíl, 192, 403; *Ruslan and Lyudmila*, 313
Gnesin Institute, 190, 331n53, 502
Gnostics, 12, 52n14, 53n19
Goethe, Johann Wolfgang von, *Faust*, 457
Gogol, Nikolai, 58n63, 82, 113n69, 377–79, 384; *Dead Souls*, 186n82, 551
Golschmann, Vladimir, 428
Gorbachev, Mikhaíl, 285, 331n49
Gorbman, Claudia, 387
Gorelik, Mordukh, 220, 221
Gorky, Maxim, 63, 113n67, 251, 288, 555
Gorodetsky, Sergey, 7
Gotgelf, Sofya, 261
Gottlieb, Ephraim, 352, 357, 424, 425, 433–34, 440, 446, 447n7, 449n74
Gozzi, Carlo, *The Love for Three Oranges*, 334, 355
Graham, Thomas, 550

Grant, Julie, Princess Cantacuzene, 348–49
Great Terror, 65, 305, 314, 329n7
Grey, Camilla, 316–17
Griffes, Charles T., *White Peacock*, 367
Grikurov, Eduard, 244, 245, 251
Grimm Brothers, 101
Gromyko, Andrei, 446
Gubaidulina, Sofia, 496–98
Gubenko, Nikolay, 320, 324, 326, 331n49
Gusman, Boris, 197, 379, 381, 397n20, 398n31, 474

Haensel & Jones, 336, 347, 348, 351, 358, 425, 431, 433, 445, 451n111
Halasz, Laszlo, 371
Hale, Richard, 444
Handel, George Frideric, *Giulio Cesare*, 319
Harris, Henry, 434
Harrison, Paul, 441
Hasselmans, Louis, 345
Haydn, Joseph, 429, 466, 534
Hayes, Helen, 437
Hébertot, Jacques, 546, 560n82
Hecht, Ben, 362–63
Heifetz, Jascha, 437
Henrich, Val P., 437
Hero of Socialist Labor, 287, 328n1, 331n50
Hindemith, Paul, 515
Hoffmann, E. T. A., 63
Honegger, Arthur, *Pastorale d'été*, 427
Huneker, James Gibbons, 341, 342, 374n17
Hungarian Revolution (1956), 301
Hynds, Reed, 428–29
Hyperion Studio, 441

Ilin, Igor, 258
immortalization (*uvekovecheniye pamyati*), 285–88; of Shostakovich, 288–90, 328n1; of SP, 293–328
International Book, 255, 256n5
International Harvester Corporation, 335, 374n29
International Prokofiev Festival, 310–12
Ivanov, Vyacheslav, 13, 52n15, n18
Ivanov-Radkevich, Nikolay, 213
Ivanov-Vano, Ivan, 394, 400n89
Ives, Charles, 531
Izvestiya, 292, 306

93, 107n13, 108n22, 110n38,
111n47, 180n1, 183n35, 286, 328,
424, 425, 430; Jubilee of, 60–62, 81,
109n30
works: *Angelo*, 114n81; "The
Awakening," 187n94; *Boris
Godunov*, 86, 109n30; *The Captain's
Daughter*, 114n80; "Cleopatra," 69,
107n9, 109n28, 196n8; *Eugene
Onegin*, 66, 69–71, 73–75, 79,
80–83, 85–87, 89, 94–102, 105,
109n26, 111n50, n52, n55,
112n64, n67, 113n77, 115–16,
180–89; "Fairy Tale of the Dead
Tsarevna and the Seven Knights,"
101–2, 115, 181n12; "I have outlived all my desires," 180n6; *Little
Tragedies*, 86; "Recollections of
Tsarskoye Selo," 180n2; *Rusalka*,
114n81; *Ruslan and Lyudmila*,
114n80; "The Snowstorm," 98
Pushkin, Natalie, 66
Pushkin, Vasily, *The Dangerous Neighbor*,
114n77, 183n38
Pushkin Commission, 61, 62, 70
Pustïlnik, Iosif, 512
Puzin, Alexey, 253
Pyatigorsky, Gregor, 442, 446

Rachmaninoff, Sergey, 255, 336, 339–40,
368, 402, 410, 423, 532, 552;
Prelude in C-Sharp Minor, 358
Radek, Karl, 455
Radin, Yevgeniy, 212, 215, 218, 221, 222
Radlov, Sergey, 415, 469
Rafalovich, Sergey, 11, 50n7; *Women's
Letters*, 7–8, 31, 50n7, 51n8, n9, n12
Ranger, Ralph, 441–42
Rappoport, Lidiya, 511
Ratgauz, Daniil, 8, 33, 51n13
Ravel, Maurice, *Chanson espagnole*, 499
Raymond, Emil, 354, 356
Red Army, 295, 302
Red Banner of Labor, Order of, 328
Reid, Susan, 507
Reisenberg, Nadia, 434
Revolution of 1905, 513
Richter, Svyatoslav, 203n4, 208n2,
224n1, 238, 242, 243, 247n3, 250,
305–6, 330n18, 331n53, 497,
523n21
Rimsky-Korsakov, Nikolay, 103, 286,

325, 382, 398n38, 403, 404, 437,
546–47, 560n80; *Snegurochka*, 103
Robin, Leo, 441–42
Robinson, Edward G., 442–43, 445
Robinson, Gladys Lloyd, 442–43
Robinson, Harlow, 11
Rogal-Levitsky, Dmitriy, 226n2
Romanticism, 88, 97, 112n67, 181n16,
531, 552
Romm, Mikhaíl, 61
Room, Abram, 207n1, 208
Roosevelt, Franklin D., 432
Rosing, Vladimir, 369–71
Rossini, Gioacchino, *Il Barbiere di Siviglia*,
313; *William Tell*, 343
Rostropovich, Mstislav, 242, 243, 247n3,
250, 264, 265, 267, 270n5, 331n53
Rousseau, Jean-Jacques, 553
Rozanov, Vasiliy, 9, 52n14
Rozhdestvensky, Gennadiy, 237n1, 485
Rubinstein, Arthur, 529n138, 532
Rubinstein, Nina, 550
Rubtsova, Valentina, 314
Rummel, I., 397n21, 398n36, n42
Russian Association of Proletarian
Musicians (RAPM), 221, 222n8
Russian Association of Proletarian
Writers (RAPP), 459, 486
Russian Civil War, 457, 460, 489n5, 490
Russian Orthodoxy, 9, 52n14, 81, 386,
389, 390, 456, 548, 559n57
Russian State Archive of Literature and
Art (RGALI), 62, 67, 81, 192, 401,
403
Russian Symphony Orchestra, 336, 341

Saar, Louis Victor, 428
Sabaneyev, Leonid, 13
Sabashnikova, Margarita, 13
Sabinina, Marina, 330n25, 505, 525n48
Sade, Hugues de, 186n77
St. Leger, Frank, 357
St. Louis Symphony Orchestra, 428–29
St. Petersburg Conservatory, 4, 239n6,
560n82
Saint-Saëns, Camille, 502
Sakharov, Andrey, 314
Sakva, Konstantin, 254
Salmanov, Vadim, 511
Samosud, Samuil, 203n4, 211, 212n3,
n4, 214, 215, 217, 220, 251–52, 255,
256n2, 260n4, 261n6, 273, 275, 276,

Index

330n18, 503–4
Saradzhev, K. S., 472
Satie, Erik, 401
Savintsev, Pyotr, 311, 312
Schindler, Anton, 530
Schindler, Kurt, 335, 338, 373n12
Schindler, Vera, 334, 335
Schirmer family, 335, 338
Schmelz, Peter J., 493–29
Schmidthof, Maximilian, 17
Schnittke, Alfred, 496–97, 509, 512, 515,
    516, 524n36, 528n134; First
    Symphony, 516; *Hommage à Igor
    Stravinsky, Sergey Prokofiev and Dmitry
    Shostakovich*, 501
Schnitzler, Arthur, 8, 51n11
Schoenberg, Arnold, 342, 359, 402, 442,
    499, 506–7, 511, 514–15, 526n79;
    Five Orchestral Pieces, 361, 375n52
Schoop, Trudi, 426
Schopenhauer, Arthur, 2, 6, 22–24,
    58n59, 536; *Aphorisms on the Wisdom
    of Life*, 14, 16–20, 27n61, 47, 57n51,
    n52
Schubert, Franz, 359, 531; "Death and
    the Maiden," 429
Schumann, Robert, 342, 373n13, 532
Schuré, Edouard, 2, 53n20; *The Great
    Initiates*, 12–13, 14, 15, 17, 19, 37,
    53nn20–22, 54n25, nn27–30, 55n33
Schwarz, Boris, 508
Scriabin, Alexander, 13, 336, 339, 340,
    532, 552
Semyonova, Marina, 238, 239n7
Serafin, Tullio, 369
Serebryakov, Pavel, 497
Sergeyev, Konstantin, 271
Seroff, Victor, 371
Shakespeare, William, 60–62, 86, 87, 99,
    107n13, 112n59, 114n82, n87, 380,
    411, 413; "Academia" edition of
    Collected Works, 63; *Antony and
    Cleopatra*, 69, 109n28,196n8; *Hamlet*,
    69, 263 (*see also SP Works Index*);
    Measure for Measure, 114n81; *Romeo
    and Juliet*, 415 (*see also SP Works
    Index*)
Shaporin, Yuriy, 202, 297, 505; *The
    Decembrists*, 305
Shaternikova, Nina, 381
Shaw, George Bernard, 63, 107n13,
    112n59, 380; *Caesar and Cleopatra*,

69, 109n28, 196n8
Shcherbak, Nikolay, 315
Shebalin, Vissarion, 192, 209, 213, 252,
    276, 277, 496, 499; Second
    Symphony, 197n1
Shepilov, Dmitriy, 307
Sherman, Isay, 226
Shlifshteyn, Semyon, 202–4, 206, 208,
    210, 212, 214, 217, 224, 472–73,
    503, 505
Shlugleyt, Ilya, 268
Shmitko, B. V., 244
Shneyerson, Grigoriy, *194*, 235, 236n1
Shostakovich, Dmitriy, 192, 213, 224,
    241–42, 297, 304–5, 312, 317, 318,
    331n 46, n54, 375n78, 398n41, 402,
    410, 493, 523n21, 526n66, 528n120,
    532, 550, 552, 554, 556n15, 559n57;
    in Communist Party, 290, 292, 307;
    death of, 516, 517; immortalization
    of, 288–90, 294; influence on young
    composers of, 496–99, 501–3, 505,
    509, 512–15, 524n31; prizes
    awarded to, 287–88, 290, 328n1
    works: *The Fall of Berlin*, 305; *Golden
    Mountains*, 387; *The Great Citizen*,
    305; *The New Babylon*, 383; *Love and
    Hatred*, 387; Symphony no. 4, 496;
    Symphony no. 5, 474, 491n32;
    Symphony no. 7, 226n1; Symphony
    no. 8, 496, 497; Symphony no. 9,
    496, 497; Symphony no. 10, 305,
    496, 497; *The Unforgettable Year 1919*,
    305
Shostakovich, Irina, 289
Shostakovich, Maxim, 319
Six, Les, 380
Skorik, Miroslav, 506–7, 511, 513, 515
Slonimsky, Nicolas, 445
Slonimsky, Sergey, 452, 499, 503, 515
Sloper, L. A., 430
Smallens, Alexander, 345, 351, 354, 357,
    358
Smirnov, Dmitriy, 502, 503, 514
Smith, Warren Storey, 444
Socialist Realism, 63, 113n67, 271, 306,
    453, 455, 482, 484, 485, 488, 489,
    490, 508, 513, 554
Socrates, 41, 55n32
Sokhor, Arnold, 512–15, 528n131
Sokolsky, Mattias, 504–5
Solovyov-Sedoy, Vasiliy, 213

Solzhenitsyn, Alexander, 314, 315
Souvtchinsky, Pyotr (Pierre), 470, 548,
    549
Sovetskaya kultura, 313, 331n53
Sovetskaya muzïka, 271, 297, 327, 331n53,
    399n55, 495, 497, 504, 505, 509,
    511, 512, 514, 526n72
Sovetskoye iskusstvo, 292, 297, 472, 474, 495
Spangler, George M., 352
Spawn of the North, 441
Stal, Alexey, 335, 344
Stalin, I. V., 61, 107n9, 196n7, 222,
    235n1, 286, 296, 304, 307–9, 314,
    320, 330n36, 331n54, 424, 435, 455,
    456, 459, 486, 490n8, 493–94, 499,
    508, 522, 542, 550, 551, 554; death
    of, 287, 290–91, 328n5, 303n37,
    485, 493, 495–96, 498, 503, 522n1,
    524n37
Stalin Prize, 213, 216n1, 220, 224,
    257n6, 271, 287, 294, 296, 297, 304,
    306–8, 311, 313, 328n1, 484, 485
Stalinism, 60, 69, 293, 295, 298, 299,
    335, 370, 453, 454, 456, 489,
    492n46, 532, 547–51, 555
Stanislavsky, Konstantin, 66, 107n9,
    558n54
Stanislavsky Theater, 201, 213, 214, 217,
    231, 246n3, 282, 306, 319, 505
Stark, Inez, 436–37
Stasevich, Abram, 267
State Planning Committee (Gosplan),
    318, 320–21
State Symphony Orchestra of
    Cinematography, 191
Still, William Grant, *Afro-American
    Symphony*, 427
Stinson, Eugene, 426
Stock, Frederick, 336, 337, 373n6, 425,
    446
Stockhausen, Karlheinz, 502
Stokowski, Leopold, 336–38, 361, 371
Strauss, Richard, 375n78, 559n60
Stravinsky, Igor, 375n78, 402, 423, 468,
    496, 499, 502, 506, 515, 532, 547,
    559n57; *Apollon musagète*, 491n23;
    L'Histoire du soldat, 560n82; *Les Noces*,
    552; *Petrushka*, 497; *Oedipus Rex*, 497;
    Le Sacre du printemps, 313, 337, 497;
    Symphony of Psalms, 470
Stravinsky, Vera, 369
Struchkova, Raisa, 256

Sudeykin, Sergey, 369, 370
Supreme Soviet, 204n2, 290, 315,
    331n46; Fourth Session of, 293
Surin, Vladimir, 225
Sviridov, Georgiy, 306, 503, 515, 525n59
Swanson, Gloria, 376, 377
Swift, Jonathan, 63
Symbolism, 7, 9, 11, 50n7, 52n15, 84,
    92, 402, 532

Tabernakulov, Vladimir, 252, 260–62,
    266, 275–78, 284
theosophy, 12–13, 53n20
Thompson, Oscar, 359, 364
Thompson, Virgil, 390
Tinyanov, Yuriy, 377–79, 384, 385,
    387–91, 394, 395, 396n8, 397n12,
    n18; *Second Lieutenant Kizhe*, 378
Tolstoy, Alexey, 288
Tolstoy, Leo, 17, 58n64, 60, 84, 286;
    Jubilee Collected Works of, 60;
    Resurrection, 9; "What Men Live By,"
    64
Tomoff, Kiril, 329n13, n16, 508
Toporov, Vladimir, 113n69, n72
Trotsky, Leon, 93, 456, 487, 490n8,
    492n46
Troyanovsky, Alexander, 432, 443
Tsukkerman, Viktor, 472
Tumanova, Zoya, 317
Tureman, Horace E., 438
Turgenev, Ivan, 17; *Smoke*, 58n64
Turnbull, Polly, 430
Twain, Mark, 535, 557n21
Tyulin, Yuriy, 511, 512
Tyutchev, Fyodor, 9–10, 52n15

Ulanova, Galina, 239n7, 256, 305, 307,
    308, 330n18, 331n53
Union of Soviet Composers (SSK), 194,
    197, 198, 203, 204, 206, 207, 226,
    227, 229n4, 257, 295, 314–16,
    329n13, n16, 331n42, n53, 492n40,
    504, 508, 512; Board, 290, 310–12,
    320; Congresses, 303, 305, 509;
    Foreign Affairs Commission, 321;
    and immortalization of SP, 291, 292,
    294, 295, 298–301, 305, 309, 322,
    323; International Commission, 315;
    Leningrad, 195, 331n53, 512;
    Moscow, 200, 204, 208, 222n8,
    331n53, 485; Musical Fund

Notes on the Contributors

Mark Aranovsky is professor and director of the music division at the State Institute for Art Research in Moscow. He has published extensively on Glinka, Prokofiev, Shostakovich, and other Russian composers. His broader studies of musical language, *Sintaksicheskaya struktura melodii* and *Muzïkal'nïy tekst: Struktura i svoystva*, appeared in 1991 and 1998 respectively.

Kevin Bartig is assistant professor of music at Michigan State University, where he teaches courses on nineteenth- and twentieth-century music. He is at work on *Composing for the Red Screen*, a book that explores Sergey Prokofiev's involvement in the Soviet film industry. His work has been recognized by fellowships from the Andrew Mellon Foundation and the American Council of Learned Societies.

Elizabeth Bergman is assistant professor of music at Princeton University specializing in twentieth-century and American music. She has published articles on Aaron Copland and Leonard Bernstein in the *Journal of the American Musicological Society*, *The Musical Quarterly*, *Journal of Musicology*, and *Cambridge Opera Journal*. Her book *Music for the Common Man: Aaron Copland During the Depression and War* (2005) received an honorable mention for the Lowens Award from the Society for American Music; she also co-edited (with Wayne Shirley) *The Selected Correspondence of Aaron Copland* (2006).

Leon Botstein is president and Leon Levy Professor in the Arts and Humanities at Bard College. He is the author of *Judentum und Modernität* (1991) and *Jefferson's Children: Education and the Promise of American Culture* (1997). He is the editor of *The Compleat Brahms* (1999) and *The Musical Quarterly*, as well as coeditor, with Werner Hanak, of *Vienna: Jews and the City of Music, 1870–1938* (2004). The music director of the American and the Jerusalem symphony orchestras, he has recorded works by, among others, Szymanowski, Hartmann, Bruch, Toch, Dohnányi, Bruckner, Foulds, Chausson, Richard Strauss, Mendelssohn, Popov, Shostakovich, and Liszt for Telarc, CRI, Koch, Arabesque, Chandos, and New World Records.

Pamela Davidson is professor of Russian literature at University College London, School of Slavonic and East European Studies. Her books include *The Poetic Imagination of Vyacheslav Ivanov* (1989), an anthology of poems dedicated to Anna Akhmatova (1991), *Vyacheslav Ivanov: A Reference Guide* (1996), an edited collection of essays, *Russian Literature and its Demons* (2000), and *Vyacheslav Ivanov and C. M. Bowra: A Correspondence from Two Corners on Humanism* (2006). Her research interests embrace comparative literature, the legacy of Symbolism, bibliographical databases, and the publication of archival materials. Her current project focuses on the role of the image of the writer as a prophet in the construction and dynamics of the Russian literary tradition.

Caryl Emerson is A. Watson Armour III University Professor of Slavic Languages and Literatures at Princeton University, where she chairs the Slavic Department with a co-appointment in Comparative Literature. A translator and critic of Mikhail Bakhtin, she has also published widely on nineteenth-century Russian literature (Pushkin, Dostoyevsky, Tolstoy), on the history and relevance of literary criticism, and on Russian opera and vocal music. Recent projects include *The Cambridge Introduction to Russian Literature* (2008).

Marina Frolova-Walker is senior lecturer in the Faculty of Music and fellow of Clare College. She studied musicology at the Moscow Conservatory, receiving her PhD in 1994. Before coming to Cambridge, she taught at the Moscow Conservatory College, the University of Ulster, Goldsmiths College London, and the University of Southampton. She has published articles in *The Cambridge Opera Journal*, *Journal of the American Musicological Society*, and *Twentieth-Century Music*, as well as contributing some of the Russian entries in the *Revised New Grove Dictionary of Music and Musicians* (2001). Her most recent publication is *Russian Music and Nationalism from Glinka to Stalin* (2007).

Nelly Kravetz is assistant professor of music at Tel Aviv University. She has published articles in *The Journal of Musicology*, *Muzïkal'naya akademiya*, *Three Oranges: The Journal of the Serge Prokofiev Foundation*, and several collections. Her research focuses on Prokofiev, Scriabin, Shostakovich, and the twentieth-century piano concerto; she is currently working on the volume *L. T. Atovmyan: Vospominaniya, pis'ma, dokumentï*.

Leonid Maximenkov is an independent scholar and senior fellow at the Council of the Humanities, Princeton University, in 2008–09. He is the author of *Sumbur vmesto muzïki: Stalinskaya kul'turnaya revolyutsiya, 1936–1938* (1997), and editor of *Bol'shaya tsenzura: Pisateli i zhurnalistï v Strane Sovetov, 1917–1956* (2005) and *Kremlyovskiy kinoteatr, 1928–1953* (2005).

Simon Morrison is associate professor of music at Princeton University specializing in Russian and French music. He is the author of *Russian Opera and the Symbolist Movement* (2002) and *The People's Artist: Prokofiev's Soviet Years* (2008). In 2007–08, he restored the original 1935 version of the ballet *Romeo and Juliet* for the Mark Morris Dance Company.

Stephen D. Press is assistant professor of music at Illinois Wesleyan University in Bloomington, Illinois. His book, *Prokofiev's Ballets for Diaghilev*, was published by Ashgate in 2006. He is at work on a reception study of Russian music in the United States.

Peter J. Schmelz is assistant professor of music at Washington University in St. Louis. He is the author of *Such Freedom, If Only Musical: Unofficial Soviet Music and Society During the Thaw* (forthcoming). Founder and chair of the American Musicological Society's Cold War and Music Study Group, his current project investigates Alfred Schnittke and late Soviet culture.

Jason Strudler is a graduate student in Slavic Languages and Literatures at Princeton University. He received a BA in Russian from the University of Rochester in 2006. His research interests include Russian and German modernist poetry, conceptualist art, opera, the decadent novel, and the theater of the absurd. He is currently working on an article on Vyacheslav Ivanov and Khlebnikov's early poetry.